RELIGIOUS MOVEMENTS IN THE MIDDLE AGES

HERBERT GRUNDMANN

Religious Movements in the Middle Ages

The Historical Links between Heresy, the Mendicant Orders, and the Women's Religious Movement in the Twelfth and Thirteenth Century, with the Historical Foundations of German Mysticism

translated by

STEVEN ROWAN

with an introduction by

ROBERT E. LERNER

UNIVERSITY OF NOTRE DAME PRESS
Notre Dame London

Manufactured in the United States
Typesetting by AeroType, Inc.

Library of Congress Cataloging-in-Publication Data

Grundmann, Herbert, 1902–1970.

[Religiöse Bewegungen im Mittelalter. English]

Religious movements in the Middle Ages : the historical links between heresy, the Mendicant Orders, and the women's religious movement in the twelfth and thirteenth century, with the historical foundations of German mysticism / Herbert Grundmann ; translated by Steven Rowan.

p. cm.

Translation of: Religiöse Bewegungen im Mittelalter.

Includes bibliographical references and index.

ISBN 0-268-01649-6 (alk. paper)

1. Europe—Church history—600–1500. 2. Heresies, Christian—History—Middle Ages, 600–1500. 3. Friars—History. 4. Monasticism and religious orders for women—Europe—History. 5. Mysticism—Germany—History—Middle ages, 600–1500. I. Title.

BR270.G713 1994

282′.4′09021—dc20 94-15466

CIP

∞ *The paper used in this publication meets the minimum requirements of the American National Standard for Information Sciences—Permanence of Paper for Printed Library Materials, ANSI Z39.48-1984.*

CONTENTS

TRANSLATOR'S NOTE

The basis of this translation is the second edition of Grundmann's book, published by the Wissenschaftliche Buchgesellschaft of Darmstadt in 1961, which added an extensive review of research, published in 1955, to what was published in 1935. The text and notes are translated into English insofar as they were originally in German or another modern European language. Long quotations of Latin in the text have been translated, but extensive Latin quotations in the notes drawn from readily available standard editions have been excised, though the locations have been noted. The numbering of the notes in the original text has been preserved. Amendments to specific notes made by Grundmann in an appendix to the edition completed in 1960 are incorporated into the original annotations, with the additions placed in brackets [ ]. It was only after completing the translation that I was able to refer to the faithful Italian translation by Maria Aussenhofer and Lea Nicolet Santini published in 1980.

The citations of the 1935 edition have been amplified in keeping with modern editing principles, wherever possible. Christina James Fritsch is to be thanked for helping me revise the wording of the translation and reedit the notes.

This translation is dedicated to my own *Doktorvater*, Professor Giles Constable of the Institute for Advanced Study, Princeton, New Jersey, in observance of his sixty-fifth birthday.

Steven Rowan
St. Louis, Missouri

INTRODUCTION TO THE TRANSLATION

Robert E. Lerner

Six toweringly impressive works of medieval history were published by German-speaking historians between 1927 and 1939: Ernst Kantorowicz, *Kaiser Friedrich II.* (1927); Percy Ernst Schramm, *Kaiser, Rom und Renovatio* (1929); Herbert Grundmann, *Religiöse Bewegungen im Mittelalter* (1935); Carl Erdmann, *Die Entstehung des Kreuzzugsgedankens* (1935); Gerd Tellenbach, *Libertas: Kirche und Weltordnung im Zeitalter des Investiturstreits* (1936); and Otto Brunner, *Land und Herrschaft* (1939). Perhaps this list confirms the adage that Minerva's owl flies at dusk. Be that as it may, Grundmann's *Religiöse Bewegungen* is now the fifth of the six to be made available to an English-language readership, after far too long a wait.[1] This introduction will attempt to explain why Grundmann's masterwork remains fresh and exciting sixty years after its initial publication, but first a brief account of Grundmann's career (never previously described in English) seems in order.

1. Herbert Grundmann (1902–1970): A Biographical Sketch

Herbert Grundmann was born in 1902 in Meerane, an industrial town of Saxony, and grew up in Chemnitz, Saxony's largest industrial city.[2] Upon graduating high school in 1921 he entered the university in nearby Leipzig, where he majored first in political economy on the assumption that he would succeed his father as the owner of a stocking factory. After several semesters, including one each in Heidelberg and Munich, the young man made up his mind not to pursue a business career, and, after flirting with philosophy and literature, decided to specialize in medieval history. Grundmann chose to write a dissertation under the Leipzig historian Walter Goetz and took as his subject the thought of the neglected twelfth-century theologian of history, Joachim of Fiore. One can only marvel at the young Grundmann's daring and energy. Very little useful scholarship on Joachim existed before he went to work; not only that, but Joachim's mode of expression was notoriously difficult and his major writings were available in print only in execrable and sometimes barely legible editions published in the early sixteenth century. Nevertheless, Grundmann forged ahead and within about a year and a half had completed a brilliant dissertation that earned him a doctorate *summa cum laude*.[3] The year was 1926 and Grundmann was all of twenty-four years old.

If the doctorate was the work of a prodigy, more prodigious accomplishments were soon to follow. Grundmann's supervisor Goetz was sufficiently impressed with the dissertation to encourage the young man to qualify for a professorial career by "habilitating" (i.e., producing a book of substantial breadth and girth). Goetz hence arranged for Grundmann to receive a two-year fellowship to support research and writing. In those years (1926–1928) Grundmann engaged in manuscript studies in Germany, France, and Italy toward the goal of editing the works of Joachim of Fiore and familiarizing himself with hitherto neglected works in the Joachite prophetic tradition. Since the xerox machine had not yet been invented and photographic reproduction was prohibitively expensive, Grundmann often stayed in one or another poorly lit and unheated library for days at a time transcribing texts longhand.[4] Nevertheless, in the same two years, he also managed to write six pathbreaking articles, four of which might easily have been published as a unit and counted as an impressive second book.[5] When his grant expired in 1928 he made ends meet by taking a position on an editorial team working on the acts of the Augsburg Diet of 1530 and proceeded concurrently to write his *Habilitationsschrift*. His "habilitation" was granted him by the University of Leipzig in July 1933, and the *Habilitationsschrift*—the book here presented as *Religious Movements in the Middle Ages*—was published in 1935.

1933 was a poor year for Grundmann to begin looking for a professorial position because he did not belong to the Nazi party or any of its affiliated organizations. Directly after the Nazi seizure of power, in March 1933, he signed his name to a public declaration of support for "Adolf Hitler and the National-Socialist State,"[6] but after that he seems to have avoided public positions about politics and to have resisted opportunism. Thus in an essay of 1936 on Meister Eckhart he insisted with some courage that "today some shoot far beyond the mark when they seek evidence in Eckhart's thought for a characteristically German, or, yet more, a pre-Christian-Germanic faith that cannot be found in his Christian-Catholic consciousness."[7] Apparently Grundmann's greatest professional problem was that he ran afoul of a Nazi watchdog for a severely critical review he wrote in 1935 of a book on Eckhart by Erich Seeberg, an author then in high standing with the Nazi regime; a zealot writing for *The National-Socialist Monthly* branded Grundmann as a "reactionary" and warned implicitly that no one should hire him.[8] Nor did it help that Grundmann's academic patron, Walter Goetz, had lost all of his influence during the Nazi era because he had served in the legislature of the Weimar Republic as a representative of the moderately Leftist Democratic Party. (In the summer of 1933, when Goetz was hospitalized as the result of an accident, Nazi students sent him the message: "What a pity you did not die!"[9]) The result was that Grundmann remained for eleven semesters as an unsalaried *Privatdozent* in Leipzig, eking out his livelihood primarily from his editing job, until he finally received the "call" in the spring of 1939 he had deserved much earlier.[10]

The call was to be professor of medieval history at the University of Königsberg. Grundmann took up this position with enthusiasm, for he loved the East Prussian landscape of lakes and rain-wet forests and was stimulated (finally, at the age of thirty-seven) by the challenge of lecturing. But 1939 was hardly more auspicious a time to begin sinking roots in the German East than 1933 had been to begin looking for a job. When war broke out he was at first deferred from military duty because of his age and poor eyesight, but in the fall of 1942 he was drafted into the army, where he was assigned a desk job. Discharged in 1943, he was drafted again in 1944 and sent to officer-training school, and then, in January 1945, attached to an anti-tank unit in East Prussia. In February he was wounded in the left wrist, sent for recuperation behind the lines, and soon thereafter taken prisoner in Wismar by the British, who released him in July.[11] By this time Grundmann had a wife (he married in 1937) and three small children. Since he had accepted a position as professor in Münster in Westphalia in the summer of 1944, his family had moved there just before the frightful Russian march into East Prussia.

Grundmann served fourteen years as professor of medieval history at Münster, a period of serenity and renewed productivity. During this time he published four short books: a second volume on Joachim of Fiore (1950); an interpretation of the origins of medieval universities (1957); a survey of medieval history-writing (1957); and a treatment of the "Cappenberger Barbarossa Head" (1959).[12] In collaboration with Hermann Heimpel he produced the only German translation of a group of medieval Latin sources published under the auspices of the Monumenta Germaniae Historica, a facing-page edition of the writings of Alexander von Roes (1949); then, also with Heimpel, he brought out a masterful critical edition of the works of the same author (1958).[13] In addition Grundmann wrote several dazzling articles, the most influential of which has been "Litteratus—Illiteratus: The Transformation of an

Educational Standard from Antiquity to the Middle Ages," and he oversaw a new edition of the four-volume standard handbook of German history ("Gebhardt"), to which he himself contributed a long section on the period between 1198 and 1378.[14]

A sense of the genial mood of Grundmann's Münster years is conveyed by lore surrounding the "Moon-Circle" (*Mondkreis*) established by Grundmann together with the historian Kurt von Raumer and the Germanist Jost Trier. Professors of different disciplines met regularly in the evenings once a month to discuss their scholarship "over the discipline-dividing fence." Since most of the streetlights in post-war Münster were still out of function, the circle met on the night of the full moon, hence its name. In imitation the university's academic assistants started meeting too and gained the name of "Mooncalves." Grundmann's affection for his Münster associates appears wistfully in the dedication of his book on the Barbarossa Head, published on the eve of his departure: "To the Moon-Circle, in leave-taking" (*Dem Mondkreis zum Abschied*).

The last station of Herbert Grundmann's career was in Munich, where he held the position from 1959 until his death from cancer in 1970 of President of the Monumenta Germaniae Historica, the renowned institute for publishing medieval historical sources. Although Grundmann felt ambivalent about assuming an administrative post and looked forward greatly to a retirement that never came, he nevertheless engineered two major accomplishments for the Monumenta. When he arrived in Munich the institute was housed in terribly cramped quarters in a former "Führer-building" that once housed offices of the Nazi party. (Ironically this was one of Munich's few downtown public structures that had survived Allied bombardments unscathed.) Grundmann saw to the resettlement of the institute in an ideal location in the Bavarian State Library. Not only did this offer far more space, but it made available three magnificent libraries under the same roof: the rich specialized medieval history collection of the Monumenta; the general collection of the Bavarian State Library; and the medieval manuscript collection of the Bavarian State Library, the largest in Germany. Secondly, after delicate negotiations, Grundmann gained from the state of Bavaria legal recognition of the Monumenta's corporate independence, thus rescinding a subordination to state ministries that had been initiated by the Nazis.

Busy as he was with administration, Grundmann offered Saturday-morning seminars in his capacity as "honorary professor" at the University of Munich and served as editor of two journals: the *Archiv für Kulturgeschichte*, and the house organ of the Monumenta, the *Deutsches*

Archiv für Erforschung des Mittelalters. How he found time for more is difficult to say, but his scholarly output hardly slackened. During his Munich years Grundmann wrote a superb short book surveying medieval heresy.[15] In addition he wrote during this eleven-year period some seventeen or eighteen substantial articles, including two long articles that thoroughly reestablished the biographical data regarding Joachim of Fiore, a long article on Robert of Liège (Rupert of Deutz) that some experts consider the best original contribution about Robert in recent times, and a methodological discussion regarding protocols of heresy trials that has become very influential.[16] To make the accomplishment even more impressive, the articles of Grundmann's last period cover a very wide range of subjects and many of them introduce hitherto unknown documentation, often edited in appendices. The harvest of Grundmann's work in article form was published after his death by the Monumenta in three volumes; had he written nothing else this would still represent an extraordinarily rich career in scholarship.[17]

Arno Borst mentions in his short biography of Grundmann that during the Munich years Grundmann engaged in discussions with many different partners, including members of the learned academies to which he belonged, research associates of the Monumenta, visiting professors, students from his seminars, and "foreign doctoral candidates." I by no means know all of those in the last category, but I do know that doctoral candidates from the United States who were welcomed warmly and offered guidance by Grundmann included Eleanor C. McLaughlin, John B. Freed, and myself. When I came to Germany in 1962–63 I was beginning work on a dissertation on a "Grundmann" topic, "the Heresy of the Free Spirit," and had obtained little direction from my doctoral supervisor in Princeton. Since I was learning German virtually from scratch, I postponed introducing myself to the President of the Monumenta until a few months before my departure in the hope that I would then be able to utter a few approximately correct sentences and understand at least the drift of whatever he might have to say. When I decided I could delay no longer I was petrified, for the distance in status, age, and erudition between us was immense; I began to wonder whether this might not be the equivalent of dropping in on Charles de Gaulle.

To my great relief Grundmann immediately put me at ease with his cordiality. I suppose he may have regarded me at first as a curiosity, for I was the first young American to cross his path; in addition, I was twenty-three, halting at his language, and if not skinnier than a drain-pipe, not necessarily heftier than one either. But I was ready for shop talk: I came primed with research questions and had brought some data I thought might interest him. Not only did the meeting go well, but he insisted on more. Then, to my complete surprise, he invited me, together with a young Englishman who had also sought his advice at the Monumenta, for supper at his home with his family. I had never taken a meal with any professor at Princeton, and German academics were notorious for keeping their distance from students.

The Grundmann apartment was in a turn-of-the-century building located in the stately neighborhood of Bogenhausen, where Thomas Mann used to walk his dog. It is impossible to describe the tremendous impression of civilized comfort created by the high ceilings, book-lined walls, and old-world furnishings. Frau Grundmann seemed the embodiment of cultivated charm, another Elisabeth Schwarzkopf. She did not wince at whatever ungainly impression I may have made, but immediately drew me and my companion into conversation, as did Grundmann and the children, who were roughly my age. When the evening ended it had started to pour, and Grundmann insisted on lending me an umbrella for my walk home through the English Garden. In a way I regret that I did not just keep that umbrella as a souvenir, but I did return to the U.S. with an even more marvelous trophy, a signed and inscribed copy of *Religiöse Bewegungen im Mittelalter*.

2. THE RELIGIOUS-HISTORICAL BRANCH OF CULTURAL HISTORY

Needless to say, I am not an impartial critic of Grundmann's most important book. Nevertheless I will endeavor to set it in its historiographical context, summarize its arguments, and discuss its reception as fairly as I can.

When the young Grundmann began to set his scholarly course in the Leipzig of the 1920s, he initially was inclined toward philosophy or the study of literature (then mostly philology), but wavered since he thought neither was rooted sufficiently in historical reality.[18] A seminar in the winter of 1923/24 with a young *Privatdozent*, Johannes Kühn, nudged him over to history since the topic was fourteenth-century German mysticism and Grundmann came to see that by pursuing research in such an area he could unite his tastes for thought, literature, and real-life experience. Kühn's seminar also showed him that he was more interested in historical source-criticism than he had thought. Supposedly the first time he spoke in this seminar it was to say: "I believe the translation here is wrong."

Once Grundmann had opted for history, the Leipzig environment proved to be ideal for allowing him to develop a personally congenial approach. The dominant style in the German academic historiography of the 1920s was a rigorous positivism applied to politics and diplomacy. In Leipzig this orthodoxy was exemplified by Erich Brandenburg, who, while Grundmann was beginning his studies, had opposed the establishment of a chair in sociology on the grounds that sociology was not a distinct discipline, and was finishing an exhaustive treatment of Germany's foreign policy from 1870 to 1914.[19] Grundmann took some courses with Brandenburg and impressed him favorably enough: it was Brandenburg who appointed Grundmann to the editorial job that tided him over financially during the 1930s. Yet while Grundmann had come to realize that he wanted to root his scholarship in real events, he was not interested in Brandenburg's purely political history or in the minute reconstruction of who said what to whom on which day and hour.

Had Grundmann studied elsewhere he would have had few alternatives, but at Leipzig he was able to work under the auspices of the "Institute for Cultural and Universal History," founded by Karl Lamprecht and directed in the 1920s by Walter Goetz. Lamprecht had been the main opponent of regnant event-oriented political and diplomatic history in the German historical world at the turn of the century.[20] He wanted to recapture "historical totality" (*Gesamtgeschichte*), particularly in regard to "mutually fructifying material and spiritual forces"; in this regard he was the one academic historian before the rise of the *Annales* school who paid close attention to conditions of every-day life such as diet and dress.[21] On the other hand, much unlike the later "Annalistes," Lamprecht's desire to master "totality" was oriented toward the goal of discovering humanity's "stages of development." He had written a nineteen-volume history of Germany (completed in 1909) in which he traced the development of the national psyche (*Volksseele*) in a highly schematic fashion ("age of symbolism"; "age of subjectivism", etc.); and in his lectures on *Modern Historical Science*, he offered instruction on such topics as "The General Mechanisms of Spiritual Transition Periods," and "Universal-Historical Problems from the Social-Psychological Standpoint."[22] Lamprecht fought furiously in defense of his controversial ideas and methods, never backing down about the existence of historical laws or the validity of behaviorist collective psychology. Consequently by the time of his death in 1915 he had become discredited.

Nevertheless Lamprecht had at least managed to establish a well-endowed institute in Leipzig, and when this was taken over after the First World War by Walter Goetz it became the only academic institute in Germany dedicated to a broad, culturally oriented view of the human past. Goetz disavowed Lamprecht's belief in laws and collective national-psychological stages, but he held programatically to the position that inquiring into the "total history of humanity was the proper task of the historian" and that studying "the development of the life of the mind" was the best strategy for inquiring into such a "total history."[23] Goetz himself never produced a major work, but he lectured during his Leipzig years on cultural history of all periods and wrote articles on the ideals of St. Francis, the revival of Roman Law in the Middle Ages, and the relationship of the Middle Ages to the Renaissance; he also produced the standard edition of Burckhardt's *Civilization of the Renaissance in Italy*. Under his aegis young scholars thrived in an institute that had its own old building (once visited by Goethe) with a commodious open-stack library and an atmosphere that encouraged non-doctrinaire discussion.[24]

Grundmann was a disciple of Goetz in three respects. First, he became a cultural historian in the sense that Goetz conceived of that calling: "cultural history is total history with an emphasis on intellectual history." As Grundmann elaborated on this point in a necrology for Goetz, although cultural history emphasizes the life of the mind, it should not be thought of in opposition to political history but should "embrace political events as well as religious, literary, artistic, economic, and social activities."[25] This certainly was Grundmann's program too. Secondly, Grundmann followed Goetz in assuming that good history of any sort had to be based on solid source criticism. Lamprecht had exposed himself to attack by eschewing documentation in his *Deutsche Geschichte* (the work was meant for the general public), relying for long stretches on secondary sources, and making frequent mistakes ("as many mistakes as sentences" said his most hostile critics[26]), whereas Goetz wrote a critical review of the sources for St. Francis before writing on Francis's ideals, and stated in a postulate fully accepted by his disciple that "the study of documents and records is the necessary prerequisite for historical science."[27]

Thirdly, however, Grundmann followed Goetz, and in this respect also the spirit of Lamprecht, in holding to the quest for synthesis. The young Grundmann was an engaged reader of Oswald Spengler and wrote a paper for one of Goetz's seminars comparing Spengler to Joachim of Fiore.[28] Grundmann assuredly was never convinced by the categorizations of either a Lamprecht or a Spengler, yet only someone who was sympathetic to the goal of broad generalization could have written a book called "Religious Movements in the Middle Ages."[29] One of Grundmann's characterizations of Goetz could just as well apply to Grundmann himself, that of the "keen-sighted, tough-minded [reviewer] of the evidence" who aims at "the understanding of the life of the past in all its conditionalities and interrelations."[30]

It can hardly be maintained that Grundmann's dissertation, *Studies on Joachim of Fiore*, for all its worth, was methodologically innovative. Certainly Grundmann's reading of Joachim was original, but the dissertation remained in the traditional genre of intellectual history. *Religious Movements in the Middle Ages*, however, was a new kind of study, one that might be called "cultural history, religious-historical branch." Before Grundmann's book appeared the dominant approach to religious history had been doctrinal. One treated religions or currents within religions by exposing the tenets or canons they upheld. In the area of medieval Christianity students of the Investiture Controversy might analyze the letters of Gregory VII and the Concordat of Worms, students of Cistercianism the *Carta caritatis* and the letters of Bernard of Clairvaux, and students of Catharism the pertinent doctrinal polemics and inquisitorial records. A monument of the doctrinal approach to medieval heresy was a survey by Felice Tocco (1884) that opened with a detailed treatment of the early twelfth-century debate on universals and interpreted Catharism as a coherent doctrinal system regardless of whether it was located in Orléans in 1022 or Ferrara in 1269.[31] Even the masterpiece of religious history written in Germany in the generation before Grundmann, Ernst Troeltsch's *Social Teachings of the Christian Churches and Groups* (1911), albeit written by a sociologist, was primarily a doctrinal history; as the title suggests, Troeltsch was more interested in mapping out "teachings" than in studying the historical contexts that produced his "teachings."[32] Ultimately doctrinal studies were oriented to locating pedigrees: the Cathars were "Manicheans," the Lollards "forerunners of the Reformation."

The sole alternative to the doctrinal approach before Grundmann was the materialist one. This had gained little momentum in Germany because of its association with Marxism, a doctrine that was anathema in almost all of German academia. The only sustained German account of medieval Christian religious movements that pursued a materialist approach was *Forerunners of Modern Socialism* by Karl Kautsky (1895), a Marxist politician and publicist, and Kautsky's amateurism did nothing for his cause among the professoriat.[33] (If Grundmann knew Kautsky's work he never said so in print.) More scholarly, and hence more respectable, was the work of the Italian socialist (and Catholic modernist) Gioacchino Volpe and that of Volpe's disciples Antonino De Stefano and Luigi Zanoni. In the first three decades of the twentieth century these men treated currents in medieval religion as products of economic and power-political circumstances, specifically as expressions of class struggle.[34] Volpe and his disciples were as little interested in doctrinal systems as Tocco had been in social strata, but saw movements of religious dissent as "religious transpositions of economic and political problems."[35]

Clearly what was needed was a historiography of religion that lay between the extremes of doctrinal classification and materialistic analysis, and this was what Grundmann accomplished in *Religious Movements in the Middle Ages*. For him understanding the doctrines that lay behind religious commitments and also the material contexts that fostered them was essential. But above all he wished to recapture the dynamism of the commitments themselves and identify the non-deterministic contingencies that carried them along their various paths. His resolve to "take religion seriously" was not, as is sometimes thought, the product of personal religious belief. When Grundmann wrote *Religious Movements* he was formally without religion; though raised a Protestant, he had officially withdrawn from the German Protestant Church many years earlier and never rejoined it. According to Alexander Patschovsky (Grundmann's last student) the author of *Religious Movements* was "an authentic free spirit who thought in a secular manner."[36]

Grundmann's epigraph, taken from an article by the Leipzig sociologist Hans Freyer dedicated to Walter Goetz, expresses pithily Grundmann's own determination to avoid anachronism in approaching his religious subject matter: "The historian restores history to the complex situation which prevailed when it was still in the course of being decided." Religious ideals are not to be measured by later standards of orthodoxy or theoretical sophistication; still less are they to be reinterpreted as veiled expressions of social protest. To grasp commitments and decisions the historian has to "make them happen again."

3. *RELIGIOUS MOVEMENTS IN THE MIDDLE AGES*

The greatest synthetic daring of Grundmann's book was to emphasize the common point of departure of groups that ultimately became located on either side of papally defined orthodoxy. Hitherto scholars had discussed either high medieval heresy or new orders within the Church, but never the common inspiration that lay behind both. Even Volpe, who had written on "Religious Movements and Heretical Sects," was concerned alone with expressions of anti-hierarchical dissent. Grundmann, however, proposed to identify a single "religious movement" of the twelfth century that subsequently issued into "religious movements," orthodox and heretical. The twelfth-century movement had been inspired by the Gregorian Reform movement of the late eleventh century; once the Gregorians began to accomplish their goals in reforming the ecclesiastical hierarchy, uncompromising idealists began to ask "whether the ecclesiastical ordination of a priest should be the sole entitlement for carrying out the work of Christian salvation."[37] The answer of those who adhered to the new religious movement was that the work of salvation could be accomplished outside of ecclesiastical orders by a strict imitation of the life of the apostles (the *vita apostolica*), with special emphasis on the practice of poverty, itinerant preaching, or both. The ideal of the apostolic life was the catalyst in all twelfth-century religious ferment. Even the Cathars, so often thought to have been doctrinaire dualists who were committed to an imported exotic ontology, were motivated most of all by desires to retrieve evangelical piety (inevitably ascetic).

The religious movement of the twelfth century was channeled in two different directions in the thirteenth century as a result of the policy of Innocent III. Seekers of evangelical perfection functioned outside of the hierarchical Church until Innocent's reign because prelates and popes had refused to offer them recognition; indeed they had usually attempted to drive them out of existence. When the Waldensians had volunteered to become a lay preaching arm of the Church in the last quarter of the twelfth century they were first ridiculed and then proscribed. Innocent III instituted an about-face in policy by recognizing clearsightedly that the Church could profit from appropriating the energy of the religious movement in its own behalf—so long as it could enforce the principle of strict obedience to ecclesiastical mandates. Immediately on becoming pope Innocent reconciled an Italian apostolic group, the *Humiliati*, with the Church, and later gave permission to a group of converted Waldensians to preach against heretics. (As Grundmann observed, the Waldensians concerned were hardly "converted" because they continued to do what they had always done; rather it was the curia that was converted.) Far more fatefully, Innocent patronized two fledgling apostolic groups that were to become the two major "mendicant orders" of the Church, the Franciscans and the Dominicans.

Because Innocent III persecuted more ruthlessly than ever before those adherents of the apostolic ideal who refused obedience, the lines between heresy and orthodoxy soon were drawn more sharply than ever before. Now there were antagonistic "religious movements" on either side of the divide. A more conventional historian might have ended *Religious Movements* by recounting in detail the thirteenth-century outcome: the organizational and doctrinal hardening of sects and the institutionalization of the mendicant orders. Instead Grundmann put those matters aside and offered an entr'acte in which he concentrated his argument (repeated elsewhere throughout the book) that the social dimension of the quest for apostolic poverty was not a reaction of poor people against increasing economic injustice but a response from within the ranks of the wealthy against the corruptions of wealth. (''Weavers did not become heretics, heretics became weavers.'') Then he devoted the rest of his book (in fact more than half of it) to a hitherto greatly neglected aspect of thirteenth-century religious history: the ''religious women's movement.'' Since so little work had been done in this area, Grundmann had to gather and scrutinize bits and pieces of evidence from a wide variety of underutilized sources such as synodal decrees, foundation charters of female religious houses, nuns' *vitae*, secular-mendicant polemics, and vernacular devotional handbooks. Since synthesis was out of the question, *Religious Movements* became more ''a series of connected essays'' than a coherent whole.[38] Nevertheless, the intellectual excitement of the second half of the book is probably even greater than that of the first.

Although a few scholars before Grundmann had written on nuns and beguines, for practical purposes he discovered the high medieval ''religious women's movement''; almost certainly he was the first to employ the term. As Grundmann demonstrated, many women in northwestern Europe during the late twelfth and early thirteenth centuries sought avidly to practice versions of apostolic perfection that encompassed not only voluntary poverty but a penitential asceticism oriented toward identification with the sufferings of Christ. The zest of these women for affective religious experience easily could have led to heresy; recognizing this, some sympathetic male officers of the hierarchical Church attempted to integrate them as best they could into the institutional life of the Church. After the mendicant orders took shape they created women's affiliates. Alternatively, religious women organized themselves as ''beguines'' in semi-religious sisterhoods.

The fact that beguines were charged with lack of discipline and propensity to theological error led Grundmann to inquire into the interrelations between the religious women's movement of the thirteenth century and heterodox mysticism. In an original reconsideration of the ''heresy of the Free Spirit'' he discredited the received assumptions that there was an organized sect of that name and that such a sect maintained a continuous clandestine existence since the time of the Amaurians, whose leaders were burned in Paris in 1210. Instead he showed that although there never was a ''free-spirit'' sect there was indeed a ''free-spirit'' style of affective mysticism particularly congenial to thirteenth-century religious women. The condemned Amaurians, learned clerics dabbling in pantheistic theological speculation, had already gained a following among such women; the female response probably helped influence the shape of Amaurian teachings. Later in the century religious women, often beguines, appropriated and refashioned similar Neoplatonic-pantheistic theses to animate their meditations and devotions. The outcome was a daring affective mysticism that hovered between orthodoxy and heresy and might seem more the one or more the other depending on the speaker or viewer. Mechthild of Magdeburg, the "new spirits" of c. 1270 in Swabia, and Marguerite Porete espoused no "particular heretical doctrine," but they had a family resemblance based on "a measureless escalation of religious experience whose spiritual assumptions [were] found time and again in the religious movement of the time."

The subject of women's affective religion led naturally to Grundmann's last topic, "the origins of a religious literature in the vernacular." His entirely original thesis on this subject was that a vernacular religious literature in prose could only arise when "a new stratum formed between the laity and the clergy—one which, like the clergy, wanted to read and even to write religious works, sermons, prayers, and not least Holy Scripture, but, like the 'laity,' could not read or write in Latin." As Grundmann maintained, this happened in the thirteenth century when religious women, mostly in cloisters or beguinages, demanded an accessible religious literature. By a minute examination of the sources Grundmann proved that the earliest vernacular religious prose writings arose side by side with the northern religious women's movement in the Low Countries and Germany; sometimes vernacular works were written for women by male spiritual supervisors, and sometimes such works were written by women themselves.

Grundmann put down his last ace when he observed that the flowering of German mysticism in the fourteenth century was intelligible only against this background. Not only were women writers such as Mechthild of Magdeburg forerunners of Eckhart, but Eckhart formulated his thought and language (the two obviously being inseparable) in order to communicate with religious women under his spiritual guidance. Grundmann thus demonstrated the enormous importance of women for a central chapter of German religious history and further substantiated his methodological premise that it is necessary to examine context as well as doctrine, audience as well as works, in order to account satisfactorily for changing cultural configurations. These, then, were "the historical foundations of German mysticism" mentioned in the last clause of his book's long subtitle.

4. The Scholarly Reception

Religious Movements received little attention when it first appeared. So far as I am aware, the only contemporary reviewer who recognized its monumental importance was Hermann Heimpel, writing in 1938 in the *Historische Zeitschrift*, but Heimpel was a friend and research collaborator of Grundmann's (at the time the two were both located in Leipzig).[39] Indeed one wonders whether the book would have been reviewed in the *Historische Zeitschrift* at all had Heimpel not seen to it because the review was quite late; in fact the book was ignored by *The English Historical Review, The American Historical Review*, and *Speculum*. Arno Borst proposes that *Religious Movements* was "too far-reaching, too explosive, too far-removed from the royal road of political history" to be appreciated by German medievalists in the 1930s;[40] doubtless much the same can be said to explain the indifference to the book in other countries. So far as I know, the only writer in the English-speaking world to call attention to the importance of Grundmann's work promptly was the non-specialist Arnold Toynbee.[41]

After the war the book came into vogue. Plausibly the rise of Christian Democracy in Western Europe made the study of reformist Christian religion—and particularly of lay movements and interrelations between orthodoxy and heresy—appear no longer so far removed from the royal road.[42] At the Tenth International Congress of Historical Sciences held in Rome in 1955 Grundmann's book of twenty years earlier offered the central conceptual framework for the section devoted to "Popular Religious Movements and Heresies in the Middle Ages," and Grundmann gave two papers for the section in which he commented on work done between 1935 and 1955. In 1961 the demand for *Religiöse Bewegungen im Mittelalter* became so great that the author oversaw its reprinting with corrections and annexes consisting of the papers he had given in Rome. The 1961 edition has remained in print in German ever since. In 1974 it was translated into Italian,[43] and now (better late than never) it appears in English.

As John Van Engen observed in an article in 1986 on the historiography of the Christian Middle Ages, Grundmann's *Religious Movements* "has become the foundation for the historical study of medieval religious life."[44] To offer just a few examples to support that statement, Grundmann's conceptualization of high medieval heresy has dominated the field; Malcolm Lambert the author of the standard English survey, writes: "to my mind, the late Professor H. Grundmann is the best single guide to popular medieval heresy."[45] Regarding early Franciscan studies, David Flood reports that "leading Franciscan historians have relied on

[*Religious Movements*]; I have seen and held the dogeared copies of [Grundmann's] study which belonged to two eminent Franciscan historians, K. Esser and S. Clasen."[46] As for the institutional history of beguines, E. W. McDonnell, the author of what remains the standard account in English, acknowledges Grundmann's "invaluable guidance and penetrating insight."[47] Finally, Grundmann's accomplishments have helped enrich one of the currently most flourishing areas of medieval studies, women's religion. Caroline Walker Bynum draws heavily on Grundmann in her *Holy Feast and Holy Fast*, and Ursula Peters states that "virtually all the recent studies of women's mysticism are pervasively endebted to Grundmann's account."[48]

To recognize that *Religious Movements in the Middle Ages* has become "foundational" of course is not to say that it is infallible. Indeed, like any stimulating good book, it has animated some lively debate. Readers coming to *Religious Movements* for the first time may wish to be cognizant of some of the criticisms it has received. By far the most frequently expressed reservation about Grundmann's work has been that it is excessively "idealistic" and pays insufficient attention to economic and social explanations for religious decisions. In the postwar period the most concerted attack along these lines came from East German Marxists of the "Leipzig school," led by the holder of the Leipzig chair in medieval history, Ernst Werner. (Ironically the university whose scholars led the attack on Grundmann was the same wherein Grundmann had created the basis for this attack.) Committed to the proposition that "the methods of historical materialism point the way as an infallible compass," Werner and his camp argued that "no one, not even in the Middle Ages, can free himself from the bases of his material existence," that the High Middle Ages, as all historical periods, was torn by "class struggle," and that "the wishes and hopes of classes were necessarily expressed in the guise of religious demands because there was not yet any secularized lay ideology."[49]

At the height of the cold war Percy Ernst Schramm in the West answered Ernst Werner in the East, by saying that someone who agrees with Marx that "religion is the opium of the masses," writes about religion "as the blind write about color and the deaf about music."[50] Grundmann avoided this polemical tone, and certainly never wanted to imply that one has to experience a personal commitment to religion in order to write about religion. While well cognizant, however, of the materialistic criticism of his line of approach he never backed away from it. Instead, he reaffirmed his view that there was indeed "a close connection between the religious movement and the economic and social changes of the twelfth century," but that this did not consist of a movement "of aspiring classes in opposition to the ruling strata," let alone a "class struggle," but rather that "a religious movement [took] hold of persons of all strata who, in the midst of economic upswing, desired to take seriously the demands of the gospels and the apostles."[51]

Now that the European Marxist regimes have collapsed it is especially important to grant that economic interpretations may have their validity whatever one's view of doctrinaire Marxism. Werner was surely warranted in maintaining that even if people who joined a given movement came from all classes the movement may have expressed the needs of one class more than another, and even if the leaders of a movement came from the wealthier classes, it does not necessarily follow that the movement did not primarily express the dissatisfactions of the oppressed. Some non-Marxists have attempted to go farther and challenge empirically Grundmann's contention that high medieval volunteers for poverty came preponderantly from the prosperous ranks of society and were driven exclusively by religious motives. With reference to beguinages, it has been argued that thirteenth-century beguines came from a greater diversity of economic backgrounds than Grundmann proposed, that some male founders or donors certainly wanted to make proper provisions for unmarried daughters, and that Grundmann overlooked the close relationship of the beguine movement to the need for tending the sick.[52] Readers ultimately will have to decide for themselves how to judge motives—how far, that is, they wish to lend credence to the explicit statements of those who opted for religious lives that they were doing so for religious reasons. It appears, though, that in terms of the social composition question Alexander Murray adjudicates the matter correctly when he states that "recent research, even where it has sought to reverse Grundmann's findings, has in effect usually only confirmed them."[53]

A different line of general criticism of Grundmann's work has been expressed less frequently. This comes at the other extreme from the economic critique, namely that Grundmann underrated the importance of doctrine. To say that the Cathars offered merely a persuasive theoretical "superstructure" for apostolic commitments may be to resist taking Catharism seriously, just as Grundmann taxed his socially oriented opponents for "not taking religion seriously." Such a criticism may be weightier now than when Grundmann wrote because new source discoveries have proven the existence of rigorous eastern dualism in Catharist circles before 1200; Waldensians who fought Cathars before 1200 accused them of promulgating unchristian teachings.[54] All told, R. I. Moore does well to remind us that deep and bitter rifts existed among different adherents of Grundmann's twelfth-century "religious movement," and that "for the Christian niceties of doctrine were important."[55]

Two other general criticisms are perhaps supplements to Grundmann rather than rejections of what he proposed. Moore recently has argued for an approach to the study of high medieval persecution from anthropological and sociological perspectives, thereby placing official responses to apostolic movements on a different plane than personal decisions made by individual popes such as Innocent III.[56] Other recent scholars regret that Grundmann ignored mundane religious practice. Doubtless Grundmann himself would have been the first to acknowledge this, for it was not his subject, although whether he would have granted that he considered daily religious practice "unworthy of treatment" is less certain.[57]

A final group of criticisms deal more with particulars. David Flood proposes that early Franciscan history should be approached from the narrower angle of the communal context of Assisi rather than broad religious currents.[58] Nevertheless, Flood concedes that Grundmann's conceptualization provides "the most compelling case for the specific role of the Franciscans in the larger religious happening of the age." John Freed has fine-tuned Grundmann on male direction of religious women by showing that Cistercians as well as Franciscans and Dominicans actively supported the thirteenth-century religious women's movement and that the mendicants sometimes preferred to oversee beguinages rather than mendicant nunneries.[59] And Ursula Peters has criticized aspects of Grundmann's account of the emergence of vernacular religious prose literature. According to her, Grundmann placed too much weight on small bits of evidence and sometimes on what she considers literary fictions. Yet Peters does not deny Grundmann's main argument that a new literature came into being because of the emergence of a new stratum of religious women who demanded it.[60]

Readers of *Religious Movements in the Middle Ages* will want to judge some of the foregoing issues for themselves. Grundmann would have wished it that way, for he never wanted to seem "canonical." But there is no doubt that he wrote what has come to be regarded as a classic. Watching Grundmann coax forth meaning from refractory sources, point out revealing details, juxtapose events, argue with prevailing scholarship, and mount conclusions with "forward-rushing power"[61] ought to be an invigorating experience for anyone who enjoys the pleasures of superb historiography.

PREFACE TO THE REPRINTED EDITION

The present book first appeared in 1935 as volume 267 in the series "Historische Studien," from the Verlag Dr. Emil Ebering, having been accepted as a *Habilitation* thesis by the Philosophical Faculty of the University of Leipzig in July 1933. Those times did not favor its theme, at least not in Germany, and the times were also hostile to its marketing abroad. Since the warehouse supply was destroyed in the War, and the book could no longer be obtained, it could not be found in many libraries and historical institutes. That would be a pain capable of enduring if so much research on the history of heresy and religious orders in the Middle Ages did not rely on it and refer to it, whether positive or critical, confirming or correcting. As a result, the demand increased rather than decreased. Despite that, the author long hesitated, doubting whether an unaltered reprint could be justified, for research had clarified many of the questions dealt with here, discovering new sources and relying on better editions. But research up to now has not led to conclusive results which would make a complete reworking of the subject possible. The lively interest the book excited outside of Germany was further demonstrated at the Tenth International Congress of Historical Sciences in September 1955, in Rome. In the section, "History of the Middle Ages," one of the primary themes was the problem of "Popular religious movements and heresies of the Middle Ages." The basis for discussion was a report prepared by medievalists from various countries and religious convictions, printed and presented to the participants, treating the state of research and questions needing further clarification (*Relazioni*, vol. 3, 305–537). E. Delaruelle of the Catholic Institute in Toulouse offered an introduction on "Popular Piety in the Eleventh Century" (309–32), as well as the final essay on "Popular Piety at the End of the Middle Ages" (515–37), along with a treatment of the influence of Francis of Assisi on popular piety (449–66). Raffaello Morghen, leader of the Istituto storico Italiano per il Medeo Evo, who edited the general report, also wrote on "Popular Religious Movements" in the era of the reform of the Church (333–56), L. Salvatorelli (Rome) on Francis of Assisi and Franciscans in the first century of the order ("Movimento francescano e gioachimismo," 403–48), and R. R. Betts (London) on "National and Heretical Religious Currents" from the end of the fourteenth century to the middle of the fifteenth century, particularly on Hussitism (485–513). Two further articles on "Heretical Sects and New Orders in the Twelfth Century" (357–402) and on "German Mysticism, Beguines, and the Heresy of the 'Free Spirit' " (467–84) were written by me and republished with a few additions in the *Archiv füKulturgeschichte* 37 (1955), 129–82. At that time I believed that this report on research would suffice to supplement my book, now twenty years old, without its reprinting. Yet the discussions on this theme at the Roman Congress (see its *Atti*, 344–71) showed many of the questions I touched on were still in dispute, such as the origin and character of the Western heresies in the eleventh century or the social-economic element of the religious and heretical movements of the Middle Ages. On the other hand, other questions on which I concentrated had been little noted or developed, particularly the rise of new orders, as well as their links to the women's movement and heresy. For these reasons, it appeared to me that we still could not do without my book, written twenty-five years before, and I perceived nothing substantial in it to change. If one were to understand the title "Religious Movements in the Middle Ages" in broader terms than intended—since in fact it was limited by its more prosaic subtitle—then a great deal more could have been included which is ignored here. Alongside the rise of new orders and sects, their further development and accomplishments could have been included, their schisms and reforms, their inner crises and conflicts—particularly in the Franciscan Order (Joachites and Spirituals); the rise of the further mendicant orders such as the Augustinian Hermits, the Carmelites, the Capuchins, etc., all the way to the popular piety of the *devotio moderna* and the "Brethren of the Common Life," as well as Hussitism and much besides, could have been covered. Yet I was never interested in giving a narrative account of *all* religious movements of the entire Middle Ages. Rather, I had intended to investigate certain connections in the creation of new communities, both inside and outside the Church, all of which intended to live and act according to the same or related impulses, coming from the counsels of the gospels and the example of the apostles. This investigation reached from the first itinerant preachers around 1100 through the Waldensians and other heretical groups, the mendicant orders and beguines of the thirteenth century, ending with the mystical "Poor in Spirit" and the heretical "Free Spirit." The manner in which this movement branched out and evolved, how it found its place under ecclesiastical and monastic rules or led to new sectarian groups, how much they were influenced by decisions of the Church and the papacy, and what importance must be attributed to Innocent III in particular—these perceptions from my book appear to me not to have been rendered obsolete by newer research, or even adequately reviewed, and they are still worth considering. What needs to be corrected or added is partly provided by the review of research added to the book, partly by still more recent material placed at the end. It seems to me that a thoroughly new treatment of this theme would be premature so long as research is either very much in flux or so very uneven in its results. It will perhaps be helpful to the progress of research to have available again the book which first sought to gain insight into these interconnections.

So I am very thankful to the Wissenschaftliche Buchgesellschaft for deciding to undertake this reprinting in response to its membership, a reprint in which only printing errors and oversights have been corrected, supplemented with the review of research ("New Contributions . . .") and some notices on more recent literature [added to notes in the English-language edition]. The bibliography was expanded in keeping with these additions.

Herbert Grundmann
Munich, December, 1960

ABBREVIATIONS

AASS	Acta sanctorum
AB	Analecta Bollandiana
ADA	Anzeiger für deutsches Altertum
AF	Analecta franciscana
AFH	Archivum franciscanum historicum
AFP	Archivum fratrum praedicatorum
AHDL	Archives d'histoire doctrinale et littéraire du Moyen Age
AHR	American Historical Review
AKG	Archiv für Kulturgeschichte
ALKG	Archiv für Litteratur und Kirchengeschichte des Mittelalters, Heinrich Denifle and Franz Ehrle, eds., Berlin, 1885–
AMSL	Archives des missions scientifiques et littéraires
AOP	Analecta ordinis fratrum prædicatorum
AP	Analecta præmonstratensia
ASL	Archivo storico Lombardo
ASOC	Analecta sancti Ordinis Cisterciensis
BEC	Bibliothèque de l'École des Chartes
BISI	Bollettino dell'Istituto storico italiano per il Medio Evo
BZTS	Bonner Zeitschrift für Theologie und Seelsorge
Cel.	Thomas of Celano. See Frequently Cited Works
COCR	Collectanea ordinis Cisterciensium reformatorum
CRCSIC	Compte rendu du . . . congrès scientifique international des Catholiques
DA	Deutsches Archiv für Erforschung des Mittelalters
DHGE	Dictionnaire d'histoire et de géographie ecclésiastique
DVLG	Deutsche Vierteljahrsschrift für Literaturwissenschaft und Geistesgeschichte
EHR	English Historical Review
Ep.	Epistolae Innocentii III (PL, 214–216)
FDA	Freiburger Diözesans-Archiv
FF	Forschungen und Fortschritte
FS	Franziskanische Studien
GWU	Geschichte in Wissenschaft und Unterricht
HJ	Historisches Jahrbuch der Görres-Gesellschaft
HV	Historische Vierteljahrschrift
HZ	Historische Zeitschrift

ISISS	Istituto storico italiano, Studi storici
KD	Kirchengeschichte Deutschlands, Albert Hauck, ed.
MA	Le Moyen Âge
MF	Miscellanea franciscana
MG Scr.	Monumenta Germaniae Historica, Scriptores
MIÖG	Mitteilungen des Instituts für österreichische Geschichtsforschung
MOPH	Monumenta ordinis praedicatorum historica
NEM	Notices et extraits des mss. de la Bibliothèque Nationale
PL	Jean-Paul Migne, Patrologiae cursus latinus
PRE	Protestantische Real-Enzyklopädie, 3rd ed., ed. A. Hauck
QF	Quellen und Forschungen zur Geschichte des Dominikanerordens in Deutschland
RAM	Revue d'ascétique et de mystique
RH	Revue historique
RHE	Revue d'histoire ecclésiastique
RHPR	Revue d'histoire et de philosophie religieuse
RHR	Revue de l'histoire des religions
RM	Revue Mabillon
RQ	Römanische Quartalschrift
RQH	Revue des Questions historiques
RSCI	Rivista di Storia della Chiesa in Italia
RSI	Rivista Storica Italiana
RSR	Ricerche di storia religiosa
S.-B.	Sitzungsberichte
SC	Studia Catholica
SG	Studi Gregoriani
SMGB	Studien und Mitteilungen zur Geschichte des Benediktinerordens
SRGUS	Scriptores rerum Germanicarum in usum scholarum
TLZ	Theologische Literatur-Zeitung
Urk.-B.	Urkunden Buch
VMKVA	Verslagen en Mededeelingen der kon. Vlaamsche Academie voor Taal- en Letterkunde
VS	Vita seraphica
ZB	Zentralblatt für Bibliothekswesen
ZDA	Zeitschrift für deutsches Altertum
ZDP	Zeitschrift für deutsche Philologie
ZGO	Zeitschrift für die Geschichte des Oberrheins
ZKG	Zeitschrift für Kirchengeschichte
ZKT	Zeitschrift für Katholische Theologie
ZRP	Zeitschrift für romanische Philologie

Introduction

> The historian restores history to the complex situation which prevailed when it was still in the course of being decided. He makes it into the present once more, reviving its acute alternatives. In the true sense of the word, he makes it happen again, that is, he has it decided again. He dissolves the content, the product, the form of the completed work or the done deed, at the same time appealing to the will, to the living power of decision, out of which these works and deeds grew.
>
> Hans Freyer[1]

All religious movements of the Middle Ages achieved realization either in religious orders or in heretical sects. The Middle Ages themselves knew no such concept as "religious movement." The words *religio* and *vita religiosa* meant the same then as "monastic order" or "monastic life" do now. Following a conviction resting upon the doctrine of *ordo* in the medieval Church, a "religious life" dedicated totally to the service of God could only take place within the stable ranks of the monastic estate, where it was assured that rule and discipline would protect the religious person against all backsliding or degeneracy, and the person would be solidly anchored in the general structure of the Church. Every religious stance which did not recognize these rules as binding and submit to them, every religious movement which did not issue in an order, cut itself off from the Church and from "true religion," becoming a sect, a "pseudo-religion," a heresy. All the religious movements of the Middle Ages were thus confronted with the alternative of either adopting the ecclesiastical forms of the *vita religiosa*, which is to say, becoming an order of monks, or separating itself from the ecclesiastical rules altogether and breaking with the Church itself, which is to say it became a sect, a heresy.

So the religious movements of the Middle Ages present themselves to the observer in the guise of orders and sects. The study of medieval religious history begins with these fixed forms; all the more so because historical research itself had its point of departure from these institutions or in a living connection with them, to a great extent. From the beginnings to the present day, the history of religious orders has been most effectively researched by members of the orders themselves; Protestant historical research has been most penetratingly involved with the history of sects and heresies, because Protestants believe they inherit and perfect the religious goals toward which sects strove. The historiography coming from the orders, as well as the Protestant historiography on heresy, must be commended for extraordinarily important contributions precisely because they combine the factual interests of the historian with the lively sympathy of those involved in something which is their own. On the other hand, their contributions have limits and weaknesses with weighty consequences for comprehending historical development as a whole. Historical investigation into a particular order is interested in the history of other orders or spiritual movements only insofar as they are necessary to understand the history of their own order. Their essential task is always that of knowing their own founder, his goals and accomplishments. This is always seen as the "first cause" of the rise of their order. The connections the founder had with contemporaries and religious or intellectual forces of the time are evaluated as mere "influences" which might have helped shape the efforts of the founder, but which are of secondary importance when compared with the founder's concrete historical and religious act, which was to found an order.

On the other side, confessional historiography, whether from the Protestant or the Catholic side, has always tended to seek out those aspects of the history of medieval sects and heresies which distinguish them most dramatically from the Catholic Church. Protestant histories of heresy continue Catholic anti-heretical polemics, but with the values reversed. They are interested primarily in doctrinal differences, and they assume that individual sects are mirror-opposites to the Catholic Church and its orders in their organization, their doctrine, and their "founders." They, too, are interested in the differences between the Church and its orders on the one side and heresy and sects on the other, rather than in their common positions and parallel evolution in the course of historical development.

This sort of historical research, conditioned by its religious and ecclesiastical standpoint, directs its efforts largely at institutions which continue to have living importance in the religious and ecclesiastical constitution of the present day, or at least—as is the case with the sects—can be seen as "forerunners" of later developments. The more important an order is today, the more we know for certain about its history; the more intensely a medieval sect can serve Protestants as a "witness to the truth" or a demonstration of the failure of the medieval Church to fulfill its religious mission, the more thoroughly historical research has concerned itself with it. On the other hand, those orders and sects which won no permanent, independent importance sink below the threshold of historical interest.

Surveys of church history have certainly fitted all the detailed research on the history of orders and sects into a general framework and sought to make the relationships among them visible. But they have depended on the results of a research which works from differing points of view with different questions, so they can only fill the white spaces between researched areas of religious development with connecting lines. The question is seldom posed whether the picture would not be essentially different if research perceived the history and character of the individual orders anew in all details through a panoramic vision of religious development in the Middle Ages, rather than starting with individual sects and their special experiences and then passing on to matters of detail.

There have been many attempts since the end of the nineteenth century to conceive the religious movements of the Middle Ages as a general historical process. But in each of these cases, interest in the social and economic significance of those movements has been made so primary that their religious sense and content were virtually ignored, or were distorted into mere subterfuges of the times to cover genuine motives and goals. If these attempts had not been left merely as a new "concept" of history in grand contours, if this "concept" itself had been used to interpret the tradition and explain historical developments in detail, then the prejudice that religious movements were basically social or even "proletarian" movements would have corrected itself.

The investigations which follow will cut a different path. They do not seek to prove and apply a preconceived "concept" of the importance and development of religious movements in the Middle Ages, but rather to describe the historical course of events and the historical connections themselves. They will attempt to grasp the original peculiarity, the historical forces and the religious goals of those movements from which the individual forms of religious orders and sects grew; they will consider the question of what events and decisions determined the development of religious movements into the various orders and sects. These investigations derive from the assumption that the rise of orders and sects was not a series of isolated, mutually independent developments formed only by the will and deed of a founder, nor by the accidental reception of a heretical doctrine; rather they belong together in historical relation to the total religious development of the West. This entails a double duty: on the one hand, the historian must show this common heritage, this emergence from a single religious movement in which religious forces and ideas originally operated in a similar manner, before forming into various orders and sects; on the other hand, the historian must recognize the factors which determined the articulation of the religious movement into its various forms, consisting of orders and sects. The goal of this labor will be to perceive what decisions brought these religious movements under the rules and forms of life of the medieval Church. This investigation will pursue developments only up to the point where the religious movement generated new forms and structures, and either orders or sects gain their independent evolution and forms. After so much study of the lives and peculiarities of individual orders and sects, the whole religious movement will be studied here as a common family tree, with the expectation of winning new conclusions about its religious nature and importance.

These purposes cannot be attained through a summary view which relies on the results of earlier detailed research and simply gathers it into a general framework. Rather, such a method of perception only proves its value when it places the course of development, the connections between the events, the historical facts and their importance in a new light, thus making them more comprehensible in all their details. Every individual step in the history of orders and heresies can demand a new interpretation and afford a new understanding if one considers it not merely in relation to the rise and development of individual orders and sects but rather in connection with the total religious movement in the course of which the various entities became differentiated. If this comprehensive interconnection of religious development is to be demonstrated and the series of decisions determining their evolution into special forms of religious life to be disclosed, research must penetrate into all the details of the history of orders and sects. Once an understanding better than that generated by traditional histories of orders and sects is won for all individual developments, while preserving a vision of the larger interconnections among religious developments not visible before, only then can we be sure that even such a thoroughly researched area as the medieval history of orders and sects is finally subject to a critical analysis which better explains the particular. This places the whole in a new light and perceives it from a different point of view.

It is impossible to summarize the results of this investigation in a few words at the outset. Only a few particularly important points will be mentioned here. Since the history of heresy has been primarily interested in dogmatic content, it has usually completely overlooked the fact that after the beginning of the twelfth century heretical movements burgeoned and were formed chiefly by the idea of evangelical poverty and apostolic preaching. As a result, the history of religious orders has not only failed to recognize the connection between the formation of orders in the twelfth century and the general religious movement, but it has been unable to evaluate the importance of the mendicant orders in their proper historical context. The result is that the decisive role of the policy of Innocent III, blazing the trail for the absorption of the religious movement into the structure of the hierarchical Church and hence first making possible the birth of the mendicant orders and the organization of the religious poverty movement and apostolic itinerant preaching into orders, has remained hidden. Before Innocent III, the hierarchical Church was stubbornly hostile to the entire religious movement; during his papacy, the transformation of the ecclesiastical rules was begun which made it possible for the ecclesiastical poverty movement, now organized in mendicant orders, to take over the struggle against heresy in the thirteenth century.

In the same way, research has overlooked the importance—even the existence—of the women's religious movement in the thirteenth century. It is significant that the women's religious movement has attracted attention only in the case of institutions similar to orders which still survive in scattered remnants in the beguinages of Belgium. In most cases this women's religious movement did not create its own autonomous orders, but rather was absorbed into the women's houses of the mendicant orders. Research on the history of orders has been content to see the initiative of individual founders of orders as the determining factor in the rise of these female orders, resulting in complete neglect of the existence of an autonomous, spontaneous religious movement among women, particularly in Germany. It has even overlooked the fact that the fate of the women's convents in the two mendicant orders was closely bound together; it has also been utterly unable to understand the struggles the two mendicant orders waged against accepting convents. This has led to misinterpretation of the original distinctiveness of the women's religious movement, which did not arise from propaganda for the mendicant orders at all. From an insight into these relationships, not only will many puzzling details of the history of orders be explained, but the preconditions will also be created for understanding the historical foundations of "German Mysticism" at the beginning of the fourteenth century. Denifle pointed the way a half-century ago, but despite all the zeal of subsequent research on mysticism, his suggestions bore little fruit. The following investigations will show how important a knowledge of the religious movement of the thirteenth century is for understanding the ecclesiastical preconditions, the religious content, and the linguistic form of "German Mysticism." They are intended to supplement the philosophical and philological research into mysticism through reference to the historical relationships from which "German Mysticism" arose and from which the connections between orthodox and heretical mysticism can be understood.[2]

CHAPTER 1

The Religious Movement in the Twelfth Century: "Apostolic Life" and "Christian Poverty"

The movement for ecclesiastical reform under Gregory VII completed the structure or *ordo* of the hierarchical Church, which rested on the idea of apostolic succession, reserving the execution of Christian salvation to those who had been ordained to it either directly or indirectly by the successors of Peter and the apostles. At the same time, the monastic reform movement originating in Cluny had begun to transform monasticism from a plethora of separate religious houses relying on their own efforts into a unified, centralized association, integrated within the ecclesiastical hierarchy by placing the leading houses directly under the curia. Both movements, the hierarchical as well as the monastic reform of the eleventh century, did not prevail in a struggle against other religious ideas, but they did assert themselves in struggles against the claims and force of temporal powers. Gregory VII himself made use of the same weapons which would later be turned against the hierarchical Church. He held that only worthy priests had the power to carry out their religious functions, so that he branded simoniac priests, who had not been called by the Church alone, as well as married and unchaste priests, to be illegitimate, ineffectual usurpers of the priestly office.[1] He also had such simoniac and unchaste priests as dared perform the mass or the other duties of ecclesiastical office prosecuted as heretics.[2]

Yet as soon as the hierarchical *ordo* of the Church had been perfected and prevailed, the idea of the "worthiness of the priest," having penetrated the consciousness of other groups, began to be turned against the concept of ecclesiastical ordination itself. Many who had been awakened by the Gregorian Reform Movement began to ask whether the ecclesiastical ordination of a priest should be the sole entitlement for carrying out the work of Christian salvation; whether the Church alone was called and ordained to realize the divine plan for salvation proclaimed by the gospels and the apostles solely through ecclesiastical representatives; whether each and every Christian might not be called by the command of the gospels and the example of the apostles to model his or her life on the gospels and apostolic standards; and whether anyone who was ordained by the Church but did not live as the gospels demanded and as the apostles had in fact lived could be a true priest. Out of such questions and doubts arose a religious consciousness which no longer saw the essence of Christianity as fulfilled in the Church alone as an order of salvation or in the doctrine of the Church alone as its dogma and tradition. Instead, this new consciousness sought to realize Christianity as a religious *way of life* immediately binding upon every individual genuine Christian, a commitment more essential to the salvation of his soul than his position in the hierarchical *ordo* of the Church or his belief in the doctrines of the Fathers of the Church and its theologians. The ecclesiastical order of salvation and the theological doctrinal structure had rather to prove their validity and commitment in terms of those biblical norms of Christian life obligating every true confessor of Christianity to follow the example of the apostles, meaning to abandon the goods of this world and work for the gospel in the discipleship of Christ, just as the apostles had done. These two concepts, the demand for Christian, evangelical poverty, as well as for apostolic life and work, became the foci of a new conception of the essence of Christianity, criticizing the Church order and doctrine which had obtained up to that time, supplying a new standard for evaluating the truly Christian life. Heretical phenomena in the region governed by the Roman Church before the Investiture Controversy, so far as we know, had demanded neither voluntary poverty nor apostolic preaching.[2a] The monastic reform movement, in its effort to renew Benedictine monasticism, had also demanded the renunciation of private property in all strictness, but it had never subscribed to an ''ideal of poverty'' or a renunciation of property on the part of the monastic community, but instead had sought substantial wealth for the houses.[3] Gregory VII fought simony and priestly marriage in order to win the day for the concept of *ordo*, but he never demanded either voluntary poverty of a Christian or the apostolic life of an individual.

Yet with the turn of the eleventh to the twelfth century, these two ideas emerged simultaneously in widely separated places, and they proceeded to determine the course of the religious movement. At the same time that a French preacher for the first time labeled as heretics people who asserted they were living the apostolic life, though they also proclaimed the dualistic doctrines of the Manichees and the ascetic implications that entailed,[4] the itinerant preacher Robert of Arbrissel[5] was wandering through northern France barefoot, with wild hair and beard and in poor clothing, gathering about him through his preaching the ''poor of Christ,'' who renounced all the goods of this world to join their master in wandering and poverty. A few years later (1114) two men were arrested in Bucy near Soissons who were believed to be heretical leaders; they admitted to holding *conventicula*, but not to propagating heretical doctrines. Although they swore that they neither taught nor believed other than the Church, and although they gave orthodox answers to all the questions of the episcopal inquisition, Guibert of Nogent, who participated in the investigation, accused them of holding the errors Saint Augustine had imputed in his polemical writings to the Manichees. Guibert added that matters which had once interested the learned alone had now descended to the unlearned, who had come to boast of leading the life of the apostles![6] At almost the same time, however, Norbert of Xanten was wandering the same region, having given up his promising career with the Imperial court and the archbishop of Cologne after a sudden conversion to ascetic rigor. He now trudged through France, gathering about himself the "poor of Christ" in the same manner as Robert of Arbrissel.

There was obviously a common motivation behind these contemporary episodes: the model of the apostles had become an ideal, expressing itself in a demand for evangelical itinerant preaching and voluntary Christian poverty. For the time being, however, no unified religious movement arose from these themes. In some cases, they led to novel forms of monasteries or orders following a brief transitional stage of apostolic itinerant preaching; in other cases, when tied with heretical ideas in open opposition to the hierarchical Church and persecuted by it to the death, they would come to conjure up the great heretical challenge to the twelfth-century Church. These two developments can only be studied separately, but their common motivations have to be kept in mind in order to understand the course and destiny of the movement for religious poverty, in which the two strands eventually reconverged into a single force after developing separately throughout the twelfth century.

1. The Heretical Movement of the Twelfth Century

The special character of the heretical movement of the twelfth century and the importance which the ideas of the apostolic life and Christian poverty had within it can best be illustrated by two letters from the middle decades of the century. In one of them, Abbot Evervin of Steinfeld reported to Bernard of Clairvaux about heretics interrogated in Cologne in 1143.[7] In the second, a monk named Heribert reports on heretics in the region of Périgueux under the leadership of a man named Poncius, otherwise unknown, probably around 1163.[8] These two letters are an improvement on many other documents about heresy in the twelfth century because they do not repeat the usual fantasies of Manichaean doctrines derived from old polemics against heresy but rather describe heretics on the basis of their own knowledge—in the case of Heribert the monk, with superstitious exaggeration, but in Abbot Evervin's case with thoughtful openness. The abbot had attended the interrogation of the heretics discovered in Cologne, and he gives their testimony without hostility or literary prejudice, in fact providing an honest account which shows he was deeply impressed by the religious content of their testimony.[9] Most of the heretics had returned to the Church and done penance, but the "heretic bishop" and his companions demanded a public disputation, under the presidency of the archbishop, in which learned representatives of their party were to participate. They declared themselves ready to give up their errors if disproved, but otherwise they intended to be faithful to their beliefs until death. The Cologne clergy did not submit to a disputation, preferring to attempt to convert them, but, as so often with heresy trials in the twelfth century, the mob intervened before matters were decided and dragged the heretics to the pyre. The heretics had sought to convince their judges by citing the gospels and the apostles to support their convictions. Because they were convinced they lived in keeping with the gospels and the example of the apostles, they claimed to represent the true Church, the true followers of Christ. Having no need for the goods of the world, like Christ's apostles they possessed neither house nor field nor cattle. In contrast to this, the Catholic clergy piled house upon house and field upon field, heaping up wealth. Even if the members of orders, monks and canons, did not have these goods as private property, still they held them in common. They, the heretics, were the "Poor of Christ" who moved restlessly and painfully from place to place like the apostles and martyrs, in the face of persecution, satisfied to have only enough to live on. The heretical words recorded by Abbot Evervin were filled with the unshakable certainty and security of faith:

> We hold this, that we are not of this world. You, who are lovers of this world, have the peace of this world, since you are of this world. You and your fathers have become pseudo-apostles, adulterating the word of Christ—we and our fathers, having become apostles, dwell in the grace of Christ, and shall remain in it unto the end of the age. To distinguish them, Christ tells us and you, "By their fruits you shall know them!" Our fruit is the way of Christ.[10]

The goal of these heretics is to follow Christ through an apostolic life in poverty and ceaseless religious activity, in keeping with the counsels of the gospels and the writings of the apostles.

Yet these thoughts are not peculiar to the heretics in Cologne. The monk Heribert portrays heresy in Périgord in Southern France with less understanding for their doctrine and way of life, but showing the same characteristics. They, too, assert they are living the apostolic life,[11] and they also believe they achieve this not simply by renouncing meat, by moderation in drinking wine, and by external compliance with other biblical counsels, but particularly through complete poverty, renouncing the use of money.[12] Just as was the case with the heretics of Cologne, they judged ecclesiastical life strictly by the norms of the Bible, and they accepted only what Scripture demanded.[13] They were thus intensely concerned with their own knowledge of Scripture,[14] and they were ceaselessly occupied as preachers, undertaking their wanderings barefoot.[15]

In Cologne as well as in Southern France, the idea of Christian poverty and apostolic life as a wandering preacher is essential to their stance as "heresy," and this idea indeed remains the main theme of heresy until the start of the thirteenth century, among Cathars as well as Waldensians. Leading the life of the apostles, being true followers of the apostles, is the heretics' basic claim, and their break with the Church followed from that.[16] Hence, the heretics were called "Good Christians," or simply "Good People," by all those who came in contact with them.[17] No impartial observer can doubt their genuine and passionate conviction that they were reviving and realizing true evangelical and apostolic Christianity in their lives. They demonstrated this through their readiness to suffer martyrdom for these convictions far too often for it to be considered a mere phrase. The first condition for understanding the religious movements of the Middle Ages is to take these convictions and claims seriously.

All the same, the Church combated these devotees of the apostolic life with all its might. There were three grounds for this. First of all, the idea that the counsels of the gospels and writings of the apostles were the uniquely binding measure for the Church as well as for every Christian[18] generated a decisively negative critique of the doctrines and usages of the Church, leading to rejection not only of the sacraments in their Catholic form, but also of the veneration of saints, prayers for the dead, the doctrine of purgatory, and so on. Secondly, the heretics who asserted they were leading the apostolic life in poverty did not recognize the *ordo* of the hierarchical Church, placing the legitimacy of ecclesiastical ordination in question. On the basis of their consciousness of having been called to carry out the gospels, they brought into being a competing church of "good Christians" with "perfect" or "elect" as clergy, and their "faithful" as congregations in precise analogy to the

Catholic Church, even developing a sort of episcopal organization.[19] Thirdly and last, in the course of the twelfth century the idea of poverty and apostolic itinerant preaching had come to be combined with dualistic doctrines in many areas, especially in Southern France. Increasingly influenced by speculative ideas from the Greek East, it yielded a strange rebirth for much of Manichee cosmogony and mythology. After the end of the twelfth century, Catholic polemic against heresy placed the greatest emphasis on this third point, on dualistic speculation and its abuses, particularly because the Cathars at least tried to justify themselves with citations from the New Testament. This tactic has so influenced perception that dualism has been stressed as the foundation of heresy ever since, with everything else seen to derive from dualism. To tell the truth, before the end of the twelfth century it is not the speculative problem of dualism which constituted the central conflict between heretics and Catholicism, but rather the questions of religious life and the Church. So far as we know, at the time of the emergence of heresy in the West in the first half of the eleventh century, dualistic doctrine was nowhere to be found. To be sure, Catholic literature designated the heretics as Manichees from the very beginning.[20] This often enticed ecclesiastical writers to read St. Augustine to discover what Manichees taught, then simply to ascribe their doctrines to the heretics of their own time.[21] When this did not happen, when they unmistakably dealt with the convictions and doctrines of contemporary heretics (even in official ecclesiastical documents on heresy), dualistic speculation either leaves little trace,[22] or it fades entirely into the background in comparison to the major question: whether the true Church of Christ resides with those who claim the apostolic succession, and thereby the full and exclusive right to ordain all Church offices, or whether it belonged to those who lived like the apostles as the gospel demanded.[23] In the twelfth century, dualistic speculation provided the philosophic "superstructure" for heresy's religious and moral demands. Dualism tells people more clearly what has to be done[24]—and this was the service dualism performed for the heretical movement in the twelfth century. For persons aroused by religious and ethical inclinations to think about the nature of the world, the Catholic doctrine of the world was infinitely harder to understand, much less comprehensible than the Manichaean doctrine. The Catholic world-picture, largely influenced both by Augustine's intellectual commitment against neo-Platonic monism on the one side and Manichaean dualism on the other, is neither monistic nor dualistic, since it recognized neither the unity and identity of all being with God nor the division of all being into the two principles of light and darkness, good and evil. Thus Augustine does not deny that evil exists, but he does deny it to be part of real existence: he interprets evil as a negation of the good. Neither of the two intellectual powers which had once struggled for the future of Christianity, monistic neo-Platonism and dualistic Manichaeism, disappeared from the scene. On the contrary, they have threateningly shadowed Christianity throughout the years. During the crisis of the hierarchical system which took place in the twelfth and thirteenth centuries, both of these threats returned to the Christian West from the Greek East. But that return was only possible because primitive religious movements with newly awakened spiritual needs were seeking speculative doctrinal systems and were capable of absorbing new religious and ethical drives.

In any case, dualistic speculation emerged more clearly after the end of the twelfth century. As a result, the religious movement split. In contrast to the Cathars, who followed Manichaean dualism and in turn were repeatedly divided by speculative sectarian disputes, there stood groups within the movement for religious poverty and apostolic itinerant preaching who not only did not follow the transition to dualism, but in fact combated it. Yet the old concept of a singular religious movement continued to pursue them, and the Church continued to persecute them, not as dualists, but for their "apostolic" claims. Even before this division over speculative problems took place, the major concerns of the religious movement were not dogma but questions of the proper religious life and the true Church. To overlook this is to misunderstand the coherence the religious movement had in this period.[25] The driving idea of the heretical movement of the twelfth century was to live according to the model of the apostles, to renounce all the goods of this world in voluntary poverty, to renew Christian life and pursue Christian doctrine by ceaseless wandering and preaching. This also entailed attacking the hierarchical Church and Catholic clergy as illegitimate successors to the apostles, insofar as they did not live in a truly Christian, evangelical and apostolic manner. All detailed criticisms of ecclesiastical institutions, of the sacraments (particularly marriage as a sacrament, the baptism of children, and the sacrament of the altar in the form of the Catholic mass), of purgatory, and the veneration of saints, arose from this basic idea of the heretics. Everything the heretics themselves used to replace the ceremonies of the Church (particularly the *consolamentum*, the laying on of hands according to the model of Paul, which communicates the Holy Spirit and has the claim to be legitimate ordination) also arises from that basic principle.

Some further remarks are needed in order to clarify the social foundations of the twelfth-century heretical movement. According to an assertion constantly repeated and seldom disputed or doubted, heresy, including the Cathar movement in the twelfth century,[26] spread primarily within the lowest social strata, particularly among "craftsmen." As a result of this perception, since the end of the nineteenth century, historical research[27] has tended to see heretical movements and associated phenomena as a sort of "proletarian movement." But such an assertion is false, applying in no sense to the religious movements of the twelfth century, and only marginally to the thirteenth.

Two things have caused people to believe that heresy spread primarily in the lowest social classes, particularly among artisans. The first is that Catholic writers often described heretics as *rusticani* or *rustici*, or as *idiotæ et illiterati*. The second is the frequent description of Cathars as *texterants*, weavers.

If the heretics are called *rusticani* or *rustici*, that does not mean they were peasants, but rather that they did not have academic training.[28] The term *idiotæ et illiterati* means exactly the same thing. It really says nothing about the social origins of the persons designated, nothing more than that they were not trained clerics. *Rusticanus* and *rusticus* are antonyms of *doctus* or *sapiens*.[29] Clerical writers[30] all denigrated the fact that people without academic, literary training dared to assert they knew better than a theologically trained clergy, which is why they stressed that the heretics were *rusticani* or *idiotæ et illiterati*.[31] They did not stop to consider that the apostles themselves, the heretics' supreme model, had once been called *idiotæ et sine literis* by the priests and scribes.[32] When Francis, the son of a wealthy merchant, called himself an *idiota* and even a *pazzus*,[33] citing the model of the apostles, he silenced learned mockery of pious simplicity for a time—at least until learned theologians from his own order took the field against heretics they called *idiotæ et illiterati*.

Even if the titles of *rusticani, rustici, idiotæ*, and *illiterati* tell us nothing at all about the social position of the heretics, still the French term for the heretics, *texterants*, weavers, would seem to indicate a social level where heresy was at home. The notion that heresy spread extensively among weavers was never asserted in sources of the twelfth century; rather, the term "weavers," *texterants, textores*, was simply the proper name for heretics in the French-speaking area, equivalent to different names used in other areas: Cathars in Germany,[34] Arians in Provence,[35] Patarenes in Italy. Just as was later the case, these names, along with those of "Waldensians" or *pauperes de Lugduno*,[36] described only the "perfect," the actual preachers of heresy, who wandered through the world in keeping with the example of the apostles.[37] These words were never used for their adherents, their congregations, the *credentes* or *fautores*. The question then, is why these wanderers traveling as preachers in the apostolic model were called "weavers." "From the practice of weavers," Eckbert of Schönau responds, "since they say that the true faith of Christ and the true worship of Christ does not exist save in their gatherings, which they hold in cellars and weaving-sheds and in underground dwellings of this sort."[38] Why did these heretical wandering preachers come to be weavers? Because they were already weavers by profession and origin? Stephan of Bourbon[39] tells about a priest in the bishopric of Toul who had been seduced by the heretics and set out for Milan together with forty members of his parish to have themselves completely trained in heresy. There he surrendered his priestly status and took up weaving. In this case a weaver was not made into a heretic, but rather a heretic became a weaver. There is nothing against the assumption that most heretical "weavers" had similar origins[40]—and the precedent of Saint Paul, who supported himself on his journeys as a rug-weaver, might have played a role as well.[41] It was part of the heretics' apostolic ideal to live from the work of their own hands, without earning more than was needed to satisfy the basic needs of life.[42] Weaving, the very craft which was the first to develop into an industry demanding labor in exchange for subsistence wages, was obviously the "chosen profession" most suited to heretic preachers, who seldom stayed in one place for long. In the chief region for heresy, in Southern France and Provence, this heretic's craft grew by the end of the twelfth century to become a true "heretic industry," with its own enterprises for the preparation of wool and the making of broadcloth, and its own merchandising. In this manner the activities of members and adherents (including female) were organized, economic links were created, and support assured for the wandering preachers.[43] All of this clearly indicates that the designation of heretics as "weavers" had nothing to do with origins among artisans, nor with any particularly strong participation of the lowest social groups in heresy. Weavers and artisans did not become heretics, heretics became weavers. It became the occupation of choice in which they could most conveniently unite their religious activities with their economic needs.[44]

If general terms for the heretics give us no information about the connection of heresy to particular social levels, it is necessary to collect and sift individual reports in the sources concerning the social origin of particular heretics. This produces an entirely different picture. Guibert of Nogent names one of the two heretics condemned in 1114 as a mere *rusticus*, uneducated, but the other, *frater Ebrardus*, was probably a monk. Under Archbishop Bruno of Trier (1102/24) two clerics and two laymen were arrested as heretics at Iwers in the Ardennes (*Gesta Trev*. c. 20, *MG Scr*. 8, 193–94). The monk Heribert writes on heresy in

Périgord: "In this seduction were many, including not only nobles who abandoned their property, but clerics, priests, monks and nuns also joined in." Bernard's secretary Gaufred (*Recueil* 15, 599) relates that, not long before Bernard's arrival in Toulouse (1145), the heretics "seduced one of the judges of the city together with his wife, so that they left their property and resettled in a village which was full of heretics, and none of their neighbors could convince them to return." Bernard himself says (Sermon 65, *PL* 65. 1092): "Clergy and priests are to be found among them, untonsured and bearded, having abandoned their ecclesiastical flocks." According to Evervin's account, the heretics of Cologne in 1143 asserted that "many of our clerics and monks" (*plures ex nostris clericis et monachis*) belonged to them. Archbishop Hugh of Rouen (died 1164) directed his writing *Contra hereticos* particularly against all those "who left the clergy and went over to heresy."[44a] In 1172 a cleric Robert, "rather subtly literate, but to no use" (*subtiliter quidem, sed inutiliter litteratus*) was burned in Arras because he was unable to purge himself through the ordeal of the hot iron against the accusation "that he not only was a heretic, but that he also favored and defended heretics."[44b] According to the Annals of the Monastery of Anchin, "Nobles, non-nobles, clerics, knights, rustics, virgins, widows and married women"[44c] were accused of heresy at the Council in Arras in 1183. In 1206 Bishop Diego disputed in Servian (between Montpellier and Béziers) with an Albigensian Theoderich, who had earlier been named William and had been a canon of the church in Nevers, but who had been seduced into heresy by his uncle, the knight Evrard of Châteuneuf. After his uncle's condemnation in Paris in 1201 he had gone to Provence and there played a large role among the heretics.[44d] A *miles* answered the question posed by Bishop Fulko of Toulouse why he and his like did not drive the heretics out of the region: "we cannot, since we were raised with them, and we can see many relatives living decently among them."[44e]

In each of these cases, it was not a question of adherents or friends of heretics, of *credentes* or *fautores*, but of "heretics" themselves, preachers wandering in apostolic poverty. And these witnesses are not selected by any special criteria, since hardly any sources have been found saying anything more about the social origins of heretics among the documents until the start of the thirteenth century.[45] These documents tell us heresy did not recruit primarily out of the lowest social levels, the "proletariat." Rather, wealthy townsmen, priests, and monks often joined the ranks of wandering heretic preachers; it was this participation of clergymen as well as prominent and wealthy persons in the heretical movement which was remarkable to contemporaries. It was already noted that women, in keeping with the apostolic model, were at work among the heretics as well, for they believed they could say with Paul: "Don't we have the power to bring along a sister, as do other apostles?"[46]

If the social composition of adherents to heresy is examined,[47] there is just as little evidence the lower classes were inclined to heresy, either exclusively or even predominantly. This is clearest in Southern France. When Bernard of Clairvaux tried to preach against heresy in Verfeil in 1145, the members of the higher classes (*qui majores erant*) left the church, and the rest of the people soon joined them. Bernard followed them outside to preach in the street, but the wealthy went into their houses, leaving only the commoners (*plebecula*) to listen, but these could hardly understand a word, since the *majores* sought to drown him out with their own noise.[48] Bernard confirmed that it was the upper strata of the townsmen and the nobility which sympathized with the heretics in other towns as well.[49] One chronicler expressly notes that heresy in the County of Toulouse about 1177 had not only blinded the simple folk, but also the clergy and the secular grandees,[50] and that it only took one look at the situation in Southern France to see that it was precisely the leading classes and a great portion of the nobility which sided with heresy against the ecclesiastical hierarchy.[51] Bernard of Clairvaux[52] already asserted what has often been repeated ever since,[53] that the upper classes in general and the nobility in particular promoted and protected the heretical doctrine of religious poverty out of greed, a lust for money and land, not for religious reasons. They desired to enrich themselves at the expense of the goods of the Church. Such motivations might have actually played a role with many of the politically interested lords of Provence, but it could not have led to the participation of virtually the entire nobility, the close attachment of the wives of nobles to heretical preachers, and the conversion of many wealthy nobles into voluntarily poor wandering preachers. Religious ideas and demands were always decisive, and insofar as our sources can answer the question of the impact of these ideas on various social levels, it is certain that many clerics, nobles and wealthy burghers adhered to heresy. There is not the slightest trace of a "proletarian" membership.[54]

2. Apostolic Itinerant Preaching and the Rise of New Orders

In his sermons on heresy, Bernard of Clairvaux raised the question of how the Church should proceed against heretics if it wanted neither to approve error nor to be overcome by it. He recommended a very simple measure: the men and women who live with one another and travel in the strictest chastity should form communities separate from one another in which they could fulfill their vows of chastity in common and under observation without providing opportunity for suspicion and offense, as had been the case before. Whoever was not ready to agree to this arrangement could justly be ejected from the Church as a heretic.[55] This proposal makes it clear that, in Bernard's eyes, the heretical movement was primarily a problem of ecclesiastical life, not dogma: he did not see his most pressing mission to be fighting or disproving the erroneous doctrines of the heretics; rather his chief task was preserving ecclesiastical order against novel and suspicious forms of life embodied in the religious movement, incorporating the religious movement into existing structures of religious houses and orders.[56]

We shall see that to a high degree this principle actually determined the attitude of the Church toward the religious movement. For nearly a half-century before Bernard's sermon, the tactic of incorporation had proved decisive whenever there was a question whether the movement for apostolic poverty was of the Church or heretical.

At the beginning of the twelfth century, when "Manichee" heretics emerged, other representatives of the idea of apostolic life and Christian poverty arose as well, wandering through the land, renouncing all possessions in imitation of the apostles, exhorting to penitence and peace, as well as agitating against the sins of the clergy.[57] These wandering preachers are distinguishable from the heretics described by contemporary witnesses only by the fact that their efforts were legalized by authorities of the Church, and that they guarded themselves against any contact with heterodox teachings such as Manichee dualism. In several cases, the Church in fact did grant such wandering preachers license to function. Robert of Arbrissel, once advisor to the bishop of Rennes, then leader of a hermit community in the forest of Craon, received permission from Urban II to be an itinerant preacher in February 1096.[58] Bernard of Thiron, who joined Robert in 1101, was supposed to have received the office of a *predicator publicus* from Paschal II in Rome.[59] In 1101, a former monk from Lausanne named Henry received permission from Bishop Hildebert of Le Mans to preach in his diocese.[60] Norbert of Genepp, a canon of Xanten[61] from a baronial family, who had once been accused of illicit preaching at a synod in Fritzlar,[62] was empowered by Pope Gelasius II to act as a wandering preacher in November 1118.[63] Yet in all of these cases, there were soon second thoughts and protests, and the Church always moved against the free exercise of wandering preaching. This is because the same troubles accompanied those wandering preachers, licensed by the Church, as did the heretical preachers. On the one hand their apostolic preaching always scourged the sins of the clergy with reckless abandon, stimulating opposition from groups favoring the hierarchy as well as threatening to undermine general respect for the hierarchical order.[64] On the other hand, the preachers gathered a crowd of male and female followers whose unregulated, unstable common life offended the principles of a stable ecclesiastical order in the same way as had the efforts of the heretics. It was particularly the participation of women in this novel type of apostolic life which demanded the intervention of the Church, just as had been the case with the heretics.[65]

After a few years as wandering preachers, Robert of Arbrissel, Bernard of Thiron, Vitalis of Savigny, and Norbert of Xanten all settled down to found orders. It is not easy to prove their ecclesiastical role in each case,[66] but the facts make a connection appear highly likely. Robert traveled the country for four years as an itinerant preacher with a crowd of followers; everywhere his advent offended the higher clergy. At the end of 1100 he appeared at a synod in Poitiers, presided over by two cardinals. Immediately afterwards, he established the house of Fontevrault, placing his female followers under strict enclosure and laying the cornerstone for a new congregation. It is to be presumed that this matter was discussed at the synod, and that Robert calmed accusations raised there by assuring the synod that he would no longer allow his adherents to follow him in mixed groups. He would henceforth separate the sexes and house the women in convents.[67]

Norbert of Xanten became the founder of an order for similar reasons. After he had wandered for a year through France, at a synod at Reims he asked the new Pope Calixtus II for a renewal of his license as an itinerant preacher.[68] It is not entirely certain that this request was granted. It appears that neither the pope nor the bishop of Laon were ready to allow Norbert to continue to wander with his retinue as a free itinerant preacher. After the end of the Reims synod, Norbert began looking for a new area of activity which would put an end to his unstable, itinerant preaching and place him and his entourage in a secure niche within the Church system. Norbert approved these plans only with the condition that he should continue to be able to remain true to his principle of living an apostolic life, in harmony with the gospels.[69] After an attempt to transfer control of a community of Augustinian canons in Laon to him failed due to the canons' opposition to Norbert's religious demands, the bishop of Laon helped Norbert to found a house in keeping with his ideas. Thus arose Prémontré.

It is unknown whether any attempt was made to neutralize Henry of Lausanne by guiding his group into monastic orders. He himself was obligated at a synod in Pisa in 1134 to surrender his activities as a wandering preacher and become a monk in Cîteaux,[70] but he did not keep this commitment. So far as we know, he never attempted to enclose his followers in monastic communities. He was pursued anew as a heretic, violently attacked by Bernard of Clairvaux,[71] and finally imprisoned.[72]

Without being able to discover all the details, it can still be determined that only those itinerant preachers found a place in the Church who—whether on their own decision or as a result of the Church's command—created a new, stable form of life for their members through founding religious houses, congregations, or orders, in which the fulfillment and pursuit of religious principles and vows could be strictly controlled.[73] Itinerant preachers who did not create a regulated existence for followers they had wrenched from the paths of worldly life were persecuted by the Church with full severity. The principle Bernard of Clairvaux came to recommend against the apostolic heresy of his own time had been already determining the attitude of the Church toward the apostolic movement since the beginning of the twelfth century.

The new religious houses and orders thus established by itinerant preachers in France preserved the mark of their origins to a remarkable degree. Unlike all earlier new monastic creations, orders and congregations (particularly the Cistercians) which arose from the bosom of established monasticism, they were not reforms of Benedictine monasticism arising from Benedictine houses. Instead, they were truly novel creations, attempts to capture in a new form of cloistered life a religious movement which had originated outside the monastery. Since this religious movement had not been exclusively male (as had been the case with all reform movements within Benedictine monasticism),[74] these new houses could not be purely masculine affairs. Housing the female followers of the itinerant preachers in religious houses became a particularly pressing need. This explains the novelty of the new religious establishments, the Fontevraulters as well as the Premonstratensians. Robert,[75] as was the case with Norbert, established houses for men and women together, so that within the houses themselves a particularly strict division was introduced. The women's houses, or double-houses, which arose in this manner from the itinerant preaching movement were, for a long time, the only places where women swept up in the religious movement could live the common life in the strict asceticism and discipline of an order. In Robert's establishment of Fontevrault and its branches, where the Rule of Benedict served as the basic rule, amended and intensified by novel statutes,[76] the female element predominated. Leadership was even vested in the hands of a woman, and male members served primarily to take care of the religious and economic needs of female communities. This female leadership was probably the chief reason for the rapid decline of Robert's community of Fontevrault. Its origin and rapid expansion was due to Robert's itinerant preaching, and after his death (c. 1117), this stimulus was gone. Robert did not know how to create a monastic congregation which could develop through its own efforts, and his female houses equally lacked support for significant future development and growth. Without a link to a dynamic male order, female houses were never able to enjoy strong, steady development.[77]

The participation of women gained far greater importance in the houses of the order founded by Norbert of Xanten. The most important and dependable witness for Norbert's efforts in founding Prémontré, Herman of Laon,[78] is particularly careful to praise Norbert for placing women as well as men under the strict discipline of his order. Herman sees Norbert's greatest accomplishment precisely in the fact that he did not take in men alone, as did the Cistercians, but also women, prescribing for them a life even harsher than the men—without stemming the influx of women desiring to enter his houses.[79] The beginnings of the house of Prémontré and its daughters are still too uncertain to be able to recognize clearly the female role.[80] They were not the dominant element in the religious communities, as was the case at Fontevrault, but they instead lived as *inclusi* or *conversi* in strict enclosure at male houses, under the leadership of abbots, providing domestic services for the brothers; initially they did not even participate in the choir service.[81] The stream of women of all classes, particularly from the nobility,[82] must have been surprisingly great, since Herman of Laon can speak of a thousand women in Premonstratensian houses in the bishopric of Laon by the middle of the century, and ten thousand in the entire order.

The order of Norbert of Xanten followed a course of development which took it further and further from its original conviction and closer to that of the older monastic orders, particularly the Cistercians. Just as the obligation to care for souls declined as their monastic duties rose, they soon surrendered the other peculiarity which arose from the origin of the order in itinerant preaching: they began to exclude women, at first by banning the establishment of new double houses,[83] and finally by excluding them from the order altogether, barring the establishment of new female houses. But it was precisely this feminine branch, rejected by the order as it grew more truly "monastic," which gained in importance for the religious movement, and would profoundly influence the destiny of the religious movement in the northern lands.[84]

3. Ecclesiastical Measures against Heresy and the Religious Movement of the Twelfth Century

If the heresy of the twelfth century had been a "sect" with a "founder" and particular dogmatic errors like the heresies of earlier times, the Church would have been able to combat it as it had others before. But heresy in the twelfth century was a religious movement without a "founder" and hence without a single name, lacking a solid organization and the universal mark of earlier heresies, namely, a particular heretical doctrine defining the nature of the heresy. Instead, there was an emphatic concept of religious life, thought authorized by the gospels and apostolic writings, and it was here where it parted company with the Catholic Church.

This characteristic of the new heresy profoundly disturbed Catholic contemporaries,[85] which is the only possible explanation for the confused, indecisive, and uncertain stance the Church took toward the religious movement throughout the twelfth century. Not only was there no unified, clear standard for punishing heresy,[86] but there were not even any clear, unambiguous guides for judging which phenomena were to be regarded as heretical. Before Innocent III, the Church did nothing to recapture religious forces developing within the heretical movement and incorporate them into its own orders.

In the first instance, it was the bishops who should have made the necessary decisions concerning heresy and the religious movement.[87] Yet their attitude during most heresy trials of the twelfth century demonstrates to an almost frightening degree the ecclesiastics' confusion and indecision. Virtually none of them knew where to commence on his own authority when confronted with someone suspected of heresy. Either he asked another for advice, or he passed the decision to the "judgment of God," delaying it so long that it was only resolved by the lynch-justice of "the people."[88] One may search these episcopal measures in vain for any indication that even one prelate was aware that these questions demanded religious decisions with profound implications for the destiny of the Church.

The curia did not take a principled position on the question of heresy and the religious movement until almost the end of the twelfth century. The curia provided neither guidance nor standards to the bishops by which they were to punish heresy, nor did the curia indicate how the religious movement was to be treated;[89] it had not even done anything to prevent the apostolic-poverty movement from falling into heresy. Before Alexander III, all decisions made at the councils in the twelfth century concerning heresy concentrated on the special conditions in Southern France—Gascony, Toulouse, and Provence—where heresy had won general importance due to its ties with the rank and file of the nobility; ecclesiastical measures were aimed less at the heretics than at their allies in a struggle between the Roman Church and the nobles and rulers.

At a synod held in the presence of Calixtus II in Toulouse in 1119, all who denied the eucharist, baptism of children, ordination of priests, and marriage were excommunicated as heretics and delivered over to worldly powers for punishment. Their *defensores* were threatened with the same penalty. The decree of the council neglected to give these heretics a name. It established the rejection of those four sacraments as a criterion for heresy, but to designate the heretics it added the words that they simulated the appearance of a religion (*religionis speciem simulantes*).[90] This formula had always proved useful to the Church when stripping heresy of its claim to religious legitimacy. During the entire twelfth century, however, the Church shirked its obligation to set the limits between valid, genuine religiosity and "simulated" *speciem religionis*.

The ruling of Toulouse was repeated word for word at the Second Lateran Council in 1139 under Innocent II, without being supplemented by further definitions.[91] The primary concern remained the situation in Southern France, which had also preoccupied the Council of Toulouse. In the same way a council at Reims under Eugenius III threatened protectors of heretics in Gascony and Provence alone with excommunication and interdict, without bothering to describe the heretics themselves in greater detail or giving them a name.[92] A council which met in Montpellier under Alexander III in 1162 threatened secular princes with excommunication if they did not heed bishops in acting against heretics,[93] but since this ruling cited the corresponding decision at the Lateran Council of 1139, it was just as completely fixated on Southern French conditions. Likewise a council held at Tours in the pope's presence the next year dealt only with heresy in the region of Toulouse, in Gascony, and bordering areas.[94] Finally, the Third Lateran Council of 1179 under Alexander III did not deal with the question of heresy or the religious movement in general, but only passed measures dealing with heretics in the region of Albi, Toulouse, *et in aliis locis.*[95] At the urging of Abbot Henry of Clairvaux, Southern French bishops, and Count Raymond of Toulouse, it was decided to be severe with the Southern French heretics: the council went so far as to invoke a crusade of secular princes against the heretics, ordering the confiscation of the property of heretics, denying them Christian burial, even forbidding anyone—as the synod of Tours had already done—from trading with them or giving them lodging. Yet the council once more failed to deal with the question of who was being pursued as a heretic. The enumeration of a few common terms for heretics was supposed to suffice to describe those against whom the measures were directed.[96] The curia still had not accepted its obligation to intervene on its own against the religious movement, leaving it to ecclesiastical and political authorities in Southern France to intervene as they wished against whatever they might think heretical.

As was the case with conciliar decisions made with papal cooperation, all attempts to restrict heresy through papal legates and missionaries were restricted to the Southern French theater.[97] Before Alexander III, only the conditions in Gascony, southern Languedoc, and Provence, where heresy had also become a political problem, attracted the attention of the curia to the question of heresy. No attempt, however, was being made to deal with heresy or the religious movement as a whole, in all countries and in all its forms.

Twice during his pontificate, Alexander III took an independent position on the religious movement and heresy. It is precisely these two cases which reveal most clearly the curia's indecision and confusion toward these phenomena, as well as the fact that this indecisiveness could not continue indefinitely.

Toward the end of 1162, between the two councils where strict measures against the heretics of Southern France were taken in Alexander's presence, a number of people from the towns of Flanders who had been accused as heretics by the archbishop of Reims came to the curia in Tours.[98] In a letter, King Louis VII of France supported accusations against the heretics, calling them Manichees or the "more common" term of *populicani*, mentioning that their way of life could give the false impression that they were better than they were.[99] He also made the strange remark that the archbishop could have earned the sum of 600 marks of silver had he let these people off.[100] Since the archbishop had not agreed, the accused turned to the curia, which had been informed in the meantime by both the archbishop and then by King Louis. As a result they were received by Alexander III severely and in an unfriendly manner, as he himself informs us. They insisted, in fact, they had nothing to do with heresy; they offered some letters in their favor, the content of which remains unknown. The decision of what to do with these Flemish burghers, accused of heresy because of their religious manner of life, rested with the pope, but the pope was unable to reach a decision. At first he tried to pass the case back to the archbishop, sending letters along with the accused which would improve their position before the archbishop. But the accused would not agree; they did not want to have their case judged in Reims but at the curia. On the other hand, the pope did not want to make a decision until he had consulted with the French king, the archbishop of Reims, and other men. What happened then is unknown. Particularly telling is a statement of Alexander III in a letter to the archbishop of Reims. The question of whether or not the Flemish burghers were heretics would simply be left open, and he gave no guidelines for how the matter should be clarified. He only warned in general terms against harsh measures, for it was better to release the guilty than to condemn the innocent, and men of the Church were better advised to use excessive caution than excessive strictness.[101]

Although the outcome of this case is not known, it is remarkable for two reasons. First, it deals with persons whose appearance and even their seemingly praiseworthy way of life had excited suspicion of heresy, but who expected to win recognition of their orthodoxy at the curia. Second, it shows how undecided the curia was toward such religious phenomena, insofar as they were not implicated in the politically sensitive situation in Southern France. It was a precise foreshadowing of the events at the Third Lateran Council in 1179.

Just as the burghers of Flanders went to the curia at Tours in 1162 to justify themselves against the accusation of the archbishop of Reims, so Waldes and his companions came to Rome[102] in 1179 after the bishop of Lyon had expelled them from his diocese for violating a ban on their preaching.[103] In this case, however, we are better informed about the origins, attitudes, and goals of the men the curia was judging than we are with the Flemish burghers of 1162. We also know exactly how the case turned out. The wealthy merchant Waldes in Lyon was by no means the first person to choose living according to the teachings of the gospels as the surest way to perfection, giving up his riches, his family, and his social position to live as a poor and homeless man as the apostles had lived. Many others had made this conversion from bourgeois prosperity to religious poverty in order to join heretic preachers.[104] In all likelihood, Waldes underwent his conversion with some knowledge of forerunners, and in any case he acted in an atmosphere influenced by heresy. It was his own desire not to separate from the Church and its faith which made a difference. He sought advice not from heretical masters but from priests and theologians of the Roman Church. He had the Holy Scriptures translated by clerics in order to discover on his own how he could truly lead his life in keeping with the gospels.[105] As a result, he began to live precisely as the heretics did, committing himself to voluntary poverty and apostolic itinerant preaching. Soon companions, who had also distributed their goods to the poor, joined him, preaching along with him against the sins of the world and exhorting to penance.[106] When this was forbidden by the archbishop of Lyon, they disobeyed him, because this ban appeared to contradict the biblical counsel to preach the gospel to all creatures. Like the apostles, they wished to obey God more than men (Acts 5:29). They still did not believe they had by any means separated from the Roman Church. Instead, they went to the curia, convinced that the successor of Peter would not forbid them what Christ himself had commanded all those who followed him to do. They hoped Alexander III and the council would recognize their life of voluntary poverty, and that he would grant them license for itinerant preaching of the gospels on the basis of the biblical translation Waldes had hired a priest to prepare in Lyon. He presented this translation to the curia for examination.[107] This act of the Waldensians presented the highest authority in the Church, the pope and council acting together, with the decision of how the Church was to treat the idea of voluntary poverty and apostolic itinerant preaching. Heretical doctrines against the sacraments, which were asserted as grounds for fighting poor itinerant preachers, did not apply to Waldes and his companions. Through their conduct, they had clearly stated their desire to submit themselves to the Roman curia.

The pope and the council completely failed to rise to the challenge of this decision, and they were incapable of grasping its significance. The curia had no objections to their commitment to voluntary poverty. Alexander was said to have praised Waldes for it and embraced him.[108] They do not appear even to have investigated the translations presented for their correctness and orthodoxy. The right to preach was made dependent on a theological examination. So far there was nothing objectionable in the curia's procedure, except for the fact that the curia did not take the matter seriously, as Walter Map, spokesman of the investigating commission, demonstrated beyond a doubt. The curia had no idea of the importance of the matter, and it showed no understanding of the nature and intention of the religious movement. This was already demonstrated by the choice of the man to lead the investigation by a commission of theologians and jurists. Walter Map, representative of the English King Henry II at the council, was a man of the world with a good eye for what was amusing or interesting, but he had no perception of what was spiritually important and politically essential. When he was inexplicably given this responsible office, he himself declared it had seemed laughable to carry out an examination at all.[109] As it was, he turned it into a comedy, letting his prideful, mocking laughter sound. After the persons examined agreed they believed in God the Father, the Son, and the Holy Spirit, Walter Map asked them if they believed in the

Mother of Christ. They naturally answered "yes." This answer provoked a peal of laughter in the learned assembly which was as incomprehensible to the itinerant preachers from Lyon as it is even today for any layman without special knowledge of the history of dogma. The examination was thus at an end, and the theological incapacity of the Waldensians was taken as proved. They were not given general permission to preach, and Alexander III instructed them that they were only permitted to preach if they were asked to by priests.[110]

The frivolity with which such a weighty matter of Church policy was decided should not cause one to overlook the fact that the rejection of the Waldensians by the pope and council was not due merely to the incapacity or pride of individual participants. Rather, the cause lay deep in convictions then held concerning the nature of the Church and its order. To be sure, the attitude of the curials Walter Map represented emerges from his writing, filled with pride for their theological training and membership in the hierarchy of the Church. Of course they conceived nothing but contempt, mockery, and disdain for these presumptuous laymen, these *idiotœ et illiterati*, who felt themselves called to preach and who believed they could be clerics without being theologians. Even such a man as Walter Map could not avoid the impression that there were deeper questions involved, and that the entire hierarchical Church in its accepted form was threatened with disruption. Significantly enough, he expressed this impression only as anxiety over his own position. "They are still humble and shy today and act as if they barely dare to come in. If they ever get in, they will throw us out."[111] This expresses not only concern for his own job, but concern for the unchanging, untouchable order of the hierarchical Church itself. As taciturn as the sources on the Church's Waldensian decision and its motivation are, the sense and the motivation of this decision can be recognized and understood as soon as one remembers the vision of the hierarchical *ordo* of the Church as it was seen by the entire Church in the days of Alexander III. This vision would be sacrificed by Innocent III in favor of the mendicant orders, but it was still being stubbornly defended in the middle years of the thirteenth century by representatives of older ecclesiastical views, particularly William of St. Amour. It was precisely in this late defense of a hierarchical *ordo* abandoned by the curia, in the polemics of William of St. Amour, that it became particularly clear what was meant when the Lateran Council forbade the Waldensians to take up the office of preaching, "insofar as they are not called on by the priests to do so." William of St. Amour once more presents that entire rigid system of ecclesiastical order which had been undisputed until Innocent III. The right to preach and care for souls was exclusively reserved for those called to it by God. God called not just the twelve apostles and their successors, the bishops, and the seventy-two disciples of the Lord and their successors, the priests, but also their deputies, the archdeacons and vicars—but no one else, neither monks nor laymen. And no one, not even the pope, could license anyone to preach and care for souls outside of this immutable order of those God called to it—unless persons called by God ask someone else to preach in their area of office.[112] Bishops and priests had always been warned precisely against permitting alien preachers to come in.[113] At the most, a few men had been able to break this strict structure of ecclesiastical office and serve as itinerant preachers in exceptional circumstances, with special papal licenses and the concurrence of local bishops and pastors. Since itinerant preaching by the religious poverty movement and heretics had spread, even such special licenses were no longer granted. When the Lateran Council of 1179 told the Waldensians they should not dare to preach *nisi rogantibus sacerdotibus*, this meant in practice only he could preach who had been called by the immovable hierarchical order, *qui vocatus est* according to the perceptions of the old Church. Walter Map had not rejected the claim of the Waldensians to a public role in the Church casually or out of mere personal pride or concern for his own position. Rather he did so out of his consciousness that he was one of those—even if one of the least[114]—"who had been called" to act on behalf of the genuine, valid order of the Church. Thus a stubborn clinging to the old ecclesiastical hierarchical form had the result of excluding new religious forces from the Church.

The representatives of a second religious congregation had to depart from the Lateran Council with the same defeat the Waldensians endured, after having presented similar wishes there. These people from the towns of Lombardy, called the *Humiliati*, distinguished themselves from the itinerant preachers of Lyon by the fact that they sought to live in an evangelical way without giving up their lives as burghers, including family and home, while renouncing fashionable luxury, lying, oath-taking, and litigiousness. On account of their evangelical form of life, the *Humiliati* were denounced as heretics—*patareni, boni homines*.[115] Yet they not only rejected heresy, they actually desired to combat it actively. The idea of combining the confession of the evangelical life with struggle against heresy, strengthening the defense of Catholic faith by conceding nothing to the heretics for living the evangelical life, first clearly appeared with the *Humiliati*. For that reason, they not only asked the curia and the council for permission to lead an evangelical way of life, but they also requested license to work against heretics in preaching and congregating. Alexander III treated them exactly as he had the Waldensians. He approved their religious way of life, but he strictly forbade them to preach publicly or to hold gatherings of their supporters.[116]

Through these decisions against Waldensians and *Humiliati*, the curia demonstrated it was not ready to tolerate the religious poverty movement, which expressed itself in apostolic itinerant preaching or congregations, within the structure of the Church. Rather it preferred to ban them, and when groups did not submit, to persecute them as heretics even if they did not vary doctrinally from the Church, even if they distanced themselves expressly from heresy, even if they were willing to place themselves in the service of the Church. New congregations of Waldensians and *Humiliati* (and possibly many others of which we do not know), who wanted to live like heretics but teach like the Church, who wanted to combine orthodox faith with evangelical life, were rejected by the curia in 1179. The curia was not spared the opportunity to see the error of this policy later and to make it good, so far as could be done. Yet before this turn of curial policy was made toward the religious movement, the curia made one more effort to execute their old policy in full force, sweeping away all the manifold entities which had arisen from the religious movement.

The actions of Alexander III at the Lateran Council did not cause the Waldensians and *Humiliati* to cease preaching and creating congregations. After at most brief hesitation, both groups continued their earlier activities in full awareness of their higher calling.[117]

Alexander's successor Lucius III found this situation on his accession and drew logical conclusions from it. When the strength of the curia was freed for the first time, after the conclusion of the struggle with Frederick I, and was able to address the pressing internal needs of the Church, Lucius published a major decree on the treatment of heresy with the agreement of the Emperor, in Verona on 4 November 1184. This decree represented the first systematic, general position of the curia on the heresy question.[118] For the first time the curia dealt not with heretical phenomena in a particular area, but rather made the attempt "to destroy the depravity of various heresies which have arisen in many parts of the world in modern times."[119] For the first time, also, guidelines were provided describing which phenomena were to be persecuted as heresy, how they were to be discovered, and how they were to be punished. The first point is the most important for our purposes. To comprehend all heresies, of whatever name (*quocumque nomine censeatur*), by their characteristics, the decree first gives a series of names of heresies, including Cathars, Patarenes, *Humiliati*, and Waldensians, along with several others which had never before appeared in the sources.[120] But there was, of course, no guarantee all existing heresies were comprehended under these names. For that reason, characteristics of heresy were listed immediately after the names. First on the list was unlicensed preaching. Whoever preached in public or in private against the ban without the permission and license of the curia or local bishop was condemned as a heretic. This ruling did not deal with a particular type of preaching, such as preaching on the articles of faith or the sacraments, nor with the spreading of error through preaching, but with all preaching by those who are not ordained to do it by the Church. All unlicensed preaching was branded as heresy. Five years earlier, the curia had declared it did not wish to issue special permission to preach to representatives of the movement for apostolic poverty, even if their orthodoxy was not in doubt. This rule totally rejected all efforts by the religious movement to break through the ecclesiastical hierarchy, even in order to reinforce it through the preaching by "successors of the apostles," whether the dogma and authority of the Roman Church were questioned or not.

It was only secondarily that Lucius III's decree on heretics declared every contradiction to the Catholic doctrine of sacraments to be heretical, opening the possibility that the Church—or individual bishops with the counsel of their clergy—could declare certain persons to be heretics. All of those guilty of unlicensed preaching, erroneous doctrine concerning the sacraments, and specific persons accused of heresy were henceforth to be persecuted and punished as heretics in a uniform manner. In fact, if that was not a definition, then at least it was a characterization of what was regarded as heresy, and there is no doubt it could have found wide application. Since the decree went on to describe carefully how open heresy and those suspected of it were to be treated, since care was taken to publish the decree in all dioceses, and since procedure against heresy was not to rely on accidentally discovered cases but to be investigated for the first time through a regular inquisition carried out by the bishops, the heresy decree of 1184 must be considered the first general act against heresy fulfilling all the preconditions for a unified, thorough struggle against error.

The weak policies of the successors of Lucius III did not continue this struggle, however. At the end of the twelfth century the hierarchical Church and the religious movement confronted one another stubbornly, tensely, and with mutual hostility, each disputing the other's right to claim itself the true Christian Church, each declaring the other heretical. A compromise appeared impossible.

CHAPTER 2

The Religious Movement under Innocent III: The Rise of New Types of Orders

The decisive turning-point in the relationship between the hierarchical Church and the religious movement took place during the pontificate of Innocent III. Until that time, the religious movement had grown on its own strength, outside the Church and in increasing opposition to it. Except for relatively paltry attempts at the start of the twelfth century, this proceeded without the curia seeking ways to accommodate within the Church the new forms of religious life represented by voluntary poverty and itinerant preaching. All attempts to win ecclesiastical recognition for these forms of life had been answered by the curia with a condemnation whose violation was to be treated as heresy. On the other hand, the Church lacked the means and energy to carry out this condemnation effectively and suppress the religious movement altogether.

This was the tense situation which prevailed when Innocent III ascended the papal throne at the start of 1198.[1] He did not respond at once with a comprehensive program, indeed he never sought to transform the situation universally or through thoroughly planned, creative measures. Yet from the outset of his pontificate until his death, Innocent invariably took a consistent position, pursuing goals representing a principled reversal of the policies of his predecessors in all measures taken by the curia in response to the religious movement and to heresy. He endeavored to bridge the gap between the religious movement and the hierarchical Church by conceding demands of apostolic preachers and devotees of evangelical poverty for a place within the Church itself, so long as orthodox doctrine and papal, hierarchical authority continued to be recognized in principle. In this way, those who held to the evangelical life, voluntary poverty, and apostolic preaching were confronted with the choice between the Church and heresy, but without the earlier dilemma in which preferring the Roman Church had entailed renouncing the ideals of the religious movement. He persecuted heresy which could not be fitted into the order of the Church under those conditions with ruthless strictness, using all his strength and means. Finally, in his struggle against heresy, he even made use of groups which participated in the religious movement right along with the heretics, but which had been able to find a place within the Catholic Church. This policy led to the formation of a series of associations, congregations, and orders in which the movement for religious poverty found orthodox forms, recognized by the Church. This applied particularly to the mendicant orders, but there were also new forms of persecuting heretics, including war against the Albigensians, and eventually the Inquisition. This does not mean that Innocent created these new entities and methods, or had simply willed them. The vital forces which led to their creation originated with him, and he at least participated in them. His policies did not express a religious change in the leadership of the Church; rather they arose from a clear understanding of the duties of the Church toward the religious movement of the time. The religious movement was not to be overcome by bans and condemnations alone, without constructive effort on behalf of the Church. Innocent III did not experience the religious forces of his time from within, but he understood them, and it is his lasting accomplishment that he understood how to bond them with the hierarchical Church through his cleverness and ability, foresight and energy. He not only dispelled the peril that the hierarchical Church might have become hopelessly isolated from the living religious forces of its times, but he also smoothed the way for the new form which Christian life was to take in the Catholic Church of the thirteenth century. As a result of his policies, the formless fermentation of the religious movement would bring forth great new orders and rules.

1. The *Humiliati*

The first steps the pope took in relation to the religious movement are inadequately documented and can only be inferred from later sources. A decree must have been issued at the beginning of his pontificate offering reconciliation with the Church for elements of the religious poverty movement, but threatening unrepentant heretics with severe penalties. We do not know whether this decree was addressed to the Church as a whole or only to a few North Italian bishoprics. Its effects can only be traced in Northern Italy,[2] particularly in Verona. There the papal decree, which had been directed to the archpriest and canons, was executed in a manner which compelled Innocent III to intervene a second time.[3] He had demanded energetic prosecution of heretics, but he had also demanded a careful *distinctio* between those who were really to be seen as heretics and the orthodox. It is unknown whether Innocent ever defined this difference more precisely. Despite this demand for a *distinctio*, the clergy of Verona had excommunicated all adherents of the religious poverty movement, whether Cathars, Arnoldists, Waldensians, or *Humiliati*. The result was that in keeping with the decree some *Humiliati* had been affected who had expressly sworn obedience to the Roman Church in the presence of the bishop and been reconciled with the Church. As a result, Innocent empowered the bishop of Verona to examine the beliefs of these *Humiliati* once more and gather information about their way of life. If suspicions about their orthodoxy proved ungrounded, the bishop was to declare them to be Catholic and cancel all measures against them. On the other hand, if the examination showed that they varied from the true faith of the Church on many points, but that they were ready to admit their errors and obey the Church, then the bishop should absolve them after they publicly renounced their errors using the oath usual in such cases. They should commit themselves to combat those errors, promising to defend the correct faith in the future, giving obedience and due veneration to the papal see.[4]

This papal letter does not permit detailed reconstruction of the earlier measures, but it clearly indicates the standards Innocent used to deal with the religious movement and heresy. He demanded harsh prosecution of heresy, but he also demanded care and consideration in deciding who was to be persecuted as a heretic. The letter justified this treatment with a preface which went far to define the new turn in papal policy.[5] It spoke of two responsibilities of the curia: strictness toward heretics, so that the truly guilty could not escape unpunished, but with *discretio* in identifying heresy, so that the innocent would not be damned. The statement of Alexander III in 1162 that it was better to acquit the guilty than to punish the innocent[6] comes immediately to mind, yet in comparing these two similar pronouncements, the significant difference of position between these two popes becomes clear. Alexander used this principle to justify his own indecision in the case of the Flemish heretics being tried by the archbishop of Reims. Innocent, on the other hand, insisted on a decision between heresy and orthodox piety. He often repeated similar formulas in later years, and all his measures in the question of heresy corresponded to this principle. His entire effort was dedicated to distinguishing between those elements which had fallen into heresy beyond recall or correction, and those who would remain in the Church or be regathered into it. All of the bans, expulsions, and anathemas had only made the situation in the religious movement more perilous. The two primary goals of his policy toward the religious movement were to persecute heretics with all possible harshness while bestowing on the others a right to exist within the Church.

Innocent's letter to the bishop of Verona also shows that his policy had already succeeded in reconciling at least some of the *Humiliati* of Northern Italy who had been restricted by Alexander III in 1179 and excommunicated as heretics by Lucius III in 1184. This success was not limited to Verona.[7] As early as 1198 or 1199, two leaders of the *Humiliati*[8] came to the curia to negotiate with Innocent III on behalf of the entire community to determine the forms in which they could develop within the Church.[9] They presented the pope with statutes the *Humiliati* had used in their houses in the past and intended to use in the future. These *proposita*, which have not survived, were handed over by Innocent to a commission,[10] which was to compose a *propositum regulare*. This proposal was then presented to a commission of cardinals[11] for examination and correction, and finally to Innocent for his definitive review. After this lengthy procedure,[12] which took almost two years, the rule of the *Humiliati* was confirmed in June 1201. This rule consisted of a combination of clauses from the rules of Benedict and Augustine, supplemented by a few elements peculiar to the *Humiliati*.[13] The original statutes presented by the *Humiliati* had obviously only served as a foundation insofar as the new rules had to be adjusted to the way of life of these communities. Otherwise, existing rules were used wherever possible. The rules were to apply to two distinct types of *Humiliati* communities, to each of which both men and women belonged: the so-called second order consisting of lay communities living in religious houses,[14] and communities of clerics living as canons and canonnesses.[15] Communities of this sort, leading a "common life" and using this new rule, were not just coming into existence as *Humiliati*; they had long been in existence. Even before the Lateran Council of 1179, communities of men and women could be found in Milan, living and working together in one house.[16] There were doubtless similar communities of *Humiliati* in other Lombard cities, and these lay communities were organized as a secondary order under the new rule. Communities of clerics among the *Humiliati* are known as early as the 1170s,[17] and these were organized as the first order. It is only due to the fact that such communities of lay people and clerics were already flourishing prior to 1200 among the *Humiliati* that a rule could be developed to apply to just such a community, living the cloistered life.[18]

But this rule could not be applied to those *Humiliati* who lived not in communal houses but with families in their own houses, both the oldest and strongest branch of the community.[19] This "lay brotherhood" could not be comprehended by the new rule any more than by any other existing rule, since it lacked the basic common denominator of all "regular" lives, the common life. When the curia sought to incorporate the *Humiliati* into the Church as a legitimate corporation, it was confronted with twin obligations. The first obligation was to find a legal form which could comprehend a religious community without a "common life," and the second obligation was to join them into a form of community with other *Humiliati*, living as lay people or clerics according to the rules of Benedictine monks or Augustinian canons, in such a way as to preserve the original unity of all *Humiliati*. The first attempt to solve this twofold obligation was only a partial success, since it was carried out while preserving old forms of organization as much as possible, supplemented by new forms only where it was unavoidable. Yet precisely because this was the first attempt to solve a novel problem, the organization of the *Humiliati* is particularly important and interesting.

The third group of *Humiliati*, lay persons living outside of common houses, did not even receive a rule of its own. In order to comprehend their way of life in a legal ecclesiastical form and to prevent the regulated portion of the *Humiliati* from splintering away and excluding the remnant from the organization, Innocent developed a form which had been unknown before, but which would win a certain importance in the following decades. He did not bestow a "rule" on the *Humiliati* living by themselves, but he did approve their *propositum*. This brief summary of religious and ethical norms of life which the *Humiliati* presented to the curia had been examined by the pope and the cardinals, and it had been altered in some points before being confirmed by a bull on 7 June 1201.[20] It recognized the moral and religious principles which even Alexander III had not denied in 1179: the avoidance of luxurious clothing, earning a living by the work of their hands, rejecting usury and returning goods obtained illegally, distributing excessive income as alms to the poor, keeping marital duties and maintaining a peaceful, moral life in humility, patience, and love. Beyond that, these lay associations were permitted to keep the seven canonical hours of prayer, with seven Our Fathers each time. They had to swear obedience to the prelates of the Church, and they were also subject to the payment of the ecclesiastical tithe as laymen.[21] None of these rules constituted a concession either for the curia or for the *Humiliati*. The permissibility of oaths was much more difficult. The *Humiliati* wanted to forbid their members to swear oaths of any sort,[22] just like the Cathars and Waldensians. In the *propositum*, the curia permitted them only to avoid unnecessary, unreasonable, or voluntary oaths not demanded by anyone, while requiring them to recognize the duty to take oaths in pressing circumstances. The *propositum*, as well as the bulls for the first and second orders,[23] cited many scriptural passages, establishing which type of oathtaking was permitted to Christians and which forbidden. The thoroughness of the justification for these rules demonstrated that the curia was willing to go as far as possible to accommodate the *Humiliati*, but not so far as to approve their rejection of all oaths, and it felt compelled to give a special explanation for this decision.

By far the most important regulation of the *propositum* permits the *Humiliati* to hold gatherings every Sunday at a suitable place, tentatively allowing the preaching of qualified brothers with the permission of the bishop, under the condition that these sermons be restricted to moral exhortation to just living and active piety. The preachers were not permitted to deal with theological questions (*de articulis fidei et sacramentis ecclesiæ*).[24] As a result of this ruling, what had been forbidden the *Humiliati* in 1179 was now permitted, namely, the right to hold assemblies and to preach at them. The restrictions which accompanied this permission did not limit its importance for the *Humiliati* in any substantive way. The bishops' permission was required for a gathering, but this does not say the same thing as the instruction Alexander III gave the Waldensians in 1179, which was that they could only preach if asked to do so by bishops; in the *propositum* the bishops are specifically instructed not to deny this permission. Permission of assemblies was thus not left up to the bishops' judgment, and agreement concerned only the time and place of gatherings. In the same way, the restriction to moral preaching and the ban on sermons concerning the articles of faith did not have so much importance for practice as for canon law. It is very unlikely that the *Humiliati* had ever tried to gain permission to preach on matters of faith. Doubtless it had always been moral questions of religious life, not matters of faith, which had interested them. In any case, in 1179 they applied for permission "to support the Catholic faith," but the ban on preaching "on articles of faith and the sacraments" certainly did not prevent them from fighting for the Catholic faith after 1201. This is because they had won the highest respect of the men of the Church as bulwarks of the faith and fighters of heresy. By dividing moral preaching from dogmatic preaching, which is first found in the *propositum* of the *Humiliati*, the curia clearly sought to designate the difference between the preaching reserved for ordained priests and that permitted to religious laymen in their own assemblies. Since a new variety of preaching was here recognized for the first time, a new art of preaching had to be developed. Yet this does not alter the fact that the *Humiliati* won papal recognition in 1201 for forms of community forbidden them in 1179 and for which they had been ejected as "heretics." Through this concession, not only did the curia manage to reintegrate the *Humiliati* into the community of the Church, but for the first time it also demonstrated that it was ready to abandon its blanket condemnation of the religious movement, permitting the formation of religious lay associations, even lay penitential preaching in the Church. The principle that no one was allowed to preach who had not been ordained to it was preserved, but it was essentially modified when a lay community for the first time received full papal permission to set up their own preachers—an event of wide-ranging importance for the future.[25]

Alongside such an important result of negotiations between Innocent III and the *Humiliati*, the question of the organizational unity of the three orders is less significant but still needs clarification. The articulation into three orders had arisen from the fact that the *Humiliati* did not present a homogeneous body from the point of view of the Church, since there were lay people as well as clerics, and since some lived the *vita communis* and some did not. None of the previous legal forms could be applied equally to the whole of the *Humiliati* community. There was hesitation to meet the challenge of a novel situation with a fundamentally novel order by organizing a heterogeneous whole under a single common rule. Old forms were preserved wherever possible, although this meant that the whole fell into three groups, of which one was organized as canons, the second as monks, and the third not organized under a real "rule" at all. The *Humiliati* would not have agreed to this new organization if measures had not been taken to prevent the complete collapse of their community into three individual groups by establishing an organization binding them all together. Doing this required something not found in any of the traditional forms of organization, for no one had ever tried to tie together a community of canons, lay persons living monastically, and lay persons living with their families. A new form of association had to be found which could combine the individual groups, themselves hammered together out of old and new elements. Such an organization was so imperfectly achieved in the negotiations of 1199–1201 that the result is not totally clear, and whatever emerged functioned for a short time and soon had to be replaced by new rules. It remains worthy of attention, however, as a first solution to the problem.

There is nothing about a common organization for all three orders in the *propositum* of the third order, nor in the bull for the second order, and very little is said about the inner organization of the individual orders. The only information is that the leaders of the third order were called *ministri*, those of the second order *prælati*.[26] The bull for the first order, however, describes exactly the interior organization, leadership of the order and mode of their election.[27] We are told that, parallel to the four *præpositi majores* of the first order, four officers headed each of the other two orders.[28] At least once a year the twelve leaders of the entire order were to meet in "general chapter" to discuss concerns of the order (excluding laymen when *spiritualia* were being discussed). In this way the continued association of the three "orders" was to be assured, but in 1246 a General Minister was elected for the entire order of the *Humiliati* who was to have leadership and right of visitation over all three orders.[29]

From the very beginning, the conference of twelve was assisted by further ties between the three orders which preserved their originally close connections. The common rule for the first and second orders, specifically, contain rules for the election of the leader of houses in the order. They express these rules so imprecisely, however, that it is not even clear what position the person elected would occupy. It obviously was not an election for the provosts of the houses of the first order, although the rule which declares this is also valid for the first order. Unlike the *præpositi* of the first order, the *prælatus* elected here was voted in (or reelected) for only one year, and the mode of election was entirely different.[30] It could hardly apply to the head of all the community houses of the second order (as the title *prælatus* would indicate). First, such an office would have no place in the regulations common to the first and second order, but would have to be found in the special bull for the second order (as is the case with the rules for the election of the *præpositi* of the first order). Secondly, only members of the second order would have been able to participate, since the third order had its own ministers, just as the first order had its own provosts. According to the express statements in the rule, however, electors of the "prelates" include not only members of the second order, or even of the two orders covered by the rules; lay people of the third order were also called on to participate. These lay people were only mentioned in the rule at this point.[31] Since members of all three orders participated in this election, it could hardly be intended only for the *præpositi* of the first order, the *prælati* of the second, or the *ministri* of the third order (who were never said to be elected only for a year). The most likely resolution is that it was a leader of the local community of all *Humiliati* who was elected, taking the title of *pater omnium* alongside the leaders of the three orders. The new organization of 1201 had to pay some respect to earlier times, recognizing a common leadership for the local *Humiliati* community in the form of an annual leader, who persisted alongside the individual leaders of order houses and lay brotherhoods and alongside the general chapter, to which each order sent four supreme leaders. The unclarity of this rule was probably due to the fact that it was not dealing with a new institution requiring a precise juristic description, but rather was simply giving ecclesiastical sanction and juristic function to established custom among the *Humiliati*.[32]

Despite the greatest possible preservation of old forms, all of these regulations still created a new entity supposed to correspond to the novel religious and sociological conditions of the *Humiliati* community. The new form of the order utterly lacked the clarity, simplicity, and direction which could have made it a model for the future. For this reason no community would ever be organized imitating the *Humiliati*. The curia never completely rejected this first attempt, however, and many measures which are first encountered here will survive into the future. Much more important than specific forms in ecclesiastical law is the new attitude toward the religious movement the curia expressed in them. The *arenga* of the bulls Innocent issued for the order of the *Humiliati* attest to his awareness of the fundamental importance of this case. To test spirits, to separate sheep from goats as a result of careful thought, neither to call evil good nor good evil, neither to condemn the just nor leave the guilty unpunished, to let *discretio* reign and to amputate hopelessly diseased limbs as would a physician—all this the pope intended to take up with the reorganization of the *Humiliati*. These principles are so cleverly garbed in their biblical costumes that they give Innocent's new policy on the religious movement a clear foundation without directly abandoning the policies of his predecessors. It was correct in his time "not to believe every spirit" (1 John 4:1); but now the prodigal son should be received again with joy, the wandering sheep returned to the herd, and in keeping with the counsel of the apostle "not extinguish the spirit."[33] These thoughts and images return time and again in Innocent's later statements on the religious movement. If one disregarded them as mere biblical window-dressing, then he would pass up the key to understanding Innocent III's policies on heretics and orders. His decisions in Church policy correspond precisely to this program.

This first step to recovering the religious movement for the Church was a real success. While not all *Humiliati* entered the new order at once,[34] most *Humiliati* were able to find a new lease on life in their ecclesiastically sanctioned form. Fifteen years after reorganization, James of Vitry, whose understanding for the religious movement had been honed through extensive experience, reports that the *Humiliati* were about the only ones fighting heresy in the heretic city of Milan. According to a witness from 1216, there were 150 houses of these pious men and women in the bishopric of Milan alone, not including members of the third order, who lived in their own houses. They had left everything behind on behalf of Christ, living by the labor of their hands, preaching and hearing the Word of God—for they had permission from the pope to preach and fight heresy.[35] In a larger context, James of Vitry later sounded yet another song of praise to the *Humiliati*,[36] praising their humility in external appearance and inner life, glorifying their successful work against the heretics. Other sources from the middle of the century join in this praise.[37] The curia had virtually no further trouble with the *Humiliati*.[38] Later they were to play a larger role in the economy and in municipal administration than in the religious movement.[39] Yet their role in the religious movement at the turn of the century remains important, since the curia for the first time succeeded in wooing adherents to the religious movement away from heresy and in incorporating them into the Church with juristic reforms, exploiting them as weapons against the peril of heresy. It was the first attempt to bridge the gap between the hierarchical Church and the religious movement.

2. THE WALDENSIANS

Innocent III had succeeded in reconciling the *Humiliati* with the Church by granting in 1201 what had been denied them in 1179, the construction of communities, lay preaching, and the practice of their ideals of evangelical poverty within the Church. Because of that, it must have seemed possible to arrange the return of the Waldensians with the same hope of success, since they had been expelled from the Church after making similar demands. If the same concessions the *Humiliati* received had been granted them, would not the grounds for their separation from the Church have collapsed, and could they not have been recognized as an ecclesiastical community in a form similar to the *Humiliati*?

Two conditions rendered this outcome difficult. The *Humiliati* were sedentary, living off their own labor, and even before 1201 they consisted mostly of closed communities living in houses. The Waldensians, in contrast, were a band of homeless, wandering preachers without possessions or income, desiring to live from the alms of their listeners. Organizing such a band of preachers according to Church law and incorporating it into the hierarchical Church without friction was a much more difficult and novel problem than regularizing the *Humiliati*. Further, as a result of its nature, Waldensianism had developed much more dramatically in the twenty years since the Lateran Council than had the *Humiliati*. Itinerant Waldensian preachers had spread their ideas across whole countries. The Waldensians could not be encompassed in a locally limitable organization. At the same time their doctrine and consciousness had been so strongly shaped by their fate and activities during these twenty years that it was doubtful that a simple suspension of the ban of 1179 and a concession of their right to create communities and preach could have reversed their separation from the Church.

Even before the Lateran Council, Waldes and his companions had cited the word of the Lord against the archbishop of Lyon's ban on their preaching: "Go out to the whole world and preach the gospel to all creatures" (Mark 16:5), as well as the Apostle, "One must obey God more than people" (Acts 5:29).[40] When the curia joined in forbidding what Waldensians believed the gospel itself had called them to do, Waldensians were presented with a choice of whether to obey the command of the Church or what they held to be the command of the gospel. It was their conviction of a vocation from the gospel which won out; it was their trust in the Church which had been shaken. Since Waldensians held the gospel to be the sole norm of life, they now sought to justify disobedience to the Church and continued activities despite papal ban by citing scripture. Conflicts between the Waldensians and Catholics in the last two decades of the twelfth century[41] demonstrate clearly how differences grew more intense, precisely because both parties constantly, honestly tried to found their convictions in the scriptures. In opposing the Catholic demand for unconditional obedience to the Church, the pope and prelates, Waldensians sought to demonstrate on the basis of the gospels how a Christian was bound to obey God alone, and that this obedience was owed to priests only insofar as they lived in accordance with God's commands, like the apostles.[42] Against the Catholic thesis that only he could preach who had been ordained to it by the pope or bishops, Waldensians proclaimed that anyone could preach in accordance with the will of the gospels, even laymen, even women, requiring no ecclesiastical ordination to do so.[43] The same question had become crucial for the performance of sacraments. As excommunicates, the Waldensians could not participate in the sacraments of the Church. Since they did not hold their excommunication to be valid, believing they were acting in accordance with the counsels of the gospels and apostles, the Waldensians asserted that pious lay persons could bind and loose, perform the sacrament of the altar, and hear confessions, in opposition to the Catholic claim that only ordained representatives of the hierarchical Church had the right and power to perform the sacraments validly.[44] During these decades, Waldensians never disputed the right of Catholic priests to dispense the sacraments, but they did demand a "good priest" for the sacraments to be valid, asserting further that "in necessity" a "good lay person" could hear confession and perform the Lord's supper.[45] These differences intensified with time and became increasingly dramatic the more they were discussed. Alan of Lille perceived the decisive difference: to Catholic opinion, there was *ordo* and *officium*, while in the opinion of the Waldensians, *meritum* alone granted the right to administer the sacraments and preach the Word of God.[46] The idea of imitating the apostles stood in contrast to the apostolic succession in the hierarchical *ordo*.[47] This dichotomy would have to be overcome before the Waldensians and the movement for apostolic poverty could ever be reincorporated into the Church.

In comparison, the other questions which separated the Waldensians from the Church played no essential role. Just as the *Humiliati*, they declared every oath and lie to be a mortal sin, equal to killing.[48] Further, they doubted the effectiveness of prayers for the dead, perhaps at first only because they were offered through unworthy priests.[49] Yet in all truly dogmatic questions the Waldensians continued to agree with the Church, and just as was the case with the *Humiliati*, they fought shoulder to shoulder with Catholic priests against "heresy," specifically the dualistic errors of Cathars.[50] Reunification with the Church was thus more difficult than with the *Humiliati*, but it did not lie outside the realm of the possible.

A. *The Waldensians in Metz, 1199*

From the outset Innocent III pursued tactics toward Waldensians similar to those used with the *Humiliati*. So far as we know, he never systematically attempted to reunify all Waldensians with the Church. He appears never to have taken any steps in this direction on his own initiative. On several occasions, however, he had to decide how to deal with Waldensian groups seeking reconciliation with the Church on their own initiative, and the new attitude of the curia under Innocent emerged with ever greater clarity, winning continually more visible form in his responses.

A local episode of little intrinsic importance provided Innocent the opportunity to take a position on Waldensians in the summer of 1199. The bishop of Metz informed the curia that secret gatherings of lay people were being held in the diocese and town of Metz, consisting of men and women reading French translations of Holy Scriptures aloud to one another and preaching. These people denied obedience to priests' commands that they cease by citing the Bible, holding in contempt all who did not belong to their circle. They even declared an ability to communicate the words of salvation better than simple priests. The request of the bishop of Metz for advice[51] was answered by Innocent's letter to the bishop and chapter of Metz, as well as by a mandate to his diocese. Although he recognized their efforts to learn scripture and live the evangelical life, Innocent declared their gathering in secret conventicles and allowing persons not installed as preachers to assume the office of preaching was intolerable; he threatened those who acted against these rules with harsh punishment. This position was identical with Alexander III and the Lateran Council of 1179, but Innocent also asked the bishop of Metz for information about where the sectarians got their biblical translation and what its tenor might be, about the beliefs of the people who used these translations, why they used them, and whether they showed the pope and the Church due esteem.[52] The pope justified his questions by citing his own ignorance of the sectarians, their lives and views, adding that one had to assume the translators as well as the preachers who used these translations could not be entirely unlearned persons. In a second report,[53] the bishop of Metz informed him the sectarians had refused obedience to the papal orders, declaring both in secret and in public that their sole obligation was to obey God. They intended to continue to meet and preach despite the ban, and they declared that they would keep and use their French Bible despite all commands of bishops and popes to the contrary. Innocent was not satisfied with this information, however, and he made no final ruling. He continued to insist on discovering what these people actually believed, who they were, and how they lived. Since he had not yet received any certain information from the bishop, he commissioned three Cistercian abbots with this investigation. They were to decide whether the sectarians were heretics—so far as the pope was concerned, the bishop of Metz had not provided enough for him to decide—and they were either to proceed energetically against them in concert with the bishop or to give the pope an adequate declaration of what sort of sectarians they might be. The three abbots determined the sectarians were indeed heretics, their biblical translation was burned, and heresy was declared uprooted from the diocese.[54] Any "conversion" of the Waldensians of the bishopric of Metz had been without success. It is the painstaking restraint Innocent used in dealing with this case and the criteria by which he sought to decide it which are worthy of remark. He declared that the formation of conventicles, unlicensed preaching, and disobedience to the commands of the bishop were not permitted, but so far as he was concerned that was not the end of the matter. He investigated the sectarians' beliefs and religious attitudes before he was willing to decide whether they were heretics. He justified this in programmatic terms in a letter to the bishop of Metz: the Church certainly had the duty to catch foxes which destroy the vineyard of the Lord, meaning an obligation to obliterate heretics, but they could not imperil true, simple piety in so doing, crippling and confusing the religious sensitivities of unsophisticated believers. They must guard against driving the religiously simple into the arms of heresy.[55] So Innocent, as these words demonstrate, recognized from the very outset of his pontificate that the entire religious movement could be driven into heresy through a stubborn attitude on the part of the Church. He wanted to deal with this peril through an intelligent, energetic distinction between heresy and a religious movement true to the Church. This policy can be followed through the following years, step by step, from the negotiations with the *Humiliati* through the reconciliation of some Waldensian groups, to the rise of the mendicant orders.

B. Durandus of Huesca and the Catholic Poor: New Directions in the Struggle against Heresy

At the beginning of 1207, one of those great disputations between Catholics and heretics, of the sort that the Church used to suppress heresy in a peaceful manner, took place at Pamiers in Southern France. The occasion was a visit by Bishop Diego of Osma, who had been tirelessly engaged in preaching and disputation against the heretics of Southern France over the previous months. Diego was returning to his Spanish bishopric for what he believed would be only a temporary interruption in his mission to the heretics which his friend and companion Dominic, subprior of Osma, was to continue. Diego would never return to France, and he would die before the end of 1207; what he had begun would pass entirely into Dominic's hands.

As he was passing through Pamiers,[56] a disputation with the Waldensians was held in the presence of the bishops of Toulouse and Conserans and several abbots; one participant was another Spaniard, named Durandus of Huesca. Although Bishop Diego had had little palpable success in his disputations with the Cathars of Southern France,[57] his fortunes with the Waldensians of Pamiers were considerably better. As contemporary sources relate, the Waldensians were overcome and confounded, and the people present, particularly the poor, sided largely with the Catholics; some Waldensians, led by Durandus, petitioned the curia, did penance and received permission to live *regulariter*.[58] Nothing further is known of the course of the discussion, or what caused this Waldensian group to make its way to the curia. It appears likely, however, that one cause of this move was the altered policy of the curia under Innocent.

This is because the methods of combating heresy had undergone decisive change in these very years. Bishop Diego had been at the curia in 1206 with his companion Dominic.[59] On their return journey they met in Montpellier with three Cistercians who had been active for two years as papal legates working against the heretics,[60] but since they had been completely unsuccessful in their efforts to convert heretics, they had been trying to resign their missions in despair.[61] The arrival of Diego and his companion, however, moved them to take up their mission again with new tactics. Diego presented the legates with a new program:[62] apostolic itinerant preaching in the same manner as the heretics, without the pomp and marks of authority of the hierarchical Church, living like heretics, but teaching as the Church teaches. Bishop Diego himself and his subprior Dominic placed themselves at the head of this new-model mission to the heretics[63] and traveled for months through the towns of Southern France as poor preachers, living from alms, challenging the Albigensian preachers to disputations, and trying to win the people back to the faith of the Church by fulfilling demands for an apostolic life which had previously been asserted only by the heretics.

It is a matter of dispute how much these new tactics for combating heresy arose from Diego's initiative. Nothing is known of any papal commission to Diego for the legates at Montpellier. Despite that, it can be inferred that the question of combating heresy was discussed by the pope and the bishop of Osma at the curia, and that Innocent gave some sort of advice. This is because what Diego presented to the legates at Montpellier corresponded precisely with what Innocent had already recommended for action against the heretics. When he entrusted the Cistercian abbot Arnald and two monks of Fontfroid with the mission against the heretics, he pressingly admonished them at the close of the message to present a modest appearance so as to blunt all foolish objections, avoiding all words and deeds which could give a heretic grounds for accusations.[64] The Cistercian legates obviously had not followed these admonitions very seriously. When Diego came to Montpellier directly from the curia, however, he advised and acted entirely in the sense of these earlier directives. Innocent probably also took the opportunity to win the two Spaniards visiting the curia for a more energetic prosecution of his plans.[65] The pope also sent the legate Raoul of Pontfroid a special letter on 17 November 1206 outlining how the new method should be applied, which was to send qualified persons to mingle with the heretics simply clothed, imitating the poor life of Christ, to win the heretics back through example and argument.[66] Of course it is impossible to determine how much the new methods of the heresy mission of Diego and his companion Dominic originated with the pope. It can be shown that even before Diego's visit, Innocent conceived of opposing the heretical poverty movement and itinerant preaching with ecclesiastical preachers living in apostolic poverty, as had been the case years before with the *Humiliati* in Lombardy. There can be no doubt he was pointing the way to applying this new method to the struggle against heresy in Southern France.

The success of the disputation at Pamiers in 1207 first becomes understandable in view of these facts. The "conversion" of the Waldensians under Durandus of Huesca would not have taken place if they had not expected to be able to return to the Church without surrendering their religious activities as itinerant preachers; somehow, they would be able to continue to pursue their religious goals within the Church. In fact, a year after the disputation of Pamiers they received papal permission to continue functioning as poor apostolic itinerant preachers, while expressly recognizing ecclesiastical authority and doctrine. In all likelihood this had already been promised at the time of their conversion. Such an approval could not be made to Durandus and his companions by Catholic disputants at Pamiers without prior empowerment by the curia, or without their being sure that such approval would be forthcoming.[67] The new orientation of curia policy under Innocent III was the precondition both for new forms of combating heresy as well as for reintegrating the religious movement into the Church.

In 1208, a year after the disputations at Pamiers, the former Waldensian, Durandus, was at the Roman curia[68] together with several companions, and their return to the Church was formally completed and their future status regulated. They were subjected to an examination of their faith, and they had to swear a thorough formula of belief in which Catholic doctrine was clearly distinguished from the heresies of the time.[69] On completing that, they received papal confirmation of their *propositum conversationis*, defining their position and future activities in the Church.

This *propositum* is not the rule of an order, and the community of the "Catholic Poor" created by it cannot be called a religious order.[70] Rather it is a first attempt to create an organizational form for a band of itinerant preachers. It shares with the *propositum* of the third order of the *Humiliati* the characteristic that the oath and organizational form of a religious association was ecclesiastically approved without adopting one of the older rules, suited only for the *vita communis;* it did not deal with the question of leadership, inner composition, reception of new members and similar matters. Yet the new association lacked the support of and connection with monastically or canonically regulated communities, and thus the new group represented an even more clearly novel form of religious association than the *Humiliati*.

Members of the group who had earlier served as itinerant Waldensian preachers were mostly clerics, almost all of them educated,[71] who became itinerant preachers of the Church after reorganization. The fundamental precondition was their recognition of the hierarchical, sacramental Church. They had to swear to obey and respect the pope and the bishops, recognize the validity of the sacraments as independent of the worthiness of the priest, confess that only priests ordained by the bishop for that purpose could administer the sacraments, and that anyone else who presumed to do so was a heretic, and oblige themselves to receive all sacraments from the proper bishops and priests alone. The Church made no concessions whatsoever to the former Waldensians on these points. Those were precisely the heresies which had developed only after separation from the Church and because of that separation. In several subordinate questions they also had to abandon fundamental Waldensian positions: like the *Humiliati* before them, they had to concede oaths to be permissible in serious situations, and to view the shedding of blood by secular powers in situations of necessity as no mortal sin. The curia compromised to some extent with earlier Waldensian convictions by freeing adherents of these "Catholic Poor" from the obligation to bear arms against Christians or from swearing in secular matters, so far as it could be done with the agreement of secular powers.[72]

The curia did offer extensive concessions to the new association concerning their religious life and work. The "Catholic Poor" had to give up almost nothing of their earlier Waldensian way of life; they could continue as before, with ecclesiastical approval.[73] They were permitted to renounce possessions and property of every form, living on the gifts of believers,[74] to preach freely, to recruit like-minded persons through their preaching and gather them in special communities. They conceded that the right to preach depended on the commission and license of the pope or a bishop, but they received papal permission to preach as a community, without any individual members having to receive special papal or episcopal license.[75] They were permitted on the one hand to preach against heretics, the enemies of the Church and papacy, then to teach a confused public and return it to the Church, and on the other hand they could also preach in their own "schools"[76] for brothers and friends. This distinction of two different manners of preaching doubtless derived from their activities as Waldensians. It is important that the curia granted them the right to preach in the "schools" for their own adherents, who were always described among the Waldensians as "friends," people remaining in civil life, in the "world," but placing themselves under the care and leadership of the "Catholic Poor," just as they had earlier been under the Waldensians.[77] Just as he had permitted itinerant preaching, so Innocent also permitted the Catholic Poor "the building of conventicles," while Alexander III had forbidden them both.

An episode in Milan shows us how unaltered and directly the "friends" of the Catholic Poor continued the life of Waldensian communities. When Durandus and his companions appeared in Milan on his return from the curia in early 1209, about a hundred Waldensian preachers declared themselves ready to be reconciled with the Church under the condition that the "school" they had formerly used be returned to them. They had been accustomed to holding their assemblies there as Waldensians, preaching before brothers and friends. Once they had been excommunicated as heretics, Archbishop Philip of Milan (1196–1206) had taken the property and destroyed the building. They made their reconciliation with the Church dependent on its return and rebuilding, so that they might again preach the Word of God in their school as they had been accustomed.[78] Despite Durandus' support, the current archbishop, Ubertus, and Innocent III did not immediately fulfill this condition. The pope, however, settled the matter in a diplomatic letter to Ubertus:[79] certainly reconciliation with the Church should not be tied to such objective conditions, but it should take place for the sake of eternal life. If the Waldensians were ready to reconcile themselves with the Church for the good of their souls, under the conditions accepted by Durandus, the archbishop should grant them the property, or another one suitable to the purpose. This should be done insofar as it appeared to him to be consonant with the honor of the Church and the salvation of the newly converted, so that they could gather for mutual encouragement and teaching.[80]

There could be no clearer proof that Innocent was conceding to these "converted" Waldensians precisely that for which they had once been excommunicated and persecuted. In this case the true "convert" was the curia.

The new, papally recognized community of preachers did not, of course, restrict itself to reconciling earlier Waldensians preachers and communities. Then as before, their chief mission was to win ever more persons for a truly Christian, evangelical life through their penitential sermons. An episode in the Southern French diocese of Elne shows that they had some success in this as well, showing that the "Catholic Poor" sought new organizational forms besides associations of active itinerant preachers and loose gatherings of "friends" living in the world. Their preaching in Elne moved several people to "do penance," make a special confession of sins, return all unjustly acquired goods, and join a community in which they renounced private property, dressed in simple clothing, and obligated themselves to chastity under the leadership of the "Catholic Poor."[81] In early 1212, when Durandus was back at the curia, he sought papal confirmation of this form of life. On 26 May, Innocent commissioned the bishop of Elne to investigate conditions to determine whether purity of faith and morals was being preserved in this new community, since he would grant papal approval if this were the case. The community in Elne contained both men and women, and clerics also belonged. They must have been persons of means, since one of them had promised to build a house for the community on his own property, to contain separate divisions for men and women, along with a hospital and a church, and there would also be provisions for outfitting the house. They all desired to place themselves at the service of the poor, caring for the sick, supporting orphans, helping poor pregnant women, and supplying the indigent with clothing in the winter—"since six works of piety suffice for salvation." But these social goals only supplemented religious duties they assumed—fasting,[82] prayer, and preaching[83]—as well as the renunciations they had accepted.

The forms of this new community do not need to be investigated any further here.[84] It suffices to show that the "Catholic Poor" pursued the same activities under the aegis of the Church as they had done when they were Waldensians. They preached penitence, intending to convert the rich to move them to surrender their "unjustly acquired goods" and lead a life of poverty in harmony with the gospels. They sought to organize their adherents and friends into communities, whether conventicles or "schools," where they gathered for edifying preaching, or separate communities organized like monasteries, where they could dedicate themselves exclusively to pious works.

It is no marvel the bishops were unable to distinguish between these "Catholic Poor" and the heretical Waldensians, and they could not understand papal recognition of this community. As early as the summer of 1209, probably immediately after Durandus' return to Southern France, the bishops sent two Cistercians to the curia to complain about the activities of the "Catholic Poor."[85] They accused the "Catholic Poor" of admitting to their gatherings and services Waldensians not reconciled with the Church, and of accepting escaped monks into their communities. Further, the "Poor" were accused of not having altered their former costume in the least, though it offended Catholics, and of preventing many from attending regular religious services through their preaching to brothers and friends in their "schools," so that even ordained clergy of their community did not regularly perform their duties. Lastly, they were accused of repeatedly saying that no secular power could carry out a death sentence without mortal sin. In response to these complaints, Innocent sent a very earnest letter to Durandus and his companions[86] admonishing them on all points and reminding them of their own assurances. In order not to excite future suspicion, Durandus and his followers were to join experienced preachers when appearing among heretics. More interesting and informative for Innocent's policy and attitude toward the poverty movement, however, is the answer he sent to the archbishops of Narbonne and Tarragona.[87] Innocent generously answered their warning that Durandus had defrauded the Church to avoid proper punishment by stating that even if this were the case, the heretics would catch themselves in their own coils. The attitude of the Church had to start from different assumptions: first of all, the Church must be concerned to separate the evil from the good, the *perversi* from the *justi*. As Innocent declared repeatedly, the Church had two duties, which was to lead those in error back from heresy, but also to preserve believers in the Catholic truth. The second duty, however, was the more important! The mistaken could be permitted to go to ruin with their error—that would be less terrible than allowing the just, the believers, to be separated from their right belief.[88] This was the same as saying, if the policy of the curia were unable successfully to combat heresy, that would be more tolerable than if, through its treatment of heresy, the curia was responsible for excluding from the Church as heretics believing and just persons, estranging them from the true faith. For that reason, Innocent admonished bishops to treat the "Catholic Poor," newly won for the Church, in a careful and forgiving manner. If the "Catholic Poor" would only adhere to the *substantia veritatis*, one could concede them many customs from their time as heretics. Perhaps this would make them more successful at winning back more heretics for the Church, and perhaps this would make the transition to their new way of life all the easier.[89] Innocent did not defend Durandus' companions against the bishops' complaints, but he did admonish them to proceed carefully: friendly counsel was always more effective than threatening harshness. Once more he used the image of the physician who treated a wound first of all with oil and then, only when necessary, with wine (cf. Luke 10:34). With "sick persons" such as these, treatment had always been with "wine," that is, with harshness, and that was all the more reason to deal with them with "oil," with mildness.[90] These sentences, clothed in biblical allegory, contained Innocent's opinion of the policies of his predecessors, whose precipitate strictness and harshness against the religious movement had caused piety to develop into heresy. To be sure, Innocent follows with another metaphor which makes earlier acts of the curia comprehensible and justifiable. By so doing, however, he is only justifying his own intention to recover carefully and cautiously what had been neglected before, to smooth the road of return to the Church for those who had once been excluded, and to create a place where the poverty movement and itinerant preaching could function within the Church. This is the significance of novel creations such as the *Humiliati*, the "Catholic Poor," and soon the community of Bernardus Primus.

The community of the Catholic Poor did not experience extensive growth, and it did not last for long. The resistance of prelates in Spain, Southern France, and Northern Italy, with their old-fashioned policies on heresy, prevented the complete application of the pope's plans. There were continual new problems. In Aragon the preachers were persecuted by the civil authorities. Almost everywhere attempts were made to take away the alms on which they intended to live. They were perennially suspected as heretics. There were efforts to impose leaders on them against their will. For four years Innocent intervened on behalf of the community time and again, admonishing the bishops to receive Waldensians back into the Church under the same conditions as had been granted Durandus and his companions, at least for those Waldensians who sought it. All was in vain, however, and the bishops did not follow the new policies of the curia on the religious movement. In a letter to the bishop of Tarragona on 12 May 1210, Innocent accused the bishops of withholding divine mercy from many persons spurred by the grace of God, which is as much as to say that they were excluding religious persons from the Church as if they were heretics.[91] After 1212 the "Catholic Poor" cease to be mentioned in Innocent's letters, and the curia gave up its efforts to support the community. Perhaps Innocent had come to the conviction that he could better reach the same goal by another route.

The community continued in existence for a few decades more. In 1237 the "poor preachers" in the provinces of Tarragona and Narbonne asked Gregory IX to confirm their association as an order under the name of the "Catholic Poor" or to permit the rule of another approved order. Gregory commissioned the Dominican provincial to visit the community, reform it and move it to adopt an established rule—the approved *propositum* of 1208 was hence not seen to be the rule of an order.[92] It does not appear a basic reorganization actually took place in 1237, for the archbishop of Narbonne and the bishop of Elne complained in 1247 of unlicensed preaching by the "Catholic Poor," who did not have an approved rule and were spreading errors. Innocent IV forbade them to presume to preach without permission, demanding they enter an approved order.[93] That was the last trace of the "Catholic Poor" in Spain and Southern France. The Lombard branch was attached to the Augustinian hermits in 1256.[94] Resistance by bishops and a decline in papal support meant the community of Durandus of Huesca failed to be recognized as an autonomous order during the great reorganization of the orders by the Lateran Council, nor did it regain significance. It remained an experiment dropped at the moment more promising groups came to attract the attention of the curia.

C. *The Community of Bernardus Primus*

Innocent repeatedly demanded that bishops continue down the path blazed by the reconciliation with Durandus, absorbing other groups from the poverty movement and itinerant preaching, but his efforts were in vain. He was able to apply this policy two years later in two separate cases: in 1210 he approved a group of poor itinerant preachers led by Bernardus Primus and William Arnaldi, and it was probably in that same year that Francis of Assisi and eleven companions came to the curia and received papal approval for apostolic preaching and a life of complete poverty. The two episodes are profoundly unequal in historical importance. Other than the three letters in which Innocent III dealt with the preaching association of Bernardus Primus, it has left almost no traces in history; the little band of Francis has become an order of world-shaking importance. Yet, in the context of the years in which these communities arose, from the perspective of the curia which extended them ecclesiastical recognition so close together, the two events had very similar significance and are both of considerable importance in revealing the attitude of the pope to the religious movement. Before Bernardus Primus[95] and his companions came to the curia, they had been actively preaching against the heretics of Southern France.[96] They were considered to be Waldensians, since they worked as poor itinerant preachers without ecclesiastical license, and they had also frequently consecrated the eucharist without being ordained. For that reason, the clergy had often acted against them, and there had been furious confrontations.[97] Durandus and his supporters stood accused of every sort of error usually attributed to Waldensians, and they were branded heretics. As Waldes had done before them, they turned to the pope, going to the curia to justify themselves.[98] They admitted they had consecrated the sacrament on their own authority, but they insisted they had not done so out of presumption nor out of contempt for the priestly office, but only out of earnest faith and Christian love, particularly because the simple faithful who lived among the heretics could not be won without the sacrament. Still, they agreed to stop doing this, and to hinder others to the best of their powers, defending the policy that only ordained priests could administer the sacraments.[99] They further promised to venerate the clergy, after being sharply chastised by Innocent for earlier offenses. They branded all other imputations of Waldensian errors to themselves as untrue, countering with a thorough confession of faith largely agreeing with that of the "Catholic Poor" in 1208. Innocent responded by confirming that the accusations against them had been unjust.[100] Had they ever been "Waldensians" at all, since Waldensian errors had been imputed to them incorrectly? They certainly had preached, even if against the heretics, and they had even distributed the sacraments without being commissioned or ordained by the Church, and that was sufficient to condemn them as guilty of heresy according to the heresy law of 1184 and the prevailing opinion of the clerical hierarchy. Even if they shunned the dualistic errors of Cathars or the anti-hierarchical resolutions of radical Waldensians, they still inevitably attracted suspicions that as unlicensed preachers they shared such heretical convictions in secret.

The situation of the religious movement in this period is brightly illuminated by the emergence of Bernardus Primus. Waldensians in those days were locked in combat with heretics who were often popularly called "Waldensians" themselves, although not all of them represented the radical anti-hierarchical doctrines of Waldensian propaganda. All apostolic itinerant preachers were being treated as heretics by the Church and its representatives, however, without reference to their dogmatic orthodoxy. Once Innocent III assumed the tiara, an additional route had opened, since apostolic preachers could have their mission confirmed by the curia, as Durandus of Huesca had done in 1208. Even Bernardus Primus and his companions made use of this opportunity only after coming into conflict with the clergy, when accusations of heresy forced them to turn to the curia. Perhaps many other groups of apostolic itinerant preachers of similar orientation had been just as ready to make agreements with the curia in order to be able to continue their work unmolested, but whether they would actually take this step was left to the occasion and their own initiative. This situation persisted as long as no organization existed which was authorized by the Church to shunt the poverty movement in all Christian lands in an orthodox direction, drawing to itself all the forces working in the sense of evangelical and apostolic movement while shunning all heresy. The *Humiliati* had been restricted to the Lombard towns; the "Catholic Poor" had not been able to create a comprehensive organization for their society, and despite the support of the curia, the resistance of the bishops had restricted and finally foredoomed any growth. It was only the Franciscans and the Preachers of Dominic who understood the task of organization and carried it out, winning a historical importance vastly greater than earlier bands of preachers. Before they could spread across nations, individual groups within the poverty movement had only one opportunity, opened to them by Innocent III, which was that they could receive special permission from the curia for their mission and way of life.

It was Bernardus Primus who now took the path already trod by the *Humiliati* and Durandus of Huesca. Papal recognition of the new community was announced on 18 June 1210 in an encyclical to archbishops and bishops.[101] Requirements for their future way of life were stipulated in an extensive confession of faith and communicated in this form to the bishops. Only two years later these points were summarized in a special *propositum conversationis* and papally approved.[102] This *propositum* was patterned on the model of the "Catholic Poor," altering only a few points. The confession of poverty and complete lack of possessions is literally the same, but an amendment declares that, besides studying scripture and preaching, they should also work with their hands.[103] A further amendment regulates contacts with sisters belonging to their community, otherwise unknown. They were to be strictly segregated from the brothers.[104] Rules for preaching are almost precisely the same as with the "Catholic Poor,"[105] the stipulations for prayer and fasting little altered, and almost everything else is literally the same. The form of community the "Catholic Poor" had pioneered appears to have been the model for incorporating the principle of poverty, itinerant preaching, and continued evolution of the spiritual community into ecclesiastical life.[106]

Beyond the two bulls of Innocent III, the *Confessio* of 1210 and the *Propositum* of 1212, and one papal recommendation to the bishop of Cremona for Bernardus Primus and his companions on 1 August 1212,[107] not a single document on the community of Bernardus Primus has survived,[108] and nothing is known about its expansion or its fate. The silence of charters and other sources leads to the assumption that it never achieved great importance. The German provost Burchard of Ursberg, who was in Rome in 1210, saw the "Waldensians" led by Bernardus Primus as they petitioned for confirmation of their community. He heard only the accusations against them. He never learned they were acquitted, nor that Innocent III recognized their band of preachers, and he tells us nothing of their fate.[109] He misinterpreted the facts by reporting that the pope confirmed another community in their stead which presented itself at the same time, called the *pauperes minores*, later *fratres minores*, that is to say, the Franciscans, who would realize the ideal of the itinerant life in an even purer form and would not be sullied by error or dubious peculiarities. Provost Burchard tidied up historical realities to make them conform with his own ideas when he asserted that the "Preachers," the Dominicans, had been confirmed by the pope in the place of the *Humiliati*, suspected of heresy.[110] In both cases, his description does not agree with the facts, yet in a certain sense the German provost had grasped the truth: the new orders of Francis and Dominic in fact did "take the place" of the novel organizations which had emerged in the first decade of the thirteenth century. To a great degree, also, they fulfilled the missions which preaching bands derived from the Waldensians and the *Humiliati* had sought to fulfill, without success. It is probably true that Innocent III and his successors simply let those earlier experiments and creations fall, turning their energies to newer creations with all the more energy, because the new orders could more surely and more generally achieve the same goals. The new orders' mission was to embody the religious movement, the ideal of voluntary poverty and apostolic preaching, while preserving orthodoxy and ecclesiastical authority, solidly anchored within the structure of the Catholic Church and committed to the struggle against heresy.

3. Francis

When Francis and his eleven companions traveled from Assisi to Rome—probably in the same year as Bernardus Primus[111]—to seek papal permission confirming their efforts as poor wandering penitential preachers, the curia was confronted by a new situation to which previous principles could be applied only with difficulty, despite all earlier measures and experiences. Up to that point, Innocent had always dealt with groups of itinerant preachers long in existence which had been declared heretics and excluded from the Church as a result of earlier policies of the curia. To win communities of that sort back for the Church and to prevent driving the religious movement further into opposition against the hierarchical Church, Innocent conceded everything somehow tolerable to the basic concept of the hierarchical Church. When Francis and his companions appeared at the curia, the question was whether the same concessions of itinerant preaching, voluntary poverty and the formation of congregations would be extended to a community which was only just forming. Francis' community had not been marked by earlier policies of the curia against the religious movement, such as the Waldensians and *Humiliati*, had not yet been persecuted as heretics for disobedience to papal bans, and thus did not need to be rewon for the Church. It remained to be seen whether Innocent's attitude to the Waldensians and *Humiliati* had been merely a tactic in the struggle against heresy or whether it arose from a general understanding that new religious forces and ideals could no longer be excluded from the Church.

Francis appeared before Innocent just as Waldes had before Alexander III thirty years before, but the curia had learned something from the experience of a generation. Innocent recognized how fatal the expulsion and ban of his predecessor had been. He repeatedly tried to reverse or reduce the effects of that baleful decision. In any case these efforts, which Innocent himself often compared with the effects of medical treatment, were primarily intended for heretics reconciled to the Church under special arrangements, and secondarily for experiments whose success was not yet certain. Hence when such a new, autonomous, untried group from the religious poverty movement as that led by Francis challenged the curia to take a stand, there was a genuine question whether the curia would grant freedom for the ideal of poverty and itinerant preaching to develop within the Church. There was a further question of what form the new community would take, since there was no fully formed organization which now simply had to be incorporated into the Church, as was the case with the Waldensians or *Humiliati*.

Innocent did not settle these questions once and for all. He permitted the young community to exist, but without taking a legally binding position, permitting the little community of penitential preachers to take shape in the course of the following decades, developing into a recognized order. The forbearance of the curia, which decided the early fate of the Franciscan community, is understandable from the general ecclesiastical and religious situation, as well as from Innocent's attitude toward the policies of the Church.

In Rome, Francis and his eleven companions met Bishop Guido of Assisi, who had followed Francis' conversion and early activities with interest and support.[112] Through him Francis gained admission to one of the most important and influential members of the College of Cardinals, John Colonna, once a Benedictine of St. Paul's near Rome, who now represented the pope in the administration of penance. John must have learned something about the poverty movement and heresy from his legation to the region of the Albigensians in 1200–1201.[113] The Cardinal agreed to present Francis' cause to the pope. Unfortunately, it is not possible for us to follow the negotiations in any detail. John Colonna tried to get Francis to accept the rule of an order of monks or hermits, hence some form of the Benedictine Rule, and Innocent himself seems to have proposed that he follow one or another of the established rules.[114] The itinerant preachers were thus advised to become monks. Francis would not agree to these recommendations, however. He did not want to be a monk or a hermit, and he did not wish to found an order such as those which already existed.[115] The conclusion of negotiations and the reports on their course show that the curia eventually dropped its objections and gave in to Francis' wishes by making no further difficulties for the continued activity and growth of the new community of penitential preachers. Cardinal John Colonna set the pattern in the decisive negotiations with Innocent. Some cardinals objected strongly that Francis' plans were a ''novelty'' and thus unacceptable, and that they were also impractical, because a community based on such a strict use of the principle of poverty would not be viable. Cardinal John countered these objections by stating that Francis exclusively cited examples from the gospels, which could be seen neither as novel nor impractical without raising criticism of Christ.[116] With Cardinal John's weighty words, the ideal of the *perfectio evangelica* had been raised in the curia for the first time, so far as is known. This was expressed in the same manner as the ideal which inspired the entire religious movement at the time, and the ideal was recognized for the first time as a legitimate way of life within the Church. It was not merely conceded out of tactical considerations in the struggle against heresy, but for the sake of its claim in the gospels. The curia could no longer avoid the conclusion that it not only lacked the means but even the religious right to suppress the ideal of the evangelical, apostolic life.

Innocent's decision conformed with this conclusion. He did not forbid what Francis intended to do; rather, he permitted it. Francis and his companions were allowed to continue their work as penitential preachers unhindered. This permission was tied to only two conditions, which were immediately fulfilled. Francis and his companions had to receive tonsure, hence becoming clerics; Cardinal John had supported this requirement.[117] Further, Francis had to swear obedience to the pope, and his eleven brethren had to swear obedience to Francis as their leader. This settled a basic question of any ecclesiastical organization, which was leadership. The oath of obedience was the first stage of an organization similar to an order, and the oral permission of the pope was the first step to confirming it. Beyond that, Innocent prescribed nothing to the community for its future formation. He did not confirm in writing the collection of sentences from the gospels which Francis had gathered, which was called both his first ''rule'' and his *propositum conversationis*,[118] and the pope did not grant them a written license to preach, let alone a formal privilege. On the basis of this papal decision, Francis' community had much less right to be considered an approved order than the Waldensian groups being reconciled with the Church in that period, which at least had papal bulls recognizing their rule of life and their right to preach. The curia's reticence is doubtless explained by the fact that no one knew whether this little community of preachers had a future or would win enough importance to demand and justify ecclesiastical organization under papal auspices. The curia decided to wait, sending Francis on his way with its blessings. If his community grew, he was to return to the curia; then a more comprehensive, binding regulation would be developed.[119]

With all its caution and restraint in the negotiations with Francis, the curia had decided in principle to grant license to this community of poor itinerant preachers, although there had been no break with heresy; it was not an agreement reconciling heretics to the Church. Innocent himself did not take the construction and ramification of this community in hand, and he probably did not even encourage it. It was left to itself, and for years its nature and mission would remain unclear.[120] It is hard to say what role Innocent III played in the further evolution of the community of preachers into an order. Political events of greater contemporary importance claimed the first attention of the curia in the following years, giving yet another decisive turn to its attitude to the religious movements of the day.

4. The Lateran Council of 1215

Since the start of his pontificate, two thoughts had dominated the policy of Innocent III on heretics: to combat stubborn and incorrigible heresy to the maximum and with all means, but also to attempt to reintegrate into the Church groups which had fallen into heresy, reconciling them with the curia and taking care, through carefully selected ecclesiastical means, to keep more from being driven into the arms of heresy.

The advent of the Albigensian war in 1209, which Innocent had probably not sought but had also not tried to hinder, epitomized the one side of his policy on heresy with grisly intensity. It was thus all the more to be expected at the great council which was to crown his life's work that Innocent would have brought to life a grand realization of the ideas which he had developed on a case-by-case basis for the religious movement and communities of itinerant preachers.

The Council was called on 19 April 1213,[121] its first general session met on 11 November 1215, and it completed its work with two further sessions on 20 and 30 November. Alongside the recovery of the Holy Land, the reform of the Church, threatened by heresy, was the focus of the program. Was it possible for the Council to believe this could be accomplished through the elimination of abuses and the restoration of old, pure forms of life among monks and clerics? Did not increased tensions between the hierarchical Church and the religious movements demand a decisive and fundamental reordering of the Church? And did not Innocent's attitude up to this point lead one to expect that he was aware of this task and ready to deal with it?

Very little is actually known about the course of the Council. We know almost nothing about the negotiations which took place before and during the council, nothing at all about the preliminary discussions in committees, and we have no idea of the forces which influenced its outcome. Only the decrees themselves survive.

Among these decrees,[122] the treatment of heresy takes primary place. First of all there is a thorough confession of the Catholic faith, followed by a condemnation of Joachim of Fiore on the Trinity[123] and a declaration of bans against every heresy against the Catholic faith up to then. The thorough descriptions dealing with heresy contained in the Council statutes of 1215 do not contain a single new sentence. They are nothing more than a summary of older decisions, partly from the heresy edict of Lucius III of 1184, partly from the decree of Innocent III by which he regulated actions against the heretics in Viterbo.[124] The Council repeated clauses of these earlier heresy decrees either word for word or with slight changes or more detailed descriptions, adding nothing essential. No new penalties were introduced for heresy; the oath-based duty of every temporal power to struggle against heresy was only more sharply formulated than it had been; the inquisitorial responsibility of bishops in their dioceses was repeated almost literally from the heresy edict of Lucius III. In short, the method of proceeding against heretics is preserved unchanged as it had been even before 1200, without the experiences of the pontificate of Innocent III stimulating any new measures.

What is more important is how the Council dealt with the decisive question of who was to be condemned as a heretic. It should be mentioned that the Council, by forbidding clerics from participating in ordeals of fire or water,[125] definitively withdrew condemnations for heresy from the accidental "judgment of God," as Innocent had demanded in 1212 in a letter to the bishop of Strasbourg,[126] with the justification that one should not tempt God. If the magical pronouncement of the ordeal no longer decided heresy, it was all the more necessary that clear methods and rules for differentiating pious believers from heretics be spelled out. The heresy edict of 1184 had solved this problem by declaring heretical first of all a list of named groups, secondly unlicensed presumption of the office of preaching, and thirdly the spreading of false teachings on the sacraments of the Church. Lastly, it was reserved to the Church and its bishops to condemn particular cases as heresy. The Council of 1215 considerably simplified these rules by publishing a new Catholic creed, with all errors violating it declared heresy.[127] This forthrightly made dogma a criterion between orthodoxy and heresy, and there was no need to elaborate by listing the names of heretical groups or teachings. Despite this, a further criterion of heresy was adopted from the heresy decree of 1184 by the Council statutes of 1215, using the same words declaring unlicensed preaching heresy![128] Repetition of this rule is not very surprising in itself, for the Church never abandoned the notion that non-ordained preaching was heretical, and Innocent had never dropped it in his negotiations with adherents of the religious movement and itinerant preaching. On the contrary, he had always compelled Waldensians and *Humiliati* explicitly to recognize it. At the same time, however, he had always tried to compromise between the drive for apostolic itinerant preaching and the ecclesiastical ban on preaching by the unordained by recognizing preaching communities of a new type, which would receive papal authority for members to preach within certain limits. If the Council renewed the ban on unlicensed preaching, it would be expected also to take a position on this new form of preaching community, giving the question of licensing preaching an entirely new face. That did not happen, or rather, the Council approved rules which directly opposed the idea of such preaching communities.

The Council expressly recognized that bishops as ordained preachers were no longer in the position to fulfill the demand for preaching by themselves. To supply this lack, the Council approved bishops and archbishops commissioning and supporting qualified preachers to assist in preaching and pastoral care.[129] Pressures of religious groups for apostolic preaching could not be satisfied by such rules.

Further, the Council passed a decree which would have prevented the rise of preaching associations which could receive a papal commission to preach, hence placing itself in unmistakable opposition to Innocent's earlier decisions and measures. It was forbidden to create "new orders"—more correctly, to "invent" new forms of orders. Whoever wanted to become a monk (*ad religionem converti*) had to accept an approved rule, and whoever wanted to found a house had to place it under the rule and custom of one of the approved orders.[130] This rule was justified by declaring that too great a variety of orders provoked disorder in the Church.

The importance of this decree only becomes clear when one considers the situation in which it was created and for which it was created. When this ban on new forms of orders was issued, there were many projects underway for new forms of organization, but none of these new structures had achieved the status of an "approved order" in canon law. The *Humiliati* could be considered an approved order, insofar as their first and second orders were organized according to the rules of Benedict and Augustine, and insofar as they lived the *vita communis*; the third order of the *Humiliati*, however, was not an approved order and had no approved "rule," following only a *propositum* approved by the curia. The communities of Durandus of Huesca and Bernardus Primus, growing out of earlier associations of Waldensians and itinerant preachers, had been recognized by the curia and admitted, but they, too, lacked an approved "rule," and they were not approved orders at the time the Council's decree was issued. Later, their status as regular orders would be denied on the basis of this decree. We have already seen that the preachers' community of Francis had been legitimized on the basis of negotiations with the curia in 1210, but could not yet be regarded as an approved order. Finally, the preachers' band Dominic established in Toulouse at the beginning of 1215 to pursue a mission to the heretics in Southern France had not yet been approved as an order when the Council met. Shortly before the Council, Dominic came to Rome to have a rule confirmed by the curia and to have his group recognized as an order. He departed the curia after being assured that new orders could only be established on the basis of old, approved forms.[131]

If the Council banned the creation of new forms of orders at this moment, this was an intervention to hinder the development of novel communities. The Council's decision is not to be seen as completing and reinforcing a completed development, nor as a guide to future development, but rather as a defensive veto of new creations in the process of birth. It was to hinder the development of new sorts of orders, cloistered communities and monks, differing significantly from Benedictine monks or Augustinian canons. This would also have prevented the development into approved orders of the communities of itinerant preachers Innocent had already recognized.

There is thus no doubt that this conciliar decree clashed directly with Innocent III's earlier measures. Either Innocent took a new course in the last period of his life, or the Council's decision did not correspond to his own views. To decide this question, it is necessary to compare the pope's attitude in the last years of his life with the Council's decree. Since nothing is known of his relationship to other new communities he supported then or during the half-year before his death, this means studying how Innocent dealt with the community of Francis in the light of the Council's decree.

According to Innocent's approval of 1210, the preaching community of Francis should have been much less significant than the "Catholic Poor." The "Catholic Poor" had been legitimized with a papal bull, and they possessed a charter which confirmed their *propositum* as legitimate. Francis had only received an oral permission, nothing else. If the Council banned the creation of new forms of orders, compelling all "religious" to accept one of the old, accepted rules for monks, there can be no doubt the original "rule" of Francis approved by Innocent was not among the approved rules and his little community could not be numbered among the approved orders. This was precisely the sort of band of penitential preachers the ban on "new forms of orders" was intended to prevent.

Despite this, far from being suppressed, the community of Francis in fact developed in the following years into an order of an entirely new sort, without binding itself to one of the approved rules, as did the Dominicans. The decree on orders issued by the Lateran Council was thus not applied to Francis and his companions. How could this happen?

We are quite poorly informed about the development of the order in these specific years. Only in 1219 was the order first named in a document, a bull of Honorius III, and then, as in a papal bull of the following year, the Minorites are expressly mentioned as an approved order,[132] although the inner character of the order was still by no means settled. Since Innocent's permission of 1210 by itself could not have sufficed to win Francis' community recognition as an approved order contrary to the decree of the Lateran Council, something must have happened in the meantime granting the Franciscans the character of an approved order without their having adopted an approved rule as the Council demanded. Let us try to examine this more closely.

The leaders of all the orders were summoned to the Lateran Council. If Francis had been the leader of an approved order at that time, he would have had to participate as such. As we have seen, this was not the case.

If the community of Francis was not yet an approved order in those days, it should have been struck by the ban on new forms of orders passed by the Council—unless something happened before or during the Council to alter this factual situation. There is thus a great likelihood that Francis' community—which had been told by Innocent to return to the curia when his following had increased!—received a more effective papal confirmation than the oral promise of 1210 before the ban of the Council took effect. These considerations also encourage the inference that this confirmation took place at the same time as the decree of the Council, and that negotiations took place between Innocent and Francis with the Council's decree in mind, exempting the Franciscan community from the ban. This inference can be adequately supported in the sources.

The first source to confirm Francis being present in Rome at the time of the Council is the *Chronicle of the 24 General Ministers*, a relatively late source of the fourteenth century.[133] This passage is probably derived from a tradition of the Dominican Order concerning a meeting of the two founders of the mendicant orders at the time of the Lateran Council, written down by Gerard Frachet in 1260/2.[134] This mention is the sole, admittedly thin, trace of a visit by Francis to Rome in 1215.[135]

There is a second, independent trace found in an older Franciscan tradition. In his second legend,[136] Thomas of Celano tells us Francis and Dominic once met in Rome in the house of Cardinal Ugolino. The cardinal asked them whether it would not benefit the Church for their brethren to become bishops and prelates. Both of them declared this to be incompatible with their ideal of the religious life. When they departed from the cardinal, Dominic asked for Francis' hemp belt, which was given him, and at parting he was said to have told Francis, "Brother, I wish they would give one order to the two of us, so we could live in the Church in one manner." The tradition does not say when this scene was supposed to have taken place, but it has been noted that, if this meeting and conversation really took place as the legend describes,[137] it must have preceded papal confirmation of the Dominican Order (22 December 1216). Then was the only time Dominic could have expressed the desire to place his community of preachers and that of Francis in one order. This proposal would be most understandable at the time of the Lateran Council, when Dominic was still searching for a form of organization on behalf of the few members of his community of preachers.[138] This trace also indicates, if without any solid proof, that Francis was in Rome at the time of the Council, negotiating over the question of the future organization of his order.

The third and most certain clue shows, even without Francis being present in Rome, that *something* happened in the context of the Council which protected the order beyond the oral approval: as the tradition of the order shows with some certainty, Innocent publicly announced to the Council his recognition of the order or its rule.[139] All of this indicates that in all likelihood,[140] Francis was in Rome in 1215 negotiating with the curia over matters concerning his order, and that Innocent expressed a new recognition of the order in public which protected it from being affected by the decree of the Council or compelling it to accept one of the older approved orders.[141] We have no idea how it happened or how the relationship between the curia and the new order changed.[142] What is decisive is this: at the very moment when the Council tried to hinder the development of new forms of orders, Innocent saw to it that the Franciscan community of preachers was secured in an old form which actually had the capacity to develop into a "new form of order."

Another episode closely tied to this also ran contrary to the intention of the conciliar decree. Since 1212 Clara Sciffi had been living together with several other women in the church of St. Damian in Assisi, which had been given them by Bishop Guido. They lived in a small monastic community which obeyed none of the recognized rules, following instead the counsels of a simple *formula vitæ* given them by Francis. The pope's oral approval of Francis' community of preachers in 1210 could in no way be used to justify cloistered women organizing under the evangelical ideal of poverty. An additional approval for the community of women led by Clara did not exist. In 1215 the Council compelled all new houses to accept an approved monastic rule. This regulation would doubtless have applied to the house of St. Damian as well, forcing them to accept an approved monastic rule. Despite this, the house survived without being obligated to any rule beyond the *formula vitæ* of Francis.[143] Several years later a second rule was formally recognized, patterned after the rule of Benedict by Cardinal Ugolino for the female houses of Central Italy.[144] Despite this, the "formula of life" remained in force in the house. When all female houses under Ugolino's rule were compelled to accept corporate property, St. Clara and her house of St. Damian managed to avoid this obligation, reject the rule, and win papal recognition for their own rule after long curial resistance. Clara's rule, based on the Franciscan rule and preserving the essential elements of the original *formula vitæ* of St. Francis for St. Damian, created an entirely new type of cloistered female community without communal property.[145] All this was possible because Clara and the sisters of St. Damian could appeal over the curia to a special act of Innocent III which had made the decree of the Council of 1215 compelling all houses to take one of the old monastic rules invalid for St. Damian. Clara had received a *privilegium paupertatis* from Innocent III, a confirmation in the form of a genuine monastic privilege saying the sisters of St. Damian were allowed to live in their community without receiving property in the manner of other houses to assure their income. Since all older, approved monastic rules, particularly those for female houses, assumed that individual religious were propertyless but the houses disposed of adequate income for its inmates, the *privilegium paupertatis* guaranteed St. Damian could not ever be forced to receive one of the old, approved monastic rules.[146]

We do not know precisely when Innocent issued this important document.[147] There is, however, valuable information which shows Innocent was fully aware of the novelty and peculiarity of this privilege, which was opposed to all other privileges for religious houses, since he is supposed to have written out the entire privilege with his own hand.[148] He must have been entirely aware this privilege legitimized an entirely novel form of cloistered female community. Whether this privilege was issued before, during or after the Council, it was unmistakably, diametrically opposed to the conciliar decree, for it made possible what the Council was trying to hinder: the rise of new forms of religious communities which did not build on the foundation of an older form of order.[149] Under the protection of this privilege, the community of St. Clara survived as a new form of female house, despite the ban of the Lateran Council. Clara had it repeatedly confirmed by subsequent popes,[150] until the new form of life was finally recognized by the confirmation of the rule composed by Clara herself before her death, preserving the original counsels St. Francis had given the sisters of St. Damian.[151]

Through his confirmation of the Franciscan community at the Lateran Council and his privilege of poverty for Clara and the sisters of St. Damian, Innocent III demonstrated his continued, lasting loyalty to the principle which his policy toward the religious movement had pursued since the beginning of his papacy. In so doing, he asserted a right for the ideal of itinerant preaching and voluntary poverty to exist, creating an area of activity within the Church so as not to permit it to fall into heresy. He further recognized, created and promoted new forms of the religious life for this purpose. New communities created after 1200, from the *Humiliati* to the Franciscans, owed their existence to the pope's insightful, careful policies, which permitted them to develop as ecclesiastically recognized associations. The survival of the community of Francis and the house of Clara Sciffi in St. Damian's in their primitive, self-selected forms beyond the time of the Lateran Council was probably due to Innocent's will alone.

The Council's decree on orders completely contradicts this policy, so it must be assumed that it did not correspond with the pope's desires, but was adopted against his will.[151a] We have no sure basis for determining who it was who passed this decree in opposition to the policies of the pope. It is most likely that bishops and prelates on one side, whose resistance to the papal policy on the religious movement had already made itself known,[152] saw a threat to their rights of pastoral care. On the other side, the old orders, particularly the Cistercians, did not want to see new orders arise alongside themselves, and they wanted to stymie the canon law measures taken by Innocent during the previous fifteen years.[153] The matter will never be fully clarified, since almost all information on the activities of the Council is lacking. But the opposition between the will of the Council and the will of Innocent is obvious: the Council's decree not only contradicts the earlier measures of the pope, but Innocent also consciously acted against the effects of this decree in establishing Francis and the religious house of St. Damian. The desire of the Council to smother the "novel" orders in their cradles, before they had been recognized as proper orders, was thus frustrated. Innocent III opened the way for the transformation and renewal of the Church over the resistance of the prelates.

Resistance of the prelates and clergy to apostolic preachers recognized by the papacy was made as palpable with the Franciscans as it had been against the *Humiliati* and the Catholic Poor, once they expanded their efforts into all countries after 1217. Papal protection, however, quickly broke the opposition. Once one knows the character and connections of the poverty movement, it is no surprise that the Franciscans in France as well as in the Rhineland were first seen as heretics,[154] since there was in fact no basic or visible difference between them and "heretical" itinerant preachers. A Paris synod in 1207/8 under Bishop Otto had already strictly forbidden all preachers to allow unlettered preachers to speak on streets and squares. Parishioners were penalized for listening to such preachers, since there was danger that they were spreading error and heresy.[155] When Franciscan friars came to France about ten years later, these unlettered preachers were naturally treated with the same suspicion as all the others. They were regarded as Albigensians. The bishop and masters of Paris, before whom they had to answer these charges, were not completely convinced by the examination of their rule, and they sent a petition to the curia and were only instructed of the orthodox, ecclesiastical character of these poor itinerant preachers by a bull of Honorius III.[156]

Things turned out even worse for the Franciscans on their first attempted mission to Germany in 1219. Just as in France, their ignorance of languages meant they were unable to defend themselves against the suspicion of heresy; they were imprisoned and chastised, and in the end they had to be happy to get back to Italy alive without having accomplished anything.[157] Even when they returned two years later with greater success, better prepared and led by German friars, they were again accused of being heretics by the clergy of Cologne—just as were the Dominicans. They were thought to be the "false prophets," the "erring people" against whom Hildegard of Bingen had warned the Cologne clergy in word and writing half a century before.[158] Indeed, all the signs Hildegard had prophesied for the coming *populus errans*[159] applied to a startling degree to the mendicant orders. The sole difference was the decisive change that had come about in the leadership of the Church as a whole, drawing the line between error and Catholic faith differently than representatives of hierarchical thought had done in the twelfth century. When William of St. Amour presented the same arguments the curia had once used to combat the religious poverty movement from the standpoint of the old hierarchical Church, calling the mendicant orders the "false apostles" of the last times, harbingers of Antichrist, he was himself condemned as a heretic. "Heresy" had come to have a different sense and content, for the Church had received a different structure, since hierarchy and religious movement no longer opposed one another but had rather coalesced into a new whole.[160]

CHAPTER 3

The Social Origins of *Humiliati*, Waldensians, and Franciscans

In order to counter the misunderstanding that the religious poverty movement drew its membership from the lowest social classes, from lowly artisans or the "urban proletariat," which is to say that it was a "social movement" born out of economic need and directed against the higher classes, we will proceed to cross-examine the witnesses for the social origins of the *Humiliati*, Waldensians and Franciscans in the first days of these associations.

In the fifteenth century, the *Humiliati* themselves traced their origins back to Lombard nobility who founded these communities as early as the start of the twelfth century, introducing them to the working of wool. This tradition is opposed by critical research[1] in favor of the proposition that the *Humiliati* movement arose about 1150 among members of the lowest social levels as a reaction to economic oppression. For the lowest proletariat, degraded into a miserable, oppressed, and helpless existence of economic dependence by the rise of capitalistic methods of production, organization as a religious community was the only way out of their situation, as well as the only way it could "strike." Workers in the Lombard wool industry not only protected themselves against oppression and exploitation on the part of entrepreneurs by forming religious-economic associations, but they also thereby became economically powerful, and after a few years they entered the ranks of capitalist enterprises.

These interpretations,[2] seeking to understand spiritual and religious movements as secondary phenomena of social and economic processes in the sense of the materialist concept of history, rest on the following assumptions: that the *Humiliati* participated in the wool industry from the very beginning, and that they emerged at the very moment the wool industry of Northern Italy developed capitalist forms, splitting entrepreneur from worker, making them capitalist and proletariat. The *Humiliati* are thus seen as a reaction against this development, and it is clear (!) that most of them were not capitalist entrepreneurs but proletarian workers.[3] Using much more recent materials, Zanoni has composed a picture of the situation of this proletariat,[4] forbidden to band together economically to better their position, their only escape to associate as religious communities in order to control their own production.[5] The first problem with this thesis is that when capitalism began in North Italian wool production, in the form of the division between worker and entrepreneur (about which we know very little), many involved in wool production were neither entrepreneurs nor workers. People who worked in the older craft forms long persisted, and they were more likely than economically powerless workers to struggle against new forms of production. Secondly, the protest against capitalist development represented by the *Humiliati* made no sense for persons from the unpropertied proletariat. As early as 1179 the *Humiliati* committed themselves to wearing simple clothing made of undyed cloth.[6] Their *propositum* of 1201 expressly prescribed proper clothing: "They are not to wear clothing which is neither too splendid nor too vile, but such that betray nothing irreligious, for neither love of the sordid [!] nor the exquisite become a Christian." That is certainly a protest against offensive luxury in fashion,[7] but a religiously based protest, a declaration on behalf of Christian simple clothing which would never have been raised by a propertyless proletariat, which could never have been able to afford anything else. Furthermore, the way of life to which the *Humiliati* committed themselves did not conform to the economic goals this theory postulates. When Zanoni (169) believes that ceaseless labor by *Humiliati* combined with their thrifty, modest way of life would have to lead to a rapid accumulation of mobile capital—he overlooks the fact that stipulations of the *Humiliati* rule directly forbade accumulating capital, making this procedure impossible. The rule demands that members of the Third Order return all "property acquired unjustly"—the common theme of all religious movements at this time![8]—and that any excess in income should be given to the poor.[9] In the same spirit, the *propositum* requires that all income beyond minimal need should be distributed as alms.[10] The *Humiliati* could not have confessed such principles if it was the purpose of their associations to make rich entrepreneurs out of poor proletarians. This leaves out of consideration the requirements for canonical prayer, fasting two days of the week, participation in sermons in their communal assemblies, for whose sake they accepted expulsion from the Church and persecution as heretics.

As early as the 1170s, clergymen were joining the *Humiliati*, and even in the early days rich and prominent persons were doing so as well.[11] According to the chronicle of the *Humiliati* by Friar Marcus Bossius,[12] "certain other nobles of the city of Milan" joined Guido de Porta Orientali on his journey to Rome to win approval of the statutes in 1199. James of Vitry, incidentally, described the *Humiliati* in 1216, clergy and lay, as "almost all literate."

These sources are incompatible with the assertion that the *Humiliati* were an economic association of the lowest proletariat in religious camouflage. Even Zanoni attributed the influx of clergy, nobles, wealthy and educated elements to the attraction of the religious ideas which the *Humiliati* had made their own, and he also felt compelled, in contradiction to his main thesis, to declare that the deepest root of the *Humiliati* movement was the religious question.[13] We know for a fact that rich burghers, nobles, clerics, and women belonged to the communities of the *Humiliati*; of the participation of "proletarians" there is not a trace. We know the religious goals which mandated them to live by the labor of their hands, to be satisfied with a "just" return, to gather no treasure, to give the surplus to the poor, and to obtain no "unjust goods"—but we hear nothing about specifically economic goals.

Zanoni seeks confirmation for his perception of the nature of the *Humiliati* in the notion that other groups in the religious movement derived from the same social class he believed gave birth to the *Humiliati*.[14] His opinion that the Cathars belonged exclusively to the lowest classes has already been shown to be false; the beguines will be discussed presently.[15] The same has often been asserted about the Waldensians,[16] but this assertion does not apply to its beginnings or until the middle of the thirteenth century. Waldes himself was a burgher who had grown rich through usury, with extensive holdings in land.[17] The first companions who joined him gave their entire property to the poor in order to live in voluntary poverty, so they could not have been propertyless either.[18] General information on the social origins of the earliest Waldensians is lacking; the description of them as *idiotæ* and *illiterati* only tell us that we know nothing about their social standing, and several sources prove even this definition does not apply to all Waldensians. The leader of the Waldensians who provoked the intervention of the bishop in Metz in 1199 was a *magister presbyter Crispinus*.[19] The Waldensians who returned to the Church after the disputation at Pamiers in 1208 under the leadership of Durandus were *ex magna parte clerici et pene omnes litterati*, as were the companions of Bernardus Primus, who had been active before 1210 as a "Waldensian."[20] The bishops of Southern France complained to Innocent III that monks had even left their cloisters in order to join the wandering preachers of Durandus, the "Catholic Poor."[21] The religious community which joined the "Catholic Poor" in the bishopric of Elne included clergy.[22] Just as in the case of Cathars and *Humiliati*, so also with Waldensians and those who split from them to rejoin the Church as itinerant preachers, those converted to voluntary poverty included the wealthy as well as a large contingent of clergy.

In his book against the Waldensians, Abbot Bernard of Fontcaude discussed what sort of people were most likely to be seduced by them. For the most part he lists psychological rather than social characteristics: inexperienced, innocent, simple, upright, and weak persons were the most likely to fall, particularly women. It is remarkable that he applies the biblical quotation of the "generation which shall devour the poor of the earth, and the poor of men" to the Waldensians, but through allegorical interpretation he quickly excludes the interpretation that it is the needy or poor who are being seduced by the Waldensians. To him, the "poor of the earth" should be understood more as "some deprived of sense," and the "poor of men" as "humble in heart."[23] Only one category of the easily seduced is defined in terms which also had a social meaning; that is the greedy![24] This could only mean that the Waldensians often converted rich persons, which is in harmony with the fact that Bernard of Fontcaude accuses heretics of often possessing several houses for their enjoyment.[25]

Everything vouches for the fact that Waldensian itinerant preachers before the start of the thirteenth century did not recruit largely from the "lowest levels of society"; we cannot show a single example of a poor convert, and we have many examples to the contrary.[26] It is certain that this situation changed from the thirteenth century on. During that period, not only did the adherents of Waldensian preachers draw more and more from little people, from artisans and peasants, but the preachers themselves came to be drawn increasingly from these ranks.[27] Still, these later characteristics cannot be applied to understand the origins of the sect.

These observations of the social foundations of the poverty movement and the social origins of itinerant preachers are completely confirmed by the corresponding data for the first Franciscans. Franciscans are also frequently cited, without much proof, as a religious vanguard of the lowest social levels.[28] Just as in the case of Francis himself, the first companion to join him, Bernard of Quintavalle, came from the same milieu as Waldes: a wealthy merchant from a respected family, *de nobilioribus, ditioribus et prudentioribus* of Assisi.[29] The next companion was Petrus Cattaneo, *vir litteratus et nobilis*, who had studied law in Bologna[30] and had perhaps been a canon of Assisi cathedral. Of the first twelve friars who were present in Rome in 1210, there was also an elderly priest, Silvester,[31] and two nobles;[32] the origins of the others were unknown.[33] Insofar as we know anything at all, this first Franciscan band of preachers represented precisely the same social groups found everywhere as supporters of the religious poverty movement: rich burghers, nobles, and clerics. Thomas of Celano, whose legends provide only the thinnest information on some friars, still remarks in general: "Many began to gather about Saint Francis, nobles and non-nobles, clergy and laymen, driven to remorse by divine inspiration."[34] James of Vitry wrote of the first Franciscans he saw in Umbria in 1216: "Many of both sexes, wealthy and worldly . . . fled the world."[35] Lastly, an anonymous legend has Francis prophesy concerning his first six companions, that "in a short time, many wise, prudent and noble will come to us and be with us," and he saw this prophecy fulfilled, when on the occasion of the Saint's canonization "many great men and nobles left everything and were converted to the Lord."[36] A search through the sources of earliest Franciscan history for the social origins of friars finds all classes represented, nobles[37] and clerics,[38] scholars (especially jurists)[39] and rich merchants,[40] artists[41] and artisans.[42] In the missionary fields precisely the same picture emerges: the friars working in Germany were joined by Emanuel of Verona; in Hildesheim a son of the Count of Poppenburg joined, who was himself a canon of the cathedral church, besides Albert the *magister puerorum* (schoolmaster) as well as a knight. Jordanus further mentions among the friars won in Germany a Hermann of Weissensee, formerly chaplain in Eisenach, then a Teutonic Knight, Nicholas de Reno, a priest learned in the law, and several *viri probi, honesti et litterati*.[43] The first English Franciscans were similarly drawn from nobles, the wealthy, clerics and the educated, so far as is reported by Thomas of Eccleston.[44]

If it is possible to typify the social origins of Franciscans at all, the common denominator must be that members of all estates and levels entered the order without distinction, but the largest contribution was from the wealthy burghers, the nobility and clergy—not the poor, neither artisans nor the industrial proletariat. In this regard there is little difference between the composition of the original Franciscans and any other group in the poverty movement, whether Cathars or Waldensians or *Humiliati*.

It must be conceded that this conclusion rests on too few scattered, statistically palpable data to produce a proper picture of the facts without preconceptions. It should be stressed all the more decisively, however, that one gets the same result by working from the spiritual and religious content of the poverty movement to determine participation, and it would be a gross misunderstanding of the sense and importance of the movement to see it as an undertaking of the lowest social classes, the poor.[45] A commitment to voluntary poverty would be a lie if poverty were already compelled by need; a confession of *humilitas* would be an empty joke in the mouth of someone who was unable to lower himself any further than need had already placed him. Yet in the religious poverty movement, poverty and humility were chosen and experienced as religious values because they meant overcoming and renouncing the goods and honor of the world, demanding a conversion, a turning away from secular prosperity and social position to another way, which was that of the gospel.

That does not mean that economic and social phenomena were a matter of indifference for the rise and development of the religious movement, but they are important in a different way from the usual perception. The movement is not a reaction of the disinherited, the impoverished, the excluded against the leaders of the Church, society, and economy of the time, but rather a religious reaction among the leaders themselves against social, economic, and cultural development. It does not seek a "bettering of social relations"[46] but its precise opposite: for the sake of religion, it opposed the opening up and flourishing of a worldly, profane culture and sensibility.

The economic and cultural rise in the clergy, nobility, and mercantile bourgeoisie in the course of the twelfth century, the splendid flourish of life, the joy in the treasures of worldliness which filled the heart in monasteries, episcopal courts, castles, and towns, imperiled the rank of religion as the highest and most essential purpose, rendering it a mere framework for earthly works and joys. The religious movement was directed against this development. The gospel won new power over the spirit at the very moment other powers threatened to replace it—similarly to what happened in the German Reformation—and it found its new adherents precisely among those who were most deeply involved in the temptations of secular culture. This return to religion expressed itself in revulsion against this culture through voluntary poverty and voluntary humility. The most essential demand of the gospel was to be poor and hated by the world, particularly in a world which seemed about to lose itself in the enjoyment of earthly riches and honors to a degree never before seen. To preach this demand tirelessly to the whole world, as the apostles had, now appeared the highest duty of every "good Christian."

CHAPTER 4

The Origins of the Women's Religious Movement

Innocent III, who opened the way for the religious movement to join the Church and work within the limits of the Catholic hierarchy, died in Perugia on 16 July 1216. On the very next day, a man appeared in the curia who not only sought consecration as bishop of Acre, but who had further business concerning not only himself, but the entire religious movement in Flanders, France, and Germany: James of Vitry. Since the election of Honorius III took place on 18 July and the coronation six days later, James was able to have his wishes fulfilled by the new pope in the course of a brief stay in Perugia. On 31 July he was consecrated bishop, and at the same time he obtained papal permission for the "pious women in the bishopric of Liège and in all of France and Germany" to live together in communal houses and strengthen one another to do the right thing through mutual "exhortations."[1] That is to say, they were permitted to form female cloistered communities without being joined to an existing order and without accepting an approved rule, and they were further permitted to preach or to exhort in an edifying manner within these communities. Honorius appears to have given his approval only in oral form, without further directions; it is known to us only from the letters of James of Vitry.

This was the first appearance at the curia of a form of the religious movement with which it had never dealt before. All of the measures and decisions of Innocent III with respect to the poverty movement, itinerant preaching, and heresy had dealt almost exclusively with the Romance countries, and always in the first instance with male associations of preachers, to which religious women occasionally belonged as marginal phenomena or among the broader following. Now, however, female religious communities from a German and Northern-French region, the bishopric of Liège, sought recognition from the curia. At the same time conflicts raged between the Church and heresy in the South, in Italy, Southern France, and Spain, and the formation of new associations of preachers approved by the Church neared completion; a new form of religious movement was unfolding in the North. This movement would soon overlap with the mendicant movement spreading from the South, intermingling and influencing the religious development of the thirteenth century in peculiar ways.

James of Vitry, who appeared at the curia as a representative of this female religious movement in Belgium, Northern France, and Germany,[2] was probably the first to recognize not only the breadth and complexity, but also the common nature and unitary importance of the religious movement in various European countries at the outset of the thirteenth century.[3] For years he had lived as an Augustinian canon, the protégé, confessor, and "preacher" in the company of Maria of Oignies, who constituted the center of the religious movement in Belgium. She had once conceived the plan to go to Southern France, to the land of the Albigensians, "to honor God there, where so many have abandoned Him."[4] After her death (23 June 1213), James wrote this woman's biography in order—as Bishop Fulk of Toulouse requested—to be able to present to the Southern-French heretics an effective portrait of a "modern saint."[5] As he traveled through Italy to the curia, he saw the same image everywhere: he observed how the *Humiliati* in Lombardy and the Franciscans in Umbria realized the ideal of voluntary poverty and chastity in much the same way as the religious women in Belgium, and how they, too, were slandered as heretics by the ignorant or hostile, despite the fact that he was convinced that they were the sole living religious force in the Church capable of restraining heresy as well as combating decline and stagnation. He reported his experiences to his friends in Belgium, and without doubt he also described the related movement of the women of Belgium to religious circles in Italy. In this way, he contributed more than any other to drawing individual groups of the religious movement out of their local narrowness and isolation, filling them with a consciousness of an ubiquitous spirit of new piety reigning throughout the Church. James of Vitry probably also met Francis himself and spoke with him.[6] At the Whitsun chapter the following year the Franciscan Brotherhood decided to expand their activity to the entire Christian world, and in the distribution of mission regions, Francis reserved for himself the Northern French province, *Gallia belgica*, since the Body of Christ was revered there by pious people more than in the rest of Christendom.[7] Francis probably came to this decision due to knowledge of the religious movement among Belgian women which he had obtained from James of Vitry.[8] Cardinal Ugolino, who was just beginning at this time to pay attention to pious female communities in Central Italy, the community of Francis, and the preaching association of Dominic, probably also received his first information about new forms of female piety in Belgium from James of Vitry.[9]

The "religious women" for whom James of Vitry obtained permission from Honorius III in 1216 have won little attention from historical research. Only after it was realized that they gave birth to the beguines have they attracted some interest.[10] Yet it is not only the rise of the beguines, but also their own characteristics which demand closer investigation before their importance to the religious evolution of the thirteenth and fourteenth century can be recognized in its entirety.

Without having drawn the same degree of attention from the curia as the religious movement in the Romance-speaking South, the religious movement in the northern lands had grown increasingly stronger through the beginning of the thirteenth century, partly within orders and religious houses, partly in irregular, heretical circles. In contrast to the Latinate countries, here it was women who were most strongly seized by new religious ideas. In the religious movement in the North, it is always the female element which is central. Again in contrast to the South, most of them managed to find a place during the twelfth century within orders and monastic houses. The Northern French orders established at the start of the twelfth century had shown a distinctive way. As we have already seen, the movement of itinerant preaching had led to new orders only in Northern France, while in the South the movement shared the fate of heretics. The most significant order created in the South, the Cistercians, did not arise from the itinerant preaching movement, but rather developed from religious houses as a renewal of Benedictine monasticism in the twelfth century. As a result, the Cistercians neither sought care of souls nor female religious groups. Certainly the Cistercian reform began under the influence of the apostolic ideals of the time, particularly the ideal of poverty, but these ideas were placed utterly at the service of the reform of religious houses. Cistercians through the entire twelfth century, from Bernard of Clairvaux to the pontificate of Innocent III, would zealously combat the concept of religious renewal outside the cloister, one that followed apostolic models or evangelical austerity. Cistercians were always the most accommodating tool of the curia in opposing the religious movement.

An early observer remarked on the great importance of the Premonstratensians, who grew out of the itinerant preaching movement, contrasting them to the monastic Cistercians, since Norbert's order attracted religious women into the regular life.[11] In fact the numerous convents for women founded by the Premonstratensians in northeastern France and in Germany through the start of the thirteenth century[12] show that Norbert's creation met a need which no religious order at all was fulfilling in the Romance lands—a need nurtured there only by heresy. In later times, to be sure, the Premonstratensians did little further to carry on this mission, and they even tried to withdraw from it. Just as the order gave up its aim to care for souls in favor of a purely monastic life similar to the Cistercians, it also tried to free itself from the participation of women, first by excluding them from communities of double houses, later by trying to exclude them from the order altogether.[13] What is decisive, however, is that through participation in the Premonstratensians, using the Rule of St. Augustine, religious women of all social levels for the first time were offered the opportunity to realize the religious ideals of the day through strict enclosure and a chaste, poor, contemplative life. When the order ceased to promote forming such communities and even rejected them, it became clear for the first time that these Premonstratensian convents had never simply been a product of the propaganda of the order. Rather they had been the precipitate of a strong religious women's movement, arising from its own pressures and needs, which would not subside when the Order of Prémontré excluded them, but would grow ever stronger, seeking new forms. This is not the place to review in detail how, in response to the refusal of the Premonstratensians, the new women's houses arising after the end of the twelfth century joined the Cistercians. When the Cistercians in their turn refused to take on any more,[14] these women formed communities belonging to no order at all, following no specific rule, but binding themselves in all strictness to commandments of female piety in chastity and poverty, prayer and fasting.[15]

Heretical developments outside the orders and houses in Northern France, Flanders, and the Rhineland are every bit as important for understanding the religious movement in the North as the history of the orders sketched by Joseph Greven. Heresy in this region had an essentially different character from Southern France or Lombardy. There had always been complaints about heresy, and heretics were occasionally burned.[16] By the end of the century it was even possible to say that Cathars or Patarines were particularly strong in Flanders.[17] Only on one occasion did a chronicler report that heretics in Flanders, burned by the archbishop of Reims in 1183, represented dualist teachings.[18] Otherwise heretics were always accused of rejecting the sacraments in the accepted ecclesiastical form, particularly marriage, child baptism, and the eucharist. Time and again it was declared with special strength that the heretics acted "under the appearance of the Catholic religion and in the clothing of the spiritual life."[19] Even in the second half of the century, several episodes demonstrate beyond a doubt that acts were perceived and persecuted as heresy which have nothing to do with the dogmatic and philosophic errors of Southern French heretics. Instead, these "heresies" arose from religious and ethical demands which they met themselves and wanted to see fulfilled by the clergy, thus attracting the suspicion of heresy. As early as 1145 the clergy of Liège sent a heretic to the curia at his own request, while his companions were kept at various religious houses until the pope could rule on their treatment.[20] In a similar manner several people who came under suspicion as heretics in Flanders and Belgium frequently appealed to the curia in the subsequent years in order to free themselves of accusations of heresy by the clergy and to witness to their desire for ecclesiastical orthodoxy. Just as Alexander III could not determine whether to condemn the burghers from Flanders, accused by the archbishop of Reims and the king of France as Manichees and "Publicans," who appealed to the curia to justify themselves,[21] so did Calixtus III take the priest Lambert of Liège under his protection against accusations by the bishop and clergy. They accused him of heresy because—as always was the case with the accusation against "heretics"—he had spread erroneous doctrines on baptism and penance, and because his adherents were supposed to have neglected church services and rejected communion. Lambert not only appealed to the curia, he defended himself against the accusations in writing, declaring that he had only been accused of heresy because he had relentlessly preached against the sins of the clergy, calling the lay people of the city of Liège to religious contemplation and reflection. He had gathered them together into pious congregations on Sunday to counter growing forces of worldliness through a realization of Christian teachings.[22] There can be no doubt that Lambert and his adherents were unrelated to anything properly called heresy. His zeal was for a reform of the clergy and a renewal of Christian life through following the example of the gospel and apostles, and it was precisely this effort which made him suspicious as a heretic to the clergy and the bishop. Certainly this particular case cannot be generalized without caution, but other sources give the same picture. An intelligent and courageous contemporary, the Parisian master Peter the Chanter, waged a dramatic, open polemic against the nonsense of the ordeal,[23] which was widely used in the North to determine the heretical character of religious phenomena, due to the lack of other ways to obtain clear rulings. It can be no accident that he leveled his best arguments against the unjust senselessness of ordeals with the example of pious women in Flanders who were accused of heresy simply because they were rumored to have had ties to Cathars, or because they resisted indecent efforts of clergymen and tried to defend their chastity.[24] The decision to live chastely out of religious commitment made women subject to the suspicion of heresy, and the ordeal of the hot iron or dunking in cold water then determined whether those suspected were to be burned as heretics or esteemed as saints. Such examples as Peter the Chanter gives are believable and such cases could not have been unique. A Cistercian chronicler of the same period reports the burning of a maiden in Reims who was held to be an adherent of the *Publicani* because she had not permitted herself to be seduced by a cleric, equating the loss of her virginity with eternal damnation. This fixed idea had been justified by her "mistress" with citations from the scripture showing an astonishing knowledge of the Bible.[25]

Just as individual religious women were accused of heresy due to their confession of the ideal of chastity, and were burned for it, the entire women's religious movement in the bishopric of Liège was suspected of heresy by the diocesan clergy until James of Vitry won them recognition from the curia. For this very reason, they called the women who lived in voluntary poverty and chastity to follow the gospel, whether individually or in groups, by the same heretical name they gave the Cathars in Southern France: beguines.[26]

When the women's houses of the Premonstratensians and Cistercians were no longer able or willing to absorb into their own ranks an ever-increasing women's religious movement, and women could no longer endure the secular clergy's blind, hateful treatment of evangelical piety practiced outside the cloister as if it were a heretical menace, the beguines emerged as a new form of religious life, beseeching the curia for protection. As Joseph Greven showed, the later form of the beguines was decisively formed by events in the little town of Nivelles in Brabant (diocese of Liège), where Maria of Oignies was long active, and where a series of members of orders and clergy, particularly James of Vitry, had taken up the cause of religious women. Still, the entire movement did not derive from there, and for decades it had been operating with similar appearance and conditions throughout the northern and Germanic lands. The pressure, first on the Premonstratensian female houses, then on the houses attached to the Cistercian Order or living according to its rule, was no less in West or Northwest Germany than in Northern France and Belgium.[27] Since the start of the thirteenth century, non-cloistered forms of female religiosity had spread wide across the whole European North, and this had not simply been an expansion from Nivelles to Germany and France. For that reason James of Vitry could present himself in 1216 as speaking for the "pious women" in France[28] and Germany. The knight Philip of Monmirail, who had established several Cistercian women's houses and beguinages in his pious zeal, knew of religious men and women in all the lands from Lombardy to Flanders and Brabant, even in Greece.[29] We know of one example of religious activity among women from the early thirteenth century which is very informative. Cæsarius of Speyer, before he became a Franciscan, had been active as a secular priest in Speyer, and his sermons had caused women to renounce all worldly luxury in a spirit of humble piety. He obviously was trying to realize ideas similar to those used earlier by the priest Lambert of Liège. In precisely the same way as Lambert, he was slandered and threatened with death by fire, which he only managed to escape by the intervention of his influential teacher, so that he had to leave Speyer.[30] We would know nothing about this episode if Cæsarius had not continued to work within the Franciscan Order according to the same ideals which had led to his being accused of heresy before, and if a fellow Franciscan had not written memoirs of his earlier activities. There must have been attempts of this sort to awaken and gather religious forces among women everywhere in those days. Only a little is known about these developments, and the mutual links among these religious women's movements cannot be pursued with any precision; it is only the general religious direction and broad distribution of this conviction among the women of Belgium, Northern France, Germany, and even across the Alps to Central Italy, which is unmistakably clear.

Sister Hadewich, who probably lived among the beguines of Nivelles in the first half of the thirteenth century, created the most intellectually important form of this religious commitment in her "Visions." She also gave the most penetrating expression of consciousness of the interconnections of the new feminine piety far across international borders in her "List of the Perfect." Among the "Perfect" she names beguines in Flanders and Brabant, in Zealand, Holland, and Frisia. She also was in contact with an enclosed hermitess "who lives far away in Saxony," she was visited by pious women from Cologne, she knew like-minded women and virgins "beyond the Rhine," in Thuringia and Bohemia, in England and Paris.[31] Hadewich lived to see one of these religious women, a beguine, burned in 1235 by the inquisitor Robert le Bougre,[32] "for the sake of her just love." Robert was a man who was believed able to recognize heretics from their speech and ways because he had once been one of the heretics in Milan. It is no wonder that his madness caused so much injury that the Church finally recalled and punished him, since the religious movement in Northeastern France and Belgium only superficially resembled the heresy of the South.[33]

To Hadewich, the title of "beguine" for the pious women does not retain a stain of heresy, and this transformation of the word "beguine" shows how much the perception of the religious character of the new feminine piety had clarified in the course of the first decades of the thirteenth century. In 1215, it still raised suspicion of heresy for a woman to be called a "beguine," since that was the name of the heretics of Southern France, but as early as 1223 the Cologne town council records speak without hesitation of religious women as beguines. In the 1230s, the charters begin to speak of the women "called beguines by the people," and after 1245 the women called themselves that name.[34] The old meaning of the word had been forgotten,[35] and the new had lost all hint of heresy.

The general character of this feminine religious movement radiating from the North can only be correctly grasped by not restricting investigation to the beguines alone, who distinguished themselves clearly from other forms of feminine piety only in the course of time. It is even less proper to take knowledge from the beguines of later times and apply it to the movement as it was at the start of the thirteenth century. It is more effective to describe the common content and equal importance of the entire religious women's movement of this time in order to make it comprehensible. Beginning from this point of origin, it will be possible to trace how, as a result of measures and decisions made by the curia, the religious orders, and the women's communities themselves, the movement evolved into various types of organizations which then proceeded to develop autonomously.

The women's movement shared with the religious movement in general the goal of a Christian way of life in the sense of the gospels, which they believed could be achieved particularly through voluntary poverty and chastity.[36] This women's piety distinguished itself from the heretical poverty movement primarily through its renunciation of apostolic activity as well as its dropping of the demand that the clergy and Church fulfill apostolic norms in order to administer their ecclesiastical offices legitimately. It would also grossly misunderstand the sense of this feminine piety and its goals for the religious life if we tried to understand its ideals, its confession of poverty and chastity as nothing but a reflection or elaboration of earthly demands in response to the conditions of the time. The frequently expressed opinion that the religious women's movement of the thirteenth century can be explained entirely in terms of the economic and social distress of women in lower, poorer social levels,[37] that it originated with women who could not marry due to a shortage of men and hence had to seek some other "means of support," not only contradicts all the sources, but utterly misunderstands them and their sense of religiosity.

The women's houses of the Premonstratensians—the first form of the religious women's movement which developed—contained, as one chronicler reports summarily, women of all levels, particularly from noble and wealthy families, as well as all ages.[38] The Cistercian women in Belgium as well as Germany came for the most part from the nobility or the urban patriciate. The notion they did not become nuns simply to find a "means of support" can be proved sufficiently from the few sources we have on these houses.[39] James of Vitry had much the same to say about the social motives of the early beguines as was said of the Cistercian women; he stressed that he saw many women among them who renounced their parents' wealth and rejected marriages with wealthy and prominent men in order to live in poverty by the work of their own hands, humble in food and clothing, dedicated totally to their religious goals.[40] Insofar as the social origins of religious women in the time of the earliest beguines can be established, there can be no doubt it was not lack of wealth but rather the flight from riches which precipitated their decision for voluntary poverty. It was not the access to marriage but the will to marry which was lacking. Maria of Oignies herself, model and center of female piety in the bishopric of Liège about 1200, was the child of wealthy and respected parents of burgher status, and she was married at the age of fourteen. Yet she renounced marriage along with her spouse, giving her property to the poor, as Francis would later do, in order to take seriously demands of the gospel by dedicating herself to helping lepers, and also to converting others to a religious life. She later lived in a cell in evangelical poverty at the canonry of Oignies, the spiritual center of a pious community of sisters.[41] Many other women in the first half of the thirteenth century separated from their husbands, who entered an order, so that they could join a beguinage. Later they would enter one of those Dominican women's houses which continued the traditions of the beguinages, particularly in Southern Germany.

James of Vitry mentions such cases in general when he describes the female Cistercians, as well as when describing the beguines in the prologue to his *Vita* of Maria of Oignies: "Many married persons abstained from licit embraces, leading a celibate and truly angelic life, all the more worthy of a greater crown, since they did not burn even though placed all the deeper in the fire" [*AASS*, June, 4, 637]. Many individual cases of this sort are reported from the oldest South German Dominican women's houses, often from their "beguine-style" onset: in Engelthal there lived Adelheid von Trochau, whose husband entered the Teutonic Knights [*Der Nonnen von Engelthal Büchlein von der Gnaden Überlast*, ed. Karl Schröder (Tübingen, 1871), 14]. In Unterlinden, one of the first to enter in 1232 was Benedicte of Muhlhouse ("a noble girl, who had had all the pleasures and delights of this world") with her little sister, whose husband ("a noble and knight") became a Cistercian, besides Adelheid of Rheinfelden ("who enjoyed many riches and honors in the world; born of a noble lineage; supplied much from her riches to the poor sisters in the early period") whose young husband ("a knight with great fame in secular things") became a Dominican, and the husband of Gertrude of Westphalia, the niece of the Dominican

Provincial Hermann of Havelberg ("of noble and famed lineage"). Reinlind of Riseck entered Unterlinden with two daughters, as four other daughters entered other Dominican women's houses, and her husband became a Teutonic Knight together with two of his sons [*Vitæ sororum*, ed. Jeanne Ancelet-Hustache, *AHDL* 5 (1930), 347ff., 394ff., 481, 464–65]. Elsbeth of Stoffeln became a nun together with two daughters in Diessenhofen-Katharinental, her husband and four sons became Knights of St. John. Agnes von Wangen also lived in this house after separating from her husband, who at first did not wish to consent, but later became chaplain in that very cloister [*Alemannia* 15.167, 171]. Gisela of Umkirch attended a veiling at Adelhausen, and she nagged her husband to consent to a separation for the next four years. In the end, she entered the house with her daughter, while her husband and son entered the Teutonic Knights [*FDA* 13.164]. Johann von Ravensburg, founder of the house of Löwenthal near Buchhorn (now Friedrichshafen) became a Dominican, his wife became prioress in Löwenthal [*FDA*, new series, 2.47]. The Advocate of Gera, Heinrich, entered the Teutonic Knights at the same time that his wife founded the house of Cronschwitz and became a nun there [*Urk. -B. der Vögte von Weida, Gera und Plauen (Thüringische Geschichts-Quellen*, 5), 1 (1885), 34–35 n. 71 and 69]. In his *Vita s. Claræ* [*AASS*, August II, p. 757], Thomas of Celano says of the Italian women's movement: "Many . . . joined in matrimony but abstaining by mutual consent, preserved the law by the men going into orders while their wives went into religious houses."

It is as often reported from the sources that young girls, particularly from the nobility, rejected an advantageous marriage, usually to the mighty scorn of their parents, because they desired no bridegroom but Christ. They would rather not be "cared for," but preferred to live in poverty and outside their own social world as a result of their religious conviction. James of Vitry not only reported this conduct among Cistercian nuns, he even promoted it in his preaching to beguines: "When a girl seeks to preserve her virginity and her parents offer her a husband with riches, whom she despises and rejects, they take this most poorly." [See above, n. 39] This was not moral preaching divorced from reality, for many pious women conducted themselves precisely in this manner. We know that Ida of Nivelles was betrothed by relatives to a burgher of Nivelles when she was nine, after the death of her father in 1209, who had left her with an inheritance, and that she fled in order to be able to "serve the Lord in chastity," "glorying more in the poverty of Christ than in affluence of worldly things and fecundity of numerous children." She joined a community of seven "poor virgins living religiously'' in Nivelles, and six years later she became a Cistercian at La Ramé [*HJ* 35.57]. Hedwig von Gundolfsheim entered Unterlinden in 1239, whose father (''adequately celebrated for goods, family and progeny'') wanted to have her formally betrothed. All efforts on the part of the family could not change her determination to enter the convent. Adelheid von Müntzenheim, who lived in the same house, remained true to her *propositum virginitatis* despite all attempts of relatives and friends to move the thirteen-year-old orphan to marry a rich, respected man. Further, there was Stephanie of Ferrette, daughter of the count of Ferrette (''born from high blood''), who prayed for the loss of her beauty when her parents wanted to marry her off, so she could avoid marriage and be able to enter a convent [*Vitæ sororum*, ed. Ancelet-Hustache, 374, 464–65, 369–70]. The most telling is the biography of Countess Jolande von Vianden, in which her high-noble family (which included Konrad von Hochstaden, Archbishop of Cologne) vainly tried for years to move the girl to accept an advantageous marriage, but how her religious desires, expressed since she was nine, always won out, finally leading her to the Dominican sisters in Marienthal. The *Vita* of the beguine Christine of Stommeln (born to wealthy peasants in 1242) also reports: ''When she was twelve, when her parents wished to give her in marriage, this handmaiden of Christ refused, and unknown to her parents she fled to Cologne''—to the beguines [*AASS*, 22 June, 5 (1867), 368].

Just as is the case with renunciation of marriage, so also religious women renounced wealth, possessions, and social position, not as a result of compulsion and need, but as a result of free choice, and it is always this voluntary commitment to poverty and humility which is praised as a religious act, not poverty derived from need. Insofar as we know anything about the social and economic situations of those women who lived as beguines or in the women's houses of the Cistercians and Franciscans in voluntary poverty, they were not poor women of the lower classes, but rather wealthy or at least prosperous women of higher estate, from the higher nobility, the ministerials, urban patriciates, and prosperous merchants. All the women who played a role in the religious movement in Belgium at the start of the century came either from the estate of knights or of merchants.[42] Noble women lived in the beguinage established by Louis IX in Paris,[43] and the Provençal beguines who joined Douceline of Digne at mid-century belonged largely to the high nobility.[44] It is largely women from the nobility and the wealthy urban patriciates who are to be found in the religious communities of South Germany, usually among the Dominicans.

While it is impossible to give all the individual proofs, a few examples will suffice. The *Vitæ sororum* of Unterlinden declares: ''Many of them came from the nobility, preëminent in great wealth and the dignity of the world: they rejected all of this for Christ, following voluntary poverty as if they were truly poor in spirit, adhering to Christ with all their strength.'' Approximately half of the women mentioned in the nuns' book can be shown to have noble descent, and in many cases their wealth is specifically mentioned. In the case of the others, noble descent is not certain, but it is often said, ''they abounded with considerable things and riches,'' ''they abounded with many possessions and riches,'' ''too many riches and rarities.'' [*Vitæ sororum*, ed. Hustache-Ancelet, 336; cf. also 381, 419, 412, 428, 466] In Ötenbach near Zürich, it is almost only women from the higher and lower nobility who are represented [*Die Stiftung des Klosters Ötenbach und das Leben der seligen Schwestern daselbst*, ed. H. Zeller-Werdmüller and J. Bächtold, (1889), 235]; in St. Gertrude in Cologne, in contrast, it is mostly urban patricians [Gabriel Löhr, ''Das Necrologium des Dominikanerinnenklosters St. Gertrud in Köln,'' *Annalen des Historischen Vereins für den Niederrhein* 110 (1927), 90, 87–88, 91–92, 96ff.] as well as in the seven houses of Dominican sisters in Strasbourg [Wilhelm Köthe, *Kirchliche Zustände Strassburgs im 14. Jahrhundert*, Dissertation, Breslau, 1902, 46]. The French Dominican sisters were exclusively noble women from their origins until the seventeenth century [Marie-Dominique Chapotin, *Histoire des Dominicains de la province de France* (Rouen, 1898), pp. x–xi], and when Cardinal Ugolino took up the organization of Italian women's houses in 1218, he was amazed to find mostly women and virgins who by human measures were wanting for nothing, due to their noble status, had they not rejected the glory and riches of the world in order to lead a religious life in poverty [Bull of Honorius III to Cardinal Ugolino, 27 August 1218, Johannes Hyacinthus Sbaralea, *Bullarium Franciscanum* (Rome, 1759ff.) 1.1]. Clara Sciffi, the only one of these Italian women whose life we know well, was in fact from wealthy urban nobility, as her biographer tells us. She was followed into the cloister by ''the famous and noble, in contempt of the palace'': ''The highest pinnacle of nobility followed her steps, lowering itself from pride of blood to holy sanctity. Not a few worthy of marriage to dukes and kings followed Clare's invitation to penance, and those the mighty wished to marry took on the garb of Clare.'' In 1268 the pope could speak of the order of St. Clare as including the daughters of kings and other magnates [*AFH* 3.672].

Only with these conclusions can we correctly see the essential outlines of the religious women's movement in the first half of the thirteenth century and understand their real themes. Just as is the case with the religious movement as a whole, the reaction against wealth and economic-cultural trends does not come from outside, from those injured by them, but from the very persons who have participated in this development of wealth and earthly prosperity. It is thus significant that the Belgian and German poverty movement produces precisely the same themes of renunciation of wealth found in the Waldensians and *Humiliati*: they wanted no part of "ill-gotten gains." The new possibilities for prospering and rising socially were seen as incompatible with the spirit of the gospel and the will of God, and for that reason, many women voluntarily chose a life in poverty rather than live off the wealth of their parents or spouses.[45] Waldes' first act after his conversion was to return his "unjust gains" to those he had exploited as a merchant.[46] In the same way the *Humiliati*[47] and the adherents of the "Catholic Poor" converted by Durandus of Huesca[48] were obliged to return "ill-gotten gains." Nothing is more characteristic of the tie between the religious movement and economic-social evolution than this flight from wealth and social position into poverty and a way of life disdained by society,[49] but particularly the denunciation of enjoying "ill-gotten gains."[50] This shows with particular clarity that the religious movement is not a protest of the "poor and oppressed" against economic development, against the accumulation of wealth and luxury, against the beginnings of capitalism and "exploitation." On the contrary, the religious protest against these developments came from the same circles originating the development and profiting from it. Just as in the case with Waldes, the *Humiliati*, and Francis, so also the beguines did not protest the wealth of others; they renounced their own wealth for the sake of a religious, evangelical ideal, giving up the goods of this world and choosing voluntary poverty and deprivation. On the other hand, one should never overestimate the economic element of the religious movement, as if it were the sole or the dominant cause of the entire phenomenon, as if the religious movement itself were only a reaction to economic conditions, perhaps a companion phenomenon of the birth of capitalism. The idea of voluntary poverty had already begun to work outside religious houses and draw support at a time when economic and social causes could not be found, and its polemic was not at first turned against economic matters but against the Church. The internal contradiction between the clergy's way of life and the demands of the gospel was the first stimulus for development. As time went on, however, economic development gave it an important dynamism and direction. It could be no coincidence that the movement for religious poverty developed most powerfully and independently in areas where trade and industry made the most progress in the twelfth century, in Lombardy, Southern France, and Belgium. It was in these places that the idea of voluntary Christian poverty sharpened into the demand to renounce the enjoyment of "ill-gotten gains." People were to live from the labor of their own hands or from alms,[51] since the contradiction between the life of a prospering urban society or a saturated noble society had the same effect on persons with religious commitments as had the earlier contrast between the life of the clergy and the gospels. They turned away from economy and society and renounced its goods in order to realize Christian ideals by living in voluntary poverty.

CHAPTER 5

The Incorporation of the Women's Religious Movement into the Mendicant Orders

When Honorius III permitted pious women of Belgium, France, and Germany to live together, he could hardly have conceived of the scale or importance of the women's movement. We also do not know the form in which this permission was issued or the area for which it was intended. In any case, the curia had not yet made a sufficient nor definitive response to the question of how, or in what form, these religious female communities would take their recognized place in the Church.

It has always been a curial principle that "religious life" in the proper sense, the complete and exclusive commitment to religious purposes and forms of life, must be bound to specific rules and assured by solid ordinances in order to endure within the structure of the Church. Hence the concepts of *religio* and *ordo* could become almost equivalent in meaning, as in the term "religious order," since a true "religion" should always be a true "order" as well.[1] At the very moment the curia was confronted with the novel and difficult problem of how to fit the lay religious movement into the structure of the Church, Cardinal Ugolino, later Pope Gregory IX, a man with a particularly clear understanding of the matter, stated the decisive principles with utter clarity. He held that every true *religio*, every way of life recognized by the Church, had to rest on particular rules and norms, prescriptions and penalties; without precise, strict regulation of common life and communal discipline, every *vita religiosa* was in peril of losing its right way and sure foundation.[2] In keeping with this principle, the curia was always concerned with structuring all religious movements as regulated orders. This policy was neither predicated on making religious movements useful, nor on forming them to the Church's purpose, as is so often declared by modern research on the Franciscans. Rather, the curia's position arose out of the conviction lying at the deepest level of the medieval outlook, which was that religious life can only realize its true value, can only have security and endurance, when placed within the universal, proper *ordo* of the Christian world through stable rules.

Hence ecclesiastical recognition of a religious movement always entailed the duty of creating rules, ordinances, and forms of life suited to it.

Yet the Lateran Council of 1215 had banned the creation of new forms of religious life. After that, a religious movement could only find ecclesiastical recognition if it could be fitted into an existing form of life. No order actually existed which was suited to receive a larger women's religious movement. Women's *vita religiosa* was always regulated only when joined to male houses, in coalition with monastic orders. The women's religious movement could thus only be incorporated into ecclesiastical rules by joining it with an existing male order.

In truth, the curia had always pursued this goal when treating women's religious communities, but it could never be attained without tedious effort. Male orders were persistent and stubborn in resisting the obligations which accepting the women's religious movement entailed. Throughout the entire thirteenth century a conflict raged back and forth over the organizational form of the women's religious movement. The women themselves sought to join the large orders, and the curia was concerned to make this possible; the orders, however, fought it, trying by all means available to avoid the obligation of receiving and administering women's communities. Although historians of the Church and of particular orders often mention this in passing, they have never understood the actual links, for they have always dealt piecemeal with the history of the individual women's branches of various orders, never with the women's religious movement as a whole. Still, the evolution of relations of the individual orders with their female branches interconnects so strongly, joining them together so closely in their mutual cause and effect, that this pattern is no longer to be understood as a matter of the individual order, but rather as a confrontation of the women's religious movement as a whole with all the male religious orders. All efforts to elucidate the development of the Clarissans in their relations to the Franciscans, to comprehend the development of their various rules, have failed because of a lack of knowledge of the fate of Dominican women in their relations to the Order of Preachers at the same time—and vice versa. Further, the relationship of the Dominicans and Franciscans to their female branches will only become comprehensible when one knows how the Premonstratensians and Cistercians dealt with quite similar questions of incorporating female branches. Particularly, it is only after a review of all the individual "histories of orders" that the role the curia played in all these conflicts becomes visible. As long as one investigates each of these problems in isolation, the measures of the curia as well as the orders will seem full of contradictions, without continuity, often absurd. Yet in combination with the general conflict between the women's religious movement and the various religious orders, each fact resolves into a sensible, understandable event in ecclesiastical policy. For that very reason these processes will be rather thoroughly treated here: first of all, because this approach will suddenly shed full light on the women's religious movement as a whole;[3] secondly, because the decades-long efforts to incorporate them into existing orders is the clearest possible demonstration of the inner connections, the peculiarity and the historical importance of the women's religious movement. All of the forces at work, the women's religious movement itself, the curia and the religious orders, try to assert their own wills. Despite all, the strength of the women's religious movement was still great enough to achieve incorporation into the orders, against the will of the orders themselves, through the mediation of the curia.

1. The Cistercian Order and Women's Houses

The Premonstratensians had withdrawn from the obligation to maintain a women's branch even before 1200.[4] Further, women's religious communities had tried everywhere to make connections with the Cistercians, since they were the sole order available to them.[5] Yet shortly thereafter, the order of Cîteaux declined to accept the trouble and responsibility which went with the organizational leadership and pastoral care for new women's communities.[6] There were complaints about the women's houses at the general chapter of the Cistercians from 1212 on. The first problem was their location, too close to men's houses,[7] and they often did not maintain complete enclosure, although women's houses could only belong to the Cistercian Order under the stipulation of strict enclosure. Even leaving the house for the purposes of founding new branches was only permitted with prior approval of the general chapter, and any violation of this procedure was regarded as flight from the convent.[8] Soon overpopulation of these houses became obvious, precipitating the establishment of maximum numbers of nuns for each house, which could never be exceeded.[9] As early as 1220 the decision was made not to incorporate any more women's houses into the order.[10] This ban applied at first only to existing women's houses which desired to enter the order. It was still possible to establish a Cistercian convent if it were adequately endowed to permit the nuns to live in strict enclosure without subsidies or alms.[11] The order only wished to free itself of the duty of its own members having to reside in women's houses and administer their worldly affairs.[12] In 1228, however, the general chapter decided not to accept another women's house into the order, neither existing houses nor new establishments. While it was impossible to forbid women's houses to follow Cistercian customs, the order refused to provide them with pastoral care or visitation,[13] strictly barring members of the order from doing anything to undermine this decision in any way. The order still had to consider the possibility the pope might direct the order to incorporate further women's houses,[14] and in fact many women's communities managed to find their way into the Cistercian Order via a detour through the curia.[15] In principle the order could not reject such papal directives, but it could inform the curia of its resolution not to accept any further women's houses, so the pope could not order any further incorporations without knowing the will of the order. For this reason the general chapter of 1230 resolved to send the curia a memorial and ask for assurance that future papal directives incorporating women's houses would only take effect if the resolution in question were expressly suspended.[16] This request was fulfilled, without doubt: just as would later be the case with the mendicant orders, the Cistercians were assured the incorporation of women's houses by papal *fiat* would only be valid with the inclusion of an "abrogation clause" specifically suspending resolutions passed by the order against receiving new women's houses.[17] The abrogation clause was intended to prevent the papal chancery from satisfying the desires of incorporation on the part of particular women's houses without being conscious in each case of the order's disapproval.

Perhaps the curia would still have attempted to overcome the order's resistance and organize the religious women's movement under the Cistercians, as they would later do with the mendicant orders. The curia might at least have forced an organizational incorporation of those women's houses already following Cistercian customs[18]—if the opportunity of reaching these goals more effectively had not presented itself at this very moment through the aid of the new orders of Dominic and Francis. These young orders were still in the course of formation, only beginning to spread internationally, and their goals certainly stood closer to the religious peculiarities of the women's movement than did the Cistercians. There was all the more hope that the religious movement among women could be brought into the regulated paths of the orders, since at their birth the new orders were contemplating ways to generate new forms of life for women's religious communities within their bounds.

2. The Dominican Order and Women's Houses in the First Half of the Thirteenth Century

From the earliest days of his work with Bishop Diego of Osma, long before he tried to create his own order, Dominic had sought a proper form of life for religious women's communities. The foundation of a women's house at Prouille in 1206 was closely connected with the struggle against heresy in Southern France which Diego and Dominic were trying to carry through with novel means. That foundation served the purpose of leading the religious movement among women of the higher classes into ecclesiastical paths, offering them a possibility of realizing religious goals within the limits of the Church which they had hitherto only sought and found among heretics. The preaching of Diego and Dominic, it is believably reported, opened the eyes of many women for the first time to the fact that those they had revered as their masters, whom they had followed and honored as "good men," *bons hommes*, were heretics. Since these people had led an evangelical life in Christian poverty as apostolic preachers, the women had been swept away by the religious currents of the day, seeing the efforts and teachings of those persons as identical with the Christian belief of the Roman Church.[19] They "converted" straight-away, and Diego and Dominic gathered them into a community at Prouille. Thus arose the first of the women's houses which would later belong to the Dominican Order.[20] The community was led by Dominic and his companions, who used Prouille for the next few years as home base for their mission to the heretics. At first this community was not distinguished in any way from similar women's houses of the Premonstratensians or other Augustinian congregations. It is not even certain whether the women were bound to monastic oaths.[21] It is likely that Dominic based discipline at Prouille on the Rule of St. Augustine,[22] adding some directives which have been preserved to us only in a later version (as the Constitutions of S. Sisto[23]).[24]

At the end of 1214, Dominic passed control over Prouille to his colleague Natalis, who remained in Prouille for the pastoral care and support of the women. During negotiations with Innocent III in Rome in October 1215, Dominic arranged for the house to be taken into papal protection.[25] When the Order of Preachers was founded, the women's house of Prouille came into its possession; the friars who had remained to care for the spiritual and material needs of the women in Prouille[26] formed an autonomous house of friars under its own prior.[27]

Prouille did not remain the sole women's house bound in this manner to the Order of Preachers during Dominic's lifetime. On a journey to Spain in the winter of 1218 Dominic laid the foundations for a women's house in Madrid, later entrusted to his brother Manes and cared for by several friars, as was the case in Prouille. Little is known about the origin and arrangements of the house or the background of the nuns in Madrid.[28]

In December 1219, Dominic was entrusted by Honorius III with the reform of a women's house in Rome. To carry out this task, he called some nuns to Rome from Prouille, assigning a few friars to lead as well. As a result, the Benedictine sisters of S. Maria in Trastevere were transferred in 1221 to the newly founded house of S. Sisto in Rome, endowed by the pope and reformed according to the principles of Prouille.[29]

The Order of Preachers had been entrusted with these three women's houses—Prouille, Madrid, and S. Sisto in Rome—by the time Dominic died. Efforts were underway to found a fourth house of this type in the last year of his life, but it was not carried out. When the friars preacher first came to Bologna in 1218, their efforts were most successful with two groups, the teachers and students of the university, and the womenfolk of the urban nobility. Their preaching influenced leaders of society to support the new congregation economically,[30] but their impact was even greater as a call to the religious life. First Diana d'Andalò, then about eighteen years of age, followed by other women of the Bolognese nobility, permitted their entire lives to be permeated by the religious spirit the friars preacher had proclaimed.[31] When Dominic himself visited Bologna in 1219, Diana made her vow before him in the church of St. Nicholas in the presence of friars preacher and of other women—a vow whose content cannot be precisely specified, but which moved Diana to determine to found a women's house which would be supervised by Dominicans in the manner of Prouille. She discussed this with Dominic, and despite many friars' objections to considering founding a women's house even before the convent of friars had been completed, Dominic decided to begin building at once, commissioning four friars to locate a suitable site (1220). This plan never developed beyond this preliminary stage. It was said that the bishop of Bologna refused to consent to build the convent on the site chosen, since it was too close to town. This does not explain, however, why the friars let the matter drop without seeking another site. Diana herself was prevented by her parents' opposition from carrying out her plans. She appears to have given up hope for the plans being carried out in reasonable time, for she entered the Benedictine house in Ronzono near Bologna on 22 June 1221.[32]

It is likely that the foundation of a women's house in Bologna in the manner of Prouille failed due to more than the resistance of the bishop of Bologna and Diana's parents. There is much evidence that Dominic himself came to think differently about incorporating more women's houses to his new order in his last days. On his deathbed, in his last conversations on the order, he pressingly warned his brethren against association with women, particularly with young women.[33] Was he only warning against the moral attitude of individual friars? Is it possible that the founder, preoccupied with questions about the future of his order in these last utterances, had been discussing whether the order should incorporate further women's communities, placing friars to oversee and supply them, thus withdrawing them from the order's primary duty of preaching? It was in Dominic's last years, when Cistercians were refusing new women's houses and Francis fought against accepting women's houses into his own order, when this question also became important to the Order of Preachers. Conditions forced the order to make new commitments on the women's question. In fact, opposition to incorporating women's houses prevailed immediately after the founder's death, precisely against the plan of Diana d'Andalò to raise a women's house in Bologna under Dominican leadership.

After Dominic's death, Diana revived her plan, and the Dominicans, particularly the new minister general, Jordan of Saxony, who as the provincial minister of Lombardy had earlier favored Diana, supported her strongly at first. During the week of Ascension, 1223, Diana and four other sisters entered the newly founded house of S. Agnes in the presence of Jordan and several friars. Three weeks later (29 June) the minister general solemnly clothed the sisters in the habit of the order, and preaching by the friars quickly won more women for entry into the house.[34] After some difficulties, the minister general was able to move Honorius III to approve the transfer of four sisters from S. Sisto in Rome to S. Agnes in Bologna, "so that they may teach them the order and mode of religion."[35] Yet despite everything, the new house did not have the same relationship to the order as those in Prouille, Madrid, and Rome, since the order had not committed itself to protect, minister, and oversee S. Agnes through a special community of friars in the same manner as the older houses.[36] The order soon demonstrated it was not about to treat the new house in the same manner as the other three. This was not due to personalities. The immediate successor to Dominic as minister general had a close, friendly relationship to Diana and her house from the beginning to his death, visiting it as often as he could and writing to it while on his journeys, demonstrating a close, personal tie to the women in Bologna.[37] It also appears—if the report of the origins of S. Agnes are dependable on this point[38]—that Jordan personally supported the complete incorporation of S. Agnes into the order. Resistance to the incorporation of further women's houses into the order had grown so strong, however,[39] that intervention by the curia was required to compel the order to accept the same duties toward S. Agnes that it already fulfilled in Prouille, Madrid, and Rome. In a bull phrased in rather abrupt tones,[40] Honorius III ordered the minister general to receive S. Agnes under the same conditions as the three other houses.[41] With the support of this bull, Minister-General Jordan obtained approval and completed incorporation at the general chapter in Bologna in 1227.

For the first time papal intervention had been used to overcome an order's opposition to receiving a women's house into its organization. Similar procedures would come to be repeated time and again. Before this could occur, however, the order moved to protect itself against the incorporation of more women's houses.

At the *Capitulum generalissimum* in Paris in 1228, where the first comprehensive collection of the order's constitutions was promulgated—the very same year in which the Cistercians banned receiving any new women's houses—all brothers were forbidden, on penalty of excommunication, to support accepting new women's houses, nor could they receive women's oaths or veil them.[42] General Jordan revealed the motivation for this decision in two letters to Diana d'Andalò and the provincial of Lombardy. In Bologna, it was believed the chapter decision of 1228 was directed against the house of S. Agnes and would ruin the labors of Diana, completed with such difficulty. This is because it was believed that if friars were forbidden from receiving the oaths of women, no new sisters for S. Agnes could be received or veiled by Dominicans. On the contrary, the minister general assured them when he heard these concerns, this decision had no effect against women's houses which already belonged to the order, particularly since such acts would conflict with papal directives. No action had even been considered by any chapter or by anyone else against the women's houses presently within the order. The new decision by the chapter was directed at entirely different problems. In many provinces of the order, especially in Germany, friars preacher had been taking oaths from young women or prostitutes who wanted to convert to religion and swear themselves to chastity, veiling them at once. The decision of the order was directed against this.[43]

This explanation by the Dominican minister general shows clearly the true basis of the troubles the order was having in its relations to women's communities. The order was not forced to change its attitude on incorporating houses of nuns because of the few women's houses which existed in the Romance countries. Rather it was the fact that women were flocking to the order in the northern provinces, particularly in Germany, which forced the order to take a principled stand. It is possible Dominic himself in his last days had second thoughts whether to continue to receive women's communities into the order, probably due to reports reaching him about conditions in Germany. The German situation to which Jordan referred in 1228 had been obvious for a long time, ever since the Dominicans arrived in Germany. The unusual conditions were demonstrated in Jordan's reports on his friend Henry, the first prior in Cologne,[44] whose efforts had enjoyed particularly great success among virgins, widows, and female penitents, and whose early death was especially mourned by the women of Cologne.[45] The advent of the Dominicans had found this strong female echo only because a religious movement among these pious women had not awaited the Dominicans' penitential propaganda in order to begin. Rather, it was here that the waves of the mendicant movement spreading from the South met those of the women's religious movement of the North. The result was massive pressure on the order from religious women which the order itself did not desire, which it resisted with all its might, and to which it was forced in the end to succumb. This process profoundly influenced the course of the history of the orders throughout the thirteenth century.

A Dominican chronicler of Colmar in the later thirteenth century did a striking job of describing the situation the Dominicans found on their arrival in Germany. Enclosed communities of women were often located near chapels of one sort or another, and the order accepted the task of turning them into convents. Further, before the arrival of the mendicants in Germany, communities of "poor sisters" had formed, wearing religious habits without belonging to any particular order and without being recognized as monastic houses. Such communities of sisters also became women's houses through the assistance of the Dominicans. Beyond that, virgins and widows, particularly noble and wealthy women, joined the Dominicans and were gathered into noble convents.[46]

This portrait of a melding of the Order of Preachers and the religious women's movement in Germany, drawn by a Dominican chronicler,[47] can be confirmed in all its details by observing the origins of those houses which eventually joined the Dominican order. In many cases these origins are shrouded in darkness, but the oldest preserved charters still manage to give some information on the origins of many houses, if they are combined with the thorough house traditions which most Dominican women's houses collected in the first half of the fourteenth century. To be sure, these origins cannot be portrayed in chronological order, since these houses all joined the Dominican order at virtually the same moment in the second quarter of the thirteenth century, even if not always to the same degree in any one area in Germany. This process is best illustrated with a few well-documented, typical examples. There were two prime possibilities. On the one hand, women's communities arose before the arrival of the mendicants in Germany, or arose independent of their influence, organizing themselves more or less in monastic fashion before the Dominicans accepted them. On the other hand, communities arose under Dominican influence, developing into houses under their guidance. In either case, the order's relationship to the women's community was roughly the same, and when the question of incorporating these communities arose, as a result of the women's request, origins no longer played any role.

In a great number of German women's houses later incorporated into the Dominican order, all that is known about their origin is that they arose from a free association of religious women seeking to realize religious ideals of poverty and chastity on their own initiative and strength, with neither a specific rule nor membership in an order. In such cases, it was usually said that a community of women had arisen in the place of the later convent, living "in the manner of the beguines"; the house was said to have grown out of a "gathering of beguines."[48]

The best-known example of such an evolution from a spontaneous association of women "in the beguine style" to a house of Dominican sisters is the house of Engelthal near Nuremberg. The nuns' book of the fourteenth century[49] and the surviving charters provide a thorough, reliable portrait of the beginnings of the house which is extremely fruitful for the history of the order in the thirteenth century. Its origins went back to a datable episode. When the young Elizabeth of Hungary passed through Nuremberg in 1211 on the way to her betrothal with the son of the Landgrave of Thuringia, one of her entourage, the harp-player Alheit, remained behind in the city, converting to a life of penance and the love of God. She "sat at Nuremberg in a house and was truly a beacon, just as she had once been widely known for her sinful way of life." It was probably not long after that there came to be a small "gathering of beguines," a community of pious women seeking to win God's grace through chastity and voluntary poverty in keeping with the religious tenor of the times.[50] This community asked the penitent Alheit to join them and become their mistress.[51] Under her leadership, they commenced their common life, contributing all they had to the common property, though this was still not at first enough to endow a religious house.[52] They ordered their lives in keeping with the life of a religious house without following a particular rule or withdrawing from the spiritual control of the local parish priest (of S. Lorenz). They elected a sub-prioress who read the hours as well as she could understand them; the mistress held the dinner readings in German. The pious life of these women, the *sorores Rottharinne*, as they were called after their mistress, the *Rotterin* (= harp-player) Alheit,[53] was soon widely known. From the very earliest days of this community we hear of special gifts of grace and ecstasies experienced by the sisters. Gifts and endowments flowed to them. A lay brother would go to receive gifts from far away. The pride of the community was a valuable gift made by Queen Kunigunde of Bohemia (1230/48). The house's further evolution was disturbed, however, when Nuremberg was placed under interdict in 1239, after the excommunication of Frederick II by Gregory IX. The women thought it best to seek another location, if only temporarily. They turned for lodging to Ulrich von Königstein, an Imperial ministerial, and they received from him the gift of three estates in Engelschalkdorf in the summer of 1240.[54] This donation proved to be an important turning-point in the history of the community. Now they had a "founder," making it possible to remain permanently at the new site, called Engelthal. The first thing they did was to erect a chapel (named for St. Lawrence, recalling their parish in Nuremberg), then they went on to establish a cloister. When a grandson of the seigneur von Königstein, his sole male heir, died in an accident near the Engelthal estate, the lord bequeathed to the sisters all he had in the village of Schweinach, receiving it back from them as a fief for life.[55] In this manner this community of women, which had managed to struggle through the first years of its existence in Engelthal, supporting themselves by doing their own domestic and agricultural work,[56] was finally sufficiently endowed to satisfy the requirements for founding a religious house. Only after this women's community had prevailed on its own strength, growing to the status of a house, did religious orders begin to play a role. The nuns' book tells us that seven abbots from the "gray order," the Cistercians, came and asked this "holy assembly" to join their order straight-away. Thus even in the 1240s, Cistercian abbots were still at work winning houses with good endowments like Engelthal for their order, despite the ban on receiving new women's houses.[57] The founder, Ulrich von Königstein, did not want his Engelthal to join the Cistercians; he wanted the sisters to continue to dress "in the garb of womenfolk," resisting any idea of his sisters becoming nuns in the true sense or belonging to any order.[58] This resistance to "nunning" religious women was not unique in those days in Southern Germany.[59] If Engelthal wished to become a religious house with all rights, it would have to join an order. If it resisted being incorporated into the Cistercian Order, there was hardly any other route left but to join the Dominican Order,[60] which was what soon happened. We do not know how or when the women in Engelthal first came in contact with the Preachers. When Bishop Frederick of Eichstätt confirmed the house in 1244 and took it into his protection, he committed the sisters to the rule of Augustine and the statutes of S. Sisto in Rome.[61] Whether or not the Dominicans then took over the care of souls in Engelthal cannot be learned from the bishop's charter. At about the same time, however, the Dominicans in Regensburg must have accepted the house.[62] In 1248 the women of Engelthal achieved reception into the order through the mediation of Innocent IV.

We are pursuing the history of the house of Engelthal this far in order to use a case typical of many others to demonstrate how women's religious communities grew from "beguine-style" origins to independent houses even before the arrival of the mendicant orders, and for a long time afterwards without their assistance. They had often won economic endowment from noble founders, and it was only after they had reached this advanced stage of development as religious houses that they made contact with the Dominicans and were received into the order.

Still, the women's religious movement in Germany was continuing to ferment when the mendicant friars arrived, and only a fraction of the movement had yet achieved solid form as monastic communities. Often the preaching and example of the new orders, especially the Dominicans, showed the women's groups the way, providing them with a shape. "Tinder which took fire as soon as the spark of Dominican preaching fell on it," is how a Dominican poet[63] described the spiritual state of German women in those days, when the women's movement collided and combined with the mendicant movement. The biography of the very woman for whom this phrase was coined illustrates the destiny of the women's religious movement in contact with the Order of Preachers. Even as a child of nine, the daughter of the Count of Vianden wanted to enter a Cistercian convent in order to be bound eternally with her bridegroom, Christ, never to submit to a mortal spouse. Her high-noble family hindered her, hoping for an advantageous marriage, and they almost succeeded in overcoming Jolande's pious longing for the convent, preparing the way for a splendid betrothal. Then the Dominicans entered Jolande's life, and from that moment on there was no wavering. Against the opposition of influential relatives, she entered the severe, impoverished community of women[64] forming under the influence of the Preachers. The preaching of the Dominicans had the same impact on hundreds of German women, giving the last push for the decision to realize the desire of their age for a religious life in voluntary poverty, showing the way in which this way of life could be found. So under the influence of Dominican preaching in Germany—despite the fact friars were forbidden to encourage or support the formation of women's religious communities, although they were not permitted to receive any woman's oath—an extraordinary number of such communities still arose. The houses were endowed either by the women joining them or by the donations of wealthy supporters, and though they were supported and advised in spiritual matters by the Preachers, they were economically and organizationally independent.

A description of the foundation of the house of Ötenbach near Zürich gives the clearest possible portrait of such a community and its development into a convent.[65] The "great holiness" of the friars preacher gave the impetus and model for these pious women to gather into the common life in voluntary poverty about 1234,[66] starting in a "derelict, collapsing house" in Zürich. They lived on bread and water and "throw-aways"—although they were daughters of prominent Zürich families. Within three years, however, they had grown numerous enough to be able to build a house on the Ötenbach brook.[67] Dominicans assisted these sisters as advisers, confessors, and preachers, and it was for the sisters "the greatest consolation, for they always had good and holy doctrine from them." Despite this, the Dominicans neither participated in the sisters' organization nor in the house's economic organization. In contrast to Engelthal and many other communities of this type, the women of Ötenbach never had the benefit of a patron to endow their house.[68] They were essentially forced to rely on what the sisters brought with them into the community,[68a] and on alms. It was precisely their "good reputation for a blessed life," that they were "the poorest and best people," which drew to them many women from the richest and most prominent families.[69] It was precisely the idea of poverty, to which so many women sacrificed "honor and goods" in Ötenbach, which ended up making the convent rich, so that the continuously growing numbers—already 120!—required the building of a new convent of stone on the site of the old wooden structure about 1285. The endowment book still records movingly that the community truly lived "in great poverty and need, great poverty of worldly goods, but rich in divine love and true humility" in the first period, particularly before it was incorporated into the Dominican Order in 1245. In all of this, the Dominicans provided only spiritual support. They accepted the community half against their will and contrary to the ban of the order, but the community developed on the strength of its own dynamism.

All over Germany, just as in Ötenbach, women gathered together in the common life under the influence of Dominican preaching, and if they were numerous or well enough endowed, they founded convents. Incorporation into the order came later, as we shall see, and everywhere by means of the same stages.[70] Probably the earliest and in some ways the most significant foundation of this sort was the convent of St. Mark's in Strasbourg. Unfortunately, there are no early narratives, but the surviving charters permit us to recover the essentials. Dominicans were in Strasbourg starting in 1224. The following year a chapel which had been used for poor people and pilgrims was passed to some pious women who had decided to "give themselves to God and to lead a regular life,"[71] conceding to them the election of a mistress and the reception of lay brothers to care for the place. The influence of Dominicans on the formation of this women's community is not imputed simply on the basis of chronology, but from other facts. According to the charter of 1225, if a dispute arose over the election of a mistress, the dean of St. Thomas was to present the election to the prior of the Dominicans, and he was also to have the responsibility of overseeing the mistress. There was thus a loose organizational tie between this community of women and the Dominicans from the very beginning. In 1230 three canons of St. Thomas and three Dominicans witnessed a charter of the bishop permitting the St. Mark community to transfer to a more protected location near the Dominican house.[72] Thereafter the Dominicans appear to have taken continually more exclusive control of the house. This is demonstrated particularly by the statutes which were followed in St. Mark's. The women had declared in 1225 that they desired to live under a rule, but the rule was not specified. From 1233 on, several other women's houses adopted the regulations which were followed in St. Mark's, the "Constitutions of the Sisters of St. Mark." These constitutions have not survived, and they are never described in greater detail, but since Gregory IX numbered St. Mark's as part of the *Ordo sancti Sixti de Urbe*,[73] there can be no doubt the constitutions of St. Mark's generally agreed with those of S. Sisto in Rome, which is to say, with the rules of the women's houses in the Dominican Order. There is an assumption this women's community, stimulated by the Strasbourg Preachers, lived according to the rules which women's houses under the order used and in which the Strasbourg Dominicans would have instructed them. It is impossible to determine whether or how the constitutions of St. Mark's differed from those of S. Sisto, but one can suppose that it left out the formula which demanded that six friars living according to the Augustinian Rule had to be in residence. It is known this requirement was not followed in St. Mark's, any more than in other women's houses, not even later (after 1245) when they had properly joined the order.

The Strasbourg house of St. Mark's, with its rules adopted indubitably with the advice of the Dominicans, was a model for many other women's houses which entered into a similar relationship with the order. This was particularly the case with the houses of the South and Southwest, in whose organization the Dominicans of Strasbourg and Zürich were involved. Whoever asked for their advice in establishing a women's house was given St. Mark's of Strasbourg as a model. In a charter of 19 December 1233 the bishop of Constance, acting on the petition of Count Hartmann of Kiburg, directed the sisters in Töss near Winterthur to use the Rule of St. Augustine and the constitutions of the Sisters of St. Mark's in Strasbourg in their new house.[74] In the same manner, Adelhausen accepted the customs of St. Mark's.[75] The nuns of Husern (Klingenthal) near Basel were actually described in 1236 as "Sisters of the Order of St. Mark's in Strasbourg."[76] A letter written by the Strasbourg prior Volknand on behalf of the provincial chapter at Trier in 1236 shows that the houses of St. Mark's in Trier and Mersch (Marienthal) were established by sisters of St. Mark's in Strasbourg and overseen by the Dominicans.[77] Kirchheim and its dependency Sirnau,[78] as well as Diessenhofen-Katharinenthal,[79] also followed the constitutions of St. Mark's.

Other women's houses which were advised by the Dominicans, but were not in the sphere of influence of the house of St. Mark's or of the Dominicans of Strasbourg or Zürich, simply adopted the constitutions of S. Sisto in Rome, perhaps with certain modifications. There was no substantial difference between the constitutions of the two houses.[80] In this manner, the house of Altenhohenau on the Inn was endowed by Count Konrad von Wasserburg for "Sisters of the Order of St. Sixtus" on the advice of the Preachers;[81] the convent of the Holy Cross at Regensburg was also attributed to the same "order" in 1237,[82] as was the convent of St. Lambrecht near Luxembourg in 1244.[83] The nuns of Ötenbach established their house according to the constitutions of S. Sisto in 1237,[84] as did the wife of the Advocate of Gera, Jutta von Weida, for the house she endowed at Cronschwitz.[85] In 1244, Engelthal also committed itself to these constitutions.[86]

Following the constitutions of St. Mark's in Strasbourg or those of S. Sisto in Rome still did not assume an organizational tie between women's houses and the Dominicans, nor did it create an association according to the law of the Church or the order. It could be assumed that any house observing the constitutions of St. Mark's was under the influence of the Dominicans and followed their advice, though many women's houses adopted the constitutions of S. Sisto without any Dominican participation. The papal curia, acting on its own, frequently recommended the customs of S. Sisto, directly under the curia in Rome, as the proper basis for the organization of new women's houses. This procedure is clearest in 1232, when Gregory IX committed all the houses of the Order of Maria Magdalene, operating in Germany since 1227 under Cistercian institutions, to the Rule of St. Augustine and the constitutions of S. Sisto.[87] Dominicans do not appear to have been involved at all,[88] and so far as we know they had not played any role in establishing the Penitential [*Reuerinnen*] Order. Rather it was Gregory IX's intention to impose as uniform a regulation as possible on the women's religious movement. If possible, he sought to establish new women's houses according to the pattern of existing houses, avoiding excessive variety, in keeping with the principle of the Lateran Council of 1215. In Gregory IX's day three rules were available requiring strict enclosure: 1) the rule written by Gregory himself in his days as a cardinal, for Italian convents,[89] which he sought to apply to all new women's houses in Italy; 2) the Cistercian institutions, and 3) the constitutions of S. Sisto. In Germany, Gregory supported the introduction of the latter two rules, but after the 1230s, as a result of opposition from the Cistercian Order, the constitutions of S. Sisto came to be preferred.[90]

Even while women's religious communities in Germany sought support from the Dominican Order, and the curia promoted their institutionalization by using the model of Dominican women's houses, preaching friars themselves had been playing an extraordinarily active role founding, organizing and spiritually developing women's houses from the moment they began in Germany. This is demonstrated by the histories of individual convents and documented in the charters of many houses.[91] Dominicans particularly won fame for their special zeal for religious women, especially the Strasbourg prior, Walter, described by a later chronicler of the order as the "founder" of several women's houses.[92] Even the minister-general of the order, John of Wildeshausen, began his tenure by acting in the same sense, veiling the sisters of Kirchberg at their request.[93]

Such close cooperation between religious women and Dominicans in Germany arose directly from the encounter between the two religious movements, each pollinating and enlivening the another. No one desired or planned this result, yet the course of history created a situation which was neither consciously registered nor foreseen by anyone, was neither directed nor ordered, and for which the legal organization was, as a result, lacking—it even contradicted the current legal structure. According to prevailing law, the women's religious movement, which crystallized spontaneously everywhere, was subject to diocesan bishops and the local parish clergy for pastoral care, so long as they were not recognized, exempted or incorporated into an order. Bishops fought to keep these women's communities, and the Dominican Order was even more opposed to receiving them, but by sheer determination women's communities managed to win incorporation into the mendicant orders despite resistance, with the support of the papal curia.

Nothing could demonstrate more clearly the autonomous dynamism of the women's religious movement.

The bishops' opposition to having women's communities removed from their dioceses is best documented by the Dominican chronicler of Colmar.[94] As women's communities developed, he reports, the bishop of Strasbourg was moved by hostile advice to claim his rights "in temporal and spiritual matters." Since they were not members of an order and did not derive from a valid monastic rule, the bishop believed he could claim jurisdiction, oversight, and control over these houses for himself, and to assert these rights he commissioned clergymen of the rank of canon whom the sisters were to obey. The women could not object to being subject to the diocesan bishop according to ordinary law. Still, they argued their houses' legal status was unclear, and they had no precise idea how much power the bishop had over them. The bishop was asked to suspend asserting any rights until the matter was clarified.

The Colmar chronicler who described these events derived his knowledge from the tradition of the situation in the diocese of Strasbourg, probably in Unterlinden in the first instance. Similar conflicts probably took place in other dioceses.[95] As soon as they were wealthy enough to fulfill the economic requirements of a convent, however, women's communities everywhere sought confirmation from their bishop of their privileges which formally separated them from the diocese.[96]

Yet the resistance of the Dominican Order to receiving women's houses proved to be much more intense than that of the bishops to their removal from the dioceses. Anything individual Dominicans did to promote religious women's communities in Germany violated the prescriptions of the order. At the general chapter in Paris in 1228, the order had specifically banned receiving new nun's houses and women's communities into the order, accepting their pastoral care, receiving the oaths of religious women, clothing them in the order's habit, or cutting their hair. This ruling was made with specific reference to developments in Germany. The decree remained utterly without effect. It was in fact the years after the decree that German Dominicans experienced their greatest days promoting new women's communities and associating them with the order. It is probably this very fact which stimulated a general chapter to pass even harsher measures. The wording of the decree is unknown but can be inferred from its effects. In his bull to the general chapter on 24 March 1236, Gregory IX mentions a decree "recently" passed at a general chapter henceforth removing friars from *cura mulierum*, cutting all contacts of the order with women's houses. As a result of this decree, the Dominicans at Prouille, including the prior installed by Dominic and four other *fratres clerici*, had refused to continue leading the convent. As a result, the nuns of Prouille complained to the curia. The women's house in Madrid soon added their complaint: the friars entrusted with their pastoral care by St. Dominic had been withdrawn by the minister general and the *definitores* of the order without special cause, and they had been replaced by secular priests. In both cases, Gregory directed the minister general to follow the women's wishes and command friars of the order to resume pastoral care in these houses.[97] If efforts were being made to exclude from the order the oldest convents, those founded by Dominic himself, this could only mean the order was trying to renounce all ties with the women's religious movement. The results of any such act should have been most visible in Germany, but the sources say nothing at all.[98] In fact, the decree had no effect whatsoever. German Dominicans did not allow the decree to disturb their relationships with the women's religious movement, and the act was soon canceled due to complaints to the curia by the houses of Prouille, Madrid, and perhaps Bologna. The initiative also was soon suspended because the support of the order's leadership was not unanimous. Minister-General Jordan had been unable to take part in the general chapters of 1234 and 1235 because of illness.[99] The decree must have been passed at one of these meetings,[100] and the minister general never approved it.[101] The *Capitulum generalissimum* of 1236 under Jordan's leadership failed to confirm it as a law of the order, so it lapsed—according to the order's constitution a decree only had force of law if it were passed at three successive general chapters.

As a result, the relationship between the order and women's houses remained as they were so long as Minister-General Jordan lived; Jordan sustained convents founded by Dominic, particularly S. Agnes in Bologna, whose sisters were personally dear to him. Otherwise, Jordan agreed with the leadership's general reluctance to receive women's houses into the order. Gregory IX also protected the just claims of the older Dominican convents on the leadership and care of the friars, but as long as he lived he also respected the reluctance of the order to take on further responsibilities for women's houses. During the brief generalship of Jordan's successor, the jurist Raymond of Peñaforte (1238–41), only one step was taken in this direction, leaving the prevailing circumstances unaltered, but providing formal legal assurance against future change. The order obtained a bull from Gregory IX on 25 October 1239 releasing it from the obligation to accept pastoral care of nuns' houses or other women's houses, control and visitation of religious houses or churches, nor would it be required to execute legal orders or publish bulls of condemnation, except when existing restrictions were specifically suspended by an "abrogation clause."[102] The justification for this act was that such obligations hindered the friars from carrying out their essential duties, which were preaching and contemplation. This bull, confirmed and reissued by the next two succeeding popes,[103] specifically released Dominicans from all obligation for pastoral care in women's houses. The curia could not transfer any further houses to the leadership or care of souls of the order without being aware that this was against the order's will. The Cistercians had requested this specific assurance from the curia in 1230,[104] and the Franciscan Order received a bull of precisely the same wording from Innocent IV on 6 March 1250.[105] In truth this did nothing to hinder the incorporation of further women's houses into the mendicant order by papal order, but it demonstrated with all clarity that this took place against the will of the order.

We are not sure whether efforts already had been made by women's houses to win reception into the mendicant orders through papal mediation, and whether this bull was just an effort to circumvent such attempts.[106] The situation remained static until 1241, when Gregory IX died and the German John of Wildeshausen was elected minister general. Only with this change in the leadership of the Church and the order did events resume their flow. The older generation had known and respected the will of the founder, and it also knew well the needs of the women's religious movement, but it was unable to bring these two factors together. As a result, the relationship between the order and women's religious movement had remained unclear and undecided. The older generation now made way for a younger generation, which sought to resolve the problem through decisive action, though it was only able to establish a new order against extraordinary odds.

The Dominican Order was the first to take the initiative. The first general chapter of the new minister general, meeting at Bologna in 1242, punished all friars giving last rights to nuns or other religious women, intervening in their leadership or accepting the duty of visitation; the decree forbade all further contact with them. Friars could only plead papal bulls to excuse and justify their care of women's houses if the abrogation clause required in 1239 was present.[107] In this way Gregory IX's bull of 1239 could be used to stop any friars from acting as priests and visitors of women's houses which had not been legally subordinated to the order. The new minister-general went even further, however. He recalled the prior of the house of friars at S. Sisto in Rome, forbade the friars caring for the souls of the women of S. Sisto to live in the house, and he even barred lay brethren (*conversi*) from living within the confines of the house.[108] It is obvious John the German sought to exploit the vacancy following the short pontificate of Pope Celestine IV (died 10 November 1241) in order to loosen the close ties of the order with the house of S. Sisto, controlled by the Roman see, in order to reduce obligations to all the old Dominican convents. The curia, however, vigorously objected to these measures once Innocent IV mounted the papal throne (25 June 1243), and the order was compelled to restore old arrangements at S. Sisto.[109]

The great countermove of women's houses against the order took place under the new pope. The stimulus was not given by a German house but by the sole French women's house then seeking membership in the Dominican Order, Montargis, between Orléans and Sens. There the widowed Countess Amicie de Joigny, daughter of Dominic's friend Count Simon de Montfort, established a convent for fifty women out of her enthusiasm for the religious work of the founder. To her distress, as a woman she was not permitted to join the Order of Preachers directly, so she sought to have her house accepted into the order's community.[110] The order refused incorporation to the house as well, however. While residing at the curia in Lyon starting in late 1244, Amicie used the opportunity to negotiate personally with Innocent IV, obtaining a bull on 8 April 1245 incorporating the house of Montargis into the Dominican Order.[111]

The bull broke the dam which had kept women's houses outside the order until that time. The procedure for the house of Montargis became a model for German women's communities, and one after another in rapid succession they achieved reception into the order via the curia in Lyon. Amicie de Joigny was not only pleased to incorporate her own house, but she also helped several German women's houses to the same goal. The first after Montargis was the house of St. Agnes in Strasbourg, which received its bull of incorporation on 7 May 1245 with the support of Amicie and her son Gaucher.[112] We have no idea what relations had arisen between Amicie de Joigny and the women of St. Agnes of Strasbourg. According to the report of the Dominican chronicler of Colmar,[113] Dominican friends advised South German communities of women to turn to the pope by having their relatives write letters seeking incorporation. It is not impossible that relatives of the Countess of Joigny lived among the women in St. Agnes. Other German women's houses also made use of the family of the Count de Montfort to reach Innocent IV. Amicie's son Gaucher petitioned the curia on behalf of the houses in Offenburg (Baden)[114] and Husern;[115] her cousin, Count Jean I de Montfort intervened on behalf of the house of St. Mark's in Strasbourg,[115a] for St. Margaret's in Eckbolsheim[116] and for yet another Alsatian house.[117] Such intervention is not specifically mentioned in the bulls for the many other German women's houses which were placed in the Dominican Order in these years.[118] Yet the papal action did stimulate a virtual pilgrimage of German religious women to Lyon. Many of the houses which could not rely on a powerful intermediary at the curia sent a pair of sisters on their way to Lyon in order to secure their wishes from Innocent,[119] and they were even said to have received strong support from influential Dominicans at the curia itself[120]—although the order, as we shall see, soon protested against these massive papal incorporations. At first, however, nothing could stop the development which had been begun by the episode of Montargis. In an unbroken chain, one house after another received a convent privilege and reception into the Dominican Order from Innocent IV in Lyon. On 4 July 1245, four other Strasbourg women's houses entered the order along with St. Mark's,[121] at least twenty-one more German houses before the end of 1246, and a further five through 1250.[122] In the course of five years, the order had to take over at least thirty-two women's houses,[123] not including Montargis in France. When one considers that the entire generalship of John of Wildeshausen—1241 to 1252—saw the establishment of only four new men's houses in Germany, a mere twenty-four in all the provinces of the order together, it can be seen what an extraordinary burden these massive incorporations caused the order. The fact that many bulls of incorporation had to be repeatedly issued shows the order could not take on these tasks without some hesitation or friction, and that it was often necessary for the pope expressly to order the Dominicans to carry out without hesitation the duties assigned through incorporation.[124]

The importance the events of 1245 and the following years had for the Dominican Order, creating new obligations toward women's houses, and the way the order responded to these new duties, can only be fully clarified in comparison to parallel developments in the Franciscan Order. For in these days the attitude of the two mendicant orders was interconnected in a way hitherto not noted.

3. THE FRANCISCAN ORDER AND WOMEN'S HOUSES IN THE FIRST HALF OF THE THIRTEENTH CENTURY

Unlike Dominic, Francis did not begin his work by organizing and leading religious women, and throughout his life he was concerned to hinder the incorporation of women's communities into his order. Women could have no place in the association of penitential preachers receiving papal approval in 1210, since the curia had never allowed women to preach penitence. It was natural penitential preaching would reach women, snatching them from the temptations of the world and leading them to "conversion." Yet it is obvious that Francis had not given a thought to what was to become of women following the call of Franciscan preaching and "converting." He was interested in awakening others to the religious life, not in the forms this life might take.

This lack of plan was clearly demonstrated in Francis' conversion of Clara Sciffi. On Palm Sunday, 1212, she completed her conversion in the Portiuncula, in the presence of the brethren, giving away her goods in order to serve God in voluntary poverty, putting aside the adornment of her clothing and hair, taking on the "signs of holy penitence."[125] What did this mean for her future form of life? It was obvious she could not remain in the company of itinerant penitential preachers. Rather, immediately after her conversion, Francis took her to a house of Benedictine nuns at St. Paul's in Bastia. Whether he thought of St. Paul's as a provisional residence, or whether Clara was actually to enter this convent[126] is as little known as why she had herself taken a few days later to another Benedictine convent, S. Angelus de Panso near Assisi.[127] She would remain there for only a brief time as well. Even if Clara had intended to remain with these Benedictine nuns and to make her profession there, it must soon have become clear to her that residence in this well-endowed Benedictine house was incompatible with the ideal of complete voluntary poverty and self-denying humility, the model of Francis.[128] With such a motivation, she and her sister withdrew from the Benedictine nuns, taking Francis' advice by moving into the church of St. Damian in front of the gates of Assisi, whose buildings had been made available to the saint for this purpose by Bishop Guido of Assisi. Other women soon joined them there, and this community lived according to Francis' directions without committing themselves to the rule of an order. Francis' instructions, a simple confession of evangelical poverty and simplicity, could not have differed essentially from the primitive "rule" of the first Franciscans. The instructions obviously contained no obligation to evangelical preaching, but did include strict commands to fast.[129] The decree concerning new orders given by the Lateran Council of 1215 probably moved the community at St. Damian's to seek a privilege to maintain their renunciation of all property, their assertion of the principle of strict poverty, and their right not to be required to accept a different monastic rule. At about this time, probably in connection with this effort, the inner organization of the community was formalized by Clara being named abbess.[130] At this time, strict enclosure was perhaps introduced. Thus arose a religious house, recognized by the curia, which differed essentially from all other convents in not relying on an endowment and the incomes it produced, but living instead on alms or earnings from their own work, renouncing all property, as did the Franciscan community.

Francis was especially fond of Clara's community in St. Damian's, and he wanted to keep it under the care of his order in perpetuity,[131] but it remained the sole women's house he "founded," whose creation he fostered directly, and whose membership in the order was desired and recognized by him. Other than St. Damian's, not a single women's house was desired by him to be incorporated into the order, nor was any friar to found or promote one. He doggedly resisted all attempts to transfer the care for other women's houses, and he strictly forbade friars to receive women into the order.[132]

In any case, all over Italy many women's communities arose at the same time as St. Damian's, renouncing property and possessions, living in voluntary poverty without keeping a specific monastic rule. They had neither joined any order nor attached themselves to any male house. Virtually nothing is known about the origins of these communities. It is also unknown how long these houses had been in existence, or whether they were the result of Franciscan preaching or the example of Clara. Quite possibly, such religious women's communities arose in Central Italy independently of Francis and Clara, a precipitate of a general poverty movement, just as similar communities formed in Belgium, France, and Germany independently of the mendicant orders. The similarity of the religious ideals and ways of life of the Franciscans and the sisters of St. Damian's—the sole argument speaking for direct influence[133]—is inadequate proof that the "movement for flight from the world" was only stimulated by Francis and Clara among Italian women. It is possible the poverty movement led to the formation of women's communities wishing to live in voluntary poverty, in Italy as in other countries, independent of Francis.[134] What is certain is that they were not "founded" by Francis or his brethren,[135] and that no institutional links grew up between them and the Franciscan Order at the outset. There can be no doubt Franciscan preaching and Clara's example essentially strengthened the religious movement among Italian women, giving it direction. When James of Vitry was in Perugia in 1216, he thought the Minorites and women's communities were part of a single phenomenon, but he said nothing about organizational or organic connections.[136] Only after 1218 is there anything about women's communities in reliable documents. At that time Cardinal Ugolino took up their cause as papal legate in Tuscany—he was probably asked to mediate by the women themselves[137]—and he petitioned Honorius III to take them under papal protection.[138] He described the women as coming from prominent, wealthy families, fleeing the glamour of the world and all its riches, abandoning all their goods in order to live in poverty in communities, in houses of prayer.[139] He did not even suggest these women had been converted by Franciscans, or that Clara had been their model, or that they stood in any relationship at all to the friars minor. Ugolino was protecting these women's communities against claims by bishops and secular persons, and he managed to receive the power from the curia to declare the donated houses, churches, and land to be property of the Roman Church. He then gathered these communities into an order, granting them a rule to guide their religious life along ordered pathways. In doing so, he neither used the Rule of Francis nor the *forma vivendi* of the sisters in St. Damian's. Since the liberation from the decree on orders by the Lateran Council which Francis and Clara had already achieved from Innocent III did not apply to these women's houses, they and the new order they formed had to be committed to one of the old forms of order and rule. Ugolino chose the Rule of St. Benedict for that purpose. This demonstrated once again how absurd the Lateran decree on orders had been, what a hindrance it was to compel novel religious realities into old legal forms. In order not to establish a "new form of order," Ugolino committed the women's houses to the Rule of St. Benedict, but they did not become Benedictine nuns.[140] A juristic formality was simply being fulfilled to give the Council's regulation its due. The old rule only had effect insofar as the life of the sisters was not ordered by special commands in Ugolino's new rule. In practice, all relationships in the new houses were already regulated by special clauses to suit their special nature. When the question was later raised what significance a commitment to the Rule of St. Benedict might have, it was authoritatively declared that it only applied to the three primary oaths of obedience, renunciation of private property, and chastity.[141]

Just as Cardinal Ugolino gave Italian women's houses their own constitution which was only theoretically dependent on the Rule of St. Benedict, he also placed them under a *visitator* of their own—whose competence did *not* extend to Clara's house at St. Damian's—and for the office he named a Cistercian named Ambrosius.[142] According to the rule, the pastoral care and visitation of these houses could be vested in any qualified and experienced priest[143]—there is not a word about Franciscans. These women's houses, with their own rule and their own *visitator*, constituted a congregation in their own right, designated with their own name as the "Order of the Poor Ladies of the Vale of Spoleto or Tuscany,"[144] without any organizational tie with the Franciscans or the sisters of St. Damian's.

The Cardinal had still not managed to make this group of women's houses into a congregation, bound by a common rule. These convents lacked a connection with a male order which could have taken over their regular pastoral service and visitation, and there can be no doubt Ugolino planned to join the "Poor Women" to the Minorites, bringing them into a relationship similar to that which obtained for St. Damian's. This goal was to be achieved in two ways: on the one hand, the sisters of St. Damian's were to accept the rule Ugolino had granted to the other women's houses, and on the other hand the Franciscans were to accept the same pastoral care and visitation in the women's houses that they provided St. Damian's. The Cardinal achieved the first goal quickly, but subsequent developments reversed it. At first he made no headway toward the second goal, but developments eventually brought him there, after many difficulties.

Negotiations on the problem of women's houses took place between Cardinal Ugolino and Francis as early as 1218 or early 1219, before Francis began his missionary journey to the Orient.[145] It is probable the cardinal managed to win the saint's agreement for the sisters of St. Damian's adopting the rule Ugolino composed for the other women's houses.[146] The adoption of Ugolino's rule was a matter of largely theoretical importance, since a commitment to it meant as little for St. Damian's as the obligation the other women's houses had to the Rule of St. Benedict. Clara and her sisters were able to accept Ugolino's rule in principle because at no point did it contradict Francis' *formula vitæ*, which was followed at St. Damian's: particularly, it said nothing about whether or not the house had to possess property. We know that the sisters of St. Damian's continued to live in keeping with the *formula vitæ* and the counsels of Francis, even where they differed with Ugolino's rule. For example, fasts at St. Damian's were more severe than those prescribed in Ugolino's rule.[147] Yet later, as soon as Ugolino's rule was changed so specifications on property conflicted with the principle of poverty upheld by the sisters of St. Damian's, Clara refused to recognize the rule. Thus the unity of regulation between the women's houses organized by Ugolino and St. Damian's had once more been lost.[148]

It was a matter of far greater concern to the Italian women's houses whether Cardinal Ugolino would succeed in transferring their pastoral care and visitation to the Franciscans. These efforts met with Francis' strict rejection. In his negotiations with the cardinal before departing for the orient, Francis declared: since he and his brethren had founded no women's houses other than St. Damian's, they did not desire to take over pastoral care for the other houses. He insisted there should be no relations between the women's houses regulated by Ugolino and the Minorites, and those religious women should not even claim membership in the Minorites by name: neither *minorissæ* nor "sisters"—

parallel to "brothers"—were to be allowed to them.[149] The cardinal saw Francis wanted nothing to do with ties between his order and women's houses; he had not succeeded in getting the Franciscans to take over pastoral care at the convents. Ugolino bestowed the office on a Cistercian—and in keeping with the saint's desires, he agreed the women would be known as "Poor Ladies" [*pauperes dominæ*], not as *sorores minores*.

Yet once Francis was far from Italy, the *visitator* of the women's houses, the Cistercian Ambrosius, died, and Ugolino exploited this opportunity to reorder the problem without the knowledge or consent of the founder of the order. Friar Philippus Longus, whom Francis had perhaps entrusted with the care of St. Damian's in his absence, played into the cardinal's hands. He permitted pastoral care for the women's houses to be transferred to himself, obviously becoming the successor of Ambrosius the Cistercian, accepting the papal commission to order Franciscan friars to serve in the women's houses and to excommunicate their oppressors.[150] When Francis learned of these developments, he was furious. These novelties were the ruin of the order, he believed, and he told one friar, "Until now the thorn was in our flesh, but there was still a hope we would be healed. Now it has penetrated to the bone, and it will be beyond healing."[151] He returned to Italy, negotiated with the curia, and managed to have all the decisions made during his absence revoked.[152] The sources give only inadequate information on how pastoral care and visitation was handled in the women's houses over the next few years.[153] In his draft of a new rule for the order in 1221, Francis added the stipulation that no friar was permitted to receive the oath of obedience from any woman; Franciscans could not offer anything more than "spiritual support" to a woman; women could complete their conversion to penitence wherever they wished.[154] This rule intended to forbid every tie between Minorites and religious women's communities. Friars could, of course, influence women through penitential preaching, but they could neither support nor permit women joining the order. This rule, composed by Francis, never attained the force of law, and this clause is missing in the rule of 1223, which received papal endorsement. In its place there is an order that the only friars who could set foot in convents were those who had special permission from the papacy to do so.[155] The order had been compelled to accept the fact there were friars with access to convents, and they could be active there at least in particular cases with special permission of the papacy. In fact we know of one case of 1223 in which Franciscan *visitatores* and *correctores* were given to a women's house.[156] Negotiations between the curia, the protector of the order, Ugolino, and Francis appear not to have resulted in an unambiguous settlement. No Franciscan *visitator* was named for all the women's houses,[157] and the relationship between the Minorites and the women's houses was not regulated as a whole, though the curia could still name Franciscans in particular cases to do visitations, and probably also to provide pastoral care in women's houses.

That this indecisive situation was only a compromise between Francis' desires and the curia's plans was demonstrated immediately after the saint's death. Through a bull issued on 14 December 1227, Gregory IX transferred the care of the *pauperes moniales reclusæ* to the minister general of the Franciscan Order,[158] and a Franciscan *visitator* was again installed for all women's houses, starting with Friar Pacificus,[159] who had aroused St. Francis' wrath by taking the same office in 1219/20.[160] There could be no clearer sign how thoroughly the curia had achieved what Francis had opposed and sought to prevent with all his might while he yet lived. Twenty-two women's houses of Central Italy[161] were thus subordinated to the pastoral care and visitation of the Franciscans, as only the house of St. Damian's had been before, with which they shared at least the formal use of rule and with which they would come to be joined under a common name as the *Ordo sancti Damiani*.[162]

This relationship between the "Order of St. Damian" and the Franciscans, who took over pastoral care and visitation, did not change further from the death of Francis to the death of Gregory IX. The obligations of the Minorites to the women's houses do not appear to have been more closely defined, either by the order or by the curia, but they were also never disputed. Only in the last part of the era of Gregory IX were there signs that this relationship was threatened by a new wave of women entering the Order of St. Damian. In a bull issued on 21 February 1241, Gregory ordered all archbishops and bishops to act against women moving about barefoot, belted with rope, dressed in the habit of the Order of St. Damian, insisting they were *discalceatæ* or *chordulariæ* or *minoritæ* and members of the Order of St. Damian. Since the strictest enclosure was a basic condition of belonging to this order, Gregory described the women's actions as *religio simulata*, endangering the reputation of the nuns of the Order of St. Damian and burdening the Franciscans, and for that reason he demanded that they put aside their offending habits.[163] It would be hard to conceive a correct image of these "minoresses" and their *religio simulata* if later documents did not tell us these were women desiring to profess Franciscan ideals and seek membership in the Order of St. Damian. The way to membership in the regular manner had been blocked, however, since the Order of St. Damian was erecting no new convents. In truth, not a single new foundation of a convent of this order is known between 1228 and 1245, despite demand and pressure from the women's religious movement.

These questions spring to life in the Franciscan Order, just as in the Dominican Order, shortly after Gregory's death. First of all—we have no idea of the immediate cause—the question arose whether Franciscans were obligated to have friars reside in the women's houses where they dispensed pastoral care, as was the case with the four convents originally under the Dominican Order. This practice must also have been the custom in the Order of St. Damian. The order obtained a bull from Innocent IV on 17 July 1245 confirming that Franciscans were only obligated to serve convents which had arisen under Gregory IX, before 1241, and that the order could only be compelled to serve other women's houses by express order of a papal bull from case to case—explicitly suspending the guarantees of the previous bull.[164] The new bull was obviously misinterpreted and abused by many, who interpreted it to free themselves of all obligations to pastoral care and visitation in women's houses where members of the order had not resided before 1241. For that reason, Innocent IV responded three months later to the petition of the women's houses by issuing a new bull commanding the order to carry out visitations of the *moniales inclusæ ordinis s. Damiani* without restriction, to preach, hear confession, read mass, and dispense sacraments, and to do this by entering the enclosure of the convent when necessary.[165] This created no new obligations but simply intensified the execution of previous customs.

Doubts over the duty of residence and Franciscans' obligations toward women's houses coincided with the period when Innocent IV in Lyon issued his first orders incorporating women's houses into the Dominican Order. Whether the Franciscan Order was only distressed by what was going on in the Preachers' Order and was trying to preclude the chance that they, too, would be burdened with the care of new convents, or whether there was knowledge of efforts to present them with *faits accomplis* as had occurred with the Dominicans, we have no idea. The attempts by Franciscans to secure themselves against receiving more convents were as vain as those of the Dominicans. On 2 June 1246, Innocent IV subordinated fourteen women's houses in Italy, France, and Spain in one day,[166] using the very same form by which he incorporated German convents into the Dominican Order. Innocent IV was not to be shaken from the fourteen known bulls of incorporation, however. In the following years Franciscans would often complain that the pope or the protector of the order, Cardinal Rainald, issued stereotyped bulls to women wandering the world without decency, undisciplined, calling themselves *sorores minores*, and asserting they desired to found houses of the Order of St. Damian[167]—hence women of the same type as the "minoresses" against whom Gregory IX acted in 1241. Such women, who did not yet live in stable communities and sought in vain to join the Order of St. Damian, had exploited the situation at the curia in Lyon, and Innocent issued them the same or similar bulls to those he had issued to many convents already operating under Franciscan pastoral care.

Before we pursue these events any further and ask about the effect on the orders of these acts by the curia, we must take a closer look at the relationships created by papal decrees.

COMPARISON OF TEXTS OF BULLS OF INCORPORATION OR COMMISSION FOR DOMINICAN AND FRANCISCAN CONVENTS

A = Bull for St. Agnes in Strasbourg, dated 7 May 1245, Ripoll, *Bullarium ordinis fratrum prædicatorum* 1.148, n. 85; in most cases the wording is identical with the bull for Montargis, 8 April 1245, ibid., no. 84 (with a different introduction[167a]).

B = Bulls for other women's houses subordinated to the Dominican Order.

C = Bulls for the houses of the Order of St. Damian placed under the Franciscan Order, Sbaralea, *Bullarium Franciscanum* 1.413, no. 134.

B

Innocentius episcopus servus servorum dei dilectis in Christo filiabus . . . *priorisse* et conventui *monasterii* X[a] salutem et apostolicam benedictionem.

Apostolice sedis benignitas prudentes virgines, que se parant accensis lampadibus obviam sponso ire, tanto propentiori debet studio prosequi caritatis, quanto maiori propter fragilitatem sexus indigere suffragio dinoscuntur.[b] Cum *igitur*[c] sicut ex parte vestra fuit propositum coram nobis, vos incluse corpore in castris claustralibus, mente tamen livera devote domino famulantes *de institutionibus fratrum ordinis Predicatorum illas, que vobis competunt, hactenus*[d] *laudabiliter duxeretis observandas ac committi . . . magistro et . . . priori Theutonie ipsius ordinis affectetis,*[e] nos *pium vestrum propositum in domino commendantes,*[f] devotionis vestre precibus inclinati, vos et monasterium vestrum *auctoritate presentium magistro et priori*[g] *committimus supradictis eadem auctoritate nihilominus statuentes,*[h] ut sub magisterio et doctrina *magistri et prioris provincialis Theutonie dicti ordinis,*[i] qui pro tempore fuerit, de cetero maneatis, illis gaudentes privilegiis, que ordini *predicto*[k] ab apostolica sede concessa sunt vel imposterum concedentur; ipsique *magister et prior*[l] *contraria constitutione*[ll] *ipsius odinis vel indulgentia ab apostolica sede obtenta seu etiam obtinienda nequaquam obstantibus,*[m] animarum vestrarum sollicitudinem gerentes et curam, *ac vobis de constitutionibus*[n] *eiusdem ordinis illas, que vobis competunt,*[o] *sine difficultate qualibet exhibentes,*[p] eidem monasterio per se vel *per* alios fratres sui ordinis, quos ad hoc viderint idoneos, quoties expedierit, officium visitationis impendant, corrigendo et reformando ibidem tam in capite quam in membris, que correctionis seu reformationis officio noverint indigere; *et nihilominus*[q] instituant et destituant, mutent et ordinent, prout *in aliis monasteriis monialium eiusdem ordinis fieri consuevit.*[r] Electio tamen *prioresse*[s] libere pertineat ad conventum. Confessiones vestras audiant, et ministrent vobis ecclesiastica sacramenta. Et ne pro eo, quod in monasterio vestro ipsius ordinis fratres residere continue non tenentur, pro defectu sacerdotis possit periculum imminere, *predicti magister et prior*[t] ad confessiones in necessitatis articulo audiendas et ministranda sacramenta *predicta*[u] vobis deputent aliqus discretos et providos capellanos. Ad hec liceat vobis redditus et possessiones recipere ac ea libere retinere, non obstantibus contraria consuetudine seu statuto *ipsius*[v] ordinis confirmatione sedis apostolice aut quacumque firmitate alia roboratis.[w] Nulli ergo etc.

Variant readings from B found in A and C.

a. A: = *monasterii S. Agnetis Argentin*. C: = *abbatisse et conv. mulierum inclusarum monasterii X ordinis sancti Damiani*
b. A, C: —*Apostolice dinoscuntur.*
c. A, C: —*igitur*
d. A: = . . . famulantes, *institutiones ordinis fratrum Predicatorum* hactenus . . .
e. A: *ac committi . . . affectetis.* C: = famulantes, *generali ordinis et provinciali fratrum Minorum X ministris desderetis pro vestra salute committi*
f. A: = nos *ad supplicationem dilecte in Christo filie nobilis mulieris Amicie domine de Jovignaco et Galcheti nati eius familiaris nostri*
g. C: = *generali et provinciali ministris*
h. A: = vos et monast. vestr. *incorporantes Ordini supradicto, predicta* auctoritate *statuimus,*

i. C: = *ministrorum generalis et provincialis fratrum Minorum provincie pretacte*
k. C: = *pretacto fratrum ipsorum*
l. C: = *generalis et provincialis ministri*
ll. A: = *consuetudine*
m. C: —*contraria . . . obstantibus*
n. A: = *vobis constitutiones*
o. A; —*illas . . . competunt*
p. C: —*ac . . . exhibentes*
q. A: —*et nihilominus*
r. C: = prout *secundum deum viderint expedire.*
s. A: = ipsius C: = *abbatisse*
t. C: = *pretacti generalis et provincialis ministri*
u. C: = *pretacta necnon divina officia celebranda*
v. A: = *predicti* C: = *vestri*
w. A: + *Quorum administrationi prefati magister et prior preficiant aliquos viros idoneos ipsosque inde removeant et substituant alios prout viderint expedire.* C: = roborato

---

4. THE REORDERING OF RELATIONS BETWEEN THE MENDICANT ORDERS AND WOMEN'S HOUSES, 1245

Relations between the Dominican Order and the German convents on the one hand and the Franciscan Order and houses of the Order of St. Damian on the other were regulated in utterly similar fashion by the papal orders of 1245 and following, and negotiations between the two orders and the curia often intersect. It is only by treating the problem of the two orders simultaneously that the significance of the new order achieved in these years becomes apparent.

The bulls which place German women's houses under the Dominican Order and the houses of the Order of St. Damian under the Franciscans all share wording:[168] the women are placed *sub magisterio et doctrina* of the minister general of the order and the provincial in question; they participate in all the privileges granted to the order. The minister general and the provincial are to assume the *sollicitudo et cura animarum* in the women's houses, either fulfilling the obligations of visitation themselves or through suitable deputies; the free election of the prioress or abbess, however, was reserved to the convent itself. They were to hear confessions from the nuns and dispense sacraments. Since the friars are not obligated to reside continuously in the women's houses, the order's leadership was to name suitable chaplains to hear confessions and give sacraments in pressing need. The convents were allowed to have possessions and incomes, even if the customs or statutes of the order in question had ruled otherwise before.

Those are the regulations which applied to all women's houses Innocent IV subordinated to the mendicant orders. Bulls for the women's houses of the Dominican Order contained two additional stipulations which are missing from the bulls for the houses of the Order of St. Damian: first, clauses in the constitution of the order or papal bulls opposing obligations to provide pastoral care to women's houses are suspended; secondly, the leadership of each order was commissioned to see to it the constitutions of the order were introduced into the women's houses, so far as they were relevant. Both these amendments were superfluous in the bulls for women's houses subjected to the Franciscan Order, since express rules against accepting *cura monialium* had neither been decreed by the order nor approved by the curia. Since women's houses were henceforth to live under the rule of the Order of St. Damian, Franciscans had no need to introduce their own special rules, as had been the case with the German convents, since the houses already lived according to similar rules (the constitutions of S. Sisto or of St. Mark's), though they had never formed an order with common institutions.[169]

It is only the bulls for the two convents subjected to the Dominican Order, Montargis and S. Agnes in Strasbourg, which differ in other ways from all the other bulls. At the conclusion, they add that the minister general and the provincial should vest administration of the house's goods and property in a few suitable men, who could be removed and replaced when necessary. While, in the case of the other convents subordinated to the Dominicans, it is said they had followed those rules of the order *quæ vobis competunt*, this restriction is not present in the bulls for Montargis and S. Agnes. Finally, in the first two bulls, the house is said to have been "incorporated" into the Dominican Order as a result of its own wish; all the other women's houses were "committed" to the Franciscans or Dominicans.

These differences among the various bulls were neither accidental nor pointless. The differences were the result of the shifting attitudes of the curia toward women's houses desiring reception into an order, or they are to be explained by the order's resistance to incorporations. The differences were the starting point for the first efforts the Dominicans made to oppose the papal orders. Since the various bulls—for S. Agnes and Montargis on the one hand, for the remaining German convents on the other—did not agree completely, at the beginning of 1246 the order asked the curia for clarification of what obligations toward convents the papal command had actually imposed on them. There is no doubt this petition informed the curia how the order wished to see these new relationships.[170] Innocent IV responded with a bull to the minister general and provincials of the Dominicans assuring the order it would receive no obligations through the papal "commission" of convents beyond visitation, pastoral care, and organization, enumerated in the "commissioning" bulls and repeated word for word in the new bull. But the bull significantly made no mention of any duty of friars to administer the holdings of women's houses, included in the bulls "incorporating" Montargis and S. Agnes.[171] The introductory formula of this bull also shows the arguments Dominicans used against complete incorporation of women's houses, insisting on reduction of their duties to the nuns. They feared the chief mission of their order, preaching, would be hindered.[172]

Soon after papal orders bestowed a great number of new women's houses on them, the Franciscans sought assurance once more (12 July 1246) that this and all future papal "commissions" of convents would not require them to assume more obligations than enumerated in the original bulls of commission.[173]

The actual reason for these negotiations only becomes clear in a protest lodged by Amicie de Joigny and her son Gaucher on behalf of the houses of Montargis and S. Agnes in Strasbourg against the assurances the papacy had granted the Dominicans. According to Amicie de Joigny, if the order only performed the functions described in the bulls of "incorporation" and the bull of 4 April 1246, then their plans had been frustrated and robbed of their true sense.[174] They believed the houses they were fostering had not been helped by mere "commission"; they insisted on complete "incorporation." In effect, they did not feel the women's houses being served by the Dominicans *in spiritualibus*, through visitation and pastoral care, was enough. They also desired care *in temporalibus*, the administration of the houses' possessions and income by Dominican friars assigned on behalf of the order. Such care was precisely what the order would not concede, since this would distract members from their true calling, which was preaching. It is probable the order protested against "incorporations" of this sort earlier, after the incorporation of Montargis and S. Agnes. That protest had led Innocent IV to grant all convents seeking association with the order only the weaker "commission," which dealt only with *spiritualia*, rather than "incorporation," which included *temporalia*.[175] With the bull of 4 April 1246, the Dominicans must have believed they had succeeded in reversing the "incorporation" of Montargis and S. Agnes, turning it into mere "commission." Protest by the Countess de Joigny, however, asserted the claims of both houses to full incorporation. Even women's houses already belonging to the Dominicans had to be concerned lest the reordering of ties between the order and women's houses should come to apply to them as well, so that they insisted on their old rights. Prouille had its claim to *rectores* Dominic had granted them to lead the house *in spiritualibus et temporalibus* confirmed.[176] S. Agnes in Bologna had an incorporation bull issued on 13 February 1251.[177]

The response to the events of 1245/46 brought even more dramatic change to the order of St. Damian. As we have seen, the Franciscans had sought to have their obligation restricted to pastoral care, visitation, and placing chaplains in women's houses, as had the Dominicans.[178] They also had themselves released in advance from having to place any friars in residence in convents which were newly assigned to the order.[179] These stipulations did not clash with the rule Ugolino had composed for the Order of St. Damian, since nothing was said about the relationship of the women's houses to the Franciscan Order. Yet individual women's houses, particularly St. Damian's itself, believed they had earned the claim through prescription to have Minorites in residence,[180] and insofar as this "customary right" had arisen under Gregory IX, it was recognized by Innocent IV in his bull of 1245.[181] As a result, the relationship of Franciscans to the women of the Order of St. Damian was not the same for each house.

The problem of house property stood in much the same situation. All of the bulls of incorporation and commission issued in 1245/46 and after expressly stated that the women's houses should have possessions and income, negating all conflicting rules. The rule of the Order of St. Damian left this question open, but Gregory IX was concerned to have women's houses accept property. Several houses of the order, particularly St. Damian's, did not follow Gregory's desires on this matter, asserting a "right to lack property,"[182] meaning there was disunity among the women's houses of the Order of St. Damian in this matter as well.

The joining of many new women's houses to the order in 1246 precipitated a reorganization which aimed at bringing the conditions for all houses into line, simply and universally, in terms of the bulls of "commission" of 1245/46 and the bull of 12 July 1246 setting the ties of Minorites to women's houses. On 6 August 1247 Innocent decreed a new rule for the *moniales inclusæ ordinis s. Damiani*,[183] which was intended to establish uniform conditions in all the women's houses belonging to the order.[184] Ugolino's rule, retained as the basis, was altered in some details, in view of the fact that Gregory IX had already altered it and reduced its severity (year of novitiate, fasts). The rule was amended to deal with two questions left open in Ugolino's version which had not been treated uniformly in the houses of the order. These two questions had even been ordered in yet another way in the "commission" bulls of 1246: the relationship between women's houses and the Franciscan order, and the acceptance of property for religious houses. All the houses of the Order of St. Damian were henceforth placed under the visitation and pastoral care of Franciscans, who were not compelled to reside in the houses, but who could name special chaplains empowered to exercise pastoral care in pressing cases. All the houses should also accept possessions and incomes, despite earlier stipulations to the contrary. In these two points the new rule agreed completely with the bulls of 1246. An additional point demanded by new circumstances was added: the Franciscans were to install a procurator, whose actions were to be controlled by the *visitatores*;[185] this official was to oversee matters *in temporalibus*. Moving beyond the "commission" bulls of 1246, relationships between the Order of St. Damian and the Friars Minor were more precisely defined: the abbess elected by women's houses had to be approved by the minister general and provincial; the foundation of new women's houses had to be approved by the general chapter of the Franciscans, and the women's houses had to use the Franciscan breviary.

This attempt to introduce unified regulation for all the women's houses subordinated to the Order of St. Damian failed due to the fact the new rule was not universally adopted. Only a few of the German women's houses placed under the order after 1250 are known to have committed themselves to the new rule.[186] We do not know of a single house in Italy, France, and Spain which accepted the new rule; many had their right to follow the old rule, written by Ugolino, confirmed in writing.[187] Resistance to the new rule was so strong that Innocent IV was forced to declare to Cardinal-Protector Rainald as early as 6 June 1250 that the houses of the Order of St. Damian were not to be compelled to observe the rule.[188]

What determined this result was the attitude of the house of St. Damian and of St. Clara herself. Accepting the new rule would have compelled this house to accept property and would have loosened its ties to the Franciscans. This peril awoke once again the Franciscan rage of Clara Sciffi and cried out for a decision. She not only rejected Innocent's new rule, she also took the opportunity to create a new rule of her own renouncing all organizational compromises, without any relationship to Ugolino's old rule, which had formally obligated St. Damian up until then. The new rule would adhere as closely as possible to the Franciscan rule. Clara's rule's essential characteristic, setting it apart from Innocent's rejected rule, was its confession of the strictest poverty, in keeping with the counsels of St. Francis. There was also a claim of Franciscan pastoral care on the scale Francis had guaranteed the sisters of St. Damian: besides a chaplain, a cleric and two lay brothers were to be continually in residence in St. Damian's.[189]

Nothing is known of the negotiations which led to papal recognition of the rule drafted by Clara. On 16 September 1252 Cardinal-Protector Rainald confirmed Clara's rule for St. Damian's. Soon after, when Innocent IV returned to Italy following more than a seven-year absence, he visited St. Clara's deathbed. Innocent issued a bull confirming the *privilegium paupertatis* which had sustained her through all efforts to change the house.[190] Soon thereafter, the pope approved her rule—two days before the saint's death on 9 August 1253. In this, the final achievement of St. Clara, the spirit of primitive Franciscan poverty once more won out over the curia's policy of Church orders, as well as over the organizational goals which had long dominated the Franciscans. The homogenization of orders for women's houses Gregory IX had pursued throughout his career as a cardinal failed when Innocent IV tried to carry it out in too thorough-going a manner before the religious power of the Franciscan ideal had been entirely extinguished.

5. THE QUESTION OF THE *CURA MONIALIUM* IN THE DOMINICAN ORDER

Basic reorganization was an even more pressing necessity for the Order of Preachers than for the Franciscans in the wake of the incorporation or commissioning of new women's houses by Innocent IV. The subordinated houses did not yet constitute a common order and followed no common rule as had been the case with the houses of the Order of St. Damian. The houses were committed to the Rule of St. Augustine, but that rule was only the foundation for regulating a convent. More precise "enabling acts" were needed in the form of special constitutions. Many of the women's houses placed under the Dominicans followed the constitutions of the house of S. Sisto in Rome, others that of St. Mark's in Strasbourg. Yet those constitutions of S. Sisto could not simply be transferred to all houses without modification, for they stipulated that each women's house had to have a community of at least six Dominicans in continual residence. The order wanted to avoid the obligation of residency in the new houses Innocent had bestowed on

Dominicans. The order could not allow the constitutions of S. Sisto to continue in force where they were already followed, nor could it tolerate the constitutions'' introduction to new houses. For that reason, the papal bulls of ''commission'' granted the order the right to introduce constitutions of the Dominican Order into women's houses, ''insofar as they were relevant.''[191]

The order was unable to fulfill this mission. It is impossible to say how the order conducted itself toward women's houses in the first years, or how hard it tried to carry out the papal orders.[192] In any case, there were extraordinary difficulties in carrying out the mandates. A few years later an effort was launched to free the order entirely of the obligations imposed on it. A chronicle of the order says that under the generalship of John the German (1241/52), great efforts were made at the curia to free the order of responsibility for women's houses.[193] Decisive discussions took place at the general chapter in Bologna in May 1252, the last held under Minister-General John of Wildeshausen, and the order's resolutions were presented to the curia.[194] The first success came in a bull dated 15 July 1252, in which Innocent IV promised the order not to impose another women's house for twenty years.[195] The order was still not satisfied. It not only wanted to bind the future, it wanted to avoid the situation created by measures taken in the past. Just as Innocent IV had earlier fulfilled the desires of the women's houses for incorporation without restraint, now he capitulated to the opposite demands of the order without restriction. In a bull of 26 September 1252 he declared he had become convinced the order had been hindered in its essential function of preaching, especially against heresy, by obligations Innocent himself had imposed on the order in response to the demands by women's houses. Since the great mission of the order should have precedence, and the needs of the women's houses could be fulfilled in other ways, the pope released the order from all obligations to the women's houses incorporated or committed to it, with the exception of Prouille and S. Sisto in Rome.[196] In one act, women's houses lost all they had achieved after so many years. They were assured they would not lose any rights obtained through incorporation, but in the future they would have no claim on Dominican *cura*.[197]

This situation, where prior arrangements had been suspended without anything new being put in its place, was utterly untenable. As was to be expected, the sisters effected by the act stormed the curia with passionate complaints and protests, and they summoned up the massed influence of their prominent and wealthy relatives to support their demands. Innocent IV saw himself deservedly pressed from both the sides he had favored in turn: on the one side was the order, which he had just guaranteed against assuming further obligations to women's houses, and on the other side there was a mass of women's houses and their influential, powerful advocates, raising demands on the pastoral care of the order.[198]

In this difficult situation, the curia was aided by two conditions which made the duty of reorganization between the Dominicans and the women's houses easier. Minister-General John the German died on 5 November 1252, and with him the order lost its most zealous agent of resistance to accepting the obligations of *cura*. For a year and a half Dominicans lacked any official leadership at all; in 1253, in the wake of the death of the minister general, the constitution stipulated there would be no meeting of the general chapter. The curia, however, knew well how to make use of this interval to construct a new situation more in keeping with the desires of the women's houses. Secondly, in the summer of 1253, Cardinal Hugh of St. Cher returned from Germany, where he had served as legate for more than two years. He was the man best suited to reorder the relations between the order and women's houses. Himself a Dominican by origin, he had been active as cardinal (since 1244) in promoting Dominican interests, and he could serve as guarantor of the order in the college of cardinals.[199] On the other hand, during his legation in Germany he had passionately defended the women's religious movement, supporting women's houses and communities to the best of his strength. He had come to understand the importance and needs of the women's religious movement as had few others. In Rome he participated in painstaking negotiations, in the end receiving a commission from Innocent IV to negotiate with the order to win a just agreement in the interests of both the order and the women's houses.[200] The cardinal started with a truce. He commanded Dominicans to practice pastoral care in the established manner in all the women's houses currently attributed to them until other arrangements were agreed to between the order and the minister general to be elected at the impending general chapter.[201] It is not known whether there were discussions of relations to the women's order at the general chapter meeting in Buda (Budapest), where Humbert of Romans was elected minister general. At the chapter the following year in Milan, such negotiations doubtless took place, but they led to no final result. The order obviously could not agree to the new order Cardinal Hugh was promoting. In opposition, the chapter passed a resolution making future reception of any new women's houses more difficult and placing the houses under fixed standards. Henceforth a women's house could only be placed under the pastoral care and leadership of the order after the approval of three successive general chapters—while the constitution of the order required the approval of only one general chapter to establish a new Preachers' house. The chapters of the two subsequent years, in Paris and Florence, gave this resolution the force of law.[202] Nothing was decided about the attitude of the order to women's houses already incorporated or attributed to the order; it was only the reception of new houses in the future which was made more difficult. In any case the resolutions reveal the order had become convinced complete rejection of all obligations to provide pastoral care could not be sustained.

By the time of the Paris general chapter of 1256, the cardinal's negotiations with the order had advanced enough for the order to declare itself ready to accept pastoral care in those houses accepted into the order's community by either the minister general or general chapter before 1254, when Hugh of St. Cher had been entrusted with reform.[203] In a letter to the general chapter, the cardinal declared the order could not withhold pastoral care from these houses with a good conscience. Two further houses, S. Dominicus in Imola[204] and the island house in Vestrim (Hungary)[205] were also to be placed under the order, in keeping with the cardinal's recommendation. The order would not be obligated to provide pastoral care to any further women's houses.[206]

It appears the cardinal did not have a proper grasp of the actual scale of concessions the order had made. The number of women's houses accepted into the community by the minister general or general chapter before 1254 eligible to receive pastoral care from the order was obviously much smaller than he believed. The agreement clearly applied to the three houses established by Dominic himself. S. Agnes of Bologna had a papal bull of 22 April 1257 expressly confirming that it was also one of the "houses accepted by a minister general or a general chapter," so that the Dominican prior of Bologna had been commissioned by Cardinal Hugh to take over the obligations of pastoral care.[207] The other houses, particularly those in Germany, could not fulfill the conditions of 1256: with the exception of the house of Paradies near Soest, received into the order in 1252 by John the German himself,[208] not one of the German women's houses had been accepted by minister general or general chapter. Their reception had instead been in response to a papal command. Despite that, Cardinal Hugh used the resolution of 1256 to commission the German provincial to resume providing pastoral care to all of the women's houses where the conditions had been fulfilled.[209] He also gave special orders to resume pastoral care in several houses which had been attributed to the order by papal order alone, still asserting the resolution of 1256 as his authority.[210]

It soon became obvious there was an error, that the resolution of 1256 did not provide a legal basis for the recovery of the German women's houses into the order, and that there needed to be further regulation to achieve this goal. At the general chapter of 1257 in Florence, Cardinal Hugh, who was present,[211] managed to gain acceptance, *propter quasdam causas*, that the order would finally pass a resolution to approve what the cardinal had erroneously believed had been approved the year before. The order was to resume providing pastoral care in all women's houses which had once belonged to the order, even if they had not originally been accepted by the minister general or general chapter.[212] Three general chapters in sequence approved this resolution.[213] In 1259 the chapter finally decided all women's houses earlier placed in the order had a claim on its pastoral care. The chapter in Florence in 1257 also validated the law that new women's houses could join the order only after the approval of three general chapters.[214] In the same year the order once more had Alexander IV confirm that incorporations of women's houses through papal bull would only be effective if the abrogation clause was included.[215]

These decisions of 1257 essentially brought the trying conflict between the order, the curia, and the women's houses over the question of *cura* to an end. The order's counterattack had failed, the women's houses had achieved their claim to Dominican leadership and pastoral care.[216] There would hardly be any change in this relationship until the Council of Trent. Under the generalship of John of Vercelli, Clement IV sanctioned the arrangement brought about by the resolutions of 1257 in a bull dated 6 February 1267, expressly suspending the bull of Innocent IV of 26 September 1252, absolving the order of all obligations of *cura*, as well as all other earlier rulings. Further, the relationship of the Dominicans to all the houses placed in the order were regulated precisely as they had been in the papal commission-bulls of 1245. There was only one added stipulation—already used for the Franciscans: the provincial prior had to confirm the election of the prioress in women's houses.[217] Legislation of the order soon came to recognize women's houses could enter the order by papal order, when stipulating the conditions for acceptance.[218] These were both purely formal acts confirming relationships created by earlier decisions.

Two goals for the order grew from this new situation: uniform constitutions had to be created for all the women's houses associated with the order, and the new stipulations had to be used to determine who had a legitimate claim to membership. The bulls of 1245 had demanded that the order resolve the question of local rules of life, but the order had not taken up the challenge. The order believed it would be able to shrug off the new obligations. When this hope was gone after the negotiations of 1257, the order's minister general,

Humbert of Romans, was commissioned by Alexander IV to create unified statutes for women's houses,[219] and the minister general submitted these new statutes to the general chapter of 1259, which was to complete reintegration of women's houses into the community of the order. The statutes were then transmitted to individual women's houses through the provincials.[220] These statutes were not a reworking of the constitutions of S. Sisto, they were an application of the constitutions of the Dominican Order, insofar as they could apply to women.[221] The order's minister general admonished women thus bound to the order to prove themselves worthy of this membership, so that friars assigned to duties in women's houses would do so not with sighs but with joyful good will.[222]

In order to establish which convents had a right to the Dominicans' *cura*, the general chapter of 1257, meeting in Florence, sent all provincial priors an order to report precisely how many women's houses there were in each province. They were to tell how many sisters lived in each house, what incomes they disposed of, and how their claim to belong to the order was established.[223] This was intended to settle without ambiguity the legal status and scale of the order's obligations to women's houses. This survey was plainly not so simple as to be carried out before the chapter of the following year. The general chapter at Valenciennes in 1259 stressed once again that only those women whose houses had been received by the minister general, the general chapter, or papal order to the relevant provincial prior could be considered sisters of the order. The chapter also repeated the demand to provincial priors to report the number of convents by the time of the next general chapter.[224] At the start of 1262 Cardinal Hugh resorted once more to writing the order's leadership to clarify what had been decided. By power of a new papal commission, he declared the leadership could rule to accept or reject those cases where the claim of women's houses to be members of the order was doubtful, always reserving the cardinal's final right to decide.[225] We do not know of any specific cases in which the claim of women's houses to belong to the order was disputed at that time.

The next concern of the order was the economic security of the women's houses attached to it. The measures which were taken in this matter allow us to see what importance the incorporation of women's houses into the order had for the fate of the women's religious movement. Minister-General Humbert of Romans had been fully aware of the religious content and spontaneous power of this movement at the time they were introduced to the order.[226] At the same time, however, he declared it necessary to place religious women's communities on a secure economic foundation. The order demanded that all women's houses subordinated to it have the means to support nuns held in strict enclosure. Humbert had a precise audit made of the wealth, property and incomes of all the houses brought to the order by the reorganization of 1257. He intended to establish the maximum number of sisters who could be accepted in each house. The maximum number was to be exceeded only in extraordinary circumstances—when particularly prominent or especially wealthy women sought entry, whose rejection would bring economic injury to the order or the enmity of influential groups.[227] Houses with more sisters than permitted by these audits were to refuse new admissions until the quota had been reached.[228] No new women's house was to be admitted to the order or subordinated to the *cura* of the Dominicans which did not adequately assure the economic support of the sisters. Both friars and nuns were still forbidden to support the foundation or reception into the order of new women's houses—unless they received special permission from the minister general or prior consent of the general chapter.[229]

Thus, joining the Dominican Order meant economic security for German convents. Under the leadership of the order, the poverty movement passed into communal forms assuring individual members a secure income while ordering and disciplining religious life. A large part of the women's religious movement in Germany thus received a new and definitive shape.[230] Later we shall see how this also created the conditions for the unfolding of ''German mysticism.''

6. THE QUESTION OF THE *CURA MONIALIUM* IN THE FRANCISCAN ORDER

Shortly after Cardinal Hugh of St. Cher's arbitration settled the relationship between the Dominican Order and the women's houses placed under it, there was an entirely similar crisis in the Franciscan Order. The relationship of Franciscans to their women's houses threatened to break down entirely, but in the end a lasting new order emerged as it had with the Dominicans.

So long as Cardinal Rainald held the double office of protector of the Order of St. Damian as well as of the Franciscan Order—which he did not surrender even when he ascended the papal throne as Alexander IV—disordered, splintered conditions continued. The abortive effort of Innocent IV to create uniformity in the Order of St. Damian and clarify its relationship to the Minorites only further confused the issue. Three rules persisted alongside one another in the Order of St. Damian. Ugolino's rule, which was given the most credence, said nothing about convent property or about pastoral care by the Minorites. Innocent IV's rule of 1247 demanded house property and income, bestowing visitation and pastoral care on the Franciscans, but commissioning chaplains and procurators to take care of routine spiritual and temporal functions. Last of all, Clara's rule, kept by St. Damian's and a few other houses,[231] banned house property and committed Franciscan friars to continuous residence in the house.

The Order of Friars Minor was primarily concerned that no more women's houses join the Order of St. Damian and come under Franciscan pastoral care. For that reason, on 6 March 1250, the order obtained the privilege from Innocent IV the Dominicans had earlier received,[232] restricting the accumulation of further obligations of visitation and pastoral care over women's houses by papal decree.[233] When Innocent IV went ahead and bestowed on the Franciscans the pastoral care of the house of Paradies near Constance, founded by the bishop there,[234] they had Cardinal-Protector Rainald assure them that no existing or newly founded houses would be placed under their care in Germany beyond the four houses of the Order of St. Damian which already had a claim on the order.[235] In an act paralleling the Dominicans, the general chapter in Narbonne passed constitutions in 1260 banning Franciscans from acting in any way to found or foster women's houses, receive religious oaths of chastity from religious women, or to receive oaths of obedience.[236] In short, Franciscans were forbidden to assist in any way in increasing the number of women's houses or promoting the women's religious movement. Finally, the order repeatedly asked the curia to intervene against women obtaining papal commissions under the pretext that they wished to found houses of the Order of St. Damian without living in strict enclosure. Since these *sorores minores* claimed to belong to the Minorite Order, bishops had come to make the order responsible for them, leading to conflicts.[237] For this reason the order sought assurance that it would only be asked to assume pastoral care in exempt houses.[238]

The relationship of the Minorite Order to the houses of the Order of St. Damian which already received Franciscan *cura* remained as it ever had been. Only when Alexander IV died on 25 May 1261—precisely in the period when the struggles over the relationship of the Dominican Order to its women's houses were finally settled—did the development of the relations between the male and female branches of the order enter a new stage. When the protectorship of the Order of St. Damian and the Minorite Order united in the hands of the pope himself lapsed, it probably would have taken little to cause the differences between the women's houses and the Franciscans in the question of *cura* to break out again, since these differences had only been carefully patched over but not finally and legally settled.[239] A common protector for both was not named, as had been the case with Cardinal Ugolino and Cardinal Rainald/Alexander IV. Now each order received its own protector. Immediately Franciscans were recalled from women's houses where they had been continually resident, and the *cura* at other houses was also revoked—the order broke all its ties with women's houses. The conflict sharpened even more when the protector of the Order of St. Damian, Cardinal Stephanus Hungarus, had himself commissioned by Urban IV to compel Franciscans to perform their obligations to women's houses, by ecclesiastical sanctions if necessary. The protector of the Minorites, Cardinal John Gaetano Orsini, protested, since this harmed the rights and freedoms of the order. As the confrontation worsened, Urban IV intervened personally and demanded from the cardinal-protector of the Minorites and Minister-General Bonaventure that they should keep everything as it was until the next general chapter at Pentecost 1263. Franciscans were to perform their wonted services to women's houses. If there was no settlement of conflict by then, the order would be free to terminate its obligations to the women's houses. On the other hand, Cardinal Stephanus, the protector of the women's houses, was deprived of all jurisdiction over Franciscans, and decrees he had issued were repealed. The women's houses were ordered to state they would comply with the arrangement Urban IV had announced.[240] In fact many women's houses did make such reports,[241] but there was no basic agreement between the two orders and their protectors before the general chapter of 1263. As a result, in keeping with Urban IV's ruling, the Franciscans should have won a free hand. In a letter to the general chapter, however, the pope exhorted the order not to dissolve its ties to the women's houses,[242] and it appears the chapter did not make any decisive ruling.[243] It is probable the resolution was already being prepared by which Urban IV gave the matter a different direction. On 14 July 1263 the protector of the Minorites, Cardinal John Gaetano Orsini, also became the protector of the Order of St. Damian.[244] Once he had united the two offices in one hand, he had what it took to settle the conflict. He turned first to the minister general, Bonaventure, commissioning him to name visitors for the women's houses.[245] Bonaventure declared himself ready to do so, under the condition that the women's houses which the order was to visit and provide pastoral care would first declare openly that the order was not legally bound to perform these services, and that no obligation would result.[246] The order thus made the point that Franciscan pastoral care and visitation in women's houses would only be voluntary, not legally obligatory. As a result of their recognition of this legal situation, however, women's houses in fact retained pastoral care and visitation from Minorites.

The situation created entailed a change of the rule of the Order of St. Damian. The rule of 1247 had declared the legal obligation of the Franciscans to perform pastoral care and visitation, which was not compatible with the new agreements. For that reason, the new version of the rule confirmed by Urban IV on 18 October 1263 transferred the *cura monialium* to the protector.[247] At the same time, however, it was stipulated that the protectorship for the women's order and the Order of Friars Minor would always rest in the same hand. The protector was to install suitable visitors and to see to the pastoral care in women's houses. To do this, he was primarily to use Franciscans, but it was not legally stipulated that they had to be Franciscans. The protector could entrust others with the duties, should he wish. In all other points, the new rule differed little from the rule created by Innocent IV in 1247. Only the name of the Order of St. Damian was altered, after the death of the holy Clara, to the official title of *Ordo sanctæ Claræ*.

This rule was adopted by the various Clarissan houses after long resistance;[248] only St. Damian's and a few other houses continued to follow Clara's rule. Some Franciscan houses followed another rule which Isabella, sister of St. Louis of France, had composed about 1254 for the house she founded at Longchamps near Paris with the assistance of five Franciscan theologians.[249]

This conflict did not alter the relationship which had developed over the years between the Franciscans and women's houses.[250] The order had only achieved a formal legal concession that its efforts for women's houses rested not on a legal obligation but on a voluntary readiness of the order. The order had probably placed so much importance on this definition so as to hold open a possibility of change in the future. In fact, in the time which followed there had to be continual negotiations and agreements to preserve the *status quo*, since there would never be a definitive legal arrangement. So long as the protectorship of John Gaetano Orsini lasted, the order was assured that it was not obligated to provide *cura monialium*; on the other hand, despite some opposition, the order always found itself ready to provide its "voluntarily assumed" obligations to the women's houses.[251] The longer the *de facto* relationship of the order to women's houses continued unaltered, deepened and tested, the less likely a suspension became and the more unimportant the order's legal reservations became. At the end of the thirteenth century, it was dropped entirely without the Minorites protesting. On 4 June 1296, Boniface VIII renewed the bull with which Innocent IV had first imposed visitation and pastoral care of women's houses on the Franciscans.[252] On 8 April 1297 the new cardinal protector, Matteo Rosso Orsini, solemnly transferred the obligation of *cura* over all Clarissan houses to the minister general and provincials of the Minorite Order. He commissioned them to introduce the Clarissan rule of 1263 to all houses where it was not yet being followed.[253] New relations were not created by that act; conditions which had long prevailed were simply declared to be legally binding. Protests and reservations of Franciscans against these obligations had become ineffectual.

So in the course of the thirteenth century, all attempts on the part of the two mendicant orders to avoid obligations to women's houses ended in failure. The women's religious movement and its demand for organizational guidance and pastoral care by the orders had proved itself more powerful than the negative policies of the mendicant orders. Women had achieved the greater part of what they had sought. The countermeasures of the mendicant orders remained without success. The curia, called to arbitrate, was concerned from the very beginning to incorporate women's communities into the new orders. Though momentarily turned to another policy by the arguments of the orders, in the end the curia had to take account of the wishes and needs of the women's religious communities. The curia had to compel the mendicant orders to take over the organizational and spiritual leadership of women's houses, even against the orders' will. About 1300 a situation was achieved whose complexity witnessed to a long, dramatic conflict. The autonomous, aggressive movement of religious women had, to a large degree, managed to find solid shape as ecclesiastical orders, despite all the efforts of mendicant orders against it. It remains historically significant that the women's religious movement did not gain its organizational form on its own, but from an outside power, the policy measures of the curia and the mendicant orders. As a result of this process, a relatively large part of the women's religious movement was not included, but developed on its own, subject to the temptation of heretical obsession. On the other hand, religious women organized by the mendicant orders never really found their religious needs fulfilled; they took "the route to the inside," away from evangelical, apostolic poverty and toward an inner, spiritual poverty, away from an external renunciation and toward an inner peace, away from the religious poverty movement and toward German Mysticism.

7. STATISTICS ON WOMEN'S HOUSES IN THE MENDICANT ORDERS IN THE THIRTEENTH CENTURY

Some information on the number of women's houses joined to both the mendicant orders in the thirteenth century, as well as the number of sisters living in these houses, would supplement this investigation and give a numerical picture of the importance of the religious women's movement so far as it had its being in these mendicant convents.

The story of the conflict between the orders, the curia, and women's houses shows that it was German women's communities and convents which were the primary concern for the Dominican Order, while for the Franciscans it was those of Italy and the other Romance countries which were in the forefront of concern. According to a Dominican list of houses from 1277, the order then had fifty-eight women's houses, of which forty belonged to the German province, while the remaining eighteen were scattered among the eleven other provinces.[254] At that time there were fifty-three communities of friars in the German province, while there were 414 in the entire order! In the following decade the number of German women's houses under Dominican leadership rose even higher. The provincial prior Herman of Minden gave the figure of seventy for 1287.[255] In 1303, after the partition of Germany into two provinces (Teutonia and Saxonia), a list of houses enumerated seventy-four German women's houses (sixty-five in Teutonia, nine in Saxonia); but seven more houses can be shown to have belonged to the order which were not listed.[256] In all, in 1303 there were 141 women's houses in the order;[257] according to this list, there were still more in the German provinces alone than in the other seventeen provinces together. Alongside the sixty-five women's houses in Teutonia there were only forty-six (or forty-eight) men's houses.

In contrast, in the Upper German province there were still only four women's houses in 1255,[258] and at the end of the century eighteen (or nineteen) women's houses alongside sixty Minorite houses.[259] At the general chapter of 1316 in Naples, a review of the number of houses in all the provinces was presented. The three German provinces then had 40 women's houses alongside 203 men's houses,[260] but all the provinces of Italy had 198 women's houses alongside 567 men's houses,[261] and the five provinces in the region of modern France had 47 women's houses alongside 247 men's houses.

These statistics gain in interest when they are joined with the number of nuns in the individual houses.[262] There are no comparable numbers for German Clarissan houses, and only a few for Italian: in 1238 there are supposed to have been fifty sisters in the house of St. Damian's in Assisi, in 1236 there were forty sisters at S. Apollinaris in Milan,[263] in 1264 there were fifty-five at Monticelli near Florence, and in 1262 there were only seventeen at S. Maria de Marca near Castello Fiorentino.[264]

Statistics for the number of nuns in Dominican houses are richer and more interesting. In Prouille, the first foundation of Dominic, Minister

General Humbert of Romans believed it necessary to reduce the number of sisters until it reached a hundred, in keeping with the effort to establish a maximum number consonant with disposable house income.[265] His successor John of Vercelli was able to increase this number to 160, since the economic base of the house had improved in the meantime.[266] In any case, Prouille was the sole Dominican convent in Provence until the end of the thirteenth century. The number of sisters in S. Sisto in Rome was supposed to have risen to 104 while Dominic yet lived.[267] Fifty sisters are documented in S. Agnes in Bologna in 1237,[268] while Montargis, the first Dominican convent in Northern France (until 1263 the only one) was constructed for the same number of sisters.[269]

Much more astonishing are the numbers for German women's houses, which were often close together and usually placed outside of large towns. In 1237, according to Gregory IX, almost 300 women lived in the five newly-founded houses of Strasbourg, though the incomes barely sufficed to support a hundred![270] In 1245 seventy sisters of noble lineage lived in Adelhausen near Freiburg;[271] in Kirchberg near Sulz ten years after its foundation (about 1240) there were more than sixty and at the end of the century eighty nuns.[272] The house of Medingen had over seventy sisters in 1260 and had to erect a branch-house in Obermedlingen due to this overcrowding.[273] Ötenbach grew from sixty-four sisters in 1237—three years after the house began!—to 120 sisters in 1285.[274] The women's houses themselves sought to stem this tide and protect themselves from receiving more sisters.[275] It was especially the Dominican Order which intervened once it had finally accepted leadership and pastoral care for the women's houses, restricting the number of sisters until each could receive a certain amount from the available house property. We unfortunately do not know the maximum numbers set for German convents by order of the minister general.[276] We only know that they were not kept in the following decades, either,[277] since available houses and maximum numbers did not equal the number of religious women pressing to get in. There were almost 120 nuns in Marienthal near Mersch (Luxembourg) in 1299,[278] and over a hundred in Wederstede about 1303. The fact that these numbers dramatically exceeded the scale corresponding to the economic strength of the houses is shown by the fact that the upper limits were reset, usually at a much lower level.[279] Ötenbach is the best example where the real level can be compared with the norms: in 1285 120 sisters lived there; in 1310 the provincial prior, Egnolf of Stoffen, declared that the property and income of the house would only suffice for sixty sisters. Even then, many more nuns were living there, and the provincial imposed a genuine program of reduction to shrink it. A new sister could only be received after two had died, and this was to continue until the house had reduced to sixty members.[280] Higher numbers were only permitted in a few houses, and in most cases the number was reduced even more.[281] If one knows how to read them, these numbers not only express the scale of the religious women's movement in the thirteenth century, but they also tell us of the nature and the inner life of women's houses. Despite inadequate economic foundations, they could hardly support the mass of women who wanted to live in them. Using resources which careful calculation of the mid-thirteenth or early-fourteenth century declared could support a limited number of nuns, indeed probably with even smaller means, twice as many sisters led voluntarily meager lives. They loved poverty, a genuinely harsh poverty, which would later be transmuted into "spiritual poverty" and "internalized" in well-endowed women's houses. They saw the sense of their existence in renouncing all the goods of the world with their own strength, joining together with like-minded women to form a life which had only religious goals. They had found a mission for their spiritual and psychological powers, a mission outside the social world in whose coils the women of this social class had always been enthralled without being able to develop. They had lost their sense for this social striving once they were seized by the religious sense of poverty and chastity. Therein lay the essential content of the women's religious movement in the thirteenth century.

CHAPTER 6

The Beguines in the Thirteenth Century

Despite their astonishing number and their being filled to overflowing, women's houses of the Cistercians, the Dominicans, and the Franciscans, were in no position to include all the women swept up by the religious movement and to find them a place in the life of their orders. As we have seen, only special circumstances made it possible for religious women's communities to win recognition as autonomous convents and win access to an order. The orders only accepted houses or communities wealthy enough to support all its members in strict enclosure with secure incomes, without relying on alms. Only when religious women's communities found a donor to place enough land at their disposal, or when wealthy women joined, bringing extensive property with them into the house, could they win recognition as convents and achieve membership in an order. Influential connections were also needed to seek incorporation with success. Once the Dominicans finally took over the leadership of the women's houses entrusted to them, virtually universal overcrowding meant these houses only opened their doors to very influential or wealthy women.

Many women who had decided on a religious life in voluntary poverty and chastity could not fulfill these conditions, so that they found entry into the house of any order barred to them. Yet in 1216 Honorius III permitted them to join pious communities, and although it was questionable how this could be squared with the conciliar decree of 1215 banning new forms of the *vita religiosa*, the Church continued to tolerate religious women's communities which were neither regulated convents nor belonged to orders. By the 1230s, the name for these women, accepted throughout Europe, was "beguine."

Beguines thus never represented a planned form of religious life; rather they were the result of the women's religious movement insofar as it did not find reception into the new orders. Some efforts were in fact made from the other side to organize these women's communities outside the large orders, but this had a positive result only in one case. A canon of Hildesheim active as a crusade preacher organized a special branch of the women's religious movement in Germany into an order which managed to receive papal recognition as early as 1227. This *Ordo sororum pœnitentium Mariæ Magdalenæ*—called the *Reuerinnen* in Germany—included primarily, if not exclusively, fallen women who had converted to a life of chastity and poverty. According to the council decree of 1215, it had to commit itself to an old, approved rule, such as the Rule of St. Benedict and the institutions of the Cistercians, but five years after foundation it turned to the Rule of St. Augustine and the constitutions of S. Sisto in Rome. It owed recognition as an autonomous order to the efforts of its founder, Rudolph of Hildesheim.[1] Other men made their marks by promoting religious women outside the orders, such as James of Vitry at the very start of the movement, John of Nivelles and John of Lier, and later James Pantaleon, the archdeacon of Liège who composed a rule for the beguines of the town and diocese of Liège,[2] Master Rainer, archdeacon in Tongern, *conservator et custos begginarum* in Tongern,[3] or the Osnabrück canon John in the archdiocese of Cologne.[4] Yet the efforts of such men never went beyond promoting and supporting beguinages in limited areas. They neither gathered beguines into an organization with a single rule, nor did they win them recognition as an autonomous body. As a result, beguines constituted a strange transitional form between the ecclesiastical orders of the day, never belonging to the monastic community of *religiosi*, since it was not an approved order. Beguines belonged just as little to the lay world of *sæculares*, since beguines had left the *sæculum*, sworn chastity, and led a *vita religiosa* permitted by Honorius III and recognized as legitimate in letters of protection and privileges from popes, legates, and bishops. Furthermore, they had been organized under house statutes peculiar to individual communities, which all members swore to uphold.

This position athwart the ecclesiastical categories became a problem for beguines. It caused contemporary opinion to turn against a phenomenon which found no niche in the system of ecclesiastical estates; it also brought on decline for beguines as a group, beset by moral scandal and heretical tendencies. The conviction of the medieval Church that forms of religious life for large numbers of people, particularly women, could last only if there were strict discipline, secured against the intrusion of moral, religious, and dogmatic perils through clear, explicit standards, was most dramatically confirmed with the history of the beguines.

Contemporary opinion, orders of provincial synods, papal bulls, and other efforts to bring beguines to order all present the same picture of the development of the beguines in the course of the thirteenth century. At the outset, James of Vitry praised beguines as the hope of the Church, promising a new flowering of Christian piety.[5] At about the same time James was celebrating this new form of religious life in his preaching to beguines, the learned and important English Franciscan Robert Grosseteste, later bishop of Lincoln, proclaimed the beguine way of life to be the highest level of Christian perfection, the greatest degree of Christian poverty (since it did not rely on alms but on earnings from their own labor).[6] Not long thereafter, the Parisian theologian Robert de Sorbon argued beguines would be more likely to survive the last judgment than many learned masters, jurists, and theologians.[7] Suddenly, after the middle of the century, beguines began to appear to contemporaries in a different light. It should be remarked that the man who set the tone for this change was anything but an impartial observer. William of St. Amour, stubborn defender of the old hierarchical order of the Church, bitterly fought all new forms of religious life. His polemics were aimed primarily at the mendicants, but when he fell into ominous conflict with the curia, which recognized and protected the mendicants as a new form of monastic life, he slyly shifted his target and continued his earlier assault against those forms of the religious poverty movement which had not made themselves legitimate and invulnerable by finding a place in the ecclesiastical order. In truth the beguines were more vulnerable to his attacks than the mendicants, for they were not an ecclesiastically recognized order. William of St. Amour stood solidly on the principles of ecclesiastical legality when he concluded beguines could not live as members of the monastic estate, could not wear a distinctive habit, and could not cut their hair. When worldly people did that, they were sinfully violating the order of the Church and deserved excommunication.[8] This formal censure of the legitimacy of beguines only constitutes the framework for further accusations and suspicions, which can be reduced to three essential points: beguines were young and capable of work but did not work, desiring to live from alms; they were too young to take an oath of chastity without strict discipline; and they stood in intimate, lively contact with the Dominicans, who were in the process of usurping the rights of the parish clergy,[9] hearing their confessions, preaching to them, conversing with them, exchanging letters with them, and promoting alms for them. What is more, the entire nature and activity of these religious women was hateful to this reactionary enemy of the religious movement of his day, from the name used for this form of religious life, *beguinagium*, through their new way of talking,[10] all the way to the arrogance of their pride in voluntary poverty and their intolerance of the possessions and wealth of others.[11] Yet William's polemic against beguines cannot be explained simply by his passionate resentment of the new religiosity. In many points his accusations indicate changes in the beguines themselves, changes which were moving contemporaries less prejudiced than the Parisian theologian to condemn beguines. Even before William of St. Amour, Gautier de Coincy treated beguines in his poems with nothing but contempt, rejection, and distrust of their religious propriety.[12] Even if one cannot take French poets of the thirteenth century as dependable witnesses, since they allow William of St. Amour to set the tone (particularly Ruteboeuf, who never spares beguines as targets of mockery and suspicion in his satires),[13] they do show what different eyes were being used to see beguines in mid-thirteenth century and how much their reputation had deteriorated.

It is more significant that concern was being raised over the same abuses of which William of St. Amour accused the beguines, but in totally different places and contexts. To combat abuses, German synods decreed beguines could neither live from alms nor beg. Young, morally unripe women were not to belong to the beguines, and beguines were not to withdraw from the oversight and pastoral care of the established parish clergy, establishing excessively intimate ties with mendicants. In the archbishopric of Mainz, whose legislation is the best known, it was already decreed in 1233 that women who had made a vow of chastity and wore a special habit without following a specific rule should not travel from village to village but should live in their houses, either supported by their property, or, if they had nothing, from handcrafts or services. They should also be subject to the proper local clergy and follow their direction.[14] The statute did not call them "beguines," but a synod in Fritzlar in 1244 repeated this statute, adding two amendments in which these women were called beguines and in which the reason for these measures was more dramatically presented.[15] Since it was too common for young beguines to violate their oaths of chastity, the synod ruled only women of good character over forty should live as beguines, and for the same reason monks and clerics were strictly forbidden to enter beguinages. Only in churches were they permitted to address beguines. All these measures proved necessary because the moral order among beguines was secured neither by a strong rule with strict enclosure nor by severe discipline.

Complaints over abuses were also raised by beguines themselves at this time, who did not blame any special character-flaw of beguines, but rather clergy and laymen who took advantage of the beguines' unprotected condition. Beguines themselves even appealed to the curia for help, and after 1235 Gregory IX frequently commissioned bishops and canons to protect beguines against harassment and seduction by clergymen, monks, and laymen, ordering them to punish the guilty.[16]

These inner problems of beguines left their traces in the work of the most important figure among these religious women, the "Flowing Light of Divinity" by Mechthild of Magdeburg. Mechthild herself lived among the beguines in Magdeburg for forty years,[17] perhaps even as the leader of a beguinage,[18] and she dramatically developed the spiritual content of this piety while not being blind to its perils. She was concerned that the beguine life could degenerate into a habit without inner experience[19] drift into a religious eccentricity incapable of conforming to Christian rules and liable to fall into confusion due to a lack of secure discipline.[20] For that reason she demanded a religious life as bound by rule and order as ecclesiastics ever had, and while still living as a beguine,[21] she had personally followed the rules and guidance of Dominicans, including both her confessor and spiritual leader, even prior to her entering a convent at an advanced age.[22]

By the second third of the century, the abuses and perils of the beguine life were not only felt by malevolent critics or ecclesiastical officials, but also with special intensity among the beguines themselves. Opinions were divided over the means to end these problems. When the curia, bishops, or clerics dealt with protecting beguines or punishing their failings, there was no expectation that inner development would stop the spreading malady. The minimum age of forty prescribed by the synod in Fritzlar was never enforced,[23] and the application of any other general prescriptions on the way of life of beguines was perennially stymied by the fact that it was never clearly decided who was to oversee them and provide pastoral care.

On the one side, parish clergy made its claim to lead and provide pastoral care for beguines as part of their legitimate flock.[24] On the other side, beguines sought to extract themselves from the ordinary parish community, obtaining special privileges from papal legates for this purpose, attaching themselves to a collegiate church, or creating their own parish—and legates as well as bishops, even the curia, promoted such efforts.[25] Most of all, however, beguines joined the entire women's religious movement in seeking pastoral service from mendicants. Although both parish clergy and orders opposed this, most of the beguinages in France as in Germany managed to attach themselves in the course of time to the Dominicans or the Franciscans. From the beginning they were free to confess to the mendicants, and they exploited this possibility to such a high degree that mendicants everywhere had to name special confessors for beguines, penalizing those friars hearing confessions too frequently or becoming too intimately involved with beguines.[26] Dispensing other sacraments to beguines, such as communion or last rights, or entirely taking over pastoral care, was expressly forbidden their members by the orders.[27] It is thus not possible to make the leadership of the orders responsible for the close ties which developed between the mendicants and beguines, as William of St. Amour accused the Dominicans. Beguines themselves preferred Dominicans and Franciscans to the parish clergy as their pastors, usually settling near mendicant houses; finally, the new orders, particularly the Dominicans, showed themselves particularly suited to guiding such communities. In the second half of the century, oversight and pastoral care for beguines was often formally bestowed on them, usually reserving some special functions to the parish clergy.[28]

Just how confused and unclear the situation of beguines had become in the mid-thirteenth century, what problems and complaints had arisen from the lack of unified leadership and order, and how puzzled the Church was with these conditions can be seen from what occurred when the general council called by Gregory X on 31 March 1272 sought to undertake a basic reform of ecclesiastical life. The summons itself exhorted princes and prelates to prepare memorials on Church problems and the means to resolve them, and on 11 March 1273 the pope commissioned individual bishops of various countries and the leaders of the large orders to prepare detailed reports on reforms needed in the Church and how improvement was to be achieved. These reports were to be presented to the curia half a year before the council, set for 1 May 1274 in Lyon, so they could serve as the basis for the reforming work of the council.[29] Three of these reports survive: that of the Dominican Order, probably prepared by Humbert of Romans on behalf of his successor as minister general; that of the Franciscan Order, prepared by Simon of Tournai, and lastly that of the bishop of Olmütz. These three reports are of enormous importance for understanding the general condition of the Church in 1273. A Southern French Dominican, a Belgian Franciscan, and an Eastern German bishop reviewed ecclesiastical conditions at the same moment, in response to the same papal commission, to prepare the council's decisions in matters of Church policy. All three reports are also very informative about the situation of the women's religious movement and the beguines in this period. Humbert of Romans[30] deals with the matter in the context of the general problems of the religious poverty movement. After complaining about uncontrolled proliferation of mendicants, *religiosi pauperes*, a burden to the entire world, often regarded not as monks but as vagabonds, lowering the reputation of the monastic order,[31] he deals with *mulieres religiosæ pauperes*, who wander villages and towns seeking support. To eliminate this dubious, offensive phenomenon, he advised the Church only to recognize those women's religious communities observing strict enclosure without relying on alms, supporting themselves by their own means.[32] The principle which always steered the curia, the order, and German synods when treating religious communities was also at work in Humbert's opinion. To him, the basis for the *vita religiosa* of women was always an economic security which made strict enclosure possible; mendicancy had to be forbidden to women. Since women's mendicancy persisted in the Church, however, Humbert believed a reforming council was obligated to eliminate it. He does not expressly say the women in question were beguines, but we are told that by other sources.

In his own reform memorandum,[33] Bishop Bruno of Olmütz also avoids speaking of "beguines," but he describes characteristics unmistakably derived from beguines. He complains of people (men as well, but particularly young women and widows), who bear the habit and name of *religiosi* without belonging to a papally approved order. They will join no valid order, not only so as not to obey anyone, but also because they believe they can serve God better in this sort of freedom. They believed, however, that they have been released of all obedience to parish clergy, with whom they would neither confess nor receive sacraments, as if these things became impure in such hands. They wandered idly and frivolously about the towns, often endangering both reputation and virtue. Just as was the case with William of St. Amour and the Mainz synod of 1244, the bishop of Olmütz recalls Paul's saying that a widowed woman could not be elected to the congregation until she was sixty, and he advises that such women be required to choose either to marry or enter an approved order. In the East, just as in the West, problems had stimulated complaints about excesses of the women's religious movement insofar as it had not been organized into an approved order. The duty of the impending council was to move against the beguines.[34]

The memorial of the Franciscan Simon of Tournai[35] speaks directly about the perils of beguines, with the situation in Northern France and Belgium before his eyes, and he gave them their proper name. Simply fitting the beguines into the pattern of estates in his narrative caused him significant trouble, since he was not sure whether he should deal with them in the context of the spiritual or worldly estates, since they belong completely neither to the *sæculum* nor to a regulated order.[36] Yet his complaint was not this unclarity about beguines, but rather the entirely distinct peril presented by women "who are called beguines."[37] It is he who warns us for the first time of the heretical tendencies of beguines, the temptation of *subtilitates* and *novitates*, a morbid occupation with religious and theological questions. These tendencies inclined beguines to read and explicate religious writings in the vernacular, French biblical commentaries, even the Holy Scripture itself, either while hidden in corners or even in public. This willful preoccupation of uneducated women with a theological literature whose secrets would not be easy to defend even among learned theologians, was not perilous enough; the

French biblical commentaries in question were also so full of error and heresy, dubious and false readings of Scripture, that beguines reading them would inevitably retail confused and heretical opinions. This memorial knew no better way to prevent such a development than destroying these dangerous writings, so that the Word of God would not be spread in the vernacular, what was holy given to the dogs, or pearls cast before swine. Simon did not consider measures against excessive religious and theological maundering among the beguines themselves. Only one extraordinary episode draws his attention and concern. According to a rumor which was spread, one of these beguines had received the wounds of Christ; in Simon's opinion, the truth had to be verified. If the rumor was true, then it should not be spoken of in private but publicly confessed; otherwise the hypocrisy must be suppressed.[38]

We will deal later with the significance of two dangerous phenomena regarded by Simon of Tournai as originating from beguines, heretical tendencies spread by means of a vernacular religious literature and an intensification of ecstatic experiences into the marvelous. For now it is enough to establish that the Franciscan memorial demands the reform council at Lyon take ecclesiastical measures against the beguines in the same way as do the Dominicans and the bishop of Olmütz. Since these memorials were to serve as a basis for the work of the council, there was certainly discussion on how the problems described were to be combated at Lyon. Nothing further is known of these discussions. Deliberations resulted only in a repetition of the Lateran ban of 1215 on new organizational forms, with the amendment that all orders which had arisen since then, particularly the mendicant orders originating after 1215, be banned and dissolved if they had no papal confirmation.[39]

There is no doubt that the council aimed this general ban at the beguines,[40] which did not constitute an approved form of order. This fault had been stressed in all three memorials, and the ban was thought to be the most effective way of eliminating the problems described in them. This measure was so out of proportion with the actual situation of the beguines, however, that there was little chance of it being carried out. Beguines would have little trouble avoiding the ban, since they had never claimed to be a regulated order needing papal approval. Yet individual beguinages often called on letters of protection from popes, legates, and bishops. Dissolving them all, in keeping with the council's decree of 1274, was not only impossible, it was never even attempted. If the decree could not be carried out in principle, it also provided no help in combating the harmful aspects of beguine life. It would have been necessary to pass general rules regulating control over the beguines, the competence of the clergy or the order for their pastoral care, and resolving the question how beguines were to be obligated to enclosure, putting an end to wandering and begging.[40a] Instead of that, the council passed a ban which could never be carried out, in fact accomplishing absolutely nothing. Some expressions from the years after the council of Lyon showed the situation of the beguines to be much more complex than the poorly advised council had assumed in its ban.

In the 1280s a diocesan synod in Eichstätt dealt with the beguines, and the statutes it passed make it clear for the first time what had not been understood in Lyon in 1274: because beguines lacked central leadership and organization, they had evolved into such a variety of forms that no general ordinances could be issued or applied to them at all. It had become more a matter of defending honorable and peaceful beguines against the suspicions and libels to which they were exposed by using the most severe means against those beguines who were rotten and sunk in vice.[41] In the same sense the contemporary Erfurt poet Nicholas of Bibra portrayed the life of a "good" beguine as a particularly meritorious form of piety, but he chided the evil doings of other beguines all the more sharply. While good beguines work day and night, usually spinning, leading a pious and pure life, frequently going to church and hearing mass, fasting, watching and giving alms, of the others it is said, "They connive under cover of a false religious leisure, wandering through the localities."[42] In describing their undisciplined gadding about with monks, clerics, and students, Nicholas stops at nothing to create biting satire. Here it is only important to see how strongly Nicholas of Bibra stresses the difference between the beguines who lived hard at work in their houses (it is no accident that he mentions their spiritual friendship with the mendicants) and the others, who wander about all over the place, attracting such a bad reputation that they are even regarded as murderers of children. This disparity between varieties of beguines also surfaces with Humbert of Romans, who demanded in his memorial of 1274 that special measures be taken against the wandering *mulieres religiosæ pauperes*, yet in his collection of sermons addressed to various ecclesiastical estates he included one directed to "Beguines, happy and worthy of all praise . . . following a most holy life in the midst of a perverse nation."[43]

All of these witnesses reveal that beguines were divided into two groups. While one part, doubtless by far the greater part, led a regulated life in beguinages, often with ties to mendicant houses, earning their way with handcrafts, the other part stimulated complaints against women who kept no enclosure and wandered about without restraint, preferring alms to work. This dichotomy would prove fateful for the further history of the beguines. The term of "beguine" used for two such distinct phenomena, combined with the lack of a fundamental organizational division between them, would lead to measures against "unregulated" wandering beguines, dragging "regulated" beguines into a common catastrophe. A clear distinction came only after a long crisis.

Some beguine rules survive for the last decades of the thirteenth century permitting some insight into the ways beguines developed in this period insofar as they took the route to strict regulation. The most important and informative are the statutes of the three beguine "gatherings" in Strasbourg near the Dominican house. It is unknown how long these communities had existed and what form they had once had, for early information is utterly lacking. In 1276 they were given identical rules with the advice and approval of their confessor, the Dominican Frederick of Ersteheim,[44] as it says in the introduction, in order to avoid the "dubious and damaging loosening of order and to submit themselves to praiseworthy discipline." All sisters were bound to shake hands to confirm these statutes, and every new entrant was to do likewise. If any woman remained in the community for more than a year, she was regarded as being *confessa et obligata* to the statutes. In the first line, all members swore to be obedient to the orders of the *magistra*, the subprioress and the confessor concerning order and control within the house.[45] Whoever does not submit and obey the statutes, or disturbs harmony among sisters, anyone guilty of an immoral way of life will be excluded from the community. The decision to do this lies with the *magistra*, the subprioress, and the majority of the sisters. Other penalties are also mentioned for infractions, but in contrast to most orders' rules, these statutes do not contain a thorough penal code. Most of the stipulations have to do with the regulation of property. There is as little talk of an oath of poverty or renunciation of private property, nor is there a genuine oath of obedience to support the obligation to keep statutes or obey the directions of officers. There is also no talk in the statutes of an oath of chastity. It is certain that the sisters lost free disposition of property on their entering the community. If a sister were expelled for violating the statutes, everything she brought in with her remained property of the house, as did the estate of sisters who died in the house; claims of relatives were expressly rejected. However, when a sister departed after living in the community longer than a year (or, if she entered as a child, after she reached her fourteenth year), she could take only her clothing and bedding, leaving all other movable and real property behind; only if she entered a religious house was she allowed to take a monetary donation of five pounds. Leaving the community was hence not impossible in principle, since it was not prevented by a binding, eternal oath, but it entailed loss of property.[46] These rules would be incomprehensible if beguinages were really what is often asserted, hostels for propertyless, unmarried women who could leave at any time once they found a niche in bourgeois life, particularly in the form of marriage. In truth, the Strasbourg rules for beguines not only made leaving in order to be married extraordinarily hard through seizure of property, but return to the world was not even considered. Instead, only entry into a religious house, hermitage or some other religious community was considered.[47] On the other hand, these rules not only assume that all of the sisters who entered the community brought property in real and moveable goods, but women somehow incapable of inheriting were expressly excluded from being accepted into the community.[48] Entry into the community was only open to women who brought property, and leaving meant the loss of that property to the community. We know from later Strasbourg documents that only women of the Strasbourg "patriciate" and the high burgher class were to be found in the three "gatherings."[49] We will consider later what that meant for the character of regular beguines. Two important aspects of the Strasbourg statutes remain to be stressed. The statutes do not say precisely how sisters were to be supported, but marginal comments indicate the community relied on income from property brought into the community, and from the profits of their labor, which can only mean the handcraft of the sisters.[50] In the same way, little was said about the sisters' relationship to the parish clergy and the Dominicans, yet a Dominican was their confessor, and the statutes were composed with his advice and approval, his directions must be obeyed by the sisters, and in necessity he could dispense from the statutes, with the agreement of the Dominican prior, who had sealed the statutes in the first place.

These statutes applied only to the three Strasbourg beguine gatherings near the Dominican house. Its rules cannot, of course, be generalized to others. Yet we find many similar stipulations in the assizes of other beguinages in this period. In 1288 a house for twenty "poor sisters or beguines" was founded by the former chief judge of the cathedral chapter in Worms, and the founder irrevocably bequeathed his total property, including a house for the beguines, and his letter of foundation stipulated the rule of the house.[51] The rule subordinated the sisters to the leadership, control, and pastoral care of the Franciscans. No women could be received into the community who did not have adequate means to support herself (this certainly meant her own property) or was capable of supporting herself with a skill she had learned, rather than begging or alms. The founder does not wish his property to pass into weak hands.[52] On being received into the community, each sister had to present all her property to the mistress, who administered the common property and accounted for it to the Franciscans. The sisters could only dispose of their property with the mistress' approval. The foundation letter specifically justified these stipulations by arguing that otherwise rich and prominent members of the "poor sisters" would think themselves superior to the poor and lowly. Even here there was not a hint of the reception of needy women from the lower orders, but rather of women who wished to be *pauperes sorores*, even if they had once been rich and prominent.[53] Whoever was expelled for a moral offense lost her entire property to the community, but when excluded due to violation of the statutes, she would receive half her property back, just as was the case with voluntary departure, whose motives were not further examined.

No other statutes of such thoroughness are known for German beguinages from the thirteenth century.[54] Still, there are agreements between the statutes of the beguines under the Strasbourg Dominicans and the Franciscans in Worms: the Hildesheim beguines had a charter issued in 1281 stating that sisters who left their community of their own free will had no claim to recover money they donated on entry; the same is true of the beguines in Halberstadt in 1302;[55] in a beguinage established in Wesel in 1309, the entry of sisters depended on property or the ability to earn their keep with handcrafts.[56] A remark of the German provincial, Ulrich of Strasbourg, demonstrates that beguines dependent on the Dominicans also lived from handcrafts.[57]

The statutes of beguinages in the thirteenth century, so far as we know them, all agree in placing a high value on assuring the economic position of the community, partly through the sisters' property, partly through the sale of their labor. This principle is significant for two reasons. First of all, begging and gathering alms were forbidden for religious women's communities, and members were as closely tied as possible to the house in order to prevent women from wandering about the streets and houses. Secondly, women were only allowed to enter these ordered communities who were not reduced to taking alms, but who could support themselves either from their property or by their own labor. Beguinages neither wanted nor were able to offer asylum to entirely poor and needy women, nor did they provide a place for the ideal of complete poverty according to the Franciscan model, where no care was taken for what was needed tomorrow. The idea of assured support increasingly replaced the idea of voluntary poverty.

Conditions developed similarly in the male variant of the beguinages which begin appearing in the second half of the thirteenth century.

They only achieved importance in Belgium, but even there they were nowhere as numerous as beguinages. The chronicler Matthew Paris had already remarked for the year 1243 that the beguines in Cologne had won male adherents, though they had grown more dramatically among women;[58] at the same time, the letter of a French cleric mentions *quosdam novos religiosos, qui beguini vocantur*, in Wiener Neustadt.[59] In both cases, we learn nothing about the way of life pursued by this male branch of the beguines. Beghard-houses exist in Bruges from 1252, soon after in Deist and other Belgian towns, functioning just as the beguinages. They lived as religious communities performing pious works and handcrafts in common, particularly weaving, though sometimes they pursued merchant activities or even agriculture.[60] These communities were very similar to houses of the Lombard *Humiliati*, as evidenced from later statutes and the contents of charters of the dukes of Brabant, freeing most of them from taxes and dues, as well as their dealings with guilds. Little is known of their origins or the motives for their rise, but analogy with similar communities permits one to suppose that the beghard communities did not arise for economic reasons. Religious motives appeared to be the primary reason for joining together and practicing their communal labor, especially weaving.[61] From the very beginning, when they were still separately organized, these beghard houses had close links to the Franciscans and Dominicans; at the end of the thirteenth and particularly at the start of the fourteenth century, when they were included in the papal anti-beghard decrees through no fault of their own, they all became Franciscan tertiaries without enduring much change in their earlier way of life, and also without losing the popular name of "beghards." They did occasionally have some disruptive elements.[62] In general, however, these orderly, hard-working, Belgian beghard communities, overseen by the mendicant orders, remained untouched by the perils of religious radicalism and heretical decadence which threatened the survival of the beguines at the turn of the fourteenth century. Only the fact that they bore the name also used for some of the most unruly elements in the Church in the thirteenth century briefly involved them in the great crisis the beguines endured.

Without ever being recognized as a religious order, as a semimonastic group lacking a clear relationship to the Church, the beguines were able for the most part to survive by binding individual communities to stable statutes, accommodating themselves to a loose form of enclosure which was only violated when they went to church services. They withdrew from collecting alms and subordinated themselves to the control of the mendicants. Still, this development into a regulated status was not made as a unit or completely, and religious women not drawn into ordered circumstances in this way became a peril to all beguines. To understand the development of these unregulated beguines in connection with the heresy of the free spirit, our investigation must return to the beginning of the thirteenth century.

CHAPTER 7

The Heresy of the "Free Spirit" in the Religious Movement of the Thirteenth Century

1. The Heresy of the "Amaurians" in Paris, 1210

The heresy that permeated the beguines in Germany after the second half of the thirteenth century, which led the Council of Vienne to level a general condemnation in 1311, has always been associated with a heretical movement in Paris discovered about 1210 and condemned by a Parisian synod. The doctrines then rampant in Paris and those later spread among the beguines were remarkably similar in so many details that it was unavoidable to suppose a historical connection. Despite this, it proved impossible to discover the routes by which these two groups of heretics could be related, so widely separated in time and space. Beyond extensive agreement in their heretical doctrines, there seemed no way to prove their actual connection.

Sources hitherto unused[1] on heresy in Paris in 1210 show that these heretics had close contact with the women's religious movement, and they also point to the way the doctrine condemned as heresy survived through the time which followed, spreading and strengthening among religious women, particularly the beguines of Germany. By carefully listening to all the witnesses, it is possible to discover the bearers of these heretical thoughts within the religious movement of the thirteenth century. It will only be after we can see these connections that the nature, spiritual content, and historical importance of these phenomena can be correctly understood.

It has long been known from the usual accounts of the case that the spread of heresy was not restricted to the fourteen scholars the council tried and condemned in Paris in 1210. They had spread their error to many places, said Cæsarius of Heisterbach,[2] and he also said that Master Rudolph of Namur and his companion, who asserted they were members of the sect in order to infiltrate it, wandered for three months with the heretics through the dioceses of Paris, Sens, Troyes, and Langres, meeting adherents of heresy in all these places. The chronicler William the Breton[3] mentions not only heretic priests and clerics, but also lay persons and women, remarking that the Paris synod only condemned the leaders, sparing the women they had seduced and misled, along with other simple persons. A contemporary description from the Scottish Cistercian house of Melrose, ignored until now, gives a clearer picture of the historical circumstances of this heresy, from which we can learn new aspects of their spiritual and religious character. The heretics had gone into the houses of widowed women, it says,[4] and through false explication of the Holy Scriptures they had led many innocents into error. This comment is very informative. The men against whom the accusation is aimed, who were condemned as heretics, were all clerics, most of them priests, while the others had lower ordinations.[5] They had almost all taken positions as parish priests and pastors in the provinces.[6] As pastors they had spread their influence among women,[7] particularly widows,[8] scattering the seeds of their dangerous convictions. The fact that they based their efforts on an arbitrary interpretation of Holy Scripture seems likely from the character of their doctrine. The people called them "papelardi." This word appears for the first time, so far as we know, in the report of the Melrose chronicle, and its meaning is not easy to determine. Later it was used as a term of abuse for members of the religious movement, and in his sermon to beguines, James of Vitry asserts the word "papelard" was used in France for the same people who were called "beguines" in Brabant and Flanders, *Humiliati* in Lombardy and *bizocæ* in Italy![8a] Accordingly, the adherents of the Paris heretics must obviously be sought among the same sort of religious women, and we will find other witnesses for it as well. What was remarkable about them to the casual observer, what aroused sympathy with some and offense with another, was their extraordinarily pious attitude, the strange earnestness of their religious way of life[9]—these characteristics were obviously being mocked with the term "papelard."

When these activities were finally chased down, the accused clerics interrogated and their convictions and doctrines investigated, an entirely different picture emerged. It appears the clerics accused were all educated, several had even earned the master's degree, and that they were all students of one man who had died a few years before[10] in the Paris house of St. Martin des Champs, the philosopher and theologian Amaury of Béne.[11] It was recalled that Amaury's doctrines had already been attacked by the Paris theological faculty as not being orthodox, and that after vain appeals to the pope he had to recant. What the actual point of this earlier conflict was cannot be recovered with any precision. According to one chronicler,[12] Amaury is supposed to have stubbornly defended the doctrine that it was a necessary item of Christian doctrine that each Christian was a member of Christ. But this learned theologian could not have been involved in a trial for the sake of one citation from Paul (*Membra sumus corporis Christi*). It is only possible to approximate the bases of this doctrine. First of all, we are rather certain Amaury had revived the work of Johannes Scotus Eriugena, and he was strongly influenced by Johannes' neo-Platonic philosophy.[13] Second, it is at least possible that he was influenced by the writings of Aristotle in natural philosophy and his Arabic commentators, who had become known only a short time before in Paris; this is not based simply on the fact that the Paris synod of 1210 not only condemned Amaury's students, but also banned the reading of the *libri Aristotelis de naturali philosophia* and its *commenta*, but also several contemporary reports which state that the ban was due to the influence of these writings on the condemned heretics.[14] Several doctrinal propositions of Amaury do survive, and their derivation from the neo-Platonic thought of Arabic commentators of Aristotle is very probable.[15]

We do not know much more about the thinker whose students were called to answer before the Paris synod of 1210 because of the doctrine they were spreading. They show themselves to be students of Amaury the philosopher because of their dialectical training,[16] and of Amaury the theologian due to their defense of the doctrine of being members of Christ, which Amaury had once been forced to recant by the Paris theologians.[17] There is no doubt that the "pantheism" of the heretics of 1210, the doctrine of the identity of God with all being, with the essence, with the nature of all things, derives from the knowledge of the philosophy of Eriugena revived by Amaury.[18] It is likely that Amaury, the philosopher and theologian, assigned himself the task which his students sought to solve: to demonstrate the truth of the neo-Platonic philosophy of identity as the true theology with the aid of scriptural exegesis, particularly through explicating opinions of Paul.[19] For it is precisely this conviction that the right philosophy must also be the true religion which is the driving force in the thought of Eriugena.

The interrogation of 1210 was thus correct in making the philosophy and theology of Amaury the starting-point of the heresy, insofar as it dealt with the neo-Platonic foundation, along with its invocation of the theology of Paul. Despite that, it is not wholly right to make him responsible for the efforts of his students. This is because the philosophy and theology taught by Amaury only became a heresy when combined with ideas of an entirely different origin and through operation in entirely different circles. The speculative ideas of the master were reminted as "doctrines of life" by the priests, pastors, and agitators who were his students, who injected these doctrines into religious groups which totally lacked any philosophical schooling, announcing them to be promises of a renewal and elevation of religious life. Particularly, they bound their teaching with a doctrine of history which gave those thoughts their heretical-revolutionary turn. The conviction that they were standing at the dawn of a new epoch of religious development which was the age of the Holy Spirit, succeeding the Old Testament era of the Father and the New Testament era of the Son—such a conviction cannot be found in Amaury himself, was never imputed to him, and it is not even likely he ever held it. For the students, on the other hand, who were tried in 1210, this doctrine of history played a decisive role,[20] not only as a philosophical framework for their point of view, but as the driving force of their efforts. Eriugena, the philosophical source for Amaury, had expressed similar thoughts, but not in his main work upon which Amaury drew.[21] On the other hand, the historical concepts of Amaury's pupils agreed surprisingly with the doctrine of Abbot Joachim of Fiore (died 1202). Even if there is no way to establish his literary influence on the Paris heretics of 1210 beyond a doubt, it still remains highly likely that the knowledge of his ideas was the source of the Amaurian convictions on the third age of the Holy Spirit.[22] With a philosophy deriving from Eriugena and a theology calling on Paul, this doctrine of history combined into an emphatic faith that they stood at the epochal turn of the ages, in which all which had obtained heretofore would be devalued and replaced with true knowledge, which would be the highest level of religion, the revelation of the Holy Spirit himself. In the little circle of pupils of Amaury, this transformation made its breakthrough, but it would not remain bottled up in them alone, for in the briefest instant it would conquer the whole world.[23] Spreading their doctrine, making a religion comprehending all people out of a school philosophy and learned theology, must have appeared to these men to be their epoch-making task. The fact that they found receptive souls, particularly among religious women, probably moved their ideas and convictions in a peculiar direction. For as it later developed, any intermingling of philosophic and theological training of neo-Platonic origins with the women's religious movement would always produce particular spiritual tendencies with an unmistakable relation to the doctrines of the Paris heretics, even when a direct relationship cannot be demonstrated. The same philosophical attitude repeatedly produced the same patterns when it intersected with the religious movement. In the Parisian heresy, this pattern appeared for the first time, so that the details of the doctrine condemned at that time deserve close attention.

Since no statements from the heretics themselves have survived, we know their attitudes only from the assertions of their orthodox enemies in the trial, both as polemic and as reports of proceedings. Of course what is traced there is the "doctrine of dissidence," the points of breakage between heresy and ordinary Catholic doctrine in questions of dogma and moral teaching. But these fragmentary sentences, which only intend to point out variance from the faith of the Church, show convincingly enough the general conviction being expressed. The heretics did not deny their philosophical origins. It was not faith and hope, but knowledge alone, a wisdom which they themselves see as their cause, which is the leading, even the sole factor of salvation as well as the very goal of salvation. This was, of course, not just any random knowledge, but a wisdom "which they have" and which they hold to be the revelation of the Holy Spirit incarnated in them. This knowledge is the resurrection, and another resurrection does not exist; it is paradise and another paradise does not exist. Non-knowledge, on the other hand, is hell.[24]

Amaury's students perhaps believed they drew this doctrine from Eriugena, for whom heaven and hell were not places but states of consciousness, as were the resurrection and the last judgment.[25] But Eriugena sought to demonstrate the inner unity of philosophy and the faith of the Church with such interpretations; his latter-day disciples, in contrast, placed their "knowledge" in sharp opposition to current dogma. Their conviction that the knowledge they had obtained was the last end of all religious life was turned against the fundamental teachings of the Church, which placed the goal of religion in a supraterrestial future, in the afterlife, holding all knowledge obtainable by earthly people to be imperfect, unsuitable, and preliminary,[26] and reserving to the sacramental Church until the end of the world the function to administer the necessary, exclusive access to future blessedness in the afterlife. The heretics of Paris placed their true philosophy, the knowledge of "spirituals" in an Age of the Spirit, in the place of the sacramental forms of the Church, which belonged to a dying age. It was not just the veneration of saints, reliquaries, and pictures which was devalued by "knowledge," but also baptism, confession, and all the other sacraments.[27] Above all else, the eucharist lost its rank in their pantheistic philosophy, which found God in all bread and in all things whatsoever,[28] and further—probably, as ever, drawing on Eriugena[29]—they declared the doctrine of the ubiquity of the body of Christ. They could not recognize a unique and supreme importance in Christ become human, since they claimed that, as Christians, they were members of Christ, not only, as creatures, a part of the cosmos which was identical with God, but in a special sense. As spirituals of the Age of the Spirit, they were incarnated God, just as Christ once had been.[30]

This challenge to the dogma and sacramental doctrine of the Church, which did not rise from rational criticism, from the rivalry between knowledge and revelation, but rather from the claim of philosophical speculation to be a religious manifestation in itself, the revelation of the Holy Spirit, corresponds to the attitude the heretics had to Christian moral teaching. Here as well, Eriugena's philosophy is unmistakably the foundation and starting-point. Evil or sin has no place in Eriugena's neo-Platonic, optimistic world vision among those things which truly exist; evil was not created by God, as is the case with all which exists, nor does it grow out of God; in the strict sense it does not exist; it is a non-thing.[31] Eriugena did not mean to deny that evil and sin were present, but rather, in keeping with Augustine, he wanted to see sin as a lack of being, a negation of true, ideal being, and to deflate it ontologically. The heretics of 1210, on the other hand, would not stop at this speculation, but won from it a practical decision against the problem of sin. This is most clearly stated in a sermon of Johannes Teutonicus, who must have been well informed of the doctrine of the heretics as abbot of St. Victor's in Paris:[32] he said that out of the doctrine that sin was a "nothing," they derived the argument that no one could be punished by God for sin, and hence that sin was without penalty. The same derivation from the idea of the non-being of everything which was not God is preserved in a second formulation: a person, insofar as he participates in being and hence in God, could no more sin than he could be obliterated.[33] With this conviction of the non-being, non-penality, and irrelevance of sin, the Paris heretics combined, on the authority of a Pauline theology, a dynamic pantheism, a pantheism which recognized and esteemed God's will and creation not only in all that was, but also in everything which occurred and—even when done by people—what was done. "God does everything in all"—from this saying of Paul the heretics continued: "both the evil and the good." Whoever knows that whatever he does is God's doing cannot "sin," does not need to have remorse or do penance.[34] True knowledge suspends the need for any repentance,[35] for it knows that God does everything, that a person does nothing on his own, but rather that everything, even the sinful deed, comes from God.[36]

For the "spiritual person" of the last age, who has true knowledge and in whom the Holy Spirit is incarnated, there is a new ethics, which knows nothing of "sin" according to the measure of moral norms, nothing of remorse and repentance, which particularly suspend the laws of sexual morality valid until now; and the Paris heretics obviously did not leave this at theoretical contemplation.[37] In doing so they exposed themselves to the moral revulsion not only of their contemporaries but also of posterity; often it was believed possible to see this "apology for sin" as the real reason for the entire heresy.[38] This approach will win us no historical understanding. Even in the Middle Ages, no one needed to become a heretic in order to sin, and a depraved turn of life did not need any philosophical clothing. The Christian moral teaching of those days never made it impossible for anyone, least of all the clergy, to live other than they taught. A philosophical inversion of Christian morality of such enthusiastic daring as the Amaurians created is not to be explained from the same motivations as the virtually universal moral depravity of the clergy of this time.[39] Rather it is an effort to bridge the yawning gap between Christian doctrine and the way of life of most Church-Christians. But while the religious poverty movement sought to conquer this discrepancy by recognizing once more Christian moral teaching as a strict commandment for leading the Christian life, the pupils of Amaury sought through their new teaching simply to eliminate the tension between religious norm and the necessities of life. Their religious convictions played as much of a role as their faith in an epoch-making mission which found its strongest echo precisely among religious women. Their Catholic persecutors, then and later, essentially stressed the negation of the teaching and principles of the Church. But many indications permit us to recognize the positive content, the leading ideas of this heretical teaching. They spoke only of divine goodness, not of divine justice, said one chronicler, and the strength of love, *caritas*, eliminated in their eyes the distinction between good and evil, stripping the sinfulness from what moral standards called a sinful deed.[40] The peculiar attitude which prevailed in this circle is most clearly expressed in the sentence: A person who knows that God is in him can never be sad but only joyful.[41] We can doubtless draw more knowledge of the actual "ethos" of this heresy from such expressions of philosophical optimism than from the moral offense of contemporaries, but at the same time we can also see its spiritual connections with the later "mysticism of love," which emerged from the mutual interpenetration of philosophical and theological speculation and the religious movement, particularly among women, and which perennially generated heretical ideas similar to those of the heresy of 1210.

2. Preconditions for the Spread of the Heresy within the Religious Movements of the Thirteenth Century

The hypothesis that the views of the students of Amaury, combining pantheistic philosophy, Pauline theology and Joachite historical doctrine, first became a disturbing heretical peril when it joined with the religious movement, particularly among women, is completely confirmed by the sequel to the events of 1210. Insofar as it was a question of true "Amaurians," the clerics from Amaury's following who had broadcast their enthusiastic ideas in their activities as pastors, the episode could be seen as closed with the Paris trial. Some of the guilty were burned, others imprisoned for life. Two years after the Paris synod, a Master Godinus, who had played a leading role among the heretics, was condemned to the stake in Amiens.[42] In 1215 the legate Robert of Courçon, in the course of revising the statutes of the University of Paris, not only banned the reading of Aristotle's physics and metaphysics, but also "writings on the teachings of the heretic Amaury,"[43] and in the same year the condemnation of Amaury was repeated by the Lateran Council.[44] After that there are no more sources indicating that devotees of Amaury or his pupils still lived and worked[45]—it appeared that his "sect" had been obliterated.

And yet within a few decades heresies reappeared in the Church which were surprisingly similar to the views condemned by the Paris synod, once again combining pantheistic philosophy with enthusiastic deifying mysticism, spreading particularly among religious women. Was it possible that the spirit of Amaurian heresy had not been utterly erased? Hadn't the neutralization of Amaury's students been enough to prevent the spread of their views once and for all? Did the roots of heresy run deeper than the Paris theologians and heresy-judges thought when they condemned only the clerics and their errors without taking seriously the receptiveness of their largely female following for these ideas? These questions must be answered in the affirmative, particularly if witnesses can be gathered on the groups, the media, and the terms in which doctrines and attitudes condemned in 1210 survived to grow and reemerge as the heresy "of the free spirit."

Once one notices that the philosophical and theological doctrines of Amaury and his students first achieved their particularly heretical effect and vitality in the course of their "pastoral application" to groups in the women's religious movement, well beyond the limits of theoretical speculation, the problem of their influence appears in a new light, revealing the historical link between the Amaurians and the "free spirits" of the later thirteenth century which has hitherto been sought in vain. For "Amaurians" and any "sect" founded by them are not to be found after 1215, yet the groups among which Amaury's students had worked as clerics and pastors remained receptive to these pantheistic, enthusiastic ideas even after their condemnation. The result was that they remained objects of suspicion to contemporaries, and later the same heresy which had been thought destroyed in 1210 in fact did break out among them. This does not prove that an Amaurian "sect" with a solid doctrine and organization continued among them—such a "sect" certainly never existed. But the novel religious attitude and peculiar religious ways of life which had created a tendency to accept pantheistic, mystical, spiritualistic ideas at the start of the thirteenth century continued to function and even expand. These religious groups did not constitute a sect, and they were never an order. Their spontaneously generated, novel ways of the religious life were neither recognized in all their ramifications nor unambiguously condemned and banned. They were neither organized within the Church nor outside, in opposition to the Church. What would have been needed for that would have been a decision—a decision by the curia or a decision in their own attitude and feeling—on what position they were to take either within or outside ecclesiastical regulations. They did not yet have a single, certain name, but rather they were called different names in various places, usually stressing some outstanding mark. People spoke of them, depending on attitude, either in an approving or negative way, for the prevailing powers had not yet decided whether they were to be praised or rejected, and they themselves revealed contradictory natures. It is only once one gathers together the manifold and scattered sources which speak under various titles and with divided sympathies of the imprecise, unregulated phenomenon which is the religious movement of the thirteenth century that a picture of the groups is won, within which the pantheistic, spiritualist, mystical heresies first seen in the Amaurians were propagated.

According to the account in the Chronicle of Melrose, the heretics condemned in 1210 were called "Amaurians" or "Godines" by their learned judges, but in the mouths of the people, the laymen, they were "papelardes"—a word which appears then for the very first time, having the approximate meaning of "pious fool."[46] Soon after, James of Vitry asserted that the same religious women called "beguines" in Flanders and Brabant were called "papelardes" in France[47]—that is to say, women suspected as heretics in Flanders as well because of their novel religious way of life (which is why they were called "beguines" there).[48] If that is true, then both the Amaurians and their adherents as well as religious women elsewhere called beguines were called by a name, "papelardes," which was otherwise unknown; a Cologne chronicler even described the heretics discovered in Paris as *Beggini.*[49] If this uniformity of naming does not simply rest on errors and confusion of individual contemporaries, then it can be concluded that the Paris heretics and the religious groups of "beguines" were regarded as associated, equivalent, and related, and hence tagged with the same name. We now have to investigate whether the words "papelardes" and "beguines" really are equivalent, and what right one has to see those so described as related to heretics and receptive to heretical views.

Indeed the words "beguine" and "papelarde" were used in the first half of the thirteenth century, first of all in France and then elsewhere, as equivalent terms for religious groups, particularly of women, whose religiosity and way of life were novel and questionable, and whose orthodoxy was a matter of suspicion. The most revealing witness to this comes from Gautier of Coincy,[50] who included a long consideration of papelardes and beguines in one of his miracle poems composed at the latest around 1220, thus at the most ten years after the condemnation of the Amaurians. He sought to expose their dishonesty and religious pretense, their slipperiness and hypocrisy. Although Gautier was himself a monk and prior of a Benedictine house near Soissons who composed his French legends for the nuns in Soissons and Fontevrault, he lacked any understanding for the new-model piety among members of the religious poverty movement, in which he was inclined to see only false piety and hypocrisy, if not worse. He begins his polemical review with the characteristic assertion: "No one can live entirely without possessions and property, and whoever asserts to be able to do it, or does it, is a dreadful, God-forsaken hypocrite—and for that reason may the fire consume all papelardes!"[51] The entire treatment is saturated with this tone of profound hostility to the idea of the religious poverty movement, which did not come to speak of the papelardes and beguines as examples of general hypocrisy by accident, but rather dealt exclusively and thoroughly with *papelardie* and *beguinage* as a new,[52] widespread,[53] disturbing phenomenon of the times. The people against which this polemic is directed are usually called *papelarts* and *papelardes*, but often also *begins* (v. 1391 ff.) and *begars* (v. 1525/7); he describes their way of life as *papelardie* or sometimes as *beginage*[54] (v. 1531). Living in the border region between Flanders and France, he actually did use the words "beguine" and "papelarde" as equivalent terms for the same phenomenon. Once he also calls them *truanz* (v. 1349)—this word, which means generally the same as hobo, cheat, or confidence man,[55] would come to be used particularly in its Latin form of *trutanni*, as we shall see,[56] for certain unsteady elements of the religious poverty movement. At one point Gautier uses another expression (*quatinus*) equivalent to *begin* and *papelart*, which permits us to assume that the learned term *Godini*, used for the Amaurians (called "papelardes" by the people) had worked its way into the popular language as a term for groups in the religious poverty movement being attacked by Gautier![57] If that is true, we have a striking demonstration that the devotees of what could be called "old-time religion" actually believed all novel phenomena of religious life, Amaurians as well as beguines and papelardes (and at first even the mendicants) to belong together in one great category as objects of suspicion, all to be regarded with uniform puzzled hostility.

This impression is confirmed throughout by the detailed accusations Gautier makes against the papelardes. He is unable to accuse them of any specific crimes against the rules or doctrines of the Church; he can only suspect—as has been the case with every other special religious community which has ever existed—of violating in secret the abstinence they displayed in public.[58] But what irritates him about these people, repeatedly driving him to new hateful and malignant statements about them, is their claim and presumption of elevated piety in their appearance and way of life, their tireless effort to be better, more just, more abstinent, humbler, more peaceful, more spiritual, more freed of the world—in short, more Christian in being or appearance—than anyone was before or is now.[59] They run about with pale faces, soft, quiet, suffering expressions, sunken gazes,[60] eat no meat and drink no wine, hold themselves distant from the pleasures of the world, as if they thought themselves holy and perfect—and Gautier can see nothing there but hypocrisy, lying, and cheating, sheltering hidden pride and ambition. For him it is all an exaggerated and calculated attitude of pseudo-piety, making an impression and seeking to win advantage—which is aimed at high ecclesiastical office if possible.[61]

This total lack of understanding for the nature and religious motives of the new-model piety is not an isolated incident. Gautier of Coincy shares this particularly with many contemporaries from the secular clergy and old-model monasticism. James of Vitry had to defend the beguines against suspicions from this quarter, and it was precisely in France that this jealous hostility against all of them, including the orthodox and ecclesiastically permitted forms of the religious poverty movement, maintained itself longer and more stubbornly than elsewhere. The targets of this hostility, however, the much-maligned beguines and papelardes unsatisfied with traditional Church-piety, seized with the will to form their existence in evangelical terms, felt themselves all the more strongly attracted to those who understood their religious needs, had the same consciousness, and provided a philosophical and religious sense for what they were going through. They were increasingly drawn to the heretics. This continued so long as the mendicant orders could not carry out their great mission to them. This explains the receptiveness of religious women, beguines and papelardes, for the efforts of the students of Amaury. Later it would be the mendicants who would fill the gaps when the older organs of the Church failed, drawing the religious movement to itself, preventing it from leaving the path of ecclesiastical orthodoxy. But they were never able to win everyone in the northern branches of the religious poverty movement, among the pious women in Belgium, France, and Germany, among beguines and papelardes. When it seemed for a while that the two chief elements of the religious movement would be beset by reactionary spirits, both the mendicant orders and the beguines, papelardes, and others not organized into orders fought side by side for their place in the Church. In the end, however, the fringes of the movement were more drawn to heresy than the mendicant orders had believed possible, and the orders felt compelled to draw a sharper line between themselves and those elements which were undependable, unsteady, organizationally incomprehensible, and dogmatically hard-to-control.

Until the middle of the century these relationships were very unclear. Two theologians could still work alongside one another at the University of Paris, one of them, Robert de Sorbon—much like James of Vitry—saw beguines and papelardes as highly pious, despised and mocked by the worldly precisely for their genuine, zealous piety,[62] while his colleague William of St. Amour, fanatic warrior against all forms of the religious poverty movement, poured passionate taunts and mocking suspicions over beguines,[63] papelardes, and "truttani,"[64] for displaying feigned poverty[65] and imposing their Pharisee values on everyone with the temerity to walk about as finely clothed as Christ in his seamless coat. They wanted to live a life of ease behind the ruse of living on alms—although they belonged to no order and thus were not monks—wandering about begging, proclaiming themselves sick and miserable in order to receive richer gifts.[66] French poets of the passing scene and satirists, headed by Ruteboeuf and the author of the *Romance of the Rose*, inherited and intensified this tone of hatred, suspicion, and contempt against the pious striving of the papelardes and beguines, beghards and truands. In Gautier's wake the contemporaries of William of St. Amour, untouched by the thoughts and experiences of the religious movement, which to them was an irritation or a joke, composed ever new verses of insult and contempt for *begardie, papelardie*, and *truandie.*[67] These names became slogans with which the representatives of the old ecclesiastical standpoint expressed their utter disdain for the innovative religious present and future,[68] at the very moment the same names became the essence of their own way of life.[69]

Despite all of this, the much-maligned beguines, papelardes, and *trutannæ* were never accused of any specific heresy,[70] although isolated cases of heretical disturbance made themselves known at the beginning and the middle of the century.[71] It was only after the 1270s, when the Franciscan memorial to the Lyon Council first referred to heretical peril among the beguines,[72] that the contemporary Dominican memorial on the same subject complained that an excessive number of *religiosi pauperes* was inundating the entire world, who were no longer called monks but *trutanni*, so that the honor and respect of the order demanded overcoming these wandering, pious beggars.[73] This was pressing because a crass case of heresy had come to light for the first time in the groups of the religious movement in South Germany,[74] while everywhere there was the suspicion that the unsteadily wandering, non-organized, and unincorporated elements of the religious poverty movement had become a peril for right faith. Still, without being able to prove a case of heresy or the spread of specific heretical doctrines, synodical legislation in the last decades of the thirteenth century took measures everywhere against this unsteady religiosity which was so hard to name properly, since it formed no order and no organized community, appeared in the most various forms and yet possessed a certain internal coherence, disturbing the protectors of ecclesiastical order all the more.

First there was a synod in Trier, probably in 1277,[75] which passed measures against *begardi* and *conversi*, whom the clergy was never to permit to preach under any circumstances, neither in churches nor on the streets and in the villages, since they were spreading errors and heresies among the people;[76] on the other hand, they acted against *trutanni* and other vagabond scholars or goliards, who were to be forbidden by the clergy to sing songs during the mass or the services over the *sanctus* or *agnus dei*, since this disturbed the priest as he chanted the canon, and it irritated the congregation.[77] In both cases it was a matter of itinerants mixing in the business of the parish clergy; first of all, it was those called *begardi* by the synodal statute, who arrogated preaching to themselves, and the others were those called *trutanni*, who disturbed the divine service with their songs.

As we have seen, the unsteady elements of the religious movement were often accused in equal terms of being *begardi* and *trutanni*, and shortly before this, Humbert of Romans asserted that itinerant *pauperes religiosi* were slandered by many as *trutanni*. In the synodical statutes of Trier, the *trutanni* were mentioned in the same breath with the "other *vagi scolares* and *goliardi*," and one can wonder if it dealt with persons with no ties at all to the religious movement, but rather the flippant, worldly, impious gang of scholars, vagabonds, and goliards we have to thank for the "Songs of the *vagantes*."[78] But much indicates that wandering clerics and scholars in the thirteenth century were not utterly lacking in the religious thoughts and efforts which fermented in other groups of the unorganized poverty movement. In the view of contemporaries, the *vagi clerici* were often put down as beghards, *trutanni*, and the like. It is probably no accident that the same Mainz synod which banned the wandering of religious women also moved against the pointless mass wandering of begging vagabonds,[79] and later synods took similar measures against both itinerant beguines and wandering scholars,[80] who were always being accused of disturbing religious services and offending the laity, as well as of receiving runaway monks into their ranks. The synodal statutes do not give a clear picture of what their punishable attitude was or how they disturbed religious services. But just as the synod in Trier accused them of singing religious songs without license during the mass, so also a Mainz synod complained that they held religious services in villages which did not have their own pastor.[81] It is all the less likely that we are dealing with profane mockery and frivolous parody of ecclesiastical practices and duties, since the popular name for these vagabonds, Eberhardines, whose origin is obscure,[82] is also found in connection with other phenomena of the religious movement.[83] Berthold of Regensburg even said once that the word "scholar" had become a term for heretics, just as the term "the poor" or "Waldensian."[84]

It is by no means easy to gather all these witnesses to create a unified, reliable picture of the connections. Yet it is precisely their variety, hard to grasp, which reflects the genuine situation of these unsteadily fluctuating elements of the religious movement, which formed no order, held no common name, and could not be swept aside by a single measure, traveling the land, begging, disturbing order in the church during services, in the community, even in the orders, which could never prove a specific heresy and whose orthodoxy was still suspected.

A provincial synod of Eichstätt in the 1280s warned equally of unlicensed lay preaching, which arrogated preaching in secret gatherings, leading the people into error.[85] These secret preachers were never named in the synodal statutes, nor were they blamed with a specific heretical teaching.[86] Belonging neither to a heretical sect known at the time, nor to a recognized order, such preachers in the diocese of Eichstätt stimulated the same complaints as the beghards and *conversi* had shortly before in Trier. Autonomous preachers, pious beggars, people with religious missions and in religious habits to which they had no right, all were seen everywhere with distress and suspicion. They wandered through the country, called sometimes beghards, sometimes *trutanni*, sometimes scholars, and sometimes by other names, and there was no way to deal with them than to forbid contact with them or support for them. In this unsteady, irregular religiosity we must seek the bearers and communicators of heretical currents which were to lead to the great crisis of beguinism at the start of the fourteenth century.

3. Heretical Currents in Women's Religious Associations in South Germany

The first traces of heretical influences and disturbance reveal themselves in women's religious communities in South Germany in the middle of the thirteenth century. The sources for this are very faulty. Martin Crusius, a Tübingen historian of the sixteenth century, says in his *Swabian Annals* that in 1261 there appeared in some Swabian convents certain people—supposedly *Fraticelli*, beghards, and beguines—who agitated against the monastic regulation of the communities, arguing that God could be better served "in the freedom of the Spirit," without following a specific rule. As a result, a dramatic conflict arose between communities desiring to live in this unregulated freedom and others submitting to regulated monastic discipline, and it was only the intervention of bishops which finally suppressed the communities hostile to regulation.[87] Crusius goes on to tell the story of the house of Kirchheim, whose nuns petitioned the bishop of Constance several times in vain for a grant of the Rule of St. Augustine, who only fulfilled this request in 1247 thanks to the mediation of the Cardinal-Legate Petrus. In the same way the nuns of Gnadenzell—Crusius continues—"Who had previously preferred the liberty of *Fraticelli*," finally understood that they could not survive without the obligation of a set rule, winning confirmation of the Rule of St. Augustine from the bishop of Constance in 1252.[88] Crusius only mentions these two houses in this context as examples of women's houses which gave up their "freedom" after some resistance and accepted a rule. He cites as his source for this report the Ulm Dominican Felix Fabri (died 1502), confessor of the Dominican convent in Offenhausen-Gnadenzell who wrote a German-language chronicle of that house in 1499.[89] The chronicle itself does not survive, and Martin Crusius himself left us only Latin excerpts of it in his annals,[90] in which he provides no more details of the episodes in question than are to be found in the other writings of Fabri which have survived. So long as Fabri's monastic chronicle remains lost, we are left with what Crusius tells us, but that relies on sources which had the charters and the house tradition of Gnadenzell at their disposal. The reports can be verified in some details, partly by checking surviving charters and traditions of the convents of Kirchheim and Gnadenzell, partly by taking into account their links with the religious movement in general.

Crusius gives some information on the origins of the house of Kirchheim below Teck in another place, but the reliability of that account is hard to determine.[91] "Perhaps," a women's house arose as early as 986. More certain is his assertion that eighty-six sisters were living in Kirchheim in 1214, but they followed no particular rule. A rich, pious man from Augsburg named Chelidonius is supposed to have become so interested in these *pauperculæ Christi sponsæ* in Kirchheim, living in grinding poverty, that he solicited the rich and powerful to support them, so that they were able to build a convent. Duke Conrad of Teck took the house into his protection in November 1235, issuing it a privilege; he as well as those Augsburg burghers found burial in the house.[92] Whether this tradition is believable in all its details[93] is hard to say; there is no documentary support. Yet it jibes so surprisingly in its essentials with the contemporary development of other women's houses in South Germany, which also began as poor communities without a secure house, without possessions, without rule, and without membership in an order, and were only placed in the position to advance to the building of a proper house through the efforts of a wealthy supporter and the entry of wealthy members, that much speaks for the dependability of this tradition.

This community of pious women in Kirchheim is first documented on 23 June 1241. At that time a property in Sirnau (north of Esslingen) was bequeathed,[94] and a portion of the sisters resettled at once from Kirchheim to Sirnau. As early as 22 July 1244, Bishop Henry of Constance took the "Prioress and convent of sisters residing in Kirchheim, now desiring to build a house in Sirnau," into his protection, permitting them to build a convent and to follow the Rule of St. Augustine and the constitutions of St. Mark's of Strasbourg, electing their prioress freely and installing their own priest.[95] In Sirnau a true convent was established in the same manner as other women's houses attached to the Dominicans, and it was placed in the Dominican Order four years later through the mediation of Innocent IV.[96] The community in Kirchheim, from which the nuns in Sirnau derived, continued to operate without adopting the Augustinian Rule, and without being subordinated to the Dominican Order as were so many other women's houses in 1245/46. There are no documents from this period for the sisters in Kirchheim. It is more probable that Cardinal Legate Petrus obtained permission from the bishop of Constance for Kirchheim to accept the Augustinian Rule[97] than that they soon won acceptance into the Dominican Order through Innocent IV when they were already following the Augustinian Rule.[98] Why the bishop of Constance repeatedly declined the request of the sisters in Kirchheim to accept the Augustinian Rule, as Crusius reports, is not to be determined from the documents. If it is true that the community for a time resisted regulation before it decided to accept this rule, then that could only have taken place before 1247. It is conceivable that a portion of the sisters left Kirchheim in 1241 and settled in Sirnau, establishing a regulated house there, since there was a difference of opinion within the community over adopting or rejecting a rule. It is conceivable that the sisters remaining behind in Kirchheim lived for a time "in the freedom of the spirit," and that the bishop of Constance was not immediately willing to concede what had at first been denied, and that the cardinal had to settle this impasse. This would harmonize Crusius' report with the documents, though without achieving total clarity on the course of events.

The beginnings of the house of Gnadenzell, in which there was also a period in which the idea of unregulated freedom ruled, are even more completely swathed in darkness. The community is only documented in 1258, when a bequest of Count Henry of Lupfen granted them a property of his five sons in Offenhausen (near Münsingen, a good twenty-five kilometers south of Kirchheim) on the condition that the sisters should permanently settle there.[99] The donation charter does not specify what rule the sisters then pursued; it cannot even be established where the community had previously resided.[100] The tradition of the house is entirely mute on this matter, since it only reported on its "founders," who made it possible to build the house, but nothing about the earlier history of the women's community itself.[101] There is nothing to affirm, but also nothing to confute Crusius' assertion, based on Fabri, that the notion of the "spirit of freedom," hostile to every rule, prevailed in the Gnadenzell community before it was committed to the Rule of St. Augustine by Bishop Eberhard of Constance in 1252.[102]

The probability of this development is increased when it is seen in combination with the religious movement in general. We have seen that itinerant religious agitators, appearing in Swabian convents, actually brought disruption into the ecclesiastical order, raising concern for the preservation of orthodoxy,[103] and that, a bit later, the memorial of the bishop of Olmütz actually accused religious enthusiasts of this sort of the very attitude which was supposed to be maintained in the South German women's communities, which was that God could be served better in "freedom" without obeying a rule or being bound to the discipline of an order.[104] In the same period such confusion ruled in Swabian communities, David of Augsburg—while recognizing the profound piety of the religious movement so often spurned, mocked, or seen as heresy—warned against "Deceivers and deceived, who follow and are seduced by their own or another's spirit, as if it were the spirit of God";[105] and similarly a fellow member of his order, Lamprecht of Regensburg, spoke in his allegorical poem "Daughter of Zion" in astonishment and marvel at the new religious "art" among the women of Brabant and Bavaria which raised their inner senses to the vision of divine wisdom through raptures and graces.[106] Yet even he warns at the same time against the excesses and lack of restraint of this female piety, its obsession with ecstasy and visions, its exaggeration of small "graces" to howling ecstasy.[107] In fact here lay a source of peril for the women's religious movement, which is that it should believe its own spirit and the spirit of others to be the spirit of God, and for religious experiences to spiral into the limitless—the women's religious movement was subject to this temptation wherever it was not kept in secure paths by strict discipline and rule. This generated that "spirit of freedom" which is first seen in the troubles of South German women's communities, first breaking into open heresy in the Swabian Ries, and by the end of the century infecting and endangering the entire religious movement.

4. Heresy in the Swabian Ries, 1270–1273

In an evaluation which has survived,[108] Albertus Magnus collected almost a hundred statements from heretics from the Swabian Ries in the diocese of Augsburg, judging them for their heretical character without giving further information about the date of this heresy, its discovery, or disposition. The Dominican Johannes Nider informs us in his *Formicarius*, written about 1435, that he had read this evaluation himself in an autograph "manual" composed by Albert.[109] Unfortunately, this "manual" could not be found.

The same evaluation is included, without the author's name but with the title *Compilatio de novo spiritu*, in a polemical collection against Jews and heretics, once believed to be the work of the Dominican Rainer Sacchoni (died 1259), and more recently called the "Passau anonymous."[110] This compilation also contains a list of twenty-nine heretical propositions which agree in all essential points with those of Albertus Magnus, designated in the manuscripts as the doctrines of the sect *de novo spiritu* or similar, but once expressly as *heresis noviter inventa apud Nordlingen*, which must describe the same heresy in the Swabian Ries.[111] The collection of the Passau Anonymous was compiled or at least begun about the year 1260. Since it contains the *Compilatio de novo spiritu*, that is, the evaluation of Albertus Magnus, as well as the twenty-nine articles on the heresy *de novo spiritu*, the heresy in the Swabian Ries would have had to be uncovered and evaluated by Albertus Magnus prior to 1260. But this assumption is false; the ties between this heresy and the religious movement of the thirteenth century can only be clarified when this erroneous dating is corrected. For that reason there has to be some detailed consideration of the so-called Passau Anonymous.

The author of this *collatio*—as the work calls itself—gathered materials against Jews and heretics because he had come to believe on the basis of experience that such a collection of materials could serve better than any talented disputation (see the preface in K. Müller, *Waldenser*, 147). The first three parts of the work consist of polemic against the Jews; then a work on the Antichrist is inserted; only then comes the section about heretics. In the polemic against the Jews it was twice stressed that Christian doctrine had been in existence for 1260 years, so that it can be inferred that this part at least was created about 1260 (see Wilhelm Preger, *Abhandlungen* 18.19ff. against Müller, *Waldenser*, 154–55). It is also certain that the author of the chapter which has this time-measure wrote not only the part against the Jews, but also helped write the part against heretics (Preger, 21ff.).

But the work was frequently reworked and amended. Three manuscripts of the complete work are known in the Bavarian State Library in Munich (many other manuscripts contain only the heresiological portion, see K. Müller, *Waldenser*, 152). The oldest of these (Munich, Clm 2714 of the end of the thirteenth or the start of the fourteenth century) essentially differs from the others, with many items shorter, everything in an eccentric order, and lacks many pieces altogether. Preger (*Abhandlungen* 18.24) saw this as the "first edition of this work," while in the other manuscripts, "much was expanded, much supplemented, much reorganized." The two passages which set the date at 1260 are to be found in this earlier version, preserved unchanged in the later versions. On the other hand, the following items are missing in this first edition: 1) a list of centers of heresy in the diocese of Passau, deriving from the reports of the inquisition in Krems in 1266 (or 1315/16? see Müller, *Waldenser*, 154), and for which reason Preger described the entire compilation the Passau Anonymous, though he did concede that additions had been made after 1266, or that the collection had been worked on for a long time (*Abhandlungen* 18.27ff.; see also Haupt, *Waldensertum und Inquisition*, 15); 2) a series of excerpts from the *Evangelium æternum*, that is, from the writings of Abbot Joachim of Fiore and the "Introduction" of Gerardo di Borgo S. Donnino, condemned in 1255 (see Denifle, *ALKG* 1.70ff.); 3) the evaluation of Albertus Magnus on heresy in the Swabian Ries, entitled *Compilatio de novo spiritu*, and 4) the twenty-nine articles on the heresy *de novo spiritu*.

The fact that these are additions which were not foreseen in the original state of the compilation of 1260, hence not yet known to the author, can be seen from the disposition of the entire work. In the first chapter of the heresiological part, dealing with the Waldensians, the author declares that in his own time all other sects had been obliterated, with the exception of the Manichees and Patarines in Lombardy, and the Ortliebern, Runcarians, and Leonists (= Waldensians) in Germany; in keeping with that, the heresiological portion speaks first of the Waldensians, then of the *secunda secta Runcariorum*, then deals with the Ortlieber as the *tertia secta*, the Cathars as the *quarta secta*, and the Manichees as the fifth. No place was foreseen for treating the *Evangelium æternum* and the heresy *de novo spiritu*, for neither has anything to do with the five "sects"; the author must not have had an inkling about these heresies in 1260. In the later versions of the compilation, these sections were all inserted before the chapter on the Runcarians; the earlier numbering of the sects was preserved, however, causing the amendments to disturb the proper order.

In a transcription of the heresiological portion of the "first version" (Vienna, Cod. 3271, fifteenth century, fol. 68^{v}) the twenty-nine articles of heresy from Nördlingen was added at the end (while Albertus' evaluation and the treatment of the *Evangelium æternum* are still lacking here); they are easy to see as additions (as is the case in the German translation, Vienna ms. 2846).

In many transcriptions of the "later version" of this portion, these twenty-nine articles are entirely lacking, but the evaluation of Albert is added at the conclusion (Vienna, Cod. 812, 517, 1664).

It is only in the reworking of the collection of the "Passau Anonymous" which cannot be proved to have taken place before the fourteenth century, that the documents for heresy in the Swabian Ries are to be found: Albertus Magnus' evaluation and the twenty-nine heretical sentences of the heresy *de novo spiritu* in Nördlingen. The reception of these pieces into the heresiological collection thus do not tell anything about when the heresy occurred. All that is certain is that it was uncovered before the death of Albertus Magnus, who composed an evaluation of it.[112]

The annals of the Colmar Dominicans, which we have to thank for many important details on the religious movement in South Germany, report that two *viri religiosi in rufis cappis* named Arnold and Tietmar came to Swabia in 1270, spreading erroneous teachings against the Catholic faith; in 1273, the annalist says, a dispute between Dominicans and Franciscans was settled which had been caused by heresy in the Swabian Ries near Augsburg.[113]

We can discover nothing further from the other chronicles of the time about these two men or the errors they spread in Swabia, nor about the conflict they occasioned between the two mendicant orders. The two articles in the Colmar Annals probably stand in close relationship to one another. The errors spread by the two *viri religiosi* in Swabia obviously led to the heresy in the Swabian Ries, which in turn gave the occasion for a dispute between Dominicans and Franciscans. And in all likelihood, it is all the same heresy which Albertus Magnus judged in his evaluation, and whose doctrine was then described once more in the twenty-nine articles of the heresy "of the new spirit" uncovered near Nördlingen.

Albertus Magnus, who served as lector in Cologne from 1270/1, never visited South Germany in this period—so far as we know[114]—so he could probably not have participated personally in an investigation for heresy in the Swabian Ries in 1270–73. But the *Determinatio* is obviously not a protocol of heretical utterances or a statement of his own inquisitorial activity, but an evaluation in which Albertus Magnus gives a purely academic judgment, so to speak, on the heretical character of a series of assertions presented to him. Perhaps one could see differences arising between Dominicans and Franciscans over the heresy in the Swabian Ries as the reason Albertus, the most important theologian of his order in Germany, was called in as evaluator. His friend and student, Ulrich Engelberti, who had been German provincial minister of the Dominicans, had often consulted him on Order matters.[115]

Since one can search in vain for their names in other historical sources, we are left with the brief remarks of the Colmar chronicler—fortunately a thoroughly reliable reporter—to classify the two men who spread error in Swabia, formed conventicles, and taught in secret, as the first sentence of Albertus' evaluation says.[116] The Colmar writer calls them *viri religiosi*, holding them to be some sort of monks. He adds, however, that they appeared in red garments, *in rufis cappis*. This means they belonged to no approved order, since none of them had a red habit. Red monastic garments did play a strange role in the perceptions of the time, despised as irregular by some, portrayed by others as the habit of an order of the future, banned by the regular orders, yet borne by many unstable elements of the religious movement.[117] This apparel permits us to suppose that the two religious at work in Swabia belonged to those groups of wandering pious whose autonomous efforts as preachers and whose appearance as irregular monks offended the rules of the Church, disturbing the times. It is from these very years that the memorials to the Lyon Council expressed the fear that such elements could endanger the order and orthodoxy of the Church. The unclear relations of these wanderers, elsewhere often *viri religiosi* associated with the mendicants as beghards or *trutanni*, might explain the fact that disputes arose between the Dominicans and Franciscans over heresy in the Swabian Ries. The sources are too imprecise and incomplete, to be sure, but they can easily be fitted into the general pattern of the times.

The Colmar chronicler says nothing about the groups which received these preachers when they came to Swabia, or where they found their adherents. The character of the landscape where the heresy emerged, and the sort of people who supported it, can only be used with great care to explain this religious phenomenon. The Swabian Ries today lies isolated from modern traffic, a region closed in on itself like an island, whose residents, protected from the "stream of time," have preserved the customs and clothing of earlier times; their mood appears influenced by the dour landscape. Whoever knows the Ries and its people today might easily be tempted to see this "world of its own" as especially propitious soil for mystical reveries of religious eccentrics.[118] Yet in the Middle Ages, the Swabian Ries wore an entirely different face. It was the meeting place for the most important routes: the old Brenner road, running from Italy via Augsburg, Donauwörth, and Nördlingen on to Dinkelsbühl, Rothenburg, Würzburg, and on to the lower Rhine and Northern Germany—the road which brought the first Franciscans to Germany in 1221—crossed in the Ries with an equally important old Roman road which came from France through the Palatine and Swabia, passing beyond the Ries over the Danube near Ingolstadt, advancing through Bavaria on to the East—this was the road which led to the realm of the Huns in the Burgundian Saga, and along which Walther and Hildegunde fled before the Huns all the way to the Rhine.[118a] Both roads went right through the Ries, which then was anything but shut off from the world or hard to reach, but rather stood open to the transit of people and ideas from the whole world. We know from the Colmar Annals that heresy did not originate in the Ries, but that it was brought in from outside by wandering preachers, and the views of the heretics stated in Albertus' evaluation permits us to see the source of this heresy and the groups within which they were active. There are more palpable points of seizure for historical understanding in the special relationships which arose out of the intermingling of the religious movements of the time than there is in the character of this region and its people.

The foundation of Albertus' evaluation must have been transcriptions of statements by several persons. Since several sentences are repeated time and again with little variation, the same question must have been presented to many persons in series.[119] Some of those heard were women, since many statements could only have been made by a woman;[120] on the other hand, none of the statements is so formulated that it would have had to be made by a man.[121]

It is the statements which can only derive from interviews with women which betray most clearly the spiritual and religious context of heresy in the Ries. These statements do not express a particular heretical doctrine of a dogmatic-ideological type, but rather a measureless escalation of religious experiences, whose spiritual assumptions are found time and again in the women's religious movement of the time. The crass statement of the women of the Ries that Christ knew them physically (II, 28) is only to be understood as an experience of the *connubium spirituale*. The idea of the soul of the pious person as a bride, the sense of desire for God, often intensified into an erotically experienced union of the soul with God, permeated and dominated female piety in general in the thirteenth century. But the degree of spiritual intensity passed through all the possibilities from a purely allegorical phrase to an illusory physical experience. The declarations of the Ries heretics are not unique among expressions of female erotic mysticism. Even with Mechthild of Magdeburg, the Latin editors of her memoirs found it necessary to weaken her erotic, immediate experiences into mere spiritual encounters. For she speaks of God, who grasps her soul "with full force on the bed of desire, who demands to go into the lusting soul on the bridal bed . . . on which he wants to kiss her and grasp her in his naked arms."[122] And when the soul, mounted by her lover in the "bed of love" sings: "I am a full-fledged bride, I desire to go to my fulfillment,"[123] Mechthild's mouth expresses not only allegory and metaphor but erotic-religious experience. How little she was unique in this time is shown by the concerned warnings of David of Augsburg, who thought it necessary to urge against the mystical arousal of women in Southern Germany, leading them to need the experience of kissing and embracing.[124] Even under the discipline of the convent this identity as bride was not infrequently experienced in a flamboyant manner, both then and later. Adelheid of Breisach, one of the first sisters at Adelhausen, lay in a swoon for half a day under an over-turned barrel, united with God in religious ecstasy, "so that she got a kiss," and one sister of the house later described that as a special act of grace.[125] With Adelheid Langmann in Engelthal, the Lord played her courtly lover, desiring her "not to absent herself from the conjugal bed a while," and he "grasped her to His divine heart, so that she melted into him like wax into a seal."[126] Such episodes could easily be multiplied.[127] But our purpose here is not to heap up examples or exhaust their psychological content, but only to indicate the realm of experience from which the statements of the Ries heretics about erotic communion with Christ derived and can be made understandable: it is the unbridled excess of an experience of the mysticism of desire, not restricted to the spiritual, which was there unfolding in the women's religious movement of the thirteenth century.

The same applies to another statement by one of the female heretics in the Ries, which was that she had suckled Jesus. Albertus Magnus responded that this was not heresy which could be refuted but silliness which deserved a good whipping.[128] But this sort of declaration was not so unheard-of or as alienating as it might seem at first glance.[129] For alongside the thoughts and conceptions of the *connubium spirituale* lives the experience of following Mary as the feminine counterpart of following Christ, and just as the one group showed the peril of erotic experience, so the other found its depth and its peril in the experience of motherhood. To empathize with Mary, who carried the divine child, bore, suckled, and caressed it, became the wish and for many the experience of innumerable religious women. In their dreams and visions they were the mothers of the child, particularly in the Christmas season, and there were no lack of cases where such obsessions led to physical realization in the symptoms of pregnancy.[130] This reference to other cases certainly does not weaken the judgment of Albertus Magnus over these *fatuitates*; but they show the historical connections which bind heresy in the Ries with the women's religious movement of the thirteenth century and its mystical agitation.

These statements, consisting of mad exaggerations of the ideas of *connubium spirituale* and imitation of Mary, did not stand in the forefront of heresy in the Ries. They were tied rather loosely to the views and doctrines which produced the great mass of testimony. But other doctrines of the Ries heretics of essential importance for the breadth of their convictions can be brought into the same historical context. This is particularly true with the idea of personal deification. A person can become God, the heretics say, and the soul can become divine in its union with God. This person, deified and united with God, stands in the center of all the statements of the Ries heretics.[131] The experience and idea of deification is common to all mystics and is also capable of being combined with Catholic orthodoxy. The dogmatic criterion for this is the question whether this deification is seen as an act of grace, a supernatural action of the deity, who draws the person to himself and into himself, or if a natural possibility is accepted that the person can be deified by his or her own efforts or by way of a metaphysical similarity of nature with God. According to Catholic teaching, it is an error of "heretical mysticism" that a person can become God *naturaliter*, while it is an apex of orthodox mysticism *per gratiam deificari*. The experience of deification is not rare among the religious women in

South German Dominican houses, and the nuns' books of the fourteenth century have described these experiences without ever being challenged for their orthodoxy;[132] for this unification with God is always seen and experienced as an act of "grace," just as the naive desire for "grace" and "consolation" filled the religious moods of South German women's houses.[133] On the other hand, Albertus Magnus declared the statements of the heretics in Ries on the deification of the person and the soul to be "Pelagian" heresy, hence conflicting with the Catholic doctrine of grace. Without doubt the heretics themselves were asked whether they believed themselves capable of being "deified" through divine grace or through their own human effort. The answers were neither uniform nor simple. One statement even said that a person could become God in keeping with his own will; another, in contrast, avoided the question of the role of grace in deification with the paradoxical utterance, "a good person is truly able to say whether he has grace or does not have grace,"[134] hence not recognizing the dogmatic distinction between "nature" and "grace" as essential, obviously not understanding this alternative as being applicable to the experience of deification. In fact the heretics' statements are unclear and complex as regards grace.[135] These religious groups had not yet made a principled resolution in this basic question of Catholic dogma. Even in this matter, the common ground between heresy in the Ries and women's mysticism of the thirteenth century is confirmed.

Mechthild of Magdeburg also spoke of her experience of *deificatio*. She has God speak to the soul: "Lady soul, you are so much a part of me that there can be nothing between you and me,"[136] and she says of the soul, from whom the fire of love has stripped the dross of sin, she becomes "a God with God, so that whatever he wills she wills, and she would not wish to be otherwise united in a total union";[137] the person who withdraws from all things in prayer with a humble heart, with a "soul more miserable" than all creatures, and is open to God alone, is "a divine God with the heavenly father."[138] Yet because of these or similar statements, even the beguine Mechthild was accused of violating the Catholic doctrine of grace. We are fortunate enough to have from her the words with which she defended herself from her own mouth, not only through the formulation of inquisitors. "I said in one place in this book that the divinity of my father is natural; now you fail to hear that and say: 'Everything God has done with us is all from grace, not from nature.' You are right and so am I."[138a] She tries to use a simile to clarify what the eye of a loving soul enlightened by divinity can see: how the eternal divinity has done things in the soul through its nature, forming and planting and "it unites with the soul more readily than with any other creatures; God has taken the soul to himself, pouring so much of his divine nature into it that the soul cannot say anything other than that in union with her he is more than her father.''[139] That might be dogmatically irrefutable, but dogmatically simple it is not, and if it were taken down by a heresy tribunal Mechthild's answer would have sounded much like the heretics in the Ries: *homo bonus dicere potest gratia se habere et non habere—du hast war und ich han och war.*

The deep difference between the Magdeburg beguine and the heretics in the Ries lay—disregarding Mechthild's poetic and religious powers of expression and her spiritual passion—not in these foundational experiences, which were common to the entire women's religious movement, but in the intellectual expression of their experiences in regard to the doctrine of the Church. Mechthild had consciously fitted herself into the ecclesiastical order, entrusting herself to the spiritual guidance of her Dominican friends, and she later entered a convent. The heretics of the Ries, in contrast, distrusted and rejected the spiritual guidance of theologically trained leaders, since such men had no understanding of the religious experiences which filled their lives.[140] They disdained the cloistered life, since their piety of experience, which bound them to no specific rules, meant infinitely more to them,[141] and all the laws of the Church had lost all sense so far as they were concerned.

This turning of female mysticism to heresy is doubtless to be explained through the influences which operated on women's religious groups in South Germany from an entirely different direction. This touches for the first time on the role in the Ries heresy of the preaching *viri religiosi*, which can be isolated in several of the doctrinal statements the heretics made. When, alongside statements on ''deification'' of the ''good person,'' the soul uniting with God, we find other sentences of a purely pantheistic character, on the identity of God with all His creatures and the substantial identity of the soul with God,[142] then entirely different ideas appear which have nothing to do with the mystical union with God and are even basically incompatible with it. Albertus Magnus in his evaluation described all doctrines of unity with God as ''Pelagian''; but he was unable to characterize the pantheistic sentences as any specific heresy. The assertion of the identity of substance between God and the soul appeared Manichee to him, and he described the notion that the soul was as eternal as God and with God to be the ''heresy of Socrates''; in the pantheistic doctrine, that all which was created is God, he saw the heresy of late-Greek philosopher and commentator of Aristotle, Alexander of Aphrodisias, whose doctrine had been revived recently in France by David of Dinant.[143] This David of Dinant had been condemned along with the students of Amaury in Paris in 1210; it cannot be completely clarified whether any relationship existed between him and Amaury of Bène and his students.[144] Albertus' statement does not show that there was any actual link between heresy in the Ries and David and his doctrines; for Albertus is not establishing the membership of heretics in a specific sect, but rather he is assigning each specific statement to a heresy which has already been condemned. One could hardly call the Ries heretics Manichees just because Albertus called many of their propositions Manichee. Many of their propositions are not to be explained from the thoughts of ecstatic women's mysticism, but are related on the one side to the views of the Paris heretics of 1210, on the other with the doctrines of the Cathars. The Ries heretics spoke just as the Cathars when they said that Christ did not suffer at the Passion, and was not injured;[145] also they held views which were similar to those of the Cathars over the fall of the angels, though not without contradiction,[146] and they did not have anything to do with the ideas of women's mysticism or the experience of unity with God. The Ries heretics shared some other views with the Cathars as well as the Amaurians, even in part with the Waldensians: they did not believe in hell and purgatory,[147] held angels and demons only to be moral personifications of human virtues and vices,[148] and did not believe in resurrection, even the resurrection of Christ.[149] The statements of the heretics before the inquisitors permit no understanding of the relationship these views had to one another. If such doctrines could not have grown out of the practical mysticism of religious women, with whom these doctrines had never been associated, this still does not mean that the Ries heretics were members of a specific sect with a solid, marked doctrine. They were in no sense Cathars, although they shared many views with the Cathars, even though Albertus Magnus in his evaluation described thirteen of the ninety-seven propositions as Manichee. For in the place of the basic principle of Cathar Manichæism, which was the dualism of good and evil, God and material, and the ascetic ethic of perfection arising from that, the Ries heretics represented pantheistic views and moral indifferentism. They were, however, not members of any "pantheistic sect," either, which had survived the discovery of the Amaurians in Paris and had found a refuge in Swabia.[150] The heretics in the Ries had made statements of a similar pantheistic stamp to those of the students of Amaury, but these few comments were isolated and incompatible with the expressions of the experience of the divine by the individual soul; there are also spiritualist convictions on the working of the Spirit in people, causing them to be accused of the heresy "of the new spirit";[151] but the statements of the heretics in the Ries say nothing about an incarnation of the Holy Spirit or the emergence of the third age of the Holy Spirit. There is not a word in the statements of the heretics about theoretical speculations on history, which Amaury's students probably took from the writings of Joachim of Fiore. Finally, it is true that the heretics in the Ries confess the idea that all events and all acts of people were God's work and they speak like the Paris heretics with the words of Paul: God does everything in all. Yet for them this thought is not treated speculatively for events in the world in general, but experientially as meant for the person united with God, not only of a possible grade of perfection a person could achieve.[152]

Two levels can be established in the statements of the Ries heretics, one agreeing with the heretical speculation of earlier heresies, particularly the Paris heretics of 1210, the other deriving from the deifying experiences of women's mysticism, all confirming our view that the heresy in the Ries grew out of the influence of wandering *viri religiosi* on a group of religious women. There can thus be no talk of a "sect" in the proper sense. There is not a trace of a sect-like organization, and the individual expressions do not reveal a unified doctrine. Inquisitorial protocols only listed the heretical "variant doctrines" in the individual catechisms. But from them it can be sufficiently established that in the foreground of the religious views of these groups was the experience of the unification of a "good person" with God, becoming God; the intellectual implications from this experience concerning the doctrines and forms of the Church, however, are determined by tendencies of an entirely different origin.

In the presence of the divinity of the perfect person, the importance of Christ vanishes not only as an intermediary but also as the only begotten son of God, as the sole person bearing God's nature. "The person becomes equal to God, transcending the Son"[153] or at least his equal. Hence the eucharist loses its singular importance, for the blood of Christ does not deserve higher esteem than the blood of the "good person."[154] The notion that a perfect person united with God receives "God in God" when that person takes the sacrament of the altar, and that the person is personally raised with the body of the Lord on the altar, and hence that the host deserves no veneration from such a person,[155] those are only paradoxical formulations of this attitude to the eucharist: the eucharist is not actually declined or rejected, neither criticized in its ecclesiastical form nor spiritualized. It is only its uniqueness which is disputed, and its worth for the "good person," since that person has already "become God" and hence is at least the equal of God's son, if not superior.

With this, meditation on the passion of Christ, which had played such an important role in the religious poverty movement and particularly in the women's movement, also lost its rationale, and there are actually statements to that effect.[156] Alongside them, apparently incompatible, is a sentence which could have come from the devotees of the *imitatio Christi*, intensifying this idea as much as the doctrine of becoming God intensified the *unio mystica*: the soul of a person becomes like the soul of Christ when that person does the same things as Christ.[157] In this intensification of the notion of following Christ—as Mechthild of Magdeburg said, "Each person should be a Christ in himself"[158]—lies the transition to the heretical devaluation of the person of Christ as the sole son of God, and here as well the contacts of the heretical doctrine of the Ries to the experiential world of women's mysticism.

The special services provided by the saints only really collapse in the face of the claims of the deified person,[159] and it is particularly the idea of imitating Mary which is transformed in consciousness, the veneration of the mother of Christ suspended and one's own perfection elevated above her merit if a person "unites with God" and "becomes God."[160] And yet the service of saints was never criticized or rejected, either by appealing to the gospel, as was the case with the Waldensians, or mocked as idolatry as was the case with the students of Amaury; rather it was always said that the "good person" could be united with God in such perfection that that person exceeded the merit and claims of the saints, becoming absolved of their service. What was obligatory for others, the ordinary Christians, is not touched upon by the heretics' utterances.

Confessions, fasts, and prayers and all priestly mediation are things overcome by the "good person," who has been united with God, things no longer needed,[161] which would even hinder that person on the way to God.[162] If these declarations are extraordinarily foreign to a group from the women's religious movement, which had placed prayer, confession, and fasting in the forefront of piety from the very beginning, so also the moral views of the heretics of the Ries appeared hard to square with the ideal of chastity which had always been the guiding star of the women's movement. Yet it is precisely on this point that outside influences are the hardest to mistake. In Albertus' evaluation, several statements appear in which all principals of Christian morality whatsoever seem suspended, and liberation from the concept of sin was proclaimed for sexual activities, at least so far as they did not violate marriage or vows. These statements have no intrinsic relation to the convictions and experiences of most of the other propositions. On the other hand, they are to be found again virtually verbatim in very different contexts, some in certain Cathar groups, others among representatives of Averroïsm at the University of Paris.[163] If it is known, however, that such views were spread among religious women in South Germany by wandering preachers and agitators, then all the other statements by the heretics in the Ries on moral questions become more understandable, since they agree with that amoral doctrine in which the tensions between the experience of deification and consciousness of sin is suspended and obliterated. There is never so much talk about the general invalidity of Christian moral teaching in them, but always about what sin means to the perfect, those united with God, the good people. Only in isolated cases would a limitless moral liberty be recognized for one of these perfect persons.[164] Most of the statements deal with the deeper, less superficial question of whether religious perfection is achievable in this life, a perfection beyond all possibility of sin. It is impossible to speak of a specific doctrine in the statements which survive. In many it is simply the consciousness of sins committed and remorse which is rejected as a limitation on the way to religious perfection;[165] in others it says that a person who had become God who committed a deadly sin could lift himself out of that sin back to God;[166] others say that one united with God cannot sin, the perfect person is sinless.[167] These sentences are hard to bring into harmony, but all of them show in the same way the division between the Christian-ecclesiastical consciousness of sin and the religious experience of perfection. The moral concepts and norms are dissolved, emptied of their sense; the religious experience supersedes all questions of ethics and morals, robbing them of their own effect. That is expressed on the one hand in the crude paradoxes of the sort "that a person could sin without sin,"[168] and on the other hand in the signification of a religious position and consciousness in which the connection between heresy in the Ries and speculative mysticism is most clearly shown.

William of St. Amour already referred to religious groups in Paris which rejected all work with hands in order to dedicate themselves exclusively and ceaselessly to prayer.[169] This devaluation of all active work in favor of a religiously contemplative life is also found among the heretics of the Ries,[170] but in their case it intensifies into an indifference to all works of virtue, which become insignificant for the religious life,[171] and it expresses itself in a passivity on the part of any person united with God toward everything happening to him; an immunity to good and evil; a surrender of all personal desire and will to the will of God and to events which are due to His will.[172] It is easy here to think of Meister Eckhart's doctrine of passivity, often expressed in similar propositions,[173] so that the last degree of this dissolution into God in the statements of the Ries heretics points directly to the doctrines of speculative mysticism and only becomes truly understandable in its terms. The deification of a person can advance so far that it "no longer needs God"; the highest degree of religious perfection is only achieved by a person when that person "abandons God for God's sake," passing over God to the "pinnacle of divinity"; only in this final unification with "divinity" do all the norms and restrictions on one's own effort fall away.[174] All of these statements are barely understandable in the disconnected form of interrogation of heretics. In the mystical writings and sermons at the start of the fourteenth century, particularly in the case of Meister Eckhart,[175] entirely similar doctrines are found at the apex of mystical speculation. One should not be tempted to supplement the statements of the heretics in the Ries with the help of later mystical doctrines, constructing a coherent intellectual system or even the "teaching system" of a sect, making it understandable in that manner. This is because the theological system and speculative doctrines of German mystics were not the foundation, the starting-point, or the source,[176] but rather they are intellectual justifications and efforts at the theoretically ordering and theologically digesting of the religious experiences which first arose from the mystical activities of the women's religious movement. For precisely that reason, however, the statements of the Ries heretics are so important for the historical understanding of German Mysticism, since they already display the primary themes of mystical speculation without being enclosed in a scholastic didactic structure, and without being coordinated with ecclesiastically orthodox theology.

This view of heresy in the Ries is remarkably confirmed by the condemnation of Margarete Porete from the Hennegau. She wrote a book[177] which was condemned and burned by the bishop of Cambrai around the turn of the century, before 1305. Despite this, she continued to circulate it among beghards and other unschooled people, also sending it to the bishop of Châlons, and for that reason she was cited before the Dominican inquisitor in Paris. A committee of theologians once more declared her book to be heretical in a written evaluation; a committee of canonists established that she could be considered a relapsed heretic, and on 31 May 1310 she was burned in the Place de Grève.[178] Unfortunately, we only know two sentences from the book of this beguine, but they are conclusive enough. They speak of the "annihilated soul" [*anima annihilata*], which is no longer subject to the law of virtues, since all the virtues are at her service; she does not concern herself with divine gifts and consolations, since this would only disturb the complete, exclusive justification of the soul in God.[179] These propositions of the beguine, probably taken verbatim from her book, come very close to the statements of the heretics in the Ries and derive unmistakably from the same idea, which is that complete absorption in God dissolves, suspends, even "annihilates" all human ties as well as all ethical norms besides all desire for any special grace, even divine grace. On the other hand the two propositions, which—to rely on the theological evaluation—were the basis for condemning the beguine Margarete, could just as well have come from Meister Eckhart, although it is virtually impossible for Margarete Porete to have been a "pupil" of Eckhart. A contemporary chronicler reproduces the condemned doctrine in different wording, perhaps to make them clearer to his readers,[180] and only then does he demonstrate the close alliance of this mystical speculation with love-mysticism on the one hand, and with the antinomianism of the mystical experience of God on the other. When chroniclers or inquisitorial protocols attempt to describe the propositions of heretics, this mystical doctrine is always distorted and confused, as if it sought to break down all barriers against compulsion and vice. When we have even a few words from the mouth of a "heretic" such as Margarete Porete, it is mystical earnestness and religious purity which speak from them.

Contemporaries in the decades around the year 1300 became gradually more aware of the spread of these mystical doctrines. Albertus Magnus was said to have remarked on the evaluation of the heretics in the Ries in his manual that similar views had emerged in his own time in Cologne as well;[181] but there is nothing further on this. At the provincial chapter of the Franciscans meeting in Colmar in 1290, two beguines and two beghards were arrested by the lector of the Minorites at Basel on suspicion of heresy, and some were also arrested in Basel.[182] It is likely that they held convictions similar to the heretics in the Ries, the beguine Margarete Porete, and the wandering beghards and beguines, who had drawn increasing suspicions of the Church concerning their orthodoxy since the turn of the century. Whole mobs of begging beghards appeared at every provincial chapter of the mendicant orders in those days,[183] even without their having any specific relationship to the order;[184] but until the first years of the fourteenth century, neither the Church nor the orders took thorough measures against them. Only then, over thirty years after the heresy in the Swabian Ries and after the Council of Lyon, the Church acted against the begging, wandering beghards and beguines, whose actions offended the rules of the Church and whose religious doctrines endangered orthodoxy. A Cologne synod led with a ban in 1307, and a Mainz synod followed their example. The archbishop of Cologne dramatically justified the ban with three arguments.[185] First of all, he argued that they followed no approved rule and belonged to no order, but that despite that they carried on a special way of life while wearing a distinctive habit. No longer living from the work of their hands as they once had, they wander about the country under the pretext of the ideal of poverty, collecting alms which are only supposed to go to those truly in need.[186] Secondly, it had happened that they publicly contradicted Dominicans and Franciscans during preaching, making themselves suspect of heresy as a result.[187] Thirdly, he accused them of holding a series of specific heretical propositions, mostly dealing with the claim of the beghards that their way of life led to sinless justification and perfection, releasing them from obedience to the rules and demands of the Church.[188] It appears that the Cologne synod did not have specific heretical propositions before it from some heresy trial, but they simply wanted to refer to the errors propagated by the wandering beghards and beguines in order to give a general ban greater impact.

The Mainz synod of 1310 says nothing about heresies of this sort, but in the same spirit, on pain of excommunication, they forbid the beghards and beguines to pass through the streets of towns and villages in their special habits begging, or to preach in public or secret gatherings.[189]

When the ecumenical council, meeting in Vienne in 1311/12 under Clement V, once more took up the reform of the Church, it was probably on the motion of German bishops that beguines in general, the *status beguinagii*, were banned, with the justification that it was no order and the beguines no *religiosæ*, not members of the monastic order, since they had neither rendered an oath of obedience nor renounced private property nor followed an approved rule. Further, Catholic orthodoxy was confused and threatened by the tendency spread among them to dispute and preach concerning religious and theological things, such as the Trinity, the nature of God, faith and the sacraments. In contrast to forty years earlier in Lyon, the Vienne Council appeared to understand the fact that the hundred-year development of beguinages was not going to vanish in response to a general ban; the ban was mollified by the statement that pious women were not to be forbidden to lead a penitential life by living honorably in communal houses.[190] On the other hand, a special decree of Clement V, made with the approval of the council, listed the errors of beghards and beguines in Germany and damned them; the "sect of beghards and beguines" which believed and spread these errors, was to be combated by bishops and inquisitors.[191]

This legislation by Clement V and the Council of Vienne of 1311/12 against beguines and beghards did not mean the end of the history of beguines. They were so internally contradictory and so lacking in clear directions for the reordering of the beguine life that only disputes reaching across decades could bring clarification and a distinction between orthodox beguines, mostly placed under the leadership and control of the mendicants, and those heretical beguines condemned at the Council of Vienne. The decrees of Vienne did constitute a decisive turning-point in the history of the religious movement in Germany. Just as the policies of Innocent III had forced the movement of poverty and itinerant preachers to decide whether to integrate into the Church or endure persecution as heretics, so also the measures of the Council of Vienne finally compelled groups of beghards and beguines to take a final position whether they wished to abandon their free, unregulated movement and take on a stable, ordered way of life, submitting to the rules of the Church. This question was not simply one concerning organizational form, but would decide whether religious thought and mystical speculation were to be restrained by the theological norms of ecclesiastical orthodoxy. Just as it had not been the function of mendicants to launch the religious movement in Europe, particularly in Germany, but rather to guide it in ecclesiastical directions and contain it in ordered forms, so mendicant theologians did not stimulate the birth of mystical life, but they had to guide it along the path of ecclesiastical orthodoxy. And just as mendicants became the harshest enemies of the heretical poverty movement in the thirteenth century, after the Council of Vienne the representatives of "orthodox mysticism" took up the most aggressive battle against the heretical mysticism of the "free spirit." These processes always become more understandable when the whole picture of the religious movement is seen, out of whose efforts both heresy and new orders, both the errors of the beghards and the "brethren of the free spirit," as well as the profundities of "German Mysticism."

CHAPTER 8

The Origins of a Religious Literature in the Vernacular

Together with the religious movement of the thirteenth century, there arose a religious literature in the vernacular, a literature which reached its apex in what is called "German Mysticism" at the start of the fourteenth century. Sermons and prayers, religious meditations and theological discussions, narratives of religious experience and visions in the vernacular rose to prominence in the course of the century, replacing a secular poetry whose age had passed. Language was given new tasks to perform, opening new possibilities which permanently marked its vocabulary and forms of expression, immensely enriching them.

It has never been doubted that this development of writing and language went together with changes in religious and ecclesiastical life. Yet if these connections are to be described and made comprehensible, it is not enough to be satisfied with bland general assertions such as, "a newly awakened religious feeling sought expression in the mother tongue." "The religious world sought to embrace broader levels of the population, and they were not to be addressed in a language alien to them"; or even, "A retreat from crabbed learned scholasticism and a turn to immediate piety went hand in hand with turning away from the ecclesiastical language of Latin and a confession to the immediacy of the vernacular." Little is accomplished by concocting motivations which might make a likely story but remain imprecise and unprovable in historical terms. Instead, it is ours to ask what were the particular circumstances which generated a religious literature in the vernacular, and what influenced the character of this writing.

Laymen had always been preached to in the vernacular in the Christian Church.[1] To be sure, in an age of liturgical piety preaching was not a particularly important part of the service. Its content was almost completely exhausted by repeating and reworking the patristic tradition, and its effect was limited to the spoken word of the preacher. Either sermons were not written down at all, or by clergymen only for the use of other clerics in making their own sermons. These sermons were neither distributed nor read. They did not become a "literature." Also, whoever was to preach in the vernacular made use of materials written in Latin. The clergyman even wrote the script for his vernacular sermon in Latin. The texts of sermons in the vernacular which we know from the twelfth century were as little intended to be read by the faithful as were the numerous collections of Latin sermons; rather, they were an emergency aid to ease the preparation of sermons for undereducated and overworked parochial and people's priests.[2]

Just as there had always been preaching in the vernacular, so there had always been prayer in the mother tongue. But here as well, these prayers fulfilled only the pious needs of the moment and did not transform themselves into literature, as was the case with Latin prayers. If a few transcriptions of German prayers are preserved alongside the mass of Latin prayer books, this is due to special circumstances and fortunate accident. The sole German prayer-book of the early Middle Ages of any importance was, notably, prepared for a woman, and quite possibly compiled by a woman as well.[3] In the general religious context, however, there was no demand for vernacular spiritual literature, for reading and pious use of sermons, prayers or religious considerations.

Religious poetry occupies a special position; there is no doubt that it intends to impart religious "literature" to those who do not know Latin, but it does so through presentation and not "reading." It was created by clerics who put religious material into verses to be presented to people who could not read. This shows immediately why there was no parallel vernacular literature of edification to equal Latin prose. The difference in education between the two estates of clergy and lay is most dramatically shown in efforts at communicating between them. Whoever is a cleric or a monk can read, and that means reading in Latin; everything written to be read, which is to say all prose, is thus Latin. Laymen do not read, they listen, and what they want to hear has to be spoken in their language. Insofar as it is prose—a sermon—it passes away with the sound of the voice; poetry, which belongs to the higher style of life, is preserved, since it will be presented again and again; even poetry is a literature of presentation, not reading. As a result there is no religious prose literature in vernacular corresponding to the massive written and read literature of religion and theology in Latin, no popular theology, no edification literature, no collections of sermons for reading by individuals, and no translations of Holy Scripture. A vernacular literature of this sort could only arise, and arise it must, when a new stratum formed between laity and clergy, one which, like the clergy, wanted to read and even write religious works, sermons, prayers, and not least the Holy Scripture, but like the "laity" could neither read nor write in Latin. The breaching of the strict division between the Latin-trained clergy and the laity in the religious movement of the twelfth and thirteenth century was the precondition and foundation for the rise of a religious literature in the vernacular.[4]

1. Itinerant Preaching and Religious Literature

It is often assumed that the preconditions for a vernacular religious literature were first created within the religious movement of the twelfth century, which with its claim to following the apostles broke through the ecclesiastical and hierarchical order, leading to the rise of a vernacular religious literature. Yet historical sources speak against this assumption. Heretical itinerant preachers, who claimed the office of apostolic preaching for themselves without being ordained to do so, at first related to their congregations, their "believers," in a manner which did not differ from that between Catholic clergy and laity. They sought to recruit for their faith through sermons in the vernacular, and to proclaim the true apostolic doctrine to their followers. They did not yet have a reading public to which they could offer vernacular texts. In fact, it has never been established that Cathars or Albigensians of the twelfth centuries ever created a religious literature in the vernacular which would have served as reading material and edification for the faithful.

It is another question whether the heretic preachers themselves prepared at least vernacular translations of the Holy Scriptures so as to be able to preach on the basis of their own biblical knowledge. If these preachers, all or most of them, were unlearned, non-Latinate people, then a biblical translation would have been a crucial basis for their preaching. Yet there is not a trace of such a biblical translation in the hands of heretical preachers until the end of the twelfth century. It is hard to imagine they existed and were used and yet eluded all Catholic observers or were never mentioned by them. It is possible to conclude from the lack of evidence that the Cathars and Albigensians of the twelfth century had no translation of the Bible. A great portion of the Cathar itinerant preachers, the "perfect," doubtless had enough Latin to obtain their own knowledge of Scripture without a translation. The others perhaps learned the most important texts by heart in "heretic schools," of which we later hear so much in relation to the Waldensians.[5] As much as is said of the use of Scriptures, particularly of the Gospel of John in services and in the rites (*consolamentum*) of the Cathars,[6] there is never a word about translations.

From the beginning of the thirteenth century, writings of the Cathars and Albigensians are often mentioned. But these writings were probably not works of edification for the "believers," but apologetic and polemical writings which arose in the conflict with Catholic adversaries,[7] and hence in Latin. It is never said that such works were written in the vernacular.[8] None have survived. There can thus be no talk about an "extensive popular literature" of the Cathars[9] at least until the thirteenth century, there is not even a trace of a "germ of a demand for private reading of religious writings in the mass of the *credentes*."[10] It is believed that a "Cathar Bible" has been found, a manuscript of the New Testament in Provençal from Languedoc (now in Lyon), which also contains a fragment of a Cathar ritual (ceremonies and prayers).[11] But this Provençal New Testament is from the mid-thirteenth century at the earliest, the Cathar origin of the translation is not certain, and one can only say that its use by Cathars is probable. In any case, the translation could not have arisen and been used in purely Cathar groups without Waldensian influence.[12]

Waldes, the merchant of Lyon, remains thus the first certainly known to have had translations made from Scriptures due to his own lack of knowledge of Latin and his desire to read the Bible on his own. According to a believable tradition, a performance of the legend of St. Alexius by a *joculator* precipitated his conversion.[13] A work of poetry which had endlessly presented religious material to the laity for their reflection, the work suddenly struck the entirely different religious attitude of a person who no longer passively listened but actually took the sense of the poetry seriously, transforming its purpose. Waldes was inflamed into a religious act. Waldes then questioned theologians about the most perfect way for a Christian to live, and in response to their advice he alienated his property, but he still wanted to know what was in the Bible. Since he did not understand Latin, he had two clerics translate the most important books of the Bible and several theological writings, at his expense.[14] In any case, Waldes knew of no earlier translations or he could have fulfilled his wish without such trouble. These translations became the foundation of his apostolic preaching. From them, he and the companions who joined him learned the word of the Bible and spread it.[15] When in 1179 they requested permission for their apostolic labors from council and pope, they also presented this biblical translation in order to show the basis of their preaching.[16] What the curia thought about these translations is not known. It was also moot, since the Waldensians were forbidden to preach in any case, so that there was no question of recognizing their vernacular Bible as the basis of their preaching.

When the Waldensians became active in other lands, they naturally had to make translations of the Bible into other vernaculars.[17] While Catholic observers were never able to find vernacular Bibles or other writings, we have numerous witnesses through the entire thirteenth century for the Waldensians' vernacular writings. In Metz, as Bishop Bertram reported to Innocent III in 1199, Waldensians used the gospels, the letters of Paul, the psalter, the *Moralia Hiob* (of Gregory the Great), and several other books in French.[18] They were burned on the order of the bishop of Metz.[19] Three years later a papal legate in Liège ordered all "books on the Holy Scripture" written in German or French to be delivered to the bishop and only returned after his review.[20] In 1229 a synod in Toulouse banned all use whatsoever of biblical texts by the laity, even in Latin (with the exception of the canonical Latin prayer book).[21] At a council in Rheims, 1230/1, which condemned a Waldensian and had him burned, any future translation of the Holy Scriptures into French was forbidden.[22] Heretics (including Waldensians) discovered at the same time (1231) in Trier were found with German translations of the Holy Scriptures.[23] Bans by synods in Tarragona (1233)[24] and Béziers (1246) against reading the Bible in the vernacular were probably also tailored to the Waldensians. Catholic polemics against heretics declared time and again that the Waldensians had the gospels and apostolic epistles in the vernacular, and that they based their sermons on them.[25] But this entire literature, consisting of translations from the Bible and a few theological manuals for its interpretation, was only created for the preachers, not as reading material for believers, for even the Waldensians were at first only a group of listeners, not a community of readers. What Waldensian literature there was in the thirteenth century[26] probably served the same purpose. The Waldensians only exhorted their faithful to read the Bible and pious writings on their own in later times,[27] long after works of edification in the vernacular were being read in other groups.[28]

Hence Waldes cannot be regarded as the vanguard of a vernacular literature for a pious laity. The conversion experience certainly awakened in him a need to read the Bible in his own language so he could proclaim biblical teaching. He, and the companions who taught with him, read or learned the Bible in their own language, but they did not put it in the hands of the "people," the "laity." They did not promote individual reading of the Bible by the faithful. The most they did was to encourage memorizing the text of the Bible so it could be proclaimed to others. Thus Waldensians did cause biblical writings to be translated and distributed in the vernacular, but only in the service of preaching. Their community was further divided into "clergy" and "laity," into preaching "perfect" and listening "believers." Since no group developed standing between those who taught and those who listened, conditions for the development of a religious literature of edification in the vernacular was lacking with them as well.

This was precisely the situation with the mendicant orders at the outset. With them as well, there was no visible reason why the itinerant preachers should have developed a vernacular literature of edification. They wanted to convert souls through the living word and the example of their evangelical life and work. They also lacked a public which could read, and we shall see that they not only did not promote a vernacular religious literature, they even at first sought to hinder it.

The German preacher Berthold of Regensburg seems to disprove this assertion. Like all itinerant preachers, Berthold always spoke in the people's language, but he never wrote his sermons down in German or distributed them to read. Neither did his listeners write down his sermons in German in order to be able to read them again. There certainly were clerics—as had been the case with earlier famous preachers—who listened to Berthold's sermons and made notes in Latin for their own homiletic use. As a result, whole collections of such Latin notes of Berthold's German sermons were created and put in circulation to serve other preachers as the basis for their own German sermons. Berthold knew of this, and since he found the wording and meaning of his sermons distorted, and, fearing that such editions could mislead other preachers, he decided to publish Latin collections of his sermons himself—not for the edification of readers but as aids for other preachers.[29] Berthold's German sermons which are found in manuscripts of the fourteenth and fifteenth century were composed neither by him nor by his audiences. The sermons noted by him or his listeners in Latin were retranslated into German after his death (1272) and published—as pious reading matter for a public which had learned to read.

There is only a small group of six sermons which probably did not make this detour through Latin but were taken down in German by Berthold's listeners and used for edification rather than for other preachers. Yet these sermons, whose manuscripts date from the end of the thirteenth century—much earlier than the other sermons—were not sermons to "the people," rather they were "monastic sermons" for a convent.[30] It was only where Berthold did not appear as a wandering people's preacher but preached to a convent that his German sermons passed directly into German pious literature. This conclusion will be confirmed as a general proposition: it was only when the mendicants came into contact with the women's religious movement that their sermons developed into a pious literature in the vernacular. This had taken place already long before Berthold's appearance; even before the women's religious movement joined the mendicant orders, the beginnings of a religious literature in the vernacular had germinated within it.

2. THE WOMEN'S RELIGIOUS MOVEMENT AND VERNACULAR LITERATURE

At approximately the time Waldes was having the Bible translated in Lyon, the priest Lambert (died 1177) was translating the Acts of the

Apostles and the Legend of St. Agnes in Liège, not for himself or as the basis for an apostolic mission, but for the edification of others. Lambert had been seeking to combat the worldly doings of urban culture through sermons and example. Particularly, he had organized communities of pious laity who sought to return a Christian character to the Sunday celebration, instead of desecrating it with minstrels, entertainers, and comedians, through drinking, games, indecent songs, dancing, and shameless carousing.[31] He prepared his translations and pious essays in the vernacular: for women there was a version of the Legend of St. Agnes, and for all of them together there was an edition of the Acts of the Apostles, both of them interspersed with his own moral observations and in verse.[32] It is certain that these translations were not intended for the edification of individuals but for oral presentation in the pious communities. Yet, unlike Waldes' translation, they were not aids for preachers but rather were meant for the edification of the laity, who would gather after the service on Sunday to meditate together, as well as to sing psalms, hymns, and spiritual songs as a group.[33] Not only the translations of Lambert were used, but also translations of the psalms with explanations and exegetical selections by a Flemish master.[34] For the first time, in these Sunday gatherings in Liège, we find the essential conditions for the creation of a religious literature of edification: a lay community desiring to read and use religious writings itself, but with inadequate Latin to use the existing literature. As a result, spiritual advisors presented vernacular translations. In any case the first elements were present. There were no stable, organized communities, but only loose occasional gatherings. No vernacular prose literature arose, but only pious poetry for presentation. There is as yet no mention of autonomous literary creation, but these elements unfold wherever the same conditions present themselves.

Lambert's critics among the Liège clergy accused him of delivering the Holy Scriptures, the sacred writings, to the unworthy with his translations.[35] He responded with the word of Christ: "The Kingdom of God will be given to the people, which will bring forth fruit" (Matthew 21:43). The fruits of this revival of Christian piety among the laity and in groups of women would in fact ripen in the following decades, but we cannot follow the development of these first germs all the way to full bloom. Any immediate connection between the pious groups formed through Lambert's efforts in Liège and the rise of the women's religious movement around the turn of the century is questionable and obscure. In the same way a link is also missing between Lambert's first efforts on behalf of a vernacular literature for the laity and the religious works from the middle of the next century such as the treatises of Beatrix of

Nazareth and the visions of Sister Hadewich. One is forced to suppose that "perhaps an entire mystical literature arose in the first half of the thirteenth century and has been lost" from the women's religious groups in Belgium.[36] Two factors speak in favor of this supposition. It is hardly conceivable that works such as the tracts of Beatrix and the visions of Hadewich could have arisen if the development of their language and the direction of their thought had not been prepared by a literature of edification and translation. Further, at the outset of the thirteenth century all the conditions were ready in the relationship of women's religious groups in Flanders and Brabant to their spiritual advisors which should have led to the creation of a religious literature in the vernacular. Many of these religious women did, in fact, know Latin,[37] but this would only have encouraged a translated literature. Such male spiritual advisors of the Belgian women as James of Vitry, Guido and John of Nivelle, John of Lier or Thomas of Cantimpré produced no vernacular pious literature for these women. Instead they only prepared Latin biographies of pious women in order to provide models for others. Yet these writings appear to have provided bases for many vernacular transcriptions, which can be demonstrated in at least one case from a fortunate discovery made a short time ago. The Benedictine William of Afflighem, who wrote a biography of Prioress Beatrix of Nazareth, made use of her German-language narrative, begun about 1220 and closed about 1235, describing her own visions, experiences, and thoughts.[38] A portion of this narrative has been recovered from a later collection of sermons,[39] consisting of meditations of the degrees of love [*Minne*], similar in its content to Victorine mysticism, linguistically a foretaste of the visions of Hadewich, who probably knew Beatrix. Similar vernacular narratives and religious essays probably provided the basis for the Latin biographies of other women from the first decades of the thirteenth century.[40] Since none of them has been preserved or even left any evidence of having existed, we are left with mere suppositions. After the middle of the thirteenth century vernacular biographies of pious women in Belgium are provable, partly written by the women themselves, partly retranslated out of Latin.[41] In the meantime, the development of a vernacular literature of edification among religious women had received a powerful push from another quarter.

Now we must take another look at the events in Paris in 1210. The synod which condemned Amaury's students also issued a ban against "theological books" in French. Whoever did not deliver them to the bishops within the grace period would be seen as a heretic. The ban expressly included translations of the creed and the Lord's prayer; only legends of saints were excepted.[42] The confiscated books were to be burned. Nothing further is said of what sort of works these "theological books" were, but their seizure stood in connection with the trial against the heretical clerics who had carried out their mission primarily among religious women, misleading the people, especially women, "through false interpretation of the Holy Scriptures."[43] It is easy to assume these were religious works written or translated by condemned clerics for groups of laity or women among whom they were spreading their religious doctrines. This is because the relationship is strikingly similar to those in other cases: wherever men with theological training participated in the women's religious movement, the ground was readied for a vernacular religious literature. Just as was the case with Liège in the days of Lambert the Priest, so also there were prayers and legends of saints in this devotional literature from the Paris sectarians, besides books of theological content of which we unfortunately know nothing more.

All of these beginnings toward a vernacular religious literature proved as tentative and weak in potential for development as the conditions which produced them. In part banned or incinerated, in part undeveloped or dried up, this literature never acquired greater importance or influence. A lasting basis for a religious prose literature could only develop where the relationships corresponding to it grew into a solid system. This would have to be a setting where religious communities of laity or women organized themselves into lasting, regulated forms of life without clerical Latin training, but with the need for contemplation and theological training and a capacity for absorbing and imparting the treasures of Latinate theological and religious education. These conditions had never been so completely fulfilled as they were in the women's religious communities attaching themselves to the Dominican Order. The Dominicans placed the greatest stress on theological training for all members, and they were the ones called to the spiritual leadership of such communities, particularly in Germany, the center of the women's religious movement. The result was that the development of a religious literature of edification in the vernacular was strongest and most important in German convents of the Dominican Order.[44]

In this matter, too, the initiative certainly did not come from the order itself, which instead resisted taking up the task presented to it by the women's religious movement in Germany. Yet out of the close contacts between German Dominicans and religious women a vernacular literature arose from the very beginning. Henry, the very first Dominican prior in Cologne, not only won the greatest applause as a preacher among Cologne women, he also wrote letters of edification to pious women,[45] apparently related in content to the Latin letters of his friend, Minister General Jordan, to Diana and the women of the S. Agnes house in Bologna. The Cologne prior, however, wrote in German. So it was precisely the first Dominican at work in Germany, Henry, who launched the sequence of devotional and mystical correspondence which achieved such great importance in religious literature. This recognition is all the more important, since letters of this sort are only preserved from much later times.[46] Incidental reference to letters of Prior Henry by Jordan tells us that the very first contact of Dominicans with the women's religious movement in Germany produced vernacular writing. The Dominican chronicler of Colmar mentions at the end of the thirteenth century, in his account of the literary accomplishments of the Order of Preachers, one Friar Henry, prior of Basel, who composed German verses for pious women.[47] Who Prior Henry of Basel was, when he lived, and what he composed cannot be said with certainty,[48] but this witness indicates how the relation between German Dominicans and the women's religious movement developed a vernacular pious literature.

These scattered traces of German writing by Dominicans on behalf of pious women or nuns is supplemented and granted increased importance by the decree of a general chapter of the Dominicans in 1242, which forbade all friars to translate sermons, collations, or other writings with religious content from Latin into the vernacular. This ban stood in the closest relation with the exhortation to friars not to give the last rites to nuns or other pious women, neither to involve themselves in their organization and leadership, nor to accept visitation duties at their houses.[49] Not only did the order refrain from fostering the development of a vernacular devotional literature, it sought to limit or ban it. The preaching friars were henceforth not to undertake to satisfy the desire for devotional reading material through translations. It was particularly significant that it was specifically translations into the vernacular of sermons and collations which were banned. All Dominican preaching was done in the vernacular—why was a "translation" into the vernacular necessary at all? This was because such sermons were written down only in Latin, to serve as the basis for future sermons or for theological study. Retranslating such texts back into the vernacular and providing them as reading material for non-theologians, particularly for religious women, was the target of the ban of the general chapter of 1242. Entirely in the same way as the German sermons of Berthold of Regensburg would be rendered into reading material, a vernacular religious literature was being created by Dominicans in the first half of the thirteenth century by retranslating Latin sermon-drafts back into German.

On the other hand a general chapter meeting at Trier in 1249 forbade Dominicans to have nuns or other women engross psalters and other books for them.[50] According to the general chapter, the religious women in contact with the Dominicans must have included many who knew the art of the scribe, and the knowledge of Latin which was bound with it. We know that sisters in many South German women's communities learned Latin with zeal. Often a sister was active as a Latin teacher, and for many sisters, the engrossing of books became the primary activity in the house.[51]

It was only once the resistance of the Dominican Order to the reception of the German women's communities into the order had been broken that relations really solidified, and their literary reflection, which had begun developing earlier but had been restricted by the order, became a part of the organizational responsibility of the order to its women's houses. Women in the houses read at meals and in private for edification just as did monks,[52] but they needed German reading materials, since their Latin training did not suffice.[53] Further, it was necessary to preach to nuns in German as if they were part of the laity, yet they could read and write like the clergy. Preaching to religious women operated under very special conditions. Strict enclosure made it impossible for sisters to attend any public sermons, so they relied totally on the sermons of their pastors. These pastors directed their sermons exclusively to sisters within the convents and could adjust the sermons to the sisters' spiritual nature and capacity to understand. The Dominican Order, the preaching order *par excellence* as well as the order with the highest and most "modern" education, threw itself into its task with the greatest zeal, once it took over the duty of pastoral care in the German convents. A command from the 1280s by the German provincial minister Herman of Minden demanded that friars entrusted with pastoral care in convents should have learned colleagues preach frequently to sisters, corresponding to the sisters' degree of education.[54] Since Denifle's revolutionary study, this command has rightly been seen as the most important indicator of the historical and organizational foundations of mystical Dominican preaching in Germany. Yet at that time it created no new relationships, it only exhorted to the fulfillment of duties, the carrying out of assigned tasks which had come to the order because of the historical situation, and which it had been unable to avoid despite all efforts to the contrary.

The development of German religious literature and German mysticism arose from these relationships after the end of the thirteenth century, and it is only to be explained historically from these relationships. The theological learning of Dominican preachers on the one hand, the forms of life, the degree of education, and the experiential world of the nuns on the other hand, together determined the context of this development, its literary forms and its language. Research on

German mysticism, whether in terms of the history of religion, literature, or language, will have to pay more attention to this fact. I will give a few more hints in what follows.[55]

Das Fliessende Licht der Gottheit (The Flowing Light of the Divinity), an account of the visions of the Beguine Mechthild of Magdeburg, is the first great work of German religious prose literature, though it survives not in its original form but in a High-German edition from the fourteenth century. It is filled with new images and ideas, shaped through a new language and gathered into a new genre, mixing poetry and prose, novel to the vernacular but closely allied with the language, form, and content of Latin religious literature.[56] Did Mechthild create all of this by herself, from her own experience? She did not understand Latin, and she calls herself "unlearned." She probably never read any theological literature herself.[57] On the other hand, she did have Dominican pastors, who also assisted her in her literary creations. She had heard sermons by Dominicans[58] who made it their task to render theological knowledge into German; indeed we know (particularly from the decree of the order in 1242) that these Dominican sermons precipitated a literature in the vernacular even before Mechthild began writing down her visions. She did not start working an entirely unprepared field. Her language and the content of her religious experiences were formed by the preaching of the mendicant orders and the literature which had grown from it. If the roots of her mysticism and her language are sought, Dominican preaching must be seen as the medium for transmitting the mystic content of earlier Latin literature as well as the theological, scholastic language for the coinage of words and thoughts found in "The Flowing Light."[59]

But there is no lack of early witnesses to this transfer of mystical and theological ideas into German and their expression in writing. Wilhelm Preger remarked that even before Mechthild, certainly before Meister Eckhart, "individual characteristic theories of speculative mysticism had been firmly transferred into German, and individual terms became fixed for the times which followed"; thus a "root of the linguistic stock of later mysticism" was created.[60] Yet these guideposts were little regarded, and the pieces preserved of such religious verses (probably from the thirteenth century) represent the earliest formulation of the mystical manner of thinking, the first witnesses of a new vocabulary. Such verse can hardly be exploited to understand the religious and linguistic development of "German Mysticism."[61] Verse-making of this sort[62] already moves a step further than the translations composed by the priest Lambert for pious groups in Liège, since they attempt an independent creation of religious content and at the same time form the beginnings of a vernacular pious literature in prose. Also known to us is edifying German prose from the thirteenth century, numerous translations of Latin treatises first created for reading by pious groups. It is only here that the German sermons of Berthold of Regensburg have their place, as well as the German treatises of David of Augsburg and many others seldom considered. It was earlier pointed out that we have only six sermons which Berthold presented in a convent as a direct survival of the German text, probably as a hearer's notes.[63] All the other "German sermons" of Berthold rework Latin originals to provide pious reading, and many observations over the content of these texts vouch for a reading public consisting primarily, if not exclusively, of women.[64] Berthold's convent sermons, however, are preserved in manuscripts from the late thirteenth century in close proximity to other treatises of edification and mysticism, including the German writings of David of Augsburg, which were doubtless intended for women's houses. It has long been disputed whether the German treatises of this Franciscan[65] are "genuine," whether he is to be regarded as "the first mystic in the German language," who "used the German language, still scorned by Albertus Magnus, for theological investigations." The agreement of the contents of the German treatises circulating under his name with David's Latin treatises in no way proves that David himself wrote German. Rather, precisely as with Berthold's German sermons and the vernacular translations of Latin sermon transcriptions which the Dominican chapter opposed as early as 1242, they could have been translated and edited from David's Latin writings and published when the desire for a pious literature in German was making itself felt. This is all the more likely since we know nothing about David's activity as a pastor in convents. He naturally wrote in Latin for his brethren in the order, doing so even with what he had originally preached in German, and he would not have written in German any more than any other theologian of his times, due to the sheer demands of the character of the language. He was certainly a member of the first generation of mystical preachers in Germany, but he probably never wrote German himself. The German editions of his treatises survive in manuscripts of the late thirteenth century, which also contain the earliest mystical and allegorical meditations composed by religious women and nuns, in part under the direct influence of David's writings.[66] This extensively allegorical and edifying literature, whose study is only beginning, comprises a second stage, together with the verses mentioned, of the development of a vernacular religious literature. The third stage consists of the scripts of sermons, in which mystical theological doctrine becomes direct material for religious reading, without the poetic and allegorical garb, as well as without the aid of

Latin models,[67] either as notes of listeners or through the hand of the preacher himself. This literature and its transcription also began in the thirteenth century well before Eckhart, and it is to be exploited if one is to understand the fund of ideas and the vocabulary of "German Mysticism" historically. Cologne Dominican sermons survive from the thirteenth century for religious women, Dominicans or beguines,[68] including two German sermons of Albertus Magnus. What particularly deserves respect is the great sermon collection of an Upper Rhenish preacher of about 1250, probably a Dominican, from which a collection of pious sermons and texts collected about 1300 drew many bits, though only a fraction of the original is preserved.[69] These were monastic sermons of which at least a part, more likely all, were delivered in women's houses[70] and, as the preserved manuscripts demonstrate, were certainly read in convents.[71] It is believed that traces of the influence of this Upper German preacher can be traced in the language of Tauler and Suso.[72] Yet it would be premature to compare the few known texts from the dawn of this religious literature in German to arrive at immediate historical connections and "influences." If the stock of German manuscripts is reviewed as a whole, many new texts will emerge whose traditions reach back into the thirteenth century.[73] Even then, one must always remain aware that the surviving literature is only a fraction of what once existed,[74] and the language and ideas of this religious literature grew out of the concrete missions of preaching and pastoral care which the Dominican Order assumed in the middle of the thirteenth century in women's houses. For this reason, a historical understanding of mystic preaching and literature requires a sympathy for their historical bases and preconditions, besides an investigation of the language and content of the writings which have survived. Historical understanding points the proper way of investigation, and it alone can explain how and why a German religious literature of this scale and in this form arose from preaching, pious and theological tracts, reports of experiences, and letters in general.

The language and literature of "German Mysticism" did not arise as a protest against an alien language, nor as a whim which found no more pleasure in the dead language of theology or saw it as an unsuited means to express a living religious experience. Rather, the new literature arose as a reflection of the religious movement of the thirteenth century, conditioned and promoted by its relationships and the special forms of religious life which developed out of it. The use of German was actually described as a "necessary evil" for expressing and describing religious things by one of the greatest artists of language among the German mystics. Suso once said, if all written words are only a cold, pale reflection of the word received within through grace, as if one were trying to describe with words the sweet playing of a stringed instrument, it was "particularly [so] in the German language."[75] Every theologian in the Middle Ages would have agreed, since for them Latin was always the language of the Holy Scripture, and all German speech and writing only a necessary aid.

Anyone who knows how much the German language has to thank mystical preachers or is receptive to the strength, tenderness, and depth of their language will probably be unhappy to convert to the concept that it was used only reluctantly, as a means necessary for reaching where Latin speech and writing was of no avail. The strength of German preachers to create words and shape the language cannot be questioned, and it does not lose the least of its value when their special, historical mission is understood, a mission which demanded of them this reworking and reorientation of the language. It is certainly not a lesser accomplishment to fulfill a great historic task through conscious effort than to do so from pure force of heart and free, naïve excess.

After all of this, only the task which research into German mysticism still must undertake can be pointed out, and the conditions for its fulfillment clarified. The language of German Mysticism is the language in which sermons were preached to German nuns starting in the mid-thirteenth century, and in which their devotional literature was written. The spiritual content of German Mysticism is determined by the mission of communicating theological doctrine in a manner suited to their religious experiential context. The peril of German mysticism, however, as fatal to their great Master as it was for many lesser spirits, the peril for the women's religious movement in general, leading to their catastrophe at the outset of the fourteenth century, consisted in the fact that the monumental mass of their religious experiences and the theological speculation which arose from it could never conform entirely to the doctrines and rules of the Church.

APPENDIX

Heresy in the Eleventh Century

The heretics discovered in various parts of Central Europe in the first half of the eleventh century and persecuted by the Church[1] were described from the beginning as Manichees.[2] This identification probably rested on Catholic onlookers' acquaintance with St. Augustine; it was not the term the heretics used for themselves. In fact, the reported doctrines and practices of the new heretics certainly corresponded extensively with Manichee teaching, so there was undoubtedly a connection with the old Manichee sect. It is uncertain whether the Manichees somehow survived in Europe since the end of antiquity,[3] or whether missionaries of the Armenian Paulicians or Bulgarian Bogomils spread their doctrines, related to those of the Manichees, from the East after the turn of the millennium, following the paths of trade.[4] In the course of the eleventh century, their errors had been spread throughout the European lands by heretic itinerant preachers.[5] Yet they never created a "sect" with organizational cohesion, but rather they won individual, very heterogeneous groups for their convictions. We first learn of a peasant in Champagne about the year 1000 who was spreading heretical doctrine; in 1022 a group of highly educated, respected, and prominent clerics in the school-town of Orléans, including teachers of theology and friends of the French royal court, were burned because of this teaching.[6] Soon the archbishop of Milan uncovered confessors of this doctrine among the high nobility of Lombardy in the castle of Monteforte near Turin,[7] and among them the countess of Monteforte herself suffered death at the stake. In the 1040s the bishop of Châlons complained that *quidam rustici* of his diocese were spreading Manichee heresy.[8] The social position and the estate of the various groups of heretics is thus so various that we are certainly not to seek a social motivation as the basis for heresy. No mention of any specific social attitudes, other than general evangelical principles, ever come from heretical testimony, and even a polemic against the clergy is hardly to be found.[9] Neither can a trace of any organizational tie be found between the individual heretical groups in a sectarian community, or any other lasting ties among them.[10] Heretical groups do not appear to be divided like the Manichees and the later Cathars into *perfecti* and *credentes*,[11] and they were not yet active as apostolic itinerant preachers. The sole sign that it was not just a matter of spreading doctrines, but also the communication of certain heretical rites is the ceremony of laying on hands (later called the *consolamentum*). This rite was first reported among the heretics of Orléans in 1022, used precisely as among the old Manichees to transmit the Holy Spirit and bring healing enlightenment, knowledge, and consolation.[12]

All contemporaries saw the real mark of the heresy to be its strict ascetic demands—complete abstinence from meat[13] and sexual intercourse[14]—and the rejection of ecclesiastical sacraments and customs: baptism, eucharist, veneration of the cross.[15] On the other hand, the Western heretics of the eleventh century lacked any trace of dualistic theology or mythological doctrine of the world which the Manichees, and the sects derived from them in the orient, always demonstrated. Wherever speculative ideas emerge, they resemble neither the old Manichee pattern nor one another.[16] Only the relatively thorough reports on the heresies among the clergy in Orléans or the nobles in Monteforte indicate the spiritual content of the heresy at all. These reports do not reveal a dualistic view of the world, but primarily a spiritualistic faith in enlightenment through the Holy Spirit, communicated through asceticism and the laying on of hands by the purified, leading them to the pinnacle of truth and wisdom, imparting to the "inner eye" the secrets of the Christian faith and the Holy Scriptures.[17] The heretical doctrine thus claimed to bring the true interpretation of Christianity. It sought its basis and justification in the words of the Holy Scripture, or at least of the New Testament. It assumed a "spiritual understanding" of Scripture imparted by the Holy Spirit.[18]

If an effort is made to form an image of the character of the heresy in the first half of the twelfth century, one discovers neither a religious movement conjured up by social maladjustments or the decline of clergy and Church, nor does one find an organized sect. There is not yet even the idea of apostolic preaching and evangelical poverty which would dominate the heretical movement after the start of the next century. What was the attraction of this heresy which won supporters in so very different places? When a cleric named Herbert, who had come to Orléans for study, was won for the doctrine of the heretics there, he believed he had mounted "the fortress of wisdom." After returning home he raved with the thoughtless zeal of a religious novice for Orléans, the town which gleamed brighter than all others in the light of wisdom and splendor of holiness.[19] In truth, before their discovery, the heretics condemned in Orléans had been regarded by outsiders as men of special wisdom and piety.[20] With other heretics of this time as well, the promise of special wisdom and holiness played a central role. The peasant Leuthard won adherents through his reputation for piety and his pretense of higher knowledge.[21] When the bishop intervened against him, his followers were easy to win back. The heretics at Monteforte professed allegiance to rules of life for an intensified piety of evangelical strictness, but also to faith in a religious enlightenment through the Holy Spirit, which would teach a true understanding of the Holy Scripture. In their case as well, the goals of their heresy were holiness and wisdom. For the heretics of Arras, the determining factor in their heresy was a conviction that they were living truly in the sense of the gospels and the apostles, and when the bishop of Cambrai took this conviction from them through his own preaching, they returned to the Church.

But when adherents and missionaries of older sects, whether from Italy or from the Greek Orient, spread their heretical doctrines after the turn of the millennium, they were successful because they accommodated the awakened demand in the West for spiritual and religious enlightenment. All of the doctrines of the Manichee and eastern sects which did not visibly and immediately serve this demand found no response in European lands. At first it was only ascetic demands which took effect, citing gospels and essentially constituting no more than a transfer of the ethics of monasticism to non-monks: chastity and abstinence from meat, then the rejection of ecclesiastical sacraments as an excessively lax practice of salvation, and finally the promises and indications of a higher, more spiritual religious knowledge. The first demand could be directly equated with the desire for an ethical and ascetic renewal of the cloistered life in the monastic reform of the time. The second demand met the pressure for purification and renewal of the salvific practice the Church. The third was linked with the spiritual awakening of the West to new knowledge. The monastic reform which originated with Cluny, the hierarchical reform by Gregory VII and the rise of theological thought since Anselm of Canterbury would at first feed on those powers which had been falling to heresy in the first half of the century. For suddenly, at mid-century, all evidence of any further thriving of heresy ceases.[22] For several decades, there is not a word about the condemnation of heretics—save for simoniacs, turned into heretics by Gregory VII—nothing about episcopal measures or synodal decrees against heresy. The religious and theological renewal within the Church and monasticism drew all these forces to its service. When heresy reemerged at the end of the century, it had a new face: for only now had it become a religious movement whose themes had become apostolic itinerant preaching and evangelical poverty.

New Contributions to the History of Religious Movements in the Middle Ages

CHAPTER 1

The Foundation of Orders and Heretical Sects in the Twelfth Century

Many new religious orders arose in the century between Urban II and Innocent III, particularly in the two decades after 1100 and then again around 1200. In the same period, but increasingly so in the second half of the twelfth century, many new heretical sects also emerged. The rise of these new orders and sects cannot be adequately explained in terms of the personal initiative and intent of their individual "founders" alone, as extraordinary and effective as they might be. Despite all differences, their themes, ideas, and efforts were unmistakably interrelated in so many ways that they cannot have emerged entirely independently of one another, only happening to appear at the same time. Both the new orders recognized by the Church and the condemned and persecuted sects had elements in common and have some common ties. As different as their paths were, their origins and destinies are still part of the self-contradictory image of the single religious movement which stimulated all of them. They differentiated and organized into either ecclesiastically orthodox groups or heretical communities in the course of time. Even if alien influences might have had an effect on these religious movements in the West, stimulating heresy in particular, the conditions which brought this about still have to be sought in the internal development of Western Christendom.

Research, which is only beginning to see these connections and problems more clearly, is confronted with the following questions which still have to be resolved:

1. What conditions and changes, motives and tendencies brought forth the religious movement of the twelfth century, a movement which led to a variety of new religious communities both inside and outside the Church which was disquieting and confusing even to contemporaries?

2. What groups in Church or society participated in or were swept up by the movement? To what extent did this movement arise from monasticism, from the clergy, or from the laity? Is it a social phenomenon in the sense that it was borne and shaped by the striving of new social levels, perhaps the urban bourgeoisie, released by the "crisis of feudalism"? Was it perhaps differentiated for social reasons and along social lines into approved orders and heretical sects?

3. To what extent are alien influences from outside the West at work, perhaps from the Orient? Is heresy in particular only to be explained in terms of an alien body invading from outside, or did it grow from the soil of Western Christendom on its own?

4. How did the Church, the papacy, the clergy, and the old orders react to this religious movement and its new communities? To what extent did this influence the differentiation of the movement, that is, the number of new orders and the rise of new sects?

A "theory" prepared in advance cannot respond reliably to these questions, but the tradition of the twelfth century itself can. This tradition cannot deal with these questions expressly and simply. Still, after critical, comparative examination and testing, scholarly explanation of the problems in question can be hoped for. Research underway for the last two decades has already achieved important, irrefutable results, while other questions still await penetrating discussion.

1. The New Orders

Of newly founded orders, whose multiplicity and variety deeply disturbed contemporaries,[1] the two most important have also been the most highly regarded and researched, since they had the most success, the greatest size, and the deepest effect, namely the Cistercians[2] and Premonstratensians,[3] as well now as the canons regular (Augustinian canons).[4] Recent research on these orders has made it increasingly clear that their origin and development cannot be understood in isolation. Why did Norbert of Genepp, a canon of Xanten, become a hermit, wandering preacher, and finally founder of an order of his own alongside other orders of Augustinian canons, instead of entering the young Cistercian Order, as did Bernard of Clairvaux? Despite that, the Premonstratensians had a constitution and way of life strongly resembling that of the Cistercians. Norbert's life and labors deserve to be compared not just with Bernard's, but with those of many other monks, hermits, canons and itinerant preachers who formed novel religious communities from similar motives and impulses in the same years, some of these communities becoming approved orders like Norbert's, some of them becoming heretical sects. Abbot Robert of Molesme himself,[4a] left the cloister twice in the course of his long life (c. 1028–1111) to lead groups of hermits even before he founded Cîteaux in 1098. He would not remain there, either. J.-B. Mahn has fruitfully compared Robert with another Benedictine abbot, Bernard of Tiron (c. 1046–1117), who also joined the hermits in the forest of Craon after thirty years in a monastery. Bernard also went from being a wandering preacher to becoming the founder of religious houses as well as of an order of his own. In this he was similar to the leader of hermits, Robert of Arbrissel (c. 1060–1115), founder of the congregation of Fontevrault, and his companions Girald of Salles (1120) and Vitalis of Mortain (1122), founder of the congregation of Savigny.[5] Many of these smaller orders soon joined the Cistercians (as Savigny did with twenty-eight houses in 1147). Others remained independent for centuries; when the Lyon merchant Waldes became an itinerant preacher, he placed his two daughters as nuns in Fontevrault, which would remain independent until the French Revolution. Through Vitalis, once the chaplain of a brother of William the Conqueror, itinerant preaching also passed over to England. After studies in France, Gilbert of Sempringham established his distinguished women's order in England prior to 1135, the Gilbertines, which sought admission to the Cistercian Order, in vain.[6] He and many other founders of orders in this era have been all too much overshadowed by the more successful Cistercians and Premonstratensians. Yet the importance and character of these orders will only become palpable when seen and compared together with those smaller but still symptomatic orders of their contemporaries in the broader picture of the multifaceted religious movement of the early twelfth century. Even less attention has been paid to the way the Carthusians and the devotees of Grandmont must have served as predecessors or stimuli for these new orders. Their early history still awaits a careful investigation[7] which would have to elucidate their relations to earlier hermit congregations in Italy as well as to the newer orders in France. Before Bruno of Cologne, the learned *scholasticus* of Reims cathedral, founded the Charterhouse, he had entered the house of Molesme about 1081 in the company of several noble clerics of Reims following a conflict with the simoniac Archbishop Manasses. At that time the house was in the process of being reformed by Abbot Robert, who would later found Cîteaux. As was the case with Robert himself, Bruno soon left Molesme with his companions to live *eremitice* nearby, until he passed on to Chartreux to establish a community. He remained there only for five years, when his earlier student Urban II called him to Rome. It was from Urban that Bruno received permission in 1091 to establish a hermit community in Calabria (La Torre). He remained there until his death in 1101, still tied to Chartreux, whose fifth prior Guigo (died 1173) organized the Carthusian Order (*Consuetudines*, 1116). If the path of Bruno of Cologne, cathedral scholastic of Reims, led to Southern Italy after his experiences at Molesme, which would also generate Cîteaux, it was in Southern Italy that the young Stephen of Thiers from the Auvergne, who grew up in the tutelage of the archbishop of Benevento, came to know the example of Calabrian hermits[8] and imitate them. After his return (supposedly with the approval of Gregory VII) he established the community of Muret about 1076/80, from which would grow the Order of Grandmont.

In this case the tie with the Italian hermit movement of the eleventh century is obvious. More work will have to be done on the extent to which the Camuldolensians[9] and Vallombrosans[9a] operated directly as examples across the Alps, and how much the writings of Peter Damiani spread the idea of the *vita apostolica* as the office of preaching.[9b] In any case, the Benedictine-Cluniac traditions and reforms are not the only ones worth watching, but also the effect of the hermits, which did not derive from the Benedictine house alone.

Father Charles Dereine, S. J., recently directed attention to the numerous "clerical hermits" of the eleventh century in France, who attracted admirers through their ascetic reputations, gathering communities around themselves and often precipitating the spontaneous erection of buildings and orders. He even believes he can use them to explain the rise of itinerant preaching: "Such a radical practice of evangelical perfection excited great admiration among the faithful; they press into the hermitage in crowds to hear the exhortations of the hermits and receive their advice. At first a matter of the occasion, with time this apostolate took on a more systematic nature. Soon itinerant or wandering preachers are to be seen, pressing the imitation of Christ and the apostles as far as possible within public life."[10] In fact, as in the case of the founder of Cîteaux, almost all the wandering preachers known to us in the early twelfth century (some of whom had been monks, clerics, or canons) spent at least some time living in extreme asceticism as hermits before progressing through the countryside preaching. The adherents they won along the way were then placed in houses under the Rules of St. Benedict or St. Augustine, or similarly organized. The most surprising thing about this is that in the course of this, distinctions between monks, canons regular, preachers, and hermits were extinguished, since a new religious ideal arose. This ideal did not simply arise "occasionally" out of the life of hermits, canons, or monks, but as an active impulse, disrupting the old ideals. It was a new sense of the ideal of the *vita apostolica*, of apostolic action *in* the world and *on* the world, rather than just in a religious house or a hermitage. Even if this impulse often eventually led to the formation of new monastic communities, at the outset there was the principle of living and working like apostles, in keeping with the gospels, as *pauperes Christi*. The reason this idea appeared so often and in so many forms, though not yet realized in the form of an order of apostolic itinerant preachers as would be the case in the mendicant orders of the thirteenth century, can only be understood from the general course of the religious movement.[11]

In the prologue to the Rule of Grandmont, there is an idea of Stephen of Thiers-Muret (died 1124) which is found in similar form elsewhere: none of the patristic rules of Basil, Augustine, or Benedict are a "source [*origo*] of religion, but rather offshoots [*propagines*], they are not the root [*radix*], but the branches [*frondes*]. The root and inexhaustible source for us, which we live today, as for all believers, which was before us and will come after us, is the gospel alone, which was proclaimed by the Savior to the apostles and through them to the whole world."[11a] Here was announced recourse to the gospels and the apostles as the norm for all religious life, the driving force behind manifold new forms of orders and communities. It is proper to observe their "branching out" from a common root, since they are not the *origo* and *radix*, but only *propagines* and *frondes*. It is only when their growth from a common root is understood that their differentiation can be comprehended as arising from varying special circumstances.

2. NEW HERESIES AND SECTS

The religious movement of the twelfth century not only branched out into a multiplicity of new orders, it also multiplied outside the limits of the Church in the form of new heresies and sects, most of them deriving from apostolic itinerant preaching, competing intensely with those orthodox founders of orders precisely because they were so closely related in motive and tendencies. Once again there has been too much concentration—as in the case of the Cistercians and Premonstratensians—on the two most effective, dangerous primary sects of the later twelfth century, who would continue to operate into later times, namely the Cathars and the Waldensians. All other sects, even unimportant ones which developed earlier, have been related to these two in one way or another. It has become ever clearer, however, that the sect of the Cathars only entered the West from the East in the middle of the twelfth century, growing rapidly thereafter. The sect of the Waldensians was formed in polemical opposition to the Cathars in 1173, only to be proclaimed heretical by Lucius III in 1184. From the very beginning of the twelfth century, numerous heretics appeared with strong followings—not to mention individual theologians condemned as heretics, such as Abelard or Gilbert de la Porée—who, on closer examination, cannot be called Cathars or "Waldensians before Waldes," as often happened.[11b] They certainly had a great deal in common with these two and with one another, but also much in common with the orthodox groups of the religious movement of their day. When they broke away from the Church and turned against it, however, they did not stand as an organized sect community with common leaders, doctrines, rites, and cults. Rather we can observe a multiplicity of individual heretical groups operating independently from one another in various areas, each with its own leader, usually known to us by name. This differentiates them also from the heretical groups of the early eleventh century, which were flushed out and condemned in Orléans in 1022, in Arras in 1025, and in Monteforte near Turin around 1028.[11c] No recognizable sectarian connection can be found among them, no common organization, even if individual links can be discovered between France and Italy. Despite many comparable features, heresy found among the learned clergy of Orléans, the Lombard nobles in Monteforte, and the untrained laity in Arras still showed diversity, and there was never a leading thinker with his own ideas who could have given a name to the heresy. The heresy also seems not to have survived its condemnation. After the middle of the eleventh century, there is nothing to be heard of heretics of this sort. The reformers of the Church combated only simonists and nicolaists as heretics. There is nothing to show that a heretical tradition from the early eleventh century lived on secretly, only to be "revived" after a pause of two generations.

When new heresies emerged after the start of the twelfth century, first in France, then in Italy, they were no longer "anonymous" or "of unknown origin." Instead they were almost always headed by a man known to us by name, often a former cleric or monk: the priest Peter of Bruis, the monk Henry, the canon and abbot Arnold of Brescia; even the Flemish heretic Tanchelm, called a *laicus* by Abelard, represented himself as a monk (*monachum mentitus*). He was assisted by Everwacher the priest along with Manasses the smith. The little-known heretic Ponnus (Poncius?) in Périgord, was not only joined by nobles, but also *clerici, presbyteri, monachi et monachæ*. The noble Eon of Stella in Brittany was called *quidam pene laicus* by Otto of Freising. In Soissons one *rusticus Clementius cum fratre Everardo* was tried as a heretic and burned in 1114. It was only later that the wealthy merchant Waldes became head of a sect in Lyon, while the jurist Hugo Speroni was doing the same thing in Lombardy (probably in Piacenza). The following these heretics attracted was no longer limited to particular castles or towns, but scattered far across the countryside. This was because they all traveled about preaching (other than Speroni?), just as the orthodox itinerant preachers did. They seldom joined together; only in the case of the followers of Peter of Bruis, who entered the entourage of Henry the monk after Peter's death (1132/3?). Only later sectarians, such as Waldes and Speroni—and perhaps Arnold of Brescia[11d]—appeared to have organized their following well enough that Waldensians, Speronists, and Arnoldists continued after their deaths—the Waldensians being the sole medieval sect to survive to the present day.

In the meantime, shortly before mid-century, an entirely different form of heresy penetrated the West, at the outset anonymous, called the "new heretics" by horrified contemporaries. Bernard of Clairvaux found it utterly uncanny that, unlike other heretics, they could not be named after a *magister*, from whom they would have their origin and doctrine.[12] After 1163 they were called "Cathars," a Greek name which betrays their origin, even if it is not documented in the East. It is further a clear tradition, indisputably established, that the Cathars received their dualist doctrine from the Bogomils of Byzantium, Bosnia, and Bulgaria, a doctrine on which many differed in detail, as well as their rite of "laying on of hands" (*consolamentum*) and their sectarian organization with its own bishops and priests, the *perfecti*, which quickly splintered into various parties and hierarchies. All of this distinguished the Cathars dramatically from all other sects of this time. Even if a few isolated Bogomil influences might have reached the West in the early eleventh century,[12a] they could not have operated without interruption there until the dramatically Eastern foreignness associated with the Cathars set in, something of which there is not a trace in the other, earlier sects. Thus heresy in the twelfth century cannot be completely explained from the internal evolution of Western piety, since the doctrine of the Cathars is an alien import. However, heresy as a whole in the West cannot be regarded as an alien element injected from outside. That is true only for the Cathars, not for the other sects, which had been born and raised in the bosom of Western Christendom. Yet the Cathars would have had a hard time gaining a foothold and attracting so much support if the previous religious movement had not already prepared the ground. Even they did not first appear in the West as the prophets of an alien, dualistic doctrine, but rather like earlier itinerant preachers they appeared as *pauperes Christi*, living and working like the apostles, trying to be "good Christians." Such conduct won them both audiences and success. Their dualistic dogma only gradually distinguished itself from Catholic doctrine. For the mass of the believers, the *credentes*, the religious attitude and moral rigorism of their preachers, the *perfecti*, was always more impressive than their dualistic speculation. In the religious movement of the West, the question of a truly evangelical way of life as the path to salvation was always more important, more vital, than all doctrinal matters of theology or cosmology. For this very reason, the Waldensians sought to realize the ideal of an apostolic life in keeping with the gospels without abandoning the Catholic faith, in contrast to the increasingly dogmatic direction of the Cathars. Despite this, the Waldensians and the parallel movement of the *Humiliati* in Lombardy came into conflict with the Church, and out of their disobedience they became heretics. Innocent III was only able to win some of them back for the Church. He clearly recognized his mission to make the forces of the religious movement work within the Church and for the Church, so that they would not slide completely into heresy and become a real peril to the Church. For this reason, Innocent III paved the way for Dominic and Francis.[12b] Their papally recognized mendicant orders were able to become heirs and executors of the religious movement within and serving the Church, as well as undermining heresy.

3. New Sources and Research on Heresy in the Twelfth Century

Knowledge of the religious movement and of heresy in the twelfth century has been considerably increased in the last two decades by intense research and the discovery of important new sources. Progress has been made even if by no means all questions have been answered and many a new problem has emerged along the way. The individual heresies can be distinguished from one another more clearly than before, so far as origin and intention go, and it is now possible to measure with greater precision the themes and impulses they shared with one another and with elements of the religious movement within the Church, as well as what divided them. It is a blessing to research that the literary contest between learned Catholics and individual heretics started rather early in the twelfth century, later resulting in general *Summæ contra hæreticos*. Perhaps before 1134, Peter the Venerable, abbot of Cluny, wrote an epistolary tract against Petrus de Bruis and his following,[13] which had been joined by the heretical monk Henry. A book of Henry's which Peter the Venerable knew has unfortunately disappeared. A monk William disputed with Henry in person and in writing about 1133/5, and his writing was discovered by Mario Esposito and published by Raoul Manselli, who also found a variant text.[14] This informative polemic against Henry's errors was used by Manselli to investigate the relationship of this heresy to Peter of Bruis as well as to the Waldensians on the other. He did not use the *Contra hereticos sui temporis* of Archbishop Hugh of Rouen (died 1164) (*PL* 192.1131–38), which doesn't identify heretics by name. Hugh accompanied Cardinal-Legate Alberich of Ostia, who accompanied Bernard of Clairvaux on a mission to Provence against Henry.

Hugh's treatise, which still deserves closer study, has been associated with the Breton heretic Eon of Stella, though without convincing evidence. Unfortunately, no new material has appeared about Eon, nor about the Flemish heretic Tanchelm,[15] or Arnold of Brescia.[16] Still, new investigations have made their heresy more intelligible in the context of their time. In contrast, the origin of the Waldensians has been placed in an entirely new light through the surprising discovery of Father Antoine Dondaine, O.P. He discovered a thoroughly orthodox confession of faith by Waldes and a Waldensian *Liber antiheresis*,[17] as well as a hitherto-unknown conclusion concerning Waldensians to the *Tractatus contra hæreticos* by Ermengaud,[18] himself probably a converted Waldensian. Ermengaud says Waldes swore to a cardinal, *quod nunquam de cetero sectam istam teneret nec haberet socios istius erroris*. Dondaine infers that the creed he discovered was presented by Waldes at this time. This has been confirmed and clarified by an eye-witness account discovered by Father Jean Leclercq, O.S.B., in the unpublished sermons on the apocalypse of the Cistercian Godfrey of Auxerre, who had been the secretary and biographer of Bernard of Clairvaux.[19] As abbot of Hautecombe he observed Waldes' recantation shortly after the Third Lateran Council in the presence of Cardinal-Legate Henry of Albano and Archbishop Guichard of Lyon (died July 1180), and Godfrey noted how soon Waldes relapsed. Godfrey shed light on many aspects of the beginnings of the Waldensians, who become much more recognizable as a result of these discoveries. Dondaine also refers to the fact that when Waldensian groups reconciled with the Church, they had to render a confession of faith very similar to that which Waldes swore. This confession was eventually placed at the head of the decrees of the Fourth Lateran Council in 1215. In this case, the formulation of the dogmatic norm of ecclesiastical faith can be followed precisely in the course of the conflict with heresy.

No less surprising and significant was the discovery of a text against the heresy of the Lombard jurist Hugo Speroni, who is barely known despite the fact that "Speronists" are still frequently named along with other heretics into the thirteenth century. Speroni probably published a book, now lost, in Piacenza, where he was consul between 1164 and 1171. The book's contents can be largely reconstructed from the thorough refutation composed shortly before 1177 in England by his earlier fellow student from Bologna, Master Vacarius, which Father Ilarino da Milano, O.F.M. Cap., discovered and edited together with a thorough commentary comparing it with all the Italian heresies of the time.[20] Our knowledge of the heresies of the twelfth century is thus made richer by a new approach which is neither that of the heretical wandering preachers nor the Cathars nor the Waldensians, but shares many ideas and tendencies with all of them.

Lastly, the history of the Cathars is enriched by numerous discoveries of new sources, critical editions and studies, and one comprehensive narrative. A. Dondaine discovered for the first time a Cathar doctrinal tract combined with a fragmentary ritual,[21] surely from the period after 1240. It was a product of the last phase of theoretical speculative dualism, composed in Lombardy in the region of Verona and Brescia either by Giovanni de Lugio or one of his adherents, the so-called "Albanenses." In connection with this text, however, Dondaine also made a thorough investigation of the beginnings of the sect in the West,[22] aided by critical studies and editions of anti-heretical tracts of the twelfth and thirteenth centuries, including the discovery of new texts by Father Ilarino da Milano[23] and Father Thomas Kaeppeli.[24] Further, the Bogomil sect of the Balkans is now so much better known[24a] that it is no longer possible to doubt their link with the Cathars in the West. Dondaine's investigations of the Albigensian council in St.-Félix-de-Caraman near Toulouse in 1167 and on the Cathar hierarchy in Italy demonstrate conclusively how Bogomil propaganda took root in the West, spread, and split. On the basis of all this new information,[25] Arno Borst presented the history and doctrine of the Cathars in summary but definitive fashion.[26] This book also treats the other heresies of the eleventh and twelfth centuries in comparison, with many useful, critical references to sources and literature, always referring back to the Cathars.

A comparatively exhaustive, source-based treatment of the other sects, including the Waldensians, or of the entire religious movement of the twelfth century, so far as that goes, has not yet appeared.[27] The *Studi sulle eresie del secolo XII* of Raoul Manselli (1953) deals primarily with the connections between Petrus de Bruis, Henry the Monk, and the Waldensians. Father Ilarino's book on Hugo Speroni deals almost exclusively with the contemporary heresies in Italy. Father Ilarino gives a survey with wider scope of "Le eresie medioevali" from the eleventh to the thirteenth centuries with numerous sources (translated into Italian), and useful bibliographic references.[28] In so doing, he organizes the heresies according to dogmatic categories, without reference to chronology or history. As a result, Speronists are grouped with Cathars, Wyclifites, and Hussites into the first groups, "movements of the doctrinal type," the Arnoldists, Waldensians, and *Humiliati* with the apostles of Fra Dolcino and Gherardo Segarelli (around 1300) and individual heretics of the early twelfth century into the third group, "ascetic evangelism," while Tanchelm, Petrus de Bruis, Henry the Monk and Eon of Stella are in the fifth group, "reactionary movements" (following the

Flagellants of 1260)! There could not be a more drastic example of how unhistorically such a dogmatically structured rubrication of heresy obfuscates and destroys their actual relations to one another as well as to the religious movements of their time. In contrast, the programmatic attempt of Raffaello Morghen[29] to trace the common biblical and religious impulses in medieval heresy instead of the usual overestimation of dogmatic differences was still written *before* the discovery of many new sources. As a result he could not take into account the alien, speculative elements of the Cathar sect, which only penetrated from the East after 1140, nor could he adequately judge the gap between the heresies of the earlier eleventh century and the religious movement of the twelfth century. Neither of these factors negates his assumption of a spontaneous, native and essentially unified religiosity of medieval heresy, but they do modify it. These heresies cannot be reduced summarily to one common denominator, though they do have much in common. The thesis of the Austrian Friedrich Heer in his book, *Aufgang Europas*, finally, is overbearing, precipitate and inadequate since it holds that the religious movements of the twelfth century in France and Italy are to be understood as expressions of social change, "ideologies" of a rising civic bourgeoisie and the "new masses," even the "inchoate proletariat of medieval metropolises," the first European "workers' movement."[30] The complicated link between economic and social change in the twelfth century and the formation of religious communities into orders and sects is not about to be comprehended with such anachronistic slogans and sociological prejudices. Only open, critical testing of all sources can adequately answer the sociological questions posed to history.

Instead of hypothetical, generalized assertions, what follows is intended to give a few indications of the historical facts and actual motifs and tendencies of religious movements in the twelfth century in order to serve further discussion and a clarification of the problems.

4. *VITA APOSTOLICA* AND ITINERANT PREACHING

The discovery of the heresy of Ugo Speroni moved Father Ilarino da Milano to remark, "The tendency to group the various heretical currents and their factions under a common and dominant evangelical inspiration and practice of poverty . . . has been shown to be in error" (p. viii, cf. p. 435). Yet Speroni agreed with many other heretics of his time in savagely criticizing "unworthy clergy," in rejecting infant baptism, and many other theses. He shared positions taken by the Cathars and Waldensians, but Speroni justified these stances differently, neither with demands for a life modeled on the apostles nor with a dualistic doctrine of the world. After research has learned to distinguish Cathars from Waldensians and other sects as a result of long, painstaking effort, it would be wrong too readily or summarily to try to bring them all back under a common denominator, seeing them either as variant forms of expression for a basically unified, spontaneous "lay evangelism," or as the "ideology" of a coherent social movement. The differences between the sectarian doctrines which have been preserved should never be ignored, since otherwise dramatic distinctions within the religious movement become incomprehensible. On the other hand, it is remarkable, and certainly cannot be an accident, that many theses, themes, and tendencies return time and again, though with differing justifications and consequences, and they often surface among orthodox groups of the religious movement just as among heretics. With all their variety of responses, it is often the same questions and problems which disturb, move, and divide the religious spirits of this time. If an effort is made to reach the basic causes and drives behind this movement, one will not be able to stop at formulating and justifying individual doctrines in various ways. Rather, the question is to what they were responding or reacting. Using Arnold Toynbee's formula, it is not just "the responses" but particularly "the challenges" which have to be regarded. The fact of the amazing multiplicity itself of the orders and sects created in the twelfth century shows that they arose from a general disquiet whose bases and motivations have to be established. Contemporaries themselves were not unaware of such common motivation; they often formulated it in similar words, no matter how variously their paths ran within or outside the Church. There were "slogans" and "main themes" of this movement which were often differently understood, interpreted, and applied, but which tell us what questions counted in these religious conflicts. The use and meaning of such "slogans" can clearly indicate what was shared and what was different.

In this context, the leading idea at work everywhere but realized in quite various ways is that of the "apostolic life." The *vita apostolica* had always been spoken of as the model and standard for a true Christian life within the Church just as it was in many heretical sects, particularly in connection with the monastic and ecclesiastical reforms of the eleventh century.[31] In those days, however, it was understood to mean nothing other than the *vita communis* of the monks and canons regular, who were to have all in common without private property, just as the first Christians of the *ecclesia primitiva* did according to the Acts of the Apostles (2:44–45, 4:32).[32] While Gregory VII had virtually equated the word "apostolic" with "papal," identifying the *ecclesia apostolica* with the church of the apostolic city of Rome,[33] Urban II programmatically recognized the life of canons regular as equal to that of the monks as *apostolica instituta disciplinæ*. To Urban, the life of the laity was also *ab primordiis ecclesiæ instituta*, though he did not recognize it as the *vita apostolica*.[34]

After the turn of the twelfth century, however, the concept of the *vita apostolica* takes on a new sense: it becomes ambiguous and disputed, people no longer agree as to what it means or demands. M. D. Chenu, O.P.,[35] has stimulatingly and knowledgeably observed that it was not only monks and canons who disputed "diverging paths of apostolic life," but also the laity, particularly wandering preachers with their followers—and finally also the heretics of the period. As late as 1125–30 *De vita vere apostolica* (IV, 4, 11)[35a] claimed that monasticism alone was the true apostolic life: "The Church grew from monastic life," "all the apostles were truly monks." Norbert of Xanten expressed a very different sense of the apostolate when he said to the bishop of Laon in 1119, trying to recruit him to lead his community of canons: "I chose to live according to the better understanding of a life purely evangelical and apostolic" (*MG Scr.* 12.675–76). Norbert said to the companions of his itinerant preaching, "We are made imitators of the apostles," (ibid., 678) and even after the founding of Prémontré he wanted to remain true to the "apostolic life which he supported in his preaching" (*PL* 188.1292). Anselm of Havelberg praised him because he "instructed as to the perfection of apostolic life by word and example" (ibid., 1155) all those who followed him. Abelard, on the other hand, not only mocked Norbert and his *coapostolus*, but also Bernard of Clairvaux as "new apostles" [*novi apostoli*] (*PL* 178.605). As early as around 1101 the Benedictine abbot Bernard, who later founded Thiron, was supposedly empowered as an itinerant preacher by Paschal II as "vicar of the apostles and public preacher" (*PL* 172.1155), as was the priest Robert of Arbrissel as early as 1096 by Urban II. The companion of their days as hermits, the earlier chaplain Vitalis of Mortain, decided "To bear the easy yoke of Christ, [following] in the footsteps of the apostles" (Ordericus Vitalis, III, 449). Only somewhat later (an important point), the further accusation that they boasted of living as the apostles is thrown at the heretics. Guibert of Nogent first wrote this about two heretics interrogated in his presence about 1114 in Soissons.[36] Archbishop Hugh of Rouen asserted a bit later that heretics of his own day were saying in 1147, "We observe the form of the apostolic life" (*PL* 192.1289). Bernard of Clairvaux said of the heretics of Provence against whom he preached, "Where is this apostolic form and life of which you boast?" (*PL* 183.1091, cf. 1098). Eckbert of Schönau said of the Cathars of Cologne, whose interrogation he attended in 1163, "They say they are leading the life of the apostles" (*PL* 195.14). Until the end of the twelfth century Cathars are accused: "They feigned that they were keeping the apostolic life."[36a] Stephan of Bourbon also said of Waldes, "He proposed to keep evangelical perfection as the apostles did," Godfrey of Auxerre complained about the *novi apostoli* of Lyon, and Walter Map saw them appearing at the curia "like apostles." Finally Bishop Diego of Osma decided along with Dominic to fight heresy in Southern France with its own weapons, "imitating the form of apostles in all things" (Peter of Vaux-Cernay, I, 23).

Where did this new religious ideal of the *vita apostolica* originate which both orthodox and heretical itinerant preachers, founders of orders and sects alike, made their own and sought to make real in their own ways? It was obviously not first spread by heretics, nor was it smuggled into the West from the East nor received from earlier "apostolics," as earlier catalogues of heresies asserted.[36b] Even if the Cathars did bring their own ideal of the apostolic life and mission from the East, something like it was already alive in the West, providing all the stronger response. There it was not *"laïc d'origine"*[37] nor originally a *"movimento popolare,"* but first appears among monks, clerics, and hermits who became itinerant preachers (many of them heretics). Accordingly, its roots should not be sought in alien influence but "in the wake of the great movement for the reform of the Church."[38] This reform, which first fought for the "freedom" of monasteries and the Church from noble and royal lay control, for the validity of canon law, for the *vita regularis et canonica* of monks and clergy, overshot the goals achieved by Cluniacs and Gregorians. The religious forces conjured up by the reforming papacy against a simoniac and married clergy were often roused to autonomous activity, no longer satisfying themselves with the renewed application of monastic rules and canon law. The gospels and the writings of the apostles themselves became the norm of a truly Christian life, the source of their piety, calling every Christian to treat himself as a disciple and apostle of Jesus. Following their counsel and example, monks, hermits, and canons began to preach, shaking the faithful even outside the monastery and the clergy, winning them for a truly Christian life. The question was only how this apostolic effort toward the lay world, and the religious communities thus formed, would fit into the traditional rules of the Church, with its division by estates into lay persons, monks, and clergy. This question became crucial for the religious movement in the twelfth century.

As early as the investiture controversy two remarkable predecessors of the future movement appeared, the *Pataria* in Lombardy and the Hirsau reform in Swabia. The *Pataria* movement was launched by the noble Milanese clerics Ariald and Landulf, who assembled and imposed on the people an oath against simoniac and unchaste clerics without committing them to any specific way of life. Only the clerics who joined lived a common life, as canons. After Landulf's death, however, his brother Erlembald, a pious knight, took the leadership about 1064. After a pilgrimage to Jerusalem he desired to become a monk, but Ariald and the monks and hermits he asked, even the curia itself, encouraged him to continue fighting for the freedom of the Church as a layman and *miles Christi*—shocking opponents over this penetration of a layman into ecclesiastical affairs. Gregory VII announced miracles performed at the grave after his death in 1075 and had his remains translated. It is not known how long the *Pataria* lived on as an organized community, a *conjuratio* of a more political than religious character. It is only a hundred years later—in the statutes of the Lateran Council of 1179—that the Cathars are called *Patarini* in Italy.[38a]

Albert Hauck already compared the *Pataria* with the Hirsau reform movement (*KD*, 3d ed., 3.876). Here it was a question of monks working as itinerant preachers out of the monastery to promote the ideas of the Gregorian reform.[39] The chronicler Bernold of Constance reports (*MG Scr.* 5.451ff.) that under their influence many laymen, even nobles, instead of entering Hirsau as subservient *conversi*, gathered together to live the "common life in the form of the primitive Church" in many places, particularly in Swabia, including outside of religious houses and without becoming monks or clerics. Urban II expressly approved this in a bull of 1091. Not only men, but also innumerable women, even peasants' daughters, renounced marriage and life in the world (*sæculo renuntiantes*—without entering a religious house!); married couples separated in order to live *religiose* under monastic or clerical leadership in pious communities.[40] There is no other record of such religious lay communities in connection with the preaching monks of Hirsau; it is obvious that they had no long duration or lasting impact.[41] In this case, as with the *Pataria*, there is no talk of a *vita apostolica*. In the next generation, however, it will be the morning cry of apostolic itinerant preachers, who, like the Hirsau monks, work primarily on the laity, and especially on women.

Many contemporaries appear to have regarded it as an offense against the *statuta sanctorum canonum* and hence heretical that the Hirsau monks preached outside their cloisters as "Gyrovagii" (denounced by the Rule of St. Benedict), sowing discord "under the appearance of religion,"[42] as was then repeatedly said of heretics. Even such a committed Gregorian as Bernold of Constance could not conceal concerns about monks preaching, insofar as they had not been ordained to it by the bishop or licensed by the pope. Yet Robert of Arbrissel received permission to work as an itinerant preacher from Urban II, Bernard of Thiron around 1101 from Paschal II, and Norbert of Xanten from Gelasius II in 1118 after a synod at Fritzlar had condemned him for unlicensed preaching. Even Henry the Monk, later a heretic, received a license to preach from the bishop of Le Mans, a license eventually revoked. Misgivings and accusations were always being bruited about against other itinerant preachers, and not just because of their ever more frequent invectives against the abuses of the clergy. The question of whether monks were permitted to preach in public, whether the laity, even women or Christians in general, were empowered, even exhorted to preach by the word of the Lord, "Go forth into the world and preach the gospel to all creatures" (Mark 16:15), would not come to rest throughout the entire twelfth century. Even such a committed representative of old Benedictine and Cluniac monasticism as Rupert of Deutz claimed the right for monks to preach which was being disputed by others. Although Bernard of Clairvaux opposed preaching by any monk outside his religious house, he was continually underway as a preacher. Even Hildegard of Bingen, abbess of Rupertsburg, preached in public as an old woman on three long journeys, not only in religious houses and before the clergy, but in front of the people—against heretics![43] The problem only became critical when the heretics refused to be barred from preaching. Waldes became a heretic over this issue alone. Precisely as with Waldes, Henry the Monk declared over forty years earlier that one must obey God rather than people, since Christ said, "Go forth and teach all peoples." For that reason it is not necessary (as Raoul Manselli argues) to posit any influence on the Waldensians by Henry's adherents, for the *vita apostolica* had been perennially understood since the start of the century as an exhortation for all Christians to preach, as if no one could be prevented from living as an apostle. The monk William told the heretic Henry this opinion was laughable, others found it presumptive, and time and again they were confronted with the word of the Apostle, "How shall they preach if they are not sent?" (Romans 10:15). Even Rupert of Deutz stressed (*PL* 176.632) that it was not preaching, baptizing and doing miracles that made apostles, but virtue and humility. Yet Bernard of Thiron (*PL* 172.1398–99) had already responded to the accusing question, "Why does he, who is a monk and dead to the world, preach to the living?" by asserting the example of St. Gregory the Great and St. Martin. "They achieved their license to preach by virtue of mortification,'' he proclaimed, citing the words of Paul (1 Corinthians 11:1), ''Be imitators of me as I am of Christ.'' Minds were divided over whether it was religious witness in following Christ which empowered one to preach or only ecclesiastical office, the *ordinatio* and *missio*. Whoever believed himself permitted to preach autonomously, through his *vita apostolica*, and would not relent, came into conflict with the Church and became a heretic. On the other hand, itinerant preachers who came to found orders certainly continued to make use of the right to preach vested in them, though they did not claim the same right for their adherents and communities. Instead, they arranged for these followers to depart from the world in a monastic fashion, despite their own ideal of an active *vita apostolica*. This largely abandoned the field to heretic preachers.

This pattern applies to Norbert and the Premonstratensians. Even after the founding of Prémontré, Norbert continued to work as a preacher against the heresy of Tanchelm in Antwerp, in Cologne, Cambrai, and elsewhere. It is hence not necessary to doubt the assertion of his *vita* that Calixtus II at the Council of Rheims in 1119 renewed the license to preach granted him by his predecessor. Yet Charles Dereine rightly stresses[44] that the Premonstratensians were committed from the beginning, not to preaching or pastoral care, but to the *vita heremitica sub canonica professione*. In their statutes (circa 1131/4) there is no mention of preaching. The Rule of St. Augustine, which they accepted, did say ''We choose to live the apostolic life,'' but this was only used to justify the complete renunciation of property in the *vita communis*. Is this renunciation, which Norbert had already recommended to the canons in Laon when he was to take over their leadership, really ''The basis of his apostolic conception of the religious life''? (Thus Dereine, 368.) In any case, he did not create an order of preachers as is usually assumed. It was only in the Eastern German dioceses that he transferred missionary and parish responsibilities to the Premonstratensians in his role as archbishop of Magdeburg. Otherwise, they appeared to contemporaries to be hermit-canons, ''far withdrawn from people'' (*PL* 213.830), not preachers. Even the spokesmen for the ''spiritualité des Prémontrés'' interpret the *vita apostolica* not as an apostolate of preaching, but as a contemplative ''living for God alone''; it is significant that Adam Scot, who thought and wrote penetratingly about his order, moved to the Carthusians in the end. When the Church grew increasingly desperate for preachers against the heretics, no Premonstratensians were called, but many Cistercians were. Dominic could not use Premonstratensian traditions to support what he was doing when he created his Order of Preachers.

To tell the truth, the Cistercians, whom the Premonstratensians extensively imitated in their constitution, were not oriented to preaching or pastoral care at the outset, but rather to strict loyalty to the Rule in their monastery, as far as possible from people, in order "to be poor together with the poor Christ." This ideal of poverty, which renounced not only private property but also feudal monastic property and tithes, was shared by the early Cistercians with Norbert and his *pauperes Christi*. Yet Alexander III already was bitterly accusing the Order of Cîteaux of having become entirely untrue to this original ideal, barely justifying its special position.[45] As often as Cistercians went to Southern France to combat heretics, they usually had no success, since they did not make a simple and poor appearance as the preaching heretics did. Innocent III exhorted them to do so, but in vain (*PL* 215.358–59); only Dominic went a different way. Even the Calabrian Cistercian abbot Joachim, who left his order in 1188 to become the founder of a new house and order at S. Giovanni in Fiore,[46] did not contribute directly to the religious movement of his own day through his intensification of the eremitic contemplative ideal. It was only long after his death (in 1202) that his ideas of history and theology would deeply move the Franciscan Order.

With all the spiritual wealth of the Cistercian and Premonstratensian culture of the twelfth century, these orders became rich and powerful, withdrawing from the world in all too monastic a manner to satisfy the religious forces and needs of the laity. Investigation is still needed to see how far they shut themselves off socially from the lower classes. The smaller orders founded by itinerant preachers or hermit-canons did not have much influence beyond their own cloisters. The threatening growth of heresy in the twelfth century only becomes understandable through this disavowal by the new orders, which alienated them from the religious movement which had given them birth. The more monastic the orders became, the more radical grew the sects.

5. THE HERETICAL RADICALIZATION OF THE RELIGIOUS MOVEMENT

The intelligent, ever ecclesiastically minded contemporary, John of Salisbury, said of Arnold of Brescia, whom John had seen teaching in Paris and later agitating in Rome, "[Arnold] taught many things in harmony with Christian law, and many more things dissenting from a Christian life" [*MG Scr*. 20.537]. In fact, all the heretics of the twelfth century were convinced that their doctrine and views were in keeping with the gospels and apostolic writings and were thus truly Christian, while the life of the Church and of the clergy did not correspond to this norm, and for that reason they attacked the Church. There were no heretics in this period—and they would have had difficulty getting a hearing or support in the West—who did not assert that they were "true Christians," calling on the New Testament for support. Thus far one could not even call the Cathars "un-Christian," for although their dualist doctrine came out of the East, it grew there as well in Christian soil, nurtured to be sure by Iranian-Manichee traditions, but always defended with biblical arguments and claiming a true apostolic succession. All that separated and alienated the heretic from the Church was *how* Christianity was to be understood and kept. They did not seek, like the theologians of early scholasticism, to bring divergent traditions into harmony through the dialectic concordance of *sic et non*, but rather they found the ecclesiastical tradition and practice incompatible with their own insistent personal understanding of the Bible.

The reform movement of the eleventh century had also measured the dominant practice of Church and cloister against a standard, namely canon law and the Rule of St. Benedict, and found them wanting. The reformers declared the consecrations and ecclesiastical acts of "unworthy priests" null and void; but for them it was not only the simoniac priest who was "unworthy," but also the unchaste.[47]

Apostolic itinerant preachers after 1100 continued the struggle unleashed by the Gregorians against "unworthy priests," resulting in many conflicts with the clergy. Whoever continued to make the validity of the sacraments and the right of priests to perform their duties, even preaching, depend on worthiness, moral purity, and a Christian way of life, rather than the mere legitimacy of ecclesiastical office and mission, became a heretic. The Gregorian reform saw its most essential goal as having been achieved when only a canonically ordained priest could serve. The reform demanded that a priest's acts have unimpeachable validity and recognition. The criticism that office and worthiness were often not in harmony did not cease; doubts arose whether the direct counsels of gospel and apostle were not more authoritative than canon law.[48] There were questions whether Christian attitudes did not count more than an ecclesiastical office, whether the apostolic succession, the sole source of the ecclesiastical hierarchy's priestly right to perform sacraments, had not to justify and preserve itself through a true imitation of the apostles.[48a]

The heretics of the twelfth century answered these questions independently of one another in various ways, but often with quite similar consequences. Even the jurist Ugo Speroni, who appears to have had nothing to do with apostolic itinerant preaching and heretics of his day, was accused of holding as the *summa sue intencionis*, that priests should be judged by their *meritum vite* rather than their *officium*. Priests should be *spirituales et mundi et perfecti*; otherwise they were *ipso iure* not priests at all, not even Christians, but thieves and murderers. Master Vacarius responded to this with all possible harshness, "The priesthood is a matter of law, that is of a certain constitution. . . . What does the office of administration, which is in the things themselves, have to do with the merit of religion and love, which is in the mind of that person?" One could exist without the other.[49] The confrontation of conceptualization which separated the heretic from the Church could not be stated more clearly. This is almost exactly what Alan of Lille has the Waldensians say, "That merit has more to do with consecration, benediction, binding and loosing, than do order and office . . . , for merit, not office, gives power." Waldensians claimed to have the *merita apostolorum*, and so they believe they could act as priests without being ordained: "Since they say they are vicars of the apostles, they should have their offices through their merit" [*PL* 210.385]. Alanus believed that there, more than anywhere else, lay their challenge to the Church. Speroni did not use this "apostolic" argument; insofar as it can be discerned from the polemics against him, he held rather that the "inner purity," the goodness of the true Christian, was predestined, independent of external attitude or even of office. Father Ilarino sees in this (p. 417ff.) "the doctrinal nucleus" and "the soul of the religious system of Hugo Speroni"; the supposed unworthiness of priests was only a polemical excuse to dismiss this "system," a faith in predestination which did not have even the inadequacy of priests as a logical premise. Did not his contemporary, Master Vacarius, see it more correctly, in his conception—as Father Ilarino himself shows (p. 414)—"anti-sacerdotalism constitutes the provocative theme of the heresy of Speroni, the atmosphere from which the nucleus emerged which generated the other doctrinal affirmations"? Is not his doctrine of predestination called forth and created as a result of his own musings over the question of what makes people Christians and priests, good, justified and holy? The Waldensians and even earlier heretics responded to this question less theoretically than practically, with their "apostolic life." But they are still convinced that it is a question of *how* a person is and lives, not *what* he is and does on account of his office.

It is impossible to speak here of a principled anticlericalism; at least it is not there at the outset. Heretical polemic begins not against priests as such, but only against unworthy priests. Even the Cathars (Borst, *Die Katharer*, 216) assert as much, although they reject the Catholic clergy and its sacraments completely, replacing them with its own hierarchy and the *consolomentum* as the sole apostolic ones. Waldensians were long ready to receive sacraments from "good" Catholic priests, and they dispensed these sacraments themselves only in necessity; it is only after 1205 that the "Lombard Poor" separated from the "Poor of Lyon," who wanted to preserve this view. Arnold of Brescia relegated the clergy to its spiritual duties, demanding it renounce worldly goods and earthly power, taking up a life in evangelical poverty, and according to these standards almost all the priests of his time were "reprobates, following Simon, except for a very few" (*Gesta di Federigo*, 1, v. 781/3). Even Hugo Speroni was thinking only of sinful priests, "since such today are neither priests nor Christians" (p. 484). The heretic monk Henry had already said, "The priests of these days do not have the power of binding and loosing"; through their sins they have lost the *dignitas apostolatus* (Manselli, *Enrico*, 56ff.). The high standards of purity and dignity demanded of the priesthood were always the starting point and basis for criticism. Thoughtful contemporaries knew that quite well; the Premonstratensian Philip of Harvengt, for example, exhorted priests: "the more holy, the more worthy to the people," (*PL* 203.670)—but the worth of their sacraments could not be made dependent on that. The frequent charge that the heretics failed to respect the mass and sacraments, particularly the eucharist, always forces us to ask whether they disdained only unworthy dispensers of the sacraments, as was certainly the case with the Waldensians. Otto of Freising says of Arnold of Brescia, "He was said not to have a proper view of the sacrament of the altar" [*Gesta*, II, 28], but Arnoldists themselves said, "the sacraments of the Church are to be avoided due to the evil of the clerics." The monk Henry wrote before 1134, "A mass could be sung and the Body of Christ confected, if one could be found worthy of doing it" (Manselli, *Enrico*, 53); Bernard of Clairvaux later complained of him, however: "He held the sacraments not to be sacred!" (*PL* 182.434).

Certainly the heretical criticism of unworthy priests could easily lead to generalized hostility against all clergy ordained by the Church, as well as against the whole Church as a hierarchy of office. Repudiation of sacramental doctrine could lead to a rejection and devaluation of the sacraments altogether. Abelard asserts that Peter of Bruis said, "the sacrament of the altar is not to be celebrated any more" (*PL* 178.1056), and Peter the Venerable combated his fundamental objections to the "priestly nonsense" of the *officium altaris*, for which he had biblical citations (*PL* 189.787ff.). Speroni used different arguments to combat the doctrine of the eucharist and transubstantiation, holding the Lord's Supper to be a mere commemoration—as the Cathars did, too, at the outset (Borst, p. 217). The justifications are various—but were there really all that many distinct ideal reasons for so many sorts of heretics to be alienated from the doctrine and practice of the Church, and for them to oppose the Church? It is even more surprising that the baptism of infants was rejected time and again, by Peter of Bruis, by Henry the Monk, by the Liège heretics as well as by Speroni and the Waldensians. Arnold of Brescia was also cited as having had erroneous ideas about infant baptism; Cathars only bestowed their *consolamentum* on children at a late date. Although variously formulated, the same conception is always operative, namely, that children could not yet be Christians out of their own faith or merit, and that was the only thing that counted. Because they also could not be sinful on their own account, Henry the Monk as well as Speroni denied original sin. In the same way, the dead are no more to be aided with prayers, alms, and fasts; that was justified in different ways by Peter of Bruis, Henry the Monk, by the Waldensians and the Cathars, but they agree in their basic motivation. Even Peter of Bruis' denunciation of the veneration of the cross and ecclesiastical buildings was not repeated by the Cathars alone—there is no reason to speak of these as "currents of the Cathar type" (Manselli, *Studi*, 37). Hugo Speroni as well, who was accused of thinking himself a philosopher, called churches "dens of thieves" and asked, "Who taught us to build towers, sound bells, paint pictures, raise crosses, make idols to worship, adore and kiss?" (526–27). In opposition to the "externality" of the cult as well as against "good works" it is time and again the internal attitude of the Christian, his inner purity, the pursuit of evangelical and apostolic counsels, which is demonstrated and promoted.

From these observations, which could be multiplied many times over, the following conclusions emerge:

1. The agreement of individual "doctrines" of various heretics should not be taken as sufficient evidence of a sectarian tie among them, with a common doctrinal tradition, so long as this is not expressly documented historically. They could also respond independently of one another in a similar manner to the current problems of their day, and the common themes permit us to see what problems were acute, disputed, and needful of decision in the religious movement as well as within the Church.

2. Insofar as the partisan, usually polemic tradition permits, it is important to investigate what particular ways of thinking and attitudes lie at the bottom of the "doctrines" of individual heretics. In this spirit, for example, Raoul Manselli (*Studi*, 59) seeks the "nucleus of the religious attitude" of Henry the Monk, Father Ilarino (411ff.) looks for the "soul of the religious system of Hugo Speroni." Arno Borst (143ff.) searches for the "Cathar faith," etc. While searching for the essence of a

heresiarch's thought, it must always be kept in mind that the personal conviction of individual heretics was only one pole of their heresy. Heretical doctrine emerges only through interaction with the opposite pole of ecclesiastical doctrine and practice, which it abrades and inflames. As a result, heretics are continually being presented with the same or similar questions; their answers are variations on themes which they would not have chosen on their own. Even the Cathar faith, which came from outside, was able to operate in the West only because its dualism and ethical rigorism seemed to offer a radical solution to religious problems which had long disturbed many Christians there, and since it called on the same New Testament tradition as the other sects—and the Church itself.

3. Heresies are hence only to be understood in the context of the general religious movement of their time, which also produced the new orders, and in their dialogue with the development of ecclesiastical theology. Just as orthodox and heretical itinerant preachers in the first half of the twelfth century worked alongside one another, competing with one another, becoming founders of orders and sects, so also later the Dominicans and Franciscans opposed the Cathars and Waldensians—antagonists on the same stage. And just as the heretics rejected the sacraments of unworthy priests, the ecclesiastical sacramental doctrine of the *opus operatum* was being elaborated,[50]—opposite answers to the same question. It will also aid our understanding of the history of the Church and of dogma if heresy is not ignored as a mere intruder or killjoy: both of them belong dialectically together in the intellectual history of Europe.

6. SOCIAL ASPECTS OF THE RELIGIOUS MOVEMENT

The fact that many urbanized regions with precocious development of trade and industry (Lombardy, Flanders-Brabant, and the Lower Rhine) became centers of heresy in the twelfth century could lead one to assume these movements originated and developed for economic and social reasons. The political activities of the Pataria or Arnold of Brescia seem to confirm this connection with the communal movement. The promotion of poverty by the heretics sounds like a social protest against the wealthy and the growing economy of money. Since Catholic polemic often described heretics as uneducated, simple people, and Cathars are often called "weavers," their adherents are sought in the lowest social levels and the motives for their opposition to the Church in their oppressed economic position. Marxists saw this to be a confirmation of their materialist conception of history, seeing heresies as class struggles. These perceptions, with many modifications, have been presented by Gioacchino Volpe and Antonino De Stefano, and Friedrich Heer made it his own after his fashion. Austin P. Evans spoke more cautiously of "possible social bases for the growth of heresy," without overlooking religious causes.[51]

If one looks at heresy in the context of the religious movement, the picture changes at once, for this movement did not arise from the cities, nor did it originate in the lower social levels, not even among the laity. It was monks, hermits and canons, often of noble origins, who brought the religious movement to the laity as itinerant preachers, and they did not speak in the first instance to the urban population and not primarily to the lower levels. Towns, to which Cluniac monks had seemed too attached, were rather avoided in the beginning. Just as the Cistercians placed their monasteries in forest valleys far from people, Norbert said: "I do not wish to linger in towns, but rather in deserted and uncultivated places" (*PL* 156.991). Other itinerant preachers were of the same mind, and they usually founded their houses for their following in isolated woodland areas. They all had highly placed noble patrons, promoters, and founders. To be sure, they were often accused of preaching to the "rude people," the "vulgar mob," but they did not turn primarily to the "scum of the people"[52] rather, contemporaries were surprised at how many noble men, and particularly women, joined them and entered religious houses. On the Lower Rhine, where Norbert converted the powerful, wealthy Count Gottfried von Kappenberg together with his brother and wife, many Premonstratensian foundations remained reserved exclusively to the nobility[53] It has not been adequately investigated how similar the situation was in the case of Cistercians or the smaller orders of Fontevrault, Savigny, etc. Perhaps it was the specific classes which could not gain reception to these orders that turned to the religious movement in other forms. Yet even heretic preachers did not attract only the lower people, who were more likely to resort to lynch-justice against them if the ecclesiastical courts hesitated. On the other hand, heretics often found support in the nobility. Even the *rusticus* Clementius was supported by the count of Soissons before the "people" killed him in 1114, and Tanchelm was probably protected by the count of Flanders, Henry the Monk by the count of Toulouse, to whom Bernard of Clairvaux wrote in alarm because of that protection (*PL* 182.434–36). In Périgord, besides clerics and monks, "nobles abandoning their goods" also followed the heretic Ponnus (*PL* 181.1721). In Toulouse, Bernard found that it was precisely the prominent, wealthy burghers who were infected by heresy; they sabotaged his preaching and only the poor listened to him. It is well known that the Cathar contingent among the nobility and the wealthy, cultivated burghers of Provence remained dangerously strong until the Albigensian crusade. Yet Waldes himself was also a wealthy merchant, as was Francis later; both of them desired to convert the wealthy to voluntary poverty, not to advance the poor economically. It has been proved an error that the French name of "texterants" for the Cathars betrays their origins. Their preachers went to weavers and learned the craft, either as a cover or as a living; they were so called "from their practice of weaving,[54] not from their class and calling, even if many weavers and other craftsmen did rise in the sect hierarchy. It is certainly a misunderstanding to see the itinerant preachers of the twelfth century as the messengers of a social program since they wanted to be *pauperes Christi*. This concept, once reserved for monks and beggars, which the Cistercians sought to take seriously, was carried by the itinerant preachers, together with the ideal of the *vita apostolica*, right out of the cloister and hermitage to the laity, who were exhorted to a pious rejection of the goods and temptations of the world. Just as was the case with Robert of Arbrissel, as with Norbert of Xanten and the Premonstratensians, the Cathars also called themselves *pauperes Christi*, bringing many nobles and wealthy burghers to renounce their goods and possessions without going into a monastery, as Waldes would do after them. Yet there is never anything in the heretic doctrines in favor of the social or economic demands of the lower classes, never a slogan of "class struggle." That "cursed gain" and "ill-gotten goods" were reprehensible was only more bluntly stressed and more seriously accepted by Arnold of Brescia,[54a] Waldes, and the others than by the ecclesiastical ban on usury and interest. Whether a handcraft of one's own was part of a truly Christian life, as the Cistercians believed, or whether the preacher was allowed to "live of the gospel" from the gifts of listeners and believers, neither the heretics nor the orders were in agreement. The Lombard and French Waldensians split over this question, but to them it was not a social but a religious question.

More surprising than the participation of certain social strata is the strong representation of women in both the orders and in the sects. A contemporary remarked with amazement (*MG Scr.* 12.657–59) how many women streamed into the strict order of Prémontré; thousands of maidens and widows, even quite noble and rich, were converted by Norbert. In fact, most of the early Premonstratensian establishments were double houses for men and women. Other orders founded by itinerant preachers, such as the Gilbertines in England, could be predominantly female; in Fontevrault the women led the double houses. The Premonstratensians soon cut off their female branch; resembling the Cistercians in this, who could not continue to fend off the many women's houses coming their way[54b] finally blocking them out altogether. This is the clearest demonstration of how both orders closed themselves against the religious movement which had originally brought them to life. The results were indicated in a letter by Hildegard of Bingen, who proudly reserved her own house for nobility alone. She warned of heretics who would say to the women: "Since you do not have your own doctors, obey us!" (*PL* 197.251). For the sects were all too happy to take the women in. Women traveled the land with their preachers, often preaching themselves. Bernard of Clairvaux was the most offended by this feminine accompaniment (*PL* 183.1091–92), but the heretics cited the words of Paul in 1 Corinthians 9:5, "Do we not have the power to take a sister with us, as other apostles?" Even Arnold of Brescia found that in Rome, where he was all too much regarded as a political agitator, he found a response and support for his ascetic demands particularly among pious women, as the eyewitness John of Salisbury reports.[54c] On his first appearance in Le Mans in 1116, the heretic Henry was accused of marrying his adherents to whores, whom he intended to convert from their lives of vice. Yet it was also Vitalis of Savigny who concerned himself to find *legitima conjugia* for *meretrices*, and Robert of Arbrissel accepted them at Fontevrault, alongside women of the high nobility! This "women's question" arose both from the reforming zeal against the unchastity of priests as well as a growing pressure from women of all social strata for active participation in religious life. The Waldensians, too, won for their cause many women who could reproach a clergy they had once serviced at their carousals.[55] What was to become of such women remained a disturbing problem throughout the twelfth century. Innocent III finally gave the counsel, "It is meritorious to make prostitutes into pious wives" (*PL* 214.102), and the *Reuerinnen*, the Order of Magdalene, sought another solution by taking prostitutes into cloistered communities.[56] The searching, unsteady general piety of women only achieved a high level of creativity in such isolated figures as Hildegard of Bingen or Elizabeth of Schönau. The mendicant orders, with their female branches, would point a new way for women, and even for the orders it was not merely a social undertaking, but a preeminently religious mission.

Despite all, it would be impossible to assert there was no close connection between the religious movement and the economic and social changes of the twelfth century. The growth of prosperity, the appearance of a monetary economy, the increase of an urban population, and the beginnings of industrial enterprises, and also the altered position of women in society did not unleash a "social movement" of aspiring classes in opposition to the ruling strata, or a "class struggle." Yet a religious movement did take hold of persons of all strata who desired to take seriously the demands of the gospels and the apostles, in the midst of an economic upswing. For that reason, many persons pressed into the new orders, which shut themselves off from the world all too soon. No one took up the mission of apostleship to the laity, particularly in the towns, abandoned to an inadequate parish clergy and a much more active class of heretic preachers. Even where pious communities gathered about their own preachers, such as the *Humiliati* in Lombardy, they fell under the same ecclesiastical condemnations as the Waldensians, until Innocent III offered them a way back into the Church. The drive to realize Christianity according to one's own biblical understanding was stimulated in all social strata, particularly in the towns, but neither the new orders nor the clergy could do it justice. The heretics did seek to meet the needs of the times, with all the more perilous success. Only the mendicant orders would master the tasks the twelfth century had left unsolved.

CHAPTER 2

German Mysticism, Beguines, and the Heresy of the "Free Spirit"

At the moment the conflict over poverty became a crisis in the Franciscan Order, culminating in the removal of the entire leadership of the order by John XXII, who condemned as heresy their doctrine of the complete poverty of Christ and the apostles, the crisis over "German Mysticism" broke within the Dominican Order, leading to the trial of Meister Eckhart. Michael of Cesena, the Franciscan minister general, Bonagratia of Bergamo, the procurator of the order, the English provincial minister, William of Ockham, and their like-minded associates were arrested in Avignon in 1323. They all fled to Louis of Bavaria at the time of his expedition to Rome in 1327, afterwards finding asylum and support at Louis' court in Munich for a common struggle against the Avignon papacy. At the same time, the leader of the Cologne Dominican school, the former North German-Saxon provincial master Eckhart of Hochheim, was being admonished for the worrisome effects of his German sermons in 1325. Eckhart was cited for heresy by the archbishop of Cologne in 1326, and after unsuccessful appeal to the curia (which he visited in person), twenty-eight propositions from his writings and sermons were condemned by the pope as heretical or suspect of heresy in 1329. Meister Eckhart died soon after. At a chapter of the order, his student Heinrich Suso was also accused of having saturated the entire country with heresy, and he was stripped of his office as lector in Constance.

There was no direct connection between these two contemporary events. Meister Eckhart, whose strongest accusers were Cologne Minorites, did not stand in a united front with the Franciscans condemned by that same pope. His adherents and other Dominican mystics did not become partisans of Louis of Bavaria, as did the Franciscans, but during the long interdict they remained neutral or pro-papal. Despite that, the fact that these two crises took place at the same time in different places cannot be seen as an accident, but rather as a symptom of the religious situation. In a certain sense German Dominican mysticism parallels the Franciscan struggle over poverty in Italy and Southern France, both tracing their roots far back into the thirteenth century. As various as their religious intentions, forms of expression, and spiritual content might seem, both episodes grew from the religious movement as it came to be institutionalized in the mendicant orders, developing in distinct ways in various orders and lands.

The fact that the question of poverty became a matter of dispute within the Franciscan Order can be explained from the original impulses and ideals of its founder, which his testament assured would never be forgotten. The Dominicans, in contrast, never regarded poverty as a religious end in itself, only as a condition, a means serving effective preaching and heresy-fighting, in the same way as did learning. What is surprising, what requires explanation, is the fact that Franciscan poverty-radicalism only made headway in Romance countries such as Italy, Provence, and Spain, although the order had been established in Germany and England at an early date and had spread dramatically there. Even when the Franciscan leaders deposed by John XXII spent two decades at the court of Louis of Bavaria in Munich working for their ideal, they found little echo or following there. The lands north of the Alps remained remarkably immune to the zeal for poverty of the Spirituals, the Fraticelli, and the Joachites.

In contrast, the speculative mysticism of Eckhart, Suso, Tauler, and other Dominicans grew out of scholastic theology, to which the order had been more inclined than the Franciscans from the beginning. Only in Germany and the Netherlands did a vernacular and popular mysticism develop in which many Franciscans were involved. As early as the thirteenth century, the movement attracted David of Augsburg, companion to the great popular preacher Berthold of Regensburg; in the fourteenth century there was Marquard of Lindau among others, though they certainly remained far behind the Dominicans in importance and influence.[1] In other countries, however, Dominican theology and preaching did not cause a vernacular mysticism to arise; although great Franciscan theologians such as Duns Scotus and Ockham lived for a while in Germany, their doctrine stimulated no religious literature in the vernacular there. The theology of Bonaventure, of which it could be expected, or the spiritualism of Peter John Olivi, also proved inert. The German mystics of the order arose instead primarily from the school of Albertus Magnus and Thomas Aquinas, his student in Cologne, more influenced by Aristotle than by Augustine.

It would be premature to try to explain this remarkable distribution of spiritual and religious movements between the Dominican and Franciscan orders totally in terms of the characters and mentalities of the various countries where they recruited and worked. Why poverty moved Italian, Provençal, and Spanish Franciscans so much more than the German or English cannot be read simply from national variations.

On the other hand, German mystics, particularly Meister Eckhart, have often been excessively celebrated as the prophets of a specifically German or Teutonic piety and worldview since their rediscovery in the nineteenth century. Even from the point of view of critical impartiality, it is impossible to deny they share many "typically German" characteristics with later German thinkers such as Nicholas Cusa, Jakob Böhme, Angelus Silesus. At the same time, they differ in a distinctive way from the Romance-Latin mysticism of Bernard of Clairvaux, the Victorines,[1a] Bonaventure, and others. Yet eighty years ago, Father Heinrich Denifle, O.P.,[2] emphatically demonstrated that these "German Mystics" as Dominicans (or Franciscans) were in the first instance scholastically trained theologians and preachers, who had no "German faith" or philosophy to proclaim, but rather proclaimed Christian doctrine on behalf of their order. He saw the peculiar forms of expression found in their German sermons and tracts to be grounded not in national character and inclination, but rather in the mission imposed on them by their order to care for a large number of women as pastors and preachers. These women were Dominican nuns and beguines, without a knowledge of learned Latin, but especially receptive of and interested in religious information and theological depth. Precisely why it was in Germany that so many women's religious communities joined the Dominicans and developed a mystical literature out of their preaching cannot be derived from any spiritual or psychological character or from the social structure of this country and people, but only from the total course of the religious movement of this time. It is only the joining together of Dominican theology and pastoral care, vernacular preaching, female piety, and the special position of Germany in the religious movement of the thirteenth and fourteenth centuries which created the conditions for the rise of a "German Mysticism."[3]

This complicated phenomenon has usually been treated all too one-sidedly in terms of its theological or literary aspects. Hegelians saw German mystics as forerunners of their own philosophy, Eckhart as the "founding father of German idealism" or the "patriarch of German speculation and Christian philosophy in general." This interpretation of the great mystic as philosopher continued in many forms, to the point where some rediscovered the existentialist philosophy of Heidegger in Meister Eckhart.[4] Since Denifle's discovery of Eckhart's Latin writings,[5] the close connection between mysticism and scholastic theology became continually clearer, with a place in the history of dogma. Yet where Denifle thought he could detect a pantheistic variation of Eckhart from Thomism, later Catholic researchers have sought to demonstrate his complete orthodoxy,[6] and Protestant theologians have stressed the neo-Platonic shading of his mysticism.[7] Suso's relationship to scholastic theology was recently given a thorough investigation, in which also his Latin *Horologium sapientiæ* proved to be a more reliable witness to his orthodoxy than his German writings.[8]

While theological research on mysticism dealt primarily with dogmatic interpretation and evaluation, distinguishing between orthodox and heretical mysticism, Germanists were hard at work trying to gather the scattered tradition of German mystical texts, ordering the remnants to create the most reliable editions possible, evaluating them for the history of language,[9] literature, and intellectual development. Interest was concentrated on the great masters of mysticism as well as on the "authenticity" of sermons or tracts circulating under their names or anonymously. Whatever could not be shown to be by Meister Eckhart,[10] Suso, or Tauler,[11] Rulman Merswin[12] or Jan of Ruysbroeck[13] was separated out and paid relatively little heed. The numerous nuns' books of the fourteenth century, the most expressive witnesses for the mystical life in those houses where mystical doctrine was preached, have been very irregularly published.[14] The most important early work of German mysticism, the "Flowing Light of the Deity" by the beguine Mechthild of Magdeburg (died 1282) is available only in an inadequate edition of 1869. The visions and letters of Mechthild's older Brabant contemporary, Sister Hadewich, have been splendidly edited and commented upon,[15] but it is still largely unknown to researchers on German mysticism.

As justified as a theological, dogmatic distinction between "authentic" and "false," orthodox and heretical mysticism might be, and as useful as it is to distinguish "authentic" mystics' texts from "inauthentic" and anonymous—a historical consideration of mysticism as a religious movement cannot allow itself to narrow its gaze and look only at the great masters and their genuine writings. In their intellectual and literary accomplishment they certainly rose far above the others, not as isolated individual thinkers, but as the most important figures of a mystical piety and way of thinking which had long moved many of their contemporaries. The strong echo they received, but also their own difference from the traditional theology of the schools, can only be understood if one already knows the living religious forces and needs which they satisfied through their teaching and preaching, to which they sought to give expression and form. Despite their incontestable will to ecclesiastical orthodoxy, it is indeed no accident that they came under suspicion of heresy, not simply a matter of malicious libel. By trying to bring the homespun religious movement of their own time into harmony with Church doctrine and scholastic theology, it was not only necessary for them to protect the frontier between ecclesiastically recognized mysticism and heretical "pseudomysticism," they had to draw the frontier itself. Their doctrine could be heretically misunderstood or misused, because more radical currents of the same movement felt themselves confirmed and encouraged by it. Meister Eckhart had to guard himself against the dubious, and for him fatal, following of beguines and beghards who broke through all the restraints of Christian doctrine and morals as the "Brothers and Sisters of the Free Spirit," in their reverie of the sinlessness and deification of the "passive person." In his "Little Book of Truth," Suso warned pressingly against a "false freedom" which appeared as a "nameless wild-man," conjuring Meister Eckhart as the "high master eliminating all difference" between God and people, grace and nature, good and evil. As decisively as Suso defended himself and his master against this heresy, he was still repeatedly suspected of it. Ruysbroeck and his group, despite all similarities, remained distrustful of Eckhart's dangerous influences, but Gerson would place even Ruysbroeck's orthodoxy in doubt.[16] "Genuine" mysticism was obviously not as easy to distinguish from the heresy of the "free spirit" as modern theologians believe, for both of them arose from the same religious movement and had too much in common not to be confused and combined by many contemporaries. They are easier to distinguish after the fact, but it is harder to distinguish them historically in terms of their origins and effects, connections and oppositions. Even the significance of orthodox mysticism and its great masters for their time can only become palpable through their "shadow side" of heretical peril and degeneracy.

Just how hard it was to find the line between orthodox and heretical mystics is shown by the fate of the decrees of the Council of Vienne (1311)[17] excommunicating and banning all beguines and beghards in Germany for falling prey to the *spiritus libertatis*, the delusion of sinless perfection. The beghards and beguines were accused of spreading errors on the Trinity, the nature of God, and the sacraments. John XXII, who published these decrees in 1317, had to modify them the very next year so that pious and honorably living beguines were not affected by them. It was soon shown to be an error to call all beguines heretics. Anxiety over suspicion and condemnation had already forced several beguinages to establish genuine ties with the mendicant orders, especially the Dominicans, who in turn attracted the suspicion of many overzealous contemporaries, as if they had promoted the heretical tendencies of these groups, even to the extent of sparing and protecting them. This delusion disturbed spirits for decades. As early as the thirteenth century, several German provincial synods issued similar decrees against the beguines. William of St. Amour polemicized against them in Paris as much as he ever did against the mendicants,[18] and beguines were repeatedly warned against the dubious practices of vernacular debating and pursuing speculative theological and religious questions in a self-willed manner. Even the name "beguine" arose around 1200 as a rebuke which was supposed to mark them as heretics.[19] The fact that both the Cathar Albigensians and the Parisian Amalricans were called on occasion by the same name, which was domesticated in Flanders, Brabant, and elsewhere to describe *mulieres religiosæ*, shows how hard the various streams of the religious movement were for many contemporaries to distinguish. The Augustinian canon James of Vitry, later bishop of Acre and cardinal (died 1240), energetically supported these early beguines as pastor and preacher, in order to defend them from suspicions of heresy. He wrote the life of the "new saint" he befriended, Maria of Oignies (died 1213), expressly as a counter-image to the heresy of Southern France. On the other hand he himself thought the *Humiliati* of Lombardy, and the first Franciscans of Umbria which he saw on his journey to Rome in 1216, were related in their hearts to the pious women of the Netherlands, Germany, and Northern France for whom he had won papal permission for communal residence and mutual *exhortatio*. He observed and witnessed most clearly to the fact that, even before any intervention of the mendicant orders, an equivalent piety was drawing innumerable women together into a life of voluntary poverty and chastity. Despite his petition to the curia, no order of their own developed; the Fourth Lateran Council had just forbidden the "invention" of new orders, only permitting rules which had already been approved. Since Premonstratensians closed their ranks to the reception of new women's houses before 1200, and Cistercians in 1220, a greater wave of female piety arose to meet the mendicant orders on their arrival in Germany than they would have aroused otherwise. The mendicant orders struggled against taking over the leadership and pastoral care of so many women's communities. In the course of the thirteenth century, noble relatives managed to get the curia to incorporate more than eighty women's houses into the German Dominican Order (regarded as the more prestigious), more than in all seventeen of the other provinces of the order combined. In the same period, Clarissan houses in Germany (about forty by 1316) remained less numerous than in Italy. Yet this meant that by no means all the women's religious communities in Germany managed to enter these orders. Many continued to be left to themselves as beguines without a single rule or leadership, often loosely associated with the mendicant orders. The English chronicler Matthew Paris estimated there to be about two thousand such beguines in Cologne and environs, in Germany as a whole "a thousand thousands";[20] in Strasbourg alone there were about eighty-five beguinages alongside seven Dominican convents, in Cologne at least 169.[21]

Since the studies of Joseph Greven on the beginnings of the beguines (1912), the earlier concept of the beguines as a charitable institution to care for unmarried women of the lower burgher classes has been disproved; at the most this applies to the beguinages of the later Middle Ages, when the religious movement which created them had long since lost its momentum. According to James of Vitry, the origins of this movement are to be found in those Netherlandish and German women's groups, usually of noble-patrician origins, which had renounced the goods and joys of the world, marriage, and family to lead a religious life in humility, poverty, and chastity, without being organized or received into an order as nuns. When compared to the religious movement of the time in Italy, their piety had shared many characteristics; it was less concerned with external apostolic work than with the inner experience of the love of God and Christ, influenced both by the mysticism of the Victorines and the courtly lyric of love. This piety rose to an intense bridal mysticism of desire which has its most eloquent expression in the works of Beatrix of Nazareth, Sister Hadewich, and the beguine Mechthild of Magdeburg. Many of these women found spiritual advisors, literary helpers, and admiring biographers in the Cistercian or Dominican Orders.[21a] Time and again the suspicion is heard that their pious mystical excesses, without rule or discipline, could estrange them from Christian doctrine and morals, leading them into heresy. Many actually did succumb to this peril.

A thorough exposition of this beguine piety by the Dutch Capuchin Father Alcantara Mens[22] places it in the context of the religious movement of the twelfth and thirteenth century, also ascribing to it a large influence on "German Mysticism," particularly on Meister Eckhart. Mens, however, denies (147ff., 198ff.) that the pantheistic, antinomian "pseudo-mysticism" of the heretical beguines and beghards, the "Brothers and Sisters of the Free Spirit," grew from the same root. He would prefer to derive it from spiritualist and pantheistic tendencies of the Cathars, who came from the East and made an appearance with the Parisian Amalricans in 1210. There is no doubt this is an error: the dualism and the ethical rigorism of all Cathars entails positions diametrically opposed to the pantheistic monism and libertinism of the beghards "of the free spirit," who have as little to do with the Cathars and Bogomils as do the students of Amaury of Bène.[23] A further accusation made against the philosophically trained clerics burned in Paris in 1210, namely that they particularly seduced women to their doctrine through false explications of the Bible, is of greater significance. The description of the women as "papelardes" is surprising, for James of Vitry tells us the pious women mocked as "papelardes" in France were called beguines in Brabant.[23a] It is easy to suppose in this case the piety of beguines was combined with philosophical-theological speculations which seduced them into an enthusiastic delusion of religious perfection in divine freedom from all earthly and human commitments. Similar ideas appear perennially when the mystical piety of women and the laity were combined with neo-Platonic and spiritualist musings about God and mankind. Much the Amalricans said in Paris in 1210 can be found again in Albertus Magnus' evaluation of the heresy *de novo spiritu*, being spread by two *viri religiosi* in the Swabian Ries near Nördlingen around 1270–73,[23b] in the condemnation of German beghards and beguines by the Council of Vienne in 1311, and by the bishop of Strasbourg in 1317. The propositions of Meister Eckhart condemned in 1329 could be understood, or misunderstood, in a similar way. His doctrine of the "passive" or "isolated" person, a "pure nothing" like all creatures, who for God's sake "abandons" the virtues and all good works, sounds hardly any different from a citation of a theological evaluation from the book of the Hennegau beguine Margarete Porete, burned in Paris in 1310 for saying, "The annihilated soul gives license to virtues; . . . such a soul cares neither for the consolations of God nor His gifts, since it is totally upon God." It appears this attitude was shared by the heretical woman Ruysbroeck rejected, Bloemardinne of Brussels. If Meister Eckhart were only known to us from the polemics of his opponents or from the bull of condemnation, as is the case with most of the heretics "of the free spirit," it would be hard to distinguish him from them.

From such agreements, as well as many similar sources, it should not be concluded that there was an organized "heresy of the free spirit" continually spreading a particular doctrinal tradition from the start of the thirteenth to the middle of the fourteenth century. Without any relationship to one another, without the efforts of a heretical sect, it is obvious the mystical drive to complete unification with God repeatedly drove exuberant spirits into the temptation and peril of defying all dogmatic and moral barriers, dissolving themselves completely in the divine unity of all. Philosophical monism and pantheism from ancient tradition, which became known again in the thirteenth century, could have strengthened, confirmed, or confused this religious drive; all-too-human obsessions for loving union, not just with God, could misuse and distort it. Yet the oft-scorned immorality of the "Brothers and Sisters of the Free Spirit" cannot unmask their religious enthusiasm—for which they went into the flames—as a mere pretext which they hardly would have needed. It is not what they did but what they believed and thought which made them heretics, despite their spiritual and psychic connections to mystics within the Church. Radical followers demonstrated the extremes to which mystics could lead, dissolving all norms and discipline, and how narrow was the line between orthodoxy and heresy on which they balanced.

The history of this heresy of the "free spirit" has still not been placed in its context, despite many useful preliminary studies. "The origin of the movement is obscure," declared one person who knows the material well.[24] Alcantara Mens excluded them from his treatment of the beguines, and they were maligned by the scholars of mysticism as "pseudo-mysticism"; the heresy of the free spirit is still the most painful gap in our knowledge of religious movements and heresies of the Middle Ages. Since the dualism of the Cathars has been completely researched, the opposite extreme of monistic pantheism should be as thoroughly and openly investigated, without theological or moral qualms, and compared with the Franciscan spiritualism of the day. This phenomenon is harder to grasp, since it was not organized in a sect or order, but rather haunted the mystical movement of the beguines, endangering it. It is not to be explained by alien influences or social causes,[25] nor from simple moral depravity or lay misunderstanding and abuse of philosophical and theological speculations. All of these factors might have contributed, but they are only symptoms of a crisis in Christian life and thought wherein traditions were no longer accepted as such. Instead, all possibilities contained within the tradition were being exploited to the extreme, ostensibly to find new paths to higher religious perfection—all the way to the ultimate goal of the deification of the individual. It is only when these pathways and traps have been precisely entered into the chart of medieval spiritual history that we will be able to measure correctly what ecclesiastical scholasticism and mysticism—the Inquisition, for that matter—had to do to overcome this crisis. It will still be necessary to ask whether spiritual and psychic impulses or potentials emerge which only came to full development later. The heresy of the "free spirit" continues to appear occasionally even after new persecutions of beguines and beghards under Charles IV, in Bern in 1375, in Eichstätt in 1381, in Valenciennes around 1400, among the *homines intelligentiæ* of Brussels in 1410, in Constance in 1434, in Mainz in 1458, etc., perhaps even among many "Picards" and "Adamites" in the Hussite era. Sectarian connections between them have not been found, nor any influence on subsequent sects of the Reformation period. Whether the ideas and tendencies of those heretics lived on in other forms, or whether they dissolved into later intellectual history without a trace, will only emerge from the thorough study which remains a task for future research.

NOTES

Introduction to the Translation

1. The other four translations, in chronological order, are: Ernst Kantorowicz, *Frederick the Second, 1194–1250*, trans. E. O. Lorimer (London, 1931); Gerd Tellenbach, *Church, State and Christian Society at the Time of the Investiture Contest*, trans. R. F. Bennett (Oxford, 1940); Carl Erdmann, *The Origin of the Idea of Crusade*, trans. M. W. Baldwin and W. Goffart (Princeton, 1977); Otto Brunner, *Land and Lordship: Structures of Governance in Medieval Austria*, trans. H. Kaminsky and J. v. H. Melton (Philadelphia, 1992).

2. The following sketch depends heavily on Arno Borst, "Herbert Grundmann (1902–1970)," *Deutsches Archiv für Erforschung des Mittelalters* 26 (1970), 327–53, reprinted in Herbert Grundmann, *Ausgewählte Aufsätze, 1: Religiöse Bewegungen*, Schriften der Monumenta Germaniae Historica 25,1 (Stuttgart, 1976), 1–25. (Borst was Grundmann's academic assistant in Münster from 1952 to 1957.) Where not otherwise indicated my biographical information derives from this account.

3. A bibliography of Grundmann's writings by Hilda Lietzmann is attached to the Borst biography: *Deutsches Archiv* 26 (1970), 354–65; repr. *Ausgewählte Aufsätze*, 26–37. Henceforth I will cite writings by Grundmann by their "Lietzmann number." The dissertation on Joachim is Lietzmann #1. Testimony to the enduring value of Grundmann's dissertation on Joachim of Fiore are the facts that it was reissued in 1966 (Lietzmann #77) and then translated into Italian more than sixty years after its initial appearance: *Studi su Gioacchino da Fiore* (Genoa, 1989). A recent appreciation is A. Patschovsky, "Studi su Gioacchino da Fiore di Herbert Grundmann," *Florensia* 3–4 (1989–90), 113–19.

4. I saw several such transcriptions among Grundmann's papers in 1973. (I remain grateful to Frau Anneliese Grundmann for allowing me access to her husband's papers at that time.)

5. The six articles are Lietzmann #2–7. Articles #4–7 could have been published as a unit as "Studies in Late Medieval Prophecy." (Of these, #5 and #7 are exhaustive path-finding short monographs, respectively on the medieval pope prophecies and the Pseudo-Joachite *Liber de Flore*.) Grundmann's first article, "Der Typus des Ketzers in mittelalterlicher Anschauung" (Lietzmann #2), has been one of his most enduringly influential. For its influence until the present day, see Peter Biller, "Les Vaudois dans les territoires de langue allemande," *Heresis* 13–14 (1989), 209.

6. On the "Bekenntnis der Professoren an den deutschen Universitäten und Hochschulen zu Adolf Hitler und dem nationalsozialistischen Staat," signed (among many others) by "Dr. Herbert Grundmann," see Klaus Schreiner,

"Wissenschaft von der Geschichte des Mittelalters nach 1945," in *Deutsche Geschichtswissenschaft nach dem Zweiten Weltkrieg (1945–1965)*, ed. E. Schulin and E. Müller-Luckner (Munich, 1989), 145, and Jürgen Miethke, "Die Mediävistik in Heidelberg seit 1933," in *Geschichte in Heidelberg*, ed. J. Miethke (Berlin, 1992), 100.

7. "Dante und Meister Eckhart," *Deutsches Dante-Jahrbuch* 18 (1936), 183–84, reprinted in Grundmann, *Ausgewählte Aufsätze, 1* (as n. 2, above), 308–309: "Sicherlich schiesst man heute manchmal weit über das Ziel hinaus, wenn man in Eckharts Denken gar zu handgreiflich nach den Spuren eines arteigenen deutschen oder gar eines vor-christlich-germanischen Glaubens sucht, die nun einmal in seinem christlich-katholischen Bewusstsein nicht zu finden sind." Grundmann continues by saying that Eckhart nevertheless had something special to say to the Germans of his day as proven by the fact that his work did not circulate beyond German territories.

8. *NS-Monatshefte*, Jahrgang 8, Heft 87 (1937), 395, cited by Borst, 334: "Sind eigentlich derartige Erzeugnisse einer nun einmal wirklich der Substanz nach reaktionären Wissenschaft . . . noch immer Empfehlungen für Berufungen oder Beförderungen?" Borst observes tellingly that Grundmann's rigorously scholarly standpoint seemed political in an environment where ideology was dominant. In fact neither Seeberg's book, nor Grundmann's review had any discernible political content; indeed Grundmann's review concluded by taking for granted the goal of looking in Eckhart's work for what was "unique and German" (das Eigene und das Deutsche): see *Historische Zeitschrift* 152 (1935), 572–80.

9. See the autobiographical account in Walter Goetz, *Historiker in meiner Zeit: Gesammelte Aufsätze* (Cologne, 1957), 79.

10. An unpublished letter of 13 June 1937 from Grundmann to Beatrice Hirsch-Reich discusses the plight of the latter's being unable to publish an edition in Germany under her own name because she was Jewish. Grundmann states in this letter that he had no political "connections," but volunteers to see whether his colleague, Hermann Heimpel, who did have "connections," might accomplish something in Hirsch-Reich's behalf. (The letter is in the Hirsch-Reich papers in the archive of the Monumenta Germaniae Historica, Munich.) N.b.: Since I wrote this introduction I have learned of very disturbing expressions made by Grundmann in 1940 about medieval Germany's "völkische Kraft," etc. in a survey article on high medieval political history published in the *Neue Propyläen Weltgeschichte*. Still more dismaying is a lecture Grundmann delivered between 1941 and 1944 to "Germanic Führer-candidates" in an "SS-Junkerschule," which includes statements about Germany's "natural *völkisch* und political superiority" and its heroic role in preserving eastern lands from "Russian-Asian" domination. The lecture was published in 1944 in a volume entitled *Germanische Gemeinsamkeit*, but does not appear in the "official bibliography" (as n. 3, above). The source of this new information is Karen Schönwälder, *Historiker und Politik: Geschichtswissenschaft im Nationalsozialismus* (Frankfurt, 1992), 226–28, 247–48.

11. Details about Grundmann's military career not provided by Borst were conveyed to me verbally by his son, Thomas Grundmann.

12. Lietzmann #25, 40, 42, 50.

13. Lietzmann #24, 43

14. Respectively, Lietzmann #49 and #35.

15. Lietzmann #66.

16. Respectively, Lietzmann #58, 68, 78, 74. The first of Grundmann's two biographical articles on Joachim has been called by Bernard McGinn, "the basis for all subsequent investigations of the abbot's career"; see McGinn, *The Calabrian Abbot: Joachim of Fiore in the History of Western Thought* (New York, 1985), 19. The view that Grundmann's piece on Robert of Liège is the best original recent study was expressed to me by America's leading expert on Robert, John Van Engen. Grundmann's methodological article has influenced my own work and that of Alexander Patschovsky; see Patschovsky, "Gli eretici davanti al tribunale: A proposito dei processi-verbali inquisitoriali in Germania e in Boemia nel XIV secolo," in *La parola all'accusato*, ed. J. C. Maire Vigueur and A. Paravicini Bagliani (Palermo, 1991), 252–67.

17. Grundmann, *Ausgewählte Aufsätze,* Schriften der Monumenta Germaniae Historica, 25, 1–3 (Stuttgart, 1976–78). The subtitles of the three volumes reflect Grundmann's breadth: Religious Movements; Joachim of Fiore; Education and Language.

18. My source for this paragraph is Borst (as n. 2, above), 328–29.

19. A brief notice of Brandenburg is in Goetz, *Historiker in meiner Zeit* (as n. 9, above), 376–77. On Brandenburg opposing a chair in sociology in 1923, Jerry Z. Muller, *The Other God That Failed: Hans Freyer and the Deradicalization of German Conservatism* (Princeton, 1987), 138; Brandenburg's massive *Von Bismarck zum Weltkriege*, based on documents of the German Foreign Office, came out in 1924.

20. Most useful on Lamprecht in English is Karl J. Weintraub, *Visions of Culture* (Chicago, 1966), 161–207. See also Luise Schorn-Schütte, *Karl Lamprecht, Kulturgeschichtsschreibung zwischen Wissenschaft und Politik* (Göttingen, 1984).

21. Lamprecht preceded Jacques Le Goff in noticing such details as when urban clocks began to strike the quarter hours: see Weintraub, 200 and Le Goff, *Time, Work, and Culture in the Middle Ages*, trans. A. Goldhammer (Chicago, 1980), 29–52.

22. Lamprecht, *Moderne Geschichtswissenschaft* (Freiburg, 1905), with lectures on "Allgemeine Mechanik seelischer Übergangszeiten" and "Universalgeschichtliche Probleme vom sozialpsychologischen Standpunkte."

23. For Goetz on Lamprecht, see Goetz, *Historiker in meiner Zeit*, 296–312; also 46–47: "die eine grundlegende Anschauung wollte ich nicht verändern: dass nämlich die Erkenntnis der *Gesamtgeschichte* des Menschengeschlechts die wahre Aufgabe des Geschichtsforschers sei und dass die unzerreissbare, wenn auch schwer zu greifende Totalität dieser Geschichte von der Entwicklung des geistigen Lebens her am ehesten einheitlich zu meistern sei."

24. See Grundmann's reminiscences in "Walter Goetz: Zum achtzigsten Geburtstag am 11. November 1947," *Die Sammlung* 2 (1947), 584–89, at 587. A full-length biography of Goetz is Wolf Volker Weigand, *Walter Wilhelm Goetz* (Boppard am Rhein, 1992); this work, however, is concerned almost exclusively with Goetz's political career and is rather superficial in its analysis.

25. "Walter Goetz," *Archiv für Kulturgeschichte* 40 (1958), 271–75, jointly authored with Fritz Wagner; see 273.

26. See Goetz, *Historiker in meiner Zeit*, 303: "so viel Sätze, so viel Irrtümer" (Goetz is attributing this dictum to Lamprecht's critics Johannes Haller and Max Lenz).

27. Ibid., 310: "Wenn ein staatlicher Teil der deutschen Geschichtslehrer Urkunden, Akten und Geschichtsschreiber herausgaben und diese Technik lehrten, so war und ist das eine notwendige Voraussetzung der Geschichte als Wissenschaft—die Schulung in der rein kritischen Forschung und in der Editionstechnik ist die Grundlage aller historischen Ausbildung."

28. The paper (I assume but am not certain that it was written for a seminar) was in the Grundmann papers when I reviewed their contents in 1973; Grundmann thanks Goetz for having brought him to hear Spengler when he was a beginning student. In 1933 Spengler was nominated to be Goetz's successor as director of the Leipzig Institute for Cultural History by a faculty committee that included Goetz; see Muller (as n. 19, above), 238. When Spengler declined, the sociologist Hans Freyer (the author of the epigraph to *Religiöse Bewegungen*) was named in his place.

29. Grundmann's critical stance regarding Lamprecht is evident from his necrology for Goetz (as n. 25), 273.

30. Necrology for Goetz, 272–73: "Immer stand dabei die scharfblickende, unbefangen-nüchterne Sichtung der Überlieferung voran . . . aber sie war ihm nicht das letzte erreichbare Ziel, sie sollte zum Verständnis des geschichtlichen Lebens in allen seinen Beziehungen, Bedingtheiten und Zusammenhängen führen." The same necrology points out that in post–World War II Germany there no longer was a chair anywhere for cultural history. (The building that housed the Lamprecht-Goetz Institute in Leipzig was levelled by bombs, the library destroyed, and the Institute itself discontinued by the East German Communist regime.)

31. *L'eresia nel medio evo* (Florence, 1884). To my knowledge Grundmann, in the appendix to *Religious Movements*, was the first to deny continuity between early eleventh-century western dualists and later Catharism.

32. *Die Soziallehren der christlichen Kirchen und Gruppen* (Tübingen, 1911), translated as *The Social Teaching* [sic] *of the Christian Churches* by O. Wyon (London, 1931). See my "Waldenser, Lollarden und Taboriten: Zum Sektenbegriff bei Weber und Troeltsch," in *Max Webers Sicht des okzidentalen Christentums*, ed. W. Schluchter (Frankfurt, 1988), 326–54.

33. *Die Vorläufer des Neueren Sozialismus: Von Plato bis zu den Wiedertäufern* (Stuttgart, 1895).

34. Volpe's main statement was *Movimenti religiosi e sette ereticali nella società medievale italiana (secoli XI–XIV)* (Florence, 1922); the main section of this book, on "religious movements and sects," first appeared in the form of articles published between 1907 and 1912. See also Luigi Zanoni, *Gli Umiliati nei loro rapporti con l'eresia, industria della lana ed i communi nei secoli XII e XIII* (Milan, 1911), and Antonino De Stefano, *Riformatori ed eretici del medioevo* (Palermo, 1938), reprinting articles first published between 1906 and 1923.

35. The quotation is from De Stefano, *Riformatori*, 381: "trasposizione religiosa di problemi economici e politici." Volpe also voiced his preference for treating his material from the point of view of "istituzioni politiche ed economiche," and "contrasti di classe," see *Movimenti religiosi*, xi.

36. Patschovsky (as n. 3, above), 119: "L'autentico spirito libero che pensa in maniera secolare." Misunderstanding about Grundmann's personal convictions has arisen because of Arno Borst's statement that a private search for the Christian Gospel was the "deepest root" for Grundmann's life's work; see Borst, 328. Nevertheless Professor Patschovsky informs me that his view of Grundmann as completely secular derives from his reading of Grundmann's private correspondence as well as his published work. Moreover, Grundmann's son Thomas (in a conversation with me of 12 August 1992) agrees with Patschovsky about his father's religious stance. Thomas Grundmann informs me as well that his father left the Protestant Church sometime in the 1920s.

37. Here, and throughout this section, my quotations are from the present translation of *Religious Movements*.

38. The observation that *Religious Movements* is "really a series of connected essays" is made by John Van Engen, "The Christian Middle Ages as an Historiographical Problem," *American Historical Review*, 519–52, at 524.

39. *Historische Zeitschrift* 158 (1938), 363–67. The other original German reviews of which I am aware are in *Deutsches Archiv* 1 (1937), 256–57 (short and rather critical), and *Historische Vierteljahrsschrift* 30 (1935), 808–809, which I have not seen.

40. Borst, 333; Borst sees a greater initial appreciation outside Germany than I am unable to observe.

41. See Arnold J. Toynbee, *A Study of History*, vol. 4 (Oxford, 1939), 652–56, an "annex" on "Innocent III's Response to the Challenge of Catharism," drawing exclusively on "an illuminating work from the pen of a modern Western scholar" (viz. Grundmann).

42. A classic article that interrelated directly with Grundmann's views on the twelfth-century religious movement was M.-D. Chenu, "Moines, clercs, laics au carrefour de la vie évangelique (XII s.)," *Revue d'histoire ecclésiastique* 49 (1954), 59–89. (For an English translation of this article, see Chenu, *Nature, Man, and Society in the Twelfth Century*, trans. Jerome Taylor and L. K. Little [Chicago, 1968], 202–38.) In the same year Chenu's article was published the author "came into conflict with ecclesiastical authorities for his participation in the worker-priest movement within French Catholicism"; see Chenu's

necrology in *Speculum* 66 (1991), 722–23. Professor Armando Petrucci has recalled to me in conversation that when he was a student in Rome in the 1950s a latter-day "*ecclesia spiritualis*" was represented there by Raffaello Morghen, Arsenio Frugoni, and Raoul Manselli, all of whom were working on subjects close to Grundmann's and very sympathetic to Grundmann's approach.

43. *Movimenti religiosi nel medioevo*, trans. L. Ausserhofer and L. Nicolet Santini, with an introduction by Raoul Manselli (Bologna, 1974).

44. Van Engen, "The Christian Middle Ages" (as n. 38, above), 523. See also John B. Freed, *The Friars and German Society in the Thirteenth Century* (Cambridge, Mass., 1977), 13, who states that "Grundmann's examination of the connections between the successive religious waves in the twelfth and thirteenth centuries has formed the basic analytical framework of most subsequent studies of the religious life of the high Middle Ages."

45. Malcolm Lambert, *Medieval Heresy: Popular Movements from Bogomil to Hus*, 2nd. ed. (Oxford, 1992), xiv. Specific studies of heresy that are endebted to guidelines set down by Grundmann are Arno Borst, *Die Katharer* (Stuttgart, 1953); my own *Heresy of the Free Spirit in the Later Middle Ages* (Berkeley, 1972; repr. Notre Dame, 1991); and Alexander Patschovsky, "Strassburger Beginenverfolgungen im 14. Jahrhundert," *Deutsches Archiv* 30 (1974), 56–198.

46. David Flood, "The Grundmann Approach to Early Franciscan History," *Franziskanische Studien* 59 (1977), 311–19, at 311.

47. Ernest W. McDonnell, *The Beguines and Beghards in Medieval Culture* (New Brunswick, N.J., 1954), viii.

48. Caroline Walker Bynum, *Holy Feast and Holy Fast: The Religious Significance of Food to Medieval Women* (Berkeley, 1987), see esp. 17, and 18 where the author refers to Grundmann as the "most distinguished historian" of the religious women's movement. Ursula Peters, *Religiöse Erfahrung als literarisches Faktum: Zur Vorgeschichte und Genese frauenmystischer Texte des 13. und 14. Jahrhunderts* (Tübingen, 1988), 5–6. Grundmann's review of the literature on medieval religious movements that appeared between 1935 and 1955 had no subheading for the women's religious movement because of the paucity of scholarship; times have changed.

49. A review of the Leipzig school's attack on Grundmann is by Peter Segl, "Mittelalterforschung in der Geschichtswissenschaft der DDR," in *Geschichtswissenschaft in der DDR, II: Vor- und Frühgeschichte bis Neueste Geschichte*, ed. Alexander Fischer and G. Heydemann (Berlin, 1990), 138–40; Segl, 139 n. 218, cites Werner's statement: "die Methode des historischen Materialismus als untrüglicher wissenschaftlicher Kompass den Weg weist." My other quotations are from E. Werner and M. Erbstösser, "Sozial-religiöse Bewegungen im Mittelalter," *Wissenschaftliche Zeitschrift der Karl-Marx-Universität Leipzig*, 7 (1957/58) Gesellschafts- und sprachwissenschaftliche Reihe, Heft 3, 267.

50. Cited by Segl, 139.

51. This is the peroration of his review of 1955 of "The Social Aspects of the Religious Movement," translated in the present volume. In a discussion of "heresies and societies" held in France in 1962 Grundmann summed up

his position by stating: "il faut distinguer entre un phénomène social, celui des conditions d'apparition et de l'influence des sectes et l'hérésie, phénomène religieux et intellectuel." See *Hérésies et sociétés dans l'Europe pré-industrielle* (Paris and the Hague, 1968), 218.

52. Criticisms along these lines are reviewed and reformulated by Robert Büchner, "Religiosität, Spiritualismus, Geistige Armut, Bildung: Herbert Grundmanns geistesgeschichtliche Studien," *Innsbrucker Historische Studien* 1 (1978), 239–51, at 241–42. In addition Büchner advances the methodological criticism that the absence of poor families issuing documents of donation does not mean that poor women were absent in beguinages.

53. Alexander Murray, *Reason and Society in the Middle Ages* (Oxford, 1985), 349.

54. See the results of research on twelfth-century Catharism summarized by Lambert, *Medieval Heresy* (as n. 45, above), 125–29; on the Waldensian *Liber antiheresis* that attacked Catharist dualism, Lambert, 74–75.

55. R. I. Moore, *The Origins of European Dissent* (New York, 1977), 264–65.

56. R. I. Moore, *The Formation of a Persecuting Society* (Oxford, 1987).

57. Cf. Van Engen, "The Christian Middle Ages" (as n. 38), 524.

58. Flood, "The Grundmann Approach" (as n. 46). Flood, 313, raises a specific problem that Grundmann was aware of but never answered quite satisfactorily: why it was that the legislation of the Fourth Lateran Council does not reflect any of the policies regarding the apostolic movements that Innocent III had done much to implement until then.

59. Freed, "Urban Development and the 'Cura Monialum' in Thirteenth-Century Germany," *Viator* 3 (1972), 311–27.

60. Peters, as n. 48, above.

61. Heimpel in *Historische Zeitschrift* 158 (1938), 367: "vorwärtseilende Kraft."

Introduction

1. Hans Freyer, "Diltheysches System der Geisteswissenschaft und das Problem Geschichte und Soziologie," *Kultur- und Universalgeschichte. Festschrift für Walter Goetz* (Leipzig; Berlin, 1927), 499.

2. I have recently summarized my research on German Mysticism in "Die geschichtliche Grundlagen der Deutschen Mystik," *DVLG* 12 (1934), 400–29. I hope to deal with German Mysticism and its connections with the heresy of the "Free Spirit" at a later time on the basis of the results obtained from this study.

Chapter 1

1. Carl Mirbt, *Die Publizistik im Zeitalter Gregors VII.* (Leipzig, 1894), 267ff., 447ff.; Gioacchino Volpe, *Movimenti religiosi e sette ereticali nella*

società medievale italiana (secoli XI–XIV) (Florence, 1926), 6ff. [Cf. Ernst Werner, *Pauperes Christi, Studien zu sozial-religiösen Bewegungen im Zeitalter des Reformpapstums* (Leipzig, 1956), which tries to explain the religious movement of this period in terms of social and economic causes; see also the thorough review of the Roman Congress by Ernst Werner and Martin Erbstösser, "Sozial-religiöse Bewegungen im Mittelalter," *Wissenschaftliche Zeitschrift der Karl-Marx-Universität Leipzig, Gesellschafts- und sprachwissenschaftliche Reihe* 7 (1957–58), 257–82. HG/1960.]

2. Hermann Theloe, *Die Ketzerverfolgungen im 11. und 12. Jahrhundert, ein Beitrag zur Geschichte der Entstehung des päpstlichen Ketzerinquisitionsgerichts* (Berlin; Leipzig, 1913), 27ff.; cf. Paul Fredericq, *Corpus documentorum inquisitionis hæreticæ pavitatis Neerlandicæ* (Ghent; The Hague, 1889ff.), 1.10ff. Most telling is the following case: in 1077 the bishop of Cambrai had a heretic burned who had answered all doctrinal questions in an orthodox manner, but who refused to receive communion from the bishop or his clergy, since they *aut symonie aut alicuius avaritie noxa adstricti tenerentur*. Gregory VII empowered the bishop of Paris to place Cambrai under interdict, since an opponent of simony had been burned there as a heretic; see *Chronicon S. Andreae, MG Scr.* 7.540; *Epistolæ Gregorii VII*, 4.20 (ed. Caspar, *MG. Epist. select.* 2.328), Fredericq, *Corpus*, 1.1ff., and 2.1.

2a. Cf. the appendix on heresies in the eleventh century. Heretics in Arras, 1025, certainly stress that their doctrines do not contradict the gospels and the apostolic writings, but they do not mention apostolic life or apostolic preaching. They support themselves by their own labor, and in this they see a religious precept, but they do not know the ideal of voluntary poverty, see Fredericq, *Corpus* 1.4. [Cf. Jean Leclercq, "La crise du monachisme aux XIe et XIIe siècles," *BISI* 70 (1958), 19–41. HG/1960.]

3. Some statements of the Cluniac Rodolphus Glaber on this are telling. To him, piety and wealth are not contradictory, but rather he sees the wealth of a religious house as the just reward for strict piety. On the Cluniacs in general, he says (*Historiæ*, ed. Maurice Prou, Collections de textes pour servir à l'étude et à l'enseignement de l'histoire [Paris, 1886], 67): *Qui quoniam his, quae dei sunt, videlicet justiciæ et pietatis operibus incessanter adheserunt, idcirco bonis omnibus repleri meruerunt*. He praises Abbot William of St. Benigne in Dijon, who introduced the Cluniac reform there and in Normandy, because (p. 66) *ultra cetera divitiis et sanctitate ipsius patrocinio assumpta cernebantur excellere monasteria. Ipse quoque firma testabatur assertione, quia, si huius institutionis tenor quocumque loco a monachis custodiretur, nullam omnino indigentiam cuiusque rei paterentur. Quod etiam evidentissime declaratum est in locis sibi commissis*. When Abbot Maiolus of Cluny was taken by the Saracens and had to pay ransom, Rodolphus Glaber had him say (p. 10), *se in hoc mundo nil proprium possidere nec peculiaris rei se fieri possessorem velle; sua tamen ditioni non negans plures teneri, qui ampliorum fundorum et pecuniarum domini haberentur*, and the monks of Cluny in fact raised a ransom of a thousand pounds of silver.

4. Radolphus Ardens in Poitiers (died after 1101, see *Histoire littéraire de la France; ouvrages commencé par les religieux bénédictines de la Congrégation de Saint Maur, et continué par les membres de l'Institut*, 12 vol. (1733–1763) 9.254ff. and 11, p. xxxi f.) in his *Homilia in dominicam VIII post Trinitatem* (*PL* 155.2011). [Ardens has since been dated to the late twelfth century.]

5. Johannes von Walter, *Die ersten Wanderprediger Frankreichs, Studien zur Geschichte des Mönchtums*, I: *Robert von Abrissel* (Leipzig, 1903), II: *Neue Folge* (Leipzig, 1906). On this see Heinrich Böhmer, *TLZ* 29 (1904), 330ff., and 396.

6. Guibert of Nogent, *De vita sua*, 3, 17, ed. Bourgin (1907); *PL* 156.951–52 = *Recueil des Historiens des Gaules et de la France*, ed. Léopold Delisle (Paris, 1869ff.) 12.265. What Guibert tells us about their doctrines (he includes traditional accounts of ritual sexuality and child murder) was obtained by him from the literature, including Augustine, and not from the heretics themselves.

7. *PL* 183.676ff. On dating, cf. E. Vacandard, "Les origines de l'hérésie albigeoise," *RQH* 55 (new series 11)(1894), 51; Theloe, *Ketzerverfolgungen*, 56.

8. *PL* 181.1720; also *Recueil* 12.550; Edmund Marténe and Ursinus Durand, *Thesaurus novus anecdotorum* (Paris, 1717) 1.453; Jean Mabillon, *Vetera Analecta, sive collectio veterum aliquot operum et opusculorum omnis generis* (Paris, 1723), 483; Bertrand Tissier, *Bibliotheca Patrum Cisterciensium* 6 (Paris, 1664), 136–37. The annals of Margan (ed. Luard, *Rerum Britannicarum medii ævi scriptores* [Public Records Office, The Rolls Series] 36: 1.15) put the contents of the letter at the year 1163, with a few variations. It is usually dated to the period before Bernard's mission against the heretics of Southern France, but on unconvincing grounds. The author is probably the Cistercian abbot of Moris, who was later archbishop of Torres in Sardinia (c. 1178/1180; Pius Bonifacius Gams, *Series episcoporum Ecclesiae catholicae quotquot innotuerunt a beato Petro apostolo*, 2d ed. [Leipzig, 1931], 839). This is the position of Tissier but without any authority. Cf. Carolus de Visch, *Auctuarium ad Bibliothecam Scriptorum ordinis cisterciensis*, ed. Canivez (Bregenz, 1927), 41. [Raoul Manselli, *Studi sulle eresie del secolo XII*, ISISS 5 (1953); idem, "Per la storia dell'eresia del secolo XII," *BISI* 67 (1955), 189–264; Raffaello Morghen, *Medioevo cristiano* (2d ed., Bari, 1958), 204–81: eresia nel medioevo; also Arno Borst, *Die Katharer* (Stuttgart, 1953), 81ff., and "New Contributions," chapter 1, section 2: "New Heresies and Sects." HG/1960.]

9. Cf. M. C. Slotemaker de Bruine, *Het ideaal der navolging van Christus ten tijde van Bernard van Clairvaux* (Wageningen, 1926), 96ff.; afterwards, also, Johannes Lindeboom, *Stiefkindern van het Christendom* (Ghent; The Hague, 1926), 66ff., whose book is without independent value in the parts dealing with the religious phenomena considered here, barely leaving the trail blazed by Gottfried Arnold and developed by Protestant research on heresy in the nineteenth century.

10. Ibid.

11. *Hæretici qui se dicunt apostolicam vitam ducere*; Annals of Margan: *qui vitam se apostolicam ducere moresque imitari mentiebantur*.

12. Ibid.

13. In the place of mass and communion they prescribe the simple celebration of the breaking of bread, hence: *communionem sacram accipere renuebant, missam nihil esse dicebant*. At the end of the Lord's Prayer, they did not recite the *gloria*, but rather the doxology, "For thine is the Kingdom . . ." (cf. J. Haussleiter, *Zur Vorgeschichte des apostololischen Glaubensbekenntnissses* [Munich, 1893], 13). They rejected the veneration of the cross and images, invoking Psalms 113:4 and 134:15, against the "images of the gentiles." That they *centies in die genua flectunt* (Annals of Margan: *septies in die et toties in nocte*) was probably also based on a biblical counsel.

14. This is how to explain the sentence: *Nullus enim tam rusticus est, si se eis conjunxerit, quin infra octo dies quam sapiens sit litteris, ut nec verbis nec exemplis amplius superari possit*.

15. *Sine intermissione praedicabant, nudipedes incedebant*; only in the Annals of Margan are added *cibos datos sobrie accipiebant*, at the same time that they decline alms in money, as the other version says, see n. 11 above. At the close, the Annals of Margan say, *Duodecim fuere magistri, excepto principe eorum, qui Poncius vocabatur*.

16. Since this is intended as an outline rather than a complete survey of the history of heresy, a few citations of the sources will suffice: Bernard of Clairvaux, Sermon 66, *PL* 183.1098: *Jactant se esse successores apostolorum et se apostolicos nominant*; Sermon 65, col. 1091: *Ubi apostolica forma et vita, quam jactatis?* The heretics (*publicani*) who came to England from Flanders in 1160 and were interrogated at a synod in Oxford, declared themselves *Christianos se esse et doctrinam apostolicam venerari* (Fredericq, *Corpus* 2.8). Eckbert of Schönau, Sermon 1, *PL* 195.14 on heresy in the Rhineland about 1160: *Apostolorum vitam agere se dicunt, sed contrarii sunt fidei sancte et sane doctrine, que a sanctis apostolis et ab ipso domino salvatore nobis tradita est*. Also see below at n. 46. As late as the Acts of Carcassonne (c. 1318) it says, *Recepti in sectam bonorum hominum dicebant, quod ipsi tenebant viam et vitam dei et apostolorum* (Ignaz Döllinger, *Beiträge zur Sektengeschichte des Mittelalters* [Munich, 1890] 2.27), as in the *Practica inquisitionis* of Bernard Gui, ed. Guillaume Mollat, Les classiques de l'histoire de France au moyen age (Paris, 1926–27) 1.22–3): . . . *quod ipsi tenent locum apostolorum*.

17. The Council of Lombez, 1165, condemned *eos, qui faciunt se nuncupare boni homines*, Giovanni Dominico Mansi, *Sacrorum conciliorum nova et amplissima collectio* (Venice, 1779–82) 22.159. The *Gesta Henrici II. Angliæ* (*Recueil* 13.173) for 1178 speaks of the *gens perfida, que se bonos homines appellari fecerant in terra Tolosana congregata*. Peter of Vaux-Cernay, *Historia Albigensis*, c. 4, ed. Achille Luchaire, *Bibliothèque de la faculté des lettres* 24 (Paris, 1908), 19: *Heretici enim a fautoribus suis boni homines vocabantur*; ibid., c. 2, p. 19, *quidam inter hereticos dicebantur perfecti sive boni homines*. Stephan of Bourbon, ed. A. Lecoy de la Marche,

Anecdotes historiques, légendes et apologues tirés du recueil inédit d'Étienne de Bourbon (Paris, 1877), 35: The women Dominic converted in Provence said of the heretics: *Illos homines, contra quos predicas, usque modo credidimus et vocavimus bonos homines*. Jean Guiraud, *Cartulaire de Notre-Dame de Prouille, précédé d'une étude sur l'albigéisme languedocien aux XIIe et XIIIe siècles* (Paris, 1907), p. lxxii: *Erant de illis bonis hominibus, qui dicebantur heretici* [!] *et vivebant bene et sancte et jejunebant tribus diebus in septimana et non comedebant carnem*. Cf. the questionnaire of the inquisitors (in Charles Molinier, "Rapport sur une mission exécutée en Italie," *AMSL*, 3rd series, 14 [Paris, 1888], 163): *Queratur primo a quolibet et occulte, si vidit unquam hereticos aut bonos homines*. The term is used extraordinarily often in heresy trials and polemics, see Döllinger, *Beiträge*, 2, index. It is the actual term the heretics used for themselves. Catholic polemic opposed it with the maxim, *Omnis homo peccator et solus deus bonus*, see Charles Molinier, "Un traité inédit du XIIIe siècle contre les hérétiques cathares," *Annales de la faculté des lettres de Bordeaux* 5 (1883), 239; Célestin Douais, *La somme des autorités à l'usage des Prédicateurs mêridionaux au XIIIe siècle (Paris, 1896), 107* (with the conclusion, *Igitur male faciunt Paterini, qui se dicunt bonos homines et sine peccato*). Cf. also Theloe, *Ketzerverfolgungen*, 71; Bernard Gui, *Practica inquisitoris*, ed. Mollat, 1.20, 24. It is all the more remarkable that St. Francis would not address the physician Bonus Johannes of Arezzo by his name, but created another name for him, *nam . . . nolebat aliquem nominare qui nomine vocaretur Bonus, propter reverentiam Domini, qui dixit: Nemo bonus nisi solus deus* (Luke 18:19); see *Legenda antiqua s. Francisci*, ed. Ferdinand-M. Delorme, Éditions de la France Franciscaine 3 (Paris, 1926), 38 n. 65; *Speculum perfectionis ou mémoires de frère Léon*, ed. Paul Sabatier (Manchester, 1928/31), 342 n. 122.

18. Cf. Bernard of Clairvaux, Sermon 65, *PL* 183.1090: *De quonam mihi evangeliorum loco producitis istam exceptionem, qui ne jota quidem, ut falso gloriamini, preteritis?*

19. Cf. Edmond Broeckx, *Le Catharisme* (Hoogstraten, 1916), 132ff. [On Cathar bishops, see Antoine Dondaine, "La hiérarchie cathare en Italie," *AFP* 20 (1950), 278–306; Borst, *Die Katharer*, 231ff. and more uncritically Savino Savini, *Il Catarismo italiano ed i suoi vescovi nei sec. XIII e XIV* (Florence, 1958). HG/1960.]

20. See the appendix "Heresy in the Eleventh Century" below.

21. This is particularly clear in the case of Guibert of Nogent, n. 6 above, and a later account (about 1180) in the chronicle of the Cistercian Rudolf of Coggeshall (*Recueil* 18.92–93), which gives a list of heretical errors and crimes on an occasion which certainly had nothing to do with Manichaeism. Eckbert of Schönau also adds an appendix to his sermons against the Cathars containing excerpts from Augustine's writings against the Manichees, *PL* 195.18 and 98 (see particularly the final section of the sermons). It is also probable that Radolphus Ardens (n. 4 above) did not obtain his views of the doctrines of the "Manichees" in Agen from the heretics themselves, but from literature. Cf. Paul Alphandéry,

"De quelques faits de prophétisme dans les sectes latines antérieures au Joachimisme," *RHR* 52 (1905), 189: "With Catharism, the Catholic clergy equated it all too readily with Manichaeism, so that they fought dualism, which mattered little to most Cathars."

22. This is the case with the heretics described by the monk Heribert in Périgord (see above), as well as in the account of the cleric of Liège to Lucius II in 1145 concerning the heresy spreading from Montwimers, purportedly to the whole of France, see Fredericq, *Corpus* 1.31–32. The heretics of Cologne described by Evervin of Steinfeld (see above) confessed to the moral implications of Manichee dualism, but the speculative foundation was alien to them. They would not consume milk products *et quidquid ex coitu procreatur*—but they have no scriptural authority nor any philosophical reason. They rejected marriage, *sed causam ab eis investigare non potui, vel quia eam fateri non audebant, vel potius quia eam ignorabant*—while Evervin otherwise gives their authority for every other point in their testimony. Bernard of Clairvaux also says nothing about the heretics he knew promoting dualistic doctrines. Hildegard of Bingen, who preached to the clergy of Cologne in 1165 about the failings of pastoral care and the perils of heresy (Letter 48, *PL* 197.249ff.) draws a picture of a looming *populus errans* which will be sent by the devil as punishment for the neglectful clergy, which bears precisely the same form as the description of heresy in another letter. Cf. the 47th letter, to the clergy of Mainz (col. 232), where Hildegard accuses the heretics of denying the *humanitas Christi* and the *sanctitas* of the sacrament of the altar, that they do not follow the command "Be fruitful and multiply," on the advice of the devil, and that they weaken their bodies through fasts *et postea omnem voluntatem incesti desiderii eorum perficiant*—but she says nothing about the *populus errans* following a dualist doctrine. Elizabeth of Schönau even asserted that the Cathars, who *quasi religiosi et innocentes apparent* in the eyes of people, rejected the eucharist and other sacraments, despite the fact that they knew that God created everything! See F. W. E. Roth, *Die Visionen der Hl. Elisabeth von Schönau und die Schriften der Aebte Ekbert und Emedo von Schönau* (Brünn; Vienna, 1884), 76.

23. Eckbert of Schönau obviously derives his knowledge of the dualistic "secret doctrine" of the heretics (*PL* 195.14: *in occultis suis dicunt* . . . though they do not declare dualism *manifestius*) from Augustine alone (Sermon 1, 3/4 is entirely drawn from Augustine's *De haeres*., c. 46), reviewing them quickly as "the familiar doctrine of Mani" (Sermon 6, 8/9, col. 40–41). He is extraordinarily penetrating and informative about the objections Cathars have to the Catholic system of hierarchical ordination (Sermon 10, col. 69ff.) and Catholic moral teaching. The entire second book and a part of the eighth book of *Contra hereticos* by Bishop Hugh of Rouen (died 1164; *PL* 192.1273ff.) is devoted to defending the ecclesiastical hierarchy, and the rest deals particularly with the heretical arguments against the sacraments (baptism, marriage). The heretics described by the cleric of Liége to Lucius II in 1145 (Fredericq, *Corpus* 1.32) taught: *quod neminem spiritum sanctum accipere credunt nisi bonorum*

operum precedentibus meritis, rejecting the sacraments of baptism, communion, and marriage in their Catholic forms, as well as the oath. There is no mention of dualist doctrine. Cf. also Bernard of Clairvaux, Sermon 66, *PL* 183.1100. At the disputation in Lombez (near Albi) in 1165, the heretics placed the question of the legitimacy of evangelical ordination in the center of debate, while their Catholic opponents placed all their stress on the doctrine of the sacraments (baptism, eucharist, marriage, penance), the recognition of the Old Testament, and the allowability of oaths—there is no mention of dualistic doctrine (Mansi, *Sacrorum Conciliorum*, 22.157ff.; *Recueil* 14.431ff.). At the disputation in Montréal in summer, 1206, between Bishop Diego of Osma and the Albigensian leader Arnald Hot, the heretics' *fundamentum disputationis* is: *ecclesiam romanam non esse sanctam neque sponsam Christi . . . eiusque ordinationem non esse sanctam neque bonam nec statutam a domino Jesu Christo;* and secondly: *quod nunquam Christus neque apostoli ordinaverunt aut posuerunt ordinem misse sicut hodie ordinatur* (William of Puy-Laurens, *Cronica*, ed. Beyssier [Paris, 1904], c. 9, p. 128).

24. See H. H. Schaeder, "Urform und Fortbildung des manichaeischen Systems," *Vorträge der Bibliothek Warburg* (1924–25), 114, 132.

25. While Heribert Christian Scheeben, *Der heilige Dominikus* (Freiburg i. B., 1927), has seen the "history of the apostolic idea in the twelfth and thirteenth century" as "an accomplishment worthy of gratitude . . . of greater importance for the history of the Church than, say, the history of the temporal authority of the Papacy" (440), but he completely misunderstands the great role of Catharism (which Scheeben sees as "profoundly heathen [!] and anti-Church," 115) in his study of the history of the apostolic idea. This explains the false thesis which dominates his vision of the origins of the Dominican Order: "Superficially Diego and Dominic appeared to be adversaries of the Albigensians. Actually they were confuting the doctrines of Waldes. Their formulation of the apostolic idea did not respond to Albigensian doctrine, but to the formulations of Waldes" [441]. Since he did not understand the character of the Cathar-Albigensian heresy, he believed that the apostolic preaching and the idea of poverty which had been promoted by the Cathars since the beginning of the twelfth century were actually created by Waldes.

26. On the social foundations of heresy in the eleventh century, see the appendix below.

27. See particularly Friedrich Engel-Janosi, *Soziale Probleme der Renaissance*, (1924), 40–41. [Alcantara Mens, "Innerlijke drijfveeren en herkomst der kettersche bewegingen in de Middeleeuwen, Religieus ofwel sociaal offmerk?" *Miscellanea L. van der Essen* (Brussels; Paris, 1947), 299–313; see also "New Contributions," chapter 1, section 6, "Social Aspects of the Religious Movement." HG/1960.]

28. In this sense *rusticus sermo* was contrasted to Latin, similarly *rusticum carmen* as early as the Carolingian period, see Eligius of Noyon, *Homil.* 6, *PL* 87.612; *MG Scr. Rerum Merov.* 5.193. [On the significance of the concepts "illiteratus" and "idiota" in the Middle Ages, see H. Grundmann, "Litteratus—

illitteratus, Der Wandel einer Bildungsnorm vom Altertum zum Mittelalter,'' *AKG* 40 (1958), 1–65. HG/1960.]

29. This is clearest in the letter of Heribert (see n. 8 above): *In hac seductione quamplures jam non solum nobilies propria relinquentes, sed et clerici, presbyteri, monachi et monachae pervenerunt; nullus enim tam rusticus est, si se eis conjunxerit, quin infra octo dies tam sapiens sit litteris, ut nec verbis nec exemplis amplius superari possit.* Cf. Guibert of Nogent, n. 6 above; the example he gives of ''heretic Latin,'' where ''*Beati eritis*'' is replaced with '*Beati heretici*'' and *heretici = hereditarii Dei*, is certainly his own creation, since no heretic has ever declared himself a heretic, since they all reserved that term for the Roman Church and its clergy. Bernard of Clairvaux, Sermon 65 (*PL* 183.1093): *Vile nempe hoc genus est et rusticanum, ac sine litteris, et prorsus imbelle*, and their erroneous doctrines are *non tam subtilia quam suasibilia, idque dumtaxat mulierculis rusticis et idiotis, et quales utique omnes sunt, quotquot adhuc de secta hac esse expertus sum*; Sermon 66, col. 1094: *Rusticani homines sunt et idiotæ et prorsus contemptibiles.*

30. Probably the most arrogant was Walter Map speaking of the Waldensians, *De nugis curialium*, ed. James (Oxford, 1914), 60.

31. Among the Cluniacs, *idiotæ* or *illiterati* were terms for monks who had not received any scholastic training, unlike the *literati*, usually raised in the cloister; E. Hoffmann, *Das Konverseninstitut des Zisterzierordens*, Dissertation Fribourg, Switzerland, 1905, 13–14.

32. Acts 4:13.

33. Francis, Testament, c. 4: *Et eramus idyote et subditi omnibus*; Thomas of Celano, *Vita prima* [= I. Cel.] *S. Francisici*, ed. a patribus collegii s. Bonaventurae (Quaracchi, 1926–), c. 10, n. 25 on friar Philippus, the sixth disciple of the saint: *Scripturas quoque sacras intelligens et interpretans, cum non didicerit* (cf. John 7:15), *illorum imitator effectus est, quos idiotas et sine litteris fore Judaeorum principes causabantur*. The chronicler Thomas of Spalato also calls Francis a *homo idiota*, contrasting him with the *literati* (*Historia Salonit., MG Scr.* 29.580).

34. Eckbert of Schönau, *Adversus Catharos, sermo* 1, *PL* 193.13: *Hos nostra Germania Catharos, Flandria Piphles, Gallia Texerant ab usu textendi appellant* (this is the first appearance of the term *Cathari*). A Council in Reims in 1157 moved against the *abjectissimi Textores, qui sepe de loco fugiunt ad locum nominaque commutarunt*, and the canon was entered in the statutes with the rubric: *De Piphlis*, see Mansi, *Sacrorum conciliorum* 21.843; cf. Charles Schmidt, *Histoire et doctrine de la secte des Cathares ou Albigeois* (Paris; Geneva, 1849) 2.281.

35. Cf. the letter of Gaufred, the secretary of Bernard of Clairvaux, on his activities against the heretics in Toulouse (*Recueil* 15.599): *Paucos quidem habebat civitas illa, qui heretico faverent; de Textoribus, quos Arrianos ipsi nominant, nonnullos; ex his vero, qui favebant heresi illi, plurimi erant et maximi civitatis illius*. Translated this says that the heretic Henry (of Lausanne) had few adherents in Toulouse; but there were some heretics who are called

Textores by us, but *Arriani* in Provence, in Toulouse, and these heretics had very many adherents, even among the most important residents. This is how Bernard's sermon 65 (*PL* 183.1092) is to be understood: *Clerici et sacerdotes populis ecclesiisque relictis intonsi et barbati apud eos inter Textores et Textrices plerumque inventi sunt.* The name "Arriani" for the heretics in Provence is frequently documented: cf. the citations in Döllinger, Beiträge 1.91, n. 5, as well as the Annals of the Monastery of Anchin (*Recueil* 18.536) on the proceedings of the Council of Arras in 1183 against the heretics: *quidem dicunt eos Manicheos, alii Cataphrygas, nonnulli vero Arianos, Alexander vero papa vocat eos Patarinos.* William of Puy-Laurens, *Chronicon*, ed. Guillaume de Catel (Toulouse, 1623), 119: *Erantque quidam Arriani, quidam Manichaei, quidam etiam Waldenses sive Lugdunenses*; William recalls a childhood memory of a heretic converted in 1170 who was called *Bernardus Ramundi Arrianus* (121). Cf. also Berthold of Regensburg, *Deutsche Predigten*, ed. Franz Pfeiffer and Joseph Strobl (Vienna, 1862–1880) 1.402; 2.70, 186, 216. The name was probably just transferred from the old Arians; see Henry of Clairvaux, letter to Alexander III in 1177 (*Recueil* 15.959) on heresy in Gaul, against which he convokes the *rigor apostolicæ disciplinæ: Revixit et Arrius in partibus occidentis, qui ab orientali judicio in propria persona damnatus, nunc in successoribus suis fines ultimos occupavit.* Döllinger's opinion (Beiträge 1.91) that the "weavers at Toulouse and environs were called Arrians in the local language" and that this was why the heretics were so called, rests on a false interpretation of the letter of Gaufred cited above. Guiraud (*Cartularium*, 1, p. ccxxxi) wants to derive it from the Latin name for the town Castelnaudery, *Castrum novum de Arrio*; cf. Theloe, *Ketzerverfolgungen*, 67; Vacandard, "Les origines de l'hérésie albigeoise," 76.

36. Cf. Karl Müller, *Die Waldenser und ihre einzelnen Gruppen bis zum Ausgang des 14. Jahrhunderts* (Gotha, 1886), 11ff.

37. See n. 34 above, statutes of the Council of Reims in 1157: *Textores, qui sepe de loco fugiunt ad locum.*

38. *PL* 195.13; he also plays on *textrinæ* in col. 19 and 90; he admonishes the heretics: *Age opus consuetudinis tue, fac discurrere panuliam cum trama per medium straminis.* Caesarius of Heisterbach says in his homilies (1225; see Joseph Greven, "Engelbert der Heilige und die Bettelorden," *BZTS* 2 [1925], 387) that Hildegard of Bingen preached in Cologne in 1165/6 against the *pseudoprophetas, id est hæretici*; when she was asked where they were to be found, she answered: "*in speluncis terræ,*" *domos vocans subterraneas, in quibus textores et pellifices operantur.*

39. Lecoy de la Marche, ed., *Anecdotes historiques*, p. 215 § 253: *Quidam sacerdos, perversus ab hereticis . . . recessit cum 40 parrochianis suis apud Mediolanum ad discendam ibi plenius doctrinam hereticorum, qui eciam ibidem abjecto sacerdotio faciebat artificia texencium*; cf. Bernard of Clairvaux, n. 35 above.

40. The Bishop of London, Gilbert Foliot, called upon Bishop Robert of Worcester (1164/79) to take action against *textores . . . vestram nuper ingressi*

dioecesim . . . qui corde conceptas hereses in vulgus spargendo praedicant (*PL* 190.936); that is, wandering preachers who say they are weavers, meaning, non-sedentary weavers in whose circles heresy has been spread. Balderich's chronicle of Arras and Cambrai reports as early as 1077 on the anti-simonists burned in Cambrai (see above, n. 2): *De cuius secta per quedam oppida multi manent usque adhuc, et eius nomine censentur textrini operis lucrum exercentes*; that is probably to be interpreted that his adherents practiced weaving, not that he had weavers for adherents. Cf. J. van Mierlo, "Het Begardisme," *VMKVA* (Ghent, 1930), 287: the Albigensians were called *texterants*, "not that they were weavers, but rather that they became weavers, after the example of St. Paul," and van Mierlo surmises the same about the later beghards, see below.

41. Acts 18:3; cf. 20:34; 1 Corinthians 4:12; 1 Thessalonians 2:9.

42. This is already the case with the heretics of Arras, see below. Evervin of Steinfeld on the heretics of Cologne, see above. Also Bernard's Sermon 65 (*PL* 183.1092): *panem non comedit otiosus, operatur manibus, unde vitam sustentat*. The *Humiliati* later operated in Lombardy in the same way, as did the beguines in Belgium, see below.

43. Cf. Guiraud, *Cartulaire*, 1, p. cclxxiii ff.

44. It is something different, to be sure, when Berthold of Regensburg later makes frequent mention in his sermons that heretics were shoemakers and weavers who could not read. That was intended to make the same impact on the audience as *idiotæ et illiterati*; but apparently it also appears to apply to the actual Waldensians after the mid-thirteenth century.

44a. *PL* 192.1284.

44b. *Chronica regia Colonensis*, ed. Georg Waitz, SRGUS (Hanover, 1880), 122.

44c. *Recueil* 18.536.

44d. Petrus of Vaux-Cernay, *Historia Albigensis*, c. 3, p. 13. On other *milites* among the heretics, c. 6, p. 22; c. 7, p. 23.

44e. William of Puy-Laurens, *Cronica*, c. 8, pp. 127–28.

45. The heretic Tanchelm, at the start of the twelfth century, a layman who first preached in *maritimis locis rudi populo*, winning first the women, then through them the men (see the following note), and whose most intimate adherents included Everwacher, a former priest, and Manasses, a smith (see Fredericq, *Corpus* 1.16ff.), does not belong in this context. Insofar as we can judge him through the highly polemic sources, he was influenced by the apostolic ideal, but he is a strange loner following fantastic ideas. The same is the case with the heretic Eude or Eon de la Stella in the mid-twelfth century, see William of Newbridge, *Recueil* 12.558; Otto of Freising, *Gesta Friderici*, ed. G. Waitz and B. von Simpson (Hanover; Leipsig, 1912) 1.56–57 (*quidam pene laicus; vir rusticanus et illitteratus*).

46. Cf. Hugh of Rouen, *Contra hereticos*, *PL* 192.1289. Bernard of Clairvaux, Sermon 65/6 (*PL* 183.1091ff.) attacked this apostolic argument of the heretics with special fervor; cf. ibid. 1092. Cf. the Council of Reims of 1157 (Mansi, *Sacrorum conciliorum*, 21.843): *Textores, qui sepe de loco fugiunt ad*

locum nominaque commutarunt, "captivas ducunt mulierculas oneratas peccatis" (a citation of 2 Tim. 3:6, hence less a description than a classification, "They are those described by Paul as coming in the last days.") The gloss to the text *"captivas ducunt mulierculas oneratas peccatis"* says: *subdolis et versutis verbis seducunt mulieres et per eas viros earum*—as the Devil seduced Adam through Eve. This formula is often applied to the "description" of the heretics, for example with Tanchelm, see n. 45 above. In 1163, alongside four men *de secta Catarorum*, a *juvencula* was also burned, see *Chronica regia Colonensis*, ed. Waitz, p. 114; Cæsarius of Heisterbach, *Dialogus miraculorum*, ed. Joseph Strange (Cologne; Bonn; Brussels, 1851) 1.298–99.

47. Cf. the careful investigation of Charles Molinier, "L'église et la société cathare," *RH* 94 (1907), 266ff., which only follows the social stratification of heresy from the beginning of the thirteenth century.

48. William of Puy-Laurens, *Cronica*, ed. Beyssier, c. 1, p. 120.

49. In Toulouse: *Ex his, qui favebant heresi illi, plurimi erant et maximi civitatis illius* (see above, n. 35), *Recueil* 15.599.

50. Gervasius, *Dorobernensis monachus, Chronicon de regibus Angliæ, Recueil* 13.140: *heresis . . . non solum vulgus simplex, sed et ecclesie dei sacerdotes et episcopos cum principibus laicis tabe confecit nefanda.*

51. Peter of Vaux-Cernay, *Historia Albigensis*, c. 1, p. 6: *Barones terre provincialis fere omnes hereticorum defensores et receptatores effecti ipsos amabant ardentius et contra deum et ecclesiam defendebant.* Cf. Guiraud, *Cartulaire*, 1, p. ccxxxvi ff., cclx; Guiraud gives lists of adherents of heresy in the cities of Provence, and the whole nobility of the region often appears; see also Molinier, "L'église et la société cathare."

52. See n. 49 above and Sermon 66, col. 1101–02; see also Guiraud, *Cartulaire*, 1, p. cclxi.

53. Cf., for example, Engel-Janosi, *Soziale Probleme der Renaissance*, 40–41.

54. On the contrary, it is surprising how often the "people" take a position hostile to heretics in trials of the twelfth century in violation of law and order, satisfying its passions with lynch justice, whether approved by the episcopal courts or not; see Theloe, *Ketzervervolgungen*, 23–24, 28, 31, 33, 35, 38–39, 43–55, 63; see below.

55. Sermon 66, *PL* 183.1102.

56. Hence Bernard's views of imitating Christ pursues an entirely different path than do the apostolic itinerant preachers, who follow it to Christian poverty; cf. C. M. Slotemaker de Bruine, *Het ideaal der navolging van Christus*, 16ff., especially 66: "Bernard preferred monastic life in keeping with the principles of Benedict to forms of life which sought to follow Christ in detail. He always felt himself a monk." Bernard never speaks of an *imitatio Christi*.

57. Cf. von Walter, *Die ersten Wanderprediger Frankreichs*, I (Leipzig, 1903), and II (Leipzig, 1906); also Heinrich Böhmer, *TLZ* 29.330ff. and 396. Concerning Robert of Arbrissel, there is no express documentation that he had professed the imitation of the *vita apostolica*, but his appearance as a barefoot,

bearded, coarsely clothed itinerant preacher (von Walter, I, 128) betrays this apostolic example, just as does the description of his followers as *pauperes Christi* (*PL* 162.1053; von Walter, I, 125). Bernard of Thiron, who was closely connected with him, was said to have been named in 1101 by Pashal II as no less than *vicarius apostolorum* and was empowered to live from the gifts of those to whom he preached (see below, n. 59). On Vitalis of Savigny, who also came from Robert's circle (von Walter, II, 66ff., 83), Ordericus Vitalis says (*Historia ecclesiastica*, ed. Augusre Le Prévost [Paris, 1838–55], 3.449): *leve jugum Christi per apostolorum vestigia ferre decrevit*. Henry of Lausanne went about in the same apostle's costume as Robert (*Gesta pontificum Cenomannensium, Recueil* 12.547); Bernard of Clairvaux wrote of him (*Recueil* 15.598): *factus gyrovagus et profugus super terram; cumque mendicare cepisset, posuit in sumptu evangelium (nam literatus erat) et venale distrahens verbum dei evangelizabat ut manducaret* (cf. von Walter, II, 133–34). Norbert of Xanten expressly stated it to be his principle in his negotiations with the bishop of Laon in 1119: *secundum saniorem intellectum pure evangelica et apostolica vita præelegi vivere*, and made it a condition of accepting the office of abbot of the canons of St. Martin of Laon that they should take on the *modus evangelicæ institutionis*, becoming *imitatores Christi* and *voluntarii pauperes* (*Vita*, c. 9, *MG Scr.* 12.678). The *Vita* (p. 675–76) describes his *novum genus vitæ* in the following terms: *in terra degere et nil de terra quærere; juxta mandatum evangelii neque peram neque calciamenta neque duas tunicas portabat*, and it has Norbert say: *Nos . . . non nostris meritis, sed sola dei superabundanti gratia imitatores apostolorum effecti sumus*. Anselm of Havelberg (*Dialogus*, I, 10, *PL* 188.1155) has Norbert appear *in apostolicæ vitæ verbo et exemplo informavit*. Even the choice of the Rule of St. Augustine as the basis of his order is determined by the idea that it made it possible for him to remain true to his principle of *vita apostolica* (*Vita*, c. 12), cf. also Abelard's *Sermo de S. Johanne Bapt., PL* 178.605, on Norbert and *coapostolum eius Farsitum* and *Historia calamitatum*, c. 12 (ibid., 164) on the *novi apostoli* Norbert and Barnard. [Cf. R. Niderst, *Robert d'Arbrissel et les origines de l'ordre de Fontevrault* (Rodez, 1952); Ernst Werner, "Zur Frauenfrage und zum Frauenkult im Mittelalter: Robert von Arbrissel und Fontevrault," *FF* 29 (1955), 269–76. On the monk Henry (of Lausanne), see Raoul Manselli, "Il monaco Enrico e la sua eresia," *BISI* 65 (1953), 1–63, and *Studi sulle eresie del secolo XII* (1953), 54ff.; Manselli holds him to be a forerunner of the Waldensians. On Norbert of Xanten, see Charles Dereine, "Les origines de Prémontré," *RHE* 42 (1947), 352–78; D. S. Santa, "La spiritualità di S. Norberto," *AP* 35 (1959), 15–56. HG/1960.]

58. Cf. the *Vita* of Robert by Balderich of Dol, *PL* 162.1050–51. It is not known within which limits this license to preach operated; cf. von Walter, I.

59. Cf. the *Vita* of Gaufridus Grossus, *PL* 172.1403: *Papa . . . ei huiusmodi officium iniunxit scilicet ut populis prædicaret, confessiones acciperet, pœnitentias injungeret, baptizaret, regiones circuiret et omnia quæ publico prædicatori sunt agenda solliciter expleret. At postquam ei vicem apostolatus tradidit, nolens ut apostolorum vicario, quem sine pecunia ad præ-*

dicandum destinabat, victus deficeret, monuit ut ab illis cibum corporis acciperet, quos verbo salutis reficeret. It is doubtful that the *Vita* gives the true content of the commission, see von Walter, II, 4–5; but the citation is still important for its estimation of itinerant preaching.

60. *Gesta pontificum Cenomannensium*, *Recueil* 12.548 (also ibid., 15.281, note e.).

61. Cf. Joseph Grevens, "Die Bekehrung Norberts von Xanten," *Annalen des Historischen Vereins für den Niederrhein* 117 (1930), 151ff.

62. *Vita*, c. 4, *MG Scr*. 12.673.

63. *Vita*, c. 5, p. 674: *liberam prædicandi facultatem obtinuit, quam ei dominus papa litterarum suarum auctoritate firmavit*; cf. Chronicle of Melrose (Mailros), *MG Scr.* 27.434: *1118 dominus Norbertus papam Gelasium adiens officium ab eo prædicationis accepit*; Anselm of Havelberg, *Dialogus*, I, 10, *PL* 177.1150: *propter suam religionem et multas enormitates et schismata, quæ tunc fiebant in occidentali ecclesia, a romano pontifice Gelasio litteras et auctoritatem prædicandi accepit*. According to Rupert of Deutz (*PL* 170.492), Norbert is supposed to have claimed *quod cum auctoritate apostolica undecim suscepisset prædicationis remedio curandos episcopatus*.

64. For Robert of Arbrissel: von Walter, I, 121ff.; especially the letter of Bishop Marbod of Rennes (ibid., 181ff.), which is all the more important for Robert's activities as an itinerant preacher because the hagiographical *Vita* (as in the case with Norbert's *Vita*) passes over this period in silence, for obvious reasons: *In sermonibus, quibus vulgares turbas et imperitos homines docere soles, non tantum præsentium, ut decet, vitia reprehendis, sed absentium quoque ecclesiasticorum non solum ordinum, sed etiam dignitatum crimina, quod non decet, enumeras, carpis, laceras . . . At enim tibi forte conducit, ut cum vulgari opinione ecclesiæ ordo viluerit, tu solus cum tuis habearis in pretio etc*. On Bernard of Thiron, cf. von Walter, II, 53. On Henry (of Lausanne), cf. *Gesta pontificum Cenomann., Recueil* 12.548 and 551; von Walter, II, 130ff. Even before 1118 in Xanten, Norbert offended others with his powerful sermons against the sinful clergy (*Vita*, c. 2, p. 672), influenced by the model of the hermit Liudolf, *qui tam in fratribus suis quam in se cædes et minas sustinuit a pravis sacerdotibus et clericis, quorum vicia reprehendere consueverat*. The hagiographic sources on Norbert's efforts as an itinerant preacher in France are too sparse to give a precise picture.

65. Robert's *Vita* by Balderich, *PL* 162.1051: *sexus utriusque adjuncti sunt ei; . . . mulieres cum hominibus oportebat habitare*. This fact gave the bishops the most grounds for complaint; see particularly Marbod's letter to Robert (von Walter, I, p. 182ff.), similarly Godfrey of Vendôme (ibid.); cf. the letter of Roscelina to Abelard (ibid., 31): *Vidi dominum Robertum feminas a viris suis fugientes viris ipsis reclamantibus recepisse, et episcopo Andegaviensi, ut eas redderet, præcipiente inobedienter usque ad mortem obstinanter tenuisse*. On the female following of Henry (of Lausanne), see *Gesta pontificum Cenomann., Recueil* 12.548 A and 549 C, also 550 A and Bernard's letter, *Recueil* 15.598; just as was the case with Robert, he was accused of having

"seduced" *matronæ*, married women of the higher classes, as well as prostitutes through his sermons, and he was regarded as suspiciously as was Robert. On the following of Norbert of Xanten during his itinerant preaching, we learn nothing from the sparse sources. The peculiar nature of his order permits an assumption that he, too, had great success in preaching to women.

66. Biographers naturally had no interest in having the founding of new orders appear to be concessions by "founders" to the demands of the Church.

67. In the *Vita* of Bernard of Thiron the links between his activity as an itinerant preacher, his negotiations with the curia (see n. 59 above) and his foundations of religious houses are as obscure as is the case with Robert of Arbrissel (cf. von Walter, II, 31ff.). But not long after the negotiations with Paschal II, he withdrew to the island of Chausey as a hermit, and when he returned to action as a preacher, he also founded houses for men and women.

68. The *Vita* says (c. 9, MG Scr. 12.678) that he *renovari postulavit et renovatas accepit* the license to preach originally received from Gelasius in 1118. Herman of Laon, on the other hand, says (*Mirac.* 3, 2, ibid., p. 655): *quia nimis ibidem papa occupatus non ex integro desideriis eorum vel colloquiis satisfacere poterat*. He promised the bishop of Laon, who had accepted him, that he would return to Laon after the end of the council and discuss the matter there. Cf. on this Albert Hauck, *KD* 4 (Leipzig, 1913), 372, n. 9.

69. *Vita*, c. 9, p. 678: *secundum saniorem intellectum pure evangelica et apostolica vita præelegi vivere*. Perhaps in the words *secundum saniorem intellectum* the attempt can be seen to distinguish his ideas of the evangelical and apostolic from the heretical forms of apostolic imitation. The words of Robert of Brittany probably have a similar meaning (1109/1112, ed. Petigny, *BEC* 5/3 [1854], 225): *Sunt quidam adulterantes verbum dei . . . non iudicantes evangelium et decreta et sacros canones*.

70. See Gaufred's letter, *Recueil* 15.599.

71. In 1145 on his missionary journey with Cardinal Alberich, see *Recueil* 15.597ff.; Gaufred always distinguished precisely between Henry and his followers on the one side and the heretics (*arriani, textores*) and their supporters on the other.

72. *Recueil* 14.373, and 15.610; cf. von Walter, II, 132; Theloe, *Ketzerverfolgungen*, 167ff.

73. The question, disputed between von Walter on the one side and Böhmer and Hauck on the other, over whether free itinerant preaching was always issued in the foundation of religious houses and orders, can be resolved by saying that Robert of Arbrissel and his comrades as well as Norbert of Xanten preached even after their foundation of houses, but without their followers. In the necrology of Vitalis of Savigny (ed. Léopold Delisle, *Rouleaux des morts du 9ᵉ au 15ᵉ siècle* [Paris, 1866], 284) it says specifically: *Nec tamen in regimine positus* (after the foundation of the house of Savigny in 1112) *pristinam paupertatem deseruit, predicationi nihilominus incubuit*.

74. Cf. Stephanus Hilpisch, *Die Doppelklöster, Entstehung und Organisation*, Beiträge zur Geschichte des alten Mönchtums und des Benediktinerordens

15 (Münster i. W., 1928), 60; Heinrich Kirchesch, *Die Verfassung und die wirtschaftlichen Verhältnisse des Zisterzienserinnenklosters zu Namedy* (Bonn, 1916), 4–5.

75. The colleagues of Robert of Arbrissel almost all founded not only male houses, but also female houses and double houses; cf. von Walter, I, 108–09, on Radulph of La Fûtaie; 111 on the monk Salomon; 116 on Girald of Salles.

76. Cf. von Walter, I, 144ff.

77. Yet on his conversion in 1173, the Lyons merchant Waldes sent his daughter to the house of Fontrevault; see the *Chronicon universale anonymi Laudunensis*, ed. A. Cartellieri and W. Stechele (Leipzig-Paris, 1909), 21.

78. *Miracula s. Mariæ Laudunensis*, 3, c. 6 (written 1149/50, *MG Scr.* 12.657): *non solum autem virorum, sed etiam feminarum cohortes idem Norbertus ad deum convertere studuit, ita ut hodie in diversis eiusdem ecclesie* (that is, the bishopric of Laon) *locis plus quam mille videamus conversas tanto rigore et silentio deo servire, ut in distinctissimis cœnobiis monacorum vix similem religionem possit aliquis invenire.*

79. Ibid., 2, c. 7, p. 659, comparing Norbert of Xanten with Bernard of Clairvaux. He described the strictness of the enclosure and the harshness of the way of life, continuing: *Et in tanto districtione et vilitate cum silentio sciantur esse reclusæ, miro tamen modo Christi operante virtute cotidie videmus feminas non modo rusticas vel pauperes, sed potius nobilissimas et ditissimas, tam viduas iuvenculas quam etiam puellulas, ita conversionis gratia spretis mundi voluptatibus ad illius institutionis monasteria festinantes et quasi ad mortificandum teneram cardem currentes, ut plus quam decem milia feminarum in eis hodie credamus contineri.*

80. There is nothing about this in the biographical sources, save the reference that the wife of Gottfried von Kappenberg took the veil at the same time, in 1122, probably in one of the three Premonstratensian houses established by Gottfried.

81. Cf. Hugues Lamy, *L'Abbaye de Tongerloo depuis sa fondation jusqu'en 1263* (Louvain-Paris, n.d.), 92ff; A. Erens, AP 5.14–15.

82. See Herman of Laon, n. 79 above; cf. also Lamy, *L'Abbaye de Tongerloo*, 100, on noble women in Tangerloo; a letter of the bishop of Laon in 1141 (in C. L. Hugo, *Annales Ordinis Præmonstratensis*, 1, *Probationes*, p. cccviii) mentions the wife of *dominus Andreas de Baldimento* (Beaudemont), who entered Prémontré. Innocent III directed the order to take care that the sisters belonging to their order *de bonis ecclesiæ vestræ, quorum non modica pars eidem loco* (Prémontré) *per eas noscitur pervenisse, sine cuiusquam contradictione nunc et semper in sustinantione temporalium necessaria consequantur* (J. Le Paige, *Biblioteca Præmonstratensis Ordinis* [Paris, 1633], 427; repeated by Celestine II in 1143 and Eugene II in 1147); in 1154, Hadrian IV wrote: *Sed et hoc intuitu charitatis præcipimus, ut sorores sub tutela vestra congregatæ, a quibus beneficia, quæ præmissa sunt, ex magna parte vobis provenerunt, ab ecclesia vestra congruam sustentationem accipiant* (ibid., 428). Many women

from the higher nobility also entered the houses founded by Robert of Arbrissel, cf. von Walter, I, 156–57.

83. The decision to forbid double houses was made in 1141, see Lamy, *L'Abbaye de Tangerloo*, 96–97; A. Erens, *AP* 5.8. In the statutes composed in the second half of the twelfth century, in Edmund Martène, *De antiquis eccl. ritibus* 3 (Antwerp, 1737), 925.

84. See below chapter 4, nn. 11–15.

85. Bernard of Clairvaux, Sermon 66, *PL* 183, col. 1094: *Omnes ceteræ huiusmodi pestes singulæ singulos magistros homines habuisse noscuntur, a quibus orginem simul duxere et nomen. Quo nomine istos titulove cenebis? Nullo.* Cf. the letter of the Liège clergy to Lucius II in 1145 (Fredericq, *Corpus* 1.32): *hæresis . . . quæ adeo varia et multiplex est, ut sub unius certo vocabulo minime comprehendi posse videatur*. Concerning the names used for heretics in various places, see above; the generic name *hæreticus* became popular later; at the start of the thirteenth century the term *hæretici et Valdenses* became common for both groups of heretics, see Célestin Douais "Les hérétiques du comté de Toulouse dans la première moitiè de XIIIe siècle d'après l'enquète de 1245," *CRCSIC* (Paris, 1891) 5.150–51. Joseph Greven, *Die Anfänge der Beginen, ein Beitrag zur Geschichte der Volksfrömmigkeit und des Ordenswesens im Hochmittelalte* (Münster, 1912), 56, justly saw the lack of a proper name as a "sign of the character of the movement . . . which either completely lacked an organization or had not yet formed solid organizations."

86. Cf. Theloe, *Ketzerverfolgungen*, 107ff.

87. Cf. Bernard of Fontcaude, *Liber contra Waldenses*, c. 2, *PL* 204, col. 803: *Liquide apparet, quod presbyterorum est, non aliorum, discernere qui sint sancti, id est Catholici, et qui profani, id est heretici*.

88. All three methods are found with the heretics captured at Soissons in 1114: after they were "indicted" by the ordeal of water, Bishop Lisiard held them until he could get advice from a synod in Beauvais on how he was to proceed against them. In the meantime, the *fidelis populus, clericalem verens mollitiem*, seized them from prison and burned them outside the town; Guibert of Nogent (*PL* 156.952; *Recueil* 12.265) justifies this with the words: *Quorum ne propagaretur carcinus, justum erga eos zelum habuit dei populus*. Similarly in Cologne in 1145 (see Evervin of Steinfeld, *PL* 183, col. 676ff.) and in Vezelay in 1167 (*Recueil* 12.343ff.). Bishop Roger II of Chalons sought advice from Bishop Wazo of Liège (*MG Scr.* 7.227–28), Bishop Roger of Worcester from the bishop of London (*PL* 190.935–36); cf. also Theloe, *Ketzerverfolgungen*, 15 and 27; on interventions of "the people" in heresy trials, see n. 54 above.

89. On the inactivity of the curia in heresy trials of the eleventh century, see Theloe, *Ketzerverfolgungen*, 22.

90. Mansi, *Sacrorum Conciliorum* 21.226–27, § 3; Fredericq, *Corpus* 1.29.

91. Mansi, *Sacrorum Conciliorum* 21.532.

92. Mansi, *Sacrorum Conciliorum* 21.718 § 18; Fredericq, *Corpus* 1.33.

93. Mansi, *Sacrorum Conciliorum* 21.1159; Fredericq, *Corpus* 1.36.

94. Mansi, *Sacrorum Conciliorum* 21.1177–78, § 4; Fredericq, *Corpus* 1.39. The heretics are not named in the text. In the title they are called *heretici Albigenses*; that would be the earliest appearance of this name of the Albigensians if the title were not possibly a later addition. Here for the first time an economic and social boycott is recommended as an effective means to combat heresy, *ut solatio saltem humanitatis amisso ab errore vie sue resipiscere compellantur*. Further, here is the first reference to the heretics' *conventicula*, which are to be sought out and forbidden.

95. Mansi, *Sacrorum Conciliorum* 21.331ff. § 27; Fredericq, *Corpus* 1.46f.

96. *In Gasconia, Albegesio et partibus Tolosanis et aliis locis . . . hereticorum, quos alii Catharos, alii Patrinos, alii Publicanos, alii aliis nominibus vocant, invaluit damnata perversitas.*

97. Cf. *Histoire générale du Languedoc,* ed. Claude Dèvic and J. Vasséte (Toulouse, 1872–1904), 2d ed., 6.79ff., 217ff., 225; Guiraud, *Cartulaire*, 1, p. ccxcii ff.

98. Three letters are preserved on this: Alexander III to Archbishop Henry of Rheims of 23 December 1162 (answer not preserved); undated King Louis VII to Alexander III, and the pope's answer of 11 January 1163; see Martène and Durand, *Thesaurus novus anecdotorum*, 2.683–84 *Recueil* 15.790; Fredericq, *Corpus* 1.36ff.

99. Letter of Louis VII to Alexander III cited in n. 98: *Per quasdam observationes, quas habent, meliores apparent quam sint.*

100. Ibid.

101. Ibid.

102. According to the anonymous Chronicle of Laon, Waldes was personally in Rome, see n. 108 below. Walter Map, *De nugis* (ed. James, 60), who led the questioning of the Waldensians in Rome himself, speaks only of two *Valdesii, qui sua videbantur in secta precipui* and explained their name *a primate ipsorum Valde dicti*, as if this *primas* were not along with them in Rome.

103. The Chronicle of Laon only states that the archbishop forbade Waldes to beg for his necessities of life in Lyon, and his wife had complained to the archbishop about the ban. Stephan of Bourbon (ed. Lecoy de la Marche, 292) reports, however, that the archbishop had forbidden Waldes and his companions from interpreting the Bible and preaching, and when they did not obey, they were expelled. Whether they turned to the curia on their own, or whether they appealed on the basis of their dispute with the archbishop is not entirely clear. Stephan of Bourbon says: *post expulsi ab illa terra, ad concilium quod fuit Rome ante Lateranense vocati* (which could only mean the Council of 1179). The two oldest and more reliable sources, the Chronicle of Laon and Walter Map, say nothing about an appeal to Rome. According to Map's account, the initiative of the Waldensians is more likely; cf. K. Müller, *Waldenser*, 9. [On the beginnings of the Waldensians, see "New Contributions," Chap. 1, nn. 17–19, as well as L. Verrees, "Le traité de l'abbé Bernard de Fontcaude contre les Vaudois et les Ariens," *AP* 31 (1955), 5–35. All sources of early Waldensian history are in Giovanni Gonnet, *Enchiridion Fontium Valdensium, Recueil*

critique des sources concernant les Vaudois au moyen âge (1179–1532); the first volume (through 1218) appeared in 1958 (Torre Pellice). HG/1960.]

104. One recalls the *nobilies propria relinquentes* who joined the heretics in Périgord, according to the letter of the monk Heribert, as well as the account of Bernard's secretary Gaufred that shortly before Bernard's arrival, one of the richest burghers of Toulouse went over to the heretics along with his wife, see above.

105. *Chronicon Laudunensis*, 20–21 for 1173; Stephan of Bourbon, ed. Lecoy de la Marche, 291.

106. *Chronicon Laudunensis*, 28. The first companions of Waldes were hence not poor people, but voluntary poor who had distributed their goods.

107. Walter Map, *De nugis*, ed. James, 60. Also David of Augsburg (*Tractatus de inquisitione hereticorum*, ed. Preger, 205), who was told of the origins of the Waldensians by converted members of the sect, says: when Waldes and his companions asked the pope for a confirmation of their *forma vivendi* (literally: *omnino vivere secundum evangelii doctrinam et illam ad literam perfecte servare*), they were *adhuc recognoscentes primatum apud ipsum residere apostolice potestatis*.

108. *Chronicon Laudunensis*, 29: *Waldensium amplexatus est papa, approbans votum quod fecerat voluntarie paupertatis*. The other sources do not mention this.

109. Walter Map, *De nugis*, ed. James, 60.

110. *Chronicon Laudunensis*, 29: *Inhibens eidem (Waldesio), ne vel ipse aut socii sui predicacionis officium presumerent nisi rogantibus sacerdotibus*. Walter Map says nothing about the formulation of the ban, though his narrative left no room to expect that the Waldensians had any right to preach. Stephan of Bourbon does not mention the negotiations at the council at all; we do not know any other original sources. Catholic research (especially Gustav Schnürer, *Kirche und Kultur im Mittelalter* (Paderborn, 1924–29) 2.338; idem, *Franz von Assisi* (Munich, 1907), 45; Karl Bihlmeyer, *Kirchengeschichte auf Grund des Lehrbuchs von F. X. von Funk*, 2: *Das Mittelalter*, 8th ed. (Paderborn, 1930), 149; J. Hollnsteiner, "*Sacrum imperium*. Eine Auseinandersetzung mit Alois Dempf," *HJ* 49 [1929], 591) presents the matter as if the Waldensians had been "conceded the right to preach morals under the oversight of the Church" in 1179. "The pope . . . permitted preaching, but only within precise limits. Laymen were not to preach without the request of priests, and they were to restrict themselves to moral preaching. Dogmatic preaching, that is, that which presents the doctrines of the faith, continued to be closed to them. That was a considerable concession. But the compromise with the clergy which Alexander III assumed when he granted the Waldensians the right to preach never was forthcoming. The archbishop of Lyon soon accused Waldes' companions of preaching on doctrines of faith without permission and attacking the institutions of the Church in their manner" (Schnürer). This view cannot be justified from the sources, in which there is never a mention of the distinction between "moral preaching" and "dogmatic preaching." The *Humiliati* were

also forbidden *districte* in 1179, *ne in publico predicare presumerent*, without such a distinction. It was only with their reception back into the Church in 1201 that they were permitted moral preaching, excluding preaching *de articulis fidei et sacramentis ecclesie* (see below). The unequivocal distinction between dogmatic and moral preaching, preaching for repentence or exhortations (cf. Hilarin Felder, *Geschichte der wissenschaftlichen Studien im Franziskanerorden bis um die Mitte des 13. Jahrhunderts* [Freiburg i.B., 1904], 33ff.) emerged only in the course of the conflicts between the Church and the religious movement. If it had been so common and obvious to contemporaries and even to the clergy alone as is often assumed by historians today, then the rulings on the license to preach for the Waldensians, *Humiliati*, Catholic Poor, Franciscans, etc., would not be so unclear, so lacking in simplicity as they are. Only decisions on Church policy developed in confrontation with movements demanding the right to preach created the distinctions in the law of the Church which are used today. For that reason it is not proper to assume these distinctions when explicating the sources. A simple juxtaposition of the papal decisions on the license to preach for the various groups within the poverty movement (such as that in Pierre Mandonnet, "Les Origines de l'Ordo de poenitentia," *CRCSIC*, vol. 5, 196–97) shows clearly that there was still no fixed terminology or unambiguous distinction among the types of preaching, but that it was only created in the decades around 1200 out of the political needs of the Church.

The statement of later witnesses (Moneta Cremonensis, *Adversus catharos et valdenses*, ed. Thomas [Rome, 1743], 402, § 4; statements of Strasbourgeois preachers in Timotheus Wilhelm Röhrich, *Mitteilungen aus der Geschichite evangelischen Kirche des Elsasses* [Paris, 1855] 1.51; cf. K. Müller, *Waldenser*, 10) that Waldes received the *officium prædicationis* from the pope cannot be found in the older sources; there, as well, there is no mention of any restriction to moral preaching.

111. Walter Map, *De nugis*, ed. James, 61.

112. William of St. Amour, *De periculis novissimorum temporum* in M. Bierbaum, *Bettelorden und Weltgeistlichkeit an der Universität Paris, Texte und Untersuchungen zum literarischen Armuts- und Exemtionsstreit des 13. Jahrhunderts*, FS, Beiheft 2 (Münster i. W., 1920), 9, on the *pseudoprædicatores*. Those "elected" are the *episcopi*, the *presbyteri* and the *diaconi*, while the three *gradus* of the *ordo perficiendorum*: monks, laymen and catechumens, *prædicare publice non possunt*; this is irrevocably established by God and *non est veresimile, quod prædictam sacratissimam hierarchiam liceat homini mortali immutare* (p. 13). Neither pope nor bishop can authorize them to preach, save *ubi ad hoc fuerint invitati* (p. 10). *Non est veresimile, quod dominus papa contra doctrinam apostoli Pauli infinitis vel pluribus licentiam concedat prædicandi plebibus alienis, nisi a plebanis fuerint invitati.—Si una persona vel infinitæ personæ habeant potestatem prædicandi ubique non invitati, cum hoc sit potissimum officium episcoporum, iam erunt infiniti episcopi universales, quod est contra jura*. William of St. Amour directs these arguments against the licensing of the mendicants to

preach; he was not successful, since in the meantime Innocent III had altered the very structure of the *sanctissima hierarchia* which had prevented the "admission" of the Waldensians and *Humiliati* in 1179, as Walter Map said. Cf. on this Burkhard Mathis, *Die Privilegien des Franzinskanerordens bis zum Konzil von Vienne* (Paderborn, 1928), 92ff.

113. Cf., for example, Bernard of Clairvaux, Ep. 242, *PL* 182.436–37.

114. Walter Map, *De nugis*, ed. James, 60.

115. Luigi Zanoni, *Gli Umiliati nei loro rapporti con l'eresia, industria della lana ed i communi nei secoli XII e XIII* (Milan, 1911), 39ff. Zanoni's suspicion against the orthodoxy of the *Humiliati* before 1179 is unfounded, in my opinion.

116. *Chronicon . . . Laudunensis*, 29–30.

117. *Chronicon . . . Laudunensis*, 30.

118. Mansi, *Sacrorum Conciliorum* 22.476ff.; Fredericq, *Corpus* 1.53ff.

119. Those are the opening words of the decree. A special edition with several additions was sent to Bishop Peter of Arras on 4 March 1185, see Fredericq, *Corpus* 1.56ff.

120. On the last three names, *Passaginos, Josepinos, Arnaldistas*, see Theloe, *Ketzerverfolgungen*, 125. Many believe that the manner of citing the *Humiliati* and the Waldensians (Poor of Lyon) indicate that the two groups had joined together as early as 1184, cf. Theloe, *Ketzerverfolgungen*, 125; Johann Baptist Pierron, *Die katholischen Armen, ein Beitrag zur Entstehungsgeschichte der Bettelorden mit Berücksichtigung der Humiliaten und der wiedervereinigten Lombarden* (Freiburg i. B., 1911), 14; K. Müller, *Waldenser*, 10–11. I agree, however, with Zanoni, *Umiliati*, 29ff., that this text is not to be read in this manner, as if they were two names for the same thing. Alongside heresies with current proper names, other groups were named with confusing designations, such as the *pauperes*, despite the fact that they did not embody true poverty, and the *Humiliati*, despite the fact that they were not really humble. This does not say that the two shared a common organization. In 1179 that was certainly not the case, and even in 1210 Burchard of Ursberg spoke of the *Humiliati* and the Poor of Lyon as two entirely separate congregations.

CHAPTER 2

1. On the whole I agree with Luigi Zanoni, *Gli Umiliati nei loro rapporti con l'eresia, industria della lana ed i communi nei secoli XII e XIII,* Bibliotheca Historica Italica, 2d series, 2 (Milan, 1911), 74ff. (in opposition to Paul Sabatier, *Vie de S. François* [Paris, 1894], 106–07), and Achille Luchaire, *Innocent III. La croisade des Albigeois* (Paris, 1905), 69ff., in their evaluation of the policies of Innocent III. I also believe I can support their views with important new arguments against the views of Heribert Christian Scheeben as he summarized them: "Innocent III threw no new ideas into his struggle with heresy. To him as well, the preaching of Catholic doctrine and the reform of the clergy

were the sole weapons, together with expropriating the heretics" (*Der heilige Dominikus* [Freiburg i. B., 1927], 28). [Helene Tillmann, *Papst Innocenz III.* (Bonn, 1954); cf. forthcoming Michele Maccarrone, "Riforma e sviluppo della vita monastica e claustrale con Innocenzo III," paper at the Eleventh International Historical Congress in Stockholm, 1960, summarized in its *Communications,* 122–23. HG/1960.]

2. The measures taken by Archbishop Philip of Milan (1196–1206) against the Waldensians, whose "school" was confiscated and destroyed, was probably related to these measures. The episode cannot be precisely dated, since it is only known from later negotiations between Archbishop Ubertus and Durandus of Huesca, the leader of the "Catholic Poor" (see below) for the restoration and return of this school to those Waldensians reconciled to the Church in 1209, see Ep. 12, 17, *PL* 216.29–30; cf. n. 7 and nn. 78–79 below. [On the *Humiliati*, cf. Alcantara Mens, *Oorsprong en betekenis van de nederlandse Begijnen- en Begardenbewegung* (Antwerp, 1947), 45–58; E. Gruber, "Die Humiliaten im alten Tessin," *Zeitschrift für Schweizerische Geschichte* 18 (1938), 268–304; P. Guerrini, "Gli Umiliati a Brescia," *Miscellanea Pio Paschini* 1 (Rome, 1948), 187–214. HG/1960.]

3. Letter of Innocent to the bishop of Verona on 6 December 1199, Ep. 2.228, *PL* 214.788–89; cf. Zanoni, *Umiliati*, 72ff.

4. *PL* 214.789.

5. *PL* 214.788–89: *Licet in agro patris familias evangelici zizania sepe pullulent inter messes, et vineam domini Sabaoth interdum nitatur tinea demoliri, sic tamen prudens agricola vinitorque discretus salubre debet remedium invenire, ne vel triticum evellatur inter zizania vel in dejectione tinee vinea corrumpatur. Similiter etiam, licet ad abolendam hereticam pravitatem invigilare debeat sollicitudo pastoris, sollicite tamen debet attendere, ne vel damnet innoxios vel nocentes absolvat.*

6. See test at chapter 1 above n. 101.

7. That leads me to conclude that Innocent's first decree was addressed to other bishoprics as well; see above.

8. Jacobus de Rondenario (Rondineto) in Como and Lanfrancus from Lodi.

9. Zanoni, *Umiliati*, 89, 92, 341 (Chronicle of Giovanni di Brera of 1421), 350–51 (the Chronicle of Marcus Bossius of 1498, who has the two *Humiliati* going to Rome in 1198).

10. Consisting of Bishop Albert of Vercelli and two Cistercian abbots from houses in Vercelli and Lodi. The Abbot of Lodi died before their mission was completed.

11. Consisting of Petrus Capuanus (St. Marcelii) and Gratianus Pisanus (Saints Cosmas and Damian), as well as the Cistercian Rainer, perhaps the later Cardinal Rainer of Viterbo, cf. Elisabeth von Westenholz, *Kardinal Rainer von Viterbo,* Heidelberger Abhandlungen zur mittleren und neueren Geschichte 34 (Heidelberg, 1912), 168. [On Brother Rainer, who was not identical with the later Cardinal R. of Viterbo and who was also not a Cistercian after 1192 but a hermit on the island of Ponza, see Herbert Grundmann, "Zur Biographie Joachims von

Fiore und Rainers von Ponza," *DA* 16 (1960), 437ff. The intimate trust of Innocent III in this Brother Rainer is indicative of the pope's religious sensibilities. HG/1960.]

12. Zanoni, *Umiliati*, 92, says that Innocent followed a similar procedure with the Trinitarian Order in 1198, cf. Ep. 1.481, *PL* 214.444.

13. For the shared rule for the first and second order of the *Humiliati*, see Zanoni, *Umiliati*, 352ff.

14. Innocent III issued this group a letter of protection on 12 June 1201, addressed to *dilecti filii de Braida, domo nova Mediolanensi, Modœciensi* [= Monza] . . . *aliisque prelatis eiudem ordinis et eorum frantribus et sororibus*. The term *Humiliati* was not used, and the membership in a particular order not mentioned; see Hieronymus Tiraboschi, *Vetera Humiliatorum monumenta* 2 (Milan, 1767), 185ff.

15. Letter of protection dated 16 June 1201, in the form of a "great privilege" with signatures of cardinals, see Tiraboschi, *Vetera Humiliatorum monumenta* 2.139ff. Remarkable is the permission to tonsure new entering members (*laicos litteratos, qui apud eos habitum susciperint regularem*) by the *præpositus* of the congregation; they also received the exemption from interdict, cf. Georg Schreiber, *Kurie und Kloster im 12. Jahrhundert* (Stuttgart, 1910) 1.158–59.

16. Zanoni, *Umiliati*, 33.

17. For example, the canons in Viboldone, near Milan; cf. Zanoni, *Umiliati*, 88; Johann Baptist Pierron, *Die katholischen Armen, ein Beitrag zur Entstehungsgeschichte der Bettelorden mit Berücksichtigung der Humiliaten und der wiedervereinigten Lombarden* (Freiburg i. B., 1911), 17; Tiraboschi, *Vetera Humiliatorum monumenta* 2.117–18, 123.

18. Pierron, *Die katholischen Armen*, 16–17, who relies only on the three bulls of 1201, sees the distinction of three forms of community among the *Humiliati* as the work of Innocent; Zanoni as well, *Umiliati*, 90ff., thinks that it was only Innocent's regulation which divided the first from the second order, since not all the *Humiliati* living in the community could be made clerics. It appears to me that the threefold organization had reality only because sociological reality demanded it. There were three groups among the *Humiliati*: married persons, who lived in their own houses; unmarried lay persons, who lived in communal housing; and clergy. So long as there was no regulation according to the law of the Church, these groupings did not have to be expressed in terms of any organization. If they were to be comprehended under the law of the Church, then the married persons and the individuals living alone could not be "regularized" at all according to existing forms of life, but the lay persons could be seen as monks and the clerics as canons. Hence the formation of the *Humiliati* in three "orders."

19. The Chronicle of Laon says specifically: *Fuerunt tunc cives quidam in civitatibus Lumbardorum, qui in domibus cum familia sua degentes quendam modum religiose vivendi eligentes,* etc., see text above at ch. 1, n. 106. The choniclers of the order in the fifteenth century always spoke of this group of *Humiliati*, the "third order," as the *primum membrum ordinis.*

20. Tiraboschi, *Vetera Humiliatorum monumenta* 2.128: *Cum vestrum nobis fuisset propositum presentatum, illud coram nobis et fratribus nostris perlegi fecimus diligenter et correctis quibusdam illud in favorem vestrum curavimus approbare.* The bull is addressed to the *ministri* of Milan, Monza, Como, Pavia, Brescia, Bergamo, Piacenza, Lodi, Cremona *aliisque ministris eiusdem ordinis [sic] eorumque fratribus et sororibus*. In the case of the bulls for the first and second orders (Tiraboschi, *Vetera Humiliatorum monumenta* 2.136, 140–41) the proposals the *Humiliati* submitted to the curia were described as *proposita*, the draft of a general rule as *unum regulare propositum*, and the fully developed general rule as *institutio regularis* (in keeping with that, the first order was *ordo canonicus secundum deum et institutionem vestram per sedem apostolicam approbatam*).

21. The stipulations on the payment of tithes shows the threefold organization of the *Humiliati* in the clearest form: the canons of the first order received the traditional liberation from the tithe on first fruits: *Sane novalium vestrorum, que propriis manibus aut sumptibus colitis* (cf. Schreiber, *Kurie und Kloster im 12. Jahrhundert,* 1.270ff.), *sive de fructibus hortorum aliarumque possessionum, que sunt infra clausuras ecclesiarum vestrarum, seu de nutrimentis animalium* (cf. Schreiber, *Kurie und Kloster* 1.291) *nullus a vobis decimas exigere vel extorquere presumat, sed vos potius decimas, que a laicis in feudum perpetuum possidentur, ab ipsis cum episcopi diœcesani consensu redimere de concessione nostra presentis privilegii auctoritate possitis, redemptas pacifice possidere.* Members of the second order had to pay tithe on their possessions, but their incomes from the work of their hands, their gardening and cattle-raising are free of tithe (bull of 12 June, Tiraboschi, *Vetera Humiliatorum monumenta* 2.136ff.). Members of the third order, as lay people without a common life, could naturally own no tithes, but rather they were duty-bound to pay all tithes without restriction (*propositum* of 7 June 1201, Tiraboschi, *Vetera Humiliatorum monumenta* 2.131). The justification of this obligation through biblical texts leads one to suspect that the wishes of the *Humiliati* were not fulfilled on this point.

22. *Chronicon universale anonymi Laudunensis*, ed. A. Cartellieri and W. Stechele (Leipzig; Paris, 1909), 29: *juramentis et causis abstinentes*.

23. Tiraboschi, *Vetera Humiliatorum monumenta* 2.129 ff., 137–38, 145–46.

24. Tiraboschi, *Vetera Humiliatorum monumenta* 2.138–39. There is nothing similar in the rule and the bulls for the first and second orders.

25. This interpretation indicates the incorrectness of Scheeben's assertion, 126: "The order of the *Humiliati* created no new forms of order, just as they sought no new goals for their order.

26. In the prefaces of both bulls in Tiraboschi, *Vetera Humiliatorum monumenta* 2.128, 135.

27. Tiraboschi, *Vetera Humiliatorum monumenta* 2.143–44. As was the case with all collegiate churches, individual houses had provosts. The provosts of four particular houses (after the Cistercian model) were set above the others as *prepositi principales or majores;* one of them served in turn every year as the

general leader of all the houses of the order, including the duty of visitation. If one of the four was guilty of an offense, the other three could remove him. The election of a provost was subject to a rather complex procedure: the whole of the house would choose an *arbiter,* he would choose three electors (two clerics and a lay brother), and after a fast of three days by the entire group, they would poll all the "brothers and sisters" and, if there was no unanimity, they would decide which was "the best choice." Naturally, only a cleric could be elected. The four *majores prepositi* had to approve the person elected; the local bishop had to confirm him formally, but could not withhold this confirmation. The person elected served for life or until removed.

28. The four *prepositi majores* in the first order, the four *prelati majores* in the second, and the four *ministri majores* in the third order. The first precise distinction of *prelati, prepositi,* and *ministri* after the three bulls of Innocent III is found only in a bull of Innocent IV of 1246 in Tiraboschi, *Vetera Humiliatorum monumenta* 2.198; cf. Zanoni, *Umiliati,* 132.

29. Bull of Innocent IV, 13 October 1246, Tiraboschi, *Vetera Humiliatorum monumenta* 2.198ff.

30. It took place by means of the so-called *via compromisi*: all the electors (see below) chose three electors, and these elected the prelate directly, two votes deciding against one. If two electors could not agree on a candidate, three new electors were chosen. Nothing is said about approval or confirmation of the person elected. After the election he would be installed as *pater omnium* in an *oratorium* by a priest, with a *Te Deum* and a liturgical mass. Cf. the text of the rule in Zanoni, *Umiliati*, 354–55. The two electoral procedures, the polling of the community by three electors and election by a few electors chosen for the task, were two methods approved for a canonical election by the Lateran Council of 1215.

31. See the rule in Zanoni, *Umiliati*, 354.

32. This interpretation is supported by the fact that this entire passage of the rule is only to be found in the older version, preserved by a bull of Gregory IX of 7 June 1227, but removed in later copies of the rule. After the unity of the three orders was reordered by the election of a *magister generalis totius ordinis Humiliatorum* in 1246 by Innocent IV, it appears that the earlier regulation fell into disuse. Or another interpretation is that the *Humiliati* asked for permission to elect a general for all three orders to preserve unity because the older rule was no longer effective. Zanoni, *Umiliati*, 58 and 131–32, sees the election provision of the rule as a sign of the original unity of the *Humiliati*, but he has no notion what its inclusion in the rule means and whose election it describes, which means that Zanoni also did not see that it could not describe the election of a leader within the particular orders but rather a prelate for the local community of all three orders.

33. Bull for the first order, 16 June 1201, Tiraboschi, *Vetera Humiliatorum monumenta* 2.139. The *propositum* of the third order says nothing of earlier heretical peril, only confessing it to be its duty to protect, strengthen, and secure religious training.

34. On 12 December 1206 Innocent III commissioned the magistrate of Faenza with driving out *Humiliati, Pauperes de Lugduno seu quilibet pravitatis heretice sectatores* (Ep. 9, *PL* 215.1042–43), mentioning *Humiliati* who have not yet been reconciled with the Church. In a bull of 10 March 1206 to the same city, the heretics were described as *qui vocantur Pauperes de Lugduno vel etiam Patarini* (Ep. 9, 18, *PL* 215.819–20). So Innocent was still using *Patarini* and *Humiliati* as equivalent concepts, as had been the case earlier (Zanoni, *Umiliati*, 39ff., 42, 272), and which according to a letter of James of Vitry in 1216 was still being done then by persons of bad will. At the start the *Humiliati* reconciled with the Church did not officially bear the title, had even rejected it (see text at n. 3 above). It is only in 1211 that we find them designated as *Humiliati* in the letter of a papal legate, and in 1214 in a letter of the pope himself, see Tiraboschi, *Vetera Humiliatorum monumenta* 2.155–56. Without knowledge of this source, many scholars assert that a portion of the *Humiliati* separated in 1201 from those who reconciled with the Church, joining with the Waldensians and becoming known as the "Lombard Poor." Cf. Wilhelm Preger, "Beiträge zur Geschichte der Waldensier im Mittelalter," *Abhandlungen der historischen Classe der bayerischen Akademie der Wissenschaften* 13/1 (Munich, 1877), 210ff.; Karl Müller, *Die Waldenser und ihre einzelnen Gruppen bis zum Ausgang des 14. Jahrhunderts* (Gotha, 1886), 58ff.; Pierron, *Die katholischen Armen*, 15, and elsewhere; Antonnio De Stephano, "Le origini dell'ordine degli Umiliati," *Rivista storico-critica delle scienze teologiche* 2 (Rome, 1906), 861–62; Scheeben, *Dominikus*, 117, 126. Even Zanoni (*Umiliati*, 79ff.), who does not identify the *Humiliati* before 1201 with the Italian Waldensians as others do, holds it likely that a portion of the *Humiliati* rejected the new rules and joined the Waldensians. According to the report of Salvus Burce (circa 1235; Ignaz Döllinger, *Beiträge zur Sektengeschichte* 2 [Munich, 1890], 64, 74) the Lombard Poor emerged at the same time (circa 1199) when the *Humiliati* reconciled with the Church, and many of the characteristics which distinguished them from the French Waldensians were shared with the *Humiliati* (manual labor, participation of married persons, etc.). But Salvus Burce specifically says that the Lombard Poor were "in the Roman Church" before joining the Waldensians, which does not apply to the *Humiliati* before 1199. The agreement in characteristics does not prove a connection (no more than the other arguments advanced by Zanoni). If the Lombard Poor were more radical than the French Waldensians in 1218, desiring its own hierarchy to place against the Catholic, refusing to receive the sacraments of the Church, etc., that does not speak for origin among the *Humiliati*.

35. James of Vitry, letter of 1216 in Heinrich Böhmer, *Analekten zur Geschichte des Franciscus von Assisi* (Tübingen, 1930), 65.

36. *Historia orientalis et occidentalis*, 335ff. (cited by Zanoni, *Umiliati*, 259–60).

37. Cf. the sermons of Humbert of Romans, cited by Zanoni, *Umiliati*, 261ff. Burchard von Ursberg, *Chronik*, ed. Oswald Holder-Egger and Bernhard von Simson (Hanover; Leipzig, 1916), 108, has a different judgment of the

Humiliati, but gives a very similar description. Burchard probably gained his knowledge of the *Humiliati* during his visit in Italy in 1210, but obviously from the sort of people James of Vitry described in 1216: a *maliciosis et secularibus hominibus patroni nuncipantur*, who accused them of being heretics long after their papal approbation. Zanoni's assumption (*Umiliati*, 86) that Burchard's description described those who had not been reconciled with the Church in 1201 and had joined the Waldensians (the "Lombard Poor" in Zanoni's estimation) is incapable of being proved and unlikely.

38. In a bull of 13 December 1226, Honorius III had to enforce the use of the rule approved by the papacy because he had heard that some still thought the statutes from the time before the reform were still valid which *non solum in quibusdam predecessoris nostri regule obviabant, sed etiam quiddam minus catholicum sapiebant* (G. Giulini, *Documenti illustrativi della storia della città e campagna di Milano* 7 [1857], 155). But the papal bull says itself that this took place *ex simplicitate potius quam ex fastuose presumptionis malitia*.

39. The importance of the *Humiliati* for the wool industry and municipal administration is thoroughly treated by Zanoni in the second and third part of his book.

40. Stephan of Bourbon, ed. A. Lecoy de la Marche, *Anecdotes historiques*, 202.

41. The most important sources are: the *Liber contra Waldenses* of Bernard of Fontcaude (died 1193; *PL* 204.793–840; *Bibliotheca maxima veterum Patrum*, 24 [Lyon, 1677], 1585ff.; cf. K. Müller, *Waldenser*, 141), based on a disputation between Catholics and Waldensians in the bishopric of Narbonne about 1190, which followed an unsuccessful attempt of Bishop Bernard of Narbonne (1181–1191) to convert the Waldensians. The last chapters of Bernard's book deal not with the Waldensians, but with other heretics (cf. the foreword, *PL* 204.795: *adjectis etiam quibusdamn aliis tractatibus contra alias hereses*); according to the title of the book (in the edition of the *Bibliotheca maxima*) they are *Arriani*. The final chapter deals with the (Cathar) "blasphemy," that God did not create the world and does not direct it. The two chapters before that (10–11) deal with various errors on the fate of the soul after death. It is uncertain whether the ninth chapter, on the errors that alms, fasts, masses, and prayers for the dead are without effect, applies to Waldensians. These errors do not appear to have been a part of the disputations which form the basis of the eight previous chapters. The work *De fide contra hereticos* by Alan of Lille (died 1202) is of equal value, and its second part deals with the Waldensians (*PL* 210.377ff.). Alan lived for a long time in Montpellier, and his book is dedicated to Count William VIII of Montpellier (died 1202). Alan was also at the Lateran Council of 1179: an anecdote describes a disputation between him and a heretic in the presence of the pope, *PL* 210.15; Barthélemy Hauréau, *Mêmoirs de l'Académie des inscriptions et belles lettres* 37 (1886), 5; Maximilianus Manitius, *Geschichte der lateinischen Literatur des Mittelalters* 3 (Munich, 1931), 794–95, 802; the doubts of Charles Schmidt, *Histoire et doctrine de la secte des Cathares ou Albigeois* (Paris; Geneva, 1849) 2.233ff. about

Alan's authorship are incorrect. Also remarkable are the accusations against Bernardus Primus and his companions before 1210, which sought to brand them as Waldensians (in a bull of Innocent III, Ep. 13.94, *PL* 216.292–93) and the assertions of Peter of Vaux-Cernay (*Historia Albigensis*, ed. Luchaire, c. 2, p. 10), who can only list four *errores* of the Waldensians: they wore sandals like the apostles, they held swearing as well as killing to be sinful under all circumstances, and they believed themselves capable of performing the eucharist in necessity without being ordained. The evaluation of Waldensians by Joachim of Fiore, written probably around 1200–1202, is also interesting (*Tract. super IV. Evang.*, ed. E. Buonaiuti [1931], 187): *Non minus timeat homo non secundum preceptum, sed ex proprio arbitrio facere illa opera que videntur esse bona, quam facere etiam pura mala. . . . Hinc arguendi sunt supra hereticos* (that is more than the heretics, the Cathars) *Pauperes de Lugdunensium*; he accuses them particularly (ibid., 151, 319) of *circa hoc exerceant omnem disputationem suam et omnino dicant fideles Christi non debere operari cibum qui perit, sed qui permanet in vitam eternam*—a demand which was continually raised by Joachim himself, but he saw the Waldensians as those *qui habent zelum Dei, sed non secundum scientiam* (p. 318), and that they acted on their own, *ex proprio arbitrio*, not *secundum preceptum*, which is worse than heresy.

42. Bernard of Fontcaude, c. 1, 2 and 6; Alan, c. 2–6; *Confessio fidei* of Bernardus Primus and his companions of 1210, Ep. 4294, *PL* 216.292: *soli deo esse obediendum, et si homini, soli justo, qui deum habet in se*.

43. Bernard, c. 4, 5 and 8 (cf. comments of Alphandéry, "De quelques faits de prophétisme dans les sectes latines antérieures au Joachimisme," 216–17); Alan, c. 1; *Confessio* of Bernardus Primus: *licere laico ac illiterato* [in Migne incorrect: *litterato*] *sine licentia cuiuslibet hominis predicare; mulieribus evangelium in ecclesia licitum esse docere*.

44. Bernard, c. 2; Alan, c. 7–8; *Confessio* of Bernard Primus: *bonum laicum conficienti eucharistiam potestatem habere, malum autem sacerdotem nequaquam; justum laicum confitentes sibi absolvere posse*.

45. Cf. Alan, c. 7; Peter of Vaux-Cernay, *Historia Albigensis*, c. 2, see n. 41 above. As late as 1218 the French Waldensians represented their own position against the Lombard Poor that they received the sacraments, penance, and communion from good Catholic priests, and that they only administered them themselves "in necessity," see the declaration in Preger, "Beiträge zur Geschichte der Waldensier," 237; K. Müller, *Waldenser*, 42ff. The Lombard Poor had only abandoned this position shortly before 1218.

46. Alan, c. 8, col. 385. In opposition, for example, Bernard of Fontcaude, c. 2, col. 800.

47. Cf., for example, Bernard of Fontcaude, c. 2, col. 799.

48. Alan, c. 15–23; *Confessio* of Bernardus Primus: *juramentum in quolibet articulo sub ecclesie forma factum peccatum esse mortale*; Peter of Vaux-Cernay, *Historia Albigensis*, c. 2, see above, n. 41; cf. also Philippe de Grève (in a sermon after 1230, in Charles Homer Haskins, *Studies in Mediaeval Culture* [Oxford, 1929] 250).

49. Alan, c. 12–14; *Confessio* of Bernardus Primus: *orationes aut missas mali sacerdotis viris vel mortuis non proficere.*

50. William of Puy-Laurens, *Chronicon*, Prologue, 119: *Erant quidam Arriani, quidam Manichei, quidam etiam Waldenses sive Lugdunenses. Qui licet inter se essent dissides, omnes tamen in animarum perniciem contra fidem catholicam conspirabant. Et illi quidem Valdenses contra alios acutissime disputabant. Unde et in eorum odium aliquando admittebantur a sacerdotibus ydiotis.* Cf. the statement of a witness to the Inquisition trial in Toulouse, 1245, concerning the period 1215–20 (in Douais, "Les hérétiques," 150): *Valdenses persequebantur dictos hereticos . . . et ecclesia sustinebat tunc dictos Valdenses et erant cum clericis in ipsa ecclesia cantantes et legentes, et credebat (testis) eos esse bonos homines.* Bernardus Primus also preached as a Waldensian before 1210 against the heretics, see below.

51. The letter of Bishop Bertram of Metz is not preserved, but its contents can be inferred from the letter of Innocent to the bishop and chapter of Metz of 12 July 1199 (*PL* 214.698–99) and from the pastoral letter to the city and bishopric of Metz (undated, probably the same date, 695ff.). The documents on this episode are best orchestrated and analyzed by Hermann Suchier, "Zu den altfranzösischen Bibelübersetzungen," *ZRP* 8 (1884), 418ff.; cf. also G. Voigt, "Bischof Bertram von Metz," *Jahrbuch der Gesellschaft für lotharingische Geschichte und Altertumskunde* 5 (1893), 51ff. Also Cæsarius of Heisterbach, *Dialogus miraculorum* 5.20 (ed. Strange, 1.299–300), tells of the *hæresis Valdosiana, ab uno eorum sic dicta*, in Metz under Bishop Bertram, who claimed to recognize two of the itinerant preachers who were *propter hæresis damnati sunt et eiecti* in his presence in Montpellier. In response to the question as to who had empowered and appointed them to preach, they answered: *Spiritus*. The bishop, however, could do nothing against them, *propter quosdam potentes civitatis, qui eos in odium episcopi fovebant.*

52. *PL* 214.699.

53. Its content can only be inferred from Innocent's letter to the three abbots of Cîteaux, Morimond, and La Crîte on 9 December 1199 (*PL* 214.793ff.).

54. This is known from the report of Alberich of Troisfontaines, *MG Scr.* 23.878, who correctly identifies the heretics as Waldensians. Statements of the pope, the bishop, or the three abbots on the matter are not preserved.

55. *PL* 214.698–99; cf. my essay on "Der Typus des Ketzers in mittelalterlicher Anschauung," *Kultur- und Universalgeschichte. Festschrift für Walter Goetz* [Leipzig; Berlin, 1927], 100). The start of the letter to the three Cistercian abbots of 9 December 1199 is similar, *PL* 214.793, where Innocent also demands *discretio*.

56. It has never been documented that Dominic was present at the disputation in Pamiers; it is pure speculation that he "accompanied his bishop at least as far as Pamiers," Scheeben, *Dominikus*, 51, 127; Pierron, *Die katholischen Armen*, 24–25.

57. Peter of Vaux-Cernay, *Historia Albigensis*, c. 6, p. 22, summarizes these missionary efforts: *parum aut nichil predicando sive disputando proficere*

potuerant; also c. 9, p. 30: *eadem predicatio . . . non multum profecit, immo pene penitus fructu frustrata est exoptato*; cf. also William of Puy-Laurens, *Chronica*, c. 10, p. 129.

58. Two accounts: Peter of Vaux-Cernay, *Historia Albigensis*, c. 6, pp. 20–21; William of Puy-Laurens, Chronica, c. 8, p. 127; cf. Pierron, *Die katholischen Armen*, 26; Scheeben, *Dominikus*, 51ff. [Cf. A. Dondaine, "Durand de Huesca et la polémique anti-cathare," *AFP* 29 (1959), 228–76; Ch. Thuozellier, "Le 'Liber antiheresis' de Durand de Huesca et le 'Contra hereticos' d'Ermengaud de Béziers," *RHE* 55 (1960), 130–41. HG/1960.]

59. This is according to the chronology of Scheeben (agreeing with the information of Peter of Vaux-Cernay, *Historia Albigensis*, c. 3, p. 11), who promises to justify it in his new edition of Jordanus. The assignment of these events to 1205 in Pierron, *Die katholischen Armen*, 24f., does not appear convincing.

60. Abbot Arnald of Cîteaux and Peter of Castro Novo and Radulfus, both from Fontfroid.

61. Peter of Vaux-Cernay, *Historia Albigensis*, c. 3, p. 12.

62. Ibid., c. 3, p. 12.

63. For the legates, ibid., c. 3, p. 12. [On the beginnings of Dominic, see Pierre Mandonnet and Marie Humbert Vicaire, *Saint Dominique: l'idée, l'homme et l'oeuvre* (Ghent, 1937), and—over the objections of Heribert Christian Scheeben—"Dominikaner oder Innocenzianer?" *AFP* 9 (1939), 237–97. Marie Humbert Vicaire, *Histoire de Saint Dominique*, 2 vols. (1957); idem, "Fondation, approbation, confirmation de l'ordre des Prêcheurs," *RHE* 47 (1952), 123–41; idem, "Saint Dominique en 1207," *AFP* 23 (1953), 335–45. HG/1960.]

64. Ep. 7.76, *PL* 215.358ff.

65. Achille Luchaire, *Innocent III,* 189–90, suspected a papal commission for the actions of Diego and Dominic in Montpellier, as did Pierre Mandonnet, *Saint Dominique: l'idée, l'homme et l'oeuvre* (Ghent, 1921), 33–34; Jean Guiraud, *Cartulaire*, p. cccvii; Pierron, *Die katholischen Armen*, 24. Scheeben, *Dominikus*, 27 n. 19, 429, violently denounced these assertions, describing them as "empty imaginings" which were only possible "with a more than superficial analysis of the sources and a gift for combination which can only cause trouble." "There is not a trace of a proof for this thesis." Perhaps even Scheeben will regard the letter passages cited in the previous note as such a trace, which escaped him as well as all earlier researchers. There are two arguments against Scheeben's version of these events (pp. 32ff.): 1) Bishop Diego went to Rome to receive permission from Innocent to resign his bishopric and go as a missionary to the Saracens. This permission was refused, and according to Scheeben, the sole result of negotiations between Innocent and Diego was that the pope gave the bishop "the simple command to return to Osma" (as Peter of Vaux-Cernay says: *precipit ei, ut ad sedem propriam remearet*). Instead of obeying this order, Diego is supposed to have made himself the head of the mission to the heretics of Southern France on his own, using methods which

arose from his initiative and without papal approval. Only three-quarters of a year later did it appear to him proper "to recall the binding papal command and begin to think of returning to his diocese" (51; cf. 68). The incoherence of this version of the events is overlooked by Scheeben because he wants to show that Diego "conceived of the idea of the order of preachers" in summer 1206, in Montpellier, "without any traceable influence of Innocent III." 2) Scheeben knows nothing about the political attitude of Innocent to the religious movement and heresy. This is the only way he can portray such a wide gap between the pope and his legates on the one hand and Diego and Dominic on the other, opposing the Cistercian abbot Arnald "as the representative of the political power of his lord," Diego dramatically as the "representative of the apostolic love of the divine savior," repeatedly portraying "the pompous legate of the powerful Pope Innocent" in contrast to the "simple Bishop Diego" (28, 32–33), seeing in this conversation in Montpellier "apostolic freedom toward the representative of the pope." This presentation might satisfy psychological needs, but it does not promote historical understanding.

66. Ep. 6.185, *PL* 215.1024–05. Luchaire, *Innocent III*, 89, sees in this letter "the exact and precise expression of the current of ideas which produced St. Dominic and created the first mendicant order." In opposition to this, Scheeben, *Dominikus*, 431, says that Luchaire "does not correctly present the causal connections." Yet Luchaire asserts no "causal connections" whatsoever. Scheeben, on the other hand, asserts that the letter contained "an approval of Diego's idea without naming the bishop" and presents (68) the letter as an answer to a request for the pope's opinion on the new missionary method. That is not only unprovable, it is false: the letter contains a commission, neither an approval nor an answer. Scheeben reveals the cause of his misapprehension in the sentence immediately following: "Dominic develops his idea independently of Rome," or as he says in another place (441): "In the intellectual struggle with heresy, the curia only took over the leadership once the mendicant orders had already been founded."

67. Scheeben can only suppose "that the stimulus for founding this society [of the 'Catholic Poor' of Durandus] originated with Dominic and Diego," so that he continues to believe the two men were acting on their own without advance papal approval.

68. A letter of Innocent of 12 May 1210 (Ep. 13.78, *PL* 216.274) names six others besides Durandus, and mentions further *socii eorum* who were with him at the curia in winter 1208. That this was only a delegation can be seen from the fact that they negotiated *tam pro se quam pro fratribus suis* (cf. Ep. 11.196, *PL* 215.1510). Then the bishops of Tarragona and Narbonne were commissioned to complete the formalities of taking oaths from the other brethren, Ep. 13.78, *PL* 216.274–75.

69. As early as his letter to the bishop of Verona on 6 December 1199 (Ep. 2.228, *PL* 214.74, n. 4), Innocent III demands a *iuramentum iuxta formam ecclesie, quod solet a talibus exhiberi* for the return to the Church of those suspected of heresy. The wording of this oath is first preserved in the case of

Durandus of Huesca, then of Bernardus Primus. [The formula which Durandus of Huesca and Bernardus Primus were required to swear agrees extensively with the oath performed by Waldes himself after 1179, which Antoine Dondaine found (''Aux origines du Valdéisme,'' *AFP* 16 [1946], 191ff.); the texts are now in Giovanni Gonnet, ***Enchiridion Fontium Valdensium***, 31ff. and 129ff. The vow of poverty cited below in n. 74 is also in Waldes' oath. HG/1960.]

70. Pierron, *Die katholischen Armen*, 53, believes the ''Catholic Poor'' of Durandus would have constituted an ''order of preachers recognized by the Church,'' not just a *societas*, and that they were later described by Alexander IV as an order (*ordo pauperum catholicorum*); according to Scheeben (p. 129), they were a ''religious order, . . . not a loose association, but rather a solidly organized community of preachers.'' But in 1237, Gregory IX expressly said that Innocent III gave them *nullam de approbatis regulis*, so that he did not see the *propositum* of the ''Catholic Poor'' to be a ''rule'' and saw the association not as an approved order (according to the guidelines of the Lateran Council of 1215) but directed them to accept *unam de religionibus approbatis*, as did Innocent IV in 1247. Pierron, *Die katholischen Armen*, 53, says: ''Observing the evangelical counsels as commandments, keeping the canonical hours, fasting in common, electing their overseer themselves, etc., gives the entire community the character of a religious order such as was common in the Church at the time.'' This analysis misses the real problem. Such associations of preachers, which were not organized according to the principles of Benedict or Augustine, were an entirely novel phenomenon of that time, and they had nothing of the ''common'' about them. The question of whether they were to be considered as ''orders'' or not depended on their further developments and future decisions. In fact the ''Catholic Poor,'' unlike the Franciscans, were not able to assert their identity as an order. Formal characteristics which were regarded as essential in canon law before or after that time, did not decide the matter, for this canon law was only determined by the decision over which entities were approved orders and which not. Innocent III was responsible for developing new forms for religious communities which were not comprehended by earlier concepts in canon law.

71. Whether they had been made clerics and tonsured before papal recognition, as Pierron, *Die katholischen Armen*, 59, asserts (cf. Scheeben, *Dominikus*, 129), is not known.

72. *Pro rebus secularibus veluti pro pretendo cummuni*; Ep. 11.198, of 18 December 1208, *PL* 215.1514. Durandus later gave occasion to complaints that he continued to argue that no secular power could carry out a death sentence without moral sin, see below.

73. Pierron, *Die katholischen Armen*, chapter 3, pp. 51ff., shows the agreements between the *propositum* for the ''Catholic Poor'' and the customs of the Waldensians in detail.

74. The formula of poverty in the *propositum* is in Ep. 11.196, *PL* 215.1512–13; Pierron, *Die katholischen Armen*, 173. This is repeated almost word for word in the *confessio* and *propositum* of Bernard Primus and his companions,

Ep. 13.94 and 15.137, *PL* 216.290 and 648; Pierron, *Die katholischen Armen*, 176 and 177–78.

75. License to preach before brethren and friends, which is to say within the community, was granted with the condition, *cum prelatorum licentia et veneratione debita*; but in a later version of the *propositum* (12 May 1210, *PL* 216.224 and 215.1513) these words were altered to *cum prelatorum conscientia et assensu, ita quod ab eis propter hoc nec ecclesiarum frequentatio nec clericorum predicatio postponatur*; only a long-term agreement was wanted; cf. Pierron, *Die katholischen Armen*, 173 and 62.

76. The *scholæ* were a form of religious gathering in Milan, for example, which had already been taking place in the first half of the twelfth century, see Zanoni, *Umiliati*, 114–15.

77. Ep. 11.198, of 18 December 1208, *PL* 215.1514. They were exempted from military service against other Christians, as well as from oaths in secular matters, which was obviously to spare their formerly Waldensian sensitivities.

78. *PL* 216.29: *ad proponendum in schola prefata more solito verbum dei.*

79. On 3 April 1209, Ep. 12.17, *PL* 216.29–30.

80. Cf. on this Luigi Zanoni, "Valdesi a Milano nel secolo XIII," *ASL* 4/17 (1912), 5ff.

81. Letter of Innocent to the bishop of Elne, 26 May 1212, Ep. 15.82, *PL* 216.601–02: . . . *sub disciplina et visitatione catholicorum pauperum permansuri*.

82. Abstention from meat on four days of the week, abstention from fish and meat in Lent and on all holidays from All Saints to Christmas, save Sundays and festivals.

83. *Singulis diebus dominicis exhortationis verbum convenient audituri.* The bishop of Elne was supposed to check particularly *ut, quod de verbo exhortationis singulis diebus dominicis audiendo predicatur, taliter et a talibus fiat, quod derogari non possit fidei orthodoxe seu canonice discipline.*

84. Pierron's identification of the community of Elne with the third order of the *Humiliati* (*Die katholischen Armen*, 42) is incorrect, since chastity was praised here, and there is no mention of working with the hands; men and women live apart and in a *vita communis*, which makes it more like the second order of the *Humiliati*, but without an obligation to an approved monastic rule.

85. The letter has been lost, and it can only be reconstructed in part from Innocent's answer.

86. Ep. 12.69, of 5 July 1209, *PL* 216.75ff.

87 Ep. 12.67 and 68, of 5 July 1209, *PL* 216.73–74. In the letter to Durandus, Innocent says that complaints had been received from the archbishop of Narbonne and the bishops of Béziers, Uzès, Nîmes, and Carcassonne.

88. *PL* 216.74.

89. Ibid.

90. The image of oil and wine was frequently used in this time, cf. the statutes of the Lateran Council of 1215, c. 21, Mansi, *Sacrorum conciliorum* 22.1010; letter of James of Vitry, 1216, in Böhmer, Analekten, 2d ed., 65.

91. Ep. 13.38, *PL* 216.275.

92. Pierron, *Die katholischen Armen*, 167–68; Thomas Ripoll, *Bullarium ordinis fratrum Prœicatorum*, ed. Antonius Bremond (Rome, 1729–.) 1.96.

93. Innocent III to the archbishop of Narbonne and the bishop of Elne, 5 June 1247, see Barthélemy Hauréau, *NEM* 24/2, 203 (cf. Elie Berger, *Les Registres d'Innocent IV* (Paris, 1884–97) 1.410, n. 2752; Pierron, *Die katholischen Armen*, 170).

94. Pierron, *Die katholischen Armen*, 168ff. and 49–50; L. Torelli, *Secoli Agostiniani* 4 (1675), 544; Zanoni, "Valdesia Milano," *ASL* 4/17, 19ff.

95. Pierron, *Die katholischen Armen*, chapters 6 and 7, who treats this the most thoroughly, gives a completely erroneous portrayal which no one has corrected. He believes that Bernard and his companions were Lombard Waldensians, thus calling them "reunited Lombards." Since he further believes that the *pauperes Lombardi* were "those *Humiliati* who had refused to return to the Church with their brethren in 1201," he tries to demonstrate the identity of these "reunited Lombards" at every point with the *Humiliati*. To understand the actual situation, it is necessary to ignore his narrative entirely and to follow what few documents exist. I will correct Pierron's errors only in a few of the most important points.

96. Statement of the notary Pons Amiel of Miravel (Aude) in an inquisitorial trial of 5 December 1245: *dixit, quod vidit apud Lauracum* [Laurac-le-Grand, Aude] *in platea Isarnum de Castris hereticum disputantem cum Bernardo Prim Valdense presente populo eiusdem castri . . . et sunt 37 anni* [hence in 1208]; Douais, "Les hérétiques du comté de Toulouse dans la première moitié de XIIIe siècle d'après l'enquête de 1245," *CRCSIC* 5 (Paris, 1891), 150; cf. Guiraud, *Cartulaire*, 1, p. cxlix. Douais misprints *Valdensem*, which is correctly translated in the text. Pierron, 172, prints this item but interprets it as meaning that Bernard "led an apostolate against the Waldensians" in 1209, "preaching against the Waldensians" (pp. 12 and 121). The *Confession* of 1210 shows clearly that Bernard and his companions worked against heretics before 1210, see below, text at n. 99.

97. Ep. 13.94, *PL* 216.292.

98. Ep. 15.146, *PL* 216.668, to the bishop of Cremona.

99. *Confessio fidei* of Bernardus Primus and his companions of 1210, Ep. 13.94, *PL* 216.291 (Pierron, *Die katholischen Armen*, 177): they would only receive the sacraments from ordained priests.

100. According to the extensive "confession of faith" in Ep. 13.94, *PL* 216.292–93. It was thus not a matter of things "Bernard had believed heretofore," and his earlier actions should not be judged from this, as K. Müller, *Die Waldenser*, 17, and Pierron assert. On the contrary, Innocent officially declares that the accusations were false in all particulars. Their declaration on the eucharist (n. 99 above) excludes the possibility that they ever taught: *bonum laicum conficiendi eucharistiam potestatem habere*, as they were accused.

101. Ep. 13.94, *PL* 216.289ff.; partly in Pierron, *Die katholischen Armen*, 176ff.

102. Ep. 15.137, 23 July 1212, *PL* 216.648ff.; in Pierron, *Die katholischen Armen*, 179ff., as "the second rule of the reunited Lombards." This letter from Innocent to Bernard begins: *Ne quis de cetero vestrum valeat calumniari propositum, sicut olim diligenter examinavimus fidem vestram, ita nunc conversationem vestram prudenter investigare curavimus et utramque litteris apostolicis fenmus comprehendi, ut illas in testimonium habeatis.*

103. Work with the hands thus was not intended to secure all the preachers' support. They were not forbidden to beg or receive alms, cf. above. That is, by the way, the sole point which permits the supposition that Bernard and his companions came from Lombardy, for the principle of work with the hands was found everywhere in the Upper Italian poverty movement, but among the Waldensians of France it was rejected. It is impossible to discover why Achille Luchaire (*Innocent III*, 105) sees Bernard as a German Cathar, or Luigi Zanoni ("Valdesia Milano," 5) and Paul Alphandéry (*Les idées morales chez les hétérodox latins au début du XIII*[e] siécle [Paris, 1908], 31–32) see him as a German Waldensian.

104. Bernard and his companions already had renounced the participation of women in preaching in their Confession, which states that they had been accused of "suspicious relations' with women. There is never a mention of women participating in preaching or of their membership in the community proper among the "Catholic Poor," so this point is missing from their *propositum*.

105. Cf. above. In this case there is no mention of a *schola*, where preaching among brothers and friends is regulated. On the other hand, the comment is added: (. . . *fratribus et amicis*), *clericis et laicis, ut discant necessaria pro hereticis convertendis*, hence preaching "in the congregation" should also serve the struggle against heresy. All that is required is the *conscientia et consensus* of prelates, as is later the case with the "Catholic Poor" as well (see above).

106. In the assertions concerning the way of life of the community, there is no essential difference between the *Confessio fidei* of 1210 and the *Propositum conversationis* of 1212. Most of the provisions are literally identical, including that on working with the hands, which does not support Pierron's assertion (*Die katholischen Armen*, 126 and 151–54) that work with the hands "withdrew significantly into the background" in the interim. Pierron places too much stress in general on differences between the "rules." The only distinction is in the question of preaching. In 1210 it is described rather indistinctly: *Habemus autem mandatum orare, et deus mittat operarios in messem suam, id est predicatores in populum suum, qui debent benigne et humiliter impetrare sibi dari ex licentia summi pontificis et prelatorum ecclesie, ut possint admonere et exhortari in doctrina sana et adversus omnes hereticos, gratia dei adjuvante, cum omni virtute animi et studio, ut eos ad fidem catholicam convertant, desudare et credentes eorum privatis et publicis admonitionibus sicut decet ab eorum credulitate et heresi separare et ab omnibus vitiis et peccatis compescere tam seipsos quam suos auditores, a superbia scilicet et*

inani gloria, invidia, ira, cupiditate et avaritia, gulositate, luxuria, mendacio, destractione, blasphemia, odio, fraude, periurio et homocidio. Pierron, *Die katholischen Armen*, 124, asserts that the preaching of the "reunited Lombards" was restricted "to exhortation and warning"; "since they were as yet inexperienced in the matters of the faith, the Holy See could hardly permit them to dispute with heretics, since the truths of the faith of the Church were primarily what was discussed there." But the text says precisely the opposite, and the preaching against the heretics which Bernard had practiced with his companions even before 1210, just as two years later in the *propositum*, was primary; the *propositum* of 1212 only formulates more precisely what was said before (imitating the *propositum* of Durandus). It is only the close tie between the choice of preachers and the prelates which stands at the conclusion of the *Confessio* (*precipientes eisdem ne passim sibi presumant predicationis officium arrogare, sed preterquam ecclesiarum rectores in fide recta et sana doctrina noverint esse probatos, licentiam eis tribuant exhortandi horis et locis*) which was lost. Instead of mentioning the extensive agreement of the *proposita* for Durandus and Bernardus Primus, Pierron tried to compare the agreement of the "rules" of the "reunited Lombards" with the customs of the *Humiliati*, since it was his thesis that these two groups derived from the same community, the Lombard Waldensians = *Humiliati*. This false thesis perverts his entire narrative. Just the fact that the "reunited Lombards" venerated the evangelical counsels as commandments and renounced property completely distinguished them utterly from the lay brotherhood of the *Humiliati*, living in the world. The *amici* or (as they are called in the *Confessio* of 1210) *auditores* are not members of the organized association of preachers, as with all Waldensian groups. Among the *Humiliati*, on the other hand, these associations of laymen (the so-called third order) constituted the community proper.

107. Ep. 15.146, *PL* 216.668, cf. above. Innocent called on the bishop to extend protection, advice, and aid to Bernard and his companions, since they had been taken *sub protectione beati Petri* on the basis of their confession of faith.

108. There is no proof that they, too, suffered from the hostility of the bishops, as Scheeben, *Dominikus*, 178, says.

109. Burchard of Ursburg, *Chronik*, ed. Holder-Egger and von Simson, 107–08, for 1212.

110. Cf. above, n. 37. Burchard of Ursburg, *Chronik*, ed. Holder-Egger and von Simson, 107, introduces the treatment on the relationship between the Waldensians and *Humiliati* and the two mendicant orders in this manner: *Que [religiones Minorum fratrum et Predicatorum] forte hac occasione sunt approbate, quia olim due secte in Italia exorte adhuc perdurant, quorum alii Humiliatos, alii pauperes de Luduno se nominabant*. Later he says (108): *Alii, videlicet Predicatores, in locum Humiliatorum successisse creduntur*. On Franciscans, he says (continuing the previous citation): *Ceterum dominus papa in loco illorum exurgentes quosdam alios, qui se appellabant pauperes minores, confirmavit, qui predicta superstitiosa et probosa respuebant. . . .*

In contrast, another German chronicler, Abbot Emo of Wittewierum (died 1237) identifies the *Humiliati* with the Franciscans.

111. It is not certain whether the first Franciscans came to the curia in 1209 or 1210. Schnürer (*Franz von Assisi*, 41) favors 1209, as does Heribert Holzapfel (*Handbuch der Geschichte des Franziskanerordens* [Freiburg, 1909], 5–6), relying on the chronology of L. Patrem (*MF* 9.91–92). The decisive argument is the account of *I Cel.*, 16, on the attitude of the brethren gathered in Rivotorto near Assisi to the procession of the Otto IV on his way to Rome to be crowned emperor. Thomas of Celano tells this story *after* his account of the visit of Francis in Rome and the first papal approval. The imperial coronation took place on 4 October 1209, and Innocent was not in Rome from May to October 1209. If Thomas of Celano is recounting events in their proper chronological order, then Francis could not have been with the pope in Rome any later than early 1209, "on 16 April, according to ancient tradition" (Schnürer). L. Patrem tries to prove that Celano's sequencing is correct by demonstrating that Francis had never been in Rivotorto before his visit to Rome. The sources cited from *I Cel.* and *Legenda trium sociorum* do not prove anything; on the contrary it is certain that Francis had stayed in Rivotorto before the journey to Rome; cf. *Legenda antiqua s. Francisci*, ed. Fredinand-M. Delorme, 1.33, 37; *Speculum perfectionis ou mémoires de frère Léon*, ed. Paul Sabatier, c. 24, 27 and 36; *Chronicle of the 24 General Ministers*, *AF* 3.5–6; Franciscus Bartolus, *Tract. de Indulg.*, ed. Paul Sabatier, 4, where Rivotorto is described as *primus locus istius ordinis . . . ubi incepit primo ordo b. Francisci*; Faloci-Pulignani, *MF* 26.51–2; M. Charmichael, *MF* 9.23; Holzapfel, *Handbuch*, 5–6. It follows that the episode in Rivotorto could have taken place in 1209 before the journey to Rome and the confirmation of the first "rule," and it is not usable for dating the episode, particularly since Schnürer (p. 134, n. 6) has shown that Otto IV did not pass Rivotorto on his approach to Rome, but only on his return in December, 1209, so that Celano's account is imprecise in any case.

Lucas Wadding, *Annales Minorum*, 2d ed. (Rome, 1731), for 1210, n. 1, Sabatier, *Vie de S. François*, 100, decided for 1210, both with not entirely convincing evidence. In the same way Böhmer, *Analekten* (1st ed., 1904), 124, and Arnaldo Fortini, *Nova vita di San Francesco d'Assisi* (Milan, 1926), 176, set the journey to Rome in 1210. Only the *Chronicle of the 24 General Ministers* (*AF* 3.6–7) sets 1210 as a precise date, but no citation of older sources contradicts this attribution unequivocally. It is confirmed by Burchard of Ursberg (see above), who was in Rome in 1210, and who could hardly have believed that Innocent confirmed Francis as a substitute for Bernardus Primus if the Franciscans had been confirmed a year before the petition of Bernardus Primus. [On the more recent state of research on Francis, see Sophronius Clasen, O.F.M., "Kritisches zur neueren Franziskusliteratur," *Wissenschaft und Weisheit* 13 (1950), 151–66; idem, "Franz von Assisi im Licht der neueren Forschung," *GWU* 3 (1952), 137–54; K. Esser, "Gestalt und Ideal des Minderbrüderordens in seinen Anfängen," *FS* 39 (1957), 1–22; idem, "Die religiüsen Bewegungen des Hochmittelalters und Franziskus von Assisi," in *Festgabe Joseph Lortz, 2:*

Glaube und Geschichte, ed. Erwin Iserloh and Peter Manns (Baden-Baden, 1958), 287–315; idem, "Franziskus von Assisi und die Katharer seiner Zeit," *AFH* 51 (1958), 1–40; L. Salvatorelli, "Movimento Francescano e Gioachimismo," X. *Congresso Internazionale di Scienze Storiche, Relazioni*, 3 (Rome, 1955), 403–48. HG/1960.]

112. It is easy to infer that Francis chose that particular moment for his journey to Rome because the bishop of Assisi was in Rome, hoping to make use of him as an intermediary.

113. Heinrich Zimmermann, *Die päpstlichen Legationen in der ersten Hälfte des 13. Jahrhunderts*, Veröffentlichungen der Sektion für Rechts- und Sozialwissenschaft der Görresgesellschaft 17 (Paderborn, 1913), 30–31; Karl Wenck, "Die römische Päpste zwischen Alexander III. und Innocenz III," *Papsttum und Kaisertum, Festschrift für Paul Kehr* (Munich, 1926), 415–74, esp. 466ff.; M. Bihl, *AFH* 19.282ff. Cardinal John died between 21 April 1214 and November 1215, *before* the Lateran Council of 1215.

114. According to *I Cel.*, c. 13, § 33, the Cardinal praised Francis' proposal, *verum quia homo erat providus et dicretus, cepit eum de multis interrogare, et ut ad vitam monasticam seu eremiticam diverteret suadebat.* The *Legenda trium sociorum*, ed. Michele Faloci-Pulignani, *MF* 7 (1898), c. 12, § 47/8 (p. 99) and the Anonymus Perusinus, "Legenda Sacti Francisci," ed. François van Ortroy, *MF 9* (1902), c. 7, § 32/3 (pp.43–44) know nothing of the cardinal's purported suggestions, who is supposed to have agreed with Francis' proposals to such a degree that he told him that he was like his own brother. At first the pope raised concerns over the strict principle of poverty, doubting its practicality. According to Angelo Clareno, "Historia septum tribulationum ordinis minorum," *Beiträge zur Sektengeschichte*, ed. Ignaz Döllinger, 2.429–30, Innocent was supposed to have exhorted Francis *quod aliquem ordinem vel regulam de approbatis assumeret.*.

115. Contrary to the assertion of Karl Müller, *Anfänge des Minoritenordens und der Bussbruderschaften* (Freiburg i.B., 1885), 33, that Francis did not want to become a member of an order, Hilarin Felder, *Geschichte der wissenschaftlichen Studien im Franziskanerorden bis um die Mitte des 13. Jahrhunderts* (Freiburg i.B., 1904), 5, declared that this misunderstood the terminology of the history of orders: the terms *vita monastica and heremetica* are only used for the old orders and their rules, "in contrast to the new orders, particularly the Franciscan Order," which is an ecclesiastical order, but neither an *ordo monasticus* nor *heremeticus*. That is a prime example of an error of interpreting historical decisions in terms of the outcome of the decisions themselves. It was only because Francis did not want to accept any of the "old" rules for orders, which were all that were available at the time, and did not want to be a "member of an order" in the sole sense which the term had at the time, and because the community of Franciscans still won recognition by the Church despite its complete novelty, that "new" forms of orders and the terminology came into existence which Felder projects back on Francis' earliest attitudes. In 1210 there was no other possibility to be a "member of an order" than through accepting a

rule for monks or hermits, that is, some variant of the Rule of Benedict, or—for clerics—the Rule of Augustine. Francis rejected that, which meant he did not want to be a monk, a "member of an order." Pierre Mandonnet, "Les Origines de l'Ordo de pœnitentia," 204, says basically the same thing with a more careful formulation, that is was not Francis' plan "to constitute a religious order imitating the old and numerous corporations already in existence in the Church." See also Walter Goetz, "Die ursprünglishen Ideale des hl. Franz," *HV* 6 (1903), 26–27.

116. These words of Cardinal John are contained only in the official legend of Bonaventure, c. 3, § 9 (*Opera*, 8 [Quaracchi, 1898], 512). On the believability of this report, see H. Tilemann, *Studien zur Individualität des Franziskus von Assisi* (Leipzig, 1914), 149; K. Wenck, "*Die römische Päpste*," 473. Older legends mention the cardinal's representations to the pope (I Cel., c. 13, § 33) only in general terms: *Coram domino papa studuit eius negotia de cetero promovere; the Legenda trium sociorum*, c. 12, § 48 (99) and Anonymus Perusinus, "Legenda sancti Francisci," c. 7, § 34 (44) have the cardinal speaking to Innocent at the outset to recommend the Franciscans: *Inveni virum perfectissimum, qui vult vivere secundum formam sancti evangelii et evangeliorum perfectionem in omnibus observare; per quem credo quod dominus vult in toto mundo fidem sancte ecclesie reformare*; according to these legends, the cardinal did not intervene in the negotiations between Innocent and Francis, and it is here (particularly in the more primitive legend of Anonymus Perusinus) Innocent himself who raises concerns about the practicability of the principle of strict poverty. Angelo Clareno, *Historia Tribulationum* (ed. Ignaz Döllinger, *Beiträge zur Sektengeschichte* 2.429–30) says: after Innocent recommended the adoption of an existing rule, due to his concerns about the practicability of the principle of strict poverty, and Francis declined, remaining with his original proposal, *tunc dominus Johannes de Sancto Paulo episcopus Sabinensis et dominus Hugo episcopus Hostiensis dei spiritu moti astiterunt sancto Francisco et pro his que petebat coram summo pontifice et cardinalibus plura proposuerunt rationabilia et efficacia valde*. This is the only source for the participation of Cardinal Ugolino of Osta, but it is not impossible, since the view that Ugolino only met Francis later has been shown to be unsustainable, see Lilly Zarncke, *Der Anteil des Kardinals Ugolino an der Ausbildung der drei Orden des hl. Franz* (Leipzig; Berlin, 1930), 104ff.; cf. below. Ugolino was continually at the curia in 1210, as his subscriptions show (August Potthast, *Regesta Pontificum Romanorum* [Berlin, 1874–75]).

117. Anonymus Perusinus, c. 7, § 36 (p. 44); *Legenda trium sociorum*, c. 12, § 52 (p. 100); Bonaventure, c. 3, § 10 (*Legenda s. Francisci*, 512).

118. *II Cel.*, c. 11, § 16.

119. *I Cel.*, c. 13, § 33: Innocent blesses Francis and his brethren, saying: *Ite cum domino fratres et prout dominus vobis inspirare dignabitur, omnibus penitentiam predicate. Cum enim omnipotens dominus vos numero multiplicabit et gratia, ad me cum gaudio referetis, et ego vobis his plura concedam et securius majora committam; almost identical, Legenda trium*

sociorum, c. 12, § 49 (p. 99): *Postulata concessit et adhuc concedere plura promisit; approbavit regulam, dedit de penitentia predicanda mandatum.* Schnürer, *Franz von Assisi*, 46, believes that the license to preach granted to Francis and his companions was explicitly limited to "moral and penitential preaching," but that there was expectation of a later authorization "to be specific, for dogmatic pulpit sermons." Innocent made that depend on whether they won more adherents, "particularly if they gained a larger number of adequately trained clerics." That is an arbitrary, certainly improper reading of the promised *majora*. At that time Francis could not have asked for anything more than penitential preaching; he could not have conceived of doing "dogmatic pulpit sermons," nor could it have occurred to the curia to promise these twelve wandering penitential preachers such a right in the future. It is not just that the sources do not say it, they directly exclude this interpretation. No one could have thought at that time that the community of Francis could have become an order in which trained clerics would have worked as dogmatic preachers. The description of the sermons of Antony in Padua in *Dialogus de vitis fratrum minorum* (ed. Leonardus Lemmens [Rome, 1902], 8) is particularly informative on the character of early Franciscan preaching. Antony was learned in the Bible and theology, but he hid his knowledge and denied it when he became a Franciscan.

120. Even after their return from Rome the brethren discussed whether to work in the world as penitential preachers or withdraw from the world as hermits; I *Cel.*, c. 14, § 35: *Conferebant . . . utrum inter homines conversari deberent an ad loca solitaria se conferre*; cf. Bonaventure, c. 12, § 1 (*Legenda s. Francisci*, 539) on the *magna dubitationis cuiusdam agonia* of Francis, who asked his companions: *Quid . . . consulitis, quid laudatis? An quod orationi vacem, an quod predicando discurram*; see also Wadding, *Annales*, 1212, n. 10ff. Even at the general chapter of 1221, when 5000 brothers were said to be gathered, one party moved for the adoption of the old rules of Benedict, Augustine, or the Cistercians, failing due to Francis' opposition, see *Legenda antiqua*, ed. Delorme, 65, no. 114 (and parallel in other sources, see Angelo Clareno, *Expositio regulæ fratrum minorum*, ed. Liverius Oliger [Quaracchi, 1912], 128). Even then the form of the order was not certain. The final rule of the order was only confirmed by papal bull in 1223.

121. Ep. 16.30, *PL* 216.823ff.

122. Mansi, *Sacrorum conciliorum* 22.981–1067.

123. In connection with this see the condemnation of Amaury of Bëne, cf. Mansi, *Sacrorum conciliorum* 23.986.

124. Ep. 2.1, of 25 March 1199 to the clergy, consuls and people of Viterbo, *PL* 214.536; in this letter, heresy was paralleled with lèse-majésté for the first time.

125. Cap. 18, Mansi, *Sacrorum conciliorum* 22.1007.

126. Ep. 14.138, of 9 January 1212, *PL* 216.502. This letter was precipitated by the condemnation of heretics (probably Waldensians) in Strasbourg in 1211, of whom the Marbach Annals (ed. H. Bloch) report. Cf. also Caesarius of Heisterbach, *Dialogus miraculorum*, 3.12, ed. Strange, 1.133, who speaks of

only ten heretics, *qui cum negarent, per iudicium candentis ferri convicti sententia incendii sunt damnati.*

127. § 3 of the heresy statute of the conciliar statute of 1215, Mansi, *Sacrorum conciliorum* 22.986, cf. Ep. 2.1, *PL* 214.537.

128. Mansi, *Sacrorum conciliorum* 22.990 (Decret. V, tit. 7, c. 13, ed. Aemilius Friedberg, *Corpus iuris canonici*, 2 [Leipzig, 1879], 787). Through *presumpserint* it is identical with the heresy decree of Lucius III, Mansi, *Sacrorum conciliorum* 22.477 (Decr. V, tit. 7, c. 9, ed. Friedberg, *Corpus iuris canonici*, 2.780); the sentence immediately preceding, which condemned Cathars, Patarines, Waldensians, *Humiliati*, etc., was not repeated in the Council statute of 1215.

129. Cap. 10 of the statute, Mansi, *Sacrorum conciliorum* 22.998.

130. Cap. 13, Mansi, *Sacrorum conciliorum* 22.1002. A partial unification of the existing forms of orders was introduced by the requirement in chapter 12 that all orders were henceforth to hold annual general chapters in imitation of the Cistercians.

131. Jordanus de Saxonia, *De initiis ordinis opera ad res ordinis Prædicatorum spectantia*, c. 27, ed. J.-J. Berthier (Fribourg, Switzerland, 1891), 14.

132. The first bull of Honorius III for the Franciscans, directed at all prelates, 11 (or 14) June 1219 (Johannes Hyacinthus Sbaralea, *Bullarium Franciscanum* [Rome, 1759ff.] 1.2; Pietro Pressutti, *Regesta Honorii papæ III* (Rome, 1888–95), vol. 1, 349, no. 2109). The next bull touching the Franciscans, on 29 May 1220, directed to prelates in France, expressly states *quod nos ordinem talium [fratrum minorum] de approbatis habemus*; Sbaralea, *Bullarium Franciscanum*, 1.5; Pressutti, *Regesta Honorii III*, 1.407, no. 2461.

133. *AF* 3.9: *Anno domini MCCXV tempore concilii generalis beatus Franciscus Romam adiit et sanctum Dominicum, qui ibi tunc erat pro sui ordinis approbatione, reperit, quem dei ostensa visio sibi favorabilem fecit.*

134. *Vitæ fratrum*, *MOPH* 1.9f. This tradition relies on the testimony of a *frater quidam minor, religiosus et fide dignus, qui socius beati Francisci multo tempore fuit.* It is also in James of Voragine, *Legenda aurea,* ed. Theodor Graesse (Leipzig, 1850), 470, relying on Gerard Franchet, and in Henry of Herford, *Liber de rebus memorabilioribus, sive Chronicon*, ed. August Potthast (Göttingen, 1859), 180, for the year 1215. Cf. Berthold Altaner, "Die Beziehungen des heiligen Dominikus zum heiligen Franziskus von Assisi," *FS* 9 (1922), 12–13.

135. B. Altaner, *loc. cit.*, holds this tradition to be "legendary," for it tells about a vision which Dominic was supposed to have had of Francis. Yet he believed that the story might have a "historical core," though the meeting of Francis and Dominic, according to Altaner (16–17) must have taken place not at the time of the Council, but rather in the years 1216/17.

136. Written 1244/46, *IIc*, p. II, c. 109/10, ed. Edouard d'Alençon, *S. Francisci Assisiensis vita et miracala additis opusculis liturgicis anchire fr. Thomae de Celano* (Rome, 1906) p. 280ff.; *AF* 10.215ff. Also see the *Speculum perfectionis*, c. 43, ed. Sabatier, 109ff.

137. Lilly Zarncke, *Der Anteil des kardinals Uglino*, 14 and 109 (along with Grützmacher, *PRE* 4.773) holds this story to be unhistorical, a tendentious legend created by zealots and Spirituals in their battles with the lax principles of Elias of Cortona, with the goal of waging a polemic against the rise of Franciscans into high Church offices. But Zarncke states this as an unprovable supposition. The final passage, which is the only one important for our purposes, is hard to imagine as a product only of the sources named. Otherwise the report can be accepted without hesitation. Cf. H. Fischer, *Der hl. Franziskus von Assisi während der Jahre 1219–1221* (Freiburg, 1907), 96ff.

138. Cf. Van Ortroy, "S. François d'Assise et son voyage en Orient," *AB* 31.461–62. This interpretation has been rejected on the sole grounds that Francis is said by *I Cel.* § 74 to have made Cardinal Ugolino's acquaintance at a meeting in Florence at an uncertain date, but certainly before 1217 (cf. Ernst Brem, *Papst Gregor IX. bis zum Beginn seines Pontifikats* (Heidelberg, 1911), 112ff.; André Callebaut, "Autour de la rencontre à Florence de S. François et du Cardinal Hugolin," *AFH* 19 [1926], 530ff.); hence the meeting of Francis and Dominic in Ugolino's house could not have taken place before 1217; see Altaner, "Die Beziehungen," *FS* 9 (1922), 9; also *AF* 10.55. Yet Zarncke's investigation has shown (105) that the assertion in *I Cel.* § 74 does not exclude the possibility "that the friendship [between Francis and Ugolino] had begun even before Florence, perhaps as early as 1210 at the curia." I will add some further citations: Angelo Clareno, 132, says that Ugolino was present in Rome for the approval of the rule, which seems highly likely anyway. The valuable *Legenda antiqua*, ed. Delorme, 47, c. 82, gives a thorough account of the meeting in Florence, but from this narrative it seems unlikely that this was the first encounter between Francis and the cardinal; for this reason, André Callebaut, "Autourde la rencontre à Florence," *AFH* 19.541, says: "No special bond united the Saint with the cardinal before their meeting at Florence, though they had known and respected one another before." The *Legenda trium sociorum*, c. 15, § 61 (p. 103) and Anonymus Perusinus, c. 10, § 42/43 (46–47) assert that immediately after the death of the first advocate of the order, Cardinal John of St. Paul (died after April 1214, *before* the Council), Cardinal Ugolino took the order under his protection, and Francis and his brethren visited him. Dominic probably knew Cardinal Ugolino in 1215, at the time of the Council, see Scheeben, *Dominikus*, 181. In the winter of 1216/17 he was often a guest in Ugolino's house, see Scheeben, *Dominikus*, 211, 224; E. Brem, *Papst Gregor IX.*, 102ff.

139. Two very good sources from Leo's circle, the *Legenda antiqua*, ed. Delorme, 39, c. 67, and the *Intentio regulæ fratris Leonis*, c. 3, ed. Leonhard Lemmens, *Documenta antiqua Francescana* (Quaracchi, 1901) 1.85, report that Innocent approved the rule in 1210 *et postea in concilio omnibus annuntiavit.* Angelo Clareno cited the passage from the *Intentio regulæ* in the *Expositio regulæ* (ed. Oliger, 16), and in another place (ibid., 6, but probably only based on this citation; cf. also 101): *Postea vero in generali concilio Roma . . . celebrato anno domini MCCXV prelatis omnibus annuntiavit se vitam et evangelicam regulam sancto Francisco et cum sequi volentibus*

concessisse; and in a letter (*ALKG* 1.556): . . . *et a papa Innocentio fuit omnibus annuntiatum in concilio generali, quod de sua auctoritate et obedientia sanctus Franciscus evangelicam vitam et regulam assumpserat et Christo inspirante servare promiserat*. Against this assertion, Liverius Oliger (*Expositio regulæ*, p. 16, n. 3) can only argue that corresponding passages in the *Legenda trium sociorum*, c. 12 (p. 100), the *Speculum perfectionis* (c. 26, ed. Sabatier [1928], 74) and the *Speculum vitæ* (c. 25, Venice, 1504, f. 20[v]) use the words *in consistorio* instead of *in concilio*, changing the sense completely. But the *Vita antiqua* discovered by F. Delorme appears to me to give preference to the reading in *concilio*, since the *Vita* text is certainly older and almost always more dependable than the *Speculum perfectionis*.

140. Wadding, *Annales*, 1215, nn. 33–34, adds other witnesses for the approval of the order at the Lateran Council, all of which either say nothing about it (Matthew Paris, Burchard of Ursberg, *Legenda trium sociorum*) or probably rely on the sources already mentioned (Marianus, Gonzaga, St. Antoninus, *Chronicon magnum Belgicum*). Sbaralea, *Bullarium Franciscanum* 1.2, asserts that the confirmation of the rule by the Council of 1215 was also confirmed by Bonaventure, Alexander of Hales, and Jordan of Saxony; I could find no such statements. Cf. also Mansi, *Sacrorum conciliorum* 22.1078. The information in a Fürstenberg Chronicle of the seventeenth century is probably independent of the rest: Abbot Berthold of Thennebach, brother of the abbot of Clairvaux (also at the Council), went to the Council in Rome in 1215 and "hilfft neben anderen den Franziscaner Orden bestättigen"; see *Fürstenbergisches Urk. -B*. (Donaueschingen, 1877–91) 1.80.

141. The interpretation of Carl Joseph Hefele and Alois Knöpfler, *Conciliengeschichte* 5 (2d ed., Freiburg i. B., 1886), 904 (already opposed by Wadding, *Annales*, 1 [1731], 82 against Abraham Bzowski, *Annalium ecclesiasticorum post illustriss et reverendiss. Caesarem Boronium*, vols. 13–20 *auctore R. P. Fr. Abraham Bzorio* [Cologne, 1616ff.], 1215, n. 6 and 1216, n. 12) is entirely wrong: if Francis actually petitioned the pope for the confirmation of his creation at the Lateran Council, "then he received an answer similar to that given to Dominic," which would be the directive to take one of the accepted rules. That certainly never happened, and this very fact requires explanation.

142. Vlastimil Kybal, *Die Ordensregeln des heiligen Franz von Assisi und die ursprUngliche Verfassung des Minoritenordens*, Beiträge zur Kulturgeschichte Meittlealters und der Renaissance 20 (Leipzig; Berlin, 1915), 13, correctly assumes the continued development of the text of the original rule in connection with reconfirmation in 1215. The sources do not permit us to follow this process.

143. There are no sources for Liverius Oliger's inference ("De origine regularum ordinis s. Claræ," *AFH* 5.204) that Clara formally accepted the rule of Benedict as a result of the Council decree of 1215. This shows how much an understanding of the process depends on comprehending Innocent's acts. [On Clara's *privilegium paupertatis*, see L. Hardick, "Zur Chronologie im Leben der hl. Klara," *FS* 35 (1953), 174–210. HG/1960.]

144. See below, chapter 5, n. 145ff.

145. See below, chapter 5, nn. 180ff. and 188ff.

146. This *privilegium paupertatis* for Clara and her sisters at St. Damian's is only preserved in a very early edition: *Firmamentum trium ordinum*, Paris (1512), 5, fol. 5a; then by Paul Sabatier, "Il privilegio di Povertà, quando S. Chiara d'Assisi l'ottene dal Summo Pontifice?" *MF* 24 (1924), 14–15. The genuineness of this document has often been disputed, cf. Edward Lempp, "Die Anfänge des Clarissenordens," *ZKG* 13 (1892), 239; Edmund Wauer, *Entstehung und Ausbreitung des Klarissenordens, besonders in den deutschen Minoritenprovinzen* (Leipzig, 1906), 2–3.; Livarius Oliger, "De origine regularum," 191; Zarncke, *Anteil des Kardinals Ugolino*, 23; Wauer and Zarncke not only doubt the authenticity of the document, but even the issuance of any *privilegium paupertatis* at all by Innocent III. All of these doubts have been authoritatively confuted by Sabatier, "Il privilegio di Povertà," 1–33. Lilly Zarncke did not know Sabatier's treatment. I rely on Sabatier in what follows. [On Clara's *privilegium paupertatis*, see L. Hardick, "Zur Chronologie im Leben der hl. Klara," *FS* 35 (1953), 174–210. HG/1960.]

147. On the basis of the *Vita S. Claræ*, Sabatier believes that this took place in Perugia in May 1216; similarly Antonio Cristofani, *Storia della chiesa e chiostro S. Damiani*, 3d ed. (Assisi, 1882), 90–91 (between the start of June and 16 July 1216). But the *Vita* does not permit precise dating; it is also possible that the privilege was already issued in 1215, in the year Clara was made abbess of St. Damian (cf. Oliger, "De origine regularum," 192); perhaps Innocent demanded that the inner organization be regulated by the choice of leadership, as he had done in 1210 on approving Francis' plans.

148. Thomas of Celano, *Vita S. Claræ*, c. 14, *AASS August II*, pp. 757–58: *Et ut insolitæ petitioni favor insolitus arrideret, pontifex ipse cum hilaritate magna petiti privilegii primam notulam sua manu conscripsit;* cf. Sabatier, "Il privilegio di Povertæ," 12–13.

149. The decisive formula of this privilege reads: *Sicut ergo supplicastis, altissimæ paupertatis propositum indulgentes, ut recipere possessiones a nullo compelli possitis*. In the solemn formula at the end of the privilege, in the place of the words *prefatum monasterium*, which appears in corresponding privileges for Benedictine houses, there is only the formula: *Vos et ecclesia vestra*; the terms for a convent were thus specifically avoided.

150. Cf. the testament of St. Clara (whose genuineness is also disputed), *AASS, August II* (12 August), 748, n. 43. We do not know any confirmation by Honorius III; there is the bull of Gregory IX of 17 September 1228, Sbaralea, *Bullarium Franciscanum*, I. 771; by Innocent IV, as Thomas of Clelano, *Vita S. Claræ*, c. 47 (*AASS Aug*. II, p. 764) reports, November 1251; this bull has not survived, either.

151. Cf. below, chapter 5, n. 188ff.

151a. That a division of such magnitude between the desires of the pope and the decision of the Council could occur is shown by the account of Gerald of Wales (*Speculum Ecclesiæ*, IV, 19, *MG Scr*. 27, 421; *Opera*, ed. J. S. Brewer, 4,

304–05) on an episode at the same council: Innocent tried to pass the ruling that every cathedral should forward a tenth of its income to the curia; the majority of the Council would not agree to this plan, so that it failed.

152. Opposition among prelates and cardinals continued after 1215. At their meeting in Florence in 1217, Cardinal Ugolino said to Francis: *multi prelati sunt et alii, qui libenter impedirent bona quæ tuæ religionis in curia romana; ego autem et alii cardinales, qui diligimus tuam religionem, libentius protegimus et adiuvamus ipsam, si manseris in circuitu istius provinciæ, Legenda antiqua*, ed. Delorme, c. 82, p. 47; cf. also *I Cel.* § 74, *AF* 10.55, with the description of the same meeting in Florence: *O quanti maxime in principio, cum hæc agerentur, novellæ plantationi ordinis insideabantur ut perderent*, which were all rendered harmless by Cardinal Ugolino.

153. Cf. P. Mandonnet, *St. Dominique*, 50–51. Also Scheeben, *Dominikus*, 176: "This decision of the Council fathers can be seen as intended as a rebuke [?] for Innocent III." But Scheeben believes Innocent recognized in advance the solidity of principles which impelled the Council to ban new orders; I believe I have shown this position to be untenable.

154. In Italy, Francis and his companions were often derided and cursed as madmen or drunkards, loafers or cheats, but, so far as we know, never as heretics; the Legend of the Anonymus Perusinus, § 17 (parallel to *Legenda trium sociorum*, § 35) remarks that the first six brethren at Assisi were badly handled by relatives and fellow citizens and laughed to scorn, *quia eo tempore nullus inveniebatur, qui omnia sua relinqueret et iret petendo elemosinam hostiatim*; for that reason it is difficult to explain Francis' conversion to the immediate influence of other itinerant preachers.

155. Mansi, *Sacrorum conciliorum* 22.683, § 41. On dating (not 1197 but 1207/8) see Theloe, *Ketzerverfolgungen*, 173.

156. Frater Jordanus, *Chronica*, c. 4 (ed. Heinrich Böhmer [Paris, 1908], 4). Against the usual assumption that this treats the mission of 1219, Callebaut, "Autour de la rencontre à Florence," 530ff., argues that this happened in summer 1217, but his proof is unconvincing; it is likely that the bull of Honorius III of 29 May 1220 (Sbaralea, *Bullarium Franciscanum*, 1, p. 5; H. Denifle and E. Chatelain, eds., *Chartularium Universitatis Parisiensis* (Paris, 1889–91) 1. 95–96, n. 37; see above, n. 132) is an answer to the request of the bishop of Paris, which could not have been sent three years earlier.

157. Jordanus, *Chronica*, c. 5, pp. 5–6; about sixty brethren went to Germany, but they did not know the language and answered all questions with "yes." Cf. Anonymus Perusinus, § 44, p. 47 and *Legenda trium sociorum*, § 62, p. 103.

158. Caesarius of Heisterbach, *Vita Engelberti*, I, 7, *AASS Nov.*, 3, 650. Cf. Joseph Greven, "Engelbert der Heilige und die Bettelorden," *BZTS* 2 (1925), 37ff.

159. Cf. above, chapter 1, n. 22.

160. I will not follow the story of the evolution of the Franciscans into an order any more than I will the work of Dominic. I think I have already ade-

quately explained the preconditions for the formation of the orders. A narrative continuing the history of the orders would concentrate on two major points: 1) the incorporation of the mendicant orders into the hierarchical Church through privileges and exemptions, and 2) the international expansion of their organizations through the foundation of houses and provincial subdivisions. The investigation up to this point has not been interested primarily in the history of the orders, but rather in the changes in relations between the Church and the religious movement, and this development is essentially complete, so far as the mendicants are concerned, with Innocent III's creation of a field for the development of the religious movement within the Church. In the twelfth century, the hierarchical Church fended off the religious movement, including its heretical elements, but in the thirteenth century the Church fought alongside the orthodox religious movement (the mendicant orders) against heresy.

CHAPTER 3

1. Even before Luigi Zanoni, *Gli Umiliati nei loro rapporti con l'eresia, industria della lana ed i communi nei secoli XII e XIII*, Bibliotheca Historica Italica, 2d series, 2 (Milan, 1911), this position was taken by Antonino De Stephano, "Le origini dell'ordine degli Umiliati," *Rivista storico-critica delle scienze teologiche* 2 (1906), 851–71.

2. Zanoni's assertions were summarized in the following way in *Civilità Cattolica*, 62 (1911) 2.443: "The *Humiliati* belong to a proletariat redeeming itself from the servitude proper to *laborantes* subjected to the whims of the *mercatores*. They discovered in the gospels the doctrine of working poverty voluntarily embraced in love, and they did not need to pretend humility or poverty, since that is what they were already." Zanoni, *Umiliati*, says of the *Humiliati* on 108: "They revenged themselves on a society which oppressed small workers, but which venerated them as soon as they were clothed in the habit of religion."

3. Zanoni, *Umiliati*, 157.

4. Despite Zanoni's assurances, it is never possible to apply automatically the data of later sources to the era of the beginnings of capitalist enterprise, a time for which there are almost no sources.

5. The sole real source for this construct is a reference to a sermon by the Dominican Humbert of Romans in the mid-thirteenth century (!), who said of the *Humiliati, humilem vitam laborantium ducunt*. Zanoni believes that *laborantes* was the normal expression for the lowest level of industrial workers. But even then this source provides nothing to support his theory.

6. *Chronicon universale anonymi Laudunensis*, 29.

7. Zanoni, *Umiliati*, 154.

8. See below, ch. 4, n. 45.

9. Zanoni, *Umiliati*, 358.

10. Hieronymus Tiraboschi, *Vetera Humiliatorum monumenta* 2.131ff.

11. See above, chapter 2, nn. 17, 18; James of Vitry, *Historia orientalis et occidentalis* 2.28, ed. Francisco Moschus (Donai, 1597), 336.

12. Composed 1493; Zanoni, *Umiliati*, 351.

13. E.g. Zanoni, *Umiliati*, 87; contrary, 169.

14. Ibid., 32, 53–54, 87, 157, 169 and generally.

15. See the appendix below; also chapter 4, nn. 38–39.

16. Cf. Müller, *Die Waldenser*, 6: "Men and women were received without distinction; they were usually members of the lowest classes of the poor." Differently Albert Hauck, *KD* 4 (Leipzig, 1913), 902–03.

17. *Chronicon . . . Laudunensis*, 20. After his conversion he gave part of his movable property to those *a quibus injuste habuerat*, part to support his two daughters, sent to Fontevrault convent, and part to the poor. The real property (*terræ et aquæ, nemora et prata, domus, reditus, vineæ, molendina et furni*) was retained by his wife.

18. Ibid., 28. Stephan of Bourbon (ed. A. Lecoy de la Marche, 291–92.) says: *Multos homines et mulieres ad idem faciendum ad se (convocavit), firmans eis evangelia, quos eciam per villas circumjacentes mittebat ad predicandum vilissimorum quorumcumque officiorum*. It is unclear to me what these last words mean, but it could hardly mean that Waldes' companions belonged to the lowest classes, the lowest professions. Rather they must have been preaching to members of the lowest classes.

19. Cf. above, chapter 2, n. 51ff.; Ep. 2.142, *PL* 214.698–99; Innocent III remarked in his letter to the bishop of Metz that the sectarians could not be *illitterati*, since they could read biblical translations.

20. Ep. 11.196, *PL* 215.1513 and Ep. 15.137, *PL* 216.648.

21. Ep. 12.69, *PL* 216.75.

22. Cf. *Chronicon . . . Laudenensis*, 29.; Ep. 15.82, *PL* 216.601–02.

23. *Liber contra Waldenses*, c. 7, *PL* 204.821ff.

24. Col. 824.

25. Col. 836.

26. David of Augsburg still remarked (ed. Wilhelm Preger, 218): *Student diligenter attrahere sibi aliquas potentes et nobiles feminas, ut per eas eciam viros vel cognatos earum sibi faceant faventes*.

27. The Waldensian burned in Reims in 1230/1 was a baker, see Haskins, *Studies in Mediaeval Culture*, 245; a heretic named Arolinus condemned in 1235 in Châlons was a barber, see Alberich of Troisfontaines, *MG Script*. 23.937. Cf. Friess, *Österreichische Vierteljahrschrift für katholische Theologie* 11 (1872), 258; A. E. Schönbach, *Studien zur Geschichte der alterdenscher Predigt* (Vienna, 1904), 120; W. Wattenbach, *S.-B. der Akademie Berlin* (1886), 51, on the inquisition among the Waldensians in the bishopric of Kammin, 1393/4.

28. I do not know of any studies of the social origins of Franciscans in the thirteenth century. [On the social origins of early Franciscans, cf. Friedrich Baethgen, "Franziskanische Studien," *HZ* 131 (1925), 434f. and A. Schäfer, *Der Orden des hl. Franz in Württemberg*, Dissertation, Tübingen, 1910, 71ff. In his commentary on the Psalms of around 1237, Cæsarius of Heisterbach writes (see

A. E. Schönbach, *S.-B. Wien*, 159 [1908], 37): *plures illorum fuerunt ecclesiarum prelati, pastores vel canonici et nonnulli fili regum, comitum, nobilium divitumque*. HG/1960.]

29. *Vita* in *AF* 2.35; cf. *I Cel.* § 24: *Franciscus de tanti viri adventu et conversatione gavisus est; Legenda trium sociorum*, c. 29: *qui erat dives valde*; cf. Fortini, *Nova vita*, 168–69, 177.

30. Cf. Jordanus, *Chronica*, 9 and 12; Sabatier, *Vie de S. François*, 258–59; idem, ed., *Speculum perfectionis seu S. Francisci Assisiensis Legenda antiquissima*, 71–72 and 112; *AF* 3.4; Fortini, *Nova vita*, 169, 178.

31. *II. Cel.*, c. 75; Bonaventure, *Legenda s. Francisci, Opera*, 8 (Quaracchi, 1898) 3.5; Anonymus Perusinus, "Legenda s. Francisci," c. 12; according to Fortini, *Nova vita*, 178, he was probably a canon of Assisi cathedral.

32. The *miles* Angelo Tancredi of Rieti, see *AF* 3.4; *Speculum perfectionis*, c. 85; *Actus b. Francisci et sociorum eius*, ed. Paul Sabatier (Paris, 1902) 9.23; and *Moricus parvulus*, according to Fortini, *Nova vita*, 178, from the "famiglia nobile" of the Morico.

33. *Frater Illuminatus* is often erroneously described as one of the twelve original friars; he was the son of *cuiusdam nobilis viri*, and was named Accarino signore della Rocca Accarina; cf. Sabatier, *Vie de S. François*, 258–89, and *Speculum perfectionis seu S. Francisci* (1898), 306–07.; Edward Lempp, *Frère Elie de Cortone, Étude biographique*, Collection d'Études et de Documents sur l'histoire religieuse et littéraire du Moyen Age, 3 (Paris, 1901), 173; Thomas of Celano, *Tractatus de miraculis*, c. 123, in *S. Francisci Assisiensis vita et miracula*, ed. d'Alençon, 407; also *Legenda trium sociorum*, ed. Michele Faloci-Pulignani, *MF* 7 (1898), 81–107.

34. *I Cel.*, c. 15 § 37.

35. James of Vitry, letter of 1216 in Heinrich Böhmer, *Analekten*, 67. In the *Historia occidentalis*, II, 32 (ibid., 70, written from 1219 on, essentially based on experience before 1216), James says of the Franciscans: *Multos non solum inferioris ordinis homines, sed generosos et nobiles ad mundi contemptum invitant, qui relictis oppidis et casalibus et amplis possessionibus temporales divitias in spirituales felici commercio commutantes habitum fratrum Minorum . . . assumperunt.*

36. Anonymus Perusinus, no. 18, p. 40; n. 47, p. 48. See also Bernard of Bessa, c. 2 (*AF* 3.671).

37. Simon Tuscus, *filius comitisse de Colazon*, s. Jordanus, *Chronica*, c. 19, ed. Böhmer, 23; *Actus b. Francisci*, c. 73. Benvenutus da Gubbio, *miles*, see *AF* 3.189. Riccieri da Muccia, *nobilis parentela*, student in Bologna, see *Intentio regulæ fratris Leonis*, ed. Lemmens, 83; *I Cel.* § 49; *II Cel.* § 44a; *Speculum perfectionis*, c. 2; *Actus b. Francisci*, c. 36–37. Rufinus Sciffi, a relative of Clara, was one of the three *socii, nobilis civis Assisii, de nobilioribus de Assisio*, see *Actus b. Francisci*, c. 31, 32, 35; *AF* 3.46–47. Angelo da Borgo S. Sepulcro, *juvenis nobilis*, see *Actus b. Francisci*, c. 29. Masseo da Marignano, *nobilis*, see *Actus*, c. 10. A *giovane da San Severino, nobile di sangue*, see *I Fioretti*, c. 41.

38. Johannes *qui erat clericus et sacerdos, AF* 3.186. Cæsarius of Speyer, *clericus*, see Jordanus, *Chronica*, c. 9. Masseo da San Severino, *plebanus*, s. *Actus*, c. 53, 3 (cf. *AF* 3.409). Antonius of Padua, from a noble family of Lisbon (*nobiliori genere progenitus*), Augustinian canon in a foundation at Lisbon, Gratianus, *sacerdos de Romagnolæ partibus oriundus; Dialogus de vitis sanctorum fratrum minorum*, 73. James of Vitry reports in 1220 that the prior of S. Michael in Acre, a master and several other clergy joined the Franciscans. Cf. also the *Legenda trium sociorum*, c. 54, and Pierrre Mandonnet, "Les Origines de l'Ordo de Pœnitentia" (Fribourg, 1897), 207.

39. Johannes Parentis, the second general of the order, *jurisperitus et judex in civitate Castellana*, joined the order together with his son, see *AF* 3.210; Jordanus, *Chronica*, c. 51. Otto Lambardus, who became the first provincial of the Rhenish province, was *jurisperitus*, see Jordanus, *Chronica*, c. 57, p. 49. Fr. Angelicus, *jurisperitus*, see Jordanus, *Chronica*, c. 32, p. 33. Niccolo di Guglielmo dei Pepoli, *judex sapiens, Actus*, c. 4; cf. Sabatier, *Vie*, 275ff. Peregrino da Fallerone, student in Bologna, *de Nobilioribus de Marchia Ancon., bene litteratus et in decretalibus eruditus*, see *Actus*, c. 36. James of Treviso and Marcus of Milan, *viri honesti et litterati*, see Jordanus, *Chronica*, c. 32, p. 33. Simon Anglicus, *vir scolasticus et magnus theologus*, the third German provincial, later reader in Magdeburg, see Jordanus, *Chronica*, c. 52, p. 47. Ambrosius Massanensis, *litterarum studiis mancipatus, divitias paupertate commutavit, cuncta quæ habuit pauperibus eroganda distraxit*, see *Dialogus de vitis sanctorum fratrum minorum*, ed. Lemmens, 51–52.

40. When the friars went to Germany in 1221, their first conversion in Trent was a burgher, Peregrinus, *vir dives*, who gave the brothers new clothes, then sold his possessions, giving the money to the poor and joining the friars. In Ylerda the friars won a prominent burgher, see *AF* 3.184–85.

41. Friar Pacificus, *qui in seculo vocabatur rex versuum, nobilis et curialis doctor cantorum*, cf. *Speculum perfectionis*, c. 59 and 100; Thomas Tuscus, *MG Script*. 22.492; *II Cel*., c. 72. Julian of Speyer had been court chaplain of Louis IX in Paris.

42. The sole early Franciscan who can be shown to have come from the artisans was Elias of Cortona, who had been a mattress-maker (*suebat cultras*, Salimbene, *MG Scr*. 32.96), but also taught children in Assisi to read (*docebat puerulos in civitate Assisii psalterium legere*) and was later a scriptor (*notary*) in Bologna (Thomas of Eccleston, *Tractatus de adventu fratrum minorum in Angliam*, ed. Andrew G. Little [Paris, 1909], 79), hence he was "an intellectually mobile craftsman," of whom it would be hard to say that "he came from the most humble ranks of society" (Sabatier, *Vie de S. François*, 233; cf. E. Lempp, *Frère Elie*). In the early days Friar Johannes Simplex also joined, the oldest son of a poor peasant, see *Legenda antiqua*, ed. Delorme, c. 19, p. 11; *Speculum perfectionis*, c. 57. Cf. also the conversion of three *latroni, Actus b. Francisci*, c. 29.

43. Marquard Longus of Aschenburg, Marquard Parvus of Mainz, Conrad of Worms; Jordanus, *Chronica*, c. 34/5, 40/1, 47, 54.

44. *De adventu minorum in Angliam*, c. 4, p. 27: in Oxford *multi probi et multi nobiles* entered the order; four *milites* who joined in London are named by Thomas, c. 2, as well as eight *magistri* and several clerics, priests, nobles from London, including the wealthy merchant Johannes Iwyn (c. 4, p. 26), who gave the friars their first lot for settlement in London, and who later entered the order himself, and finally the chancellor of Oxford, Eustachius of Normaneville (p. 64), *qui prius fuerat multum nobilis et dives magister artium et decretorum*. Thomas of Eccleston remarks (c. 10, p. 55): *Tales intrabant frequenter personæ, quibus videbatur de jure honorificentius providendum*. On the first French Franciscans I have collected no data, but I recall *magister* Alexander of Hales, who entered the order in Paris in 1222; he was from England.

45. Cf. also J. C. De Haan, *Tijdschrift voor Geschiedenis* 42.161, who opposes Gioacchino Volpes' view (*Movimenti religiosi*, 113–14) of the apostolic brethren of Segerelli and fra Dolcino (1260–1307) as a movement formed from economic and social causes and tendencies, uses telling sources and correct procedural questions.

46. Friedrich Glaser, *Die Franziskanische Bewegung* (Stuttgart, 1903).

CHAPTER 4

1. The letter of James of Vitry to his friends in Flanders, October 1216, is in Heinrich Böhmer, *Analekten*, 66: *Inpetravi, ut liceret mulieribus religiosis non solum in episcopatu Leodiensi, sed tam in regno quam in imperio, in eadem domo simul manere et sese invicem mutuis exhortationibus ad bonum invitare*. Both Greven and Hauck understand *regnum* and *imperium* as France and Germany respectively. On the addressees of James' letter, see Greven, *Die Anfänge der Beginen*, 138–39. [On James of Vitry, Maria of Oignies, and the beginnings of the beguines, see Ernest William McDonnell, *The Beguines and Beghards in Medieval Culture, With Special Emphasis on the Belgian Scene* (New Brunswick, N.J., 1954), reviewed by Alcantara Mens, *MA* 64 (1958), 305ff. and idem, *Oorsprong en betekenis*. HG/1960.]

2. Even before James of Vitry, another delegate of the religious women of Belgium had gone to the curia—perhaps to appear at the Lateran Council?—but he died on the way, in the Alps; cf. Thomas of Chamtimpré, *Vita Lutgardis*, 2, c. 1; *AASS*, 16 June 3, 245 (4, 1867, 197).

3. Cf. Philipp Funk, *Jakob von Vitry, Leben und Werke* (Leipzig; Berlin, 1909); Greven, *Anfänge der Beginen*, 54ff.

4. *Vita* II, 9, *AASS*, 23 June, 4, 658 (5, 1867, p. 565).

5. The prologue to the *Vita* of Maria of Oignies, *AASS*, 23 June 4, p. 638 (5 [1867], 549), is directed to Bishop Fulk of Toulouse, recalling his own statement from a visit in Belgium.

6. Francis was in Perugia when Innocent III died, and James of Vitry had just arrived, see Thomas of Eccleston, *Tractatus*, 119; cf. Callebaut, "Autour de la rencontre à Florence," *AFH* 19.545ff.

7. *Legenda antiqua s. Francisci*, ed. Delorme, p. 46, c. 79; cf. *II Cel.*, c. 152 § 210 (*AF* 10.245). Wadding and the Bollandists say, "He reserved Belgium to himself."

8. Callebaut, "Autour de la rencontre à Florence," 545ff., even believes that Francis might have learned of the Corpus Christi visions of Juliane of Cornillon from James of Vitry. These visions began as early as 1208, but would only precipitate the introduction of the festival of Corpus Christi in the 1240s.

9. James came to know Cardinal Ugolino during his first visit to Perugia, but it was only later, on a journey from Acre to the curia, that he presented him with the *Vita* of Marie of Oignies and a relic of her. Both of these reports come from Thomas of Chantimpré's additions to James' *Vita*, *AASS*, 23 June, 4, 672 (5 [1867], 577–78). Callebaut is incorrect when he has James giving the *Vita* to the cardinal in 1216.

10. Greven, *Anfänge der Beginen,* and Greven's article, "Der Ursprung des Beginenwesens," in *HJ* 35 (1914), 25–58, 291–318; Greven gives a short summary of his research in the journal *Der Belfried*, 1 (1916/17), 355ff. Among later work on the origins of the beguines, L. J. M. Philippen, *De Begijnenhoven, Oorsprong, Geschiedenis, Inrichting* (Antwerp, 1918) (with a complete bibliography on the literature of the beguine question, 435ff.) and several articles by J. van Mierlo.

11. Herman of Laon, see above, chapter 1, n. 78.

12. There need to be more detailed investigations on the women's houses of the Premonstratensians before sure conclusions can be drawn. For the time being, see Greven, *Anfänge der Beginen*, 112ff.; Lamy, *L'Abbaye de Tongerloo*, 92ff.; my own article, "Zur Geschichte der Beginen im 13. Jahrhundert," in *AKG* 21 (1931), 315ff., as well as the list of houses in Albert Hauck, *KD*, vol. 4, 3d and 4th eds. (Leipzig, 1913); vol. 5, 1st and 2d eds. (Leipzig, 1911/20); Schmitz-Kallenberg, *Monasticon Westfaliæ; the Verzeichnis der Stifter und Klöster Niedersachsens vor der Reformation* (Hanover-Leipzig, 1908) by H. Hoogeweg, and the *Hessisches Klosterbuch*, Veröffentlichungen der Historischen Kommission für Hessen und Waldeck 12 (Marburg, 1915) by Wilhelm Dersch. [On women's houses or double houses of the Premonstratensians (originally in Cappenberg) see Norbert Backmund, *Monasticon Præmonstratense*, 3 vols. (Straubing, 1949–1956), *passim*, esp. 1.196. HG/1960.]

13. Cf. above, chapter 1, n. 83; Johannes Le Paige, *Biblioteca Præmonstratensis Ordinis* (Paris, 1633), 354f. It is not known precisely when the decision not to admit any more women to the order was made. On 13 May 1198 Innocent III wrote to the abbots of the Premonstratensians (Ep. 1.198, *PL* 214.174) confirming this decision. After Innocent's death, Abbot Gervasius of Prémontré applied to the curia to have the renewed decision of the general chapter *de non recipiendis sororibus* reconfirmed by the new pope, see Carl Ludwig Hugo, *Sacræ antiquitatis monumenta*, 97. James of Vitry, in his *Historia orientalis et occidentalis* 2.22, pp. 324–25, without giving the date of this act. The decision must have been repeated in 1270, when it finally had the desired effect, see Greven, *Anfänge der Beginen*, 116–17; cf. the chapter *De*

non recipiendis sororibus (D. 4, c. 13) in the Premonstratensian statutes of 1290 in Le Paige, *Biblioteca Præmonstratensis Ordinis*, 826.

14. Cf. below, chapter 5, text at n. 5ff.

15. Greven, *Anfänge der Beginen*, 119ff. and "*Der Ursprung*," 316–17, where he summarizes his views as follows: "An autonomous beguine movement formed when the Premonstratensians began to relieve themselves of their female branch and the Cistercians sought to incorporate women into newly founded abbeys, though never sufficient to accommodate the stream of potential members and without persisting in their efforts to receive them. So the beguines took the place of the women's movement which the Premonstratensians had begun [?], arising first (roughly after 1199) as a prelude and stopgap alongside the Cistercian women's houses, but finally (after 1228) as an autonomous community, since the number of abbeys had become fixed." Greven correctly asserts against Hauck: "Nothing about these pious women indicates a rejection of the idea of monasticism, rather they all bespeak such a pressure on houses of orders that the limits of existing orders burst."

16. On the Lower Rhine, after the persecution of 1143/5 (see above), eight "Cathars" were burned in Cologne in 1163, including two women. They had come to Cologne from Flanders, but it is not known of what their heresy consisted; cf. *Chronica regia Colonensis*, 114; *Annales Coloniensis maximi, MG Scr.* 17.778; Cæsarius of Heisterbach, *Dialogus miraculorum*, 1.298–99. There are only traces of any persecutions of heretics in Germany in the last third of the century, see Theloe, *Die Ketzerverfolgungen*, 60.

17. Gerald of Wales, *Gemma ecclesiæ*, I, 11, *MG Scr.* 27.412 (about 1197). Cf. also the peculiar formulation of the heresy decree of Verona, 1184, which Lucius III sent to the bishop of Arras on 5 March 1185 (Fredericq, *Corpus* 1.56ff.).

18. William of Nangis, *Recueil des Historiens des Gaules et de la France*, ed. Léopold Delisle (Paris, 1869ff.) 20.741; Fredericq, *Corpus* 1.50.

19. *Annales Rodenses* for 1135, see Fredericq *Corpus*, 1.30; letter of the clergy of Liège to Lucius II, 1145, ibid., p. 32; Hildegard of Bingen, see above, chapter 1, n. 22.

20. Letter of the clergy of Liège to Lucius II, Fredericq, *Corpus* 1.32–33.

21. Cf. chapter 1 above.

22. Cf. Arnold Fayen, "L'Antigraphum Petri et les lettres concernantes Lambert le Bègue, conservées dans le manuscrit de Glasgow," *Compte rendu des séances de la commission royale d'histoire* 68 (5th series, 9) (Brussels, 1899), 255ff.; Greven, *Anfänge der Beginen*, 158f.; J. van Mierlo, "De bijnaam van Lambertus il Beges en de vroegste beteekenis van het woord Begijn," *VMKVA* (Ghent, 1925), 405–47, and "Lambert li Begues in verband met den oorsprong der begijnenbeweging," ibid. (1926), 612–60.

23. *Verbum abbreviatum, PL* 205.230; expanded version, 545ff.

24. Col. 230; the same story in a different version, col. 545. Cf. 230 and 546–47, telling the story of the recluse to whom no one would give alms because she was thought to have had dealings with Cathars. She asked a learned

cleric how she could purge herself of the suspicion of heresy, and trusting in her own innocence and his advice, she submitted herself to the ordeal. When it ruled against her, she was burned.

25. Radulph, abbot of Coggeshall, reports the story without criticism (*Chronicon anglicanum, Recueil* 18.92–93); he even relates credulously that the *magistra* withdrew from the proceedings by vanishing through the window into thin air, *malignorum spirituum ministro, ut credimus, subvecta.* Radulph lists the entire sequence of Cathar errors for this case, including rumors about subterranean orgies, for *virginitatem predicant in operimentum sue turpitudinis.*

26. Cf. Greven, *Anfänge der beginen*, 70 f.; "*Der Ursprung*," 33ff., 38–39, 44–45, 47. J. van Mierlo, "De bijnam van Lambertus," 424ff., took the word "beguine" to be a shortened form of the word "Albigenses," convincingly, so far as I'm concerned, although this has not found universal acceptance (cf. Grundmann, "Zur Geschicte der Beginen," 296). What is certain is that the Cologne chronicler used the term "Beggini" at the start of the thirteenth century as the proper term for Albigensians (*Chronica regia Coloniensis*, ed. Waitz, 185: *qui Beggini dicebantur*; 187: *heresis, cuius cultores Beggini denominabantur*; cf. ibid., 229, 233–34), hence not bestowing on the Southern French heretics a name deriving from a Belgian phenomenon on the basis of analogy, as L. J. M. Philippen believes (*Les Béguines et l'hérésie albigoise*, Annales de l'Academie royale d'Archéologie de Belgique 73 [1925], 233ff.). Secondly, religious women in Belgium and the bishopric of Liège were actually suspected of Catharism when they were called beguines. The probable though not absolutely certain conclusion is that the word "beguine" is identical with "Albigensian." Cf. also J. van Mierlo, "Ophelderingen bij de vroegste geschiedenis van het wood begijn," *VMKVA* [1931], 983ff.). On the other hand, recent attempts at the etymology of the word "beguine" from the Romance side have produced nothing new or convincing; see E. Gamillscheg, *ZRP* 40 (1920), 138–39 and 382–33; J. Bruck, ibid., 690–91; L. Spitzer, ibid., 41 (1921), 351 f. The notion that the Liège priest Lambert was called *beginus* (= heretic), which formed later into his nickname *le Bègue* (= stutterer), reported by Greven and van Mierlo, is not supported in the original sources. Lambert's nickname appears to have been developed in the middle of the thirteenth century in order to provide a less pejorative etymology for the word "beguine" and to declare Lambert the founder of the beguines; cf. "Zur Geschichte der Beginen," 297 and below in this chapter. [On the derivation of the word "begina" from "Albigen-ses" see now J. van Mierlo, "De wederwaardigheden van een etymologie: De vroegste geschiedenis van het woord 'begin'," *VMKVA* (1945), 31–51; in agreement McDonnell, *Beguines and Beghards*, 435ff.; Alcantara Mens, *Oorsprong*, 351ff. contradicts, without convincing grounds. HG/1960.]

27. Cf. my article "Zur Geschichte der Beginen," 315ff.; Johannes Linneborn, "Die Westfälischen Klöster des Cistercienzerordens bis zum 15. Jahrhundert," *Festgabe für Heinrich Finke* (Münster, 1904), 262ff. More than 150 female houses arose on German soil between 1200 and 1250 which were either incorporated into the Cistercian order or followed its constitutions.

28. Beguines are, of course, only reported later in the records in France, when the term "beguine" had become an accepted term for pious women, cf. Léon Le Grand, *Les Béguines de Paris* (Paris, 1893), 300ff.

29. Thomas of Chantimpré, *Bonum universale de apibus*, ed. Georgius Colvenerius (Douai, 1627) 2.38 (p. 391). Stephan of Bourbon (ed. A. Lecoy de la Marche, *Anecdotes historiques*, 20–21, § 11) says concerning Philip of Monmirail: *multa monasteria albarum monialium in Francia construxit*, telling the story of a beguine he had told him (see below, chapter 7, n. 124).

30. Frater Jordanus, *Chronica*, 8.

31. See the "List of the Perfect" in *De Visionen van Hadewijch*, ed. J. van Mierlo, Leuvense Studien en Tekstuitgaven 10 (Louvain-Ghent-Malines, 1924/5), 179ff. I agree with J. van Mierlo in his evaluation of Sister Hadewich's personality, who convincingly opposes equating her with the Brussels heretic Bloemenardinne, whom Ruysbroeck is supposed to have combated due to her doctrine of the free spirit (according to the *Vita* of Ruysbroeck composed by Pomerius about 1415/20). He overcomes all objections to the proposition that Hadewich probably lived and wrote in the first half of the thirteenth century, was born into a noble family in Antwerp about 1180/90. She was swept up by the religious movement from the age of eleven, but never entered a convent, living instead in Nivelles, the center of the beguines, playing a leading role in the religious-ecstatic women's movement as leader of a beguinage. She died in old age between 1260 and 1269, and out of recognition for her holiness she was solemnly buried in the Cistercian house of Villiers alongside other holy men and women of her time (including Juliana of Cornillon) in 1269. On van Mierlo's various works, see the bibliography. He summarizes his research in "Hadewijch une mystique flamande du 13e siècle," *RAM* 5 (1924), 269ff., and in the introduction to his edition of Hadewich's visions. Cf. also T. Brandsma, "Wanneer schreef Hadewych hare Visioenen?" *SC* 2 (1926), 238ff.

32. Hadewich, *Visionen* (ed. J. van Mierlo 1.189), mentions in the "List of Perfect" a contemporary who had died, a *beghine, die meester Robbaert doedde om hare gherechte minne*.

33. Paul Fredericq, *Inquisitio hæreticæ pravitatis neerlandica. Geschiedenis der Inquisitie in de Nederlanden tot aan haare hereinrichting onder keizer Karel V (1025–1520)* (Ghent, 1892–7) 1.50ff.; J. Frederichs, *Robert le Bougre, premier inquisiteur générale en France*, 1892; J. van Mierlo, *Dietsche Warande en Belfort* (1921) 1.455ff.; Charles Homer Haskins, "Robert le bougre and the Beginnings of the Inquisition in Northern France," *AHR* 7 (1902), 437ff., 631ff. = *Studies in Mediaeval Culture*, 193ff. The beguine killed by Robert the inquisitor, mentioned by Hadewich, was probably Alaydis, burned on 17 February 1236 in Cambrai. She was an older woman who had become famous for her piety over a wide area before Robert "uncovered" her; see Alberich of Troisfontaines, *MG Scr*. 23.937; T. Brandsma, SC 2.238ff.

34. Cf. Philippen, *De Begijnenhoven*, 31–32: in 1232 the women in Louvain were still spoken of as *mulieres religiosæ*, in Ghent in 1233 as *religiosæ mulieres caste et sub disciplina vivere volentes*, in 1235 in the same town they

are *pauperes religiosæ mulieres*, in 1241 in Liège they are *mulieres religiosæ*. It is only in 1239 that the bishop of Cambrai first calls them *religiosæ mulieres quæ beghinæ dicuntur*. On the same development of the terminology in Germany, see Grundmann, "Zur Geschichte der Beginen," 307; in 1233 a charter of the bishop of Osnabrück speaks of *femine religiose, quas sorores vocant die Rede*; in 1240 the same women are described as *femine, quas sorores vel beggynas vocant*. In the same way, the name asserted itself in the period between 1233 and 1244 in German synodical statutes, see chapter 6, nn. 14–15. A bull of Gregory IX of 1233 speaks of the *virgines continentes perpetuam deo vocantes castitatem*, in a bull of 1235 they are first described as *sorores conversæ, quæ Beginæ vulgariter appellantur*; papal bulls continued to preserve the circumlocution; they almost never used the term "beguine" as a true proper name.

35. In a passage for 1248, the chronicler Matthew Paris said that the meaning of the word "beguine" was as unknown as the origin of the group, *MG Scr*. 28.417. Gautier de Coincy says in his poem of 1220 at the latest (see below, chapter 7, text at n. 49 and following, Étienne Barbazan, *Fabliaux et contes des poètes françois*, ed. M. Méon [Paris, 1808], I, p. 320, v. 1516ff.): *begin, ce dient* [= *dicunt*] *se derive / et vient a benignitate. / . . . Je i sai autre derivoison: . . . Begin se viennent de begon / et de begin revient begars*. Cf. William of St. Amour, *Magistri Guillelmi de Sancto Amore Opera omnia, quæ reperiri potuerunt* (Coutances, 1632), 266: *Beginæ ideo appellantur, ut asserunt, quasi benignæ, vel quasi bono igne ingitæ*; on similar false etymologies of the word, see Alfons Hilka, "Altfranzösische Mystik und Beginentum," *ZRP* 47 (1927), 165. After as early as 1220 there were already efforts to recover the origin of the word "beguine"; because its original meaning was no longer known, invented etymologies sought to assign it a new meaning.

36. The *Annales principum Hannoniæ* of the Franciscan James of Guise (died 1399), which derives from the tradition of the Cistercian house of Fontenelles, describes the way of life of the beguinage which developed in Fontenelles in 1212 before the convent emerged from it: *Nec regula speciali aut statuta obediencialibus, habitu approbato aut ceremoniis regularibus minime vinciebantur, sed solum divinis preceptis et consiliis evangelicis et juxta collationes in vitis patrum contentas, observationes grosso et rudimodo prout melius poterant innitebantur obnixe; MG Scr*. 30, 1, 264. James of Vitry in his beguine sermon (Greven, "*Der Ursprung*," 464–47f.) portrays the women's movement and the rise of the beguines in a summary fashion.

37. Hauck, *KD* 5.382, still says of the religious-ecstatic women of the start of the thirteenth century: "They were members of the middle and lower levels of the population."

38. See above, chapter 1; detailed studies of the class origin of Premonstratensian female houses are lacking, but cf. Lamy, *L'abbaye de Tongerloo*, 100.

39. Cf. Linneborn, "Die westfälische Klöster," 340ff.; Grundmann, "Zur Geschichte der Beginen," 317; James of Vitry, *Historia orientalis et occidentalis*, 305–06, describes the flood of women into the Cistercian order. The

Leven van Sinte Lutgard also describes the Cistercian sisters in Aywières in most cases as *edele nonne, edele nonne wel geboren*, etc. (ed. Fr. van Veerdeghem [Leiden, 1898), v. 3775, 4980ff., 10581ff., 5353, etc.). In the Cistercian female houses of Southern Germany as well, almost all are noble, see G. Bruschius, *Monasteriorum Germaniæ centuria*, I (Ingolstadt, 1551) 1.101 on Pirckenfeld, 144 on Schlüsselau, 112 on Wasserschaffen-Heiligen Kreuztal, 36–37 on Himmelkron im Vogtland.

40. Greven, "Der Ursprung," 47.

41. Cf. Greven, *Anfänge der Beginen,* 89ff.; *Vita* of James of Vitry, *AASS*, June, 4, 639–40. (5, 1867, 550–51.)

42. Greven, *Anfänge der Beginen*, 92ff., 63; cf. also the *Annales principum Hannoniæ, MG Scr.* 30, 1, 264ff. on the foundation of the beguinage (later the Cistercian women's house) at Fontenelles near Valanciennes by two daughters of a "noble knight," soon joined by *virgines adulescentulæ nobilies ac potentum filiæ*. Hagiographers often stressed that Belgian religious women did not descend from nobility, but rather from *mediocribus parentibus*, which meant that they derived neither from the nobility nor from the poor, but from wealthy burghers. James of Vitry says of this Maria of Oignies: *Quæ mediocribus orta parentibus, licet divitiis et multis bonis temporalibus abundaret* [!], *numquam tamen eius animum bona transitoria ab annis puerilibus allexerunt* (*AASS*, June, IV, p. 639: Bollandists erroneously believed it necessary to insert *non mediocribus* as a correction). Ida of Léau is described in the same terms—but Ida made no use of her *dives parentela*; *AASS*, 29 October, 13, 109. Ida of Nivelles was also *mediocribus orta parentibus*, as was Beatrix of Nazareth (see C. Henriquez, *Quinque prudentes virgines* [Antwerp, 1630], 199), whose father was a very wealthy burgher of Tirlemont, who founded three houses for Cistercian women from his own wealth; cf. J. van Mierlo's introduction to Beatrix' tracts. On Christine of Stommeln, whose father was a brewer, Peter of Dacia says in his *Vita Christinaw Stumbelensis*, ed. Johannes Paulsen (Gottenburg, 1896), 111: *Eligens pocius esse cum deo in paupertate quam cum parentibus in deliciis permanere*.

43. Cf. Gottfried of Beaulieu's *Vita Ludovici* (*Recueil* 20.12) says that several beguines from the impoverished nobility were paid a pension by Louis IX; the other *mulieres honestæ* did not need one.

44. Cf. *Vie de Ste. Douceline* by Philippine de Porcellet, ed. Joseph Mathias Albanès (*La vie de sainte Douceline, fondateur des Béguines de Marseille* [Marseille, 1879]); ed. E. Gout, 1927.

45. James of Vitry, prologue to his *Vita* of Maria of Oignies, *AASS*, June, 4, p. 636 (cf. Greven, *Anfänge der Beginen*, 65). Also see James' sermon to beguines cited above. Ida of Louvaine was also a child of wealthy and respected parents, but out of her *desiderium paupertatis et abjectionis*, she made as little use of her father's goods *tamquam de perperam acquistitis*, in the face of her father's active disapproval. Instead, she earned her keep herself, spinning or weaving (*nendo*) at night, and from her earnings she could even give some alms; *AASS*, 13 April, 2, 158, 163ff.

46. *Chronicon . . . Laudunensis, 21: De mobilibus his, a quibus injuste habuerat, reddidit.*

47. Cf. the Rule in Zanoni, *Umiliati*, 354: *pro posse suo injuste habita reddentes*; cf. the *propositum* of the tertiary order in Hieronymus Tiroboschi, *Vetera Humiliatorum monumenta* (Milan, 1766–68) 2.131: *usuras et omnia male oblata reddite!*

48. Letter of Innocent III to the bishop of Elne, Ep. 15.82, *PL* 216.601.

49. The contempt and mockery many rich, prominent relatives expressed for women who committed themselves to voluntary poverty is often documented; cf. the *Vita* of Maria of Oignies, I, 15, *AASS*, June 4, 640; also 2, 3, 652 on the attitude of society against the knight Iwan of Rèves, converted by Maria. Brother Herman's biography of the Countess Jolande von Vianden, see John Meier, ed., *Bruder Hermanns Leben der Gräfin Jolande von Vianden* (Breslau, 1889), esp. verses 1615ff.

50. The Landgravine Elizabeth of Thuringia, whose life is only understandable in the context of the general women's religious movement, gave this ruling to her followers, in keeping with the advice of her confessor Conrad of Marburg: withdraw *ab illicite acquisitis*, see A. Huyskens, *Quellenstudien zur Geschichte der Hl. Elisabeth, Landgräfin von Thüringen* (Marburg, 1908), 116. Since Elisabeth Busse-Wilson, *Das Leben der heiligen Elisabeth von Thüringen; das Abbild einer mittelalterlichen Seele* (Munich, 1931), cannot see this connection in her biography of Elizabeth of Thuringia, p. 126, she interprets "the Church politics" of Conrad of Marburg as being behind this demand, sneakily taking advantage of his ward. In fact, this had been a religious demand long before either Elizabeth or Conrad lived, and one which Elizabeth sought conscientiously to pursue.

51. Just as Francis wanted his brethren to support themselves through their own labor, only permitting them to beg in cases of necessity, or as, for example, the adherents of Bernardus Primus depended on their own labor and the alms of their hearers, so also the religious women of Belgium supported themselves with their own labor, accepting alms only in special circumstances; see Greven, *Anfänge der Beginen*, 99ff.; *HJ*, 35, 53, 58, 65; cf. idem, "Der Ursprung," 47. Also Gautier de Coincy (about 1220) says of the beguines he loathed, *vilain mestier et ort* [= *art?*] *aprenent*; Barbazan, *Fabliaux et contes* 1.310, verse 1227. Cæsarius of Heisterbach, *Dialogus miraculorum*, IV, 84 (ed. Strange, 1.251). The labor of the beguines almost always consisted of spinning or weaving—exactly as was the case with the Cathars: in both cases, this activity was the most suitable source of income for religious "home workers" and "casual workers."

CHAPTER 5

1. Pierre Mandonnet, "Les Origines de l'Ordo de pœnitentia," vol. 5, 194, cites an unpublished work of Herman of Minden, Dominican Provincial of Germany: *Nota quod nominibus istis "ordo" et "religio" et huiusmodi*

indifferenter utimur; also the sentence: *religio, ordinem, ordo regulam, regula instituta genuerunt*. Cf. also Goetz, "Die ursprüngliche Ideale," 30–31.

2. Prologue to the rule for Italian women's houses, Sbaralea, *Bullarium Franciscanum* 1.263 and 395: *Cum omnis vera religio et vitæ institutio approbata certis constet regulis et mensuris, certis etiam constet legibus disciplinæ, quisquis religiosam ducere vitam cupit, nisi certam atque rectam conversationis suæ regulam disciplinamque vivendi observare studuerit diligenter, eo ipso a rectitudine deviat, quo rectitudinis lineas non observat, et ibi deficiendi incurrit periculum, ubi per discretionis virtutem certum ac stabile proficiendi collocare neglexerit fundamentum.*

3. The thoroughness of the investigations following will appear justified to anyone who knows the contradictory treatments of the *cura monialium* in the Cistercian Order (Winter, Hauck, *KD*, Gr. Müller, and others), the Dominican Order (Mortier, Danzas, Denifle, Baur, Wilms, Finke, Rother and others), or on the Poor Clares and their rule (Lempp, Lemmens, Wauer, Oliger, and others). I will abstain from correcting the many errors of detail on the history of particular orders in this literature in order to prevent my account from growing even further out of proportion. Those errors and confusions are due not only to insufficient attention paid to the general connections shared by the histories of particular orders, but to inadequate analysis and imprecise interpretation of original sources, which I will cite extensively, not through errant paraphrases. As soon as a person views historical connections from all sides, as I have done, bringing together the policy of the curia, the inclination of the women's religious movement, and the attitude of the mendicant orders, specifically the evolution of the Dominican and Franciscan orders, the events prove to be a clear, comprehensible process, whose individual acts, once so contradictory and unexplainable, interconnect like the links of a chain. All that remain unexplained are unimportant side-questions, a result of gaps in the sources.

4. See above, chapter 1, n. 81ff.; chapter 4, text at n. 11ff.

5. Gregor Müller, "Vom Cistercienserorden," *Cistercienser-Chronik* 37 (1925), 233, believes that the Cistercian Order must have expressly decided to admit women's houses to the order, since the legislation of the order first concerned itself with the *moniales* of the order in 1212, and that no nuns belonged to the order before this, but this supposition seems unnecessary to me. Women's houses joined as a result of the conditions of the time, not in response to legislation, and the order intervened formally only once there were problems.

6. The relationship of the Cistercian Order to women's houses has never been fully clarified. References are found in Franz Winter, *Die Cistercienser des nordöstlichen Deutschlands* (Gotha, 1868/71), 2, 4–5, 17; Albert Hauck, *KD*, vol. 4, 3d and 4th eds. (Leipzig, 1913); vol. 5, 1st and 2d eds. (Leipzig, 1911/20), 4, 425; Kirchesch, *Die Verfassung und die wirtschaftlichen Verhältnisse*, 4ff.; Gregor Müller, "Vom Cistercienser-Orden," 233–34, 252; Werner Ronnenberger, *Das Zisterzienser-Nonnenkloster zum hl. Kreuz bei Saalburg, an der Saale* (Jena, 1932), 24ff.; Johannes Zeimet, *Die Cistercienserinnenabtei St. Katharinen bei Linz am Rhein*, Germania Sacra, Abteilung Rhenania sacra

regularia, 1: B. Die Cistercienser-Klöster (Augsburg; Cologne, 1929), 5ff. Since the new critical edition of acts of the general chapter of the Cistercian Order, *Statuta capitulorum generalium ordinis Cisterciensis*, ed. Joseph Marie Canivez (Louvain, 1933–1941) (vol. 1 [1933], through 1220) is not yet available to me, I use the older, imprecise edition by Martène and Durand, *Thesaurus* 4.1243ff. and Hugo Séjalon, *Nomasticon Cisterciense seu antiquiores ordinis cistericensis constitutiones, editio nova* (Salesmis, 1892). [See E. G. Krenig, *Mittelalterliche Frauenkloster nach den Konstitutionen von Cîteaux, unter besonderer Berücksichtigung fränkischer Nonnenkonvente*, Dissertation, Würzburg, 1953); *ASOC* 10 (1954), 1–105; cf. also B. Huemer, "Verzeichnis der deutschen Zisterzienserinnenklöster," *SMGB*, new series, 6 (1916), 1–47. Simone Roisin, "L'efflorescence et le courant féminin au XIIIe siècle," *RHE* 39 (1943), 342–78. HG/1960.]

7. 1212 (c. 13, Martène and Durand, *Thesaurus* 4.1311–12); in 1218 the ruling was made that women's houses had to be at least six miles from male houses and ten miles from one another (p. 1322; Séjalon, *Nomasticon*, 282).

8. 1213 (c. 2, p. 1312, cf. Séjalon, *Nomasticon*, 279): *Moniales, que jam incorporate sunt ordini, non habeant liberum egressum, nisi de licentia abbatis, sub cuius cura consistunt. . . . Si que vero fuerint incorporande de cetero, non aliter admittantur ad ordinis unitatem, nisi penitus includende; Inhibetur . . . , ne presumant mittere moniales suas ad aliquem locum constituendum nisi de licentia capituli generalis; quod si presumptum fuerit, que sic misse fuerint, pro fugitivis habeantur*. The command for enclosure was made stricter in 1219 (c. 10, p. 1324; cf. Séjalon, *Nomasticon*, 282, c. 12 for 1218). The incorporation of nuns desired by the archbishop of Cologne was made dependent on whether they lived in strict enclosure (c. 23, p. 1325). In 1225 (c. 6, p. 1340) it was ordered: *Nullus preter visitatores claustra earum ingrediatur, nec detur eis licentia loquendi nisi per fenestram ad hoc honestius preparatam, et per eandem fenestram loquantur etiam de confessione*; houses in which strict enclosure had not been introduced five years after incorporation were to be excluded from the order; this rule was repeated and made more severe in 1228 (c. 8, p. 1349) and again in 1268 (c. 2, p. 1429).

9. 1219 (c. 10, p. 1324; cf. Séjalon, *Nomasticon*, 282, c. 12 for 1218): *abbas visitator taxet numerum personarum, quem transgredi non licebit*; 1225 (c. 6, p. 1340) repeats it with the addition: *quod abbatisse et priorisse, que taxatum numerum transgredi presumserint, sciant esse deponendas*; in 1239, special inspectors were named to establish the possessions and incomes of newly incorporated women's houses, setting the maximum number of nuns in proportion (c. 6, p. 1369; cf. 1267, c. 2, p. 1427 and 1242, c. 13, p. 1378).

10. 1220, c. 4, p. 1327 (cf. Séjalon, *Nomasticon*, 283, c. 9): *Inhibetur auctoritate capituli generalis, ne aliqua abbatia monialium de cetero ordini incorporetur.*

11. In 1225 (c. 6, p. 1340–41) the order was given: *Ne ulle de cetero incorporetur ordini; incorporande ad novas mittantur abbatias, donec peractis competenter edificiis ita possessionibus et rebus necessariis suffi-*

cienter dotate (fuerint), quod possint penitus includi et incluse sustentari de suo, ita quod eas non oporteat mendicare. The ban of 1220 was relaxed in 1221 (c. 27, p. 1332) in favor of the house of Pantemont, whose incorporation had already been promised to the bishop of Amiens, and in 1223 in response to the desire of the bishop of Toulouse in favor of the house of Depontio and its filials (c. 29, p. 1337).

12. 1222 (c. 12, p. 1334).

13. 1228 (c. 7, p. 1348): *Nulla monasteria monialium de cetero sub nomine aut sub jurisdictione ordinis nostri construantur vel ordini socientur. Si quod vero monasterium ordini nondum sociatum vel etiam construendum nostras institutiones voluerit emulari, non prohibemus, sed curam animarum earum non recipiemus nec visitationis officium eis impendemus.*

14. The edition of chapter decrees by Martène and Durand, *Thesaurus*, does not show any decree on the treatment of women's houses incorporated *ex precepto domini pape* was passed in 1228. This is to be found in the acts of the general chapter of 1239 (c. 6, p. 1369). In the *Institutiones capituli generalis* of 1256, dist. XV c. 1 (Séjalon, *Nomasticon*, 360) the wording of the decision is given following the order cited in the last note: *Si qua vero ex precepto domini pape aut alia necessitate suscipere oportuerit, non prius ordini socientur, donec, peractis competenter edificiis, ita possessionibus et rebus necessariis sufficienter dotata fuerint, quod possint moniales penitus includi et inclusi secundum ordinem vivere, ita quod eas non oporteat mendicare*; cf. the decree of 1225 in n. 11 above.

15. Cf. the statutes of the general chapter of 1230 (c. 7 and 11, p. 1352): 1231 (c. 11, p. 1353); 1235 (pp. 1362–63). On 26 June 1232 Gregory IX directed the abbot of Clairvaux to invest the abbot of Himmerode with the visitation and care of souls of the nuns' house of Löwenbrucken and to have them instructed in the statutes of the order *juxta eiusdem ordinis constituta. (Mittelrheinisches Urk.-B.*, 3, 360, no. 459). In 1233 the abbot of Cîteaux incorporated the nuns' house of Heiligkreuztal (near Riedlingen) *ad petitionem vestram, de mandato domini pape, cuius litteras super hoc recepimus speciales, et de assensu et beneplacito nostri capituli generalis* (Königliches Staatsarchiv in Stuttgart, ed., *Wirtembergisches Urk.-B.* [Stuttgart, 1849–1913] 3.320, no. 825; the sisters already used the Rule of St. Benedict and the institutions of the Cistercians, see ibid., 284ff., n. 790). The same in 1235 with the nuns' house of Marienborn in Ramsdorf (later Coesfeld, see *Westfälisches Urk.-B.* 3.180, no. 330). Since the chapter decrees of the following years (1235, c. 1, p. 1360; 1244, c. 7, p. 1382; 1268, c. 2, p. 1429) repeatedly mention *moniales ordini de cetero sociande*, incorporations through papal fiat were obviously still frequent. Incidentally, the ban on members of the order working for the incorporation of new women's houses was not always obeyed; cf. n. 57 below.

16. 1230 (c. 7, p. 1352): *injungitur abbatibus ad curiam profecturis, ut insinuent domino pape statutum capituli generalis de monasteriis monialium ordini de cetero non sociandis, et impetretur ab eo, quod si quas ad*

capitulum direxerit litteras, non facta mentione de prædicta statuto, non habeant firmitatem.

17. Cf. Ripoll, *Bullarium* 1.107. I do not know of a corresponding bull for the Cistercian Order. Cf. the bull of Alexander V to the general chapter in Cîteaux, 20 June 1257 (*Westfälisches Urk.-B.* 3.328, no. 621): the nuns' house of Rengering (diocese of Münster), which had pursued the institutions of the Cistercians for forty years, asked for papal mediation to be incorporated into the order. The order is to incorporate the house, *si tot redditus habeat, de quibus commode valeant sustinari, . . . gerendo curam earundem sicut aliorum monasteriorum ipsius ordinis specialem, non obstante statuto de non incorporandis amodo eidem ordini monialibus aut ipsarum monasteriis, ut dicitur, a nobis nuper facto iuramento, confirmatione sedis apostolice seu quacumque firmitate alia roborato, sive quavis alia dicte sedis indulgentia, de qua planam et expressam oporteat in presentibus mentionem fieri.*

18. Between 1229 and 1235 the bishops of Minden and Ratzeburg wrote to Gregory IX: *cum plurima sint cenobia dominarum ordinis Cisterciensis in Alamannia eidem ordini nondum adhuc incorporata vel a sede apostolica talis ordo sit confirmatus, supplicamus sanctitati vestre, ut ordinem talium dominarum, cum ordinem Cisterciensium observent, licet non incorporate, dignemini vestra auctoritate confirmare; Westfälisches Urk.-B.* 5.354–55, nos. 365–66. [See Otmar Decker, *Die Stellung des Predigerordens zu den Dominikanerinnen*, 1207–1267, Quellen und Forschungen zur Geschichte des Dominikanerordens in Deutschland, 31, 1935. HG/1960.]

19. Stephan of Bourbon (ed. Lecoy de la Marche, *Anecdotes historiques*, p. 35 § 27): when Dominic preached in Fanjeaux, nine *matronæ* approached him and said: *illos homines, contra quos predicas, usque modo credidimus et vocavimus "bonos homines"* (cf. above, chapter 1, n. 17). According to Stephan's account, Dominic achieved the conversion of these women by means of an exorcism. This should not reduce the believability of the historical situation, which was reported in a similar way in other sources; cf. Berthold Altaner, *Der heilige Dominikus, Untersuchungen und Texte* (Breslau, 1922), 36 and 124–25.

20. This agrees with the account in Jordan of Saxony, *De initiis ordinis*, c. 18 (J.-J. Berthier, 10): *Ad susceptionem autem quarundam feminarum nobilium, quas parentes earum ratione paupertatis erudiendas et nutriendas tradebant hereticis, earum miseratus approbrium servus Dei Didascus quoddam instituit monasterium . . . Prulianum* (as a result of a decision of the general chapter of 1259 the name "Dominicus" was substituted for "Didascus" in the text, *MOPH* 3.98). Further, Bishop Fulk of Toulouse, in the earliest charter for Prouille in 1206 describes the women in Prouille as *mulieres conversæ per prædicatores ad prædicandum contra hæreticos et ad repellendam hæresim pestiferam delegatos* (Guiraud, *Cartulaire* 1.1, no. 1; cf. 2.73, no. 322), and in another charter of 15 May 1211: *dominæ conversæ religiose viventes*; similarly Archbishop Berengar of Narbonne describes the women of Prouille on 17 April 1207 as *priorissa et moniales noviter conversæ monitis et exemplis fr. Dominici Oxomensis sociorumque eius* (ibid., p. 109, n. 348 and p. 158, n. 401).

Scheeben, *Dominikus*, 73, tries to interpret the words *mulieres conversæ* in the last two charters cited not in the sense of "converted heretics," but rather in the sense of "women won for the religious life." Other sources cause him to concede (80) that "if one is to believe later biographers," some converted heretics did join the community. His view is that, despite the agreement of authorities on this point, the first women were not adherents of the heretics before their "conversion." Scheeben can only document this with the remark that it was "not easy to understand Dominic believing converted heretical women to be suited to give instruction in Catholic faith and educate others to a Catholic life." Contrary to this it should be said that the women of Prouille were not entrusted with such duties at first (see n. 24 below) and that "reconciled heretics" were often used in other cases (the "Catholic Poor," Bernardus Primus) as preachers against heresy.

21. Scheeben can only support his assertion, "The women were not subjected to any monastic obligations of any sort," with the *argumentum ex silentio* that until 1211 there was no talk of a "convent" of Prouille, and that the terms "prioress" and *moniales* (found even earlier) do not necessarily indicate a monastic community living according to an approved rule.

22. Scheeben, *Dominikus*, 88, supposes that Dominic introduced the Rule of St. Augustine in Prouille in 1211 without requiring the sisters to take an oath. On 197 he says that until 1216 Prouille was a "free organization, independent of any of the older rules of orders," a community which lived "according to an entirely modern rule composed by Dominic." In 1216 the introduction of a new rule modeled on that of the Premonstratensians proved necessary (199, but contradicting it on 243: "in itself the change in the rule for the friars preacher did not entail a change in the rule of the sisters as well").

23. On the constitutions of S. Sisto, see Scheeben, *Dominikus*, 247–48; André Simon, *L'Ordre des Pénitentes de S. Marie-Madelaine en Allemagne au XIIIe siècle*, Theological thesis (Fribourg, Switzerland, 1918), 38 ff.; Ripoll, *Bullarium* 7.410.

24. Scheeben, *Dominikus*, tries to prove that Prouille was originally not a convent but part of a "preaching factory" established by Diego and Dominic, an "apostolic women's community" (76) which was "related to a large scale to the care of the lay soul" (248), whose task was the education of children and the religious education of grown persons. In his conception the women of Prouille made "missionary journeys in the environs of Prouille, visiting Catholic families, instructing children and grown persons in the doctrine of the Church and recruiting for missionary activity," and they "collected and educated the children of Catholic parents in residential schools" (74). But there is not a scrap of evidence for this "missionary" and doctrinal work of the women of Prouille. This arbitrary construct, which makes Prouille the precise analogy of the "heretic schools," is documented by Scheeben (435, no. 137) only by their confrontation with the heretics, their boarding schools, mentioned by Jordan (see above, n. 20), and by the "participation of women in the labor of missions," which Scheeben tries to document with a ("obviously badly mutilated") charter of

1207 in which two parents dedicate themselves and their goods *domino deo et b. Mariæ et omnibus sanctis et sanctæ prædicationi et domino Dominico de Osma et omnibus fratribus et sororibus, qui hodie sunt vel in futuro erunt*, causing this donation *ad sanctam prædicationem* to be confirmed by the recipients (Guiraud, *Cartulaire* 2.1 and 234). Scheeben wins his whole concept of the "missionary activity" of those men and women under the leadership of Diego and Dominic from this muddled document, an activity which Dominic himself described as *sancta prædicatio* (74, cf. 97: "this is not differentiated from a mission station in China or Africa"). But Scheeben's entire construct lacks historical foundation. Antonin Danzas, *Études sur les temps primitifs de l'ordre de St. Dominique*, 4 (Paris, 1877), 4–5, already lodged a convincing protest against such an unhistorical view of the foundation of Prouille. Scheeben concedes that after 1211 the other goal of the community of Prouille, "the monkish, ascetic life of women"—which we see as the sole goal of the community from the very beginning—"moved ever more into the foreground" due to a lack of capital! (80).

25. Cf. Scheeben, *Dominikus*, 172ff.

26. According to a bull of Gregory IX to Minister-General Jordan on 24 March 1236 (Ripoll, *Bullarium* 1.86, no. 149; Guiraud, *Cartulaire* 1.7, n. 7) a prior and four *clerici fratres* were established at Prouille for the *cura in spiritualibus et temporalibus*; a bull of Innocent IV on 18 August 1248 (Ripoll, *Bullarium* 1.183, no. 200; Guiraud, *Cartulaire* 1.8–9, n. 10) describes them as *rectores, qui curam vestri gerant in spiritualibus et temporalibus diligentem*.

27. François Balme and R. P. Lelaidier, *Cartulaire ou Histoire diplomatique de St. Dominique* 2 (Paris, 1897), 9ff.

28. Jordan of Saxony, *De initiis*, c. 39 (ed. Berthier, 19). Gerhard Frachet, *Vitæ fratrum, MOPH* 1.224. The bull of Gregory IX, 7 April 1236, to the minister general and the Spanish provincial (Ripoll, *Bullarium* 1.87, n. 153). Cf. Scheeben, *Dominikus*, 259ff, and 295. A letter of Dominic to the prioress and convent in Madrid in 1220/21 is the sole example of his handwriting, save for a few charters, see Jacobus Quétif and Jacobus Echard, *Scriptores ordinis Prædicatorum recensiti* (Paris, 1719) 1.37; Altaner, *Dominikus*, 210.

29. Ripoll, *Bullarium* 1.13, n. 23; cf. Scheeben, *Dominikus*, 290ff., 322, 328–29. The Gilbertines of Semperingham were the first to be entrusted with the reform; it was only after they did not follow through that Honorius transferred the obligation to Dominic.

30. The young Diana d'Andalò supposedly encouraged her father to give the Preachers a building site for their religious house, and as a result of the enthusiasm of the noble ladies of Bologna, *expergefacta est devotio militum nobilium et consanguineorum dominarum, qui ceperunt fratres adjuvare et venerari*. Both stories come from an anonymous narrative of the origins of the St. Agnes house in Bologna, probably written by Sister Angelica between 1264 and 1283 (ed. *AOP* 1.181ff.), which also was used as the chief source for what follows; cf. Berthold Altaner, *Die Briefe Jordans von Sachsen, des zweiten Dominikanergenerals* (1222–37) (Leipzig, 1925), 63; Scheeben, *Dominikus*, 350 ff.

31. *Ceperunt preterea multe nobiles domine et illustres matrone de civitate Bononie ipsius [Diana] exemplo cum fratribus predicatoribus familiaritatem et colloquium habere de salute anime; AOP* 1.181.

32. This was against the desires of her parents, who had her taken out of the convent by force. Afterwards, as she lay sick in her parents' house, she resumed corresponding with Dominic. After her recovery, she fled on 1 November 1222 to Ronzono, and her family finally reconciled itself to her unbendable will.

33. Jordan of Saxony, *De initiis*, c. 56 (ed. Berthier, 28–29).

34. *AOP* 1.182: *Paulo post due nobiles domine de Farraria earum collegio sociate sunt*. P. 183: *Fratres predicantes per Lombardiam et Marcham convertebant ac earum collegio sociare curabant . . . de nobilioribus Lombardie et Marchie.* [Cf. H. Chr. Scheeben, *Jordan der Sachse* (Vechta, 1937); idem, *Beiträge zur Geschichte Jordans von Sachsen* (QF 35, 1938); G. Vann, *To Heaven with Diana! A Study of Jordan of Saxony and Diana d'Andalò* (London, 1960). HG/1960.]

35. On the details, see Altaner, *Briefe Jordans*, 75ff.: *ut eas doceret ordinem et modum religionis.*

36. According to the anonymous account of the origins of St. Agnes (*AOP* 1.183) Jordan had mass celebrated daily in the convent and had lay brothers (*conversi*) placed there, *qui in eadem residerent domo ac procurarent temporalia ipsarum*, hence there were no *fratres clerici* under a prior as in the three older women's houses. The account continues: *Sed tempore procedente sororibus visum est melius, ut in domo earum residere minime tenerentur conversi vel clerici; et idcirco felix pater ordinavit hoc, . . . ut quotidie ipsis celebrarent divina, licet in domo earum residere non tenerentur*. Since the entire account is intended to show the house of St. Agnes as a *domus ordinis* and hence with a right to the *cura* of the Preachers, its assertions and motivations should be treated with care; but the basic facts are utterly reliable.

37. Cf. Altaner, *Briefe Jordans*, 119ff.

38. *AOP* 1.183.

39. *AOP* 1.183 (continuing the passage cited in n. 36 above): *Tempore autem procedente ceperunt quidam fratres questionem facere de predicta domo ac predictis sororibus molestiam inferre. Unde predicius pater instante capitulo generali apud Parisium* [according to Altaner, *Briefe Jordans*, 91, probably 1226] *una cum diffinitoribus habuit consilium cum magistris Parisiensibus, qui simul tale dederunt responsum, videlicet quod eandem domum non poterant a sua cura sequestrare absque mortali peccato. Et tunc ipse beatus pater valde duriter reprehendebat illos qui aliqualem querimoniam sive questionem movebant de predicta dono, et exhortabatur eos ac monebat valde, presens et absens, ut illam domum diligerent ac consolarentur utpote domus ordinis*. Such declarations by Jordan and the chapter are not known.

40. Altaner, *Briefe Jordans*, 92, brings the assertions of house tradition (see *AOP* 1.183) and the text of the bull into harmony if one assumes that Jordan desired the "remarkably unfriendly phrasing" in the bull in order to give himself "support to his rear and a secure position" against the opposition which

wanted to reject all pastoral care in women's houses. The sources, however, are too sparse to know this with any certainty.

41. Ripoll, *Bullarium* 7.7, dated 17 December 1226. This was not to restore an earlier situation; rather, Diana was pressing her claim to incorporation for the first time. This is shown by a letter from Jordan to Diana at the start of 1227 (Altaner, *Briefe Jordans*, 26–27). A brief time earlier the minister general had congratulated the women of St. Agnes on their success (Altaner, *Briefe Jordans*, 12).

42. *ALKG* 1.222, Dist. 2, c. 27: *In virtute spiritus sancti et sub pena excommunicationis districte prohibemus, ne aliquis fratrum nostrorum decetero laboret vel procuret, ut cura vel custodia monialium vel quarumlibet aliarum mulierum nostris fratribus committatur; et si quis contraire presumpserit, pene gravioris culpe debite subjaceat. Prohibemus etiam, ne aliquis decetero aliquam tondeat vel induat vel ad professionem recipiat.* Hieronymus Wilms, *Geschichte der deutschen Dominikanerinnen* (Dülmen i. W., 1920), 44, assumes that the general chapter as early 1224 in Paris ruled against accepting care of souls in any women's house. There is no authority for this assumption, which certainly rests on a false dating of Jordan's letters nos. 48 and 49, which relate to the chapter of 1228 (see below). Wilms puts the bull of Honorius III of 1227 in a false relationship with that supposed chapter decree.

43. Altaner, *Briefe Jordans*, 48, 49, to the provincial of Lombardy.

44. The question of whether there was another prior in Cologne before Henry is unimportant here; cf. Greven,"Engelbert der Heilige," 37; Gabriel Löhr, *Beiträge zur Geschichte des Kölner Dominikanerklosters im Mittelalter*, QF 15 (Leipzig, 1920), 1; Scheeben, *Dominikus*, 361–62.

45. Jordan of Saxony, *De initiis*, ed. Berthier, 25: *Missus pro priore Coloniam, quam copiosum ibidem et uberem manipulum animarum in virginibus, in viduis, in versi penitentibus per assiduam predicationem lucrifecerit Christo . . . tota adhuc clamat Colonia*. Here is also the narrative of the miraculous experience of a married *venerabilis matrona* in Cologne after Henry's death; before his death, Henry had written edifying letters in German to her, cf. below, chapter 8, n. 45.

46. *De rebus alsaticis ineuntis seculi XIII, MG Scr*. 17.234–35, written by the author of the large and small Colmar annals; cf. Rudolphe Ernest Reuss, *De scriptoribus rerum Alsaticarum historicis inde a primordiis ad sæculi xviii exitum* (Strasbourg, 1898), 19; H. Papst, ed., *Annalen und Chronik von Kolmar* (Colmar, 1854), p. xii. Then follows an interesting account of costuming and equipment in this particular house.

47. The Premonstratensian abbot Emo of Wittewierum (Frisia; writing 1234/7) is another one who counts the religious women's communities alongside the mendicant orders, the *Humiliati* and the beguines as a distinctive phenomenon of the the era of Gregory IX; *MG Scr*. 23.517: *Multe siquidem novitates in diebus domini Gregorii novi pelularunt. Prima est religio Predicatorum, qui ut nubes volant; item Humiliatorum seu Nidosorum vel Nudipedum* [= Franciscans]; *item quorundam simplicium, qui dicuntur Beggini; item collegia communium feminarum.*

48. Cf. Lushing Baur, "Die Ausbreitung der Bettelorden in der Diözese Konstanz," *FDA* 29, new series 2 (1900), 38–39 on Neidingen on the Danube (cf. Fickler, *Gymnasium-Programm Donaueschingen*, 1845/46); 41 on Katharinenthal; 47–48 on Löwenthal near Buchhorn (Friedrichshafen); 49 on the three women's houses in Constance; 54 on Saulgau-Siessen; 56 on S. Katharinen in St. Gallen (cf. A. Huber, ZB 31.361); 57 on Marienberg near Reutlingen; 27 on Adelhausen near Freiburg (ed. J. König, Anna of Munzingen, "Chronica," *FDA* 13 [1880], 132). Hieronymus Wilms, *Das älteste Verzeichnis der deutschen Dominikanerinnenklöster,* QF 24 (Leipzig, 1928), 24 on Vienna; 31 on Augsburg; 50 on Ammerschwihr; 63 on Koblenz. Anton Steichele, *Das Bistum Augsburg, historisch und statistisch beschrieben* (Augsburg, 1861ff.), 3, 467, on Dorf-Kemnaten. Max Josef Heimbucher, *Die Orden und Kongregationen der Katholischen Kirche*, 2d ed., 3 vols. (Paderborn, 1907–08) 1.581. Sigmund Riezler, *Geschichte Baierns* 2 (Gotha, 1880), 220ff. The house of Weil near Esslingen also grew from a community of "converts" which moved from Esslingen to Weil in 1230 (*Wirtembergisches Urk.-B*. 3.269, n. 778); links with the Dominicans can only be documented from 1245, when the house was incorporated into the order. In the same way, the house of S. Gertrud, which played an important role in German mysticism but unfortunately left no house history, also arose from a community of beguines; in 1257 the "recluse" Helwig and her fellow sisters moved to the chapel of S. Gertrud, where they received a letter of protection. They were following the Rule of St. Augustine then, but they were not yet under Dominican leadership. Incorporation with the Dominican Order was only attempted in 1263, and it was completed only in 1283; see Löhr, "Das Nekrologium," 65ff.

49. *Der Nonne von Engelthal Büchlein der Gnaden Überlast*, ed. Karl Schröder, Bibliothek des Litterarischen Vereins in Stuttgart 108 (Tübingen, 1871). The "Fundation des Frauenklosters zu Engelthal" in Georg Ernst Waldau, *Vermischte Beyträge zur Geschichte der Stadt Nürnberg* 2 (Nuremberg, 1787), 121ff. is only an extract from the *Büchlein* of Engelthal, composed by a nun of the house of the S. Katharine in Nürnberg in order to give a preface to the history of her own house, which was founded in 1294 by nuns from Frauenaurach. Frauenaurach (near Erlangen) was begun about 1269 by Engelthal nuns. Specific information in the "foundation" which does not come from the *Büchlein* of Engelthal probably relied on good oral tradition. Some documents on Engelthal are in Johann Christoph Martini, *Historische-geographische Beschreibung des ehemaligen berühmten Frauenklosters Engelthal* (Nuremberg; Altdorf, 1762); cf. Friedrich Heidingsfelder, *Die Regesten der Bischöfe von Eichstätt* (1917), 223–24.

50. *Büchlein* of Engelthal, p. 1; the women were certainly not called "beguines" at the time, since the name only appears in South Germany at a later time (see above, chapter 4, n. 34). In the documents, the name of "beguine" only appears in Nuremberg in 1280, see Andreas Würfel, *Historisch-geneologischen und diplomatatischen Nachrichten zur Nürnberger Stadtgeschichte*, 2 vols. (Nuremberg, 1765–67) 2.723; Georg Ernst Waldau, *Neue Beyträge zur Geschichte der*

Stadt Nürnberg, 2 vols. (Nuremberg, 1790–91) 1.224. These naturally have nothing to do with the "Beginen" of the *Büchlein* of Engelthal.

51. It is impossible to establish when this took place. The author of the *Büchlein* of Engelthal did not know it exactly: they resided *etliche Jahre* in Nuremberg (until 1239), she says, *der zahl waiz ich niht*. Several years could have passed between the conversion of Alheit in Nuremberg in 1211 and her joining the beguines. According to the Dominican chronicler Johannes Meyer, the house arose under Minister-General Jordan of Saxony (1222–1236), see Wilms, "*Das älteste Verzeichnis*," 71, n. 2. This could not apply to the foundation of the convent proper at Engelthal in 1240, but perhaps this relates to the development of a community in Nuremberg.

52. *Büchlein* of Engelthal, ed. Schröder, 2: *seit sie niht hetten dez guts, daz sie ein closter gestiftet mohten.*

53. See the charter of Ulrich von Königstein, 1240, in Martini, *Historisch-geographische Beschreibung*, 8–9; see the next note.

54. The foundation charter of Ulrich von Königstein is falsely dated as 1245 in Martini, *Historisch-geographische Beschreibung*, 9; the correct date of 28 June 1240 is in Heidingsfelder, *Regesten*, 224; this alone jibes with the narrative in the *Büchlein* of Engelthal and the following charter of 1243. In the *Büchlein*, however, the reference is very imprecise: *da sie da gewont heten in daz virde jar, da kam die groez vinster*, since that can only be the solar eclipse of 6 October 1241. Witnesses of the donation of 1240 to the *sorores cognomine Rottharine Norimberc quondam deo militantes* are five Imperial ministerials and five burghers of Nuremberg.

55. Charter of 1243 in Martini, *Historisch-geographische Beschreibung*, 6–7. Among the witnesses, besides nobles and burghers of Nuremberg are found the abbot of Kastel and the abbot of S. Egidien in Nuremberg. Ulrich von Königstein speaks of the *sorores in Engelthal, cuius fundator extiti.*

56. *Büchlein* of Engelthal, 3.

57. A whole series of South German women's houses arose out of groups which had been free "beguine-like" communities, becoming "capable of being convents" through gifts by noble donors, and were taken up by the Cistercian Order: Niederschönenfeld near Burgheim (east of Donauwörth), 1241, see *Monumenta Boica, Edidit Academia Scientiarum Boica* (Munich, 1763ff.) 16.259; Johann Knebel, *Chronik des Klosters Kaisheim*, ed. Franz Kittner, Bibliothek des Litterarischen Vereins in Stuttgart 226 (Stuttgart, 1902), 66ff.; Steichele, *Das Bistum Augsburg*, 2.590, 678. Oberschönenfeld, probably before 1240, certainly before 1248; see J. Knebel, *Chronik* 45ff., 67; Steichele, *Das Bistum Augsburg*, 39; Th. Wiedemann in Anton Steichele, ed., *Beiträge zur Geschichte des Bistums Augsburg*, 2 vols. (Augsburg, 1850–52) 2.193ff.; P. Braun, *Geschichte der Bischöfe von Augsburg* 2.543 and *Geschichte der Grafen von Dillingen und Kiberg*, 420; Riezler, *Geschichte Baierns* 2.220; the community is supposed to have existed since 1211, and in the 1220s the Advocate Volkmar von Kemnat endowed it to the level of a convent. Stahelsberg, founded about 1245, transfered to Zimmern in 1252, see Steichele, *Das Bistum Augsburg*

2.667ff. Heckenbach (Heppbach, Heggbach; between Biberach and Ochsenhausen), supposedly founded in 1233 *a duabus conversis feminis, Beginas vocabant, quarum una erat ex nobili gente Rosenburgiorum, altera vero ex Luadenburgensi familia*, joined by other *puellæ nobiles*, see G. Bruschius, *Monasteriorum Germaniæ centuria* 1 (Ingolstadt, 1551), fol. 67–68; Martinus Crusius, *Annales Suevici* (Frankfurt, 1593/6) 3.1, c. p. Baindt, established as a Cistercian convent in 1240 by the endowment of Schenk Konrad von Winterstetten (*Wirtembergisches Urk.-B.* 4.10, no. 964; 2.457 no. 952), had existed as a free community in Seefelden on Lake Constance and then for five years *cum summa difficultate* in Boos near Saulgau; see Bruschius, *loc. cit.*

58. *Büchlein* of Engelthal, p. 3; also the ministerial Konrad von Lauffenholz, a friend of the founder, who had been marshal of the Teutonic Knights in Prussia and had settled near the Engelthal house, *het dar umb ein leiden, daz man die frawen nunnen hies;* ibid., 5.

59. Cf. below, chapter 7, n. 87ff., and n. 140.

60. Some women's houses hesitated over which order they should join. Wonnenthal near Kenzingen, documented since 1242, joined the Dominicans in 1254, but passed to the Cistercians in 1254, see F. J. Mone, *ZGO* 8.481; F. J. Mone, *Quellensammlung zur badischen Geschichte* (Karlsruhe, 1867) 4.47; *FDA*, 2d series, 1.13ff. and 2.38–39; Wilms, *Verzeichnis*, 76; in the same way, Alzey in Hessia belonged to the Dominican Order in 1248, but by 1262 it had joined the Cistercians; Neuburg on the Neckar was Cistercian after 1224, subordinated itself to the Dominicans in 1287, but before 1300 it had returned to the Cistercians; see Wilms, *Verzeichnis*, 75–76.

61. Heidingsfelder, *Regesten*, 233–34, n. 730, 9 June 1244.

62. The process is not entirely clear in the nuns' book of Engelthal: on 5, scenes are presented which assume the presence of the Preachers in Engelthal; on p. 6 it is reported how the sisters *nach dem orden sungen* for the first time in advent, and later (7) it says: *in den selben zeiten do fugt ez sich also, daz die prediger von Regensburch in dise gengend wurden wandeln. Da gehizen sie in, sie wolten in irer gehorsam sein*. Then the mistress surrendered her office, they elected a prioress, and she went with one sister and a lay brother to Rome (Lyon) and obtained there confirmation of all the house's privileges (1248; cf. n. 119 below).

63. Meier, Bruder Hermanns Leben, p. 7, vv. 530–31: *dy zarde was ein zunder, dat al ze balde vûr entfeit*. Cf. also Thomas of Chantimpré, *Bonum universale de apibus* 2, c. 29, p. 317ff.

64. Marienthal near Mersch in Luxembourg, founded in 1232 by sisters of St. Mark's in Strasbourg. The entry of Jolande, who became prioress of Marienthal in 1258, quickly raised the house to importance and prosperity.

65. H. Zeller-Werdmüller and J. Bächtold, eds., "Die Stiftung des Klosters Ötenbach," *Zürcher Taschenbuch*, 2d series, 12 (1889), 213ff. [A. Halter, *Geschichte des Dominikanerinnen-Klosters Oetenbach in Zürich*, 1234–1525 (Winterthur, 1956). HG/1960.]

66. Zeller-Werdmüller and Bechtold, eds., "Die Stiftung des Klosters Ötenbach," 236, says that the sisters had been living together for five years when

they obtained a papal privilege of immunity, 1239. Whether the "beguinage" uniting the three women founding Ötenbach had lasted longer cannot be established. The Dominicans had been in Zürich since 1229.

67. On 13 August 1237, Gregory IX exhorted the faithful of the diocese of Constance to help build the convent; shortly afterward he took the house into papal protection; Antiquarische Gesellschaft in Zürich, ed. *Urk.-B. der Stadt und Landschaft Zürich*, 2.11–12, no. 509/10.

68. The *Klosterbuch* proudly announces, *daß si keinen stifter hetten ze anfang ires klosters noch keinen herren, auf des hilf si sich trösten.*

68a. In a charter for Wonnenthal (near Kenzingen) of 1248 it is said that the sisters built their convent *de sua substantia et fidelium elemosinis*, see F. J. Mone, *ZGO* 8 (1857), 485; cf. on this K. Bürger, *FDA*, 2d series, 1 (1900), 138.

69. Zeller-Werdmüller and Bechtold, eds., "Die Stiftung des Klosters Ötenbach," 231, 238, 219. On the families of the high nobility, the ministeriality, and the Zürich patriciate, see ibid., 235, n. 6.

70. In Adelhausen near Freiburg, noble ladies had begun a religious commune before the Dominicans settled in Freiburg in 1235; but their influence had obviously radiated there from Strasbourg, and the Strasbourg Dominicans supported the community in Adelshausen from the beginning. Very soon, when the widowed Countess of Sulz, a sister of Rudolf of Habsburg, joined the community under the influence of Dominican preaching, the community could move to the establishment of a convent; cf. the brief notice in the chronicle of Anna von Munzingen, *FDA* 13.152; on this, see Engelbert Krebs, "Die Mystik in Adelhausen," *Festgabe für Heinrich Finke* (Münster, 1904), 41ff. (50ff. on the Countess of Sulz). The Strasbourg prior Walter was a close advisor of the women who gathered together in Colmar from the very beginning; they were wealthy enough to found a convent at once; in 1232 Prior Walter veiled the first sisters in Unterlinden, most of them ladies of the high nobility; cf. A. M. P. Ingold, *Le monastère des Unterlinden* (Strasbourg, 1897), 222–23.

71. *Urk.-B. Strassburg* 1.97, no. 118: . . . *deo famulari et regularem vitam ducere*; the chapel had been founded in 1182 by the dean of St. Thomas. H. Wilms, *Verzeichnis*, 54, gives an incorrect account of the content of the charter, as if the sisters had lived in a *reclusorium* together. There is no mention of this in the charter, which says: *quibusdam mulieribus religiosis, que ibidem deo famulari et regularem vitam ducere decreverunt*, which indicates that they had just joined together. Cf. M. Harth, "Die Rolle des Dominikanerklosters St. Marx zu Strassburg in der Frühgeschichte des Ordens," *Archiv für elsässische Kirchengeschichte* 7 (1932), 101f.

72. *Urkunden and Akten der Stadt Strassburg* (Strasbourg, 1879–1919) 1.173, no. 220. The statement in Wilms, *Verzeichnis*, 54, that the house had been placed under the Dominicans in 1220 is incorrect; Johann David Schoepflin, *Alsatia . . . diplomatica* 1 (Mannheim, 1772), 365, to which Wilms refers, but he prints only the bishop's charter which deals with the transfer of the house.

73. *Urk.-B. Strassburg* 1.197, no. 252, where it is forbidden for the *priorissæ et conventui monasterii S. Marci Argentinensis ordinis S. Sixti de Urbe*

to receive more sisters, *cum monasterium vestrum sororum multitudine pregravetur.*

74. *Urk.-B. Zürich* 1.358, n. 484.

75. On 12 October 1234, the bishop of Constance issued a letter of protection for *quasdam pauperculas et religiosas sorores apud Adelhusen, que sub habitu religionis imitando regulam b. Augustini de ordine predicatorum a nobis eisdem sororibus . . . indultam secundum consuetudinem sancti Marci in Argentina deo devote famulari voverant*; see König, ed. Anna of Munzinger, *Chronica*, 234.

76. Th. Walter, *Urkunden und Regesten der Stadt Rufach* (Rufach, 1908), 19–20, n. 35–37: *sorores ordinis sancti Marchi in Argentina.*

77. *Urkunden Strassburg* 1.196, n. 251.

78. Charter of 22 July 1241 in *Wirtembergisches Urk.-B.* 4.33, no. 983.

79. Charter of 15 July 1242 in *Urk.-B. Zürich* (Zürich, 1888ff.) 2.71, no. 567.

80. As is noted above, St. Mark's itself was attributed by Gregory IX to the *Ordo S. Sixti.*

81. *Monumenta Boica* 17.1, n. 1; Count Konrad certified: *novellam plantationem sororum ordinis s. Systi consilio predicatorum et aliorum prudentum virorum in veteri Hohenawe inchoavimus.* The nuns were described in 1238 as *Dominæ s. Sixti* and in 1239 and 1242 as *religiosæ sorores s. Sixti*, ibid., 4, n. 3 and 6, n. 5. I cannot verify the tradition of the house that the first nun, Cæcilia Romana, clothed in her habit by St. Dominic himself, came from S. Sisto to Altenhohenau; Wilms, *Geschichte der deutschen Dominikanerinnen*, 35, believes it was possible that Prioress Cæcilia of Bologna briefly resided at Altenhohenau and initiated the convent.

82. Thomas Ried, *Codex chronologicus-diplomaticus episcoporum Ratisbonensis* (Regensburg, 1816) 1.381–82, n. 396, a donation to the *sorores de ordine s. Sixti* in the filial of the Holy Cross convent of Regensburg at Schwarzhofen; two Dominicans were among the witnesses. Cf. ibid., 382, n. 397 and 402–03, n. 415. The house at Regensburg originated as *pauperes sorores*, who lived outside the city, but to whom burghers donated a site within the city in 1233; the bishop confirmed this donation to the "poor sisters," *quas dudum etiam in nostram protectionem recepimus*, see Ried, *Codex*, 372–73, n. 388.

83. Stauber, "Kloster und Dorf Lambrecht," *Mitteilungen des historischen Vereins der Pfalz* 9 (1880), 209–10.

84. *Urk.-B. Zürich* 2.11, no. 509.

85. Berthold Schmidt, ed., *Urk.-B. der Vögte von Weida, Gera und Plauen*, 2 vols. (Jena, 1884–92) 1.35, n. 71.

86. See above, n. 62. On the house of Unterlinden, Antonin Danzas, *Études sur les temps primitifs de l'ordre de S. Dominique* 4 (Paris, 1877) 4.64, says that the two women founders went to Rome to learn the institutions of S. Sisto and bring them back to Unterlinden; the authority he asserts is an Alsatian chronicle, probably meaning the Colmar chronicler, whose account (see n. 119 below) is interpreted by Danzas in a confused and incorrect manner. The sisters

of Unterlinden probably followed the constitutions of St. Mark, since they were sponsored by the Strasbourg Dominicans.

87. A. Simon, *L'Ordre des Pénitentes*, 29ff. [Ph. Hofmeister, "Die Exemption des Magdalenerinnenordens," *Zeitschrift der Savigny-Stiftung für Rechtsgeschichte, kanonistische Abteilung 35* (1948), 305–29; see also below, "New Contributions," chap. 1, n. 56. HG/1960.]

88. There is no authority for the assertion of Altaner, *Briefe Jordans*, 97: "From the very beginning there were numerous contacts between this new order and the Order of Preachers." Simon, *L'Ordre des Pénitentes*, 31, shows that organizing the Penitential Order according to the constitutions of S. Sisto grew out of the initiative of Gregory IX.

89. Zarncke, *Der Anteil*, 36–37.

90. The commission of Gregory IX, 2 April 1232, to the bishop, Dominican prior and cathedral canon of Strasbourg, is significant since it directs them to reform the house of St. Stephen in Strasbourg and Eschau, occupied by Augustinian nuns. This reform was to be either on the basis of the Cistercian rule or the customs of S. Sisto; *Urkunden Strassburg* 1.177–78, n. 227; cf. 4/1, 53–54, no. 51; *Regesten der Bischöfe von Strassburg* (Innsbruck, 1908ff.) 1.60, n. 985.

91. In a bull of 26 September 1238 to the German Dominican provincial (*Mittelrheinisches Urk.-B.* 3.480, n. 630), Gregory IX says that the sisters of the house of St. Martinsberg near Trier *ad exhortacionem fratrum tui ordinis religionis habitum assumentes, se juxta ipsorum doctrinam et consilium in divine legis observantiam direxerunt*; for that reason, the provincial should permit them *in spiritualibus provideri* by the Dominicans of Trier, but *sine juris prejudicio alieni*; the house was thus not yet exempt.

92. Johannes Meyer, *Liber de viris illustribus ordinis prædicatorum*, ed. Paulus von Loë, *QF* 12.28. Prior Walter encouraged the founding of Unterlinden and led its development, often taking part in its chapter assemblies, cf. Gerhard Frachet, "Vitæ fratrum," *MOPH* 1.222. He was also active at Adelshausen.

93. Martin Gerbert, *Historia nigræ silvæ* 2 (St. Blasien, 1788), 101. Cf. Franciscus Petrus, *Suevia ecclesiastica* (Augsburg; Dillingen, 1699), 459. L. Bauer, "*Die Ausbreitung*," 2.34–35, believes it possible that Minister-General Thomas formally received the house of Kirchberg into the Dominican Order; the sisters' book reports the veiling. In fact, Kirchberg is the sole German women's house which is referred to as a *conventus ordinis Predicatorum* even before the incorporations of 1245 and the reordering of the matter of pastoral care, in a charter of the bishop of Constance, 11 March 1240 (*Wirtembergisches Urk.-B.* 4.436, n. 139). Still, the formal incorporation only took place in 1245. The participation of Minister-General Johannes in the founding of the convent of Paradies near Soest in 1252 does not belong here, since the relationship of the order to women's houses had changed fundamentally in the meantime; see below, n. 192.

94. *MG Scr.* 17.235.

95. In a few cases papal bulls approved Dominican oversight only with specific reservation of the rights of the bishop, cf. n. 91 on St. Martinsberg near Trier.

96. Most of the women's houses only obtained the privilege of protection and immunity in 1245 and the years immediately following, together with subjection to the Dominican Order, through papal intervention; the house of Ötenbach had already obtained this in 1239, see *Urk.-B. Zürich* 2.24, no. 524. They were all prepared according to the formula of the *Privilegium speciale ordinis S. Augustini*, see Michael Tangl, *Die päpstlichen Kanzleiordnungen von 1200–1500* (Innsbruck, 1894), 233; as a sign of the order to which it pertained, there was only: *secundum deum et beati Augustini regulam*, without mention of institutions or constitutions which were to be kept in the houses.

97. Ripoll, *Bullarium*, 86, n. 149 (on 24 March 1236 for Prouille; also in Guiraud, *Cartulaire* 1.7, n. 7) and 87, n. 153 (7 April 1236 for Madrid). In the first bull the wording was: *occasione cuiusdam constitutionis nuper edite in capitulo generali, scilicet ne fratres supradicti ordinis curam deinceps habeant mulierum*, the Dominicans in Prouille had relinquished their leadership; in the second, also directed to the minister general of the order: *vos paucis abhinc diebus et definitores ordinis vestri voluntarie et sine aliqua causa ipsos (fratres) ab ipsarum cura removistis*. Perhaps a bull of Gregory IX for S. Agnes in Bologna which is not preserved but mentioned in the narrative of the origins of this house (*AOP* 1.183) was related to this; cf. Altaner, *Briefe Jordans*, 104.

98. Zeller-Werdmüller and Bechtold, eds., "Die Stiftung des Klosters Ötenbach," 222–23. The *grosse capitel general* [mentioned there] is the "Generalissimum" of 1228, but the denial of the Zürich Dominicans was also—according to the chronology of the Ötenbach book as well—precipitated by the decree of 1234/5.

99. Altaner, *Briefe Jordans*, 102 and 108.

100. This decree is not mentioned in the acts of the chapters of 1234 and 1235 (*MOPH* 3.4–5), but they are not complete and not preserved in the originals; the decrees which were later repealed were obviously removed from the repertory.

101. Letter of Jordan to Diana, no. 47, ed. Altaner, *Briefe Jordans*, 47. Altaner, 101ff., dates this letter to July 1234 on cogent grounds: that decree would have been passed by the general chapter in Paris in 1234 (it is also likely that a similar decree was passed in Bologna in 1235). It is odd that complaints of Prouille and Madrid on the results of this decree were only dealt with by the curia in 1236, although Jordan would have suspended the decrees as soon as he learned of them. Altaner, *Briefe Jordans*, 105, supposes that despite Jordan's objections, the opposition to women's houses once more won out at the next chapter in 1235 because Jordan was not present.

102. Ripoll, *Bullarium* 1.107.

103. By Innocent IV on 16 November 1257; Ripoll, *Bullarium* 1.354, no. 189.

104. See n. 16 above.

105. Sbaralea, *Bullarium* 1.538, n. 319.

106. In 1239 the house of Ötenbach sent two sisters and a priest to Rome. It seems possible to me that they were already trying then to win reception into

the Dominican Order through papal intervention, just as was to happen for many houses six years later, and that this precipitated the order's reaction. The sisters of Ötenbach did receive a privilege of protection for their house (on 6 May 1239, see *Urk.-B. Zürich* 2.24, n. 524), but they were only incorporated in 1235, see the Ötenbach book, 224ff.

107. *MOPH* 3.24.

108. Letter of Innocent IV to the minister general and the *definitores* of the general chapter in Bologna on 14 May 1244, Ripoll, *Bullarium* 1.143.

109. Cf. the letter of Innocent to S. Sisto on 3 February 1244, Ripoll, *Bullarium* 1.131, with the assurance that the house *sub magistero et doctrina magistri et prioris provincialis Tusciæ . . . maneatis.* These were obligated to supply them *de fratribus suis in monasterio vestro sufficientes deputare fratres tam clericos quam conversos et priorem discretum et providum ibidem restituere debeant residentem, qui vos et eos verbo instruat et exemplo et corrigat etiam delinquentes*, as had been done under earlier ministers general. The Dominicans residing in the houses should participate in all the rights of the order.

110. *Chronicon ordinis* (probably by Gerhard Franchet), ed. B. M. Reichert, *MOPH* 1.322 (cf. also 7.2): *Filia comitis Simonis, scilicet domina Amicia de Joviniaco . . . voluit multociens, quod filius suus unigenitus . . . intraret ordinem, si fratres voluissent; et in extremis agens ipse apud Cyprum in exercitu regis Francorum* [Louis IX] *habitum nostrum suscepit et factus est frater. Ipsa quoque, sicut dixit, quia homo non erat nec poterat esse frater, ut saltem soror fieret, fecit domum sororum de Monte-Argis et bene dotavit, in qua taxatus est numerus 50 sororum, que speciali prerogativa sanctitatis et religionis fulgerent in Francia, inter quas et ipsa sepulta requiescit*. It is not known when the house was founded; *Gallia Christiana* (2d ed., 12, 256) has it founded as early as 1207 and asserts that, according to the house tradition, Dominic himself had often visited. The sole son of Amicie was Gaucher (not Jean de Montfort, as Reichert believes), whom Innocent often described as *familiaris noster* in the bulls of 1245, see n. 114 below. Amicie died in 1252. The sister of Henry III of England entered the house of Montargis; she was the widow of the brother of Amicie de Joigny, Simon de Montfort, Earl of Leicester, who usurped English rule in 1264 and fell in battle in 1265 against the pretender to the English throne. There was also a daughter of Frederick II, Blanchefleur, whose epitaph reads (*Gallia Christiana*, 2d ed., 12, 257): *Por l'amour de Dieu et sa virginité dépita l'empire et tout le monde selement de ses amis, vint en France en cette maison en habit de beguinage jusquá la fin et trespassa le 20 de Juin 1279.*

111. *MOPH* 1.322. The bull of incorporation to the minister general and the French provincial in Ripoll, *Bullarium* 1.148, n. 84. Cf. below.

112. Ripoll, *Bullarium* 1.148, no. 85 and 86, giving the corresponding directives to the minister general and the provincial of *Teutonia*; cf. Berger, *Les Registres*, no. 1252/53, for the text, see table on p. 117, below. The bull reads *ad supplicationem nobilis mulieris Amicie domine de Jovignaco et Galcheti*

nati eius familiaris nostri. In a bull of 7 August 1247 to the minister general and provincial in which he presses for the incorporation of the house of St. Agnes, Innocent says (*Urk.-B. Strassburg* 4/1, 79–80, n. 125): *idem monasterium incorporavimus ordini vestri, nobili muliere Amicie de Jovigniaco et Gualchero nato eius familiari nostro interponentibus super hoc non sine multe intercessionis instantia partes suas*. The bull of incorporation was repeated on 1 June 1247 (*Urk. -B. Strassburg*, 4/1, 76, n. 114; Berger, *Registres*, no. 2789/90), on 7 August 1247 and 12 October 1247 (Berger, *Registres*, nos. 3155 and 3329); cf. below, n. 170 and 174.

113. See n. 119 below.

114. Diocese of Strasbourg; incorporated 11 July 1246, Ripoll, *Bullarium* 1.166–67, n. 156/7; Berger, no. 2221/22. Almost nothing is known of the house, cf. Wilms, *Verzeichnis*, 77.

115. Later transferred to Klingenthal near Basel; incorporated on the same day as Offenburg, Ripoll, *Bullarium*, 1, 167, n. 158/9; Berger, *Registres*, no. 2224; Historische und antiquarianische Gesellschaft zu Basel, ed., *Urk.-B. der Stadt Basel*, 1.133, n. 190; Wilms, *Verzeichnis*, 45–6.

115a. Incorporated on 4 July 1245, Ripoll, *Bullarium* 1.151, n. 94; repeated on 21 February 1246, Berger, *Registres*, no. 1700, and on 13 March 1246, Ripoll, *Bullarium* 1.158, n. 123, where it reads: *consideratione dilecti filii nobilis viri Johannis comitis Montisfortis nobis pro vobis supplicationibus.*

116. Berger, *Registres*, no. 1827.

117. Ripoll lists bulls of incorporation for "Ebenhim," 19 March 1246 (*Bullarium* 1.159, n. 127) and for "Obenheim" on 13 May 1246 (164, n. 145); Berger, *Registres*, no. 1768 for "Ehenheam" on 13 March 1246; it is likely that all three cases are intended for Oberehenheim in Alsace; cf. Wilms, *Verzeichnis*, 77.

118. But Cardinal Hugh of St. Cher speaks in a letter of 13 March 1254 (Ripoll, *Bullarium* 7.33, no. 382) of the *monasteria, que ipse* [Innocent IV] *ad preces et interventum multorum nobilium et magnatum auctoritate sedis apostolice . . . nostro ordini univit*. The house of Himmelwonne-Löwenthal (near Buchhorn = Friedrichshafen) was placed under the Dominicans by Innocent IV at the request of the knight Johann von Ravensburg, the founder of the convent, who visited the curia for that purpose, as well as of Johann's relatives the abbot of St. Gallen and the bishop of Constance; *Wirtembergisches Urk.-B.* 4.217, 227 no. 1151/9.

119. The Colmar chronicler, "De rebus alsaticis," *MG Scr.* 17.235. The widow of the Count of Sulz went from Adelhausen near Freiburg, a sister of Rudolf of Habsburg, *zu dem concilium ze Lewen . . . umb den orden, den erwarb si da, FDA* 13.154; it was incorporated on 15 July 1246, ibid., 235–36. The first prioress, Williburg, and Sister Mechthild von Zimmern traveled from Kirchberg near Sulz *nach Rom* (that is, to the curia) and obtained a letter of protection (2 May 1245) as well as incorporation (24 October 1245), see *Württembergische Vierteljahrshefte für Landesgeschichte*, 2d series, 3 (1894), 291ff. Prioress Diemut von Gallenhausen, accompanied by a sister and a lay brother, traveled from Engelthal to *Rom*, obtaining incorporation on 20 September 1248

and protection on 10 October 1248, see the *Büchlein* of Engelthal, 7; Martini, *Beschreibung des Frauenklosters Engelthal*, 13ff.; Heidingsfelder, *Regesten*, 224, n. 720. In the *Vitæ sororum* of Unterlinden (ed. Ancelet-Hustache, 337) there is a brief mention, *quanta instancia et labore predicatorum ordinem a domino apostolico impetrarunt, curiam Romanam in persona propria adeundo*.

120. According to the report of the Colmar chronicler, Minister-General John himself supported incorporation in dealings with the pope; *Büchlein* of Engelthal, 7. It is uncertain whether this was Minister-General John or one of the two Dominican cardinals, perhaps Hugh of St. Cher, then at the curia, and who signed the privilege for Engelthal and later showed himself an enthusiastic promoter of the religious women's movement in Germany.

121. Ripoll, *Bullarium* 1.150/1, n. 89ff.; Berger, *Registres*, no. 1379/80; *Urkunden Strassburg* 1.224–25: S. Katharina (repeating the incorporation bull "with essential additions" on 20 August 1249, see *Urkunden Strassburg* 1.225, n. 1; S. Elizabeth; S. Nikolaus and Matthäus (= S. Nikolaus zu den Hunden; repeated 1248, see *QF* 3.80); S. Johannes.

122. Ripoll, *Bullarium* 1.151ff. lists bulls for the following houses: Sirnau (later Esslingen) on 14 July 1245 (cf. *Wirtembergisches Urk.-B*. 4.105–06, no. 1048; Berger, *Registres*, no. 1494/46). Weil on 9 September 1245 (cf. *Wirtembergisches Urk.-B*. 5.442–43, no. 55/6; Berger, no. 1495/96). Mendingen, Gotteszell near Schwädabisch-Gmünd (cf. *Wirtembergisches Urk.-B*. 4.130ff., Berger, no. 1069/70). S. Maria in Arena (later S. Katharina) in Augsburg, and Ebenheim (see n. 117 above) on 13 March 1246. Altenhohenau am Inn (cf. *Monumenta Boica* 17.10f., n. 11/12; Berger, no. 1814/15) and Marienbrunnen (= Wissembourg in Alsace) on 21 April (according to Berger, no. 1827, Merinbrunne, 20 April) 1246. Würzburg, 10 July 1246. Offenburg in Baden and Husern near Basel (later Klingenthal), 11 July 1246 (cf. *Urk.-B. Basel* 1.133, n. 190; Berger, no. 2221/4). Cronschwitz, 9 November 1246 (cf. *Urk.-B. der Vögte von Weida, Gera und Plauen* 1.45–46, n. 87).

Bulls with similar wording not listed in Ripoll are preserved for the following houses:

From 1245: Ötenbach near Zürich, 12 July, see *Urk.-B. Zürich* 2.129, n. 623. Adelhausen near Freiburg, 15 July, see Anna of Munzinger, 235–36; repeated on 18 May 1249, see Berger, *Registres*, no. 4523/24. Wonnenthal, 4 September, see F. J. Mone, *Quellensammlung zur badischen Geschichte* 4.47; Berger, no. 1486/87 (Wimenthal). Töss, 2 September, see *Urk.-B. Zürich* 2.132ff., no. 626/27. Kirchberg, 24 October, see *Wirtembergisches Urk.-B*. 4.114, n. 1055; Berger, no. 1770/71. Unterlinden near Colmar, 4 September, see Ingold, *Le monastère des Unterlinden*, 226, n. 5/6. Diessenhofen-Katharinenthal, see *FDA* 11.20 (without date).

20 April 1246, S. Margarethe in Eckbolsheim, later Strasbourg, see Berger, no. 1827/28. Also in 1246, Sylo-Schlettstadt, see *Annales Colmarensis, MG Scr*. 17.190; Hauck, *KD* 4.996; Johann Daniel Schoepflin, *Alsatia illustrata* . . . (Colmar, 1751) 2.381.

2 August 1247, S. Lambrecht near Neustadt on the Hardt (repeated 20 September 1248), see *Urk.-B. zur Geschichte der Bischöfe zu Speyer*, ed. Franz Xavier Remling, 1 (Mainz, 1852), 401–02, no. 435; A. Stauber, "Kloster und Dorf Lambrecht," 79. 11 September 1248, Mersch near Luxembourg, see Berger, no. 4138/39. 20 September 1248, Engelthal, see Fr. Heidingsfelder, *Regesten*, 224, n. 730. 27 January 1249, Kirchheim, see Berger, *Registres*, no. 4335/36; *Wirtembergisches Urk.-B.* 6.470, n. 30/1. 2 June 1250, Himmelwonne-Löwenthal, *Wirtembergisches Urk.-B.* 4.217, no. 1151. 1250 as well, S. Barbara in Trier, see Jacob Marx, *Geschichte des Erzstifts Trier*, 5 vols. (Trier, 1858–64) 4.457.

123. It is not unlikely that other German women's houses were placed in the order in a similar manner without the bulls having been preserved. It is a different matter with the house of Alzey in Hessia, which the Dominican prior at Worms incorporated into the *ordo S. Augustini*, in keeping with a bull of Innocent IV of 15 January 1248, *diocesani episcopi in omnibus jure salvo*. The bull is only excerpted in Ripoll, *Bullarium* 1.181, n. 193 (cf. also Berger, no. 3547), but it has nothing in common with the incorporation or commissioning bulls for the other houses, and it does not order subordination to the Dominicans.

124. *Urkunden Strassburg*, 4/1, 79–80, n. 125, to the minister general and German provincial on 7 November 1247. Cf. also the bull of Innocent IV to the same, concerning carrying out the incorporation of Himmelwonne (Löwenthal) on 1 October 1250. *Wirtembergisches Urk.-B.* 4.227, n. 1159.

125. Thomas of Celano, *Vita s. Claræ*, c. 8, *AASS*, August, 2, 756: *sancte penitentie suscipit insignia*; cf. I Cel., 8, 18, and the bull of canonization of 1255 in Sbaralea, *Bullarium* 2.81ff. [L. Hardick, "Der Orden der hl. Klara in Deutschland, Hinweise zu seiner Geschichte," *VS* 34 (1953). HG/1960.]

126. The *Vita, AASS*, August, 2, 756, says: *donec aliud provideret altissimus*, but this hardly reflects the actual thoughts of Francis and Clara.

127. Her sister Agnes joined her there.

128. *Vita s. Claræ*, c. 10, p. 756: *Ubi cum non plene mens eius quiesceret, tandem ad ecclesiam s. Damiani beati Francisci consilio commigravit.*

129. This *forma vivendi or formula vitæ*, which Francis gave the sisters in St. Damian, is mentioned in Clara's rule of 1253, c. 6 (*Seraphicæ legislationis textus*, 62–63) and in a bull of Gregory IX to Agnes of Bohemia on 11 May 1238.

130. Three years after her conversion, *cogente beato Francisco suscepit tandem tandem regimen dominarum, Vita*, c. 12, p. 757; cf. the bull of canonization in Sbaralea, *Bullarium* 2.82. Oliger, "De origine," 192 and 204, also infers a connection between the *Privilegium paupertatis* (see above, chapter 2, n. 143ff.) and the naming of Clara as abbess.

131. Clara's rule of 1253 (p. 62) draws her words from Francis' *forma vivendi* for St. Damian: *Volo et permitto per me et fratres meos semper habere de vobis tamquam de ipsis curam diligentem et sollicitudinem specialem.*

132. In his negotiations with Cardinal Ugolino in 1219, Francis declared, *preter unum illud, in quo Clara reclusit, nullum aliud se exstruxisse aut extrui procurasse atque ita huius solius curam assumpsisse tam quoad disciplinam regularem quam quoad tenuem victum mendicitate per se aut*

socios conquirendum. Neque quidquam sibi tandumdem displicere, quam ut fratres in aliis partibus monialibus domicilia constitui et per se regi impensius voluerint, see Wadding, *Annales Minorum*, for 1219, n. 44 (1 [Rome, 1731], 311) from the manuscript *Chron. ant.* of Ugolino de Monte; Marianus, I, c. 9. Friar Thomas of Pavia says, according to Friar Stephanus, a companion to the saint: *Nec unquam ipse aliud monasterium mandavit fieri, licet tempore suo aliqua monasteria constructa fuerint procuratione quorumdam;* see Oliger, "De origine," 419.

133. Leonhard Lemmens, "Zum Leben und Werke der hl. Klara," *Der Katholik* 4/12 (1913), 5–6 and 9, believes the characteristic of these convents to have been complete renunciation of every earthly possession, confirming "that the source of this great poverty movement is to be seen entirely in the example and preaching of Francis and Clara." The similar communities in the North demonstrate that this is not correct.

134. Cf. Zarncke, *Der Anteil*, 27ff.

135. See n. 132 above for the assertion of Thomas of Pavia: *tempore suo aliqua monasteria constructa fuerunt procuratione quorundam.*

136. Letter of James of Vitry in Böhmer, *Analekten*, 67: *Multi enim utriusque sexus, divites et seculares, omnibus pro Christo relictis seculum fugiebant, qui fratres minores vocabantur*; he speaks first of the Franciscans, then adds a bit on religious women: *Mulieres vero juxta civitates in diversis hospiciis simul commorantur, nichil accipiunt, sed de labore manuum vivunt. Valde autem dolent et turbantur, quia a clericis et laicis plus quam vellent honorantur*. Then he resumes his description of the Franciscans. In the *Historia occidentalis* written by James of Vitry during his residence in the orient (1220/27), he says nothing about the participation of women in his description of the Franciscans.

137. Zarncke, *Der Anteil*, 36–37.

138. Ugolino's letter is in the bull of Honorius III for Monticelli in Florence, dated 27 August 1218, Sbaralea, *Bullarium* 1.1.

139. *Quamplures virgines et alie mulieres, quibus secundum instabilitatem prosperitatis mundane prosperum statum in seculo sua videtur nobilitas polliceri, . . . desiderant fugere pompas et divitias huius mundi et fabricari sibi aliqua domicilia, in quibus vivant nihil possidentes sub celo, exceptis domiciliis ipsis et construendis oratoriis in eisdem.*

140. Cf. Oliger, "De origine," 203–04; Leonhard Lemmens, "Die Anfänge des Clarissenordens," *RQ* 16 (1902), 102ff., and *Zum Leben und Werke der heiligen Klara*, 10; Zarncke, *Der Anteil*, 43–44, opposing Lempp and Sabatier. Ugolino's rule (in the bulls of 24 May 1239 and 13 November 1245, in Sbaralea, *Bullarium* 1.264 and 395) begins: *Regulum beatissimi Benedicti . . . vobis tradimus (concedimus) observandam in omnibus, in quibus eidem vivendi formule vobis a nobis tradite . . . (secundum quam specialiter vivere decrevistis) contraria minime comprobatur.*

141. When Agnes of Prague asked for a change in the rule, particularly the elimination of the first words, *Regulam b. Benedicti vobis tradimus observan-*

dam, on the cogent grounds, *cum impertinens et impossibile reputetur, quod in ordine due regule debeant observari*, Innocent IV answered her on 13 November 1243 (Sbaralea, *Bullarium* 1.316). Gregory IX himself had said in his own day, *Regula ipsa sorores sui ordinis non ligat ad aliud nisi ad obedientiam, abdicationem proprii ac perpetuam castitatem, que substantialia cuiuslibet religionis existunt*; and Innocent IV added that the sisters were committed to the Rule of St. Benedict, *ut per ipsam quasi precipuam de regulis approbatis vestra religio authentica redderetur, nulla tamen propter hoc necessitate inducta, ut ipsam teneamini observare* [*sic*]. Innocent IV gave the same explanation to all Poor Clares on 15 April 1244, stressing, *vobis ad merendum premia perennis vite sufficit, quod solum predictam formulam* [Ugolino's rule] . . . *observetis,* hence without observing the stipulations of the Rule of St. Benedict; Sbaralea, *Bullarium* 1.350; Oliger, "De origine," 447.

142. Thomas of Pavia, Oliger, "De origine," 419.

143. Sbaralea, *Bullarium* 1.266 and 398.

144. . . . *ordo pauperum dominarum de valle Spoleti sive Tuscia*. In a formulary of Ugolino for the exemption of such women's houses, the rule is described as *forma vite et religionis pauperum dominarum de valle Spoleti sive Tuscia per dominum Hugonem . . . auctoritate domini pape eisdem sororibus tradita*, see Oliger, "De origine," 196. In charters concerning the convent of S. Apollinaris in Milan, the rule of 1244 is described as *regula ordini Spoletano a domino papa concessa, or forma vite pauperum dominarum clausarum in valle Spoliti manentium*, and the order itself ordo de Spolito, see Josephus Antonius Saxius, *Archiepiscorum Mediolanensium series* 2 (Milan, 1755), 671ff.; cf. also *AFH* 17.345 and 346–47 (*ordo Spolitanus*), 348–49 (*ordo pauperum manialium de Tuscia*), 349 (*religio monialium de Tuscia*), 351 (*ordo Spoleti*); only in 1234 *monasterium dominarum ordinis S. Damiani*, ibid., 358, 360ff. See n. 146 below.

145. See n. 149 below; hence it was at the same time when Ugolino created his rule for the women's houses, which was written between August 1218 and 29 July 1219.

146. The only source is a bull of Gregory IX to Agnes of Prague, 11 May 1238, Sbaralea, *Bullarium* 1.243: *Predictam regulam* [Ugolino's rule] *studio compositam vigilanti et acceptatam a predicto sancto necnon per felicis recordationis Honorium papam . . . postmodum confirmatam dicte Clara et sorores concesso ipsis ab eodem intercedentibus nobis exemptionis privilegio solemniter sunt professe*; cf. also the bull of Innocent IV to Agnes of Prague on 13 November 1243, Sbaralea, *Bullarium* 1.315. The fact that Francis approved the adoption of Ugolino's rule by St. Damian's before his departure for Egypt is demonstrated, to my satisfaction, in Ugolino's charter for Monticelli, 27 July 1219 (with papal confirmation, 9 December 1219, Sbaralea, *Bullarium* 1.3). The grounds given by Zarncke (*Der Anteil*, 47, 77) for St. Damian's accepting Ugolino's rule only after 1225 are not convincing, and they are contradicted by the charter of 11 February 1223 for the foundation of the convent of St. Apollinaris in Milan for *moniales, que debent ibi vivere secundum ordinem et regulam beati Damiani de valle*

Spolliti iuxta civitatem de Sixi [= Assisi, see *AFH* 17.343]. In fact, Ugolino's rule was followed (see ibid., 355 and 523); the formula of the charter assumes that this rule was already accepted by St. Damian's as well.

147. Cf. Clara's letter to Agnes of Prague, *AFH* 17.517; see Leonhard Lemmens, "Zum Leben und werke," 12; Zarncke, *Der Anteil*, 56–57.

148. On the special position of the house of Monticelli near Florence, see Zarncke, *Der Anteil*, 32–33, 45ff.

149. Wadding, *Annales* 1219, n. 44 (1 [1731], 311). Thomas of Pavia, Oliger, "De origine," 419. Brother Ambrosius, the visitator of the women's houses, died soon thereafter, so the conversation took place before Francis' journey to the orient. Lilly Zarncke's doubts (*Der Anteil*, 36, 74) about the reliability of this account seem as groundless as Oliger's assertion (201–02) that Ugolino could not have intended to entrust the Franciscans with pastoral care over the women's houses in 1218/19, since the Franciscans did not yet have stable residences. In any case the cardinal could have tried to establish the same relationship which obtained with St. Damian's. One more reason for Ugolino to support this relationship, and for Francis to oppose it, is that even if it did not assume the Franciscans were sedentary, it certainly encouraged it.

150. Thomas of Pavia, see Oliger, "De origine," 419. Jordan, *Chronica*, c. 18, ed. Böhmer, 12. Cf. Zarncke, *Der Anteil*, 72ff., who makes the situation hard to understand because of his poorly documented doubts on the dependability of Thomas of Pavia (who relied on Friar Stephanus, a companion of Francis). The appearance of a Friar Ambrosius in a bull of 1228 does not disprove this, since the visitator Ambrosius was already dead in 1219 (Zarncke, 73), as Oliger (420, n. 1) demonstrated.

151. Thomas of Pavia, minister provincial in Tuscany (died 1278/79) reports this on the authority of Friar Stephanus.

152. Jordan, *Chronica*, c. 14, ed. Böhmer, 14–15. Jordan says nothing about the removal of Friar Philippus as visitator or the suspension of his right to place Franciscans in convents, since he did not mention these novelties in the first place, but they can be drawn from the Rule of 1221 itself, noted by neither Lilly Zarncke nor Livarius Oliger.

153. Cf. below, n. 157.

154. *Regula non bullata*, c. 12, in Böhmer, *Analekten*, 9: *Et nulla penitus mulier ab aliquo fratre recipiatur ad obedientiam, sed dato sibi consilio spirituali ubi voluerit agat penitentiam*. Karl Müller, *Anfänge des Minoritenordens*, 17–18, wanted to see this as a remnant of the oldest rule of 1210, since this stipulation made no sense once the "second order" was in existence in 1212. W. Goetz, "Die ursprüngliche Ideale," 27, supposed that it was a ban against just any friar receiving new members of the Poor Clares, and he saw this as "a sign of the advancing organization of the two originally tightly connected branches of the order." Both views appear unsustainable to me, since there was as yet no "Order of the Poor Clares" in the sense assumed here. The ruling is only intelligible as a defense against any tie whatsoever between the Franciscans and women's houses (save St. Damian's).

155. *Regula bullata*, c. 11, in Böhmer, *Analekten*, 23–24: *Ne ingrediantur monasteria monacharum præter illos, quibus a sede apostolica concessa est licentia specialis*. The scope of this ruling was disputed immediately after the promulgation of the rule. In the bull "Quo elongati" of 28 September 1230 (Sbaralea, *Bullarium* 1.70), Gregory IX says: *Quamquam hoc* [the ban on entering convents] *de monasteriis pauperum monialium inclusarum fratres hactenus intelligendum esse crediderint, cum earum Sedes apostolica curam habeat specialem, et intellectus huiusmodi per constitutionem quamdam tempore date regule, vivente adhuc b. Francisco, per provinciales ministros fuisse credatur in generali capitulo declaratus, certificari nihilominus postulastis, an hoc de omnibus generaliter, cum Regula nullum excipiat, an de solis monasteriis monialium predictarum intelligi debeat: nos utique generaliter esse prohibitum de quarumlibet cenobiis monialium respondemus; et nomine monasterii volumus claustrum, domos et officinas interiores intellegi, pro eo quod ad alia loca, ubi etiam homines seculares conveniunt, possunt fratres illi causa predicationis vel eleemosyne petende assedere, quibus id a superioribus suis pro sua fuerit maturitate vel idoneitate concessum; exceptis semper predictarum monasteriorum inclusarum locis, ad que nulli datur accedendi facultas sine licentia sedis apostolice speciali.* Nothing is known of the decree of the general chapter mentioned. Cf. n. 180 below.

156. Bishop Acto of Camerino for the women's house at Sanseverino, 15 June 1223 (Oliger, "De origine," 200). In case the Franciscans did not carry out visitation, or the women denied visitation to the Franciscans, the bishop reserved the right of visitation for himself. This charter was registered and confirmed in a charter of 4 December 1224. The participation of Franciscans in the establishment of other women's houses, which Oliger (199) believed he could prove, in order to show that Francis and the order *non adeo contrarii erant curæ et visitationi etiam præter S. Damianum*, is justly doubted by Zarncke, *Der Anteil*, 70; in the first place it is not certain that the witnesses called *frater* were Franciscans, secondly, they say nothing about an organizational or pastoral relationship to the women's houses. Who was to receive the duty of pastoral care and *visitationis* was never mentioned in other exemption privileges for women's houses, cf. *AFH* 17 (1924), 345. In 1224 the *pauperes sorores ordinis de Spolito* came into possession of St. Apollinaris in Milan, given to them by the archbishop on the request of Cardinal Ugolino, introduced by the prior and priest William *scti. Nazarii in Brovio* and frater Leo *de ordine fr. Min*. (Saxius, *Archiepiscoporum . . . series*, 673). The archbishop did as suggested. There is nothing about the relationship between the Franciscans and the sisters.

157. In a charter of the archbishop of Milan, for the S. Apollinaris convent of Milan dated 2 November 1224 (in J. A. Saxius, *Archiepiscoporum . . . series*, 2, 672; cf. Oliger, "De Origine," 420 and *AFH* 15.75), a *Brunetus filius quondam Oldradi de Carmaniago, qui de mandato domini pape est provisor et rector omnium monialium ordinis de Spolito* appears among the

witnesses—obviously no Franciscan, since he is not called *frater*. Probably he was named as trustee of the women's houses in Friar Philip's place.

158. Sbaralea, *Bullarium* 1.36: *Tibi et successoribus tuis curam committimus monialium predictarum in virtute obedientie districte precipiendo mandantes, quatenus de illis tamquam de ovibus custodie vestre commissis curam et sollicitudinem habeatis.*

159. At the latest after 28 July 1227; see the bull of Gregory IX to the women's houses in Milan (*AFH* 17.349), Vallegloria near Spello (Mittarelli, *Annales Camuldolensium* 4 [1759], 296), Siena (Sbaralea, *Bullarium* 1.33–34, and Oliger, "De origine," 421).

160. Letter of the new protector of the order, Cardinal Rainald, to the women's houses, dated 18 August 1228; Oliger, "De origine," 446.

161. They are listed in the address of the letter by Cardinal Rainald already mentioned, headed by St. Damian's in Assisi.

162. The letter of Cardinal Rainald of 1228 does not describe the individually named *pauperia monasteria* with a common name, but simply groups them together as a unity. After 1234 the term *pauperes moniales inclusæ ordinis s. Damiani* wins out, see *AFH* 17.358, 360; Sbaralea, *Bullarium* 1.207, 209.

163. Sbaralea, *Bullarium* 1.290, n. 331.

164. Sbaralea, *Bullarium* 1.367–68, n. 84 (Berger, *Registres*, no. 1483).

165. Sbaralea, *Bullarium* 1.387–88 (Berger, *Registres*, no. 1960) of 16 October 1245; corresponding messages to the women's houses on 21 October 1245, Sbaralea, 388 (Berger, no. 1961). On 8 November 1245, Innocent IV sent a bull with the same wording to the minister general and the provincial of the March of Ancona for the women's houses of this province, Sbaralea, *Bullarium* 1.393. There is no contradiction between this bull and the previous one, as is always asserted. On 13 November 1245 Innocent III confirmed the rule of the Order of St. Damian, composed by Cardinal Ugolino.

166. Sbaralea, *Bullarium* 1.413, Berger, *Registres*, n. 1949). Text of the bull, see below. Three Spanish houses are addressed: in Medina del Campo, Burgos and Zamora; one in Bordeaux; the remaining ten in Italy: Ascoli; five in the bishopric of Fermo: Offida (cf. the letter of protection dated 23 October 1245, Berger, *Registres*, no. 1575), Ripatransone, Castanea (?), S. Francesco (Berger: S. Thomas) de Monte Sancto (?) and S. Maria de Virginibus in Fermo; S. Maria de Campo Martio in Verona; S. Maria Magdalena in Alessandria (letter of protection of 6 October 1245, Berger, no. 1540); S. Maria Magdalena in front of Norcia (protective letter of 15 June 1245, Berger, *Registres*, no. 1329); S. Michael de Auximano.

167. On 20 April 1250 Innocent IV wrote to the archbishops and bishops of Lombardy, the March of Treviso and Romagna: *Sicut nuper a viris accepimus fide dignis, quedam muliercule interius onerate peccatis, foris tamen sanctitatis, cuius virtutem prorsus abnegant, speciem pretendentes . . . absque jugo discipline damnabiliter evangantur circumeundo varias regiones, . . . sub nomine ordinis s. Damian . . . se velle monasteria eiusdem ordinis*

construere profitentes, super ipsorum fundationes litteras a nobis impetrant tacita veritate; the reputation of the Franciscan Order had been injured by this; for that reason the pope suspended these bulls; Sbaralea, *Bullarium* 1.541. On 30 September 1250 Innocent orders the bishop of Salamanca to act against women wandering about, claiming they were *fore ordinis s. Damiani mentiuntur*, which caused the nuns belonging to the Order of St. Damian in Salamanca to complain; the text of the bull is very close to the bull of Gregory IX in 1241; Sbaralea, *Bullarium*, 1, 556. On 8 July 1252 (ibid., 619; the date is uncertain, see Lempp, "Die Anfänge," 228), Innocent responded to a complaint by Franciscans against *moniales quamplurium monasterium, que ordinis s. Damiani fore se asserunt*, who received from Innocent and Cardinal Rainald *ut monasteriorum ipsarum sollicitudinem gerentes et curam eis correctionis et visitationis officium impendatis et ministretis ecclesiastica sacramenta*; see n. 238 below.

167a. The bull for Montargis (Ripoll, *Bullarium* 1.148, no. 84) has the beginning: *Cum sibi dilecta in Christo filia nobilis mulier Amicia de Jogviiaco et Balesibus et natus eius monasterii S. Dominici juxta Montem Argi Senocentie diecesis fundatores in nostra propria presentia constituti et dilecte in Christo filie Priorissa et sorores eiusdem monasterii incluse corpore . . . libere, secundum ordinem vestrum desiderent domino famulari, nos eorum precibus inclinati monasterium ipsarum incorporantes ordini supradicto duximus statuendum, ut eedem priorissa et sorores sub magisterio . . . .*

168. See the comparison of bulls above.

169. Hence the women's houses of the Franciscans are described as *ordinis s. Damiani*, while in the case of the others there is no term for an order; in the same way, at the close of the bull the theme, in the case of the Franciscan houses, is about their own order, while in the case of the Dominican houses there is talk only of the Dominican Order.

170. It is a bull for S. Agnes of Strasbourg dated 12 October 1247, Ripoll, *Bullarium* 1.178, n. 186, which tells us that the bull of 4 April 1246 was issued *ad magistri et priorum ordinis instantiam*, hence as a response to a petition and suggestion of the order; see n. 174 below.

171. The conclusion of the bull of 4 April 1246 in Ripoll, *Bullarium* 1.161, no. 132, reads: *Quocirca (discretioni vestre per apostolica scripta) mandamus, quatenus omnia premissa juxta constitutionis huiusmodi tenorem, cum eas vestro incorporari Ordini nos velimus, curetis diligenter et sollicite adimplere*. In the parallel bull for the Franciscans on 12 July 1246 in Sbaralea, *Bullarium* 1.420, no. 142: non [instead of *nos*] *velimus*; but Sbaralea remarks that *nos* would suit the Dominican bull better. In a bull of 12 October 1247 (Ripoll, *Bullarium* 1.178, no. 186), which completely repeats the text of that bull, in the place of that passage is, *cum eas vestro incorporari ordini nolimus*. In a transcription of the bull of 4 April 1246 in Ms. theol. lat. Oct. 109 of the Staatsbibliothek Berlin, fol. 36v, it reads *velimus*, the word *nos* is missing (the date there is *Lugd. II kl. aprilis* instead of the *II nonas Apr.* in Ripoll); I was unable to check other manuscripts. Due to the context, the correct reading must

be: *nolimus* or *non velimus*. Ripoll and Sbaralea have obviously not understood the context and corrected the reading. What is meant is that the women's houses should not be "incorporated" into their order but "committed"; the duties arising from this "commission" can be assumed by the order without abandoning its position that women's houses were not to be "incorporated."

172. Ripoll, *Bullarium* 1.160–61, n. 132.

173. Sbaralea, *Bullarium* 1.420, no. 142, text identical to Ripoll, *Bullarium* 1.160–61, no. 132, save for a different motivation: *ne sancte contemplationis otium occursu occupationum multiplicium valeat imperdiri.*

174. The bull of Innocent IV for S. Agnes in Strasbourg, 12 October 1247 (Ripoll, *Bullarium* 1.178, no. 186) and with the same wording for Montargis (ibid., 179, no. 187) begins by repeating the "incorporation bull" (7 May and 8 April 1245), then the bull for the Dominicans of 4 April 1246, by which the relationship between the order and women's houses had been regulated in the meantime in response to a petition by the order, and finally it continues so that he directed the Dominicans to fulfill all the obligations received in the bulls of "incorporation."

175. In a few cases variations of the terminology are developed here. The bull for the house of Altenhohenau on the Inn, dated 21 April 1246 (*Monumenta Boica* 17.10ff., no. 11/12; only summarized in Ripoll, *Bullarium* 1.161, no. 134) completely agrees with the "commission" bulls of other Franciscan houses, but at the conclusion there is the same sentence as in the "incorporation" bulls on the administration of properties. On the other hand, the nuns of St. Dominicus in Imola received a bull on 28 March 1252 on the petition of the bishop of S. Sabina, and it was confirmed by Innocent IV on 11 May 1252 (Ripoll, *Bullarium* 1.206, no. 252 and 7, 27, no. 367), which agree in content with the other "commission" bulls, though it says nothing about the administration of properties, and instead of the word *committere* it uses *incorporare vel unire*; this is also likely for the lost bull for S. Maria de Nazareth near Pavia, cf. the bull of 26 February 1253, Ripoll, *Bullarium* 1.226, no. 292; see below, n. 197.

176. Ripoll, *Bullarium* 1.183, no. 200; Guiraud, *Cartulaire*, 1, no. 10, 18 August 1248. Despite this, on 27 April 1249, a "commission" bull was issued for Prouille, see Guiraud, 1, 9, no. 11.

177. Ripoll, *Bullarium* 7.24–25, no. 364.

178. 12 July 1246, Sbaralea, *Bullarium* 1.420, no. 142.

179. 17 July 1245, Sbaralea, *Bullarium* 1.367–38, no. 84.

180. When Gregory IX regulated the relations of the Minorites to the women's houses of the Order of St. Damian by stating the Franciscan Rule in his bull "Quo elongati," 28 September 1230 (Sbaralea, *Bullarium* 1.68, no. 56), declaring that friars were to enter only the outer enclosure, and then only with special papal permission (see n. 155 above), Clara protested as Amicie de Joigny was to do later, see *Vita*, c. 37 (762). We do not know of this episode from documents, only from legend, so that we do not know more about the concessions to Clara. Probably the continuous residence of Minorites was conceded to the house of St. Damian's at that time. This appears to be the opinion of Oliger, "De origine,"

422–23, who shows the continual residence of Franciscans in several other houses in the Order of St. Damian in the following years.

181. Sbaralea, *Bullarium*, 1.367–68, n. 84 (Berger, *Registres*, no. 1483).

182. *Vita s. Claræ*, c. 14 (758). Instead of giving in to Gregory's request, Clara had the *privilegium paupertatis* renewed on 17 September 1228. On the other houses which preserved their renunciation of property, cf. Oliger, "De origine," 415–16.

183 Sbaralea, *Bullarium* 1.476ff., no. 227; Conradus Eubel, *Epitome et supplementum Bullarii Franciscani* (Rome, 1908), 241ff., no. 15.

184. In a bull of 23 August 1247 to the women's houses of the Order of St. Damian (Sbaralea, *Bullarium* 1.488, no. 236) commanding the reception and introduction of the new rule, all obligations exceeding those of the new rule were declared invalid, and corresponding regulations, oaths or papal decrees were suspended. The motive for this revision of the rule was, first, the unfulfillable harshness of the old rule; secondly, various and disparate dispensations had introduced variety into the way of life of the individual houses.

185. Procurators can already be documented before 1247 in many houses where no Franciscan resided, see Oliger, "De origine," 425.

186. Pfullingen on 21 October 1252, see C. Eubel, *Epitome*, 61; *Wirtembergisches Urk.-B.* 4.308, no. 1239. Strasbourg on 18 January 1255, Sbaralea, *Bullarium* 2.8; *Urkunden Strassburg* 1.291, no. 384.

187. Oliger, "De origine," 426–27.

188. Eubel, *Epitome*, 249, no. xxi. The bull of Innocent IV, 18 March 1253, beginning "*Recto assumpto tramite*" mentioned in *Firmamentum trium ordinum* (Paris, 1512) is not known in its original wording, but it obviously agrees with the bull of 6 June 1250. Oliger, "De origine," 433, wants to see it as ungenuine, but it is probably only misdated in the *Firmanentum.*

189. Rule, c. 12 (*Seraphicæ legislationis textus*, p. 74).

190. Sbaralea, *Bullarium* 1.671ff.; *Seraphicæ legislationis textus*, p. 49ff.; cf. Sabatier, "Il privilegio di Povertà," 19ff.

191. See the edition of the charters above: *ipsis de constitutionibus eiusdem ordinis illas, que ipsis competunt, sine difficultate qualibet exhibentes.*

192. It is remarkable that Minister-General John the German himself encouraged the establishment of the women's house of Paradies under Dominican leadership as late as the beginning of 1252, cf. the account of the Dominican Henry of Osthoven in Johann Suibert Seibertz, *Quellen der Westfälische Geschichte* 1 (Augsburg, 1857), 4ff.

193. *Chronica ordinis*, ed. M. Reichert, *MOPH* 1.334 and 7.10.

194. The fact that the matter was discussed at the chapter of 1252 and the resolutions brought to the curia by the *diffinitores* comes from the letter of Hugh of St. Cher dated 3 March 1254, Ripoll, *Bullarium* 7.33, no. 382; in a letter of Hugh to the German provincial dated 10 February 1257 (*Année Dominicaine ou Vie des Saints, des Bienheureux, des Martyrs . . . de l'ordre des Frères-Prêcheurs*, 2d ed. [Lyon 1886], *Mars*, 2, 888) it says that the suspension

of the obligation to cura by Innocent IV was accomplished *procurantibus hoc quibusdam fratribus dicti ordinis.*

195. Ripoll, *Bullarium* 7.30, no. 375, prints this bull with the date: *Perusii septimo kal. Junii pontif. n. anno X*, that is, 26 May 1253. However, since Innocent IV dates his documents uninterruptedly from Assisi from 1 May to 5 October 1253, where he consecrated a church on 25 May 1253, August Potthast, *Regesta Pontificum Romanorum* Berlin, 1874–5), no. 14605 corrected the date to 26 May 1252 (*anno IX* instead of *anno X*). In the manuscript Berlin, Staatsbibliothek, Theol. lat. Okt. 109, fol. 36v, the bull is dated *Perusii Idus Julii pont. n. anno X*, that is, 15 June 1252. Innocent IV issued two other bulls to the Dominicans on the same day from Perugia, see Potthast, *Regesta Pontificum*, no. 14664/5. Further, the text of the bull in this manuscript is better than that in Ripoll (see above), and the correctness of the date of 1252 is confirmed from the factual context.

196. Ripoll, *Bullarium* 1.217, no. 269. Cf. also Heinrich Denifle, "Meister Eckharts lateinische Schriften und die Grundanschauung seiner Lehre," *ALKG* 2 (1886), 642.

197. Cf. the bulls of Innocent for the house of S. Maria de Nazareth near Pavia, 26 February 1253, and for S. Dominicus in Imola, 17 June 1253, Ripoll, *Bullarium* 1.226, no. 292, and 7.31, no. 376: through the bull of 26 September 1252, which had suspended the obligation to *cura*.

198. Letter of Cardinal Hugh of St. Cher to the provincial of Lombardy and the prior of Bologna, 13 March 1254, Ripoll, *Bullarium* 7.33, no. 382: after the suspension of the obligation of *cura: ad instantiam tamen magnam et perurgentem parentum earundem sororum valde nobilium et plurimorum, qui super huiusmodi mutatione insperata et incredibili vehementer offensi domino nostro summo pontifici suas preces nuper affectuosas et validas porrexerunt, quodammodo [Innocentius] coarctatur hincinde, nolens, quod ad petitionem fratrum concesserat, tam subito retractare, nec valens bono modo tot et tantorum petitionibus et obsecrationibus non prebere consensum.* Cf. the letters of Hugh of St. Cher to the German provincial, 10 February 1257, *Année dominicaine on vies des saints et illustres personnages de l'un et l'autre sene de l'Ordre des Frères Prêcheurs distribuées suivant les jours de l'anée* (Grenoble, 1912), *Mars*, 2, 888–89: *ad devotam instantiam multorum nobilium pro ipsis sororibus domino pape supplicantium.*

199. Cf. on him J. H. H. Sassen, *Hugo von St. Cher, seine Tätigkeit als Kardinal, 1244–1263* (Bonn, 1908).

200. Letter of Hugh to the provincial of Lombardy and the prior of Bologna, 13 March 1254, Ripoll, *Bullarium* 7.33, no. 382. The commission of Innocent IV to Cardinal Hugh in the bull of 18 February 1254 in Ripoll, *Bullarium* 7.32, no. 380 (also inserted in two later letters of the cardinal, in Heinrich Finke, *Ungedruckte Dominikanerbriefe des 13. Jahrhunderts* (Paderborn, 1891), 52–53, no. 4, and *Année dominicaine, Mars* 2, 889) mentions suspending the *cura* obligations of the order; the sisters earlier placed under the order *sicut accepimus magnam exinde sustinent detrimentum.*

201. Cardinal Hugh to the provincial of Lombardy and the prior of Bologna, 18 March 1254, Ripoll, *Bullarium* 7.33, no. 382. Cardinal Hugh's letter of 10 February 1257 mentions that the same commission went to the German provincial, *Année dominicaine, Mars*, 2, 889. Cf. the bull of Alexander IV to the prior of Bologna, 22 April 1257, Ripoll, *Bullarium* 1.335: Cardinal Hugh, to whom Innocent IV *commisisse dicitur oraculo vive vocis, ut de sororibus predicti ordinis ordinaret, prout expedire videret, ordinavit, quod fratres dicti ordinis earum curam gererent, donec per Magistrum et generale capitulum predicti ordinis esset aliter ordinatum.*

202. Amendment to the chapter *De domibus concedendis* of the constitutions of the order: *Sub eadem districtione prohibemus, ne magister vel capitulum aliquod curam monialium seu quarumlibet aliarum mulierum recipiat nisi per tria capitula fuerit approbatum; MOPH* 3.75 (*inchoatio* at the chapter in Milan, 1255), 79 (*approbatio* at the chapter in Paris, 1256), 84 (*confirmatio* at the chapter of Florence, 1257). The ruling was also included in the statutes of the order edited by Raymond of Peñaforte, see *ALKG* 5.549, dist. II, c. 1.

203. Bull of Alexander IV to the prior of Bologna, 22 April 1257, 1, 335, no. 153. Cardinal Hugh to the German provincial, 10 February 1257, *Année dominicaine, Mars* 2, p. 889. Cf. Cardinal Hugh's letter of 5 February 1262, n. 206 below.

204. Cf. n. 197 above.

205. This house was founded by King Bela of Hungary for his daughter Margaret, who only gave her oath at the general chapter of 1254 (which was moved to Buda *ob devocionem regis et regine*, see *MOPH* 1.337) at the hands of Minister-General Humbert.

206. Cardinal Hugh writes, invoking his commission from Innocent IV on 18 February 1254. This letter is addressed to the minister general and the definitores of the general chapter in Florence in the two manuscripts which contain it (see H. Finke, *Ungedruckte Dominikanerbriefe*, 52–53, no. 4, and *Année dominicaine, Mars* 2, 890), bearing only the date *feria V post octavum pasche*, without year. Both editors have dated it at 1257, but this cannot be correct, since the letter could not have been directed at the chapter in Florence in 1257, for 1) the resolution which Cardinal Hugh moves was already passed at the Paris chapter of 1256 (see n. 203 above; both of the letters cited there were written before the chapter in Florence); 2) Cardinal Hugh took entirely different measures on this question at the chapter of Florence in 1257 (see below, n. 210); 3) he himself unmistakably says in a letter of 5 February 1262 (Finke, *Ungedruckte Dominikanerbriefe*, 54, n. 6; *Année dominicaine, Mars*, 2, 890) that it was done at a chapter before 1257 (see below, n. 212; the added "F" in the Berlin manuscript edited by Finke is an error; the letters in question before 1257 saw no general chapter in a town called F . . .). The letter of Cardinal Hugh was thus written to the chapter at Paris, where the resolution he was moving was actually dealt with.

207. Bull of Alexander IV in Ripoll, *Bullarium* 1.158; before the general chapter of 1257!

208. See n. 192 above; perhaps also Kirchberg, see n. 93 above.

209. Letter dated 11 February 1257, *Année dominicaine, Mars*, 2, 888–89.

210. Such directives survive for Unterlinden near Colmar, 10 February 1257 (see Bernardus Pez, *Bibliotheca ascetica antiquo-nova* [Regensburg, 1723ff.], 8, 148ff., no. xxi; A. M. P. Ingold, *Le monastère des Unterlinden*, 227, index no. 14) and for S. Lambrecht, 11 February 1257 (see Johann Friedrich Böhmer, J. Ficker, E. Winkellmann, eds., *Regesta imperii*, 8 vols. [Innsbruck, 1888–] 5, no. 9094). The house of Montargis had had its relationship to the order certified by a bull of Alexander IV on 23 January 1257 (Ripoll, *Bullarium* 1.328, no. 138), without referring to the order's resolution of 1256—obviously because it feared that it did not meet the criteria set by that resolution.

211. Cf. the encyclical of Minister-General Humbert, *MOPH* 5.43–44 (also in Joachim Joseph Berthier, ed., *Humberti de Romanis Opera de vita regulari* [Rome, 1888–89] 2.508).

212. Letter of Cardinal Hugh, 5 February 1262 (Finke, *Ungedruckte Dominikanerbriefe*, 54, n. 6; *Année dominicaine, Mars*, 2, 890–91), in which the cardinal describes the entire course of the negotiations. For that reason, doubts were later raised over the legal situation, which the cardinal sought to settle on behalf of Urban IV by this letter.

213. See the previous note. In the proceedings of the general chapter, there is nothing about it. It was not really a matter of order legislation but rather, as it were, order politics. Cardinal Hugh said in 1262 that the resolution had not been written down.

214. This regular way was used, for example, by the S. Agnes house in Freiburg, which was incorporated by the general chapters of 1281/83 (Wilms, *Verzeichnis*, 48; it was established by sisters from Adelhausen); the house at Lienz was incorporated through the chapters of 1277/79, see Célestin Douais, *Acta capitulorum provincialium ordinis fratrum Prædicatorum* 2 (Toulouse, 1895), 233. G. R. Galbraith, *The Constitution of the Dominican Order* (Manchester, 1925), 48, has been misled because he does not take note of the difference between the foundation of new houses of friars and the reception of women's houses.

215. 16 November 1257, Ripoll, *Bullarium* 1.354, no. 189 (repeating the bull of Gregory IX, dated 25 October 1239). This bull was issued again on 5 December 1259, Ripoll, *Bullarium* 1.385, no. 254.

216. Felix Fabri, O.P., in his *Tractatus de civitate Ulmensi*, 6, 4 (ed. Gustav Veesemeyer [Tübingen, 1889], 167) is profoundly in error on the age and name of pre-Dominican women's communities when he comes to summarize the entire development.

217. Ripoll, *Bullarium* 1.481, no. 59. The bull of Innocent IV, 4 April 1246, regulating the obligations of *cura* in women's houses under the order (see n. 170 above) was renewed again by Nicholas IV on 8 December 1289, Ripoll, *Bullarium* 2.26.

218. The general chapters 1267/69 added to the stipulation cited in n. 202 above: *vel nisi per dominum papam ordini committatur; MOPH* 3.137, 144. A

new version of the entire clause was passed at the general chapters of 1285/87: *Prohibemus districte, ne aliquis curam recipiat predictarum, nisis per tria capitula generalia fuerit approbatum, et nisi cura per dominum papam ordini commitatur vel per alium qui possit facere commissionem predictam;* *MOPH* 3.237, 242–3, 248. The German provincial Hermann of Minden (1286/90) stresses in one letter (*RQ* 33.164) that the obligation of pastoral care by the order extended *tam circa sorores, que per sedem apostolicam nobis commisse sunt, quam circa eas, que per aliquem Magistrorum vel capitula generalia sine cuiusquam prejudicio sunt recepte.*

219. Finke, *Ungedruckte Dominikanerbriefe*, 53, n. 5.

220. Letter of Minister-General Humbert to the *sorores curæ fratrum ordinis prædicatorum commissæ* by the general chapter at Valenciennes, 1259, *MOPH* 5.50–51.

221. It cannot be established whether the constitutions of 1259 are those published in *AOP* 3.338ff.

222. Letter of the minister general to the sisters of the order from the general chapter in Strasbourg, 1260, *MOPH* 5.57. After this reordering, the designation of *Ordo s. Sixti and Ordo s. Marci* is no longer used for German women's houses, but only *Ordo s. Augustini secundum instituta ordinis fratrum Prædicatorum* or something similar; see, for example, the charters for Paradies near Soest, *Westfälisches Urk.-B.*, 5/1, p. 253, no. 551; for Steinach, Stetten, Offenhausen, Ripoll, *Bullarium* 1.361 and 408; for Klingenthal: *Urk.-B. Basel* 1.236; for St. Lambrecht: Remling, *Urk.-B. zur Geschichte der Bischöfe zu Speyer* 1.403, no. 436; for Engelthal: Heidingsfelder, *Regesten* 2.224 (in 1267; ibid., 1271: *conventus sororum in E. sub regula s. Augustini et regimine fratrum ord. Praed.*); for Altenhohenau: 1273 *sorores inclusæ ord. s. Augustini secundum instituta et sub cura fratrum ord. Præd. viventes, Monumenta Boica*, 17, 18; Schwarzhofen: 1265 *conventus devotarum feminarum . . . domino sub habitu et regimine fratrum ord. Præd. famulantium*; 1268, *conventus sororum s. Augustini . . . secundum constitutionem fratrum prædicatorum deo militantium*, see Wilhelm Schratz, *Urkunden und Registen zur Geschichte des Nonnenklosters zum hl. Kreuz in Regensburg* (Regensburg, 1887), 150–52, cf. ibid., 152, 159.

223. *MOPH* 3.88.

224. *MOPH* 3.98.

225. Letter of 5 February 1262, Finke, *Ungedruckte Dominikanerbriefe*, 54, no. 6 (see n. 212 above).

226. Letter of the general chapter at Strasbourg to the sisters, 1260, *MOPH* 5.56.

227. See the constitutions for the women's houses in *AOP* 3.342, c. 14. Letter of the minister general to the sisters, at the general chapter of Strasbourg, 1260, *MOPH* 5.57. According to a letter by the German provincial Herman of Minden (1284/90), according to a statute of the minister general, a house was allowed to have only as many nuns as it had three marks of silver income for each (*RQ* 33.162; that corresponds, according to the figures of G. Löhr, to a value of

about 520 Marks of 1800), and the maximum number could only be exceeded if particularly prominent persons demanded entry who could not be rejected without damage to the order, or where the entry of particularly prosperous women would bring the house economic advantages, which is to say, at least 100 silver marks in money or a property of the value of 140 marks (assuming a return on money of 9%, on land of 6%), so that three sisters could be supported from the income. Many houses had observed this rule for a decade.

228. See below, n. 260ff.

229. Constitutions for women's houses, *AOP* 3.348, c. 30. The general chapters of 1285/87 amended the ban of 1228 that Dominicans not work to receive new women's houses into the order (see n. 42 above) with the phrase, *nisi de licentia magistri ordinis speciali; MOPH* 3.228, 231, 237.

230. The ordering of the relationship between the Dominicans and women's houses in Germany was particularly promoted by the provincial prior Herman of Minden, 1284/90, without changing anything essential in the circumstances which had prevailed since 1257. Cf. Denifle, "Meister Eckharts lateinische Schriften," 641ff. and 649–50; G. Löhr, *RQ* 33.159ff. A publication by Ritzinger on Hermann of Minden, announced by A. Simon, *L'Ordre de Pénitentes*, 86, has not appeared, so far as I know. At the end of 1286 the houses of the Order of Mary Magdalen, about forty of them, were placed (committed) under the pastoral care and visitation of the Dominican Order by the legate Johannes Boccamazzi, but that was only a provisional action caused by the deficiencies of the leadership of that order *quousque per sedem apostolicam aliud fuerit ordinatum* (A. Simon, *L'Ordre des Pénitentes*, 87, 251–52, 254), and they accepted neither the habits nor the rules and constitutions of Dominican nuns (ibid., 87, 254–55, no. 163, for the instructions of Hermann of Minden for the attitude of the Dominicans to the "Reuerinnen"): rather Nicholas IV confirmed them under the Rule of St. Augustine and the constitutions of S. Sisto, which they had followed since 1232 (ibid., 258, no. 169) and in 1296 they were placed under their own *præpositus* (ibid., p. 98, 260, no. 174). In a bull of 8 December 1287, Legate Johannes Boccamazzi once more summarily incorporated all German women's houses to the Dominican Order which had been placed under that order by himself, a minister general or a general chapter (ibid., 256, no. 163/6). It is neither provable nor likely that it was the legate's intention to incorporate the Order of Mary Magdalene into the Dominican Order, or that this was only reversed by the confirmation of the rule of S. Sisto in 1291, as A. Simon, *L'Ordre des Pénitentes*, 91ff., believes.

231. Cf. Oliger, "De origine" 435; the houses of S. Agnes in Prague and Breslau certainly kept this rule.

232. On 25 October 1239 and 3 September 1239, repeated again on 16 November 1257, Ripoll, *Bullarium* 1.107, 121, 354.

233. Sbaralea, *Bullarium* 1.538, no. 219.

234. Commission to the German provincial, 6 July 1250 (Sbaralea, *Bullarium* 1.545, no. 331), to take over the *cura* of Paradies, ordering at least four experienced sisters of the Order of St. Damian and, either in person or through

suitable friars, to *eisdem monialibus celebrare divina et exhibere ecclesiastica sacramenta et alia omnia, que in domibus eiusdem ordinis s. Damiani per fratres Minores consueverunt hactenus exhiberi*; the conclusion of the bull: *non obstantibus aliquibus statutis vel indulgentiis seu privilegiis eidem a sede apostolica concessis, per que id impediri vel differri possit et de quibus specialem oporteat in presentibus fieri mentionem*, canceling the bull of 6 March 1250 for this case.

235. Alexander IV to the German provincial and the provincial chapter in Esslingen, 8 March 1255; Alexander V confirms this assurance.

236. *ALKG* 6.106. These constitutions were edited and published in 1260 by Bonaventure, but contained mostly resolutions of earlier general chapters which cannot usually be dated (Franz Ehrle, "Die älteste Redactionen der General-constitutionen des Franziskanerordens," *ALKG* 6 [1892], 81). They were repeated in later editions of the constitutions.

237. Bull of Alexander IV to archbishops and bishops of Lombardy, the March of Treviso and Romagna, Sbaralea, *Bullarium* 1.541, no. 322; see above, n. 167. The same letter was sent by Alexander IV on 8 January 1257 to the archbishops and bishops of Gascony and Aquitaine, Sbaralea, *Bullarium* 2.183–84, no. 272. Cf. also the bull of Innocent IV to the bishop of Salamanca, 30 September 1250, Sbaralea, *Bullarium* 1.556, no. 345, see n. 167 above.

238. Bull of Innocent IV, 8 July 1252, Sbaralea, *Bullarium* 1.619, no. 419 (according to Potthast, *Regesta Pontificum*, 6 June 1253, Wadding, 6 June 1252; see Lempp, "Die Anfänge," 228). On 27 May 1248 the provincial of the March of Ancona was granted the cura of the house of S. Proculus in Esino near Sinigaglia *de consilio fratrum minorum*, with the explanation: *cum asseratur exemptum*, Sbaralea, *Bullarium* 1.517, no. 279.

239. The sole usable if not very dependable report on this conflict is in Philipp of Perugia (*AF* 3.710; almost word for word in the *Chronicle of the 24 Ministers General, AF* 3.329).

240. Bull of Urban IV to Cardinal-Protector Johannes Gaetanus and to Bonaventure, 19 August 1262, Sbaralea, *Bullarium* 2.574–55, no. 168, with the false date of 1264; corrections and additions to the text of the bull is given in Zephyrinus Lazzeri, "Documenta controversiam inter fratres Minores et Clarissas spectantia (1262–1297)," *AFH* 3 (1910), 670–74, who has done basic research on the course of this conflict (*AFH* 3 [1910], 664–79, and 4 [1911], 74–94). The developments described above can be drawn from this bull.

241. Cf. Lazzeri, "Documenta," 673ff.

242. 15 May 1263, Lazzeri, "Documenta," 671–72; cf. Sbaralea, *Bullarium* 2.578: since the chapter desired to close the question of the relation to women's houses, *universitatem vestram rogamus et hortamus attente, quatenus . . . sorores easdem habentes in domino commendatas more solito vestre cure presidia ministretis.*

243. In a sketch of the resolutions of this general chapter, *ALKG* 6.37 there is, in fact: *Ut omnino dimitteretur cura sanctimonialium Damianitarum sive Clarissarum*; but these sketches are not original protocols, but rather

"summarized from information obtained elsewhere" (Ehrle), and the resolution reported is probably taken from the imprecise report in the *Chronicle of the 24 Ministers General*—precisely like the previous error that the chapter of 1263 ruled *ut peteretur in protectionem ordinis Joh. de Ursinis*, who had long been protector. Lazzeri, "Documenta," 676, believes that it is possible to conclude from the results that no decisions were made at the general chapter of 1263.

244. Sbaralea, *Bullarium* 2.474–75, no. 72.

245. Cf. *AFH* 4 (1911), 81.

246. The *forma instrumenti publici seu litterarum nostre libertatis* which the women's houses were to endorse stands in a letter of Bonaventure to the *visitator monialium Tusciæ* of 29 September 1263, *Lazzeri*, "Documenta," 679, as well as in a letter of Cardinal-Protector John to the women's houses of Tuscany, 11 December 1263, *AFH* 4 (1911), 80: *Recognoscimus, quod ordo fratrum minorum vel fratres eiusdem ordinis nobis seu monasterio nostro seu personis in eo degentibus ad obsequia seu ministeria exhibenda aliquatenus ex debito non tenentur*; women's houses could never raise a legal claim on the services the Franciscans rendered *de facto seu liberalitate sua vel mera gratia*, or sue the order.

247. Sbaralea, *Bullarium* 2.508ff.

248. Cf. Oliger, "De origine," 442.

249. Sbaralea, *Bullarium* 2.477 in the confirmation bull of Urban IV, 27 July 1263; the earlier confirmation by Alexander IV does not survive; cf. Oliger, "De origine," 436ff. The rule permits house property, pastoral care and visitation is bestowed on the Franciscans, and Franciscan confessors are even required to be in continuous residence in the houses: *Confessores earum ac socii eorumdem sint de ordine fratrum minorum ibi commorantes.*

250. Cf. the letter of the cardinal protector to the Upper German provincial, 10 February 1268, ed. Ferdinand-M. Delorme, *AFH* 5 (1912), 48ff.

251. In 1276 the cardinal protector asked the new minister general, Hieronymus of Ascoli, and the general chapter at Lyon *ut fratres non ex debito, sed sui amore obsequiis insisterent sororum sancte Clare. Quod multum dicto generali et ordini fuit grave,* see *AF* 3.359; but it was approved under the condition that the Clarissan house sign the *Instrumentum libertatis* (see n. 246 above). The general chapter of 1277 resolved, following the desire of the protector, *quod serviatur dominabus sancti Damiani modo consueto ex mandato domini papa usque ad sequens capitulum generale*, see A. G. Little, *EHR* 13 (1898), 707; cf. *AFH* 7.681; Ehrle, "Die ältesten Redaktionen," 47–48; *AF* 2.89. Cf. on this the *Vita Nicolai IV* by Hieronymus Rubeus, cited in Z. Lazzeri, "Documenta," 91.

252. Sbaralea, *Bullarium* 4.396, no. 70, repeats the bull of Innocent IV, 12 July 1246 (see above, n. 173), continuing: *mandamus, quatenus omnia premissa, etiamsi eedem littere de cetero nullatenus apparerent, circa prefata monasteria et eorum personas, siue ordinis s. Clare sive s. Damiani sive Minorisse [sic] dicantur, exequi diligenter et sollicite studeatis.*

253. Sbaralea, *Bullarium* 4.431ff., no. 114.

254. Spain, 2, France, 4 (first Montargis, then Rouen—only in 1263!), Provence, 1 (Prouille), Lombardy, 3, Rome, 3, Poland, 2, Hungary, 2, Dacia, 1; there were as yet no women's houses in the provinces of Greece, England, and Terra Sancta. Cf. Quétif, Echard, *Scriptores Ordinis Prædicatorum* 1.1; H. Wilms, *Geschichte der deutschen Dominikanerinnen*, 48, and *Verzeichnis*, 5; Baur, "Die Ausbreitung der Bettelorden," 77; Pierre Mandonnet, *Catholic Encyclopedia* 12.369.

255. Finke, *Ungedruckte Dominikanerbriefe*, 46.

256. Wilms, *Verzeichnis*, 75ff., also includes eight houses which had been under the order before 1308, but were then no longer members, and p. 79ff., seven houses which already existed but only came under the order in later years.

257. Thus Wilms, *Geschichte*, 46; Denifle, "Meister Eckharts lateinische Schriften," 643, counting 160. The list (in Quétif, Echard, *Scriptores*, 1, p. iv ff.; Edmund Martène, *Veterum scriptorum amplissima collectio* [Paris, 1724–33] 6.539) is not always unambiguous. The two Spanish provinces had 8, the four Italian provinces had 41 women's houses, Hungary, 8, German-Austria, 8.

258. See n. 235 above.

259. Konrad Eubel, *Geschichte der oberdeutschen (Strassburger) Minoritenprovinz* (Würzburg, 1886) 12–13.

260. According to an anonymous chronicle by a Basel Franciscan written about 1325, ed. L. Lemmens, *RQ* 14.255: Alemannia superior, 54 male, 22 female; Saxonia, 100 male, 15 female; Colonia, 40 male, 3 female. Edmund Wauer, *Entstehung und Ausbreitung des Klarissenordens* (Leipzig, 1906), 70ff., can only show 25 Clarissan houses in the three German Franciscan provinces.

261. The most were in Central Italian provinces; Tuscia, 50 male, 22 female; Roma, 49 male, 22 female; Provincia S. Francisci, 66 male, 32 female; Provincia S. Angeli Custodis, 22 male, 20 female; Marchia, 88 male, 20 female.

262. According to Johannes Linneborn's figures ("Die westfälische Klöster des Clarissenordens," 336–37) Westphalian Cistercian convents contained on average at least 30 nuns. The number of Premonstratensian nuns in Bonoeil, where the nuns originally at Prémontré were settled after many shifts in residency, was limited at 20 in 1240; see Carl Ludwig Hugo, *Annales ordinis Prémonstratensia* (Nancy, 1734), I, col. 392.

263. *AFH* 17.364.

264. Lazzeri, "Documenta," 675 and 673.

265. Guiraud, *Cartulaire* 1.255, no. 204.

266. Ibid., 260, no. 210; in 1294 Minister General Stephan of Besançon demanded that a maximum be observed; of those *jam receptis verbo, provisione et litteris* none could be veiled so long as the maximum number was exceeded; see ibid., 264–65, no. 213.

267. A. Danzas, *Études* 4.255.

268. Giovambattista Melloni, *Atti e Memorie degli uomini illustri in santità . . . nati o morti in Bologni*, 6 vols. (Bologna, 1773–1818) 1.229, n. 4.

269. See n. 110 above.

270. 19 December 1237, *Urkunden Strassburg* 4/2, 53–54, no. 51.

271. See the statistics of the Dominican chronicler Johannes Meyer, *FDA* 13.134, n., and 136; also S. Dietler, *Gebweiler*, ed. Schlumberger, 11.

272. The nuns' book of Kirchberg, F. W. E. Roth, "Aufzeichnungen über das mystische Leben der Nonnen von Kirchberg bei Sulz, Predigerordens, während des 14. und 15. Jarhhunderts," *Alemannia* 21 (Bonn, 1898), 117; Ph. Strauch, ibid., 16, with a reference to Franciscus Petrus, *Suevia ecclesiastica* (Augsburg, 1699), 459ff.; *Beschreibung des Oberamtes Sulz*, (Stuttgart, 1862), 234–35; Köingliches statistisches-topographischen Bureau, *Das Königreich Württemberg*, 3 vols. (Stuttgart, 1882–86) 3.399.

273. *AOP* 4.560.

274. Ötenbach nuns' book, ed. Zeller-Werdmüller and Bächtold, 222, 235.

275. Cf. the bulls of Innocent IV for St. Mark's in Strasbourg, 29 March 1249, for St. Johannes and S. Katharina in Strasbourg, 8 September 1249; *Urkunden Strassburg* 1.245, no. 329.

276. *MOPH* 3.98.

277. The German provincial Herman of Minden (1286/90) writes in a letter (*ALKG* 2.650): *Quia numerum statutum sibi a magistro ordinis sunt plurimum supergresse, ipsas inducite, quod sistant et retrocedant, donec per sororum obitus priores limites attingantur.*

278. N. van Werveke, *Cartulaire du Prieuré de Marienthal* (Luxembourg, 1885), 218, no. 242.

279. The provincial Herman of Minden set a maximum for the St. Agnes house established in 1264 in Freiburg at 40 sisters; see *RQ* 33.167.

280. *Urk.-B. Zürich* 8.317, no. 3056, 12 August 1310.

281. The provincial Egnolf of Stoffen set the number of nuns at 52 at Himmelskrone near Worms, see Heinrich Boos, *Urk.-B. der Stadt Worms* (Berlin, 1886) 2.31–32, no. 47. At St. Gertrude in Cologne it was set at 46 between 1316 and 1323. The house of Weil near Esslingen was said to have been restricted to 70 nuns in 1362 (Bihlmeyer, "Mystisches Leben," 63–64), but in 1442 it had more than 130 sisters (Memminger, *Württembergisches Jahrbuch* 2 [1819], 194).

CHAPTER 6

1. Cf. Simon, *L'Ordre des Pénitentes.*

2. The later pope Urban IV (1261–64); see Joseph Greven, *Die Anfänge*, 211. He was canon of St. Lambert in Liège from 1234, archdeacon in 1243.

3. Cf. Greven, *Anfänge*, 212; H. Nimal, "Les béguinages," *Annales de la société archéologique de l'arrondissement de Nivelles* 9 (1908), 28; in 1253 Cardinal-Legate Hugh of St. Cher granted him the *officium visitationis et reformationis* in the diocese of Liège to carry out the reform statutes of the legate; later he was *scholasticus* in Tongern and *provisor in spiritualibus* for the bishop of Liège, who granted him control and leadership of the beguines and beghards in his diocese (see n. 40a below); he died the next year, leaving

testamentary donations for seventeen beguinages; see J. Paquay, "Regesta de Renier, écolatre de Tongres," *Bulletin de l'institut archéologique Liègeois 35 (1905), 1ff.; cf. Analectes pour servir à l'histoire ecclésiastique de la Belgique* 20 (Louvain, 1886), 125ff. Probably this Magister Rainer is the source of the rule for the Brussels beguines confirmed by Duke John I of Brabant, see Aubertus Miræus, *Opera diplomatica et historica*, 2d ed. (Brussels, 1886) 2.1006. [See the two newer books summarizing the history of the beguines by Mens, *Oorsprong en betekenis*, see comments in "New Contributions," n. 22; McDonnell, *Beguines and Beghards*. HG/1960.]

4. Cf. *AKG* 21.307ff.

5. See above, chapter 4, n. 1ff.

6. Thomas of Eccleston, *De adventu fratrum minorum in Angliam*, ed. Andrew G. Little, 123–24. (also *MG Scr.* 28.558). Robert Grosseteste was lector of the Franciscans in Oxford before becoming bishop of Lincoln; he died in 1253.

7. "Sermo de conscientia ad theologos," in César Égasse Du Boulay, *Historia Universitatis Parisiensis*, 6 vols. (Paris, 1665–73) 3. 232.

8. "Casus et articuli, super quibus accusatus fuit a fratribus Predicatoribus, cum responsionibus ad singula," in William of St. Amour, *Opera*, 92. All citations on the beguines to be found in the writings of William of St. Amour are also found in Johannes Laurentius Mosheim, *De beghardis et beguinabus commentarius* (Leipzig, 1790), 26ff. In the "Casus et articuli," he defends himself against the accusation that Dominicans had directed at him, stressing that his polemic was not directed against the mendicants but other phenomena, which *nullus sint religionis per sedem apostolicam approbatæ, including quædam mulieres juvenes, quas appellant Beguinas, per totum regnum tam diffusæ (quæ nulla regula canonica coercentur); Opera*, 266. [Cf. E. Faral, "Les 'Responsiones' de Guillaume de Saint-Amour," *AHDL* 18 (1950/51), 373 –95. HG/1960.]

9. "Collectiones catholicæ et canonicæ scripturæ ad defensionem ecclesiasticæ hierarchiæ," *Opera*, 267.

10. Ibid., 305, 332.

11. "Casus et articuli," *Opera*, 92.

12. See below, chapter 7, n. 50ff.

13. A summary of literary mentions of beguines in France by Hilka, "Altfranzösische Mystik und Beginentum," 121ff.; cf. below, chapter 7, text to n. 61ff.

14. Chapter 45 of the statutes, in F. J. Mone, "Kirchenordnungen der Bistümer Mainz und Strassburg aus dem 13. Jahrhundert," *ZGO* 3 (1852), 141 (cf. Carl Joseph Hefele, Alois Knöpfler, *Conciliengeschichte*, 5 [2d ed., Freiburg i. B., 1886], 1026, and Heinrich Finke, *Konzilienstudien zur Geschichte des 13. Jahrhunderts* [Münster, 1891], 29ff.).

15. Statutes of this council in Joseph Hartzheim, *Concilia Germaniæ* (Cologne, 1759 ff.), 3.603, among the statutes of the provincial council of Mainz, 1261; Finke, *Konzilienstudien zur Geschichte*, 22ff., showed that they were from 1244, referring to the synod of 1233. After an almost literal repetition of

the earlier decree, the amendment follows. Finke, *Konzilienstudien*, 35, supposes that these amendments had already been passed at an earlier Mainz synod shortly after 1233, but this appears to me to be inadequately documented.

16. Cf. *AKG* 21.303ff.; bull of 21 November 1235 to the Osnabrück canon Johannes, crusade preacher for the archdiocese of Cologne, to protect the *sorores conversæ, quæ Beginæ vulgariter appelantur*, also on 27 October 1237 to the cathedral scholasticus of Cologne, on 19 June 1246 to the bishops of Osnabrück and Münster, see *Osnabrücker Urk.-B.* 2, no. 378; 4, nos. 674 and 678. Cf. also the charters of the legate Peter of Albano (10 November 1250) and Hugh of St. Cher (5 October 1251) to protect Cologne beguines, in Leonhard Ennen and Gottfried Eckertz, *Quellen zur Geschichte der Stadt Köln* 2 (Cologne, 1863), 298, n. 295, and 306, n. 301.

17. The chronology of her life according to autobiographical testimony (particularly in *Das fliessende Licht*, IV, 2) and the information her editor and translator have, it appears to me, been definitively clarified by Jeanne Ancelet-Hustache, *Mechtilde de Magdebourg; étude de psychologie religieuse* (Paris, 1926). According to this, she was born in 1207, went to Magdeburg in 1230, remaining there forty years as a beguine; in 1250 she had the experience which stimulated her to describe her visions, which were edited by her Dominican confessor Henry of Halle (only the seventh book, which has no Latin version, was written later in Helfta). In 1270 she entered the convent of Helfta, and in 1282 she died (cf. also A. Hauck, *ZKG* 32.186ff.). It is not certain that she was of noble parentage, but it appears likely despite Ancelet-Hustache's objections, 52 ff.; cf. Hubert Stierling, *Studien zu Mechthild von Magdeburg* (Nuremberg, 1907), 27ff. and Grete Lüers, *Die Sprache der deutschen Mystik des Mittelalters im Werke der Mechthild von Magdeburg* (Munich, 1926), 57ff. In any case, she willingly gave up *die welt, weltlich ere und allen weltlichen richtum*, from a desire, *das ich ane mine schulde wurde versmähet,* see *Das fleissende Licht der Gottheit*, I, 1, ed. Gall Morell (Mainz, 1869), 4; IV, 2, p. 91; VII, 64, 279 (ed. W. Schleussner, pp. 123–24); *Revelationes Gertrudianæ ac Mechtildianæ* 2.436. She probably wanted to enter a convent but could not find an opening (IV, 2: *Do lies mich got niergen eine.*). [R. Kayser, "Minne und Mystik im Werke Mechthilds von Magdeburg," *The Germanic Review* 19 (1944), 1–16. HG/1960.]

18. *Das fliessende Licht*, II, 15, ed. Morell, 66–67, God speaks to Mechthild: *ich mus dich aber leren: die edeln juncfrowen kostet ir zucht vil sere, si müssen sich twingen an allen iren liden und müssent vil dike vor ir zuchtmeisterine bebenen, also ist minen bruten in ertriche an irem lichamen gegeben*; VI, 7, 182 (in the Latin text, *Revelationes*, 526, with the caption: *De beguina distorta moribus et conversatione): In miner gesellschaft ist ein geistlich mensch* [*Revelationes: quædam femina religiosa*], *von dem lide ich manig not dur sine bösen siten, also das mir der mensche an keinen dingen volgen wil.*

19. *Das fliessende Licht*,, II, 15, ed. Morell, 76 (cf. *Revelationes*, 610): *O ir vil torehtigen beginen, wie sint ir also vrevele, das ir vor unserm almehtigen rihter nit bidenent wenne ir gotz lichamen so dikke mit einer blinden gewon-*

heit nement. Nu, ich bin die minste under üch, ich mus mich schemen, hitzen und biben. Also V, 11, 138–39 (*Revelationes*, 591–92), where she denounces people who were only externally pious, often addressing them as *liebe swester.*

20. *Das fliessende Licht*,, V, 5, ed. Morell, 134 (*Revelationes*, 629–30), Mechthild tells of a beguine who chastized herself to death; when Mechthild prayed for her, she saw the woman's spirit *clar an im selber als die sunne, . . . das hatte si von irem reinen herzen in getruwer meinunge*; but the beguine told her that prayers would do her no good, since she had to do penance for her *eigen willen ane rat*, for, *Ich wolte in ertriche keines menschen rat volgen nach christenlicher ordenunge*. Cf. also the fragment of a dialogue between a "truly spiritual sister" and a "worldly beguine," *Fliessende Licht*, III, 24, 88–89; *die geistliche swester sprichet usser dem waren lihte des heligen geistes sunder herzeleit, aber die weltlich begine sprichet us von irem fleische mit lucifers geiste in gruwelicher arbeit* (the dialogue announced between these two representatives of the *zwöigerleie lute uf disem ertrich* does not follow; H. Stierling, *Studien*, 18 and 104, seeks it in II, 23, ed. Morell, 43, but that is a dialogue between love and the soul; cf. Heinz Tillmann, *Studien zum Dialog bei Mechthild von Magdeburg*, Dissertation [Marburg, 1933], 13). Cf. also *Revelationes*, 527: *De beguina in apparentia et non existentia: Femina quedam habitum religionis beguinarum induerat, sed tamen curiis dominorum secularium serviebat* = *Fleissende Licht*, IV, 17, 110: *Von einer vrow die ze hove gerne was: Ein vrowe hette sich begeben und wolte dennoch ze hove dienen . . .*

21. The convent of Helfta was not incorporated into any order, though it did observe the institutions of the Cistercians. Pastoral care of the house, where the visions of both Mechthild of Magdeburg and Gertrude of Helfta originated, appeared to be largely in the hands of the Dominicans. as was the case at the Cistercian convent of Overweimar, where Dominicans worked simultaneously as confessors and preachers; cf. the *Vita* of the nun Lukardis, *AB* 18.330–31, 340, 344, 352, 363, and *passim*.

22. The Latin preface to the German text of *Fliessende Licht* (ed. Morell, 1), which was probably composed by Henry of Halle about 1270 (see Ancelet-Hustache, *Mechtilde de Magdebourg*, 42–43; Ph. Strauch, *ZDA* 27.371), calls Mechthild a *begina, que fuit virgo sancta corpore et spiritu, . . . sequens perfecte vestigia fratrum ordinis predicatorum* (Henry of Nördlingen translates the word *begina* with *swester*); *Fliessende Licht*, II, 23, p. 44, in a dialogue, love says to the soul: *Ich bin in einem heligen orden, ich vaste, wache, ich bin one hoptsunde, ich nin gnug gebunden* (= *Revelationes*, 539: *ego ordinem sanctum porto, jejuno, sine crimine vivo, satis ligata sum regula et conclusa).* That is probably as little usable in an autobiographic sense as the later statement of the soul in the same dialogue: *ich wone in der wollust miner mage*, etc., but it indicates a prevailing sense. Because of this statement, Jeanne Ancelet-Hustache believes Mechthild was a Dominican tertiary, but this is unlikely; we have no evidence that there were any tertiaries in Magdeburg at that time; further, Mechthild later entered a Cistercian convent; her esteem for

Dominic as her *lieben Vater* (*Fliessende Licht*, II, 24) does not prove that she was any different from the many beguines who were very fond of the order; Christine of Stommeln, who remained a beguine her entire life, had the same relationship to the Dominicans as Mechthild; both managed to get their brothers into the order.

23. The same rule was repeated at the Mainz synod of 1310 (Hartzheim, *Concilia Germaniæ* 4.200–01). It was specifically suspended for Frankfurt beguines in 1291 by Archbishop Gerhard of Mainz on the request of their pastor, since they *aliquibus videatur onerosa, et alique puelle per huiusmodi prohibitionem a dei servicio abstrahi videantur*, see *Codex diplomaticus Mœnofrancofurtanus*, ed. Johann Friedrich Böhmer (Frankfurt am Main, 1901–05) 1. 262. The rule composed for the three Strasbourg beguinages (who also belonged to the province of Mainz) foresees the reception of girls under fourteen, who were to receive their habits when they reached fourteen and swore obedience to the rule, see *Urk.-B. Strassburg* 3.27, no. 78.

24. The Mainz synods of 1233 and 1244 demanded: *Subdite sint suis plebanus et eorum consilio regantur*. A Mainz synod of 1261, whose resolutions were repeated in 1310, banned on pain of excommunication *omnibus religiosis, ne subditos plebanorum, maxime autem Beginas et Bicornos* [1310: *Beghardos*] *aut inclusas ac alias personas huiusmodi communicent corpore domini aut alia porrigant ecclesiastica sacramenta parvulis vel adultis*; only confession could be transferred by the *subditi plebanorum*, often with permission of the pastor, *quibusdam religiosis*. The statutes of 1261 in Hartzheim, *Concilia Germaniæ 3.610–11 (cf. Finke, Konzilienstudien*, 23) need to be corrected using the text of the repetition in 1310, Hartzheim, 4.220; the reading *Molusas* instead of *inclusas*, and the explanation given in A. J. Binterim, *Pragmatische Geschichte der deutschen National-, Provinzial-, und vorzüglichsten Diözesanconcilien*, 5 vol. (Mainz, 1848) 5.204, and Hefele and Knöpfler, *Conciliengeschichte* 6.74, "Beguines from the Mühlhausen community," is wrong. A Magdeburg synod of 1261 declared: *De mulieribus que Begine vocantur, statuimus, ut plebano, in cuius morantur parochia, obediant sicut ceteri parrochiales; alioquin ad id per ipsos plebanos cum excommunicationibus sententia compellantur*; Hartzheim, *Concilia Germaniæ* 3.807; for dating, cf. Hefele and Knöpfler, *Conciliengeschichte* 6.79.

25. As early as 1230 Cardinal-Legate Otto granted to the Cologne beguines the privilege of communicating outside their parish except for the three high festivals; Cardinal Hugh of St. Cher confirmed this privilege in 1251, see Ennen and Eckertz, *Quellen zur Geschichte der Stadt Köln*, 2, no. 295 and 301. The bishop of Cambrai permitted the beguines in Valenciennes to erect their own chapel with their own chaplain, who also took over pastoral care for those beguines who lived outside the beguinage, see Miræus, *Opera diplomatica-historica* 2.855–56. In 1261 the beguines in Diest received a church of their own with a cemetary and one or more priests, because they *ex eo, quod in diversis degunt parochiis, incommoditates et pericula animarum patiuntur*, see ibid., 1.768. The bishop of Liège gathered all the beguines in Aachen

into a common beguinage, giving them a pastor of their own, a chapel, and a cemetary, *ut status becginarum nostre diocesis illibatus servetur, ut et quietius ac pacatius divine speculationi valeant intendere,* see *Mitteilungen des Vereins für Aachener Vorzeit* 5 (1892), 2ff., 63–64; Wilhelm Liese, *Geschichte der Caritas* (Freiburg i. B., 1922) 2.78. The earliest Osnabrück beguinage was controlled by the cathedral chapter (see *AKG* 21.307ff.); a burial ordinance of 1278 commanded that all beguines not living in this house of canonesses were within the burial right of the parish priest, who also veiled such beguines.

26. General chapter of the Dominicans at Paris, 1242, *MOPH* 3.26; *Priores in domibus nostris ubique confessores beginarum instituant certos, mutaros et paucos*; Metz, 1251, ibid., 59: *Quod priores solliciti sint dare beguinis confessores certos, discretos et maturos, et determinent tempus nec nimis rarum nec nimis frequens vacandi earum confessionibus*. Similar stipulations in the statutes of the provincial chapter of the Roman Dominican province in Douais, *Acta capitulorum* 2.486 (Rome, 1243), 491 (Rome, 1246), 494 (Rome, 1249), 495 (Perugia, 1249), 500 (Anagni, 1252), 513 (Naples, 1260), 518 (Viterbo, 1264). Instead of *biguinæ* they were called *bizocæ,* thus in 1246 and 1249; this name arose from the name "begine" according to Jacques of Vitry, see *HJ* 35.44–45; (in a charter about Franciscan tertiaries in Florence, 1244, there is mention of a *domus quæ dicitur Hospitale pauperum pro bizocaris, qui homines de pœnitentia nuncupatur*, see Vincenzio Fineschi, *Memorie istoriche che possono servire alle vite degli uomini illustri del convento di S. Maria Novella di Firenze* [Florence, 1790], 97). Statutes of the provincial chapter of the Dominican province of Florence, Douais, *Acta capitulorum* 1.105 (Avignon, 1264) and 319 (Avignon, 1288). Undated statutes of the Franciscan province of Francia (see *AFH* 7.452, c. 9 § 2, c. 10 § 2) and Provence (*AFH* 14.423).

27. Chapter General of the Dominicans at Bologna, 1240 (*MOPH* 3.17): *Monemus, ne fratres nostri amodo religiosis mulieribus sacramenta preter penitenciam administrent*; citing a corresponding rule of the general chapter of 1238. General chapter of 1242, ibid., p. 24; see *MOPH* 3.24; 1245, ibid., 32: *Fratres nostri nullo modo sacramentum unctionis extreme mulieribus impendant.*

28. About 1260, the archbishop of Cologne placed the beguines of Cologne under the control of the Dominicans, see Ennen and Eckertz, *Quellen zur Geschichte der Stadt Köln* 2.445–46, no. 428; the beguinages in Liège were also placed under the oversight of the Dominicans, whose prior had to name a chaplain for the beguines, see M. D. Chapotin, *Histoire des Dominicains de la province de France* (Rouen, 1898), 512ff. In 1271 the St. Peter's canonry in S. Gallen agreed with the Dominicans over pastoral care for beguines and corresponding duties: the beguines could commune with the Dominicans, and they only had to participate in services and communion and make donations in their parish church only at the three high festivals, and they were otherwise bound to obey the pastor as did other members of his flock; see *Urk.-B. Basel* 2.42, no. 73. Cf. also below, n. 44ff. An anonymous *Chronicon rhythmicum* from about

1270 (*MG Scr.* 25.305, v. 383) says in general of the Dominicans and Franciscans: *Per hos duos ordines Begine velantur.*

29. Josef Auer, *Studien zu den Reformschriften für das 2. Lyoner Konzil*, Dissertation, Freiburg i. B., 1910, 7ff.; Autbert Stroick, "Verfasser und Quellen der Collectio de scandalis ecclesiæ," *AFH* 23.3ff.

30. His memorial is the so-called *Opus tripartitum*, ed. P. Crabbe, *Concilia omnia* 2.967ff.; then by Edward Brown, *Appendix ad fasciculum rerum expetendarum et fugiendarum* (London, 1690) 2.185ff.; cf. Bertha Birckman, *Die vermeintliche und die wirkliche Reformschrift des Dominikanergenerals Humbert de Romanis* (Berlin; Leipzig, 1916); Fritz Heintke, *Humbert von Romans, der fünfte Ordensmeister der Dominikaner* (Berlin, 1933), 117ff.; K. Michel, *Das Opus tripartitum des Humbertus de Romanis*, 2d ed., 1926; his basis for the assumption that Humbert did not write on the commission of the leadership of the order (24 ff., citing Daniel Antonin Mortier, *Histoire des Maîtres Généraux de l'ordre des Frères Prêcheurs*, 8 vols. (Paris, 1902–20) 2.89ff.) and that his memorial was not precipitated by the summons to the council and the following papal request, but was precipitated earlier by a special request, is not convincing.

31. Humbert de Romanis, *Opus tripartitum*, III, 3.

32. *Opus tripartitum*, III, 3, in Brown, 224. The exerpt from the *Opus tripartitum* in Cod. Vat. Reg. lat., 880, printed in Mansi, *Sacrorum conciliorum* 24.109, altered this citation subtantially. The exerpt was probably made only at the start of the fourteenth century by Bernard Gui, often with arbitary changes; cf. Bertha Birckman, *Die vermeintliches*; Léopold Delisle, *BEC* 37.516 n. xvi, and in *NEM*, 27/2, p. 303 ff.; Karl Wenck in *HZ* 118.301; Elisabeth Kraack, *Rom oder Avignon? Die römische Frage unter den Päpsten Clemens V. und Johann XXII.* (Marburg, 1929), 36; Fr. Heintke, *Humbert von Romans*, 139ff.

33. The so-called "Relatio" in K. Höfler, *Abhandlungen der bayrischen Akademie der Wissenschaften*, 4/3 (Munich, 1846), 27. The first sentence (*religiosorum sibi habitum et nomina vendicantes*) permits us to assume that Bishop Bruno knows and means the name "beguine." [The "Relatio" of Bishop Bruno of Olmütz for the Second Lyon Council of 1274 is also in *MG*, *Constitutiones* 3 (1904/06), 589ff., no. 620. HG/1960.]

34. The bishop did not want to blame these people for heretical doctrines; continuing the previous citation (p. 28), he answered the request for a report from Gregory X, *de infidelitatibus cuiusvis secte vel ritus*, with the brief sentence: *De infidelibus vero inter nos conversantibus deo teste de hereticis nihil scimus*, and passes directly to a report on the Jews. It is thus impossible to believe that the people he attacked previously were a "Waldensian community" (Stroick, "Verfasser und Quellen," *AFH* 23.9) because they did not wish to receive communion from clerics. That is more closely related to the fact that Bishop Bruno makes his most serious charges against the mendicants in the *Relatio* for attacking the rights of the parish clergy everywhere, particularly in confessing; in the same way he accuses the "beguines" of confessing and

communing with the mendicants rather than the parish clergy; the comment *illecte forsitan ab aliquibus, per quos nubere prohibentur*, plays on the influence of the mendicants on religious women.

35. The so-called "Collectio de scandalis ecclesiæ," first published by Ignaz Döllinger, *Beiträge zur politischen-, kirchlichen- und Culturgeschichte*, 3.180ff.; new edition by A. Stroick, *AFH* 24.33ff., which the author has also interpreted (*AFH* 23.15ff. and 43ff.); from the older literature, Auer, *Studien zu den Reformschriften*, 14ff., which first recognized that the "Collectio" was a reform memorial for the Council of Lyon.

36. At the close of the review of the ecclesiastical estates (*AFH* 24.58) it says: *Et apud nos mulieres aliæ, de quibus nescimus, utrum debeamus eas vel sæculares vel moniales appellare. Partim enim utuntur ritu sæculari, partim regulari*. His discussion on the beguines is then delayed until the end of his review of the secular estates, 61–62.

37. *AFH* 24.61–62.

38. *AFH* 24.62. A. Stroick, *HJ* 50.342ff., holds it to be probable that this speaks of Elizabeth of Erkenrodt; but we know of other cases of stigmatization among religious women of this period. Ida of Louvain was supposed to have born the images of the wounds of Christ on her hands, feet, and side; since she was unable to hide them, she asked God in her humility to take the signs from her (Stroick, ibid., 344–45). The beguine Christine of Stommeln, according to the account of the Dominican Peter of Dacia, bore the stigmata or received them repeatedly, first appearing in 1256/57, of which she first spoke in 1270, then in the years 1259/60, when the rumor of stigmatization drew many curious to her. In a letter of 1273/74, Peter of Dacia told of a "spiritual daughter" in Sweden, who experienced convulsions every Friday and bore the five wounds. Stigmatization is also often mentioned in the nuns' books of many Dominican convents in the thirteenth century.

39. Mansi, *Sacrorum conciliorum* 24.96–97 (*Corpus juris canonici*, VI, lib. 3, tit. 17, c. 1, ed. Aemilius Friedberg [Leipzig, 1879] 2.1054–55).

40. At the start of the fifteenth century, the Basel Dominican Johannes Mühlberg cites in his *Materia contra beghardos* the decree of the Council of Lyon under the title, *Hic reprobatur status beghardorum et beginarum*, see H. Haupt, "Beiträge zur Geschichte der Sekte vom freien Geiste und des beghardentums," *ZKG* 7 (1885), 516.

40a. As early as 1266 (1 August), the bishop of Liège commanded the scholasticus of Tongern, Rainer, to whom he had granted the *provisio, cura ac regimen beginarum et beggardorum* (see above, n. 3) for his diocese, *quod beguinas, que habitum beguinarum deferentes, relictis curtibus et congregationibus beguinarum disciplinatarum, singulariter in seculo manent et conversantur in detrimentum animarum et scandalum aliarum, per censuram ecclesiasticam compellatis et compelli faciatis, quod habitum beguinarum penitus rejiciant et deferant secularem, omnium remanentes beguinarum privilegio denutate, nisi infra terminum competentem a vobis vel ab eis, quibus id commiseritis, prefigendum, ad congregationes et conventus aliarum se transferant beguinarum, prout statutum est in nostra synodo generali* [sic]; see *Analectes pour servir à l'histoire ecclésiastique de la Belgique* 20.127.

41. The synod took place under Bishop Reimboto (1279–1297), probably before the German national synod of 1287, according to Hefele and Knöpfler, *Conciliengeschichte* 6.228, about 1284. Statutes in the *Pastoralblatt des Bistums Eichstätt* 32 (1885), 74–75 (also excerpts in Joseph Chmel, *Die Handschriften der k. k. Hofbibliothek in Wien* [Vienna, 1840–41] 2.349): *Excrevit in ecclesia dei numerus feminarum, que nuncupantur Begine, inter quas nonnulle divina favente gratia honestatis sue et integritatis famam irreprehensilem et illesam conversant. Alie vero sunt, in quibus vicia se menciuntur esse virtutes, dum sub quadam conversationis specie et ficte religionis ymagine lascivias et vanitates infinitas exercent, fornicationis et incontinentie morbo laborant et interdum, sicut ex publica fama didicimus, quamplures insolentias ac alias enormitates committunt, ex quibus fame et honestati aliarum Beginarum sepe detrahitur et scandalum in populo generatur. Quia igitur contra tales vehementer presumendum est, quod ex corrupta quondam intentione vestem religionis, quam deferunt, assumpserint et assumant, videlicet [ut] excessus suos huiusmodi facilius et diutius palliare ac correctiones clericorum declinare valeant et vitare, ne forsitan hoc pretextu penam correctionis evadant, universis ac singulis ecclesiarum rectoribus et eorum vicariis per civitatem nostram et dyocesim constitutis districte precipiendo mandamus, quatenus si quam ammodo Beguinam per singulas vestras parrochias deprehenderitis incontinentie visio publice laborantem, ita quod excessus ipsius sit notorius, inter alia ipsum in loco communi, qui vulgariter "Schreiat"* [= the stocks] *dicitur, in presentia populi virgis cedi ac publicis subici verberibus faciatis. Quod si forsitan aliqua, postquam excessus eius manifestus fuerit et detectus, pro evitanda pena ad alium se parrochiam transtulerit, sacerdos ibidem ad denunciationem prioris, in cuius deliquit parrochia, eandem penam cum efficacia exequatur, ut saltem ex hoc huiusmodi delinquentes rubore suffuse et alie exemplo earum deterrite a consimili excessu discant et studeant abstinere. Quicunque occasione inductus in parrochia sua circa penam huiusmodi exequendam se exhibuerit negligentem, ipsum ab officio suo tamdiu volumus manere suspensum, quousque negligentiam suam purgaverit vel a nobis relaxionis beneficium meruerit obtinere.*

42. *Carmen satiricum*, ed. Th. Fischer, *Geschichts-Quellen der Provinz Sachsen*, 1/2, 92–93, v. 1605ff.: *Sunt ibi Begine, quarum numerus sine fine. Quedam perverse, quedam vivunt bene per se. Ex hiis sunt quedam, que nec turpem neque fedam rem cupiunt scire, sed ad ecclesiam libet ire, missas audire, sincero corde redire missa completa; sic vivunt mente quieta tamquam claustrales; etenim velut estimo tales plus commendantur, quam que sub clave serantur. Quamvis absque nota Christo reddant sua vota et sine clamore, spe corde fide vel amore proficiunt plus quam si starent jugiter usquam alte cantantes modicumque boni meditantes. Quavis nempe die miseris sub honore Marie mundo corde data sit ab hiis elemosyna grata.*

Jejunant, vigilant et lanea stamina filiant et mala deplorant; si nocte dieque laborant, ocia vitantes et que bona sunt Operantes. Cras hodie vel heri non cessant probra fateri fratribus et nudis verbis cum fletibus udis sompnia nocturna recitant vel facta diurna. Quamvis sit rarum, tamen accidit hoc, quod earum quedam ducuntur extra se vel rapiuntur, ut videant Christum; vulgus jubilum vocat istum. Sunt alie quedam, de quarum moribus edam, que quasi matrone sub falsa religione ocia sectantur et per loca queque vagantur. Horrentes fusum discurrunt undique lusum; nunc adeundo forum, nunc claustra petunt monachorum, et quandoque chorum perlustrant canonicorum et fortasse thorum; malus est jocus iste sororum, etc.

43. "De modo prompte cudendi sermones," lib. 2, no. 5, *Biblioteca maxima veterum patrum* (Lyon, 1677) 25.483: *felices Beguinæ et omni laude dignissimæ*, who *in medio perversæ nationis ducunt vitam sanctissimam.*

44. The rule for the house "zum Thurn," 12 April 1276, is in the *Urk.-B. Strassburg* 3.27–28, no. 78; other than the magistra and subprioress, fourteen sisters are named (most only by first names); in 1314 a total of thirteen sisters lived in the house, ibid., 234–35. The rule for the house "von Innenheim," dated 14 April, is in Mosheim, *De beghardis*, 158ff.; *Urk.-B. Strassburg* 3.29, no. 79; at that time there were nine members, as is the case with the house "von Offenburg," whose rule is dated 4 May, ibid., 3.30, no. 81. The name of "beguine" does not appear in these charters, where they are called *sorores*; the presently lost manuscript of the fourteenth century from which Mosheim published the rule had the title, *Constitutiones domuum beguinarum Argentiniensium*. On the location of the three houses near the Dominican house, see C. Schmidt, *Strassburger Gassen- und Häusername im Mittelalter*, 2d ed. (Strasbourg, 1888), 47.

45. The statutes begin: *Nos* [then the names of the sisters] . . . *volentes materiam dissolutionis suspecte et nocive diffugere et ad disciplinam commendabilem coerceri, de consilio et consensu confessoris nostri fratris Frederici dicti de Ersteheim O. F. P. in Argentina hec inter nos ordinavimus et fide data inviolabiliter nos observaturas publice profitemur, Ordinavimus itaque et fide corporali prestita observare promisimus . . . ;* each paragraph begins with the words, *Item volumus et ordinamus et fede data vallamus.* §9: *Ordimamus et promittimus fide prestita, quos in hiis que circa statum nostrum ordinanda fuerint et corrigenda, obediemus magistre nostre et subpriorisse et ei, qui pro tempore nobis confessor fuerit deputatus, et eis non submittimus ex presenti ordinatione quoad hec et quoad omnia supra memorata et ordinata, ita etiam quod confessor noster de consilio prioris fratrum predicatorum possit in quolibet articulo huius cedule nobiscum dispensare, si viderit oportunum.*

46. The Colmar Dominican chronicler (*MG Scr.* 17.235), incidentally, describes the customs of South German houses which were later placed under the Dominican Order in a quite similar way.

47. §2: *Si . . . voluntate mutata recesserit sive propter honestam causam, puta quia in reclusorio carceris permanere voluerit* [that is, if they wish to

become recluses] *sive alias ad societatem honestam transire voluerit, de omnibus secum apportatis sive in mobilibus sive in immobilibus nihil secum deportare valebit exceptis vestimentis et lectisteniis, nisi benignitas sororum eidem voluerit facere gratiam ampliorem. Item si claustrum intrare voluerit, quinque libras tantum de bonis suis accipiet apportatis*. Mosheim (163) already marvelled that this did not provide specifically for withdrawal with the purpose of marriage, and since he was persuaded that "no beguine had to forego this entirely," he thought that transfer to a *societas honesta* also meant matrimony. But this is hard to square with the loss of property.

48. §6: *Preterea nolumus, quod aliqua recipiatur, quia in bonis paternis, materinis vel peculio adventicio vel profecticio vel alias ut in seculari habitu existens valeat succedere ex quacunque causa, nisi aliquo casu renuntiemus.*

49. Cf. Charles Schmidt, "Die Strassburger Beginenhäuser im Mittelalter," *Alsatia* 7.152; W. Kothe, *Kirchliche Zustände Strassburgs im 14. Jahrhundert*, Dissertation, Breslau, 1902, 46, 49, 52.

50. §1: If a woman departed from the community before the completion of a year, she could take everything she had brought with her, but she must compensate the house for its expenses in her feeding and clothing (40 pence a month for support), and *nec opere eius nec utilitas proveniens ex his, quæ attulit, vel poterat evenire* could not be figured in.

51. Heinrich Boos, *Urk.-B. der Stadt Worms* 1(Berlin, 1886), 286ff., no. 438; also in Bihl, *AFH* 14.187ff., who holds these *pauperes sorores vel beoginæ* to be Franciscan tertiaries from the beginning. In the same year a second beguinage was established for fourteen sisters, see Boos, 1.285–6, no. 436; as early as 1275 a will mentions forty *muliebræ bekinæ* in Worms, Boos, 240, no. 372.

52. *Ne in usum malarum personarum convertam [bona mea], districte sine ulla dispensatione prelati volo, ut nulla in dictarum sororum consortium recipiatur, quam oporteat mendicare, quin aliqui modo honesto vel labore consueto et honesto valeat sibi necessaria acquirere et comparare*; the sisters are specifically forbidden to earn their living by caring for the sick. The number of sisters could only be increased with the approval of the Franciscans, if the means of the house suffice for more than twenty and if they *rebus habundaverint.*

53. Ibid.: *Et quoniam divites et nobiles humilioris condicionis socias contempnere consueverunt, nolo ut aliqua soror in curiam recipiatur nisi prius resignet omnem substanciam suam in manus magistre et efficiatur sicut pauperes que est intus. Quicquid etiam habet aliqua ultra valorem trium librarum, in manus magistre resignabit et tamen de eisdem bonis honeste de licentia magistre ipsius quidquid sibi expedit faciat, cui magistra licentiam non negabit.*

54. The rule of the Brabant beguines, confirmed by Duke John I of Brabant (Miræus, *Opera diplomatica-historica* 2.1006; cf. n. 3 above) has in mind the specifically Belgian form of beguinage, consisting of individual homes. There also, the reception of wealthy and poor women is provided for; in

general, the women, *puellæ* and *viduæ*, should build houses at their own cost, which they would occupy for life; after their deaths, the houses would fall to the community, and the heirs of the sisters would have no claim; poorer beguines, who could not afford to build their own houses, were then placed in these homes.

55. *Urk.-B. Hildesheim* 1.182–83, no. 374, 1281: *sorores que ad predictam congregationem intraverunt vel intrabunt, data ad earum necessitates pecunia, si aliquo motu proprio ab ipsis recedere voluerint, super repetitione pecunie sive in parte sive in toto eas nullatenus audeant molestare*. Similar in a Halberstadt charter of 1302, *Halberstädter Urk.-B.* 1.223, no. 294.

56. Heidemann, "Die Beginenhäuser in Wesel," *Zeitschrift des Bergischen Geschichts-Vereins* 4.94. In the beguinages in Hamburg and Lübeck, an entry-fee was even demanded.

57. H. Finke, *Ungedruckte Dominikanerbriefe*, 83, no. 52, advice for the Dominican house about to be visited: *Vitent quoque begginarum conventicula et ibi ultra quod decuerit non morentur nec sint talibus honorosi pauperculis, quibus labor manuum est pro censu.*

58. *Chronica major*, *MG Scr.*, 28, 234; cf. also *Historia Anglicana*, ibid., 417 on the *beguini sive beguinæ*. At the second mention of the Cologne beguines in the *Chronica major* at 1250 (ibid., 320 and 430), Matthew Paris speaks only of women, as does the "Abbreviatio Chronicorum Angliæ" derived from him, for 1248, ibid., 449. In Cologne charters, beghards are first mentioned in 1258, see J. Asen, *Annalen des Vereins für Geschichte des Niederrheins* 111.87–88. Even before 1237, there is mention by the Frisian Premonstratensian Abbot Emo of Wittewierum of *quidam simplices, qui dicuntur Beggini* in his chronicle (*MG Scr.* 23.517); see above, chapter 5, n. 47).

59. In the letter of the cleric Ivo of Narbonne, who fled France about 1215 because he was suspected of heresy, going through Northern Italy to Carinthia and Austria, from whence he reported to the archbishop of Bordeaux on his experiences, see Matthew Paris, *Chronica major*, *MG Scr.* 28.230.

60. The assertions of seventeenth-century Belgian historians about older beghard houses in Louvain and Antwerp cannot be tested. Such a community of *beghuini* or *beghardi* is witnessed in 1252 in Bruges when Countess Margaret of Flanders issued it a letter of protection (see Louis Gilliodts-van Severen, *Inventaire diplomatique des archives de l'ancienne école bogarde à Bruges* [Bruges, 1899]). In 1257 the *fratres obedientes dicti Beggardi* are witnessed in Diest working the land; in 1281 these *fratres Beggardi manentes in conventu eorum prope Diest* accepted the rule of the Franciscan tertiaries. In 1276 Duke John I took beghards acting as merchants in Tirlemont into his protection, and in 1277 he did the same for beghards involved in weaving in Brussels. In 1284 there is mention of a *conventus Beghardorum* in Malines, in 1293 in Louvain, where the beghard house (just as in Brussels) became a meeting-place for weavers. In 1298 the beghard house in Tournai is witnessed, in the following years houses in St. Omer, Middelburg and Bois-le-Duc. Cf. G. des Marez, "Les Bogards dans l'industrie drapière à Bruxelles," *Mélanges Paul Fredericq*, 1904, 277ff.; J.

Vannérus, "Documents concernants le Tiers Ordre à Anvers et ses rapports avec l'industrie drapiére," *Bulletin de la commission royale d'histoire, Académie royale de Belgique* 79 (1910), and "Documents concernants les Bogards de Malines," ibid., 80 (1911); Fr. Callaey, *Les Beggards des Pays-Bas*; J. Van Mierlo, "Het Begardisme," *VMKVA* [1930], 283ff.). Callaey and van Mierlo mention the following name-forms for the beghards: *beghardi, beghuini, aerme Begharde, boni pueri, goode kinder die man heet Beggarde, bigardi, beggardi, begehardi, beginhardi;* later *bogardi* and *bogaard.*

61. J. van Mierlo, "Het begardisme," 286–87, rightly asks: "Were they weavers by trade before they took up beguinism? Or did they become weavers as a result of passing to beguinism? Most historians have chosen the first alternative, although it is certain that though the earliest *beguini* included members from the nobility and the high burgher class, there were fewer than was the case with the beguines."

62. In 1285 Duke Gui de Dampierre took measures against certain beghards in Bruges *qui mainent vie deshonnete et veulent leur deshonnete couvrir par l'abyt des Begards, et par les fais de tels sunt li autre sans leur coupe souvent escandelisiet*, see Gilliodts-van Severen, *Inventaire diplomatique* 1.7; in 1286 the bishop of Cambrai issued an order against beghards who had left or been expelled from the house in Malines *propter suos excessus vel ex alia causa*, and, if they did not return, were to put off their *habitus beggardalis* under penalty of excommunication, see Vannérus, *Bulletin de la commission d'histoire* 80.237–38.

Chapter 7

1. In the newest book on Amaury, by G. C. Capelle, *Amaury de Bène: étude sur son panthéisme formel*, Bibliothèque Thomiste 16 (Paris, 1932), the citation from the Chronicle of Melrose is printed among the historical sources (111), but it is evaluated neither in the investigation nor in the narrative. Since Capelle barely dealt with the historical conditions and context of the heresy of 1210, but simply reconstructed the philosophical system of Amaury and his students (without distinguishing between them), to investigate his relationship to the philosophic tradition and to judge it in Thomistic terms, his entire study is historically sterile and factually unconvincing. [Cf. also M. Th. d'Alverny, "Un fragment du procès des Amauriciens," *AHDL* 25/26 (1950/51), 325–36. HG/1960.]

2. Cæsarius of Heisterbach, *Dialogus miraculorum*, V, 22 ed. Joseph Strange, 1.304: *Isti hereses multas et maximas excogitaverant et jam in plurimos de eorum secta invenerunt.*

3. Guilelmus Brito, *De gestis Philippi II*, ed. Delaborde, *Oeuvres de Rigord et de Guillaume le Breton*, Société de l'Histoire de France (Paris, 1882) 1.232: *Huius secte plures sacerdotes, clerici et laici ac mulieres . . . tandem detecti . . . ; mulieribus autem et aliis simplicibus, qui per maiores corrupti fuerant et decepti, pepercerunt.*

4. *Chronica de Mailros*, ed. J. Stevenson, Publications of the Bannatyne Club (Edinburgh, 1835), for 1210, 109–10 (= *Recueil des Historiens des Gaules et de la France*, ed. Léopold Delisle (Paris, 1869ff.) 19.250; John Fell, William Fulman, and Thomas Gale, *Rerum Anglicanorum scriptores vederes* 3 vols. (Oxford, 1684–91) 1.184; among the excerpts from this chronicle in *MG Scr.* 27.432ff., this passage is not to be found).

5. The list of names in the decree of 1210 (*Chartularium Universitatis Parisisiensis* 1.70, no. 11) agrees almost entirely with the more thorough account of Cæsarius of Heisterbach, *Dialogus miraculorum*, V, 22 (ed. Strange, 1.304), which I present here (in the sequence of the Paris decree, with the most important variants in parentheses): *Bernardus subdiaconus. —Wilhelmus (de Arria) aurifex (= aurifaber) propheta eorum. —Stephanus sacerdos de Veteri Curbuel (= Corbolio). —Stephanus sacerdos de Cella. —Johannes sacerdos de Uncinis (= Occines). —Magister Wilhelmus Pictaviensis subdiaconus, qui legerat Parisius de artibus et tribus annis studuerat in theologia.* —(On these six, Cæsarius says in summary: *isti omnes in theologia studuerant exepto Bernardo*). —*Dudo (sacerdos) specialis clericus magistri Almerici sacerdotis* [*sic*], *qui fere decem annis in theologia studuerat*. (Dominicus de Triangulo; missing in Cæsarius). *Odo diaconus and Elinandus acolitus (clerici de S. Clodoaldo).* (On these first ten, the decree of 1210 ordered: *isti degardentur penitus seculari curie relinquendi;* they were burned). —*Ulricus sacerdos de Lueri (= Lauriaco), qui sexagenarius studuerat in theologia tempore multo. —Petrus de S. Clodoaldo sacerdos et sexagenarius, qui etiam audierat theologiam; . . . antequam caperetur, pre timore monachus effectus est (= modo monachus S. Dionysii). —Magister Garinus (= Guarinus presbyter de Corbolio), qui conventaverat Parisius de artibus, et hic sacerdos audierat theologiam a magistro Stephano archiepiscopo Cantuarensi* (that is, he attended lectures by Stephen Langton while he was still in Paris). —*Stephanus diaconus de Veteri Corbuelo.* (Of these last four, the decreee of 1210 ruled: *degradentur perpetuo carceri mancipandi).* The *Chronicon . . . Laudunensis*, 69, names as *precipui* 3) *Stephanus presbyter parrochialis de Corbolio*; 13) *magister Garinus eiusdem castri capellanus*, and 1) *magister* [*sic*] *Bernardus*. The third continuator of the great Cologne annals says at 1210: *Hoc anno in adventu domini quidam heresiarcha Bernardus nomine cum aliis 9, quorum 4 sacerdotes erant, Parisius venientes, occulte perveretere populum nitebantur*; he does not include, then, the final four, who were only punished with prison; among the ten in the first group there actually were only four priests. The second continuator of these annals says for the same year: *Erant autem 14 tam clerici diversi ordinis quam et laici; see Chronica regia Colonensis*, 230 and 187–88. In fact there was no layman among those condemned; it is to be noted that even the "goldsmith," William of Arria—"their prophet," as Cæsarius says, who surfaced in this affair—was doubtless a cleric and had studied theology, since he was degraded along with the others. It is thus impossible to appeal to him to prove the participation of "artisans" in heresy.

6. Cæsarius, *Dialogus miraculorum*, 306: *non erant in civitate excepto uno Bernardo*. Robert of Auxerre, *Chron. (MG Scr.* 26.275): *quorum erant aliqui sacerdotes curam animarum habentes*. Two of them were already over sixty years of age, the age of the others is unknown; Cæsarius described them as *viri scientia et etate magni*.

7. Cf. also Cæsarius, *Dialogus miraculorum*, 307: *In ipsa nocte* [of the condemnation] *is, qui inter eos potior habebatur, ad ostium cuiusdam incluse* [sic] *pulsans sero suum errorem confessus est, asserens se magnum hospitem esse in inferno et eternis incendiis deputatum*.

8. The words of the Chronicle of Melrose: *qui et domos viduarum penetraverant*, depends on 2 Timothy 3:6 (see chapter 1 above, n. 46), where Paul speaks of the pseudo-prophets who will appear in the "perilous times" before the end to the world: *ex his enim sunt, qui penetrant domos et captivas ducunt mulierculas oneratas peccatis*; the "glossa interlinearis" of Anselm of Laon (died 1117) says to this: *illi penetrant domos, qui ingrediuntur domos illorum, quorum regimen animarum ad eos non pertinet*—hence those who practiced pastoral care without permission. In precisely the same sense William of St. Amour later went to war with the mendicants using this particular text and its gloss, *De periculis novissimorum temporum* in Max Bierbaum, *Bettelorden und Weltgeistlichkeit an der Universität Paris* (Münster i. W., 1920), 7.

8a. *Sermo ad virgines*, ed. Joseph Greven, *HJ* 35.44–45; see below, n. 47.

9. Cf. Robert of Auxerre, *MG Scr.* 26.275: *quibus fecerat favorem ad populum fucata species honestatis et vite gravitas superducta;* cf. below, n. 58.

10. In 1206, since Alberich of Troisfontaines (*MG Scr.* 23.890) says, *post quatuor annos sue tumulationis* the corpse of Amaury was unearthed and burned.

11. Contemporary sources (and many later authors) write the name either Amalricus, Almericus or Amauricus, Amorricus, and name his students hence Almaricani (Chronicle of Melrose), Almarici (*Chron. anon. Laud.*), Almariciani (Thomas Aquinas), or Amauriani (*Tract.*). It is only through the Chronicle of Martinus Polonus that the form Amalricus was popularized.

12. Guilelmus Brito, ed. Delaborde, 1.230, gives a general characterization of Amaury. Cf. also the description in the Anonymous Chronicle of Laon (ed. Cartellieri and Stechele, 69): *Almaricus . . . vir quidem subtilissimus, sed ingenio pessimus fuit. In omnibus facultatibus in quibus studebat, aliis contrarius inveniebatur. Item sciendum quod iste magister Almoricus fuit cum domino Ludovico, primogenito regis Francorum, quia credebatur vir esse bone conversationis et opinionis illese*.

13. Whether Amaury himself misunderstood Eriugena's ideas (thus Pierre Duhem, *Le système du monde* 5 [Paris, 1917]. 245ff.) or whether this misunderstanding should only be blamed on his students, cannot be decided, since we have nothing of Amaury's own thoughts. The doctrines ascribed to him by the canonist Henry of Ostia (see Johannes Huber, *Johannes Scotus Erigena* [Munich, 1861], 435–36.) and the chronicler Martinus Polonus (*MG Scr.* 22.438)

are verbatim citations from Eriugena's *De divisione naturæ*; cf. Krönlein, *Theologische Studien u. Kritik* 20, 1 (1847), 292ff.; Ch. Jourdan, *Mémoire sur les sources philosophiques de l'hérésie d'Amaury de Chartres et de David de Dinant*, 1870. [Cf. Maïeul Cappuyns, *Jean Scot Erigène* (Louvain; Paris, 1933). HG/1960.]

14. *Chartularium Universitatis Parisiensis* 1.70, no. 11; 72, no. 12, according to the account of the condemnation of the Amaurians: *Horum causa quosdam libros etiam ipsis sapientibus cognovimus interdictos*. Guilelmus Brito, ed. Delaborde, 233. Robert of Auxerre, *MG Scr.* 26.276.

15. The Magdeburg Centuries [Mathias Flacius Illyricus et al., *Ecclesiastica historia, integram ecclesiae Christi ideam, quantum ad locum, . . . secundum singulas centurias . . . per aliquot studiosos & pios viros in urbe Magdeburgica* (Basel, 1559–74)] (Basel, 1574, Cent. XIII, c. 5, p. 558) cited as a thesis of the Amaurians: *Deum esse animam celi*, with the source given as Thomas Aquinas, in whose works I could find nothing of the sort. Gabriel Prateolus [Du Préau], *Elenchus alphabeticus de vitis, factis et dogmatibus omnium hereticorum* (Cologne, 1569), 22–23 (and later Jacobus Thomasius, *Origines historiæ philosophicæ et ecclesiasticæ [Magdeburg, 1699], 112) cites from Gerson, Tractatus 3 super Magnificat: Amalricus et similes heretici dicebant mentem contemplativi vel beati perdere suum esse in proprio genere et redire in illud esse ideale, quod habuit in mente divina;* I cannot find this citation in the Gerson edition by Du Pin (4.269ff.). Cf. also the two other assertions of Gerson (*De myst. theol. specul. consid.*, 41, *Opera* 3.394 and *Epistola ad fratrem Bartholæum Carthusiensem, Opera* 1.79–80), cited by Krönlein, *Theologische Studien und Kritik*, 20/1, 291–92, were not used because it could not be proved that Gerson's statements on Amaury were reliable. Because these fragments have almost never been considered, and the other doctrines reported for Amaury and his students have had nothing to do with Aristotle and his commentators, any connection between the condemnation of the Amaurians and that of Aristotle has been rejected; cf. Barthélemy Hauréau, *Histoire de la philosophie scholastique* (Paris, 1872–80), 2/1 (1880), 100ff.; Otto Bardenhewer, *Die pseudoaristotelische Schrift über das reine Gute (Liber de causis)* (Freiburg i. B., 1882), 212ff.; Pierre Duhem, *Le système du monde* 5.245ff.; Martin Grabmann, *Forschungen über die lateinische Aristoteles-Übersetzungen des 13. Jahrhunderts* (Münster, 1916), 133–34. The reliability of this fragment and its philosophical origin still has to be investigated. It is obscure whether Amaury also shows the influence of the Platonic renaissance of the school of Chartres (see Hauréau, *op. cit.*, 83; Bernardus Silvester, *De mundi universitate*, ed. Barach and Wrobel, p. xix).

16. Cf. Cæsarius, *Dialogus miraculorum*, 305: *Habebant etiam miserrimi illi argumenta sua nullius prorsus valoris, quibus suos errores confirmare nitebantur*. The utterly dialectic style of this argument is clear from the treatise "Contra Amaurianos" edited by Baeumker (first in the *Jahrbuch für Philosophie und spekulative Theologie* 7 [1893], then in the *Beiträge zur Geschichte der Philosophie des Mittelalters* 24, 5/6, 1926), probably written by

Garnerius of Rochefort, in my view, after the trial. (Cited in the following as "Tract.") The author addresses that directly once: *Sed quoniam michi videor magis philosophis loqui quam theologis—nam, si vere theologi essent, magis sanctorum testimoniis quam humane rationi consentirent, scientes quia fides non habet meritum, cui humana ratio prebet experimentum—ideo facultatis ratione naturalis hoc idem probare possumus.* Tract., 32.

17. Tract., c. 8, p. 24: *Nemo, inquiunt, potest esse salvus nisi credat se esse membrum Christi.*

18. *Chartularium universitatis* 1.71: *Omnia unum, quia quicquid est, est deus*; Tract., c. 9, p. 24ff.: *Deus est omnia in omnibus*. Thomas Aquinas (*Summa theologiæ*, I, q. 3 a 8 c) formulates that with Aristotelian concepts: *Alii dixerunt deum esse principium formale omnium rerum, et hec dicitur fuisse opinionem Amalricianorum*; but it is uncertain whether the Amaurians ever actually used such terminology. Henry of Ostia and later Martinus Polonus and Gerson cited the sentence, *quod omnia sunt deus*, asserting the identity between creator and creation, as the *primus et summus error* which Amaury took from the writings of Eriugena; cf. the citations in J. Huber, *Johannes Scotus Erigena*, 435ff., P. Duhem, *Le système du monde* 5.247–48, shows how what Duhem holds to be orthodox doctrines of Eriugena became heresy in the hands of Amaury and his students due to their interpretation as real, *natura* = *physis* what Eriugena said of the ideal, *essentia* = *ousia*: their unity of being with God. Eriugena is thus, according to Duhem, not responsible for the pantheism of the Amaurians; similarly Étienne Gilson and G. C. Capelle in their book on Amaury. Yet links in intellectual history often consist of misunderstandings, both conscious and unconscious.

19. The thesis of Amaury on membership in Christ is based on Ephesians 5:30; cf. 1 Corinthians 6:15 and 12:27. For the doctrines of the identity of God with the cosmos, the ubiquity and universal activeness of God, his students cited Romans 11:36; 1 Corinthians 15:28 and 12:6; Colossians 1:16; cf. Tract., c. 9, pp. 24, 27; c. 1, p. 2ff.; c. 2, p. 9ff. There were also citations of John 1:3–4 in Tract., c. 2, p. 12. There were also, incidentally, many appeals to the Old Testament, see Tract., c. 2, p. 12.

20. B. Hauréau, *Histoire de la philosophie scolastique*, 2/1, 92, describes this doctrine of history as the "chief dogma of this religion." The opinion of Eugène Anitchkof [Evgenii Visil'evich Anichkov], *Joachim de Flore et les milieux courtois*, Collezione di studi meridionali, series 2, vol. 13 (Rome, 1931), 275ff., that this doctrine of history was only imposed on the Amaurians by later chroniclers rests on a complete ignorance of the sources.

21. Henry Bett, *Johannes Scotus Erigena: A Study in Mediaeval Theology* (Cambridge, 1925), 178, assumes that the Amaurians developed their doctrine of history directly from Eriugena's doctrine of epochs, without any influence from Joachim of Fiore. On the contrary, Eriugena dealt with this doctrine only in exegetical ancillary works (*Commentaria in Evangelium Johannis, PL* 122.308; *Expositio super Hierarchiam Ecclesiaæ*, ibid., col. 265ff.), not in the *De divisione naturæ*, which is the only writing we can be certain Amaury

knew. Concretely, the theses of the Amaurians agree much more with the teaching of Joachim than with these ideas of Eriugena. Cf. also E. Gebhard, *L'Italie mystique*, 59–60; Herbert Grundmann, *Studien über Joachim von Floris* (Leipzig; Berlin, 1927), 95.

22. *Chartularium universitatis* 1.71: *Pater a principio operatus est sine filio et spiritu sancto usque ad eiusdem filii incarnationem. —Pater in Abraham incarnatus. —Filius usque nunc operatus est, sed spiritus sanctus ex hoc nunc usque ad mundi consummationem inchoat operari*. Tract., c. 10, p. 30: *Pater incarnatus fuit in Abraham et in aliis veteris testamenti patribus, filius dei in Christo et in aliis veteris testamenti patribus, filius dei in Christo et in aliis christianis, spiritus sanctus in illis quos vocant spirituales*. It is precisely in this chapter that the dialectical argumentation of the Amaurians emerges most clearly. Guilelmus Brito, ed. Delaborde, 230ff. Cæsarius, *Dialogus miraculorum*, 305.

23. Tract., c. 12, p. 51: *Dicunt quod usque ad 5 annos omnes homines erunt spirituales, ita ut unusquisque poterit dicere: Ego sum spiritus sanctus*. The special prophecies which Cæsarius has the Amaurian William Aurifaber tell the spy Rudolph of Namur deal with events during this five years of general transformation: four plagues will descend on the people, the princes, the burghers, and the *prelati ecclesie, qui sunt membra Antichristi*; and the French king shall fulfill his eschatological role as the immortal ruler of the entire world. These are prophecies such as often appear in this period, but which have little organic connection with Amaury's ideas. Perhaps they were passed on only by this William, who ascribed to himself a special prophetic role.

24. *Chartularium universitatis*, 1.71: *Spiritus sanctus in eis incarnatus, ut dixerunt, eis omnia revelabat, et hec revelatio nihil aliud erat quam mortuorum resurrectio. Inde semetipsos iam resuscitatos asserebant, fidem et spem ab eorum cordibus excludebant, se soli scientie mentientes subjacere*. Tract., c. 7, p. 21: *Ex hac eadem cognitione fabulosum dicunt, quicquid magistri Parisienses de resurrectione asseverant, quia, ut aiunt, cognitio hec plena est resurrectio nec alia est expectanda;* pp. 39–40: *Dicunt resurrectionem corporum non esse*; c. 3/4, p. 13ff.: *Infernus nichil aliud est quam ignorantia, nec aliud est paradisus quam cognitio veritatis, quam se dicunt habere. Cæsarius, Dialogus miraculorum,* 304.

25. Cf. J. Huber, *Johannes Scotus Erigena*, 405ff., 396ff.

26. The author of the Tract., 17, accused the Amaurians: *Nec veritatis cognitio nec paradisus haberi potest in hoc exilio; cognitionem dico specificam, non enigmaticam, quia . . . quoquo modo potest hic agnosci quasi per speculum in enigmate, sed specietenus cognoscemus eum in illa beatitudine.*

27. Cæsarius, *Dialogus miraculorum*, 305 (see above) and 304: *Altaria sanctis statui et sacras imagines thurificari idolatriam esse dicebant; eos qui ossa martyrum deosculabantur subsannabant*. Cf. Tract., c. 12, p. 50: *Sine omnium obligatione sacramentorum sola veritas ista confert (scil. sanctificationem in via, glorificationem in patria);* c. 5, p. 17: *Si judeus habet cognitionem veritatis quam habemus, non oportet ut baptizetur*. An even

more thorough indifference to the Church, even to Christianity, was shown in the sentence preserved by Cæsarius (304): *Sic deum locutum fuisse in Ovidio sicut in Augustino.*

28. Tract., c. 12, p. 48: *Sed istud, quod est principium omnium sacramentorum, quantum in ipsis est, evacuant, ut hoc evacuato etiam cetera sacramenta evacuanda demonstrent. Unde dicunt, quod, si aliquis esset spiritualis et haberet illam veritatis cognitionem quam se habere dicunt, et cessarent omnia sacramenta, quia sacramenta ecclesie signa sunt sicut cerimonialia in veteri lege; et sicut adveniente Christo cessaverunt, ita nunc per spiritum sanctum advenientem in eis hec signa debent cessare.* Ibid., 47: *Sicut corpus domini adoratur in pane consecrato in altari, ita adoratur in pane simplici apposito comedenti.* Cæsarius, *Dialogus miraculorum,* 304: *Dicebant non aliter esse corpus Christi in pane altaris quam in alio pane et in qualibet re.* Cf. *Chartularium universitatis* 1.71, the complicated theological analysis of the doctrine of the eucharist; further, Tract., c. 11, p. 46, on the distinction represented by some Amaurians between the external, visible body of Christ, which was placed on the cross, and his "inner body," a divine force which is everywhere at once, identical with Plato's idea; the author of the treatise answers this with a polemic against Plato's *fictio philosophi.*

29. Cf. J. Huber, *Johannes Scotus Erigena*, 383–84. Tract., c. 11, p. 39.

30. *Chartularium universitatis* 1.71: *Filius incarnatus, id est visibili forma subjectus. Nec aliter illum hominem esse deum quam unum ex eis cognoscere voluerunt.* Cæsarius, *Dialogus miraculorum*, 305: *Concedebant, quod unusquisque eorum esset Christus et Spiritus sanctus*. Cf. Tract., c. 9, p. 24 and c. 10, p. 30: *Ecce hucusque credidimus filium incarnatum; jam isti Christum predicant "ingodinatum"* [a play on the Amaurian Godinus].

31. Cf. J. Huber, *Johannes Scotus Erigena*, 350ff.; H. Bett, *Johannes Scotus Erigena,* 68ff.

32. He was one of those Master Rudolph of Namur first informed about the heresy he had uncovered, see Cæsarius, *Dialogus miraculorum*, 306. The passage from his sermons is in B. Hauréau, *Histoire de la philosophie scolastique*, 2/1, 93–94: *Sunt profane novitates, quas introducunt quidam Epicuri potius quam Christi discipuli, qui periculosissima fraudulentia persuadere nituntur in occulto peccatorum impunitatem, asserentes peccatum ita nihil esse, ut etiam pro peccato nemo debeat a deo puniri. —Sed et, quod summe dementie est et impudentissimi mendacii, tales non verentur nec erubescunt dicere se deum esse . . . Absit autem quod fons scientiarum, urbs ista perfecti decoris in sapientia hac peste fedetur*. On Johannes Teutonicus, abbot of St. Victor from 1203, died 1229, see *Histoire littéraire de la France* 14.57–58.

33. Cæsarius, *Dialogus miraculorum*, 304–05: *Maximam etiam blasphemiam ausi sunt dicere in spiritum sanctum. . . . Si aliquis in spiritu est, aiebant, et faciat fornicationem vel aliqua alia pollutione polluatur, non est ei peccatum, quia ille spiritus, qui est deus, omnino separatus in carne* [sic] *non potest peccare, et homo, qui nihil est* [sic], *non potest peccare, quamdiu ille spiritus, qui est Deus, est in eo. Chartularium universitatis* 1.71: *Quidam*

eorum nomine Bernardus ausus est affirmare se nec posse cremari nec alio torqueri supplicio, in quantum erat, quia in eo, quod erat, se deum dicebat.

34. Tract., c. 2, p. 9: *Secundam eorum heresim sumunt ex auctoritate apostoli dicentis: Deus operator omnia in omnibus; unde inferunt; ergo tam bona quam mala. Ergo qui cognoscit deum in se omnia operari, peccare non potest. Et sic deo et non sibi attribuunt, quod peccant; et sic neminem penitentia indigere mentiuntur.*

35. Tract., c. 6, pp. 18–19: *Si quis a sacerdote longam succepisset penitentiam, si haberet eorum cognitionem, non oporteret ut ageret penitentiam.*

36. Tract., c. 2, p. 12: *Qui cognoscit deum in se omnia operari, etiam si fornicationem faceret, non peccaret. Non enim sibi attribuere debet, sed totum deo quod facit.* P. 13: *Qui aliquid sibi attribuit, quod facit, et non totum deo, in ignorantia est, que est infernus. . . . Nihil habet homo de suo in suis operibus.*

37. This is not only said by the chroniclers (see n. 40 below); a statement such as *Chartularium universitatis* 1.71–72: *De meritis presumentes, gratie derogantes [sic], mentiti sunt bonorum baptismatis non egere parvulos ex eorum sanguinibus propagatos, si sue conditionis mulieribus carnali possent copula commisceri* also points in that direction.

38. This is already found in Tract., 12: *Auctorem peccati dicunt, qui peccatum non fecit nec inventus est dolus in ore eius* (1 Peter 2:22). *Quare? Ut facilius flectant mulierculas in fornicationem.* Ibid., 9: *Quare hoc? Ut inferant impunitatem peccandi et sic procliviores faciant ad peccandum mulierculas oneratas peccatis* (cf. 2 Timothy 3:6; n. 8 above). Cf. throughout Angelo Clareno, *Expositio regulæ fratrum minorum*, ed. Livarius Oliger (Quaracchi, 1912), 219, and the *Historia septem tribulationum*, ed. Franz Ehrle, *ALKG* 2 (1886), 130; Ignaz Döllinger, ed., *Beiträge zur Sektengeschichte* 2 (Munich, 1890), 509.

39. Cf., for example, the portrayal in the Colmar chronicler, *MG Scr.* 17.232.

40. Guilelmus Brito, ed. Delaborde, 232. This is probably the source of Martinus Polonus, *MG Scr.* 22.438.

41. Tract., c. 6, p. 19: *Qui cognoscit, inquiunt, deum esse in se, lugere non debet, sed ridere.*

42. *Chronicon . . . . Laudunensis*, ed. Cartellieri and Stechele, 70 (*MG Scr.* 26.454) for 1212. The treatise *Contra Amaurianos* polemicized against this Godinus (see n. 30 above), and according to the Chronicle of Melrose (see n. 4 above), Robert of Courçon named the heretics of 1210 *Godini*, after this man.

43. *Chartularium universitatis* 1.79, no. 20. According to the Chronicle of Melrose, Robert of Courçon had a large role in fighting the Amaurians. That is all the more probable, since—as we know from Cæsarius of Heisterbach (p. 306)—he was among those first informed by Master Rudolph of Namur when he detected heresy. Robert was at that time a canon of Paris, becoming a cardinal only at the start of 1212 and returning to France as legate in May 1213, see F. J. G. la Porte-du Theil, in *NEM* 6.176.

44. Mansi, *Sacrorum conciliorum* (Venice, 1779–82) 23.986.

45. The canonist Henry of Ostia asserted that the doctrine of Amaury was not described in detail at the Council in 1215 *because Amalricus iste habuit quosdam discipulos tempore huius concilii adhuc superstites, ob quorum reverentiam suppressum exitit dogma istud, quorum etiam nomina adhuc honestius est supprimere quam specialiter nominare*, see Wilhelm Preger, *Geschichte der deutschen Mystik im Mittelalter* (Leipzig, 1874–93) 1.182; *Chartularium universitatis* 1.82, doubts this assertion without any relevant basis. Perhaps this concerned students of the philosopher and theologian Amaury who had no relation to the heresy of 1210, for it is hardly conceivable that the curia had any personal hesitation about heretics of this sort.

46. Cf. Charles Dufresne Du Cange, *Glossarium mediæ et infimæ latinitatis*, ed. G. A. L. Henschel and L. Favre (Niort, 1883–87) 6.145; Frédéric Godefroy, *Dictionnaire de l'ancienne langue française et de tous les dialectes du XI*[e] *en XV*[e] *siècles* (Paris, 1880ff.) 5.727 and 10.268.

47. *Sermo ad virgines*, ed. Joseph Greven, *HJ* 35 (1914), 44–45: *Quando autem puella virginitatem suam custodire proposuit et parentes offerunt ei maritum cum diviciis, conculcet et respuat. . . . Sapientes autem . . . huius seculi, prelati scilicet seculares et alii maliciosi homines volunt eam interficere et a bono proposito retrahere dicentes: Hec vult esse Beguina—sic enim nominantur in Flandria et Brabancia—vel Papelarda—sic enim appellantur in Francia—vel Humiliata—sicut dicitur in Lombardia—vel Bizoke—secundum quod dicitur in Italia—et Coquenunne—ut dicitur in Theutonia; et ita deridendo eas et quasi infamando nituntur eas retrahere a sancto proposito*. The sermon probably comes from James' service as a cardinal, 1229/40, but it must draw on experiences before 1216, when James was a canon regular in Oignies near Namur (after 1207?), associated with the group of religious women ("beguines") around Maria of Oignies.

48. See chapter 4 above, n. 26.

49. The second continuator of the *Chronica regia Coloniensis* (ed. Waitz, 187–88) begins his account on the discovery of the Paris heresy with the words: *Cum diabolica persuasione eorum qui Beggini dicebantur execrabilis doctrine semen paulatim irreperet et iam in plures transfunderetus eorum perversitas . . .* [then Rudolph of Namur decided to uncover them].

50. On Gautier of Coincy, died 1236, cf. Erhard Lommatzsch, *Gautier de Coincy als Satiriker* (Halle, 1913); Gustav Gröber, *Grundriss der romanischen Philologie*, 2/1 (Strasbourg, 1902), 651. The poem "De seinte Léocade, qui fu dame de Tolète, et du saint Arcevesque," in Barbazan, *Fabliaux et contes des poètes françois*, ed. M. Méon (Paris, 1808) 1.270ff. (in Poquet, *Les miracles de la Sainte Vièrge traduits et mis en vers par Gautier de Coincy* [Paris, 1857], 75ff., the excerpt on beguines and papelardes is left out, partly "in the interest of the primary action," partly for "reasons of a more elevated order"[!]). The verses on the Franciscans (= fratemeneur, v. 1419/23, see n. 57 below) show that the poem could not have been composed after 1220, since they are seen as a novel and dubious phenomenon (certainly the first mention of the Franciscans in French literature). According to Louis Petit de Julleville, *Histoire de la langue*

et de la littérature française 1 (Paris, 1896), 48, Gautier gathered his gradually completed "Miracles de Nôtre Dame" about 1220, according to Gröber about 1223. The long excursus on beguines and papelardes in the legend of the archbishop of Toledo is one of Gautier's habitual inserts or additions (*queues*) of moral and contemporary content, with no relation to the poem surrounding it.

51. V. 1147ff.: *Nul ne peut mais nul bien avoir / fors par paraige ou par avoir, / ou par molt grant ypocrasie; / mais Diex het molt si faite vie; / mal brasiers et male flambe arde / et papelart et papelarde!*

52. V. 1485/6: *Papelardie est une treuve / et une gille toute nueve.* This passage shows that Gautier is not using the word "papelardie" to describe hypocrisy in general, and that he is not writing a "general satire against hypocrisy," aimed "at all the Tartuffes in the clergy and the orders," who "display calculated piety in words and moans, of which their heart knows not" (Lommatzsch, *Gautier de Coincy*, 26, 31); rather, he is dealing with a specific phenomenon of his own time.

53. V. 1535ff.: *Il est en tant des renoiés, / que toz Artois en est noiez. / Tout ont noié jusqu'à Noion / se toz en Oyse nes noion, / touz ert, ce cuit ainz quatre mois / Noions noiez et Noiemois.*

54. This word is thus not "first documented after 1261/2," as Alfons Hilka, "Altfranzösische Mystik und Beginentum," *ZRP* 47 (1927), 122, believes.

55. Cf. Du Cange, *Glossarium* 8.201–02; Godefroy, *Dictionnaire* 8.95; Otto of Freising, *Gesta Friderici*, poemium (ed. Waitz and von Simson, 11), says of the widespread prophecy of the "Deus peregrinus": *Quisquis fuit ille propheta seu trotannus, qui hoc promulgavit.* Eberhard of Béthune, *Liber antiheresis*, c. 25 (*Bibliotheca maxima veterum Patrum* [Lyon, 1677] 24.1572) makes the strange accusation against the Waldensians that they used itinerant preaching as an excuse to see and marvel at many lands, and for that reason he calls them *trutanni: O mira novitas! Novum genus tritannorum, qui locorum varietates aliter videre non poterant aut mirari nisi se fingerent esse Christos!* Cæsarius of Heisterbach, *Dialogus miraculorum* I, 3 (ed. Strange, 1.9) speaks of a *clericus actu trutannus, quales per diversas vagari solent provincias.* The monks of Charroux (diocese of Poitiers) provide the monks staying with them from the Flemish house of Andres a *subtilis trutannus, tempore annosus, ordine munus morigeratus, . . . eorum monachum* as a travel guide on their return (*MG Scr.* 24.737), that is, a man who knew the way because he had been around. The bishop of Liège called the false Count Baldwin of Flanders who appeared in 1224 a *trutanus* (*MG Scr.* 16.358; F. Wachter, in his "Geschichtsschreiber" translates this word in keeping with its sense as "cheating vagabond"); in the same way Lambert of Andre (about 1200) calls a pilgrim and *pseudoconversus* who presents himself as Count Baldwin of Andre, who had died in Palestine, as a *trutannus* (*MG Scr.* 24.634. Robert de Sorbon, *Sermo de confessione* (*Bibl. Patr. Paris.* 5.1472) speaks of *trutanni* as crafty beggars: *Scis, quod trutanni infirmi et pauperes ostendunt transeuntibus membrum magis morbosum, ut eos ad misericordiam et compassionem sui alliciant;* in the same way William of St. Amour, see the text to n. 66 below; also similar,

Cæsarius of Heisterbach, *Dialogus miraculorum*, VIII, 50 (ed. Strange, 2.131). Albertus Magnus, *Sententiæ*, IV, 43, 7, calls those who boast of having special knowledge of the coming of the last days *fatui et trutanni*. Salimbene calls the Cologne archpoet and primate *magnus trutannus et magnus trufator et maximus versificator* (227, 572, 651); he even charges that cardinals *scripturam truphatorie et trutannice juxta suum erroneum intellectum exponunt* (228).

56. See below, n. 67ff.

57. Gautier opposes the *preudome*, the pious model Christian, to what he holds to be false forms of the religious life. V. 1409ff., it says: *Preudome pas ne sont tot cil / qui baissent l'uel et le sorcil. / Sachiez por voir* [= *vrai*] *que preudom nus / ne set faire le quatinus, / le begin, ne le pappelart, / car ne set noient* [= *nient*] *de l'art / ne riens n'en daigneroit savoir, / car riens ne prise tel savoir, / Preudome ne set, se Diex me voie, / fors que plaine oevre et plaine voie. / Je voie, se Diex me doinst honeur, / que cil las, cil fratremeneur, / qui par ces voles vont trenblant, / font bele chiere et bel samblant, / et belement as gens trenblant, / font bele chiere et bel semblant, / et belement as gens parolent. / Main cil begin d'ire m'afolent; se font plus juste / ne fu la none Sainte Juste* . . . The word *quatinus* (or *faire le quatinus*) is otherwise unknown, not even appearing in the *Roman de la Rose*; Godefroy's *Dictionnaire* (6, 489) only cites this passage, and a survey for other sources of the word among Romance linguists produced no result. For Gautier, *quatinus* is equivalent with *begin* or *pappelart*. Since the Chronicle of Melrose tells us that the Amaurians were called both *Godini* and *papelardi*, I think it highly likely that this word, used by Gautier as meaning *begin* and *pappelart*, was formed out of the word *Godini*. The word *Godini*, coined by the theologian Robert of Courçon (see n. 4 above) would have circulated by word of mouth for some time, but perceived as a word in Latin and contaminated with a word already known, *quatinus*. I would hold that to be convincing if experts (W. von Wartburg, E. Lommatzsch, G. Cohen–Paris) had not declared it etymologically impossible for the word *quatinus* to be derived from *Godinus*, and that the word *quatinus* more probably was connected with the Picardic *couatir* = hidden, *en catimini* = in hiding. Then the expression *fair le quatinus* would no longer have a historically specific meaning (as does *faire le begin, le papelart*). The analogous case of the origin of the word "beguine" from "Albigenses," which has also been proclaimed impossible by etymologists, but confirmed by historical witness (see chapter 4 above, n. 26). makes it likely to me that *quatinus* can still derive from Godinus, despite etymological worries. Dr. Skommodau of Paris is the source of the reference that the word in question is spelled "quatinus" in the Paris manuscripts, Bibliothèque Nationale, fonds français 22928 and 23111 (both from the thirteenth century), like the Laon manuscript cited by Godefroy. Other Gautier manuscripts appear not to have the passage.

58. V. 1275ff. he closes a long, hostile polemic against equating God and unnatural sexuality with the verses: *Tex gens se vont plus reponant / que gelines qui vont ponant. / Main Diex li bons Clers qui tot set / dit qui mal fait, jor fuit*

et het. / Genz de mal faire costumiere / toz tans clarté het et lumiere. / Papelart sovent se reponent . . . Further, v. 1351ff.: *Devant la gent sont simple et qui* [= *quieti*] */ mais quant il sont en lor requoi, / assez font pis que cil ne face / qui monstre au siecle riant face. / Tex fait grant senblant d'abstinence / qui paior a la conscience / et plus l'a vuide, vaine et fauxe, / que tex mengue bone sauxe / et bone char à granz buignons. /Se soutieument les esclignons / molt troverons en lor afaire / d'anglez de qoi Diex n'a que faire. / Diex aime molt la plaine voie, / Diex velt chascuns ses oeuvres voie, / Diex aime molt communité, / Diex aime pais et charité. Cf. also Gautier's accusation in another poem (in Poquet, Les miracles de la Sainte Vièrge*, 643, v. 594ff.; cf. Lommatzsch, *Gautier de Coincy*, 29) against the sinful relations of the *truants* to the *joennes papelardeles*, with the malicious word-play: *Papelardiaus et papelardeles / on a la foiz papelart d'eles.*

59. V. 1158: *tuit sont fax, et bon se font;* v. 1288: *si bon se font et si parfait;* v. 1162: *sor tote gent sont decéu / por la loenge de cest mont, / et por monter un poi amont / assez sueffrent travail et paine. / Le vin laissent por la fontaine, / et la char por les pois baiens: / Tex est pire que uns paiens, / qui par sa grant ypocrisie / moustre qu'il est de meillor vie;* v. 1199ff.: *et par senblant molt se despisent, / por ax acroitre s'apetisent / por ax acroitre s'amenuisent;* vv. 1285–86: *par lor senblant au siecle s'enblent* [= withdraw itself], */ por lor senblant seint home sanblent*. V. 1668ff.: *Nos chars nos ruevent amorter / par géunes, par abstinences; / molt blasment noz incontinences, / noz ostraiges et noz orguelz: le festu voient en noz elz, / le trastre es lor ne voient mie.*

60. V. 1174: *simple chiere* [= face] *sevent bien faire, / tuit sanblent estre esperitel. / Ge sai por seint Esperit tel, / qui tant est simples et et seriz, / ce sanble estre seinz antecriz;* vv. 1182–83.: *les sanblanz omi esperitex / faces maigres et amorties;* v. 1140 and 1426, see above, n. 57.

61. V. 1453ff.: *li pluseur, c'en est la voire* [= truth] */ font quanqu'il font par vaine gloire / pour estre avant sachié [= preferred] et trait*; v. 1543ff.: *Li papelart le mont honissent, / papelart s'apapelardissent / por estre Abbé, Evesque ou Pape.*

62. *Sermo de conscientia ad theologos, Bibliotheca sanctorum Patrum*, ed. Margarinus de la Bigne, 5 (2d ed., Paris, 1589) 1462: *Ille qui frequentat magis scholas et diligentius magistrum audit, debet melior clericus reputari; ergo beguini sive in seculo sive in religione* [!] *in libro isto scilicet conscientie sunt sapientiores, quia frequentius et pluries confitentur, sicut patet ad oculum; imo propter hoc dicuntur Papalarei* [= *Papalardi*?], *quia frequentant confessiones*. In the same sermon (1458), he rages against people who, *cum sint cum papelardis viris et religiosis*, present an appearance of piety, but are worldly when among the worldly; those who were *coram magnam beguinis* wore a spiritual garment, *coram mundanis*, however, they wore worldly splendor. In Robert's *Iter Paradisi* (ibid., 1492) it says: *Aliquis incipit agere penitentiam, irridetur ab aliquo, qui dicit: Iste est beguinus, et tunc iste tibi dicet aliquid, quia modo aliquo tibi injuriatur; ignosce ergo ei, tibi dicet aliquid, quia modo aloquo tibi injuriatur; ignosce ergo ei, et aliquid lucratus es ad*

viam tuam. In Robert's unprinted treatise, *De conditionibus matrimonii*, there is an *exemplum de illo begino, qui ultra mare locutus fuit cum rege Francorum;* more information than this cannot be gained from this in A. Lecoy de la Marche, *La chaire française au Moyen Age,* 2d ed. (Paris, 1886), 100–01 and 300. Cf. also the *Vita b. Edmundi Cantuar. episcopi* (died 1242) by the Cistercian Bertrand of Pontigny in Marténe and Durand, *Thesaurus novus anecdotorum* 3.1791: *quædam prostituta irridenti animo suis ait comitibus: Eamus ad papalardum illum;* when she approaches him, she is converted by the saint.

63. "Collectiones catholicæ," *Magistri Guillelmi de Sancto Amore Opera omnia, quæ reperiri potuerunt* (Coutances, 1632), 2664nd67, 275, 305; also William of St. Amour speaks (as does Robert de Sorbon, n. 62 above) of *aliquis beguinarum, sive regularis, sive secularis existat;* he also uses this name for members of the mendicant orders.

64. Cf. above, chapter 6, n. 8ff. William of St. Amour, "Casus et articuli," *Opera*, 91 (see Mosheim, *De beghardis*, 27), William attacks *trutanni validi corpore, quorum est in regno Francie multitudo infinita*, who are just like the beguines, *Boni valeti* [beghards] and papelards, *cum sint validi ad operandum, parum certe aut nihil volunt operari, sed vivere volunt de eleemosynis in otio corporali sub pretextu orandi, cum nullius sint religionis per sedem apostolicam approbate*; cf. n. 66 below.

65. William of St. Amour, *Opera*, 97: *Si aliquis nunc ita pretiosam vestem deferret, Papelardi in faciem eius spuerunt sicut pharisæis puerunt in faciem domini Jesu Christi sic induti;* cf. *Casus et articuli, Opera,* p. 92, the accusation against *Beguinæ et Boni Valeti dicentes, quod vestis pretiosa portari non potest sine magno periculo;* the boni valeti are beghards, see Mosheim, *De beghardis*, 37ff.

66. *Collectiones catholicæ, Opera,* 228: *Propter mendicitatem etiam, qui otiose vivere volunt, multipliciter simulatores fiunt; nam ut miserabiliores appareant et ex eo eleemosynas largiores acquirant, plerumque simulant se infirmos et debiles, cum tamen sint sani et fortes, ut videmus quotidie in trutannis; plerumque autem per hypocrisin simulant se esse sanctos, cum tamen parum aut nihil sanctitatis preter speciem exteriorem habeant, ut videmus in aliquibus papelardis*. Cf. William Peraldus, O.P. (before 1260), *Summarium virtutum: Caro decipit sicut papelardus, qui dicit se infirmum et pauperem, cum non sit* (Ducange, *Glossarium* 6.145). Robert de Sorbon says the same about the *trutanni* (see n. 55 above), but he does not describe the beguines and papelards, whom he respects, as *trutanni*!

67. Witnesses from French literature in the thirteenth century in Alfons Hilka, "Altfranzösische Mystik und Beginentum," 164ff.; Tiberius Denkinger, *Die Bettelorden in der französischen didaktischen Literatur des Mittelalters*, Dissertation, Münster, 1915, 50ff.; E. Lommatzsch, *Gautier de Coincy*, 30. Cf. also the sources for the word *papelardie* in Godefroy, *Dictionnaire* 10.268. I will cite only a few remarkable examples. In the rhyme chronicle of Philip Mouskes (written before 1244) the equation of *beghin et papolart* (v. 30733, ed.

von Reiffenberg, 2.673): *Et tout çou fisent beghin et papelart et jacobin.* In Ruteboeuf there is, particularly, the poem *Des ordres*, with the refrain: *Papelart et Beguin ont le siecle honi* (ed. A. Kressner, 1885, 56–57; ed. Jubinal [1839] 1.170) and the verses: *Il n'a en tout cest mont ne bougre ne herite* [= *hereticus*] *ne fort popelican, vaudois ne sodomite, se il vestoit l'abit où papelarz s'abite, c'on ne le tenist ja a saint ou a hermite*; also the *Dit des beguines* (26–36; 1.186) and the *Dit des regles* (63ff.; 1.194. In Gautier de Metz, *Mappemonde* (about 1247: Du Cange, *Glossarium* 6.145): *Tels sont chil à ces capes grans / Con doit bien appeler truhans [or: trutans], qui papelart nommer se font / et à droit, car Papelart sont / Adont on à nom papelart / car avoir veulent tout le art / et le plus bel de l'autre gent / par fausse chiere et faus semblent*. In Gerbert de Montreuil (ed. Ch. Potvin, *Perceval le Gallois* 6.201): *Si parement pas ne sambloient de truande ne de beguine*. The accent on the words beguine and papelard is so unstable in the thirteenth century that opponents of the religious movement often use *fausse begine* and *pseudo-papelarda* to diminish them, see Hilka, "Altfranzösische Mystik," 164, 170.

68. Particularly informative is the German poem, "Das leben der Gräfin Jolanden von Vianden," by Friar Herman (J. Meier, *Bruder Hermanns Leben*, 47, vv. 3882–83): Jolande's relatives accuse her: *ir duet uns allen schande mit ûren begardien*. When Jolande's brother married the countess of Salm in 1247, Jolande asked her sister-in-law to spare her from participating in the dancing; *nu was dy brut ein edel wif / hersch unde stolz, dat Al ir lif / zur wereltvroide herze druck. /Der suster wort sy widersluch, / sy sprach: vil lyve suster min, / wilt du mir begine sin / ar begardie driven, / so ganc zu suchen wiven, / dy des gelusten, dat raden ich, / erlaiz der truanden mich. / Du solt mir spiln, lachen / und alle vroiden machen* (57, v. 4769ff.). Berthold of Regensburg (A. E. Schönbach, *S.-B. Wien*, 147/5, 22) speaks in a sermon of *trugner, trugnerinne, trugnerius*, warning against the heretical *doctrina anguli*—probably he is trying to translate the word *trutannus*. Cf. n. 83 below.

69. Cf. particularly the poems *Qui vuet droit beguinage avoir*, published by A. Hilke (145ff.), *Savês que j'apiel beghinage?* (p. 122, completely in E. Bechmann, *ZRP* 13.72ff.), also the *proprietés de beguinage* (156).

70. Only William of St. Amour refers to heretical quietism in Parisian religious groups: "Casus et articuli," *Opera*, 91: *Et extra predictas* [= supply *trutanni, boni valeti* = *begardi, beguinæ*] *jam est quarta secta Parisius, que dicit numquam operandum manibus, sed incessanter orandum; et si homines sic orarent, plures fructus terra sine cultura afferret quam modo offerat cum cultura*. William describes as sects the most various forms of the religious poverty movement which are not organized as orders, but in fact they were not groups strictly distinguished from one another, let alone organized "sects" of any sort.

71. See below, n. 87ff.

72. Autbert Stroick, ed., "Collectio de scandalis ecclesiæ," *AFH* 24.61–62; see above, n. 35ff.

73. Humbert de Romanis, *Opus tripartitum*, III, 3; see above, n. 32.

74. See below, n. 108ff.

75. To date this synod, whose statutes are preserved in a unique manuscript of the fourteenth century bearing the date of 1227, cf. Albert Hauck, *KD* 4 (3d ed., Leipzig, 1913), 9, n. 6, and particularly the careful investigation by Fr. Arens, *ZKG* 33 (1912), 84ff.

76. Statutes of the synod in Hartzheim, *Concilia Germaniæ* 3.531, and Blattau, *Statuta synodalia archidiœcesis Trevirensis*, I, p. 24: *Precipimus firmiter et districte sacerdotibus, ne predicare permittant aliquos illiteratos, videlicet Begardos vel conversos seu alios, cuiuscumque ordinis sint, etiam extra ecclesiam videlicet in vicis vel in plateis, et sacerdotes parochianis suis precipiant, ne tales audiant, propter hereses et errores, quos seminant in populo*. The *conversi* are not a special community alongside the beghards (perhaps Waldensian preachers, as Karl Müller, *Die Waldenser*, p. vii, believes); the designation *Begardi seu conversi* is found in other sources for one and the same thing; see below, n. 133.

77. Hartzheim, *Concilia Germaniæ* 3.532; Blattau, *Statuta* 1.25: *Item precipimus, ut omnes sacerdotes non permittant trutannos et alios vagos scolares aut goliardos cantare versus super Sanctos et Agnus dei aut alias in missis vel in divinis officiis, quia ex hoc sacerdos in canone quam plurimum impeditur et scandalizantur homines audientes.*

78. Nikolaus Spiegel, *Die Vaganten und ihr Orden*, Programm Speyer, 1892, interpreted the decree of the Trier synod imaginatively : "The *Vagantes* were tolerated here and there, on festive occasions (such as Prime and the dedication of churches) to beautify the service with song, and they used this opportunity to sing frivolous ditties during the holy activities," and he adds, "These were possibly drinking and game songs, as well as reworkings of hymns (*vinum bonum et suave* instead of *verbum bonum*, etc.)." Unfortunately, there is nothing on this in the sources, and it all arises from prejudices about the *Vagantes* and Goliards in general. All valuable and datable poems of "lyrics of the *Vagantes*," incidentally, derive from the twelfth century; the precious manuscripts of the thirteenth century in which these poems are collected (*Carmina burana*, ms. in St. Omer) were not by "vagantes" but by devotees of these poems. W. Meyer, *Nachrichten von der Gesellschaft der Wissenschaften zu Göttingen*, 1907, 76 and 88, properly stresses that one should not seek the poets of these lyrics among the *vagi scholares* regulated by synods in the thirteenth century.

79. See above, chapter 6, n. 14; Statutes in Mone, "Kirchenordnungen," 141 §46: *Quia vagi scolares, qui vulgo Eberhardini vocatur, deo abhominabilem vitam ducunt, divinum officium invertunt, unde etiam laici scandalizantur, monachis dant apostatandi materiam, quippe quos de claustris suis recedentes et alibi in seculo receptaculum non invenientes ipsi in suum recipiunt consortium, statuit hec sancta synodus prohibendo, ne quis clericus eos recipiat vel aliquid det eiusdem; quod si fecerit, a superiori suo suspensus acriter corrigatur. Nullus etiam scolaris recipiatur, nisi chorum et scolas frequentans*. The statutes of the Magdeburg provincial synod of 1261

repeats this *verbatim*, Hartzheim, *Concilia Germaniæ* 3.807, §20, with the addition at the end: *sive decenti alias servitio deputatus*. In Fritzlar in 1244 the statute of 1233 was repeated verbatim, expanded by the amendment that truly poor students should not be infringed who were compelled to wander and beg: the *Everardi prefati, qui vitam ducunt reprobam et infamem*, should be admitted to eccesiastical consecrations and services only after long probation and basic improvement of their way of life. This was repeated by the synod in Mainz in 1310 with a further amendment, see n. 81 below; Hartzheim, *Concilia Germaniæ* 3.600, §17 and IV, 186.

80. At the German national synod in Würzburg in 1287, the reception and support of *vagi scholares* was placed in the closest connection with the ban of the "apostolic brethren," who were expressly dissolved as an unapproved order the year before by Honorius IV (bull of 11 March 1286, see *Bullarium Romanum* [Turin, 1857] 4.84); see the statutes of the council in Hartzheim, *Concilia Germaniæ* 3.732–33, §34. Clerics and lay were warned against these apostles, with their *intuitus religionis ac insolitus habitus*—it is utterly unknown whether there were followers of this "sect" in Germany; perhaps the papal legate was only carrying out the commission of Honorius IV at the national synod to announce the suspension of this order in all lands. They were given the strange name of *Leccatores seu reprobati apostoli* (Mansi, *Sacrorum conciliorum* 24.863 incorrectly given as peccatores). Leccatores was an actual term for wandering singers, players, and performers of non-clerical status, see Du Cange, *Glossarium, "lecator"; Die Gedichte des Archipoeta*, ed. M. Manitius (*Münchner Texte* 6), 1913, 37, strophe 23; Johann of Nuremberg, *De vita vagorum*, in Wilhelm Grimm, *Altdeutsche Wälder* 2.49. These apostles of poverty also were called *vagantes*!

81. Hartzheim, *Concilia Germaniæ* 4.186 for the year 1310, amendment to the decrees of 1238 and 1244: *Quia clerici vagabundi, qui Eberhardini vocantur, quorum vita deo est odibilis, clericos et ipsos laicos scandalizant, discurrendo per terras in villis, que carent propriis sacerdotibus, aliquando celebrare presumunt seu, quod verius est, quantum in ipsis est, divina officia prophanare, statuimus, ut tales ad mandata tum diœcesani seu loci archidiaconi teneantur in custodia carcerali, ad hoc si necesse fuerit invocando auxilium brachii secularis, salvis nihilominus constitutionibus contra tales a nostris predecessoribus promulgatis*. The text agrees in part with the bull of Honorius IV against the apostolic brethren, 11 March 1286.

82. Its derivation from Archbishop Eberhard of Salzburg (1200/1240) as a benefactor of the *vagantes* is a pure hypothesis; see Frantzen, *Neophilologus* 5 (1920), 63; J. W. Muller, *Tijdschrift voor nederlandsche Taal- en Letterkunde* 39 (1920), 137; Alfons Hilka, *Studi medievali*, 2d series, 2.417ff. The travel account of Bishop Wolfger of Passau (ed. Zingerle, 1877, 26) lists for Easter, 1208 (or 1204) a gift to an *episcopus Ebberardinorum* and to "another mime."

83. Berthold of Regensburg, in a Latin sermon (*Serm. spec.*, 33, manuscript Leipzig 496, f. 73e; see A. E. Schönbach, *S.-B. Wien*, 147/5, 81 and 107), speaks

of people who are loved neither by God nor by people, and he presented as an example: *Pikardi* [= *beghards*], *Everhardini, kusores, armigeri, falsi mendici et huiusmodi pauperes, falsi religiosi, qui miseri sunt intus in peccatis, extra miseri semper in labore, in defectu* . . . In Netherlandish literature there are more examples to be found later for the term Eberhardians: in the fragmentary popular play entitled "Truwaten" *(= Trutanni!)*, a Bruder Everaert seduces a maid to become a *truwanten*, and he describes *swesters, baghinen, lollaerde* as his companions (ed. P. Leendertz, *Middelnederlandsche dramat. Poezie*. 1907, 132ff.).

84. A. E. Schönbach, *S.-B. Wien*, 147/5, 45: *Sunt heretici, qui modo venerunt ante diem judicii, qui se vocaverunt primo pauperes, post Waldenses, post scolares, nunc bonos homines vel "wislos" vel "weglos."*

85. See chapter 6 above, n. 41; statutes are in the *Pastoralblatt des Bistums Eichstätt* 32 (1885), 74: *Item quamvis apud deum, qui est illuminans omnem hominen venientem in hunc mundum, damnata sint opera tenebrarum et reprobata in tantum, ut apostolis suis ad predicandum missis preciperit dicens: Quod dico vobis in tenebris, dicite in luce, etc., quidam tamen laici occulta conventicula celebrantes, predicationis sibi usurpant officium et, sicut timeri oportet, corda simplicium evertunt et eos in quendam cecitatis errorem abducunt. Quia igitur in ecclesia dei ordo doctorum precipuus et principalis existit* [sic] *non debet sibi quisquam nisi specialiter ad hoc missus predicationis officium usurpare; nam secundum apostolum quomodo predicabunt nisi mittantur? Quam ob rem vobis universis ac singulis committimus firmiter injungentes, quatenus plebisanis vestris presuadeatis attente et nihilominus sub pena excommunicationis inhibeatis districte, ne huiusmodi predicatores immo potius deceptores aut quoslibet eorum sermones recipiant et audiant quoquo modo, alioquin qui super hoc tertio a vobis moniti ab huiusmodi predicationibus audiendis seu proponendis abstinere noluerint, tanquam suspectos de heresi nostris auribus deferatis.* The chapter title, *Contra beghardos*, is from the editor.

86. The Waldensians cannot be treated in the section which follows.

87. Martinus Crusius, *Annales Suevici*, III, 2, c. 14 (vol. 2, 99).

88. On Gnadenzell: *quibus antea libertas illa fraticellana placuerat.* . . . The rule was confirmed: *Sic Gratiæcellenses quoque, quibus antea libertas illa fraticellana placuerat, cum jam viderent ordinem suum negligi, quod nulli regulæ astrictus esset, impetrarunt et ipsæ ab episcopo Constantiensi regulam s. Augustini anno 1252, in qua ipsas deinde pontifex Alexander IV confirmavit prædicoribusque commendatæ sunt, non tamen ordini incorporatæ; bullam is ipsis dedit cum multis privilegiis hoc 1261 anno*. The last statement is the only reason Crusius lists this entire episode under 1261.

89. Cf. Max Häussler, *Felix Fabri aus Ulm und seine Stellung zum geistigen Leben seiner Zeit*, Beiträge zur Kulturgeschichte des Mittelalters und der Renaissance 15 (Berlin-Leipzig, 1914), 6; see also p. 65 on Fabri's method of working with documents.

90. Crusius, *Annales Suevici*, III, 2, c. 8; 2.75ff.

91. Cf. also J. U. Pregizerus, *Suevia sacra* (Tübingen, 1717), 73 and 78; Felix Fabri, *Tractatus de civitate Ulmensi*, 167. The information in L. Baur, *FDA*, 2d series, 2.36–37, and Wilms, *Das älteste Verzeichnis*, 40 (and 42) are inadequate.

92. Crusius, *Annales Suevici*, III, 1 c. 11 (2, 36). Cf. I, 2, c. 15 and II, 5, c. 3. The counts of Teck were regarded as the "founders" of Kirchheim, see Felix Fabri, *Historia Sueviæ*, ed. Melchior Goldast, *Rerum Suevorum Scriptores* (Ulm, 1727), 74.

93. Crusius continues in the same citation to tell that a wealthy noblewoman came to Kirchheim who received permission from Duke Conrad *omnes eo inferre opes suas*. This is partly confirmed, partly corrected by a charter of 4 March 1249 (*Wirtembergisches Urk.-B.* 4.190, no. 1125), in which Duke Louis of Teck permits Adelheid *et quedam alie ministeriales nostre ad locum Kyricheim deo sub regulari disciplina ibidem perhenniter mulitature se suaque contulerunt*, conceding to the house its own burial and a priest of their own. Kirchheim was already regulated at that time; see below.

94. *Wirtembergisches Urk.-B.* 4.27–28, no. 978; the charter was issued in Esslingen for the *devotæ in Christo dominæ de Chirchein* by Albert of Altbach; among the witnesses is a *Prior frater H. de Basila*, indubitably the Dominican Henry of Westhofen (see below, chapter 8, n. 48), and a *procurator frater Dietericus de Colonia.*

95. *Wirtembergisches Urk.-B.* 4.33, no. 983.

96. On 14 July 1245, ibid., 104ff., no. 1047/48; cf. also 3.109ff., no. 1052; 4.137, no. 1075 and 168, no. 1105; cf. above, chapter 5, n. 122.

97. Martin Crusius calls him *Petrus Cardinalis aurei vexilii*, adding the German words "*zum güldenen Fahn*"; so Felix Fabri's German-language house history is his source; Crusius did not retranslate entirely correctly, since it is the cardinal-deacon *S. Georgii ad Velum Aureum*. On his legation in 1247/48, see Böhmer, Ficker, and Winkelmann, *Regesta Imperii*, 5/2, 1549ff.

98. *Wirtembergisches Urk.-B.* 6.470, nos. 30–31, Berger, *Les Registres* 2.42, no. 4334/36, the commissioning bull for Kirchheim, dated 27 January 1249. Crusius gives conflicting information on the incorporation of the house; III, 1, c. 11 (2.36), he says that the sisters sent a prædicator (= Dominican) to Koblenz to speak with the legate (the cardinal was indeed in Koblenz in August 1247), and he received a grant of the Dominican rule from the legate (that is, the permission to keep not only the Rule of St. Augustine but also the constitutions of St. Mark's or S. Sisto), and the house was commended to the Dominican Order by Innocent IV, Alexander IV, and Clement IV; this is correct, as the bulls cited show. However, III, 2, c. 14 (2.99, cf. n. 88 above) he says that Kirchheim was first consecrated at the Chapter General in Bologna in 1267 (as says Chr. Besold, *Virginum sacrarum monumenta* [Tübingen, 1636], 548), but that does not jibe with the other facts.

99. *Wirtembergisches Urk.-B.* 5.231–32, no. 1466, dated at Rottweil, 1258; there are no Dominicans among the witnesses. Cf. the confirmation of the donation of 4 August 1262, ibid., 6.75, no. 1673; see Trutpert Neugart,

Episcopatus Constantiensis chronologice et diplomatice illustratus, vol. 1/2 (Freiburg i. B., 1862), 271; L. Baur, "Die Ausbreitung der Bettelorden in der Diözese Konstanz," *FDA*, 2d series, 2 (1901), 53–54.

100. What stands in the charter is: *magistre et conventus in Kenhusen* (or *Kerenhusen*, or *Renhusen*); that is either Kernhausen near Spaichingen (north of Tuttlingen) or Rennehausen (now Hausen ob Rottweil), cf. *Wirtembergisches Urk.-B.* 5.232 and G. Bossert, *Württembergische Vierteljahreshefte für Landesgeschichte*, 2d ser., 2 (1893/4), 111–12.

101. Supposedly the counts of Lupfen, Zollern, Gundelfingen, and Neuffen refused to follow Emperor Frederick II on his expedition to Italy in 1237, and for that reason they were condemned by a princes' court at Rottweil to build and endow a house for seventy-two women in penance. A canon was supposed to have recommended the *pagus Offenhusus* as a site, as well as the adoption of the Rule of St. Augustine and incorporation into the Dominican Order. The Dominicans of Constance, Rottweil, and Esslingen were supposed to have helped with the construction, which began in 1250; see Crusius, *Annales Suevici*, III, 2, c. 8, v. 2, 77, based on Fabri's house history. Neugart, *Episcopatus Constantiensis*, 1/2, 271, declares this entire foundation story to be a fable.

102. This adoption of the Rule of St. Augustine in 1252 is, once again, only reported by Crusius, whose report passed through Joseph Vochezer, *Geschichte des fürstlichen Hauses Waldburg*, 3 vols. (Kempten, 1888–1907) 1.179 into the *Regesta episcoporu Constantiensium*, ed. Paul Ladewig (Innsbruck, 1886ff.) 1.205, no. 1791, without finding any other confirmation.

103. Whether the names applied to them (*qui nominabuntur Fraticelli, Beghardi et Beguinæ*) were original or applied to them later cannot be established. It is certain that there is no link with the Italian *fraticelli*, since they saw the "Rule" as strictly binding and unchangeable.

104. See chapter 6 above, text to n. 33.

105. *De ext. et int. hominis compositione*, II, 24, p. 110; probably written in 1240/5 (see Dagobert Stöckerl, *David von Augsburg* [Munich, 1914], 196).

106. *Tochter Syon*, ed. K. Weinhold (Paderhorn, 1880.) The period of composition is determined by the fact that the (otherwise unknown) *bruder Gerhart, der minnern brüder . . . provincialis minister in diutschen landen oben*, who encouraged the composition and helped in its presentation, could have had a place in the series of ministers of the Upper German province only in the years 1246–52; see K. Eubel, *Geschichte der oberdeutschen (Strassburger) Minoriten-Provinz*, 158–59 and 24. P. 430–31: *Swie tump ich doch anders si / mir ist jedoch diu wisheit bi / daz ich wol weiz Jesum Christ / daz er diu obrist wisheit ist / diu daz herze durhgrebet / und den inren sin erhebet / in die kunst, die nieman / mit rede zende bringen kan. / vür den sin sie so hohe get / daz man sie michels baz verstet / dan man iu davon kunne sagen. / diu kunst ist bi unsern tagen / in Brabant und in Baierlanden / undern wiben ufgestanden. / herre got, waz kunst ist daz / daz sich ein alt wip baz / verstet dan witzige man?*

107. Pp. 436–37, v. 2979ff. and 431, v. 2853ff.

108. Ms. I, 331 of the Stadtbibliothek Mainz, written end of the thirteenth or start of the fourteenth century, with the title (fol. 62a): *Hec est determinatio magistri Alberti quondam Ratisbonensis episcopi ordinis fratrum predicatorum super articulis invente heresis in Recia dyocesis Augustensis;* see H. Haupt, "Beiträge zur Geschichte," 556, who also gives the editorial changes to the edition in W. Preger, Mystik 1.461ff. The 88th thesis of this *determinatio* says: *in Recia est veritas.* The concept "Rhaetia" then embraced more than the Schwäbisch Ries of today; in the Marbach Annals, for example, Augsburg is described as a city of Raetia, *MG Scr.* 17.162.

109. Johannes Nider, *Formicarius*, III, 5, ed. Colvener (Douai, 1602), 215: *Reperri in libro manuali, quem pro sua persona per totum dominus Albertus manu con scripsit propria . . . unde puncta supradicta ac articulos plures quam hic notareim manu propria prefatus conscripsit dominus.* The Mainz ms. was probably transcribed directly from this manual, see Haupt,"Beiträge zur Geschichte," 375–76, 505–06. Van Mierlo appears not to know anything about either the Mainz ms. or Nider's notice, or he could not say of the 97 theses of the Determinatio, "Nothing shows that the work presented is by Albertus Magnus" (*Het Begardisme, VMKVA,* 1930, 296).

110. Since W. Preger's researches on this work (*Mystik*, 1.168ff.; *Abhandlungen der Bayerischen Akad.* 13.179ff. and 18.27ff.) believes the author was a cleric from the Austrian portion of the diocese of Passau—but the proof of that is not convincing, see below. It was partially published among the works of the Jesuit Gretser, *Opera*, 12 (1738), and in the *Bibliotheca maxima veterum Patrum* (Lyon, 1677) 25.262ff. The *Summa de Catharis et Leonistis* by Rainer Sacchoni is only part of this collective work, as Giesseler established in 1834 in his "Commentario critica de Raineri Sacchoni Summa." Cf. also K. Müller, *Waldenser*, 147ff. [Cf. also Franz Unterkircher, " 'Pseudo-Rainer' und 'Passauer Anonymus'," *MIÖG* 63 (1955), 41–46. HG/1960.]

111. These articles have frequently been published in several forms: W. Preger, *Mystik* 1.469; Döllinger, *Beiträge*, 393 and Wattenbach, *S.-B. Berlin*, 1887, 522, based on the ms. Clm 4386, which resents the *XXIX articulos de heresi novi spiritus* together with other heresiological texts, not with the "Passau Anonymous"; Döllinger, *Beiträge*, 391ff., based on Clm 14,959; Ch. Schmidt, *ZHT* 22.247ff. based on Strasbourg ms. B 147 of 1404; also in these two mss. are the *novæ hæreses de novo spiritu* are not as part of the collected work of the Passau Anonymous, but as an addition to a Strasbourg heresy investigation of 1317. Cf. further H. Haupt, *ZKG* 23.187ff. on the Vienna ms. 3271 (15th century) of the "Passau Anonymous," in which the articles are entitled: *Hec heresis noviter inventa apud mordlingen*—which should certainly be Nördlingen, since there is no Mordlingen, but Nördlingen lies in the Swabian Ries.

112. The title in the Mainz ms. (n. 108 above): *Determinatio mg. Alberti quondam Ratisponensis episcopi* speaks—unless it was not added later by a scribe—for composition after 1262, since Albertus was bishop of Regensburg, 1260/62, and after 1262 he signed and sealed as *fr. A. episcopus quondam*

Ratispon., see *Analecta Bollandiana* 20.297ff. and the seal in the *Urk.-B. Basel* 1.313, no. 426. The attempt by F. Pelster, *ZKT* 45 (1921), 624, to date the inquisition in the Ries and Albertus' evaluation of it to June 1257, is not convincing; first of all, Pelster, basing himself on an erroneous dating of the "Passau Anonymous," does not deal with the possibility of dating it after 1260; secondly, he works with the false assumption that Albertus was the author and his evaluation was only an appendix to the treatise *De inquisitione hæreticorum*, which W. Preger convincingly attributes to David of Augsburg (see against Pelster's hypothesis M. Bihl, *AFH* 18.143ff.). Pelster's assertion is based on a Regensburg Dominican in the middle of the fourteenth century who writes that the falseness and senselessness of the Manichee heretical doctrine *patet intuenti vel legenti librum domni Alberti Magni de inquisitione hereticorum, quam fecit in pluribus locis Suevie* (Clm 26 897 f. 42v). That probably refers to the *Determinatio*, in which the *hæresis Manichæi* is referred to thirteen times. Whether it can be assumed from this that Albert himself led inquisitions in several places in Swabia is questionable; the Dominican of the fourteenth century probably knew no more than we do, that is, he knew the *Determinatio* and only interpreted its title rather imprecisely.

113. *MG Scr.* 17.194 and 195; in the edition of Gérard-Liblin (Colmar, 1854), 36 and 38.

114. Cf. Heribert Christian Scheeben, *Albert der Grosse: zur Chronologie seines Lebens*, QF 27 (1931), 112ff.

115. Cf. Finke, *Ungedruckte Dominikanerbriefe*, 80, 82, 84; Scheeben, *Albert der Grosse*, 98ff.

116. The first sentence of Albertus' *Determinatio*, typical of the character of the whole as a theological evaluation, reads: *Conventicula facere et in secreto docere, contra fidem non est, sed contra modum evangelicum, ubi dicitur: ego semper palam docui (in synagoga et in templo et) ubi omnes Judei conveniunt, et in abscondito locutus sum nihil,* [John 18:20; Matthew 10:27] *quod in aure auditis, predicabitur etc.*

117. The Lateran Council of 1215, § 16, *De inumentis clericorum* (Mansi, *Sacrorum conciliorum* 22.1006) specifies for clerical clothing: *Pannis rubeis aut viridibus . . . non utantur*. At the Chapter General of the Dominicans in Florence, 1257, the habits of *conversi* should be *similis coloris capis clericorum*, *MOPH* 3.84; Reichert remarks on this (referring to Humbert de Romanis, *Opera de vita regulari*, ed. J. J. Berthier, 2.5) the habits of clerics of the order were then not yet uniform, *sed alius cappa nigra indui consueverat, alius rufa, alius grisea*. William of St. Amour says in his sermon (*Opera*, p. 501): *Cum aliquis clericus cum cappa rubea et foraminata vel cappa manicata inciperet vobis predicare aliqua nova, non de facili crederetur; sed si haberet cappam clausam sicut presbyter, magis crederetur sibi*. The monks of the "last order" seen by Mechthild of Magdeburg in her vision of the last days wear red cloaks (IV, 27, ed. Morell, 121).

118. Heinz Otto Burger, *Schwabentum in der Geistesgeschichte* (Stuttgart, 1933), 49, concerning the Ries heresy, he believes that the "quite exceptional

richness of religious life'' in the Ries can be explained by the ''effect of the blood of pre-Germanic residents'' (''Celto-Roman and perhaps also Ostian-Alpine remnants of population''). Albert Hauck, *KD* 4.309, speaks in poetic terms of the adherents of the ''clever mysticism of the nameless Ries master'' ''in the young little towns and old villages of that peculiar countryside,'' calls the man he believed responsible for Albertus' evaluation a ''thoughtful Swabian.'' At the end of the narrative on the heresy in the Ries, he asserts in general terms (p. 910) that heresy in the thirteenth century ''only moved the laity,'' and that the participation of priests and scholars was a rarity; this explains the unclarity of heretical doctrines, their lack of solid formulas and consistent structure. All of this is imprecise, overlooking the entire religious layer between ''priests'' and ''lay''; incidentally, all of the condemned Amaurians were clerics!

118a. Cf. K. Weller, ''Die Nibelungenstrasse,'' *ZDA* 70 (1933), 49ff., idem, ''Die Hauptverhehrsstrasse zwischen dem westl. und südl. Europa,'' *Württembergische Vergangenheit, Festschrift,* 1932.

119. In Albertus' *Determinatio*, propositions 4 and 34 on the oath to prayer; 9 and 41 on confession; 25, 44, and 50 on fasting and prayer; 15, 56, 22 and 39, 28 and 49, 45 and 62, 60 and 75; other statements are obviously in response to one and the same question. It does not appear possible to me to divide up the individual hearings and determine their number; it seems the same series of questions was posed to each. Many sentences read like the openings of investigations: 10, *dicitur quod familiaris fuerit suspectus et heresi infectis;* 35, *dicitur ne secreta verba alis publicentur;* 71, *non audet dicere id quod reputat malum apud hereticos*. But we do not know whether Albertus has preserved the original sequence of hearings in his own evaluation. Most frequently repeated are propositions about becoming God, 13/14, 25 and 27, 30, 36/37, 56, 58, 74. H. Haupt, *ZKG* 7.507–08, saw that it dealt with several hearings. It is incomprehensible how Albert Hauck, *KD* 4.909, can say: ''It seems to be the investigation of a single man, who had obviously achieved success in conventicles.'' In fact it is more certainly an investigation of several women. The twenty-nine articles *de novo spiritu* are also not a single hearing, since many propositions are literally repeated, cf. 108 and 115, 117 and 119 in the enumeration by Preger, *Mystik* 1.469; also 120 and the following sentence (which is missing in Preger).

In what follows, Albertus' evaluation is designated I, the twenty-nine articles as II, and the theses of II are numbered separately.

120. II, 28: *dicunt se carnaliter cognosci a Christo*; in another version: *quod pollunt se corpore Christi;* I, 90: *quod aliqua lactet puerum Jhesum cum matre usque ad lassitudinem et defectum*; I, 13: *dicere quod mulier facta sit deus*; I, 97: *quod mater quinque puerorum virgo possit esse*. Also propositions I, 31 and I, 74, which measure the perfection of people with that of the Virgin Mary, can be seen as expressions of women.

121. The participation of men in the heresy emerges clearly from many propositions (I, 53, *solutus et soluta*; I, 81, *viri et mulieres soluti*) and the moral teaching of the heretics assume that.

122. *Fliessende Licht*, II, 23, ed. Morell, 45; VI, 1, 175: . . . *mit voller maht in dem bette der minne trutet, der au der minnelustigen sele in das notlich brutbette wil gan . . . uf das er si möhte durküssen und mit sinen blossen armen umbevahen*. Cf. G. Luers, *Die Sprache der deutschen Mystik*, 50, 52–53, 47–48. Similar application of the bed of love and *brutloft*, the *minnekliche umbehalsunge* and the *mit armen umbevangen*, etc., are found throughout *Fliessende Licht*, cf. for example, I, 3, 4, 5, 8, 14, 19, 22, 44; II, 6, 15, 23, 26; III, 1, 2, 5, 9, 10 and so on.

123. *Fliessende Licht*, I, 44, Morell, 21: *ich bin ein vollewachsen brut, ich wil gan nach minem trut.*

124. David of Augsburg, *De exterioris et interioris hominis compositione* (Quaracchi, 1899), III, 66, p. 359: *non videtur autem pretereundum, quod quidam, decepti a seductoribus spiritibus vel propriis falsis opinionibus putant sibi apparere in visione vel ipsum Christum vel eius gloriosissimam genitricem et non solum applexibus et osculis, sed etiam indecentioribus gestibus et actibus ab eis demulceri etc.;* cf. Emil Michael, *Geschichte des deutschen Volkes*, 3 (Freiburg i. B., 1906), 142. Cf. also the narrative of Philip of Montirail (in Thomas of Chantimpré, *Bonum universale de apibus* [Douai, 1627], II, 38, no. 2) on the Beguine who had long foregone the *sensibilis Sponsi visitatio* and hence was anxious and nervous, until in the end Faith, Hope, and Charity sent to the *Sponsus* with the request that he once more send his *inestimabilis et durabilis consolacio.*

125. Chronicle of Anna von Munzingen, *FDA* 13.154–55: *das si kam zu dem kusse* . . . Cf. also Cæsarius, *Dialogus miraculorum*, VIII, 16; Birlinger, *Alemannia* 11.19; E. Schiller, *Das mystische Leben der Ordensschwestern zu Töss*, Dissertation, Bern, 1903, 59.

126. *Die Offenbarungen der Adelheid Langmann*, ed. Strauch, 93, 21; 93, 14; 67, 29: *ein weil nit mangeln ab dem gemahilpettlein . . . umving si und druket si an sein gotlich hertz, daz sue dauht si klebot in im als ain wahs in ainem insigel.*

127. In response to the report of Merin in Kirchberg, the nuns' book (see Roth, *Alemannia* 21.106) that she *gar zertlich mit unserm herrn koset;* cf. ibid., 118–19, on Mechthild of Waldeck, who entered Kirchberg at the age of eight (died 1305), and particularly Margarethe Ebner in her correspondence with Henry of Nördlingen, ed. Ph. Strauch, 69–70.

128. I, 90: *Dicere quod aliqua lactet puerum Jesum cum matre usque ad lassitudinem et defectum, fatuitas est verberibus potius quam verbis corrigenda.*

129. Cf. also Mechthild, *Fliessende Licht*, I, 17 (ed. Morell, 10): *o du ruwender got an minen brust.*

130. Cf., for example, on Sister Willbirch of Offeningen in Kirchberg, Roth, *Alemannia* 21.113; on the Cistercian nun Lukardis in *AB* 18 (1899), 195; on the Beguine Agnes Blanbekin in Vienna, Bernardus Pez, *Agnetis Blanbekin Vita et Revelationes* (Vienna, 1731), 244; Joseph Chmel, *S.-B. Wien* 2.89, c. 195; on Anna of Ramsweg in Diessenhofen-Katharinenthal, Birlinger, *Alemannia*

15.176; on Sister Wila and Heiltraut of Bernhausen in Weil, see the "Nonnenbuch von Weil," ed. Bihlmeyer, 72, 74; on the Beguine Gertrud von Osten, see Ludwig Zoepf, *Die Mystikerin Margarete Ebner* (Leipzig; Berlin, 1914), 125; On the entire phenomenon of the *imitatio Mariæ, see Grete Lüers, Marienverehrung mittelalterlichen Nonnen* (Munich, 1923), 28. Even Margarethe Ebner (c. 1291–1351) said she had often suckled Jesus (*Margaretha Ebner und Heinrich von Nördlingen. Ein Beitrag zur Geschichte der Deutschen Mystik*, ed. Ph. Strauch (Freiburg i.B; Tübingen, 1882), 87 and 90; cf. 120, 122, 127, 129), and she also feels herself embraced and kissed by the Christ child (p. 91; cf. Zoepf, *Die Mystikerin*, and O. Pfister, "Hysterie und Mystik bei Margarethe Ebner," *Zentralblatt für Psychoanalyse* 1 [1911], 468ff.)

131. I, 14: *homo potest fieri deus*, I, 56: *homo potest fieri deus cum deo et ipsum penetrare*; I, 36: *homo secundum voluntatem fit deus*; I, 25: *anima unita dei deificatur*; I, 27: *homo potest fieri equalis deo vel anima fieri divina*; I, 13: *mulier facta est deus*; I, 30: *aliquis prefertur* [*Christo?*] *et deo equatur.*

132. Cf., for example, "Nonnenbuch von Kirchberg," ed. Roth, *Alemannia* 21.106, 118; *Nonnenbuch von Weil*, ed. Bihlmeyer, 71–72: *in diser genad kom ir sel in sölch vereinunge und nissen gotez, daz sie sprach, daz sie nie höher noch got neher köm;* 72: . . . *da vereinet sich got alz gar mit ir, daz sie recht darfüllet ward mit götlicher süssigkeit*, 69: *"ich bin gotz vol."* "Nonnenbuch von Adelhausen," *FDA* 13.160: *"alles das an mir ist, das ist got"*; cf. also p. 165; "Nonnenbuch von Katharinenthal," *Alemannia* 15.178.

133. Particularly surprising in the nuns' book of Kirchberg, ed. Roth, *Alemannia* 21.103ff., where an entire system of individual acts of grace is listed, the *Gnade Jubilus*, the *genad contemplationis*, etc.; similarly in the sisters' book of Unterlinden, *Vitæ sororum*, ed. Jeanne Ancelet-Hustache, *AHDL* 5 (1930), 340, 347, 439, 462, 467, etc., the ever repeated "graces" (*gratia consolationis, consolationes*, etc.). Cf. the warning of Lamprecht of Regensburg against overestimating every single little "grace," *Sanct Franciscken Leben und Tochter Syon*, 437.

134. I, 2; in contrast, of another heretic it is said: *quod aliquam receperit gratiam maiorem quam homo habuerit vel habiturus sit* (I, 86), but it is not said of what these acts of grace consist. Another statement (I, 37) avoids the question through a moral interpretation of deificatio: *Cum corpore fit deus bonus homo, si intelligitur per equalitatem sanctitatis.*

135. Cf. II, 21: *boni homines non debent viris literatis revelare bonitatem suam et gratiam quam habent;* II, 25: *Quod peccata cum dolore non recogitentur, quia per hoc gratia retardatur!* Cf. the previous note.

136. *Fliessende Licht*, I, 44, ed. Morell, 22; ed. Schleussner, 144: *Frow sele, ir sint so sere genaturt in mich, das zwischent uch und mir nihtes nit mag sin.* In the Latin translation of *Fliessende Licht*, these passages are always cleansed dogmatically through slight changes; so it says here: *per unionem naturarum ineffabilis gratia nos conjunxit*, see *Revelationes*, 2, 551; cf. Grete Lüers, *Die Sprache der deutschen Mystik*, 49–50. In the excerpts of *Fliessende Licht* in the

Würzburg ms. which W. Schleussner published, "virtually everything personal about Mechthild," as well as "everything historical, particularly everything said about the Dominicans" is left out (see p. iv), besides most of the excerpts which have interested us here.

137. *Fliessende Licht*, VI, 1, ed. Morell, 174: *mit got ein got, also das er wil das wil si, und si mögent anders nit vereinet sin mit ganzer einunge*; in the translation (2, 611): *fitque una cum deo, et hec est vera unio, conformitas voluntatum.*

138. VI, 1, p. 174: *ein götlich got mit dem himelschen vatter;* in the translation: *efficatur membrum Christi*; cf. G. Lüers, *Die Sprache der deutschen Mystik*, 52.

138a. *Ich sprach an einer stat in diseme buche, das die gotheit min vatter ist von nature; das verneme du nit und spreche: Alles das got mit uns hat getan, das ist alles von gnaden und nit von nature. Du hast war und ich han och war.*

139. VI, 31, ed. Morell, p. 205: *sich allermeist mit ir vereinet under allen creaturen; er hat si in sich beschlossen und hat siner götlichen nature so vil (in si) gegossen, das sie anders nit gesprechen mag, denne das er mit aller einunge me denne ir vatter ist;* cf. on this the comment of Wilhelm Oehl, *Deutsche Mystiker* 2 (1911), 197; also Meister Eckhart, *Reden der Unterscheidung*, ed. Ernst Diedrichs (Bonn, 1913), 44.

140. I, 17: *non debet queri consilium a viris litteratis sive de devotione sive de aliis;* II, 21: *quod boni homines non debent viris litteratis revelare bonitatem suam et gratiam, quam habent, quia nesciunt litterati, quid sit, nec cognoverunt nisi per pellem vitulinam, ipsi vero sugunt ex deitate (divinitate).*

141. I, 73: *Melius est hominem unum ad talem perfectionem ducere quam centum claustra constituere.*

142. I, 76: *omnis creatura est deus*; II, 7: *omnis creatura plene est deus*; I, 7: *anima est sumpta de substantia dei*; I, 96: *anima est de substantia dei*; I, 95: *anima est eterna cum deo*; cf. also I, 77: *homo deus est et ideo non est tangendum* (certainly referring to Psalms 104:15: *Nolite tangere Christos meos*).

143. I, 76: *Dicere quod omnis creatura sit deus heresis Alexandri est, qui dixit materiam primam et deum et noym, hoc est mentem divinam in substancia idem esse; quem postea quidam David de Dinanto secutus est, qui temporibus nostris pro hac heresi de Francia fugatus est et punitus fuisset, si deprehensus fuisset.*

144. Cf. Gabriel Théry, *Autour du décret de 1210 I: David de Dinant, Étude sur son panthéisme matérialiste. II: Alexandre d'Aphrodise, Aperçu sur l'influence de sa noétique*, Bibliothéque Thomiste, 6/7 (Paris, 1925/6).

145. I, 59: *Christus non doluit in passione*; II, 2: *quod nullo modo sit credendum Christum in passione fuisse* [*di*]*laceratum* [or: *vulneratum*] *vel quicquam doluisse*; I, 91: *dicunt Christum non laniatum fuisse in passione.* On the corresponding Christology of the Cathars, see Guiraud, *Car-*

tulaire 1.lxii; Douais, *La somme des autorités*, 130; Schmidt, *Histoire et doctrine* 2.31ff.; Broeckx, *Le Catharisme*, 82ff. But even among the Amaurians there were indications of similar doctrines, see above, n. 28, which agrees particularly with the proposition I, 47: *divinitas separata est a corpore Christi.*

146. I, 60: *Angeli non sunt lapsi a celo*; I, 75: *angelus non cecidisset, si bona intentione fecisset quod fecit*; II, 8: *Quod angeli non cecedissent, si debito modo in conspiratione cum Lucifero perstetissent* [or: *processissent*].

147. I, 46: *purgatorium et infernum non esse*; II, 6: *quod infernus nullatenus sit.*

148. I, 45: *nec angelus est nec demon*; I, 62: *angelos non esse nisi virtutes et demones non esse nisi vicia*; II, 5: *quod angeli nihil aliud sunt nisi virtutes hominum; quod non sint demones nisi vicia (et peccata) hominum*; Cf. above, n. 24ff., on the Amaurians, and Guiraud, *Cartulaire* 1.lxv–lxvi; Douais, *Somme des autorités*, 127, 132 on the Cathars.

149. I, 40: *resurrectio non est futura*; II, 12: *quod non sit resurrectio (credenda)*; I, 48: *Christus non resurrexit.*

150. This conception of a "sect of the free spirit," first appearing among the Amaurians in Paris in 1210, soon after as the Ortlieber in Strasbourg, continually reappearing despite persecution and pursuing the goal "to win ground with the people as well, to form a special religious community," finally spreading their propaganda in the Swabian Ries, has dominated all earlier research, see Preger, *Mystik* 1.213; Hermann Reuter, *Geschichte der religiösen Aufklärung*, 2 vols. (Berlin, 1875–77) 2.240ff.; Auguste Jundt, *Histoire du panthéisme populaire au moyen âge et au XVIe siècle* (Paris, 1875); Heinrich Joseph Wetzer and Benedikt Welte, eds., *Kirchen-Lexikon* 2.1339ff.; Bihlmeyer, *Kirchengeschichte* 2.221 and others. Only Hermann Haupt saw the situation more correctly, as early as 1897, *PRE*, 3d ed., 3.467ff.

151. I, 78: *Homo debet abstinere ab exterioribus et sequi responsa spiritus intra se*; I, 33: *hoc non loquor ego sed spiritus in spirito*; I, 5: *quod alicui responderit omnium spiritum veritas* [Albertus remarks: *presumptionis magis et fatuitatis verbum est quam heresis*]; II, 27: *quod libertas quies et commodum faciunt locum spiritui sancto in homine*; I do not understand the proposition I, 57: *spiritus sanctus est negotiator*; that means: *spiritum sanctum esse servum vel ministrum*, says Albertus, explaining it as the *heresis Nestoris.*

152. I, 15: *Homo ad talem statum potest pervenire, quod deus in ipso omnia operetur*; I, 56: *ad hoc pervenit homo, quod deus per eum omnia operetur*; I, 66: *quidquid faciunt homines, ex dei ordinatione faciunt.* The first two sentences were declared Pelagian by Albertus; on the latter, which does not restrict the omnipotence of God to the perfect person, but declares it in general for all people, he says: *heresis est eorum, qui dicunt omnia provenire ex necessitate et nihil ex permissione divina, et est error cuiusdam Alexandri*—he refers once more to the Aristotelian Alexander of Aphrodisias, of whom, as he says elsewhere, David of Dinant was a disciple.

153. I, 59: *homo equatur patri et transcendit filium*. I, 58: *homo potest fieri altior filio dei*.

154. I, 51: *sanguis boni hominis venerandus est ut sanguis Christi*; II, 26: *quod sanguis boni hominis vel (alia) superfluitas (corporis sui) sicut sanguis Christi est tractandus* [or: *ita reverenter sit tractanda sicut corpus Christi*]; I, 65: *non oportet inclinari corpori Christi, eo quod homo deus est*; I, 28: *homo unitus deo est venerandus ut Christi corpus*; II, 32: *quod ita deo sunt uniti, quod sanguis eorum sit totum sicut sanguis Christi*.

155. I, 29: *aliquis dicit se deum in deum recipere, quando recipit sacramentum altaris*; I, 42: *homo elevatur cum corpore domini in altari*; II, 14: *dicunt se elevari cum corpore domini in missa, nec surgunt nec flectunt genua (ob reverentiam dei), quando elevatur vel portatur, nisi tantum propter homines ne scandalizentur*; II, 36, the same thesis with different motivation: *non est assurgendum corpori domini, quia deus ubiquitus est*.

156. I, 67: *non est memorandum passio Christi domini*; II, 24: *quod (boni homini est) qui volunt adipisci veram bonitatem non* [or: *nunquam*] *debent cogitare de passione domini* [or: *Christi*].

157. I, 23: *Anima alicuius etiam facientis eadem cum Christo equatur anime Christi*.

158. *Fliessende Licht*, VI, 4, ed. Morell, 180: *ein jeglich mensch sölte wesen an im selben ein christus;* in the translation the point of these words is blunted: *verum omnis homo deberet esse Christi*, see *Revelationes* 2.638.

159. I, 22: *dicit aliquis ad hoc posse devenire, quod sanctos non oporteat revereri*; I, 39: *homo unitus deo non habet sanctos revereri*; II, 1: *quod quilibet homo, quantumcumque peccaverit, possit in uno anno precellere dignitatem et meritum sancti Nicolai et Pauli et sancte Marie Magdalene et sancti Johannis baptiste et cuiuslibet sancti vel etiam genetricis dei vel etiam ipsum Christum Jesum*; II, 9: *quod homo unitus deo non deferat sanctis (honorem vel) reverentiam*.

160. I, 31: *homo in devotione potest precellere beatam virginem*; I, 93: *beata virgo digne inclinet homini*; I, 70: *parvum est beate virginis meritum, eo quod homo super deum potest ascendere*; I, 74: *homo potest transcendere beate virginis meritum et fieri deus et deo non indigere*.

161. The statements on this are once again not entirely consistent. I, 44: *Deo unitus non debet jejunare vel orare*; I, 41: *Homo unitus deo non debet confiteri etiam peccatum mortale;* on the contrary, in I, 9: *Confessio venialium non est necessaria*; I, 16: *Homo tantum proficit, quod sacerdote non indigeat*; I, 64: *Peccata non debent confiteri sacerdoti*; I, 20: *jejuniis et orationibus non est insistendum*; on the contrary I, 3: *viginti paternoster prevalent misse sacerdotis*; I, 89: *orationes cedunt bonis et non peccatoribus*; cf, II, 17, n. 170 below; I, 52: *licite comedantur tempore jejunii prohibita ab ecclesia sicut caseus et ova*; but II, 10 only says: *quod diem diei non preferunt in jejunio* [or: *in jejuniorum observantiis*], *quia unus dies sicut alter*; cf. II, 19: *quod absque pavore et sine peccato in secreto comedunt quotiescumque volunt et quidquid volunt si habent*; also I, 38: *dicit se non comedisse cum*

comedit, and I, 49: *Homine comedente deus comedit*, certainly relating to fasts, but unclearly. Somewhat varying from this on confession, II, 13: *Quod bonum hominem non oportet peccata quantumcumque gravia nisi alteri bono confiteri, sed dicant in corde: Ego peccavi*; and II, 20: *Quod non sit necesse narrare in confessione circumstancias* [or: *gestus*] *peccatorum, sed sufficit dicere: Ego peccavi.*

162. I, 50: *Orationes, jejunia, confessiones peccatorum impediunt bonum hominem*; I, 79: *Confessio impedit perfectum*; II, 15: *Quod homines impediant (et retardent) bonitatem suam per orationes suas et jejunia, flagella (et vigilias) et alia quecumque bona opera*. Cf. also I, 4: *Promisse orationes non debent solvi*; I, 34 is similar.

163. I, 63: *Hoc quod fit sub cingulo a bonis non est peccatum*; cf. on this Peter of Vaux-Cernay, ''Historia Albigensis,'' ed. Achille Luchaire, *BFL* 24 (1908), c. 2 (p. 10); Charles Molinier, ''L'église et la société cathare,'' *RH* 95.3–4: *Non credimus autem silendum quod et quidam heretici dicebant, quod nullus peccare poterat ab umbilico et inferius*; Schmidt, *Histoire des Cathares* 2.152. I, 53: *soluta conubendo cum soluto non plus peccant quam admittendo matrimonialiter conjunctum*; Albertus Magnus describes this proposition as Manichee; further I, 81: *oscula virorum et mulierum solutorum non sunt peccatum*; cf. on this the proposition of the Averroîsts condemned in Paris in 1277: *Quod simplex fornicatio utpote soluti cum soluta non est peccatum* (Pierre Mandonnet, *Siger de Brabant et l'Averrosïme latin au XIIIe siècle* [Louvain, 1908–11] 2.19, no. 205); at the same time the proposition was also condemned: *Quod non est orandum; quod non est confitendum nisi ad apparentiam.*

164. II, 11: *Quod unitus deo possit (audacter) explere libidinem carnis per quemque modum licite (et religiosus in utroque sexu sine omni peccato).* Some sentences which speak of the permissibility of perjury and theft appear to me only understandable as responses to questions intended to entrap, which sought to draw the consequences from the principle of ''sinlessness''; I, 69: *Bono homini non est peccatum periurare et mentiri*; I, 43: *Homo unitus deo licite potest tollere re alienum*; cf. I, 92 and II, 18.

165. I, 87: *Non est cogitandum de peccatis commissis*; II, 25: *Quod peccata commissa cum dolore non recognitentur [or: nunquam debent cum dolore recogitare nec dies elapsi in vanitate], quia per hoc (per hance amaritudinem) gratia magis retardatur.*

166. I, 80: *Homo translatus in deum et peccans mortaliter ex peccato adminiculum habet ad deum, si per se intelligitur.*

167. I, 94: *Homo in vita sic proficere potest, ut impeccabilis fiat*; I, 21: *Aliquis pervenit ad hoc, quod non possit peccare*; I, 24: *Homo unitus deo peccare non potest*; II, 4: *Quod homo possit ita uniri deo, quod quidquid de cetero faciat, non peccat.*

168. I, 55: *Peccatum non est peccatum*; I, 6: *Homo facit mortalis peccati actum sine peccato*; cf. also I, 94: *Ita deificitur de salute aliquis, quod peccata ei nocere non possint; I, 61: Nihil est peccatum nisi quod reputatur peccatum.*

169. See n. 70 above.

170. II, 66: *Quod boni homines non debent insistere laboribus, sed vacare et videre quam bonus et suavis est dominus*; cf. II, 17: *Quod orationes non valent que fiunt infra opera hominum.*

171. I, 85: *(Dicunt) . . . virtutibus non provehi nec peccatis impediri.*

172. II, 22: *Quod homo de malo tantum gaudeat quantum de bono (et de omni quod acciderit ei), quia deus ita preordinavit*; II, 23: *Quod boni homines non (timeant nec) doleant, si incidant in peccata qualicumque, quia deus sic preordinavit, nec talis preordinatio decebat impediri* [or: *et quia predestinationem nullus debet impedire*]; II, 35: *Quod non sit orandum pro serenitate vel aliis, que deus sic preordinavit*; I, 68: *de morte patris et matris non est dolendum nec pro animabus eorum orandum*; I, 8: *non debent suffragia fieri pro animabus determinatarum personarum, sed illis, quibus deus cupit.*

173. I will only refer to a few passages: Meister Eckhardt, *Reden der Unterscheidung*, ed. E. Diederichs, 20: *Ja, der recht wer geseczt in den willen gotz, der solt nit wöllen, sie sünd, da er ingevallen was, daz des nit gebetten, sol nit sin weder: "gib mir die tugent oder die wise" oder: "ja, herre, gib mir dich selber oder ewigs leben," dann: "herre, gib nit, dann das du wiltt, und tu, herre, was und wie du wilt in aller wise." Buch der göttlichen Tröstung und von dem edlen Meuschen*, ed. Ph. Strauch (Bonn, 1922), 14: *Ein sogetaner mensch ist so ein unt einwillig mit got, das er alles das wil das got wil unt in der wise so es got wil, unt darumb, wann got denn etliche wise wil, das ich ouch sünde han getan, so woelt ich nit, das ich si nit hetti getan, wann so wort gottes wille in der erden, das ist in missetat, als in dem himele, das ist in woltunne*. Cf. the fourteenth proposition of John XXII's bull on Eckhart, 29 March 1329, *ALKG* 2.636.

174. I, 74: *Homo potest fieri deus et deo non indigere*; I, 11: *aliquis venit ad hoc, quod deo non indigeat*; I, 19: *Homo non est bonus nisi dimittat deum propter deum*; I, 70: *Quod homo super deum possit ascendere*; II, 30: *Quod sunt in apice divinitatis*; I, 72: *Ei, qui admittitur ad amplexus divinitatis, datur potestas faciendi quod vult.*

175. Cf. Meister Eckhart, *Buch der göttlichen Tröstung*, ed. Strauch, 14–15, 25; *Reden der Unterscheidung*, 18: *Es ist kein rat als gut, got ze finden, dann wa man got last*; ibid., 42; Franz Pfeiffer, *Deutsche Mystiker des 14. Jahrhunderts*, 1 (Göttingen, 1845) 2.310: *Daz hoehste unde daz nehste daz der mensche gelazen mac, daz ist, daz er got dur got laze*; ibid., 283 and Josef Quint, *Deutsche Mystikertexte des Mitlelalters* (Bonn, 1929) 1.37. Cf. all of the sermon attributed to Meister Eckhart in A. Jundt, *Histoire du panthëisme populaire*, 275ff.: the spiritually poor *habent nit allein gegeben fründen und mage, ere, leib, sele und guot, me si sind zemal ledig aller guoter wercke, si haltent weder boesz noch guotes, wann das ewig Wort das würcket die werck; die göttlich Armen sind nit allein ir selbes ledige, me si sind och gotes ledige und sind sein als recht ledige, das er chain stat vindet in in, da er würcken muege. . . . Hie sind alle menschen ain mensch und derselb mensch ist Christus.*

176. This is the opinion of Gustave Théry, *Contribution à l'histoire du procès du maître Eckhart* (Paris, 1926), even if he conceives all of Eckhart's mystical cleverness as exaggerations of scholastic doctrines; in the same way, H. Denifle, *"Meister Eckharts lateinsche Schriften,"* 417ff., who interprets Eckhart's mysticism as a misunderstanding of the scholastic doctrine of being. Both views can be confuted by saying that similar mystic ideas were already current in religious circles where dialectical exaggeration and scholastic misunderstandings played no role.

177. Probably in Latin, since it is never mentioned as being written in another language; later chroniclers asserted that they also translated the Holy Scriptures, see chapter 8 below, n. 67.

178. See the protocol of the inquisitorial judgment of *Margarita de Hannonia dicta Porete* and the evaluation of the Paris canonists on 30 May 1310 in Fredericq, *Corpus* 1.156ff.; in the evaluation, she is called a *Beguina* and she is accused of having given her book after the first condemnation *pluribus aliis personis simplicibus, Begardis et aliis* to read.

179. See the evaluation of the Paris theologians on 31 April in Fredericq, *Corpus* 2.63; the inquisitor presented the theologians with excerpts from Margarete's book, of which the evaluation only presents two, the first: *Quod anima adnichilata dat licentiam virtutibus nec est amplius in earum servitute, quia non habet eas quoad usum, sed virtutes obediunt ad nutum*; and the fifteenth point: *Quod talis anima non curat de consolationibus dei nec de donis eius, nec debet curare nec potest, quia tota intenta est circa deum, et sic impediretur eius intentio circa deum.*

180. Continuation of the chronicle of William of Nangis, Fredericq, *Corpus* 1.160: *Quod anima annihilata in amore conditoris sine reprehensione consciencie vel remorsu potest et debet nature quidquid appetit et desiderat concedere.*

181. Johannes Nider, *Formicarius*, III, 5, ed. Colvener, 214: *Repperi in libro manuali, quem pro sua persona per totum dominus Albertus manu conscipsit propria, se eadem annotasse, videlicet quod suo tempore in Colonia fuit eadem heresis.*

182. *Annales Colmarienses, MG Scr.* 17.217, for 1290: *Lector fratrum minorum de Basilea fecit capi in Columbaria in capitulo suo duas beginas et duos begardos et in Basilea plures, quos hereticos reputabat.*

183. *Annales Colmarienses,* ibid., 227 on the provincial chapter of the Dominicans in Basel in September, 1302: *In hoc capitulo fuerunt conversi seu beghardi seu fratres non habentes domicilia LXXX in una processione mendicantes cibaria;* there were supposed to be 570 (or 500, according to the edition of the Colmar Annals by Gérard-Liblin, 1854, 190) brothers at the chapter, an improbably high number; cf. G. R. Galbraith, *The Constitution of the Dominican Order* (Manchester, 1925), 62ff. On the Minorite chapter in Colmar in May 1303, the Colmar chronicler says: *Comparuere illic centum quinquaginta fratres; conversi seu begihardi XXX bini et terni in processione per Columbariam transeuntes elymosinam mendicabant*; this is pp.

196–97 in the edition of Gérard-Liblin and Heinrich Böhmer, *Fontes rerum Germanicarum* 2.40–41; from the same ms. Jaffé reads the number 300 rather than XXX, *MG Scr.* 17.228; that is probably an error.

184. Cf. G. Bihl, *AFH* 9.169. The general chapter of the Dominicans in Bologna, 1302 (*MOPH* 3.315) expressly warned *ne studentes in generalibus studiis se occupent in beguinariis aut familiaritatibus notabilibus mulierum.*

185. The statute in Mosheim, *De beghardis*, 211ff.; Hartzheim, *Concilia Germaniæ* 4.100ff.; Fredericq, *Corpus* 1.150ff. Cf. also J. Asen, *Annalen*, 111, 105–06.

186. Because of these words and the later demand of the statute: *Quatenus infra unius mensis spatium habitu huiusmodi assumpto dimisso resumptoque priori ad genus vivendi pristinum revertantur, manibus vite necessaria justis (ut solebant) laboribus acquirentes*, it was always believed that these beghards were to be regarded as "artisans and day-workers." This is not tenable. It means, rather, that beghards and beguines were no longer to live from begging but from crafts, as was the case with all regulated houses of beguines and beghards.

187. *Eorum aliqui, laici litteras nescientes, Prædicatoribus et Minoribus in sermonibus eorum et predicationibus publicis non sine vehementi suspicione pravitatis heretice publice restiterunt.*

188. *De quibus aliqui a veritatis et fidei orthodoxe comperti sunt tramite deviare et errores et zizania seminare. . . . Mendaciter enim et falso dicunt: Qui non sequitur me, non potest salvari, quia non soleo peccare, se ex hoc divinitati similes mentientes; . . . justos se esse et sine peccato jactantes; . . . forte dicunt: Qui spiritu dei aguntur, non sunt sub lege; . . . dicunt quod hoc celitus sit eis revelatum.* Then there is a thesis from the views of the religious women's movement: *Aiunt etiam, nisi mulier virginitatem in matrimonium deperditam doleat et dolendo deploret, salvari non potest; . . . Horum etiam aliqui dicunt, quod quilibet habens uxorem legitimam, causa sequendi deum propria voluntate eam invita ea possit dimittere.* Beyond that, they are accused of the same doctrine as the heretics in the Ries: *simplicem fornicationem non esse peccatum* (see above, n. 163). I do not understand the sentence: *blasphemant deum fore in quadam perditione.*

189. Hartzheim, *Concilia Germaniæ* 4.200–01. To date this, cf. Finke, *Konzilienstudien*, 38–39; at the same synod, earlier beguine ordinances of the Mainz province (see above, chapter 6, n. 23) were repeated, directing them to join the beguines working and living in houses.

190. Clementines, III, tit. 11, c. 1, "Cum de quibusdam," *Corpus iuris canonici*, ed. Aemilius Friedberg [Leipzig, 1879], vol. 2, col. 1169; Mosheim, *De beghardis*, 621–22; Fredericq, *Corpus* 1.167–68. The conclusion reads: *Sane per predicta prohibere nequaquam intendimus, quin si fuerint fideles alique mulieres, que promissa continentia vel etiam non promissa honeste in suis conversantes hospitiis penitentiam agere voluerint et virtutum domino in humilitatis spiritu deservire, hoc eisdem liceat prout dominus ipsis inspirabit.*

191. Clementines, V, tit. 3, c. 3, "Ad nostrum," *Corpus iuris canonici*, ed. Friedberg, vol. 2, cols. 1183–84; Mosheim, *De beghardis*, 618; Fredericq, *Corpus* 1.168–69. Cf. Ewald Müller, *Das Konzil von Vienne* 1311/12, Vorreformationsgeschichtliche Forshungen 12 (Münster i.W., 1934), 577ff.

Chapter 8

1. Cf. C. Schmidt, "Über das Predigen in den Landessprachen," *Theologische Studien und Kritik* 19 (1846), 243ff.; R. Cruel, *Geschichte der deutschen Predigt im Mittelalter* (Detmold, 1879), 217; Anton Linsenmayer, *Geschichte der Predigt in Deutschland* (Munich, 1886), 10, 14, 36ff.; A. Lecoy de la Marche, *La chaire française au Moyen Age*, 233ff.; Louis Bourgain, *La chaire française au XIIe siècle* (Paris, 1879), 169ff. [Cf. also K. Boeckl, "Die Bedingtheiten der deutschen Mystik des Mittelalters," in Albert Lang et al., eds., *Aus der Geisteswelt des Mittelalters. Studien und Texte, Martin Grabmann . . . gewidmet* (Münster i. W., 1935), 1011–120. HG/1960.]

2. See the Latin preface to the German sermon collection of the priest Conrad, the sole author of such a collection from the twelfth century to be known by name, in J. Schmidt, 9. *Jahresbericht der k. k. Staatsgymnasium im 3. Bezirk in Wien* (Vienna, 1818), 1ff.; Linsenmayer, *Geschichte der Predigt*, 286, 53ff. and 245ff. The oldest source for such a collection is the note in the manuscript collection of S. Emmeram in Regensburg from the tenth century: *Sermones ad populum teutonice*, see Naumann, *Serapeum* (1841), 261.

3. Prayer book of Muri from the twelfth century, see Friedrich Wilhelm, *Denkmäler deutscher Prosa des 11. und 12. Jahrhunderts* (Munich, 1914ff.), no. xxix, 73ff., commentary 161–62; see also no. xxviii, xxx, xxxii, 69ff., 87ff., and 96ff., commentary 157ff., 179, 191. Otherwise most of the prayers in German from the twelfth century are for pious women and nuns, see Gustav Ehrismann, *Geschichte der deutschen Literatur bis zum Ausgang des Mittelalters*, Handbuch des deutschen Unterrichts an höheren Schulen 6 (Munich, 1918ff.), 2/1, 169ff.

4. Cf. on the following the survey by Helga Hajdu, *Lesen und Schreiben im Spätmittelalter* (Fünfkirchen, Romania, 1931), as well as my own essay, "Die Frauen und die Literatur im Mittelalter," *AKG* 26 (1936).

5. Friedrich Kropatscheck, *Das Schriftprinzip der lutherischen Kirche*, 1: *Die Vorgeschichte. Das Erbe des Mittelalters* (Leipzig, 1904), 152–53, 26ff; Müller, *Die Waldenser*, 77ff. The presence of biblical translations among the Cathars in the twelfth century cannot be derived from the fact that a papal legate mocked their faulty mastery of Latin after a disputation with heretics (Roger of Hoveden), although they were well-versed in the Bible; Henry Charles Lea, *Geschichte der Inquisition im Mittelalter*, ed. Joseph Hansen (Bonn, 1905–13) 1.112.

6. Schmidt, *Histoire et doctrine*, 2.127ff.; Döllinger, *Beiträge* 2.2, 5, 28, 34, 37ff.; Guiraud, *Cartulaire* 1.cxx; Douais, "Les hérétiques," 158ff. Berthold of Regensburg accuses the heretics of not being able to read, but

knowing everything by heart, see Schönbach, *Studien zur Geschichte*, 43; 93ff., for corresponding citations from Ermendardus, *Contra Catharos*. All of these sources derive from the thirteenth century. Only at the start of the fourteenth century is there evidence that the Cathars (as was the case long before with the Waldensians) used translations of the Bible; see Bernard Gui, *Practica inquisitionis*, ed. Douais, 242; Guillaume Mollat, ed., Les Classiques de l'histoire de France au Moyen Age (Paris, 1926/7) 1.26: *Legunt de evangeliis et de epistolis in vulgari, applicando et exponendo pro se et contra statum romane ecclesie*. Cf. also the statements from the inquisitions in 1308/9 on the gospels and epistles of Paul *in romancio* in Molinier, "Un traité inédit," 234 n. The statement in another trial in 1320 on the use of the Gospel of John *de latino et romano* in Molinier, "Rapport sur une mission exécutée en Italie," 290–91, is also certainly not to be attributed to Waldensians, though perhaps to Cathars.

7. As in the case of the disputation at Montréal in October 1206, when the leading heretic, Deacon [!] Arnald Hot, presented written theses and then composed a response to the counter-theses of Bishop Diego of Osma, both certainly in Latin; cf. Peter of Vaux-Cernay, "Historia Albigensis," ed. Achille Luchaire, c. 3 (pp. 14–15).

8. Cf. Molinier, "Un traité inédit," 266ff. The troubadour Robert, Dauphin of the Auvergne and count of Clermont (died 1234), was supposed to have compiled an entire collection of heretical writings, see Stephan of Bourbon, A. Lecoy de la Marche, ed., *Anecdotes historiques*, 275ff. Salvus Burce in Piacenza wrote his book *Supra-Stella* against a heretical book entitled *Stella*, see Döllinger, *Beiträge* 2.52. Lucas of Tuy (died 1249), *De altera vita fideique controversiis adversus Albigenses*, III, 17 (written before 1240; *Biblioteca maxima veterum Patrum* [Lyon, 1677] 25.247f.) tells of a French heretic active in Spain, Arnaldus, as *scriptor velocissimus*, who *corrupta sanctorum opuscula vendebat vel dabat catholicis* and in the end was executed in Léon; further, II, 2 (p. 241) a heretical book which argued with passages and citations from philosophers, *Perpendiculum scientiarum*. Moneta Cremonensis, *Adversus Catharos et Valdenses libri quinque* [written after 1240], ed. Thomas Augustinus Ricchinius (Rome, 1743), 2, 71, 79, 86, 94, 97, claims the writings *cuiusdam heretici Tetrici nomine* as the source for his knowledge of heretical doctrine. Rainer Sacchoni, O.P., *Summa de Catharis et Leonistis* (written 1250) used an extensive book of the heretic Johannes de Lugio in Bergamo, *cuius exemplarium habeo et perlegi et ex illo errores supradictos extraxi*, see Martène and Durand, *Thesaurus novus anecdotorum* (Paris, 1717) 5.1773.

9. Lea, *Geschichte der Inquisition*, I, p. 112.

10. Helga Hajdu, *Lesen und Schreiben im Mittelalter*, 6.

11. Published in facsimile by Clédat, *Le Nouveau Testament traduit au XIIIe siècle en langue provençal*, Bibliothéque de la Faculté des Lettres de Lyon 4 (1888); cf. E. Reuss, *Revue de Théologie* 5 (1852), 321ff.; idem, *Geschichte der Heiligen Schriften des Neuen Testaments*, §465ff.; Samuel Berger, *La Bible française au moyen âge* (Paris, 1884), 35ff.

12. Cf. Wendelin Förster, "La Noble Leçon," *Göttingische Gelehrten Anzeigen* (1888), 762ff.; Guiraud, *Cartulaire* 1.xxviii and cxxi f., holds the manuscript to be Cathar, but from a time when the doctrinal strictness of the Cathars had grown weak and Waldensian influence had penetrated; Edmond Broeckx, *Le Catharisme*, 200–01, joins in this opinion.

13. *Chronicon . . . Laudunensis*, ed. Cartellieri and Stechele, 20.

14. Stephan of Bourbon, ed. Lecoy de la Marche, 291. Stephan of Bourbon is a very reliable reporter on this, since he knew both the translator and the scribe, whose names he mentions, and cites their own reports. Another source has Waldes causing it to be translated. Döllinger, *Beiträge* 2.6; Bernard Gui, *Practica inquisitoris*, ed. Mollat, 1.34; cf. David of Augsburg, *Tractatus de inquisitione hereticorum*, ed. Wilhelm Preger, 209.

15. Stephan of Bourbon, ed. Lecoy de la Marche, 291–92.

16. Walter Map, *De Nugis Curialium*, ed. James, 60.

17. Cf. W. Förster, "La Noble Leçon," 765.

18. See above, chapter 2, n. 51ff. Suchier, "Zu den altfranzösischen Bibelübersetzungen," 418ff. Jostes, *HJ* 11 (1890), 7, 11ff.; Wilhelm Walther, *Die deutsche Bibelübersetzungen des Mittelalters* (Brunswick, 1889–92), 738ff. Innocent III asked for information about the men, *qui sacras scripturas taliter transtulerant, aut eorum, qui docent taliter jam translatas, quorum neutrum potest fieri sine scientia litterarum* (*PL* 214.698). Neither Innocent nor the bishop of Metz overlooked a link between the sectarians of Metz and the Waldensians. In truth asking after the translator himself was rather pointless: doubtless these were the writings Waldes had translated, now retranslated into French (as they were later to be retranslated into German). One copy of the translation of the *Moralia* of St. Gregory survives, see Suchier, "Zu den altfranzösischen Bibelübersetzungen," 422–23; Berger, *La Bible française*, 47ff. It is a matter of dispute whether other surviving translations come from this group of heretics, see Berger, *La Bible française*, 40ff.; Suchier, "Zu den altfranzösischen Bibelübersetzungen," 424.

19. Alberich of Trois-Fontaines, *Chron.*, *MG Scr.* 23.878.

20. 1202 *Omnes libri romane vel theutonice scripti de divinis scripturis in manus tradantur episcopi, et ipse quos reddendos viderit reddat;* see Aubertus Miræus, *Opera diplomatica et historica* 1.664; Wackernagel, *Altdeutsche Predigten*, 347; Suchier, "Zu den altfranzösischen Bibelübersetzungen," 422.

21. Hefele and Knöpfler, *Conciliengeschichte*, 782, no. 14; Mansi, *Sacrorum conciliorum* 23.197.

22. Haskins, *Studies in Mediaeval Culture*, chapter 11, "The Heresy of Rheims," esp. 247 (text of a sermon of the chancellor of the University of Paris, Philippe de Grève: . . . *preceptum est in Remensi concilio ne transferantur sicut hactenus libri sacre Scripture in gallicum idioma*) and p. 255.

23. *Gesta Trevirorum, MG Scr.* 24.401l; Hartzheim, *Concilia Germaniæ* 3.539: *Plures erant secte, et multi eorum instructi erant scripturis sanctis, quas habebant in theutonicum translatas.*

24. Edmund Martène and Ursinus Durand, *Veterum scriptorum et monumentorum amplissima collectio* (Paris, 1724/33) 7.123, no. 2; Hefele and Knöpfler, *Conciliengeschichte* 5.1037.

25. Passau Anonymous (*Biblioteca maxima* 25.264): *Novum et vetus testamentum vulgariter transtulerunt et sic docent et discunt*. David of Augsburg, *De inquisitione*, ed. Preger, 209: *Dociles inter suos complices et facundos docent verba ewangelii et dicta apostolorum et aliorum sanctorum in vulgari linqua corde affirmare ut sciant et alios informare et fideles allicere*; cf. also 213. Bernard Gui, *Practica inquisitionis* (ed. G. Mollat, 1.62; also Döllinger, *Beiträge* 2.13–14): *Habent evangelia et epistolas in vulgari communiter et etiam in latino, quas aliqui inter eos intelligunt et sciunt legere, et interdum que dicunt (aut predicant) legunt in libro, aliquando autem sine libro, maxime illi, qui nesciunt legere, sed ea corde tenentes didicerunt.*

26. Berthold of Regensburg (Schönbach, *S.-B. Wien*, 147/5, 43) speaks in a (Latin) sermon of a heretic of unspecified sect appealing to his "knowledge without books": he knows the *Anegenge*—that is the start of the Gospel of John, the *berchsalmen* (perhaps the Sermon on the Mount?) and the *30 gradus Augustini*, a piece also mentioned by David of Augsburg (ed. Preger, 215) and described as a moral didactic poem. In another (German) sermon, Berthold mentions heretical songs which *ein verworhter ketzer . . . die kint an der straze lerte, daz der liute deste mer in ketzerie vielen* (*Deutsche Predigten*, ed. Pfeiffer and Strobl, 1.406). That is only propaganda for oral use, not reading material. On the "tract literature" earlier attributed to the Waldensians, cf. J. Goll, *MIÖG*, 9.329ff. Whether the Provençal *Nobla Leyczon* derives from as early as the thirteenth century is uncertain; it is not reading material either, any more than later Provençal didactic poems, since they are versifications, not prose; manuscripts of this literature, by the way, survive from the late fourteenth and the fifteenth centuries, see Förster, "La Noble Leçon," 771ff. The earlier disputed question whether a Waldensian Bible is to be found in a manuscript in Tepel (citations in Walther, *Die deutsche Bibelübersetzung des Mittelalters* 1.8–9, cf. also 154ff., 197–98.) does not need to concern us here; the manuscript is from the end of the fourteenth or the start of the fifteenth century. It is hard to settle such questions from internal criteria, since a heretic's translation does not need to differ from the translation of an orthodox scholar.

27. Hajdu, *Lesen und Schreiben*, 12–13.; Herzog, *Die romanischen Waldenser* (1858), 121–22; Edouard Montet, ed., *La Noble Leçon text original*, (Paris, 1888), 19–20 and 521, vv. 287–88.

28. I have yet to find any documentation, from the origins of the Waldensians to at least the end of the thirteenth century, for the assertion, most recently made by K. Burdach, "Die nationale Aneignung der Bibel und die Anfänge der germanischen Philologie," in *Festschrift. Eugen Mogk* (Halle an der Saale, 1924), 241, that the Waldensians were the first to demand "to communicate the Holy Scriptures themselves to the broad masses and to give it into their hands."

29. See the preface to Berthold's *Rusticanus de dominicis*, in A. E. Schönbach, *S.-B. Wien*, 152, VII, p. 3 ff.; Heinrich Denifle, *ZDA* 27.303–04. The

results of Schönbach's studies on Berthold in the *S.-B. der Wiener Akademie der Wissenschaften*, v. 147 and 151–54 (1904/06) and in his older book, *Über eine Grazer Handschrift lateinische-deutscher Predigten* (1890), agrees with my own studies, though starting from different assumptions.

30. *Deutsche Predigten*, ed. Pfeiffer and Strobl, 2.258f., nos. 66–71, see below, text to n. 63.

31. Cf. Lambert's letter to Calixtus III, 1177, in Fayen, "L'Antigraphum," 349 and 351.

32. Fayen, "L'Antigraphum," 352 (corrected by Greven, *Die Anfänge der Beginen*, 177–78): *Unde et ego bonis eorum studiis cooperans, virginibus vitam et passionem beate virginis et Christi martyris Agnetis, omnibus vero generaliter Actus Apostolorum rithmicis concrepantes modulis ad linguam sibi notiorem a latina transfuderam, multis loco congruo insertis exhortationibus, ut videlicet haberent, quo diebus festis, mundo in rebus pessimis exultante, a venenato ipsius melle sese revocare potuissent.* Alberich of Troisfontaines, *MG Scr.* 23.855, also says on Lambert's translations: *Multos libros et maxime vitas sanctorum et actus apostolorum de latino vertit in romanum;* cf. also *Vita Odiliæ, Analecta Bollandiana* 13 (1894), 208, then Aegidius of Orval, *Gesta episcoporum Leodensium, MG Scr*. 25.112; the assertion under a miniature of Lambert from the thirteenth century that he translated the epistles of Paul is doubtful, see Greven, *Anfänge*, 194–95.

33. Fayen, "L'Antigraphum," 352: *Residuum autem diei usque ad vespertine laudis tempus, sollempnibus dico diebus, in psalmis, in ymnis et canticis spiritualibus expendebant, audita queque in ecclesia ruminantes et sese mutuo ad custodiendum cohortantes.*

34. Fayen, "L'Antigraphum," 353: *Est preterea apud eos liber psalmorum cum omnibus glosulis suis et auctoritatibus eas roborantibus, in vulgarem linguam a quodam magistro Flandrensi translatus*. Waldes presented a glossed psalter to the Lateran Council of 1179. On the oldest known French psalter of this type, from the start of the thirteenth century, see S. Berger, *La Bible française*, 64ff.

35. Fayen, "L'Antigraphum," 353: *Queritur iste me scripturas sacras indignis aperuisse.*

36. J. van Mierlo, "Hadewijch une mystique flamande du 13e siècle," *RAM* 5 (1924), 398, n. 36.

37. Cf., for example, on Christiana of S. Troud, *AASS*, 24 July, 5 (1868), 657: *Intelligebat ipsa omnem latinitatem, et sensum in scriptura divina plenissime noverat, licet ipsa a nativitate litteras penitus ignoraret, et earum obscurissimas quæstiones spiritualibus quibusdam amicis, cum interrogaretur, enodatissime reserebat. Invitissime tamen ac rarissime facere voluit, dicens scripturas sanctas exponere proprium esse clericorum nec ad se huiusmodi ministerium pertinere*. Ida of Léau attended the *scholas literalis scientiæ* from her seventh year; both later practiced the *ars scriptoria* in the Cistercian convent of La Ramée; see *AASS*, 29 October, 13, 110 and 113; Chrysostomus Henriquez, *Quinque prudentes virgines, sive b. Beatricis de*

Nazareth, b. Aleydis de Scharenbecka, b. Idæ de Nivellis, b. Idæ de Lovanio, b. Idæ de Lewis ord. Cist. præclara gesta (Antwerp, 1630), 10.

38. [Henry of Ghent], *De viris illustribus*, in Aubertus Miræus, *Bibliotheca ecclesiastica* (Antwerp, 1639–49), 173: *Wilhelmus dictavit etiam latine quamdam materiam satis eleganter de quadam moniali cisterciensis ordinis, que teutonice multa satis mirabilia scripserat de se ipsa*. This Latin *vita* is in Henriquez, *Quinque prudentes virgines*; also the prologue to *Analectes pour servir à l'histoire ecclésiastique de la Belgique* 7.77ff., in which the author says: *me solum huius operis translatorem existere, non autorem, quippe qui de meo parum admodum addidi vel mutavi; hec prout in cedula oblata suscepi illa vulgaria, latino in eloquio coloravi;* Beatrix had no contemporary witness who could have written her experiences. L. Reypens and J. Van Mierlo, eds., "Beatrijs van Nazareth. Seven manieren van Minne," *Leuvense Studieen en Teksuitgaven* 12 (1926), 24ff., doubt whether William of Affighem wrote the Latin *vita* of Beatrix. But if the catalogue of authors entitled *De viris illustribus* came from a monk of Afflighem, as Franz Pelster, *HJ* 39 (1919), 253ff. makes likely, his information on William of Afflighem deserves more respect than his other attributions. In Carolus de Visch, *Auctarium ad Bibliothecam Scriptorum ordinis Cisterciensis*, it is said that the *vita* of Beatrix was *scripta ab Alberico* [died 1286] et Victorico [died 1383] *monachis Thosanis* [= Doest] *in Flandria, quam in Flandricam linguam translatam penes me habeo*. De Visch insists that Beatrix also wrote a book entitled *De observantiis regularibus in Ordine Cisterciensi* in 1239.

39. Beatrijs van Nazareth, *Seven manieren van Minne*, ed. Reypens and van Mierlo. Cf. J. van Mierlo, "Beatrijs van Nazareth," *VMKVA* (1926), 51ff.; see below, n. 59.

40. This is supposed by J. van Mierlo, *Dietsche Warande en Belfort* 25 (1925), 367 and *VMKVA* (1926), 71 for the Latin *vitæ* of Lutgard of Tongern, Ida of Nivelles and Ida of Louvain.

41. The *vita* of Julianne of Cornillon (died 1258) was first written in French or Walloon, probably by her friend the recluse Eva of St. Martin (died 1264), but it is only preserved in a Latin translation; see *AASS*, April 1, 444: *Que quidem per diligentiam unius valde religiose persone in lingua gallica litteris commendata . . . adorsus sum, quod gallice factum fuerat, vertere in latinum;* cf. J. Demarteau, *La première auteure wallone, la b. Eve de St. Martin*, 1896; on this, *Analecta Bollandiana*, 16, 531–32; according to Barthélemy Fisen, *Flores ecclesiæ Leodiensis* (Lyon, 1647), the Walloon vita still survived in the seventeenth century in the library of the house of Cornillon, where Juliane was prioress. Cf. also the translation of the *vita* of Lutgard into German verse by Thomas of Chantimpré: *Leven van Sinte Lutgarde*, ed. Fr. van Veerdeghem (Leiden, 1898).

42. *Chartularium Universitatis* 1.70: *De libris theologicis scriptis in Romano precipimus, quod episcopis diocesanis tradantur, et "Credo in deum" et "pater noster" in Romano, preter vitas sanctorum, et hoc infra purificationem, quia apud quem inveniuntur, pro heretico habebitur*. Cæsarius of

Heisterbach, *Dialogus miraculorum*, V, 22 (ed. Strange, 307): *Libri Gallici de theologia perpetuo damnati sunt et exusti.*

43. See above, chapter 7, text to n. 4ff.

44. In what follows I will follow only the developments in Germany and refer only to parallel developments in other countries, which have as yet been little studied. It should be expected that a vernacular literature also developed in South France (Prouille) and Italy (Rome, Bologna) from Dominicans relations with convents, as well as due to the relations of Franciscans with the women's religious movement, but little is known about this in the thirteenth century. In Provence, the earliest prose text of any importance seems to be the *vita* of Douceline, who was the leader of the Marseilles beguines, written by one of her successors, Philippine de Porcellet, about 1300 (*La Vie de Ste. Douceline*, ed. Albanès, 1879; ed. R. Gout, 1927). The South French beguines also had translations of Peter John Olivi's postils on the Apocalypse and other tracts. The Dominican Venturino of Bergamo recommended devotional writings in Provençal to a sister of the order to read in the first half of the fourteenth century, see Giuseppe Clementi, *Un santo patriota d.b. Venturino da Bergamo dell' Ordine de' predicatori* (1304–1346) 2.107. In France the *vita* of Isabella, the sister of Louis IX, founder of the house of Longchamps (died 1270) should be mentioned, written by Agnes of Harcourt (abbess in Longchamps, 1263–91), but only published by the Bollandists in a Latin translation (*AASS*, August, 6.801; cf. Johannes Hyacinthus Sbaralea, *Supplementum* [1806], 6 and *Histoire littéraire de la France,* 20.98ff.). E. Bechmann, *ZRP* 13.34ff. and Alfons Hilka, "Altfranzösisch-Mystik," 47, 120ff. have referred to French prose and verse for beguinages or convents from the second half of the thirteenth century; otherwise, this literature of "old French mysticism" has attracted little attention. A mystic prose literature does not appear before the end of the thirteenth century among religious women (Angela da Foligno, died 1309). The oldest Italian letters surviving were written by a Fra Guidone d'Arezzo to his fellow brothers and sisters of the Order of Gaudenti (Gustav Gröber, *Grundriss der romanischen Philologie*, 2/3 [Strasbourg, 1902], 41). Whether the translations of the writings of Angelo of Clareno (see *AFH* 11.47ff.) and the legends of St. Francis (*Legenda antiqua*, ed. Minocchi [1905]) were created for the female followers of the Franciscans cannot be established. In a letter to the nuns in Unterlinden, Venturino of Bergamo drafted a plan for a model convent in Bologna in which not only all readings, but even the liturgy would be in the vernacular! See Clementi, *Venturino* 2.124; Berthold Altaner, "Venturino von Bergamo, O.Pr., eine Biographie, zugleich ein Beitrag zur Geschichte des Dominikanerordens im 14. Jahrhundert," *Kirchengeschichtliche Abhandlungen*, ed. M. Sdralek, 9/2 (Breslau, 1911), 76–77.

45. Cf. above, chapter 5, n. 45; Jordanis de Saxonia, *De initiis ordinis*, ed. J.-J. Berthier, 25–26; after Henry's death (1225 or 1227) *venerabilis quedam matrona, que ipsum fratrem adhuc viventem mira devotione diligebat*, consoled herself with his letter; there she found *verbum quoddam, cuius secundum latinam interpretationem* [sic] *hec est sententia: "Super dulce Jesu*

pectus recumbite, et anime vestre sitim extinguite." Jordan was not speaking of a letter written in Latin, but in German.

46. C. Greith, *Die deutsche Mystik im Prediger-Orden*, 58, claims to have read German prayers and contemplations by the first Cologne Dominican prior, Henry, in a manuscript in the Zürich Stadtbibliothek (Codex 178). A search of the Zürich Zentralbibliothek could not uncover the manuscript Greith indicated at the present time, but hope remains that it shall be found. Not to be confused with those are the sermons of a Cologne Dominican lector, Henry (of Louvain), a contemporary of Tauler; cf. Ph. Strauch, *Alemannia* 21 (1893), 16.

47. *MG Scr.* 27.233: *Frater Henricus prior Basiliensis ordinis fratrum predicatorum fecit rithmos theutonicos bonis mulierculis ac devotis.*

48. Perhaps it was the first prior of the Basel Dominican house established in 1233, Henry of Westhofen (died 1252), who also oversaw the pastoral care of the sisters of Unterlinden (then in Ufmühlen) for a few years (1234/8); Meyer, *Liber de viris*, 27, praises him as *hereticorum validissimus persecutor*, saying of him: *in confessionibus et predicationibus multam gratiam obtinebat*; but he says nothing about versification for pious women. Two Basel priors of later times are worth mentioning as poets: Henry of Marbach, prior 1270/3 (cf. Meyer, *Liber de viris*, 31 and Ludwig Sutter, *Die Dominikaner-Klöster auf dem Gebiete der heutigen deutschen Schweiz im 13. Jahrhundert* [Lucerne, 1893], 114) and Henry of Lauffenberg (= H. Tugendarius? see Sutter, 114), brother of a nun in Unterlinden, prior in Basel in 1281, but no longer prior in 1284. Jeanne Ancelet-Hustache, "Vitæ sororum," *AHDL* 5 (1930), 444–45, holds this Henry of Lauffenberg to be the poet praised in the Colmar chronicle and identifies him with a lector of the Basel Dominicans who was a physician, as was Henry of Lauffenberg, and from whom there survive Latin verses (*MG Scr.* 17.239f.). But the frequently documented Basel lector Henry (see *Urk.-B. Basel* 2.82, no. 149 for 1274; in 1276 a witness of the rule of the Strasbourg beguinage zum Thurn is one *Heinricus de Basilea quondam lector o. fr. Pr.*, see *Urk.-B. Strassburg* 3.28, no. 78), who composed Latin verses, is hard to equate with Henry of Lauffenberg and the Basel prior who composed German verses. Nor can it be Henry of Meissen (Frauenlob) who is meant in the passage of the Colmar chronicle, as N. Spiegel believes (*Die Vaganten und ihr Orden*, Gymnasium-Programm Speyer [1892], 44); he was in Basel for a while between 1283 and 1291, but not Dominican prior. The words of the Colmar chronicler: *bonis mulierculis ac devotis* appear to me to speak more of the earliest period of the religious women's movement, not of the period of full-fledged Dominican convents. From 1234 to 1269 Unterlinden was under the pastoral care of the Basel Dominicans, as Husern-Klingenthal was even before 1245. In a manuscript of the Basel Universitätsbibliothek from the fourteenth century (A XI 55; see Gustav Binz, *Die deutschen Handschriften der öffentlichen Bibliothek der Universitt Basel*, 1 [Basel, 1907ff.], 289) there are fragments of German verse with the signature: *ego Heinricus feci*, which—according to a courteously communicated hypothesis of W. Stammler—could be from the Basel prior Henry. Yet his poetry could not have been restricted to little pious verses if he

was thought worthy of being mentioned by the Colmar chronicler as one of the authors of the Dominican Order alongside Thomas Aquinas, among others.

49. *MOPH* 3.24: *Nec aliquis fratrum de cetero sermones vel collaciones vel alias sacras scripturas de latino transferat in vulgare.*

50. *MOPH* 3.47: *Fratres non faciant sibi scribi psalteria vel alia scripta per moniales vel alias mulieres.*

51. See, for example, Hieronymus Wilms, "Das Beten der Mystikerinnen," *QF* 11 (1916), 28ff. and 31; E. Krebs, "Die Mystik in Adelhausen," 83ff. On the writing of books in convents in general, see *AASS*, October, 13, 124ff.; for the later Middle Ages, A. Hauber, "Deutsche Handschriften in Fraunklöster des Späteren Mittelalters," *ZB* 31.341ff. The knowledge of Latin advanced so far even in relatively early times that the Dominican Peter of Verona could preach at Adelhausen in 1244 in Latin and be understood by many of the sisters, see *FDA* 13.134; see Seraphim Dietler, *Gebweiler Chronik*, 11.

52. See the constitutions of S. Sisto, c. 3, in A. Simon, *L'ordre des Pénitentes*, pp. 144–45: *In refectorio semper ad mensum legatur et sorores cum silentio devote audiant lectionem;* c. 5: *Post vesperas omnes simul ad collacionem veniant, ubi legatur lectio prout in cisterciensi ordine fieri consuevit;* c. 21 (p. 152): *Diebus festivis omnes vacent lectioni, divinis officiis et orationi, mechanicis operibus pretermissis.* Cf. the *Constitutiones sororum ord. præd.* in *AOP* 3.340, c. 6: *De collacione*. Following the model of the Rule of St. Benedict, the military orders also prescribe that there should be readings at meals, and it had to be read in the vernacular, since no one would have understood Latin; this is probably important for the rise of a vernacular literature of the order (see Fritz Karg, *Das literarische Erwachens des deutschen Ostens im Mittelalter* [Halle, 1932]), but there are two important differences with the convents: 1) readings were done only at the main meal, not at the evening *collatio* (Gustav Schnürer, *Die ursprüngliche Templerregel* [Freiburg i. B., 1903], 137, c. 9 and p. 137, c. 16; Max Perlbach, *Die Statuten des Deutschen Ordens* [Halle, 1890], 41, c. 13, and 44, c. 16, where it is stressed that there was no reading at the *collatio*, in distinction to other orders). And it is precisely the collatio which is quite important in the convents for pious reading or preaching. 2) Among brothers of military orders, the ability to read on their own was certainly a rarity (see Schnürer, 105), so that the readings were done by a cleric, and the order was not oriented to an exemplary life. A religious literature of edification did not develop within the military orders as a result. [Cf. Herbert Grundmann, "Deutsches Schrifttum im Deutschen Orden," *Altpreussische Forschungen* 18 (1941), 21–49. HG/1960.]

53. For the same reason the laws of the order were read to the sisters in German, see the *Admonitiones* of the German provincial Herman of Minden (1286/90) for convents in Heinrich Denifle, "Meister Eckeharts lateinische Schriften," 644: *Constitutiones secundum ordinationem . . . magistri ordinis correctas habeant, que frequenter legantur et aliquotiens exponantur in vulgari;* also 649, the instructions for the Dominicans entrusted with the *cura monialium: Constitutiones publice legantur in refectorio per singulas*

ebdomadas in vulgari; the nuns' book of Engelthal (*Der Nonne von Engelthal Büchlein von der Gnaden Überlast*, ed. K. Schröder [Tübingen, 1871], 2) says that before the actual foundation of a convent, while they still resided in Nuremberg as a Obeguinage,'' the mistress would read *in teutsche ze tisch.*

54. Instruction of the provincial to those Dominicans entrusted with the *cura monialium*, Denifle, ''Meister Eckharts lateinische Schriften,'' 650: *Providete, ne refectione careant verbi dei, sed sicut eruditioni ipsarum convenit, per fratres doctos sepius predicetur.* According to Denifle (*loc. cit.*, 645) the *fratres docti* are to be understood as masters and lectors of theology.

55. Cf. my article, ''Die geschichtliche Grundlagen der Deutschen Mystik,'' *DVLG* 12 (1934), 400–29.

56. Cf. Lüers, *Die Sprache;* F. Karg, *Das literarische Erwachen*; Tillmann, *Studien zum Dialog.*

57. *Fliessende Licht*, II, 3, ed. Morell, 30: *des latines kan ich nit*; VII, 21, p. 237: *ich selber ungeleret bin*; III, 1, p. 56: *ich han da inne ungehörtú ding gesehen, als mine bihter* [sic] *sagent; wa ich der schrift ungeleret bin*. Cf. Grete Lüers, *Die Sprache*, 33ff.; Jeanne Ancelet-Hustache, *Mechthilde de Magdebourg*, 17–18.

58. Cf. particularly Mechthild's vision, III, 1, p. 56ff., in which she peers into the nine heavenly choirs, consisting of *luter geistlicher megde zusammen mit den prediern*; that she does not mean just any preachers, but the preaching friars = Dominicans, is shown by the sentence (59): *Alsust singen die predier: o userwelter herre, wir han gevolget diner milten gütin in willeclichem armuoteund haben dinú wizelosen schaf ingetriben, die dine gemieteten hirten liessen gan usser dem rehten wege.*

59. It is particularly the connection of ''the mysticism of love,'' in the visions of Hadewich, the treatises of Beatrix of Nazareth and the ''Flowing Light'' of Mechthild, with the Latin mysticism of the Victorines which should be investigated. Cf., for example, *Fliessende Licht*, IV, 28, p. 127: *dis büch ist begonnen in der minne, es sol ouch enden in der minne* with Hugh of St. Victor, *Soliloquium de arrha animæ: Ego scio, quod vita tua dilectio est, et scio, quod sine dilectione esse non potes*, and with the ''Seven manieren van Minne'' of Beatrix. I cite a detail which reveals the close connections: the highest ecstatic degree of mystical love is called *Orewoet* in Beatrix (ed. Reypens and van Mierlo, 22) and Hadewich (ed. van Mierlo, 157, 159–60), for Mechthild it is *windische minne* (III, 13, p. 75; cf. I, 20, p. 10: *du bist ein sturm mines herzen*, says the soul to God; see also G. Lüers, *Die Sprache*, 46, 36, 302); the Latin root of this idea has not yet been found. Cf. also G. Lüers, 103, on the ''eyes of the soul'' in Richard of St. Victor, Hadewich and Mechthild.

60. Preger, *Mystik* 1.288ff.; F. J. Mone, *Anzeiger der Kunde des deutschen Mittelalters* 3.177, refers to several such rhymed pieces from the thirteenth century in Netherlandish libraries; many of them were believed by Preger to belong to a later period.

61. Most important is a ''Lied von der Dreifaltigkeit,'' which Preger, *Mystik*, 1.289ff., published in translation, Bartsch, *Die Erlösung imiteiner Answahl*

geistlicher Dichtung (Quedlinburg; Leipzig, 1858), 193ff., Michael Denis, *Codices manuscripti theolici bibliothecae Vindobonensis*, 2 vols. (Vienna, 1793–95) 2.1086, Friedrich Heinrich von der Hagen, *Minnesänger*, 5 vols. (Leipzig, 1838–61) 3.468 dd f., and Philippe Wackernagel, *Das deutsche Kirchenlied*, 5 vols. (Leipzig, 1836–77), 2 (1869), 238, no. 445, in Middle High German, and F. Beck, *Gymnasium-Programm Zeitz*, 1882/83 excerpted, together with a Latin commentary. Bartsch and Preger date it by language, versification, and content to the second half of the thirteenth century; cf. also Ph. Strauch, *ADA* 9.121–22. The poem, however, is so rich in its "mystical" word coinages that it has been ascribed to Meister Eckhart, with the following justification: "How would it suit an author of such gifts and originality as Eckhart to assume that he merely took so many distinctive expressions and turns of phrase from the poem before us" (F. Beck, *Gymnasium-Programm Zeitz*, xiv, which shows in detail the many parallels between the poem and Eckhart). This concept of "authorial originality" was never less applicable than to the preachers of German mysticism. It is precisely this which makes it hard to rule on the contributions of individual "authors," but it also reinforces the duty to explain the development of mystical literature not on the basis of the "original" accomplishments of individuals, but from a general historical purpose, the communication of Latin theology to religious women in the vernacular.

62. On similar versifications, see Preger, *Mystik* 2.56; Adolf Spamer, *Texte aus der deutschen Mystik des 14. und 15. Jahrhunderts* (Jena, 1912), 175ff.; Strauch, *ADA* 9.121; especially interesting is the poem "Tocher Syon oder die minnende Seele" (ed. E. G. Graff, *Diutiska* 3.3ff.; on other editions, manuscripts or versions of the "Tochter Syon" and its commentaries, see W. Wichgraf, "Der Traktat von der Tochter Syon und seine Bearbeitungen," *Beiträge zur Geschichte der deutschen Sprache und Literatur*, 46, 173ff.) and the "Rede von den 15 Graden," written in "rhymed prose" (ed. W. Dolfel, *Germania*, 6 [1861], 144ff.), whose author also produced "Die Lilie"; cf. Ph. Strauch, *Deutsche Literatur-Zeitung* 33 (1912), 994ff. We know also of a translation of the Dominican Rule into German verse in 1276 for the nuns in Marienthal near Mersch (Luxembourg), probably composed by Friar Herman (of Veldenz?), who also composed a life of Jolande of Vianden after 1283; this translation does not survive; cf. J. Meier,"Bruder Hermanns Leben," lxxvii f.; cf. J. B. Schoemann, "Die Rede von den 15 Graden," *Germanistische Studien* 80 (1930) (27, 61!); also Adolf Bach, *Das Rheinische Marienlob, eine deutsche Dichtung des 12. Jahrhundert des 13. Jahrhunderts, Bibliothek des litterarischen Vereins in Stuttgart* 281 (1934), esp. xlviii.

63. See n. 29 above; cf. also Karl Rieder, *Der sogenannte St. Georgener Prediger* (Berlin, 1908), xxiii; A. E. Schönbach, *S.-B. Wien*, 153/4 (1906), 50, 59, 75.

64. A. E. Schönbach, *S.-B. Wien*, 153/4 (1906), 73, 54, 56f., 69 and elsewhere; the manuscript tradition of Berthold's German sermons (except for the six convent sermons) does not go back beyond the fourteenth century.

65. Printed in Pfeiffer, *Deutsche Mystiker* 1 (1845), 308ff.; Preger, *Mystik* 2.9ff., only recognizes a portion of it as "genuine"; in contrast, Ph. Strauch, *ADA* 9.117, holds it all to be "genuine" and calls David the "first mystic in the German language," and Stöckerl, *Bruder David von Augsburg*, 210ff, attempts to show that all of the German works transmitted under his name derive from him by citing agreements with his Latin writings in detail. Contrary to this, the Franciscans in Quaracchi (in the edition of David's "De exterioris et interioris hominis compositione," p. xv) and E. Michael (*ZKT* 25.396 and *Geschichte des deutschen Volkes* 3.133f.) assume that David wrote nothing in German.

66. Cf. the various workings of the "orchard" allegory, probably arisen from a Latin model, in Alemannic and Alsatian versions, see Philipp Strauch, *Beiträge zur Geschichte der deutschen Sprache und Literatur* 48.349 and 360; on other versions, which include works by David of Augsburg, see Stöckerl, *Bruder David von Augsburg*, 258ff. Closely related is the tract of the *Palma contemplationis*, an allegory of *willeklichu armut* and the rise of the loving soul to God, directed at *juncfrowen, die gottes briute wellent sin*. Several mss. of this tract derive from as early as the thirteenth century, several probably from convents. It is found in Latin, French, Dutch, High and Low German, see Strauch, *Beiträge*, 335ff.; K. Christ, "La livre du paumier," *Festgabe für H. Degering* (1926), 57ff., publishes a French text from a Berlin ms. of the thirteenth century (about 1275?), in which a pious beguines' rule follows the "Palm" text: *la rigle des fins amans et li ordinaires de deus beguines*; Christ knows of six North French mss. of the tract from the thirteenth century. Also deserving attention is the tract *von 42 tugenden, als der grosz Albertus schriben;* cf. Strauch, *Beitäge*, 309; Jostes, *Meister Eckhart und seine Jünger*, 136, no. xxxi; Hauber, "Deutsche Handschriften," 344. The same applies to the "Seelenspiegel," a collection of mystical sermons and teachings for nuns in a ms. of the thirteenth century (Karlsruhe, Cod. perg. germ. 37) from which F. J. Mone, in the *Anzeiger für Kunde der deutschen Vorzeit* 4.368ff. and 8.489ff. and 612 gives brief excerpts. This collection contains pieces from the "Upper Rhenish Preacher," to be dealt with soon.

67. F. Maurer, *Studien zur mitteldeutschen Bibelübersetzung vor Luther*, 68ff., referred to the importance of Dominican convents for the translation of the Bible into German; a Dutch-German glossed harmony of the gospels, *Leven van Jesus*, probably originated in the thirteenth century in Cologne among Dominicans, created for religious women and nuns; cf. Reifferscheid, *Jahrbuch des Vereins für niederdeutsche Sprachforschung* 10 (1884), 33 and n. 52; Priebsch, *Deutsche Handschriften in England* 2.236. It should be recalled that groups of women suspected of heresy and operating outside of the orders also promoted translation of the Bible; the Franciscan memorial for the Council of Lyon in 1274 mentions that (see *AFD* 24.61–62.) and the Belgian beguine Margarete Porete, who was burned in Paris in 1310, was supposed to have translated from the Bible herself, see Jean d'Outremeuse: *qui translatat la divine escripture; Grandes Chroniques de France: qui avait trespassée et transcendée l'escripture divine*; see Fredericq, *Corpus* 2.64.

68. Ph. Strauch, "Kölner Klosterpredigten des 13. Jahrhunderts," *Jahrbuch des Vereins der niederdeutschen Sprachforschung* 37 (1911), 21ff. on a ms. of the fourteenth century from the tertiary settlement of Kamp near Boppard (just as was the case with the Prague ms. of the "Rede von den 15 Graden," see *Germania* 6.145); pp. 27–28 on the audience for the sermons. One passage (44) from a sermon of "Master Gerhard" (probably Gerhard of Minden, numbered as one of the most important theologians of the thirteenth century by the Dominican Henry of Herford, along with Ulrich of Strasbourg and Dietrich of Freiberg; Denifle, "Meister Eckharts lateinische Schriften," 240) is remarkable: *Sumeliche sprechint, dat die sele si gotlicher naturen, inde sprechint ouch dat sie wieder zu gode kume, also dat si alzemal niet inwerde. Dat sint unreine ketzere. Alleine die sele eweliche in gode gewest si, so is si doch eweliche eine creature gewest, e si got ie geschufhe, inde sal also wieder ze gode kumen, dat si ein wesen in ir selver eweliche sal behalden.*

69. K. Rieder, *Der sogenannte St. Georgener Prediger*, xxi and 10.

70. Ibid., xix; they frequently expressly refer to the sisters of a convent which is under a prioress—hence probably to Dominican women.

71. A portion of the sermons survives in a manuscript written about 1300, whose whole content is intended for a convent, as well as in a ms. of the mid-fourteenth century from the Dominican convent of Adelhausen, see Rieder, *Der sogenannte St. Georgener Prediger*, xii and xiv ff. Two transcriptions of the complete collection of sermons derive from an exemplar written in 1305. The sermons could not derive from "the first period of the fourteenth century," as Preger, *Mystik* 2.32, says. Netherlandish transcriptions of the same collection of sermons (the so-called *Limburger Sermoenen*, ed. J. H. Kern) as J. van Mierlo showed, also contained passages from the letters of Hadewich and from a mystical tract of Beatrix of Nazareth.

72. W. Preger, *Mystik* 2.32; Ph. Strauch, *ADA* 9.117.

73. Reference, for example, should be made to the listing of Netherlandish mss. by Borchling in the *Beiheften* to the *Nachrichten der Göttinger Gesellschaft der Wissenschaften* (1902), 139ff., 206 and (1913), 76, 177–78, as well as to Munich mss. CGM 9, 168, 77, 99, 101, 142, 182, 186.

74. It must be recalled that the work of Mechthild of Magdeburg was only preserved by chance; if Henry of Nördlingen had not found it seventy years after Mechthild's death and worked it into a different linguistic form, it would have been lost to us. Nothing at all is preserved of Dietrich of Freiberg or the nameless lector who was praised by the famous nuns' poem as the equal of Meister Eckhart as a mystical preacher (see Engelbert Krebs, *Meister Dietrich*, 147f.), and it is an unfounded assertion to call Master Dietrich "the first to preach in the manner of German mystics" (Denifle, "Meister Eckharts lateinische Schriften," 528; M. de Wulf, *Histoire de la philosophie médiévale*, 5th ed., 2 [1925], 236).

75. Suso, *Deutsche Schriften*, ed. Bihlmeyer, 199. Also Mechthild (*Fliessende Licht*, II, 3, p. 30) complains and regrets that she could not understand Latin, since German was inadequate: *Nu gebristet mir tütsches, des latines kan*

ich nit. Grete Lüers, *Die Sprachek*, 34, says, exaggerating, that there was a "disrespect for the German language among mystics."

Appendix

1. All sources are given in Theloe, *Die Ketzerverfolgungen,* 5ff.

2. Ademar of Chabannes [died 1034], *Chronicon*, ed. Jules Chavanon (Paris, 1897), 173; about 1018 *exorti sunt per Aquitaniam Manichei*; also 185, 194; Chronicle of Auxerre, *Recueil des Historiens des Gaules et de la France*, ed. Léopold Delisle, 10.271 on the heretics of Orléans: *Acsi denuo Manichei heretici*; letter of Bishop Roger of Châlons, 1043, *MG Scr*. 7.226–27: *perversum Manicheorum dochma sectantes; . . . heresiarche suo Mani*; Hermannus Contractus, ibid., 5.130 on the heretics at Goslar, 1052: *dogmata Manichea secta*.

3. Cf. E. de Stoop, *Essai sur la diffusion du Manichéisme* (Paris, 1909), 90ff.; Broeckx, *Le Catharisme*, 13ff., 19ff.

4. Celestin Douais, *Les Albigeois* (1879), 189ff.; Schmidt, *Histoire et doctrine*; Archimandrite Stéphane Gheorghieff, *Les Bogomils et Presbyter Kosma* (Lausanne, 1920), 56. The monk Euthymius asserted about 1050 that the Bogomils traveled through the entire Roman Empire as monks and priests, turning to all the Christians on earth, dividing the countries of the Roman Empire among themselves by lot as missionary districts and putting all their energy into the service of their propaganda; see G. Ficker, *Die Phundagiagiten* (Leipzig, 1908), 63 and 167; see J. A. Ilic, *Die Bogomilen in ihrer geschichtlichen Entwicklung*, Dissertation, Bern (Karlovci, Yugoslavia, 1923).

5. The heresy discovered in Orléans in 1022 is supposed to have been betrayed by a woman from Italy (Rodolphus Glaber, *Historiæ*, III, 8, ed. Maurice Prou [Paris, 1846], 74), according to another by an uneducated (rusticus) Southern Frenchman from the Périgord (Ademar, 184); the heretics themselves answered questions as to the origin of their doctrine that they had long existed without being discovered (Rodolphus Glaber, 75). The heretics came to Arras from the diocese of Châlons, where people from Italy had spread the heresy (Fredericq, *Corpus* 1.3). The heretics in Monteforte near Turin knew that their fellow believers were scattered across the entire world (*MG Scr*. 8.65).

6. A leader of the heretics in Orléans in 1022 had earlier been confessor to the queen; he and ten other canons of the cathedral in Orléans were convicted of heresy, degraded, and burned; three years earlier the cantor had died as an adherent of heresy, see Ademar, *Chronicon*, 184–85. The other leader headed the school at St. Peter, Rodolphus Glaber (74). *Gesta synodi Aurelianensis*, ed. Guérard (109). *Fragm. Hist. Franciæ*, *Recueil* 10.498. Rodolphus Glaber says (80) that thirteen heretics were burned; one cleric and a nun (!) avoided death by fire through conversion, see *Gesta synodi Aurelianensis*, 115.

7. *MG Scr*. 8.66; Rodophus Glaber, 94.

8. *MG Scr*. 7.226–27.

9. Only the heretics of Arras, 1025, whose social status is unknown, but who were not clerics because they did not understand Latin, based their rejection of

baptism and other matters on the *vita reproba ministrorum*, which could not communicate the *remedium salutis*; they declared it to be an evangelical and apostolic norm to earn their living with the work of their hands; Fredericq, *Corpus* 1.4. The noble heretics in Monteforte wanted to have their property in common with all people. The peasant Leuthard preached against paying the tithe. Otherwise, social or economic questions are never mentioned.

10. Only the heretics of Monteforte spoke of a more comprehensive community to which they belonged: *Ab aliis vero, qui potestatem habent ligandi et solvendi, ligari ac solvi credimus*. They also speak of a "pope," who continually visited their brethren scattered over the entire world and was sent by God for the forgiveness of sins; that was the sole true pope, who did not wear a tonsure like the Romans. But that is obviously a symbolic representation of the Holy Spirit, see Edmond Broeckx, *Le Catharisme*, 143.

11. Only the Arras heretics of 1025 described themselves as the *auditores* of their leader Gundolf, from Italy, Fredericq, *Corpus* 1.3, but it is questionable whether one can think here of the Manichee *audientes* et *electi*.

12. *Gesta synodi Aurelianensis*, 111; letter of Bishop Roger of Châlons (after 1246, *MG Scr.* 7.226–27). The rite can be discerned among the heretics at Monteforte from an unclear report by Rodolphus Glaber, IV, 2, pp. 94–95; in 1025, the heretics at Arras replaced ecclesiastical sacraments with *quædam justitia*, which was the sole way to purify a person—probably also the laying on of hands.

13. Ademar, *Historiæ*, 173 on the "Manichees" in Aquitaine about 1018: *abstinentes a cibis quasi monachi*; John of Fleury on the heretics of Orléans, *Recueil* 10.498; *MG Scr*. 8.65 on the heretics in Monteforte, ibid.; 5.130, on the heretics in Goslar, ibid., 7.226, on the heretics in the diocese of Châlons.

14. Ademar, *Historiæ*, 173: *Castitatem simulabant, sed inter se ipsos luxuriam omnem exercentes*. *MG Scr*. 8.65: *Virginitatem pre ceteris laudamus, etc.;* with complete continence *sicut apes sine coitu genus gigneretur humanum*. The peasant Leuthard left his wife *quasi ex precepto evangelico*, Rodolphus Glaber, 49. On the heretics in Orléans, John of Fleury, *Recueil* 10.498: *Nuptiis detrahebant*; cf. ibid., 212; *MG Scr*. 7.226; Fredericq, *Corpus* 1.2, on the heretics in Arras: *Conjugatos nequaquam ad regnum pertinere*.

15. Ademar, 173; Fredericq, *Corpus* 1.2; *Gesta synodi Aurelianensis*, 111; *Recueil* 10.498; Rodolphus Glaber, 49. Only the letter of the bishop of Châlons mentions the ban on killing, *MG Scr*. 7.226.

16. The heretics of Orléans in 1022 taught the eternity of heaven and earth *usque auctore initii*, Rodolphus Glaber (76) reports. In response to the question of the bishop of Beauvais whether they did not believe that God created everything from nothing, they answered: *Ista illis narrare potes, qui terrena sapiunt atque credunt ficta carnalium hominum scripta in membranulis animalium*, *Gesta synoda Aurelianensis*, 114, where, however, the heretics went on to speak of God as the *conditor omnium*. The heretics in Monteforte confessed: *(Pater) deus est eternus, qui omnia ut (= creavit?) ab initio et in quo omnia consistunt; MG Scr*. 8.66. All other sources mention no cosmological concepts.

17. *Gesta synodis Aurelianensis*, 111, 114. The heretics in Monteforte responded to a question about the trinity: *Filius animus est hominis a deo dilectus; spiritus sanctus divinarum scientiarum intellectus, a quo cuncta discrete reguntur. —Jesus Christus . . . est animus sensualiter natus ex sancta scriptura; spiritus sanctus sanctarum scripturarum cum devotione intellectus*.

18. The peasant Leuthard sought to demonstrate his convictions on the basis of the Bible (*quod non didicerat*) in the presence of Bishop Gebuin of Châlons. Rodolphus Glaber, 49; he asserted *propheta ex parte narrasse utilia, ex parte non credenda*, so that he did not recognize the Old Testament as being canonical. The heretics in Orléans presented their doctrine as biblical exegesis, see *Gesta synodi Aurelianensis*, 109: *cum divini verbi dulcedine ab eis debriatur mortifero nequitiæ austu*; also the experience of the man who declared himself to be their follower in order to betray them (ibid., 110–11) show clearly that they practiced "pneumatic exegesis"; the Catholic judges almost always portray heretics as only covering their doctrine with Scriptures at the beginning, cf. Rodolphus Glaber, 76. The heretics of Arras, 1025, appealed to the gospels and apostolic writings to justify their teaching and way of life, and they declare they uphold those writings *opere et verbo . . . nullamque preter hanc spripturam se recipere,* Fredericq, *Corpus* 1.3. On the other hand the heretics in Monteforte say: *Vetus ac novum testamentum ac sanctas canones cotidie legentes tenemus*.

19. *Gesta synodi Aurelianensis*, 109–10: *testificans Aurelianum urbem præ cæteris urbibus coruscare luce sapientiæ atque sanctitatis lampade*. That stimulated the discovery of heresy by Arefast the knight, in whose service the cleric Herbert stood; Arefast participated actively in the investigation; later he became a monk at St. Peter's at Chartres; he is the source of the report in the cartulary of this house, the so-called *Gesta synodi Aurelianensis*, so that it deserves complete confidence.

20. Cf. n. 6 above; also Ademar, *Chronicon*, 1844–85: *qui videbantur esse religiosiores aliis*; 185 on the leader of the heretics, *quem rex valde dilexerat propter sanctitatem, quem eum habere credebat*. Rodolphus Glaber, *Historiæ*, 75: *Viri hactenus in omni morum probitate perutilissimi*. These statements weaken the account in Ademar, *Chronicon*, 184–85, and in the *Gesta synodi Aurelianensis*, 112 on prayers to the devil, ritual orgies by heretics, and the use of the ashes of burned children as a medium for magic; they deserve our interest, however, in studying the migration of motifs of anti-heretical polemics from patristics via Byzantium to the West; cf. my article on "Der Typus des Ketzers in mittelalterlicher Anschauung," *Kultur- und Universalgeschichte. Festschrift W. Goetz* (Berlin; Leipzig, 1927), 91–107, esp. 104–05.

21. Rodophus Glaber, *Historiæ*, 49.

22. In 1056 a council in Toulouse once more forbade all intercourse with and all aid to heretics, on pain of excommunication, without specifying a particular type of heresy; Mansi, *Conciliorum sacrorum* 19.849, c. 13. [This

appendix has aroused the most lively controversy. Even more one-sidedly than here, Raffaello Morghen stressed the "origini neotestamentarie del pensiero ereticale"—originally without alien influences—in "Osservazioni critiche su alcune questioni fondamentali reguardanti le origini e i caratteri delle eresie medioevali," *Archivio della R. Deputazione Romana di storia patria* 67 (1944), 97–151, essentially repeated in his book: *Medioevo Christiano* (Bari, 1951), 212–86, 2d ed. (Bari, 1958), 204ff. The most decisive contradiction to him was A. Dondaine, O.P., "L'origine de l'hérésie médiévale," *RSCI* 6 (1952), 47–78. A review of the events and sources is given by Ilarino da Milano, O.F.M. Cap., "Le eresie popolari del secolo XI nell'Europa occidentale," *SG* 2 (1947), 43–89, and "Le eresie medioevali," in *Grande Antologia Filosofica* 4 (1953), 1599–1689; cf. also Borst, *Die Katharer*, 71–80. Raffaello Morghen has defended his thesis several times: "Le origini dell'eresia medioevale in Occidente," *Ricerche di storia religiosa*, 1 (1954), 1–24; "Il cosidetto neomanicheismo occidentale del secolo XI," *Accademia nazionale dei Lincei, XII Congresso "Volta"* (1957), 84–104 and 158–60; in the report of the Roman Congress, *Relazioni* 3 (1955), 333–56; cf. "New Contributions," below, n. 29. This controversy over the origin and character of heresy in the eleventh century has not yet come to a final, unanimous decision. Cf. also Eugenio Dupré-Theseider, "Problemi di eresiologia medioevale," *Bollettino della Società di Studi Valdesi* 56 (1958), 1–17; idem, *Introduzione alle eresia medioevali* (Bologna, 1953). HG/1960.]

NEW CONTRIBUTIONS, CHAPTER 1

Published in *X Congresso Internazionale di Scienze Storiche* (Rome, 1955), *Relazioni* 3.357–402 and 467–84, repeated with additions in *AKG* 37 (1955), 131–82.

1. Robert of Torigny, *De immutatione ordinis monachorum* [1154], *PL* 202.1309–20; *Liber de diversis ordinibus, qui sunt in ecclesia* [c. 1125/30], *PL* 213.807–50; Anselm of Havelberg, *Liber de una forma credendi et multiformate vivendi* [c. 1150], *PL* 188.1141–60; on this and other monastic controversial writings, cf. Georg Schreiber, "Studien über Anselm von Havelberg," *AP* 18 (1942), 5–60.

2. Dom J. Othon [Ducourneau], "Les origines cisterciennes," *RM* 22 (1932), 133–64, 23 (1933), 1–32, 81–111, 153–89, 233–52; Jean-Berthold Mahn, *L'ordre cistercien et son gouvernement des origines au milieu du XIIIe siècle* (Paris, 1945; 2d ed., 1951). On the "Carta caritatis prior," which Mahn (died 1944) did not yet use, discovered by Josef Turk in 1939 and investigated along with other documents of the Cistercian origins, see *Analecta s. Ordinis Cisterciensis*, 1, 4 and 6 (1949–50); Gérard de Beaufort, "La Charte de la Charité cistercienne et son évolution," *RHE* 49 (1954), 391–437; Jean-A. Lefèvre, "La véritable Carta Caritatis primitive et son évolution (1114–1119)," *COCR* 16 (1954), 5–29, besides other studies in the same volume; on this Alain d'Herblay, "Le problème des origines cisterciennes," *RHE* 50 (1955), 158–64; Ernst

Werner, "Neue Texte und Forschungen zur Charta Caritatis," *Forschungen und Fortschritte* 29 (1955), 25–29; Robert Folz, "Le problème des origines de Cîteaux," *Mélanges S. Bernard, XXIV*[e] *Congrès de l'Association Bourguignonne des Sociétés savantes 1953* (Dijon, 1954), 284–94; also other articles on the beginnings of the Cistercians in that volume, as well as in the collected volume *Bernard de Clairvaux*, Commission d'histoire de l'Ordre de Cîteaux, Études et documents 3 (Paris, 1953), where Bernard's relations to other orders are studied in detail. On the interior development of the order, see now Archdale Arthur King, *Cîteaux and Her Elder Daughters* (London, 1954).

3. Charles Dereine, S.J., "Les origins de Prémontré," *RHE* 42 (1947), 352–78; François Petit, O. Præm., *La Spiritualité des Prémontrés au XII*[e] *et XIII*[e] *siècles* (Paris, 1947); Norbert Backmund, O. Præm., *Monasticon Præmonstratense*, 3 vols., 1949–56; Placide Fern. Lefèvre, O. Præm., *Les Statuts de Prémontré reformés sur les Ordres de Grégoire IX et d'Innocent IV au XIII*[e] *siècle*, Bibliothèque de la RHE 23 (Louvain, 1946); Emiel Valvekens, *Norbert van Genepp* (Bruges, 1943); Georg Schreiber, "Prämonstratenserkultur des 12. Jahrhunderts," *AP* 16 (1940), 42–108 17 (1941), 5–33.

4. Charles Dereine, "Vie commune règle de St. Augustin et chanoniers au XIe siècle," *RHE* 41 (1946), 365–406; idem, "L'élaboration du status canonique des chanoines réguliers spécialement sous Urban II," *RHE* 46 (1951), 334–565; summarizing, idem, "Chanoines," *DiHGE* 12 (1953), cols. 287–98; John Compton Dickinson, *The Origins of the Austin Canons and their Introduction in England* (London, 1950).

4a. Columban Spahr, *Das Leben des hl. Robert von Molesme* (Fribourg, Switzerland, 1944), with a critical edition of the *vita*; Séraphin Lenssen, "St. Robert fondateur de Cîteaux," *COCR* 4 (1937), 2–16, 81–96, 161–77, 241–53.

5. Jacqueline Buhot, "L'abbaye normande de Savigny, chef d'ordre et fille de Cîteaux," *MA*, 3d series, 7 (1936), 1–19; Johannes von Walter, *Die ersten Wanderprediger Frankreichs* and his *Geschichte des Christentums*, 1/2 (1934), 541ff. These itinerant preachers deserve even more investigation, see above chapter 1, section 2.

6. Rose Graham, *St. Gilbert of Sempringham and the Gilbertines* (London, 1901). The *vita* and documents of the canonization of Gilbert (died 1189) was published by Raymonde Foreville, *Un procès de canonisation à l'aube du XIII*[e] *siècle. Le livre de Saint Gilbert de Sempringham* (Paris, 1943).

7. Augustin Fliche, *La réforme grégorienne*, Histoire de l'Église 8 (1946), 445: "There are no studies of a genuinely scholarly quality on the small eremitical orders." Albert De Meyer and J.-M. De Smet, *Guigo's Consuetudine van de eerste Kartuizers*, Mededeelingen van de k. Vlaamse Academie voor Wetenschappen, Letteren en Schone Kunsten van België, Klasse der Letteren, 13/6 (Brussels, 1951); Bernard Bligny, "Les premiers Chartreux et la pauvreté," *MA* 57 (1951), 27–60. On the hermits of Grandmont, see the excerpt from his unprinted thesis by Dom Jean Becquet, "Les institutions de l'Ordre de Grandmont au moyen-âge," *RM* 42 (1952), 31–42.

8. Mahn, *L'ordre cistercien*, 28f. believes, "The Calabrian hermits who taught Stephen renounced all property and practiced itinerant preaching, the preacher living from the alms given him by his listeners." That is incorrect, according to the *Vita Stephani* (*PL* 204.1013), edited by the fourth prior of Grandmont, Stephen of Lisiac between 1139 and 1163, these hermits lived without possessions, *unanimiter in claustro. . . . Milo of Benevento, who grew up with Stephen, praised their life in sermonibus quos ad populum faciebat*, aiding them with donations of food and clothing. J. Becquet (see n. 7 above) doubts the "Calabrian inspiration" of the founder of Grandmont, but without convincing reason.

9. Alberico Pagnani, O.S.B., *Storia dei Benedettini Camaldolesi cenobiti, monache ed oblati* (Sassoferrato, 1949) restricts himself to the internal history of the order in the traditional manner.

9a. D. Roger Duvernay, "Cîteaux, Vallombreuse et Étienne Harding," *Analecta s. ordinis Cisterciensis* 8 (1952), 379–495, refers to many similarities between Vallombrosans and Cistercians, holding Stephen Harding to be the intermediary, since he could have visited the Tuscan Vallombrosan houses on his journey to Rome before 1090, and he composed the *Carta Caritatis* in 1118; on him, cf. Dom Alexis Presse, "Saint Étienne Harding," *COCR* 1 (1934), 21–30, 85–94.

9b. Marie Humbert Vicaire, O.P., stresses in his new edition of Pierre Mandonnet, O.P., *Saint Dominique*, 168ff. the innovative importance of Petrus Damiani for the idea of the *vita apostolica*; unfortunately this interests neither Fridolin Dressler, *Petrus Damiani, Leben und Werk*, Studia Anselmiana 34 (Rome, 1954) nor Heinz Löwe, "Petrus Damiani, ein italienischer Reformer am Vorabend des Investiturstreits," *GWU* 6 (1955), 65–79, but see 76f.

10. Dereine, "Les origins de Prémontré," 362f,, cf. idem, "Vie commune règle de St. Augustin," 402–03, and "Chanoines," 383ff. Abbé Sansaulieu is preparing a review of all hermits in France in the Middle Ages for the École des Hautes Études; for the interim, there is Louis Gougaud, *Ermites et Reclus* (Ligugé, 1928) and *RAM* 1 (1920).

11. Petit, *La Spiritualité des Prémontrés*, 34–35, is of the opinion that, "The establishment of itinerant preachers was not yet possible; . . . neither the canon law then in force, nor the state of morals, nor the very idea people had of the apostolic life, would permit it," but this assertion has no justification. Cf. also Mandonnet and Vicaire, *St. Dominique*.

11a. *PL* 204.1136. Similar is Stephen's *Sermo de unitate diversarum regularum*, c. 2, in Edmund Martène, *De antiquis ecclesiæ ritibus* (Venice, 1783), 308: *Querentibus, cuius professionis vel cuius regulæ cuiusve ordinis vos esse, dicatis: Christianæ religionis primæ ac principalis regulæ, evangelii scilicet, quod omnium regularum fons est atque principium* . . .

11b. Borst, *Die Katharer*, chapter 1, gives the best review of the long history of research and perception of these heresies, to which the author owes many references for this report; also cf. Manselli, *Studi sulle eresie*, chapter 1, and Jean Charbonnier, "De l'idée que le protestantisme s'est faite de ses rapports avec le catharisme, ou des adoptions d'ancêtres en histoire," *Bulletin de la Société de l'histoire du Protestantisme français* 101 (1955), 72–87.

11c. On these heretical groups in the eleventh century, see P. Ilarino da Milano, "Le eresie popolare," 43–89; Borst, *Katharer*, 71ff.; Dondaine, "L'origine de l'hérésie médiévale," *RSCI* 6 (1952), 47–78 and the response of Morghen, "Le origini dell'eresia," 1–24; Morghen deals with this question anew in his report for the Roman Historical Congress.

11d. Before 1164, John of Salisbury wrote in his *Historia pontificalis* on Arnold of Brescia (*MG Scr*. 20.538): *Hominum sectam fecit, que adhuc dicitur heresis Lumbardorum*; cf. Arsenio Frugoni, "Arnaldo di Brescia nelle fonti del secolo XII," *ISISS*, 8/9 (Rome, 1954), 131ff.; on later "Arnoldists," see n. 16 below.

12. Bernard, Sermo 66, *PL* 183.1094. The letter of the clergy of Liège to Lucius II is similar, *PL* 179.937–38.

12a. That is still in dispute between A. Dondaine and R. Morghen, see 11c above. Borst, *Katharer*, 72, believes that Dondaine "conclusively demonstrated" the influence of Bulgarian Bogomils on Western heretics, but that it was only an "addition," not the decisive impulse of this heresy.

12b. On the significance of Innocent III for the ecclesiastical recognition of the religious poverty movement and its organization in the mendicant orders, with whose help the heretical branches of this movement not reconciled with the Church were combated, see above, chapter 2; in agreement is Helene Tillmann, *Papst Innocenz III.*, Bonner Historische Forschungen 3 (1954), 180ff.; see also P. Sophronius Clasen, O.F.M., "Kritisches zur neueren Franziskusliteratur," *Wissenschaft und Weisheit* 13 (1950), 156, 162, similar in "Franz von Assisi im Licht der neueren Forschung," *GWU* (1952), 144, 151.

13. *PL* 189. 719–850; Joseph Kramp, "Chronologisches zu Peters des Erwürdigen Epistola adversus Petrobrusianos," *Miscellanea F. Ehrle* 1 (1924), 71–79; Raoul Manselli, *Studi sulle eresie*, 25–43. The objections of Arno Borst, *Katharer*, 3, against dating the tract before 1134 are still to be tested.

14. Mario Esposito, "Sur quelques écrits concernants les hérésies et les hérétiques aux XIIe et XIIIe siècles," *RHE* 36 (1940), 143–62; his assertion that William of St. Thierry wrote the tracts against Henry is unprovable, see Manselli, "Il monaco Enrico," 1–63, with the text of the tract; idem, *Studi sulle eresie*, 45ff.

15. Henri Pirenne, "Tanchelin et le projet de démembrement du diocèse d'Utrecht vers 1100," *Académie royale de Belgique, Bulletin de la Classe des Lettres*, 13th series, 5 (1927), 112–19; L. J. M. Philippen, "Der hl. Norbertus en de strijd tegen het Tanchelmisme te Antwerpen," *Bijdragen tot de Geschiedenis* 25 (1934), 251–88, with sources on Tanchelm's fight against the decadent canons in Antwerp, whom Norbert replaced with Premonstratensians. [Walter Mohr, "Tanchelm von Antwerpen. Eine nochmalige Überprüfung der Quellenlage," *Annales Universitatis Saraviensis*, Philosophie-Lettres (Saarbrücken, 1954), 234–47, presents "another review of the sources" on the heretic Tanchelm; he explains many of the oddities relayed about him, and

believes that "one can see to a particular degree a unification of Pataria and itinerant preaching" in his doctrine. The large proportion of women among the followers of Tanchelm is also remarkable. According to Mohr, "it would not be improper to see here one of the roots which would lead to the flowering of the beguines." HG/1960.]

16. While Antonio Suraci, *Arnaldo da Brescia* (Turin, 1952), gives us nothing new, Frugoni, "Arnaldo di Brescia," critically explains the sources on Arnold, convincingly distinguishing his original religious intentions (in combination with the "movimento evangelico") from his later political involvement with the movement for the autonomy of the city of Rome. A gathering of biblical arguments of the "Arnoldists" was found by Ilarino da Milano, "La "Manifestatio heresis catarorum," quam fecit Bonacursus," *Aevum* 12 (1938), 301–24, esp. 308ff., on which Frugoni, 175ff.

17. Dondaine, "Aux origines du Valdéisme," 191–235, though only one chapter of the "Liber antiheresis" is published, "De statu ecclesiæ," along with a list of the chapters.

18. Antoine Dondaine, "Nouvelles sources de l'histoire doctrinale du néo-manichéisme au Moyen Age," *Revue des Sciences philosophiques et théologiques* 28 (1939), 465–88, esp. 483–84; the final chapter, "De Waldensibus," was published by Giovanni Gonnet, "Waldensia," *RHPR* 33 (1953), 202–54, esp. 252ff., also reviewing other sources on the Waldensians critically; cf. Mario Esposito, "Sur quelques manuscrits de l'ancienne littérature religieuse des Vaudois du Piémont," *RHE* 46 (1951), 127–59. Ermengaud was usually identified with the abbot of S. Gilles (1179–95), but he is probably the earlier Waldensian, *Ermengaudus Bitterensis* (Béziers; *PL* 216.274) who was reconciled with the "Catholic Poor" of Durandus of Huesca by Innocent III (Borst, *Katharer*, 9, with the support of Dondaine). That makes the intimate knowledge of the Waldensians in Provence capable of explanation, and it also raises the doubts of Manselli, *Studi sulle eresie*, 87, whether the Waldensian chapter was written by Ermengaud.

19. Jean Leclercq, O.S.B., *Analecta monastica 2*, Studia Anselmiana 31 (Rome, 1953), 194ff., where a report by Godfrey on a Cathar trial in Le Puy in 1181 by Cardinal-Legate Henry of Albano follows (cf. his letter, *PL* 204.235ff.). Leclercq unfortunately does not distinguish between Cathars and Waldensians. Of their *primus inventor*, Godfrey says, *a loco nativitatis Wandesius nominatus*; this is to be corrected by what G. Gonnet, "Waldensia," 239ff., says about the name and origin of Waldes; cf. Ph. Pouzet, "Les origines lyonnaises de la secte des Vaudois," *Revue d'histoire de l'église de France* 22 (1936), 5–37, esp. 12, but who offers no new material. The entire literature on the history of the Waldensians is listed rather unselectively in Giovanni Gonet and A. Armand-Hugon, *Bibliografia Valdese*, Bollettino della Società di Studi Valdesi 93 (Rome, 1953).

20. Ilarino da Milano, *L'eresia di Ugo Speroni nella confutazione del maestro Vacario. Testo inedito del sec. XII con studio storico e dottrinale*, Studi e testi 115 (Vatican City, 1945).

21. Antoine Dondaine, *Un traité néo-manichéen du XIIIe siècle. Le "Liber de duobus principiis," suivi d'un fragment de rituel cathare* (Rome, 1939); on this, see Borst, *Katharer* (1953), appendix 3, 254–318.

22. Antoine Dondaine, "Les actes du concile albigeois de Saint-Félix de Caraman," *Miscellanea G. Mercati*, 5, *Studi e Testi* 125 (Vatican City, 1946), 324–55; idem, "La hiérarchie cathare d'Italie, 1–3," *AFP* 19 (1949) and 20 (1950), in which 20.308–24 is the "Tractatus de hereticis" of Anselm of Alessandria, inquisitor in Lombardy about 1267; idem, "Le manuel de l'inquisiteur, 1230–1330," *AFP* 17 (1947), 85–194.

23. Ilarino da Milano, "La 'Manifestatio heresis catarorum,' quam fecit Bonacursus," *Aevum* 12 (1938), 301–24; idem, "Le 'Liber supra Stella' del placentino Salvo Burce contro i Catari e altre correnti ereticali," *Aevum* 16 (1942), 272–319; 17 (1943), 90–146; 19 (1945), 281–341; idem, "Disputatio inter catholicum et paterinum hæreticum," *Aevum* 14 (1940), 85–140; idem, "La 'Summa contra hereticos' di Giacomo Capelli OFM e un suo 'Quaresimale' inedito (sæc. XIII)," *Collectanea Franciscana* 10 (1940), 66–82.

24. Thomas Kaeppeli, "Une somme contre les hérétiques de s. Pierre Martyr (?)," *AFP* 17 (1947), 295–335.

24a. Dimitri Obolensky, *The Bogomils: A Study in Balkan Neo-Manichaeism* (Cambridge, 1948) largely renders Steven Runciman, *The Medieval Manichee: A Study of the Christian Dualist Heresy* (Cambridge, 1947) redundant; cf. Alois Schmaus, "Der Neumanichäismus auf dem Balkan," *Sæculum* 2 (1951), 271–99; Borst, *Katharer*, 66ff.

25. Luciano Sommariva, "Studi recenti sulle eresie medievali," *RSI* 64 (1952), 237–68, gives a penetrating and intelligent review of research; cf. Arno Borst, "Neue Funde und Forschungen zur Geschichte der Katharer," *HZ* 174 (1952), 17–30. Overzealous, mythological-literary hypotheses on the Cathars are presented by Déodat Roché, *Le Catharisme*, 2d ed. (Toulouse, 1947), *Études manichéennes et cathares* (Arques, 1952), *Spiritualité de l'hérésie: Le Catharisme* (Paris, 1953); René Nelli, "Les troubadours et le catharisme," *Cahiers d'études cathares*, 1 (Arques, 1949) and other participants in the "Centre d'études cathares de l'Institut d'Études Occitanes de Toulouse" cannot be reviewed here; a critical appraisal, Paul Imbs, "À la recherche d'une littérature cathare," *Revue du Moyen Age latin* 5 (1949), 289–302. Also distorted by local patriotism is Fernand Lequenne, *Le drame cathare ou l'hérésie nécessaire* (Paris, 1954) and utterly, Maria Henrietta Fonseca, "O catarismo e a cruzada contra os albigenses," *Revista de História* 8 (Sao Paolo, 1954), 79–117.

26. Arno Borst, *Katharer*, also Robert Folz, "Le Catharisme d'après un livre récent," *RHPR* 33 (1953), 322–28; Herbert Grundmann, *HZ* 150 (1955), with reference to other reviews.

27. The Swiss religious historian Walter Nigg, in his *Buch der Ketzer*, 2d ed. (1954), is satisfied with spirited remarks on the Cathars and Waldensians without bothering to evaluate the critical literature.

28. Ilarino da Milano, "Le eresie medioevali," 1599–1689.

29. Morghen, "Osservazioni critiche," reappearing with little change under the title "L'eresia nel medioevo," in idem, *Medioevo Christiano*, also including the article, "La crisi della religiosità medioevale," from *Ricerche Religiose* 18 (1947). On this see A. Pincherle in *RSI* 60 (1948), 607–19, who doubts whether medieval heresies are understandable as growing out of lay understanding of the Bible without a teaching tradition or outside influences. Cf. also Raffaello Morghen, "Medioevo e Rinacimento," *BISI* 66 (1954). [Manselli, "Per la storia dell'eresia," 189–264, discovered the original text of the "confessio" or the Cathar Buonaccorso, converted in Milan, which is at the basis of the " 'Manifestatio hæresis Catharorum,' quam fecit Bonaccursus," edited by Ilarino da Milano (see n. 23 above), as well as another recantation of heresy in a Paris manuscript from the Southern French Cluniac house of Moissac. Both of these are significant sources from the earlier period of Catharism, still without radical dualism. Manselli also researches Archbishop Hugh of Rouen, "Contra hæreticos sui temporis" (see above, text at n. 15), without assuming any connection between the heretics in Brittany combated there and any other sects. He also refers strongly to the statements of Godfrey of Auxerre, formerly abbot of Clairvaux, on the Waldensians and Cathars, published by Jean Leclercq (see n. 19 above), and he finally reviews the chapter on the Waldensians from Ermengaud's work against the heretics, published by Giovanni Gonnet (see n. 18), which he holds to be a later addition by a different author. He also rejects (pp. 261–62) without strong justification the easy supposition that it was not Abbot Ermengaud of St. Gilles (before 1195) but the Waldensian Ermengaud of Béziers converted with the "Catholic Poor" of Durandus of Huesca in 1207 who wrote the whole text. Ermengaud of Béziers would have had close personal knowledge of the Waldensians of Provence, but would have also seen Cathars as the true heretics. On this question, important for the early history of Waldensianism, see now Charles Thouzellier, "Le 'Liber antihæresis' de Durand de Huesca et le 'Contra hereticos' d'Ermengaud de Béziers," *RHE* 55 (1960), 130–41; Gonnet, *Enchiridion Fontium Valdensium*, 153–57, with the text. HG/1960.]

30. Friedrich Heer, *Aufgang Europas. Eine Studie zu den Zusammenhängen zwischen politischer Religiosität, Frömmigkeitsstil und dem Werden Europas im 12. Jahrhundert* (Vienna; Zürich, 1949), with a volume of commentary; chapter 6, pp. 384–515, "Religiöse Volksbewegungen und der Wandel Europas im 11. und 12. Jahrhundert"; see reviews by Theodor Mayer, *HZ* 171.449ff., François Louis Ganshof, *MIÖG* 61.434ff., Herbert Grundmann, *DA* 11.273f. The second part of the work, *Die Tragödie des Heiligen Reiches* (Stuttgart, 1952; commentary 1953) deals with the "political religiosity" of the Empire and the Imperial bishops as the opposition to the new spiritual and religious movement.

31. Luchesius Spätling, O.F.M., *De Apostolicis, Pseudoapostolis, Apostolinis. Dissertatio ad diversos vitæ apostolicæ conceptus decursu elucidandos. Pontificium Athenæum Antonianum, Facultas Theologica, Theses ad Lauream 35. Monachii* (Munich, 1947), 41ff.: "De Apostolicis sæculi XII" with appendix on apostles and apostolic life from the time of the original

apostles to the end of Christian antiquity; L. M. Dewailly, "Notes sur l'histoire de l'adjectif 'apostolique'," *Mélanges de science religieuse* 5 (1948), 141–52; Abbé Antoine Mouraux, "La 'vie apostolique'' à propos de Rupert de Deutz," *Revue liturgique et monastique* 21 (1935/6), 82–105; Jean Leclercq, *La vie parfaite* (1948), chapter 3: "La vie apostolique."

32. About 1075 Sigebert of Gembloux writes (*MG Scr.* 8.511) on the monastic reform radiating from Gorze, supported by Archbishop Adalbero of Metz (929–62): *monasticam disciplinam elaborabat . . . ad apostolicæ vitæ redigere normam.* At the Roman synods of 1059 and 1063 all clerics were exhorted *ut ad apostolicam communem scilicet vitam summopere pervenire studeant (MG Scr.* Constitutiones 1.547–48). Further witnesses in Dereine, "Vie commune règle," 365–406 esp. 366ff. In the first *vita* of St. Boniface by the Anglo-Saxon Willebald, it is said of the monks at Ohrdruf: *Propriis sibi more apostolico manibus victum vestitumque instanter laborando adquesierunt* (W. Levison, *Vitæ s. Bonifacii*, 1905, 433–34); the second *vita*, by Radbod, says on the Christian way of salvation: *Hanc semitam triverunt apostoli et pro suis quisque viribus omnes apostolici viri* (ibid., 63). Boniface himself does not appear to be speaking of the *vita apostolica*, but it still remains to be determined whether Anglo-Saxons in the eighth century used the word in a special sense, rather than only for the pope and the *sedes apostolica* (see ibid, index, 230), and whether (as in Willibald above) the formulation of the Rule of St. Benedict, c. 48, was influential: *tunc vere monachi sunt, si labore manuum suarum vivunt, sicut et patres nostri et Apostoli*; cf. also chapter 2: *abbas apostolicam debet ellam semper formam servare. . . . .*

33. In the register of Gregory VII (ed. E. Caspar, *MG. Epistolæ selectæ* 2, index) the word *apostolicus* is extraordinarily frequent, but never *vita apostolica* or *imitatio apostolorum*, and the like.

34. In the letter of protection by Urban II for the Bavarian canonical foundation of Rottenbuch (Raitenbuch) dated 28 January 1092, *PL* 151.338; *Monumenta Boica* 8.3ff., cf. *Germania Pontif.* 1.375, no. 2; on this, Jacob Mois, *Das Stift Rottenbuch in der Kirchenreform des XI.–XII. Jahrhunderts. Ein Beitrag zur Ordensgeschichte der Augustiner-Chorherren*. Beiträge zur altbayerischen Kirchengeschichte 19 (2d series, 6) (Munich, 1953), 75ff. The programmatic portion of the text was repeated in privileges of Urban II and his successors for other Augustinian canons, as well as with approvals of the Premonstratensian Order (*PL* 198.36), also issued independently (*PL* 151.535–36). Cf. Innocent II, Ep. 565 (*PL* 179.628): *Vita canonicorum est vita apostolica.*

35. Marie Dominique Chenu, "Moines, clercs, laîcs au carrefour de la vie évangélique (XIIe siècle)," *RHE* 49 (1954), 59–89.

35a. *PL* 176.61164; Dereine, "L'élaboration du status canonique," 550, holds the author to be Honorius Augustodunensis, others that he is Rupert of Deutz or even a Victorine. Bernard of Clairvaux also, in *Apologia ad Guillelmum*, *PL* 182.912, says that the monastic estate *primus fuit in ecclesia, . . . cuius apostoli institutores.*

36. Guibert of Nogent, *De vita sua*. III, 13, ed. Bourgin (1907), 212ff.: *qui vitam se apostolicam tenere jactantes, eorum actus solos legere amplectuntur*. They only cite the gospels and the apostles, although they are supposed to be *rustici* and *illiterati*. Guibert concedes that these answered *christianissime* in interrogation, and yet he finds them comparable to the Manichees he knows through St. Augustine. In the eleventh century, it is only said of the heretics discovered in Arras in 1025 that they desired *verbo et opere evangelicis et apostolicis mandatis*, see Bouquet, *Recueil* 10.541; otherwise there is nothing of the *vita apostolica* among earlier Western heretics.

36a. This is Radulphus Ardens on the "Manichees" in Agen, Garonne, about 1200 (*PL* 155.201; against my earlier dating, see above, chapter 1, n. 4, see B. Geyer, *Die patristische und scholastische Philosophie*, in *Überwegs Grundriss der Geschichte der Philosophie*, 12th ed., vol. 2 [1951], 248) *mentiuntur se vitam tenere apostolicam*. On the heresy of Ponnus in Périgord (before 1147? thus Borst, *Katharer*, 4) the monk Heribert says, *PL* 181.1720: *heresim suam defendentes ex verbis Christi et Apostoli . . . dicunt . . . quod ipsi soli . . . apostolice vite veri sectatores permaneant*, and the annals of Margan: *vitam se apostolicam ducere moresque imitari mentiuntur*. Further sources in Borst, *Katharer*, 102.

36b. On "apostolics" in the heretical catalogues of Augustine, Isidore, Hrabanus Maurus, Honorius Augustodunensis, etc., see L. Spätling (n. 31 above), 3ff.

37. So, for example, Petit, *La Spiritualité des Prémontrés*, 18, more correctly 211: "It is historically the movement of clerical reform which led to the development of the apostolic life."

38. This assertion of Morghen, "Le origini dell'eresia," 4, which Dondaine, "L'origine de l'hérésie," 47ff., disputes for the eleventh century, but which can be demonstrated for the early twelfth century.

38a. On the *Pataria*, which has not yet been adequately studied, see S. M. Brown, "Movimenti politico-religiosi a Milano ai tempi della Pataria," *ASL*, 6th series, 58 (1931), 227–78; also Carl Erdmann, *Die Entstehung des Kreuzzugsgedankens*. Forschungen zur Kirchen- und Geistesgeschichte 6 (Stuttgart, 1935; reprint, 1955), 127ff. [English translation, *The Origins of the Idea of Crusade*, trans. Marshall W. Baldwin and Walter Goffart (Princeton, N.J., 1977).] For the usual assumption that the *Pataria* continued to work in Northern Italian cities, preparing the way for Arnold of Brescia and other heretics, there is as yet no proof. On the name *Pataria*, see Arsenio Frugoni, "Due schede: 'pannonus' e 'patarinus'," *BISI* 65 (1953), 129–35; differing is Antoine Dondaine, *AHDL* 19 (1952), 111ff.

39. Remarkable is the account of Lampert of Hersfeld (ed. Holder-Egger, 277), that Gregory VII sent some laymen along with his legates to Germany in 1076, *qui magnis opibus relictis ultro se ad privatam tenuemque vitam propter Deum contulerant*; they were to give public witness everywhere—through preaching?—that Henry IV had been licitely excommunicated.

40. Ernst Werner, "Bemerkungen zur Hirsauer Bewegung," *Wissenschaftliche Zeitschrift der Universität Leipzig*, 1953, no. 3, 9–17, seeks to explain the

Hirsau lay movement in terms of the "economic and social changes within the feudal social order": "class hatred of the oppressed" was specifically directed by those at Hirsau against the bishops loyal to the king; in the first instance it was "adherents from the lower classes . . . a working force attached to the monastery which was cheap and willing" which were used. Yet the sole source, Bernold, stresses that even high nobles, peasant daughters, and whole villages sought the *vita communis* from religious motives. There is not a trace of the influence of older, eastern heresies, as Werner supposes.

41. G. G. Meersmann and E. Adda, "Pénitents ruraux communitaires en Italie au XIIe siècle," *RHE* 49 (1954), 343–90, see the peasant converts who leave land to the cathedral chapter of Vicenza as remnants of the Hirsau lay communities, but they would more likely be a penitential brotherhood similar to the *Humiliati*.

42. *Liber de unitate ecclesiæ conservanda*, II, 38, *MG Libelli de Lite* 2.266f.: *sub specie religionis; Annales Augustani*, *MG Scr*. 3.128; *Chronicon Laureshamensis*, *MG Scr.* 21.432. Bernold's letter to Provost Adalbert of Speyer, *Libelli de Lite* 2.98: *De predicatione monachorum quod iterum notatis, et nobis placet, ut non nisi ordinati predicent catholicoque obediant presuli, nisi ab apostolica sede fuerint emancipati.*

43. *Vita s. Hildegardis*, III, 1, *PL* 197.122; she writes to Cologne (ibid., 253): *Ego autem timida et paupercula per duos annos valde fatigata sum, ut coram magistris et doctoribus ac cæteris sapientibus in quibusdam majoribus locis ubi mansio illorum (hæreticorum) est, vivente voce ista proferrem.* Bertha Widmer, *Heilsordnung und Zeitgeschehen in der Mystik Hildegards von Bingen*, Basler Beiträge zur Geschichtswissenschaft 52 (Basel, 1955), did not even remark how unusual Hildegard's attitude was, although she deals specifically in chapter 5, 219–66, with Hildegard's attitudes to the religious and political movements of her own time.

44. Dereine, "Les origins de Prémontré," 364ff. (contrary to my own doubts, above, chapter 8); cf. Petit, *La Spiritualité des Prémontrés*, 46: "What surprises the historian of spirituality when reading the old statutes of the Order of Prémontré is that nothing is provided for the apostolate," but he still believes (510) that not all Premonstratensians renounced it.

45. Cf. the passage from the bull of Alexander III of 1170, suppressed in the Cistercian tradition and unknown until now (J.-L., 11663), which was first published by Jean Leclercq, *Revue Bénédictine* 62 (1952), 151.

46. For Joachim's relationship to the Cistercian Order, which he left, an unfinished tract *De vita et regula s. Benedicti*, written shortly before his departure, is particularly informative, ed. C. Baraut, *Analecta sacra Tarraconensia* 24 (1951), 33–122; on this, see Herbert Grundmann, *Neue Forschungen über Joachim of Fiorre* (1950), 46ff. A remarkable, but unfortunately fragmentary, remark of Gaufrid of Auxerre about Joachim (*ex Judæis orta persona est, in Judaismo . . . annis pluribus educata!*) in Jean Leclercq, *Analecta monastica* 2 (1953), 200f., needs further study. A contemporary description of Joachim's life as a Cistercian and founder of religious houses, known only

from a later reworking, which was already mentioned by E. Jamison (*The Sicilian Norman Kingdom in the Mind of Anglo-Norman Contemporaries*, British Academy, 1938), is published by C. Baraut, "Las antiguas biografías de Joaquín de Fiore y sus fuentes," *Analecta sacra Tarraconensia* 26 (1955), 1–38. See now *DA* 16 (1960).

47. Gregory VII (*Regesta*, IV, 21) in 1077 declared it to be the worst possible miscarriage of justice, worthy of heavy penalties, that a priest, Ramihrdus, was burned as a heretic simply because he had dared to say that simoniac and unchaste priests should not celebrate the mass and that the sacrament should not be received from them. The chronicler of Cambrai (*MG Scr.* 7.540) says that at his trial Ramirhdus *veræ credulitatis sanctionem per omnia profitebatur*, but that he still did not wish to receive the sacrament from any abbot, priest, or bishop, since he held them all to be simonists. There is no doubt that he was not a Cathar, as many researchers assert. The devotees of Hirsau were also accused of not wishing to hear the mass from "unworthy priests" or to receive their blessing.

48. The heretic Henry was confronted with this accusation: *Quid cornicarius inepte, tanquam si necesse sit cuncta reperiri in evangelio, que fideliter servat christiane religionis institutio ac non multa fecerint et instituterint apostoli eorumque successores, que in evangelio non reperiuntur?* Manselli, "Il monaco Enrico," 51f.

48a. The opinion of Arnold of Brescia on the pope (according to John of Salisbury, *MG Scr*. 20.538) is significant: *Dicebat quod sic apostolus est, ut non apostolorum doctrinam imitetur aut vitam et ideo ei obedientiam aut reverentiam non deberi.*

49. *Sacerdotium res juris est, hoc est constitutionis cuiusdam. . . . Quid enim commune habet officium et caritatis, que est in mente ipsius hominis?* Da Milano, *L'eresia di Ugo Speroni*, 476, 484, 550–51; 559: *Tu vero clericum non ordinis nomine, sed meriti persone esse putas*; 561, Vacarius declares against Speroni that the tonsure as well *magis ordinem ipsum significat quam persone meritum, id est religionem*. As Vacarius, 500, says: *procul dubio si sacerdotes sunt, in officio remanebunt suo, etiam si pessimi sunt et immundi*, as it was argued against the heretic Henry (Manselli, "Il monaco Enrico," 58): *nostri sacerdotes si resipiscunt et peccant occulte, si non accusantur et juditio non deponuntur, debent tollerari nec potestate sibi tradita privantur.*

50. One of the early witnesses for the doctrine of the "opus operatum" is clearly formulated against heretics: Innocent III, *De s. altaris mysterio*, III, 5, *PL* 217.844: *In sacramento corporis Christi nihil a bono majus, nihil a malo minus perficitur sacerdote . . . quia non in merito sacerdotis, sed in verbo conficitur creatoris. Non ergo sacerdotis iniquitas effectum impedit sacramenti, sicut nec infirmitas medici virtutem medicinæ corrumpit. Quamvis igitur opus operans aliquando sit immundum, semper tamen opus operatum est mundum*. That these concepts are not "a creation of our era" as in Damien van den Eynde, O.F.M., *Les définitions des sacraments pendant la première période de la théologie scolastique* (Rome-Louvain, 1950), 58, is

shown by Artur M. Landgraf, *Dogmengeschichte der Frühscholastik*, 3/1 (1954), 53ff. and 145ff., but without paying attention to the conflict with heretical doctrine; see also Ludwig Ott, *Grundriss der katholischen Dogmatik*, 2d ed. (1954), 380.

51. Volpe, *Movimenti religiosi*; Antonio De Stephano, *Riformatori ed eretici del medioevo* (Palermo, 1938); Heer, *Aufgang Europas*; Austin Patterson Evans, "Social Aspects of Medieval Heresy," *Persecution and Liberty, Essays in Honor of G. L. Burr* (New York, 1931), 93–116; cf. also William D. Morris, *The Christian Origins of Social Revolt* (London, 1949). The religious motivation of heresy (joining Grundmann, *Religious Movements*) is stressed by Alcantara Mens, "Innerlijke drijfveeren en herkomst der kettersche bewegingen in de Middeleeuwen, Religieus ofwel sociaal offmerk?" *Miscellanea L. van der Essen* (Brussels-Paris, 1947), 299–313.

52. Thus Werner, "Bemerkungen zur Hirsauer Bewegung" (see note 40), 14, on Robert of Arbrissel, who was in fact the son of a priest, but received particularly good reception among the nobles of Normandy and their wives.

53. Johannes Ramackers, "Adelige Prämonstratenserstifte in Westfalen und am Niederrhein," *AP* 5 (1929), 200–38, 320–43; 6 (1930), 281–332.

54. As late as 1244, when Catharism had already become a "middle-class church," it was testified before the inquisition in Carcassonne (Borst, *Katharer*, 228, cf. 248) that the heretics *tenuerunt operatorium artis textoris* and that one named *miles* joined with others, *addiscebant ibidem ad texendum cum ipsis hereticis*; P. Meyer, *Annuaire-bulletin de la société de l'histoire de France* (Paris, 1879), 238. In these cases, weavers have not become heretics, but rather heretics have become weavers; cf. above, chapter 1, n. 34; Alcantara Mens, op. cit., agrees.

54a. *Gesta di Federico I in Italia*, ed. E. Monaci (Rome, 1887), v. 773ff.: *Veraque miscebat falsis multisque placebat. . . . Usuras raptusque omnes et turpia lucra, bella, simultates, luxus, periuria, cedes, furta, dolos turpesque thoros, carnalia cuncta, ut Scriptura docet, vite referebat obesse.*

54b. Cf. Roisin, "L'efflorescence cistercienne," 342–78.

54c. *MG Scr.* 20.538: *Habuit enim continentie sectatores, qui propter honestatis speciem et austeritatem vite placebant populo, sed maximum apud religiosas feminas inveniebant subsidium.*

55. Gaufrid of Auxerre in J. Leclercq, *Analecta monastica* 2.195.

56. Simon, *L'Ordre des Pénitentes*, 195; Kurt Köster, "Mainz in der Geschichte des Reuerinnen-Ordens," *Jahrbuch für das Bistum Mainz* 3 (1948), 243–72.

NOTES FOR NEW CONTRIBUTION, CHAPTER 2

1. James Midgley Clark, *The Great German Mystics. Eckhart, Tauler and Suso* (Oxford, 1949) provides, 98–109, a brief survey of German Franciscan mystics; they are not discussed in Friedrich-Wilhelm Wentzlaff-Eggebert, *Deutsche Mystik zwischen Mittelalter und Neuzeit*, 2d ed. (Tübingen, 1947),

who otherwise provides the richest bibliography besides Geyer, *Die patristische und scholastische Philosophie*, 789ff. Cf. also S. Grünewald, *Franziskanische Mystik* (Munich, 1912).

1a. P. E. Croydon, "Notes on the Life of Hugh of St. Victor," *Journal of Theological Studies* 40 (1939), 232ff. disputes the notion that Hugh of St. Victor was a German and son of the Saxon Count of Blandenburg, with some impressive arguments, preferring an origin in Flanders or Lorraine; cf. Joseph de Ghellinck, S.J., *Le mouvement théologique au XIIe siècle* (Bruges, 1948), 131, 186.

2. Heinrich Denifle, O.P., *Die deutschen Mystiker des 14, Jahrhunderts. Beitrag zur Deutung ihrer Lehre*. Aus dem literarischen Nachlass, Otwin Spiess, O.P., ed., Studia Friburgensia, 2d series, 4 (Fribourg, Switzerland, 1951), written before his pioneering study, "Meister Eckharts lateinische Schriften," including the excursus "Über die Abfänge der Predigtweise der deutschen Mystiker."

3. Herbert Grundmann, "Die Geschichtliche Grundlagen der deutschen Mystik," *DVLG* 12 (1934), 400–29.

4. Käte Oltmann, *Meister Eckhart*, Philosophische Abhandlungen, 2 (Frankfurt-Main, 1935); opposed to this the idealistic reading of Wilhelm Bange, *Meister Eckharts Lehre vom göttlichen und geschöpflichen Sein* (Limburg-Lahn, 1937); Berthold Peters, *Der Gottesbegriff Meister Eckharts* (Hamburg, 1936); cf. the ontological investigation of Hans Hof, *Scintilla Animæ. Eine Studie zu einem Grundbegriff in Meister Eckharts Philosophie* (Lund-Bonn, 1952).

5. Eckhart's Latin writings have not yet been fully published; excerpts in Denifle, "Meister Eckharts lateinische Schriften"; three numbers appeared of the *Opera omnia latina* planned by the Roman Dominican Institute S. Sabina: 1. *Super oratione dominica*, ed. R. Klibansky (Leipzig, 1934), 2. *Opus tripartitum*, *Prologi*, ed. H. Bascour (1935); 3. *Quæstiones Parisienses*, ed. A. Dondaine (1936). The plan had to be abandoned because the general edition led by Erich Seeberg and, after his death, Josef Koch, surpassed it: Meister Eckhart, *Die deutschen und lateinische Werke*, edited on behalf of the Deutsche Forschungsgemeinschaft. Thus far the following incomplete volumes have appeared of the Latin works (with German translations): vol. 1, *Prologi in opus tripartitum, Expositio libri Genesis*, ed. K. Weiss (3 fascicles, 1937/54); vol. 2, *Expositio libri Exodi* (1 fascicle, 1954); vol. 3, *Expositio s. evangelii secundum Johannem*, ed. K. Christ and J. Koch (4 fascicles, 1936/53); vol. 4, *Sermones*, ed. E. Benz (3 fascicles, 1937/50); vol. 5, *Collatio in libros Sententiarum, Quæstiones Parisiensis, Sermo die s. Augustini Parisius habitus, Tractatus super oratione dominica*, ed. J. Koch (fascicle 1/2, 1936). The *Sapientia*-commentary was edited by G. Théry, *AHDL* 3/4 (1928/9), as well as the best edition of the records of the trial, with Eckhart's written defense, ibid., 1 (1926); on this Franz Pelster, "Ein Gutachten aus dem Eckhart-Prozess in Avignon," *Beiträge zur Geschichte der Philosophie und Theologie des Mittelalters*, Supplement 3 (*Festschrift für M. Grabmann*) (1935), 1099–1124.

6. Otto Karrer, *Meister Eckhart. Das System seiner religiösen Lehre und Lebensweisheit* (Munich, 1926); Alois Dempf, *Meister Eckhart. Eine Einführung in sein Werk* (Leipzig, 1934); Herma Piesch, *Meister Eckharts Ethik* (Lucerne, 1935) and *Meister Eckhart. Eine Einführung* (Vienna, 1946).

7. Seeberg, *Meister Eckhart*, on it Herbert Grundmann, *HZ* 152 (1935), 572ff. and "Eckhartiana," *ZKG* 56/7 (1937/8); Heinrich Ebeling, *Meister Eckharts Mystik. Studien zu den Geisteskämpfen um die Wende des 13. Jahrhunderts*, Forschungen zur Kirchen- und Geistersgeschichte 21 (Stuttgart, 1941), on which see Wilhelm Grebe, *Blätter für deutsche Philosophie* 18 (1944), 187ff.; more careful and very well-informed is Konrad Weiss, *Meister Eckharts Stellung innerhalb der theologischen Entwicklung des Spätmittelalters*, Studien der Luther-Akademie, 2d series, 1 (Berlin, 1953), along with the very informative survey of H. Hermelink on the state of Eckhart studies in *Studien der Luther-Akademie*, ed. C. Strange, 2d series, 1: *Eckhart-Studien* (Berlin, 1953).

8. J. A. Bizet, *Henri Suso et le déclin de la scolastique* (Paris, 1952); J. Bühlmann, *Christuslehre und Christusmystik des Heinrich Seuse* (Lucerne, 1942); biographical: Conrad Gröber, *Der Mystiker Heinrich Seuse* (Freiburg i.B., 1941). The critical edition of the "Horologium sapientiæ" being prepared by P. Dominikus Planzer, O.P. (see *Divus Thomas*, 12/13, 1934/5) has still not appeared. Suso's German writings were edited by Karl Bihlmeyer in 1907.

9. Hermann Kunisch, "Die mittelalterliche Mystik und die deutsche Sprache," *Mitteilungen der deutschen Akademie* 15 (1940), 25–33; Josef Quint, "Mystik und Sprache," *DVLG* 27 (1953), 48–76, where many specialist studies are mentioned; cf. also K. Ruh, "Die trinitarische Spekulation in deutscher Mystik und Scholastik," *ZDP* 72 (1953), 24–53.

10. The results of long critical investigation have been summarized by Josef Quint, *Die überlieferung der deutschen Predigten Meister Eckharts* (1932) and *Neue Handschriftenfunde zur überlieferung M. Eckharts und seiner Schule* (1940). The following German works are available in the *Eckhart-Gesamtausgabe*: vol. 1, *Predigten* (5 fascicles 1936/51, almost complete; 3 further volumes of German sermons will follow); vol. 5, *Traktate* (2 fascicles, 1954: *Liber Benedictus*, of which there is also a special edition by J. Quint, *Kleine Texte für Vorlesungen und übungen*, ed. H. Lietzmann and K. Aland, no. 55, 2d ed., 1952). On the date and the woman addressed by the *Liber Benedictus*, see L. L. Hammerich, *ZDP* 56 (1931), 69–98; H. Roos, ibid., 224–33; G. Théry, *Mélanges J. De Ghellinck* 2 (1951), 903–35. Cf. the selection by J. Quint, *Textbuch zur Mystik des deutschen Mittelalters (Eckhart, Tauler, Seuse)* (Halle, 1952).

11. There is still no critical edition of Tauler sermons; eighty sermons from individual manuscripts are printed by F. Vetter, *Deutsche Texte des Mittelalters*, 11 (1910), supplemented by A. L. Corin, *Sermons de J. Tauler*, Bibliothèque de la Faculté de Philosophie et Lettres de l'Université de Liège 33 and 42 (1924/29).

12. *Schriften aus der Gottesfreund-Literatur*, ed. Ph. Strauch, Altdeutsche Textbibliothek 22/23 and 27 (Halle, 1927–29).

13. Ruysbroeck, *Werken*, ed. J. van Mierlo et al., 4 vols (1932/4); a philological, critical edition is planned.

14. In addition to the older, largely flawed, and scattered editions of the German-language nuns' books of Adelhausen near Freiburg, Engelthal near Nuremberg, Katharinenthal in the Thurgau, Kirchberg near Sulz, Oetenbach near Zürich, Töss near Winterthur, Weiler near Esslingen (see Friedrich-Wilhelm Wentzlaff-Eggebert, *Deutsche Mystik,* 66ff. and 298f.) there is also the Latin "vitæ sororum" of Unterlinden (near Colmar), ed. Jeanne Ancelet-Hustache, 317–509.

15. *De Visionen van Hadewich*, ed. J. van Mierlo; *Brieven*, ed. Jan van Mierlo, Leuvense Studieën en Tekstuitgaven, 2 vols. (Louvain, 1947). Cf. also Beatrijs van Nazareth (c. 1205–1268), *Seven manieren van minne*, ed. Reypens and van Mierlo.

16. Maria Alberta Lücker, *Meister Eckhart und die Devotio moderna*, Studien und Texte zur Geistesgeschichte des Mittelalters 1 (Leiden, 1950); cf. J. van Mierlo, "Ruusbroec's bestrijding van de ketterij," *Ons geestelik Erf* 6 (1932), 304–46; André Combes, *Essai sur la critique de Ruysbroeck par Gerson* 1 (Paris, 1945).

17. Ewald Müller, *Das Konzil von Vienne, 1311/12*, Vorreformationsgeschichtliche Forschungen 12 (1934), 577ff.

18. Faral, "Les 'Responsiones'," 337–95

19. J. van Mierlo derives the word *begina* from the heretical name Al-bigenses, with good reason, see *RHE* 23 (1927), 785ff. and 28 (1932), 380ff., also "Ophelderingen bij de vroegste geschiedenis van het woord begijn," *VMKVA* (Ghent, 1931), 983–1006 and *Ons geestelijk Erf* 23 (1949), 247ff., against the objections of Alcantara Mens, who derives the word from "beige," the gray-brown of the uncolored wool of their habits, although he concedes that the name "beguine" originally had a heretical sound to it; see also Roisin, "L'efflorescence cistercienne," 362f. and McDonnell, *Beguines and Beghards*, 432ff.

20. *MG Scr.* 26.234 and 443; cf. also Asen, *Die Beginen in Köln*; Karl Zuhorn, "Die Beginen in Münster," *Westfälische Zeitschrift* 91 (1935), 1–149, and older local research on the beguines in Philippen, *De Begijnhoven.*

21. Dayton Phillips, *Beguines in Medieval Strasburg: A Study of the Social Aspect of Beguine Life* (Palo Alto, Calif., 1941), with statistics on the equal participation of women of all levels.

21a. Simone Roisin, *L'Hagiographie cistercienne dans le diocèse de Liège au XIIIe siècle* (Louvin-Brussels, 1947).

22. Mens, *Oorspong*; on it see Charles Dereine, *RHE* 44 (1949), 633ff., with references to earlier "manifestations of the beguine movement in the larger sense of the word," in Germany and France. Most recently there has appeared an even more comprehensive presentation by McDonnell, *Beguines and Beghards*, which deals directly and thoroughly with all the sources on beguines and beghards, including their heretical forms, from the twelfth to the fourteenth century, creating a reliable general picture with many notes of biographical and bibliographical content. It is irreplaceable for future research.

23. Capelle, *Amaury de Bène*, and M. Dal Pra, *Amalrico di Bena* (Milan, 1951) do not support the connection I demonstrated between the Amaurians and the women's religious movement (see above, chapter 7); a new source is provided by M. Th. d'Alverny, "Un fragment."

23a. On the term "papelarde" for the Amaurians as for the beguines, see above, chapter 7, n. 46ff.; Mens, *Oosprong*, 35–36, and 279ff; McDonnell, *Beguines and Beghards*, 418–19 and 472–73.

23b. Despite many superficial similarities, the heresy evaluated by Albertus Magnus cannot be called "Cathar mysticism" (thus Mens, *Oorsprong*, 218, cf. 198); on dating and origins, see above chapter 7, section 4.

24. Father Livarius Oliger, O.F.M., "Libero Spirito," *Enciclopedia cattolica* 7 (1951), 1277; cf. Antonio De Stephano, "Interno alle origini e la natura della 'secta spiritus libertatis'," *Archivum Romanicum* 11 (1927), 150–62. L. Oliger, "De secta spiritus libertatis in Umbria sæc. XIV," *Storia e Letteratura* 3 (Rome, 1943) works from very interesting documents on a heresy discovered by St. Clara of Montefalcone, whose leader was an earlier follower of the apostolic Gherardo Segarelli. Oliger (61–62) believes that her quietism, with its amoral consequences, derived neither from the few Franciscan adherents of the sect nor from the pantheism of the Amalricans or heretical beghards. It could hardly be an accident, however, that the "Brothers and Sisters of the Free Spirit" appear in Germany and the "secta spiritus libertatis" in Italy at the same moment, with many similar doctrines, and that often (even in papal bulls) the Provençal Spirituals and the followers of Olivi are called beguines, at a time when the German beguines and beghards were being condemned. This connection deserves further study; cf. McDonnell, *Beguines and Beghards*, 433f.

25. The assertion of Heer, *Aufgang Europas*, 261, that German mysticism was "carried by nobles" is just as one-sidedly generalized and half-true as his opinion that the religious movement of the twelfth century was bourgeois or proletarian (see above). In his *Europäische Geistesgeschichte* (1953), 189, Heer modifies his assertion: "There were women and their priests, there were nobles. . . . The movement emerged from these two 'estates' and spread, as it watered down, hereticized and vulgarized itself in the petty-bourgeois 'circles' of the late-medieval town." But does this say anything relevant or conclusive about men such as Tauler, Ruysbroeck, or Merswin? Even Willy Zippel, *Die Mystiker und die deutsche Gesellschaft des 13. und 14. Jahrhunderts*, Dissertation, Leipzig, 1935, cannot provide a sociological explanation for mysticism and its impact. Informative observations on the origins of many South German mystics from ministerial families which came into the towns can be found in Heinrich Gürsching, "Neue urkundliche Nachrichten über den Mystiker Heinrich von Nördlingen," *Festgabe für Karl Schornbaum* (Neustadt/Aisch, 1950), 42–47; on him, see also Anton Walz, "Gottesfreunde um Margarete Ebner," *HJ* 72 (1952), 253–65. Whether different social strata were at work in "heretical mysticism" remains to be seen, but social motifs and demands are not to be found here, either. The contested question of whether the beguines' movement

is to be seen in social or religious terms is most carefully considered by McDonnell, *Beguines and Beghards*, 81ff., which holds it—too summarily, to be sure—to be a "product of urban civilization," but does not deny the originally religious impulse, coming to the conclusion, "their origins must be assigned to a complex of socioeconomic and religious motivation" (p. 88). The last word has not been said on this, it appears to me.

FREQUENTLY CITED WORKS

Acta capitulorum generalium, vol. 1. Ed. B. M. Reichert. *MOPH* 3. Rome, 1896.

Actus b. Francisci et sociorum eius. Ed. Paul Sabatier. Collection d'études et de documents sur l'histoire religieuse et littéraire du moyen âge 4. Paris, 1902.

Adelhausen nuns' book. See Anna of Munzingen.

Ademar of Chabannes. *Chronicon*. Ed. Jules Chavanon. Collection de textes pour servir à l'étude et à l'enseignement de l'histoire. Paris, 1897.

Alphandéry, Paul. "De quelques faits de prophétisme dans les sectes latines antérieures au Joachimisme." *RHR* 52 (1905), 177–218.

——. *Les idées morales chez les hétérodox latins au début du XIIIe siècle*. Bibliothèque de l'École des hautes études, Sciences religieuses 16:1. Paris, 1908.

Altaner, Berthold. *Der heilige Dominikus, Untersuchungen und Texte*. Breslauer Studien zur historischen Theologie 2. Breslau, 1922.

——. *Die Briefe Jordans von Sachsen, des zweitens Dominikanergenerals (1222–37), Texte und Untersuchungen; zugleich ein Beitrag zur Geschichte der Frömmigkeit im 13. Jahrhundert* = *QF* 20. Leipzig, 1925.

——. "Die Beziehungen des heiligen Dominikus zum heiligen Franziskus von Assisi." *FS* 9 (1922), 1–28.

——. "Venturino von Bergamo, O.Pr., eine Biographie, zugleich ein Beitrag zur Geschichte des Dominikanerordens im 14. Jahrhundert." *Kirchengeschichtliche Abhandlungen* 9:2. Ed. M. Sdralek. Breslau, 1911.

d'Alverny, M. Th. "Un fragment du procès des Amauriciens." *AHDL* 25/26 (1951), 325–36.

Analectes pour servir à l'histoire ecclésiastique de la Belgique 20, 2nd series, 4. Louvain, 1886.

Ancelet-Hustache, Jeanne. *Mechthilde de Magdebourg, étude de psychologie religieuse*. Paris, 1926.

——. "Vitæ sororum." *AHDL* 5 (1930), 312–509..

Angelo Clareno. "Expositio regulæ fratrum minorum." Ed. Ignaz Döllinger. *Beiträge zur Sektengeschichte*, vol. 2. Munich, 1890, 417–516.

——. "Expositio regulæ fratrum minorum." Ed. Franz Ehrle. *ALKG* 2 (1886), 106–155, 249–327.

——. *Expositio regulæ fratrum minorum*. Ed. Liverius Oliger. Quaracchi, 1912.

——. "Historia septem tribulationum ordinis minorum." Ed. Ignaz Döllinger. *Beiträge zur Sektengeschichte*, vol. 2. Munich, 1890, 129–236.

Anna of Munzingen. *Chronica* (of the convent of Adelhausen). Ed. J. König. *FDA* 13 (1880), 129–236.

Année dominicaine ou vie des saints, des bienheureux, des martyrs . . . de l'ordre des Frères-Prêcheurs. 2nd ed. Lyon, 1886.

Anonymus Perusinus. "Legenda sancti Francisci." Ed. François van Ortroy. *Miscellanea francescana* 9 (1902), 33–48.

Armand-Hugon, A. See Gonnet, G.

Asen, Johannes. *Die Beginen in Köln*. Annalen des Historischen Vereins für den Niederrhein, vols. 111–13 (1927–29).

Auer, Josef. *Studien zu den Reformschriften für das zweite Lyoner Konzil*. Dissertation, University of Freiburg i. B., 1910.

Backmund, Norbert. *Monasticon præmonstratense*. 3 vols. Straubing, 1949–56.

Baeumker, Clemens. See *Tractatus contra Amaurianos*.

Barbazan, Étienne. *Fabliaux et contes des poètes françois*. Ed. M. Méon. Paris, 1808.

Baur, Ludwig. "Die Ausbreitung der Bettelorden in der Diözese Konstanz," *FDA* 28, 2nd series, 1 (1900), 1–101; 29, 2nd series, 2 (1901), 1–107.

Beatrijs van Nazareth. *Seven manieren van minne*. Ed. L. Reypens and J. van Mierlo. Leuvense Studien en Tekstuitgaven 12 (1926).

Berger, Élie. *Les Registres d'Innocent IV*. Bibliothèque des écoles françaises d'Athène et de Rome, 2nd series, 1. Paris, 1884–97.

Berger, Samuel. *La Bible française au Moyen Age*. Paris, 1884.

Bernard Gui. *Practica inquisitionis* [*Manuel d'Inquisiteur*]. Ed. Guillaume Mollat. Les classiques de l'histoire de France au moyen age. Paris, 1926–27.

Berthier. See Jordanis de Saxonia.

Berthold of Regensburg. *Deutsche Predigten*. Ed. Franz Pfeiffer and Joseph Strobl. Vienna, 1862–80.

———. See A. E. Schönbach.

Bett, Henry. *Johannes Scotus Erigena: A Study in Mediaeval Philosophy*. Cambridge, 1925.

Bibliotheca maxima veterum Patrum. Vols. 24, 25. Lyon, 1677.

Bierbaum, Max. *Bettelorden und Weltgeistlichkeit an der Universität Paris, Texte und Untersuchungen zum literarischen Armuts- und Exemtionsstreit des 13. Jahrhunderts*. FS, Beiheft 2. Münster i. W., 1920.

Bihlmeyer, Karl. *Kirchengeschichte auf Grund des Lehrbuchs von F. X. von Funk, 2: Das Mittelalter*. 8th ed. Paderborn, 1980.

———. "Mystisches Leben in dem Dominikanerinnenkloster Weiler bei Eslingen im 13. und 14. Jahrhundert." *Württembergische Vierteljahrshefte für Landesgeschichte*, 2nd ser., 25 (1916), 61–96.

Birckman, Bertha. *Die vermeintliche und die wirkliche Reformschrift des Dominikanergenerals Humbert de Romanis*. Abhandlungen zur mittleren und neueren Geschichte 62. Berlin; Leipzig, 1916.

Birlinger, Anton. "Leben heiliger alemannischen Frauen des 14./15. Jahrhunderts, IV: Die Nonnen von Kirchberg bei Haigerloch." *Alemannia* 11 (1883), 1–20.

———. V: Die Nonnen von St. Katharinenthal bei Diessenhofen." *Alemannia* 15 (1887), 150–84.

Böhmer, Heinrich. *Analekten zur Geschichte des Franciscus von Assisi*. 2nd ed. Sammlung ausgewälter kirchen- und dogmengeschichtlicher Quellenschriften, 2nd ser., 4. Tübingen, 1930.

Bonaventure. *Legenda s. Francisci, Opera*, vol. 8. Quaracchi, 1898, 504–64.

Boos, Heinrich. *Urkundenbuch der Stadt Worms*. Quellen zur Geschichte der Stadt Worms, vol. 1. Worms, 1886.

Borst, Arno. *Die Katharer*. Schriften der Monumenta Germaniæ Historica 12. Stuttgart, 1953.

Brem, Ernst. *Papst Gregor IX bis zum Beginn seines Pontifikats*. Heidelberger Abhandlungen zur mittleren und neurern Geschichte 32. Heidelberg, 1911.

Broeckx, Edmond. *Le Catharisme*. Universitas Catholica Lovaniensis, Diss. theol. 2:8. Hoogstraten, 1916.

Brown, Edward. *Appendix ad fasciculum rerum expetendarum et fugiendarum*, vol. 2. London, 1690.

Bruschius, C. *Monasteriorum Germaniæ centuria*, vol. 1. Ingolstadt, 1551.

Burchard von Ursberg. *Chronik*. Ed. Oswald Holder-Egger and Bernhard von Simson. SRGUS, 2nd ed. Hannover; Leipzig, 1916.

Cæsarius of Heisterbach. *Dialogus miraculorum*. Ed. Joseph Strange. Cologne; Bonn; Brussels, 1851.

Callebaut, André. "Autour de la rencontre à Florence de S. François et du Cardinal Hugolin." *AFH* 19 (1926), 530–58.

Capelle, G. C. *Amaury de Bène: Étude sur son panthéisme formel*. Bibliothèque thomiste 16. Paris, 1932.

Cel., see Thomas of Celano.

Chapotin, Marie-Dominique. *Histoire des dominicains de la province de France*. Rouen, 1898.

Chartularium Universitatis Parisiensis. Ed. Heinrich Denifle, Émile Chatelain. Paris, 1889–91.

Chronica regia Colonensis. Ed. Georg Waitz. SRGUS, vol. 18. Hanover, 1880.

Chronica de Mailros. Ed. Joseph Stevenson. Publications of the Bannatyne Club. Edinburgh, 1835.

Chronica ordinis fratrum Prædicatorum [by Gerhard Frachet?]. Ed. B. M. Reichert. *MOPH* 1 (1896), 321–38; 7 (1904), 1ff.

Chronicon universale anonymi Laudunensis. Ed. Alexander Cartellieri and Wolf Stechele. Leipzig; Paris, 1909.

Commission d'histoire de l'Ordre de Cîteaux. *Bernard de Clairvaux*. Preface by Thomas Merton. Études et documents, no. 3. Paris, 1953.

Crusius, Martinus. *Annales Suevici*. Frankfurt, 1595/6.

Danzas, Antonin. *Études sur les temps primitifs de l'ordre de S. Dominique*, vol. 4. Paris, 1877.

David of Augsburg. *Tractatus de inquisitione hereticorum*. Ed. Wilhelm Preger. Abhandlungen der historischen Classe der bayerischen Akademie der Wissenschaften 14:2. Munich, 1879. 181–235.

———. *De exterioris et interioris hominis compositione*. Quaracchi, 1899.

Delorme. See *Legenda antiqua s. Francisci*.

Denifle, Heinrich. "Meister Eckharts lateinische Schriften und die Grundanschauung seiner Lehre." *ALKG* 2 (1886), 417–615.

——. See *Chartularium Universitatis Parisiensis.*

——. *Die deutschen Mystiker des 14, Jahrhunderts. Beitrag zur Deutung ihrer Lehre*. Ed. Otwin Spiess. Aus dem literarischen Nachlass. Studia Friburgensia, 2nd ser., 4. Fribourg, Switzerland, 1951.

Denkinger, Tiberius. *Die Bettelorden in der französischen didaktischen Literatur des Mittelalters*. Dissertation, Münster, 1915.

Dereine, Charles. "Vie commune règle de St. Augustin et chanoniers au XIe siècle." *RHE* 41 (1946), 365–406.

——. "Les origins de Prémontré." *RHE* 42 (1947), 352–78.

——. "L'élaboration du status canonique des chanoines réguliers spécialement sous Urban II." *RHE* 46 (1951), 334–565.

——. "Chanoines." *DHGE* 12.287–98.

De Stephano, Antonino. "Le origini dell'ordine degli Umiliati." *Rivista storico-critica delle scienze teologiche* 2 (1906), 851–71.

——. "Interno alle origini e la natura della 'secta spiritus libertatis'." *Archivum romanicum* 11 (1927), 150–62.

——. *Riformatori ed eretici del medioevo* (Palermo, 1938).

Dialogus de vitis sanctorum fratrum minorum. Ed. Leonardus Lemmens. Fragmenta franciscana 1. Rome, 1902.

Dietler, Seraphim. *Die Gebweiler Chronik*. Ed. Joh. von Schlumberger. Gebweiler, 1896.

Döllinger, Ignaz. *Beiträge zur Sektengeschichte des Mittelalters,* 2: *Dokumente vornehmlich zur Geschichte der Valdesier und Katharer*. Munich, 1890.

Dondaine, Antoine. *Un traité néo-manichéen du XIIIe siècle. Le "Liber de duobus principiis," suivi d'un fragment de rituel cathare*. Rome, 1939.

——. "Nouvelles sources de l'histoire doctrinale du néo-manichéisme au moyen age." *Revue des sciences philosophiques et théologiques* 28 (1939), 465–88.

——. "Aux origines du valdéisme." *AFP* 16 (1946), 191–235.

——. "Les actes du concile albigeois de Saint-Félix de Caraman." *Miscellanea Giovanni Mercati*, vol. 5, *Studi e testi* 125. Vatican City, 1946. 324–355.

——. "Le manuel de l'inquisiteur, 1230–1330." *AFP* 17 (1947), 85–194.

——. "La hiérarchie cathare d'Italie, 1–3." *AFP* 19 (1949) and 20 (1950).

——. "L'origine de l'hérésie médiévale." *RSCI* 6 (1952), 47–78.

Douais, Célestin. "Les hérétiques du comté de Toulouse dans la première moitié de XIIIe siècle d'après l'enquête de 1245." *CRCSIC*. Paris, 1891. 5.148–62.

——. *Acta capitulorum provincialium ordinis fratrum prædicatorum*, vol. 2. Toulouse, 1895.

——. *La somme des autorités à l'usage des Prédicateurs méridionaux au XIIIe siècle*. Paris, 1896.

Du Cange, Charles Du Fresne. *Glossarium mediæ et infimæ latinitatis*. Ed. G. A. L. Henschel and Léopold Favre. Niort, 1883–.

Duhem, Pierre. *Le système du monde*, vol. 5. Paris, 1917.

Dupré-Theseider, Eugenio. *Introduzione alle eresie medioevali*. Bologna, 1953.

——. "Problemi di eresiologia medioevale." *Bollettino della società di studi valdesi* 102 (1958), 3–17.

Ebeling, Heinrich. *Meister Eckharts Mystik. Studien zu den Geisteskämpfen um die Wende des 13. Jahrhunderts*. Forschungen zur Kirchen- und Geistersgeschichte 21. Stuttgart, 1941.

Ebner, Margarete. See Strauch.

Eckhart. *Reden der Unterscheidung*. Ed. Ernst Diederichs. Kleine Texte, no. 117. Bonn, 1913.

——. *Buch der göttlichen Tröstung und von dem edlen Menschen*. Ed. Philipp Strauch. Kleine Texte, no. 55, 2nd ed. Bonn, 1922.

——. *Deutsche Mystiker*, vol. 2. 4th ed. Ed. Franz Pfeiffer. Göttingen, 1924.

Ehrle, Franz. "Die ältesten Redaktionen der Generalconstitutionen des Franziskanerordens." ALKG 6 (1892), 1–138.

——. See Angelo Clareno.

Engel-Janosi, Friedrich. *Soziale Probleme der Renaissance*. Beiheft zur Vierteljahrschrift für Sozial- und Wirtschaftsgeschichte 4 (1924).

Engelthal, nuns' book. *Der Nonne von Engelthal Büchlein von der Gnaden Überlast*. Ed. Karl Schröder. Bibliothek des Litterarischen Vereins in Stuttgart, 108. Tübingen, 1871. [Modern German translation by Margarete Weinhandl, *Deutsches Nonnenleben: Katholicon*, vol. 2. Munich, 1924]; Ed. Wilhelm Oehl and Christine Ebnerin. *Das Büchlein von der Gnaden Überlast*. Kempten, 1924.

Ennen, Leonhard, and Gottfried Eckertz. *Quellen zur Geschichte der Stadt Köln*, vol. 2. Cologne, 1868.

Eubel, Konrad. *Geschichte der oberdeutschen (Strassburger) Minoriten-Provinz*. Würzburg, 1886.

——. *Epitome et supplementum bullarii Franciscani*. Rome, 1908.

Fabri, Felix. *Tractatus de civitate Ulmensi*. Ed. Gustav Veesemeyer. Bibliothek des Litterarischen Vereins in Stuttgart 186. Tübingen, 1889.

Faral, Edmond. "Les 'Responsiones' de Guillaume de Saint Amour." *AHDL* 18 (1950–51), 337–95.

Fayen, Arnold. "L'Antigraphum Petri et les lettres concernantes Lambert le Bègue, conservées dans le manuscrit de Glasgow." *Compte rendu des séances de la commission royale d'histoire* 68. Brussels, 1899. 255–366.

Finke, Heinrich. *Ungedruckte Dominikanerbriefe des 13. Jahrhunderts*. Paderborn, 1891.

——. *Konzilienstudien zur Geschichte des 13. Jahrhunderts*. Münster, 1891.

Fliche, Augustin. *La réforme grégorienne*. Histoire de l'église 8. Paris, 1946.

Förster, Wendelin. "La Noble Leçon," *Göttingische Gelehrte Anzeigen*. 1888. 753–803.

Förg, Ludwig. *Die Ketzerverfolgungen in Deutschland unter Gregor IX*. Berlin, 1932.

Fortini, Arnaldo. *Nova Vita di San Francesco d'Assisi*. Milan, 1926.

Frachet, Gerhard. "Vita fratrum ordinis Prædicatorum." Ed. Benedictus Maria Reichert. *MOPH* 1. Louvain, 1896.

Fredericq, Paul, ed. *Corpus documentorum inquisitionis hæreticæ pravitatis Neerlandicæ*. Ghent; The Hague, 1889–.

Friedberg, Aemilius, ed. *Corpus iuris canonici,* vol. 2. Leipzig, 1879.

Frugoni, Arsenio. *Arnaldo di Brescia nelle fonti del secolo XII*. ISISS, 8–9. Rome, 1954.

——."Due schede: 'pannonus' e 'patarinus'." *BISI* 65 (1953), 129–35.

Galbraith, Georgina Rosalie. *The Constitution of the Dominican Order.* Manchester, 1925.

Gerardus de Fracheto. See Frachet.

Gesta synodi Aurelianensis. Ed. Benjamin Guérard. Collection de documents inédits sur l'histoire de France, vol. 1. Paris, 1840.

Geyer, B. *Die patristische und scholastische Philosophie.* In *überwegs Grundriss der Geschichte der Philosophie,* vol. 2. 3rd. ed. 1952.

Godefroy, Frédéric. *Dictionnaire de l'ancienne langue française et de tous les dialectes du XIe au XVe siècle*. Paris, 1880–.

Goetz, Walter. "Die ursprünglichen Ideale des hl. Franz von Assisi." *HV* 6 (1903), 19–50.

Gonnet, Giovanni. *Enchiridion Fontium Valdensium. Recueil critique des sources concernant les Vaudois au moyen âge*, vol. 1. Torre Pellice, 1958.

——. "Waldensia." *RHPR* 33 (1953), 202–54.

Gonnet, Giovanni, and A. Armand-Hugon. "Bibliografia Valdese." *Bollettino della Società di Studi valdesi* 93 (1953).

Greven, Joseph. *Die Anfänge der Beginen, ein Beitrag zur Geschichte der Volksfrömmigkeit und des Ordenswesens im Hochmittelalter*. Vorreformationsgeschichtliche Forschungen 8. Münster, 1912.

——. "Der Ursprung des Beginenwesens." *HJ* 35 (1914), 26–58, 291–318.

——. "Engelbert der Heilige und die Bettelorden." *BZTS* 2 (1925), 32–48.

Grundmann, Herbert. "Zur Geschichte der Beginen im 13. Jahrhundert." *AKG* 21 (1931), 296–320.

——. "Die Geschichtliche Grundlagen der deutschen Mystik." *DVLG* 12 (1934), 400–29.

——. "Der Typus des Ketzers in mittelalterlicher Anschauung." *Kultur- und Universalgeschichte. Festschrift für Walter Goetz* (1927), 91–107.

Guilelmus Brito. *De gestis Philippi II*. Ed. Delaborde. *Oevres de Rigord et de Guillaume le Breton*, Société de l'histoire de France. Paris, 1882.

Guiraud, Jean. *Cartulaire de Notre-Dame de Prouille, précédé d'une étude sur l'albigéisme languedocien aux XIIe et XIIIe siècles*. Bibliothèque historique du Languedoc 1. Paris, 1907.

Hadewich. *De Visionen van Hadewich*. Ed. Jan van Mierlo. Leuvense Studieën en Tekstuitgaven 10. Louvain; Ghent; Malines, 1924–25.

——. *Brieven*. Ed. Jan van Mierlo. Leuvense Studieën en Tekstuitgaven. Louvain, 1947.

Hajdu, Helga. *Lesen und Schreiben im Spätmittelalter*. Specima dissertationum facultatis philosophicæ Universitatis Quinque-ecclesiensis, Schriften aus dem deutschen Institut. Fünfkirchen, 1931.

Hartzheim, Joseph, and Johann Friedrich Schannat, eds. *Concilia Germaniæ*. 11 vols. Cologne, 1759–1790.

Haskins, Charles Homer. *Studies in Mediaeval Culture*. Oxford, 1929.

Hauber, A. "Deutsche Handschriften in Frauenklöstern des späteren Mittelalters." *ZB* 31 (Leipzig, 1914), 341–73.

Hauck, Albert. *Kirchengeschichte Deutschlands*. [*KD*]. Vols. 4–5. Leipzig, 1913, 1911–20.

Haupt, Hermann. "Beiträge zur Geschichte der Sekte vom freien Geiste und des Beghardentums." *ZKG* 7 (1885), 504–76.

Hauréau, Barthélemy. *Histoire de la philosophie scolastique*. Paris, 1872–80.

Heer, Friedrich. *Aufgang Europas. Eine Studie zu den Zusammenhängen zwischen politischer Religiosität, Frömmigkeitsstil und dem Werden Europas im 12. Jahrhundert*. Vienna; Zürich, 1949.

Hefele, Carl Joseph, and Alois Knöpfler. *Conciliengeschichte*, vol. 5. Freiburg i. B., 1886.

Heidingsfelder, Friedrich. *Die Regesten der Bischöfe von Eichstätt*. Veröffentlichungen der Gesellschaft für fränkische Geschichte 6: 3. 1917.

Heintke, Fritz. *Humbert von Romans, der fünfte Ordensmeister der Dominikaner*. Eberings historische Studien 222. Berlin, 1933.

Henriquez, Chrysostomus. *Quinque prudentes virgines, sive b. Beatricis de Nazareth, b. Aleydis de Scharenbecka, b. Idæ de Nivellis, b. Idæ de Lovanio, b. Idæ de Lewis ord. Cist. præclara gesta*. Antwerp, 1630.

Brother Hermann. *Life of Jolande*. See John Meier.

Hilka, Alfons. "Altfranzösische Mystik und Beginentum." *ZRP* 47 (1927), 121–70.

Huber, Johannes. *Johannes Scotus Erigena*. Munich, 1861.

Hugo, Carl Ludwig. *Annales ordinis Præmonstratensis*. Nancy, 1734.

Ingold, Augustin Marie Pierre. *Le monastère des Unterlinden*. Mitteilungen der Gesellschaft für Erhaltung der geschichtlichen Denkmäler im Elsass, 2nd series, 18. Strasbourg, 1897.

James of Vitry. *Jacobi de Vitriaco libri duo, quorum prior orientalis sive Hierosolimitanæ, alter occidentalis historiæ nomine inscribitur*. Ed. Franciscus Moschus. Douai, 1597.

Jordanus de Saxonia. *De initiis ordinis, Opera ad res ordinis Prædicatorum spectantia*. Ed. Joachim-Joseph Berthier. Fribourg, Switzerland, 1891.

———. *De initiis ordinis, Opera ad res ordinis Prædicatorum spectantia*. Ed. Heribert Christian Scheeben. MOPH 16:2. 1935.

Jordanus. *Chronica*. Ed. Heinrich Böhmer. Collection d'études et de documents sur l'histoire religieuse et littéraire du moyen age 6. Paris, 1908.

Jundt, Auguste. *Histoire du panthéisme populaire au moyen âge et au XVI*[e] *siècle*. Paris, 1875.

Karg, Fritz. *Das literarischen Erwachen des deutschen Ostens im Mittelalter*. Mitteldeutsche Studien, vol. 1; Beiheft 3 of *Theutonista*. Halle, 1932.

Katharinenthal, nuns' book. See Birlinger.
Kirchberg, nuns' book. See Birlinger and Roth.
Kirchesch, Heinrich. *Die Verfassung und die wirtschaftlichen Verhältnisse des Zisterzienserinnenklosters zu Namedy*. Dissertation, Bonn, 1916.
König, J. See Anna of Munzingen.
Kothe, Wilhelm. *Kirchliche Zustände Strassburgs im 14. Jahrhundert*. Breslau, 1902.
Krebs, Engelbert. "Die Mystik in Adelhausen." *Festgabe für Heinrich Finke*. Münster, 1904), 41–105.
Lamprecht of Regensburg. *Sanct Francisken Leben und Tochter Syon*. Ed. Karl Weinhold. Paderborn, 1880.
Lamy, Hugues. *L'Abbaye de Tongerloo depuis sa fondation jusqu'en 1263*. Recueil des travaux de l'Université de Louvain 44. Louvain; Paris, n.d.
Langmann, Adelheid. *Die Offenbarungen der Adelheid Langmann, Klosterfrau zu Engelthal*. Ed. Philipp Strauch. Quellen und Forschungen zur Sprach- und Culturgeschichte der germanischen Völker 26. Strasbourg, 1878.
Lazzeri, Zephyrinus. "Documenta controversiam inter fratres Minores et Clarissas spectantia (1262–1297)." *AFH* 3 (1910), 664–79; 4 (1911), 74–94.
Lea, Henry Charles. *Geschichte der Inquisition im Mittelalter*. Trans. and ed. Joseph Hansen. Bonn, 1905–13.
Leclercq, Jean. *Analecta monastica*, vol. 2, Studia Anselmiana 31. Rome, 1953.
Lecoy de la Marche, Albert. *Anecdotes historiques, légendes et apologues tirés du recueil inédit d'étienne de Bourbon*. Paris, 1877.
———. *La chaire française au Moyen Age*. Paris, 1886.
Legenda antiqua s. Francisci. Ed. Ferdinand-M. Delorme. Éditions de la France franciscaine 3. Paris, 1926.
Legenda trium sociorum. Ed. Michele Faloci-Pulignani. *Miscellanea francescana* 7 (1898), 81–107.
Lemmens, Leonhard, ed. *Documenta antiqua Franciscana*, vol. 1: *Scripta fratris Leonis socii s. p. Francisci*. Quaracchi, 1901.
———. "Zum Leben und Werke der heiligen Klara." *Der Katholik* 4:12 (1913).
——— "Die Anfänge des Clarissenordens." *RQH* 16 (1902), 93–124.
———. See *Dialogus de vitis sanctorum fratris Minorum*.
Lempp, Eduard. "Die Anfänge des Clarissenordens." *ZKG* 13 (1892), 181–245.
———. *Frère Elie de Cortone, étude biographique*. Collection d'études et de documents sur l'histoire religieuse et littéraire du Moyen Age 3. Paris, 1901.
Leven van Sinte Lutgarde. See William of Afflighem.
Linneborn, Johannes. "Die Westfälischen Klöster des Cistercienzerordens bis zum 15. Jahrhundert." *Festgabe für Heinrich Finke*. Münster, 1904. 253–362.
Linsenmayer, Anton. *Geschichte der Predigt in Deutschland*. Munich, 1886.
Löhr, Gabriel. "Das Necrologium des Dominikanerinnenklosters St. Gertrud in Köln." *Annalen des historischen Vereins für den Niederrhein* 110 (1927), 60–179.
———. *Beiträge zur Geschichte des Kölner Dominikanerklosters im Mittelalter*. QF 15. Leipzig, 1920.

Lommatzsch, Erhard. *Gautier de Coincy als Satiriker*. Halle, 1913.

Luchaire, Achille. *Innocent III. La croisade des Albigeois*. Paris, 1905.

Lüers, Grete. *Die Sprache der deutschen Mystik des Mittelalters im Werke der Mechthild von Magdeburg*. Munich, 1926.

Mahn, Jean-Berthold. *L'ordre cistercien et son gouvernement des origines au milieu du XIIIe siècle*. 2nd ed. Paris, 1951.

Mandonnet, Pierre. "Les Origines de l'Ordo de pœnitentia." *CRCSIC*. 5 vols. Fribourg, Switzerland, 1897. 5.183–215.

———. *Saint Dominique: l'idée, l'homme et l'oeuvre*. Ghent, 1921.

———. *Siger de Brabant et l'Averroism latin au XIIIe siècle*. 2nd ed. Louvain, 1908–11.

Mandonnet, Pierre, and Marie Humbert Vicaire. *Saint Dominique: l'idée, l'homme et l'oeuvre*. Ghent, 1937.

Manselli, Raoul. *Studi sulle eresie del secolo XII*. ISISS 5. Rome, 1953.

———. "Il monaco Enrico e la sua eresia." *BISI* 65 (1953), 1–63.

———. "Per la storia dell'eresia nel secolo XII, Studi minori." *BISI* 67 (1955), 189–264.

Mansi, Giovanni Dominico, ed. *Sacrorum consiliorum nova et amplissima Collectio*, vols. 23–25. Florence, 1759–1798.

Map, Walter. *De nugis curialium*. Ed. Montague Rhodes James. Anecdota Oxoniensia, Medieval and Modern Series 14. Oxford, 1914. [*De nugis curialium. Courtiers' Trifles*. Ed. and trans. M. R. James, revised by C. N. L. Brooks and R. A. B. Mynors. Oxford Medieval Texts. Oxford; New York, 1983.]

Martène, Edmund, and Ursinus Durand, eds. *Thesaurus novus anecdotorum*. 5 vols. Paris, 1717.

———. *Veterum scriptorum et monumentorum historicorum, dogmaticorum, moralium, amplissima collectio*. 9 vols. Paris, 1724–33.

Martini, Johann Christoph. *Historisch-geographische Beschreibung des ehemaligen berühmten Frauenklosters Engelthal*. Nuremberg; Altdorf, 1762.

McDonnell, Ernest William. *The Beguines and Beghards in Medieval Culture, with Special Emphasis on the Belgian Scene*. New Brunswick, N.J., 1954.

Mechthild of Magdeburg. *Offenbarungen der Schwester Mechthild von Magdeburg oder das fliessende Licht der Gottheit*. Ed. Gall Morell. Regensburg, 1869.

———. *Das fliessende Licht der Gottheit, nach einer neugefundenen Handschrift*. Ed. and trans. Wilhem Schleussner. Mainz, 1929.

———. *Das fliessende Licht der Gottheit*. Trans. Wilhelm Oehl. Deutsche Mystiker, vol. 2. Kempten; Munich, 1911.

Meier, John. *Bruder Hermanns Leben der Gräfin Jolande von Vianden*. Germanistische Abhandlungen 7. Breslau, 1889.

Mens, Alcantara. *Oorspong en betekenis van de Nederlandse Begijnen- en Beghardenbeweging*. Verhandelingen van de k. Vlaamse Academie voor Wetenschappen, Letteren en Schone Kunsten van België, Klasse der Letteren, 9:7. Antwerp, 1947.

——. "Innerlijke drijfveeren en herkomst der kettersche bewegingen in de Middeleeuwen, Religieus ofwel sociaal offmerk?" *Miscellanea L. van der Essen*. Brussels; Paris, 1947. 299–313.

Meyer, Johannes. *Liber de viris illustribus ordinis Prædicatorum*. Ed. Paulus von Loë. QF 12. Leipzig, 1918.

Michael, Emil. *Geschichte des deutschen Volkes*, vol. 3: *Deutsche Wissenschaft und deutsche Mystik während des 13. Jahrhunderts*. Freiburg i. B., 1908.

van Mierlo, Jan. "Was Hadewijch de ketterin Blomardinne?" *Dietsche Warande en Belfort* 2 (Louvain, 190), 267–86.

——. "Hadewijch en Eckhart." *Dietsche Warande en Belfort* 23 (1923), 1138–55.

——. "Was Hadewijch de Gelukzalige?" *Dietsche Warande en Belfort* 24 (1924), 52–67, 106–115.

——. "Hadewijch een gelukzalige Bloemardinne?" *Dietsche Warande en Belfort* 25:3 (1925), 28–49.

——. "Een hopeloos pleit." *Dietsche Warande en Belfort* 26 (1926), 468–80, 580–94.

——. "Beata Hadewigis de Antverpia." *Dietsche Warande en Belfort* 27 (1927), 787–98, 833–43.

——. "Het Begardisme." *VMKVA* (Ghent, 1930).

——. "Het ontstaan van de middelnederlandsche letterkunde." *Dietsche Warande en Belfort* 28 (1928), 582–95.

——. "Hadewijch une mystique flamande du 13e siècle." *RAM* 5 (1924), 269ff., 380ff.

——. "Hadewijch en de ketterin Blommardinne." *Tijdschrift voor nederlandsche taal- en letterkunde* 40 (1921), 45–64.

——. "Encore Hadewijch et Bloemmardine." *Revue belge de philologie et d'histoire* 7 (1928), 469–510.

——. "Hadewijchiana I-III." *VMKVA (Ghent, 1927), 195–225, 425–42.*

——. *"De bijnaam van Lambertus il Beges en de vroegste beteekenis van het woord Begijn."* *VMKVA* (Ghent, 1925), 405–447.

——. "Lambert li Begues in verband met den oorsprong der begijnenbeweging." *VMKVA* (Ghent, 1926), 612–60.

——. "Beatrijs van Nazareth." *VMKVA* (Ghent, 1926), 51–72.

——. "Ophelderingen bij de vroegste geschiedenis van het woord begijn." *VMKVA* (Ghent, 1931), 983–1006.

——. "De poëzie van Hadewijch." *VMKVA* (Ghent, 1931), 285–439.

——. "Hadewijch en Wilhelm van St. Thierry." *Ons geestelik Erf* 3 (1929), 45–59.

——. "Ruusbroec's bestrijding van de ketterij." *Ons geestelik Erf* 6 (1932), 304–46.

——. See Beatrijs van Nazareth.

——. See Hadewich.

da Milano, Ilarino. "La 'Manifestatio heresis catarorum,' quam fecit Bonacursus." *Aevum* 12 (1938), 301–24.

———. "Disputatio inter catholicum et paterinum hæreticum." *Aevum* 14 (1940), 85–140.

———. "La 'Summa contra hereticos' di Giacomo Capelli OFM e un suo 'Quaresimale' inedito (sæc. XIII)." *Collectanea franciscana* 10 (1940), 66-82.

———. "Le 'Liber supra Stella' del placentino Salvo Burce contro i Catari e altre correnti ereticali." *Aevum* 16 (1942), 272–319; 17 (1943), 90–146; 19 (1945), 281–341.

———. *L'eresia di Ugo Speroni nella confutazione del maestro Vacario. Testo inedito del sec. XII con studio storico e dottrinale*. Studi e testi 115 (Vatican City, 1945).

———. "Le eresie popolare del secolo XI nell'Europa occidentale." *SG* 2 (Rome, 1947), 43–89.

———. "Le eresie medioevali." *Grande Antologia Filosofica* (Milan, 1953), 1599–1689.

Miræus, Aubertus. *Opera diplomatica et historica*. 2nd ed. Brussels, 1723.

Molinier, Charles. "Un traité inédit du XIIIe siècle contre les hérétiques cathares." *Annales de la faculté des lettres de Bordeaux* 5 (1883), 226–56.

———. "Rapport sur une mission exécutée en Italie." *AMSL*, 3rd series, 14 (Paris, 1888), 133–336.

———. "L'église et la société cathare." *RH* 94 (1907), 225–48.

Mollat, Guillaume. See Bernard Gui.

Mone, Franz Josef. *Quellensammlung der badischen Landesgeschichte*, vol. 4. Karlsruhe, 1867.

———. "Kirchenordnungen der Bistümer Mainz und Strassburg aus dem 13. Jahrhundert." *ZGO* 3 (1852), 129–50.

Moneta Cremonensis. *Adversus catharos et valdenses libri quinque*. Ed. Thomas Augustinus Ricchinius. Rome, 1743.

Montet, Edouard, ed. *La noble Leçon, texte original*. Paris, 1888.

Morell, Gall. See Mechthild of Magdeburg.

Morghen, Raffaello. *Medioevo christiano*. 2nd ed. Bari, 1958.

———. "Le origini dell'eresia medioevale in Occidente." *RSR* 1 (1954), 1–24.

———. "Il cosidetto neo-manicheismo occidentale del secolo XI." *Accademia Nazionale dei Lincei, XII Convegno "Volta": Oriente e occidente nel medioevo* (Rome, 1957), 84–104, 158–60.

Mosheim, Johannes Laurentius. *De beghardis et beguinabus commentarius*. Leipzig, 1790.

Müller, Gregor. "Vom Cistercienserorden." *Cistercienser-Chronik* 37 (1925).

Müller, Karl. *Die Anfänge des Minoritenordens und der Bussbruderschaften*. Freiburg i. B., 1885.

———. *Die Waldenser und ihre einzelnen Gruppen bis zum Ausgang des 14. Jahrhunderts*. Gotha, 1886.

Neugart, Trudpert. *Episcopatus Constantiensis chronologice et diplomatice illustratus*, vol. 1:2. Freiburg i. B., 1862.

Nider, Johannes. *Formicarius*. Ed. Georgius Colvener. Douai, 1602.

Oehl, Wilhelm. See Engelthal.

——. See Mechthild von Magdeburg.

Ötenbach nuns' book. *Die Stiftung des Klosters Ödotenbach und das Leben der seligen Schwestern daselbst*. Ed. H. Zeller-Werdmüller and J. Bächtold. Zürcher Taschenbuch, 2nd series, 12 (1889).

Oliger, Livarius. "De origine regularum ordinis s. Claræ." *AFH* 5 (1912), 181–209, 413–47.

——. "De secta spiritus libertatis in Umbria sæc. XIV." *Storia e letteratura* 3 (Rome, 1943).

Petit, François. *La Spiritualité des Prémontrés au XIIe et XIIIe siècles*. Paris, 1947.

Petrus of Vaux-Cernay. "Historia Albigensis." Ed. Achille Luchaire. *BFL* 24. Paris, 1908, 1–75.

——. Ed. Pascal Guebin and Ernest Lyon. Société de l'histoire de France. 3 vols. Paris, 1926–39.

Petrus, Franciscus. *Suevia ecclesiastica*. Augsburg; Dillingen, 1609.

Pfeiffer, Franz. *Deutsche Mystiker des 14. Jahrhunderts*, vol. 1. Göttingen, 1845.

——. See Berthold of Regensburg.

——. See Eckhart.

Philippen, L. J. M. *De Begijnhoven, Oorsprong, Geschiedenis, Inrichting*. Antwerp, 1918.

——. *Les Béguines et l'hérésie albigoise*. Annales de l'Academie royale d'Archéologie de Belgique 73 (1925).

——. "Der hl. Norbertus en de strijd tegen het Tanchelmisme te Antwerpen." *Bijdragen tot de Geschiedenis* 25 (1934), 251–88.

Pierron, Johann Baptist. *Die katholischen Armen, ein Beitrag zur Entstehungsgeschichte der Bettelorden mit Berücksichtigung der Humiliaten und der wiedervereinigten Lombarden*. Freiburg i. B., 1911.

Poquet, Alexander Eusèbe. *Les Miracles de la sainte Vierge, traduits et mis en vers par Gautier de Coincy*. Paris, 1857.

Potthast, August. *Regesta pontificum romanorum*. Berlin, 1874–75.

Preger, Wilhelm. *Geschichte der deutschen Mystik im Mittelalter*. Leipzig, 1874–98.

——. "Beiträge zur Geschichte der Waldensier im Mittelalter." *Abhandlungen der historischen Classe der bayerischen Akademie der Wissenschaften* 13:1. Munich, 1877. 181–250.

——. "Über das Verhältnis der Taboriten zu den Waldensiern des 14. Jahrhunderts." *Abhandlungen der historischen Classe der bayerischen Akademie der Wissenschaften* 18. Munich, 1889. 1–111.

Quétif, Jacobus, and Jacobus Echard. *Scriptores ordinis Prædicatorum recensiti*, vol. 1. Paris, 1719.

Quint, Josef. "Mystik und Sprache." *DVLG* 27 (1953), 48–76.

——. *Textbuch zur Mystik des deutschen Mittelalters (Eckhart, Tauler, Seuse)*. Halle, 1952.

Recueil des Historiens des Gaules et de la France. Ed. Léopold Delisle. Paris, 1869–.

Remling, Franz Xavier. *Urkundenbuch zur Geschichte der Bischöfe zu Speyer*. Mainz, 1852.

Revelationes Gertrudianæ et Mechthildianæ. Ed. Solesmensium O.S.B. monachorum cura et opera. Poitou; Paris, 1875–77.

Rieder, Karl. Der sogenannte St. Georgener Prediger. Deutsche Texte des Mittelalters 10. Berlin, 1908.

Riezler, Sigmund. *Geschichte Baierns*, vol. 2. Gotha, 1880.

Ripoll, Thomas. *Bullarium ordinis fratrum Prædicatorum*. Ed. Antonius Bremond. Rome, 1729–.

Rodolphus Glaber. *Historiæ*. Ed. Maurice Prou. Collections de textes pour servir à l'étude et à l'enseignement de l'histoire. Paris, 1886.

Roisin, Simone. *L'hagiographie cistercienne dans le diocèse de Liège au XIIIe siècle*. Louvain; Brussels, 1947.

———. "L'efflorescence cistercienne et le courant féminin de piété au XIIIe siècle." *RHE* 39 (1943), 342–78.

Roth, F. W. E. "Aufzeichnungen über das mystische Leben der Nonnen von Kirchberg bei Sulz, Predigerordens, während des 14. und 15. Jarhhunderts." *Alemannia* 21 (1898), 103–48.

Sabatier, Paul. *Vie de S. François*. Paris, 1894.

———. "Il privilegio di Povertà, quando S. Chiara d'Assisi l'ottenne dal Sommo Pontifice?" *Miscellanea Franciscana* 24 (1924), 1–33. [The same in French in the *Bollettino della R. Deputazione di Storia Patria per l'Umbria* 24 (1920), 71–121.]

———. *Speculum perfectionis seu S. Francisci Assisiensis Legenda antiquissima*. Collection de Documents pour l'histoire religieuse du Moyen Age. Paris, 1898.

———. See *Speculum perfectionis*.

———. See Actus b. Francisci.

Saxius, Josephus Antonius [= Giuseppe Antonio Sassi]. *Archiepiscopus mediolanensium series*, vol. 2. Milan, 1755.

Sbaralea, Johannes Hyacinthus, ed. *Bullarium Franciscanum*. Rome, 1759–.

Scheeben, Heribert Christian. *Der heilige Dominikus*. Freiburg i. B., 1927.

———. "Albert der Grosse: zur Chronologie seines Lebens." *QF* 27 (1931).

Schleussner, Wilhelm. See Mechthild of Magdeburg.

Schmidt, Charles. *Histoire et doctrine de la secte des Cathares ou Albigeois*. Paris; Geneva, 1849.

Schnürer, Gustav. *Franz von Assisi*. Weltgeschichte in Characterbilder. Munich, 1907.

Schönbach, Anton Emil. *Studien zur Geschichte der altdeutschen Predigt*, vol. 3: *Das Wirken Bertholds von Regensburg gegen die Ketzer*. S-B der Akademie der Wissenschaften in Wien, philosophisch-historische Klasse 147:5. Vienna, 1904.

———. *Studien über Berthold von Regensburg*. S-B der Akademie der Wissenschaften in Wien, philosophisch-historische Klasse, 151:2; 152:7; 153:4; 154:1; 155:5. Vienna, 1906–07.

Schreiber, Georg. *Kurie und Kloster im 12. Jahrhundert*. Kirchenrechtliche Abhandlungen, 65–68. Stuttgart, 1910.

——. "Prämonstratenserkultur des 12. Jahrhunderts." *AP* 16 (1940), 42–108; 17 (1941), 5–33.

——. "Studien über Anselm von Havelberg." *AP* 18 (1942), 5–60.

Schröder, Karl. See Engelthal.

Seeberg, Erich. *Meister Eckhart*. Philosophie und Geschichte 50. Tübingen, 1934.

Séjalon, Hugo. *Nomasticon Cisterciense seu antiquiores ordinis cistericensis constitutiones*. Salesmis, 1892.

Simon, André. *L'Ordre des Pénitentes de S. Marie-Madelaine en Allemagne au XIIIe siècle*. Dissertation, University of Fribourg, Switzerland, 1918.

Slotemaker de Bruine, C. M. *Het ideaal der navolging van Christus ten tijde van Bernard van Clairvaux*. Wageningen, 1926.

Spätling, Luchesius. *De Apostolicis, Pseudoapostolis, Apostolinis. Dissertatio ad diversos vitæ apostolicæ conceptus decursu elucidandos*. Pontificium athenæum antonianum, Facultas theologica, Theses ad lauream 35. Monachii. Munich, 1947.

Speculum perfectionis ou mémoires de frère Léon sur la seconde partie de la vie de saint François d'Assise. Ed. Paul Sabatier. British Society of Franciscan Studies, vols. 13 and 17. Manchester, 1928–31.

Spiegel, Nikolaus. *Die Vaganten und ihr Orden*. Programm Speyer, 1892.

Stauber, A. "Kloster und Dorf Lambrecht." *Mitteilungen des historischen Vereins der Pfalz* 9 (1880).

Steichele, Anton. *Das Bistum Augsburg, historisch und statistisch beschrieben*. 4 vols. Augsburg, 1861–78.

Stephan of Bourbon. See Lecoy de la Marche.

Stöckerl, Dagobert. *Bruder David von Augsburg, ein deutscher Mystiker aus dem Franziskanerorden*. Veröffentlichungen aus dem kirchenhistorischen Seminar München 4:4. Munich, 1914.

Strauch, Philipp. *Margaretha Ebner und Heinrich von Nördlingen. Ein Beitrag zur Geschichte der Deutschen Mystik*. Freiburg i.B.; Tübingen, 1882.

——. See Langmann, Adelheid.

——. See Eckhardt.

Stroick, Autbert. "Verfasser und Quellen der Collectio de scandalis ecclesiæ." *AFH* 23 (1930), 3–41, 273–99, 433–66. Edition of the *Collectio, AFH* 24 (1931), 33–62.

Suchier, Hermann. "Zu den altfranzösischen Bibelübersetzungen." *ZRP* 8 (1884), 413–29.

Theloe, Hermann. *Die Ketzerverfolgungen im 11. und 12. Jahrhundert, ein Beitrag zur Geschichte der Entstehung des päpstlichen Ketzerinquisitionsgerichts*. Abhandlungen zur mittleren und neueren Geschichte 48. Berlin; Leipzig, 1913.

Thomas of Celano. *Vita prima* [= I Cel.], *Vita secunda* [= II Cel.] *S. Francisci Assisiensis*. Ed. a patribus collegii s. Bonaventuræ. AF 10. Quaracchi, 1926–.

——. *S. Francisci Assisiensis vita et miracula*. Ed. Eduardus Alenconiensis [d'Alençon]. Rome, 1906.

——. *Vita S. Clarae*. AASS August II.

Thomas of Chantimpré [Cantipratanus]. *Bonum universale de apibus*. Ed. Georgius Colvenerius. Douai, 1627.

Thomas of Eccleston. *Tractatus de adventu fratrum minorum in Angliam*. Ed. Edward G. Little. Collection d'études et de documents sur l'histoire religieuse et littéraire du moyen âge 7. Paris, 1909.

Tillmann, Heinz. *Studien zum Dialog bei Mechtild von Magdeburg*. Dissertation Magdeburg, 1933.

Tiraboschi, Hieronymus. *Vetera humiliatorum monumenta*. Milan, 1766–69.

Tractatus contra Amaurianos, ein anonymer, wahrscheinlich dem Garnerius von Rochefort zugehöriger Traktat gegen die Amalriker aus dem Anfang des 13. Jahrhunderts. Ed. Clemens Baeumker. Beiträge zur Geschichte der Philosophie des Mittelalters 24:5–6. Munich, 1926.

Unterlinden, nuns' book. See Ancelet-Hustache, Jeanne, "Vitæ sororum."

Vacandard, Elphgène. "Les origines de l'hérésie albigeoise." *RQH* 55 (2d series, 11) (1894), 50–88.

Vannérus, Jules. "Documents concernants le Tiers Ordre à Anvers et ses rapports avec l'industrie drapière." *Bulletin de la commission royale d'histoire, Académie royale de Belgique* 79 (1910).

Vicaire, Marie Humbert. See Mandonnet, Pierre.

Visch, Carolus de. *Auctuarium ad Bibliothecam Scriptorum ordinis Cisterciensis*. Ed. Joseph M. Canivez. Bregenz, 1927.

Volpe, Gioacchino. *Movimenti religiosi e sette ereticali nella società medievale italiana (secoli XI–XIV)*. Collana Storica 6. 2nd ed. Florence, 1926.

Wadding, Lucas. *Annales minorum*. 2nd ed. Rome, 1731.

von Walter, Johannes Wilhelm. *Die ersten Wanderprediger Frankreichs, Studien zur Geschichte des Mönchtums*, part I: *Robert von Abrissel*. Studien zur Geschichte der Theologie und der Kirche 9.3 (Leipzig, 1903); Part 2: Studien zur Geschichte der Theologie und der Kirche, 2nd series, 2 (Leipzig, 1906).

Walther, Wilhelm. *Die deutsche Bibelübersetzung des Mittelalters*. Brunswick, 1889–92.

Wauer, Edmund. *Entstehung und Ausbreitung des Klarissenordens, besonders in den deutschen Minoritenprovinzen*. Leipzig, 1906.

Weil, nuns' book. See Bihlmeyer.

Wentzlaff-Eggebert, Friedrich-Wilhelm. *Deutsche Mystik zwischen Mittelalter und Neuzeit*. 2nd ed. Tübingen, 1947.

Werner, Ernst. *Pauperes Christi. Studien zu sozial-religiösen Bewegungen im Zeitalter des Reformpapsttums*. Leipzig, 1956.

——. "Neue Texte und Forschungen zur Charta Caritatis." *Forschungen und Fortschritte* 29 (1955), 25–29.

——. "Bemerkungen zur Hirsauer Bewegung," *Wissenschaftliche Zeitschrift der Universität Leipzig*, 1953, no. 3, 9–17.

Westerholz, Elisabeth von. *Kardinal Rainer von Viterbo*. Heidelberger Abhandlungen zur mittleren und neueren Geschichte 34. Heidelberg, 1912.

William of Afflighem. *Leven van Sinte Lutgarde*. Ed. Frans van Veerdeghem. Leiden, 1896.

William of St. Amour. *Magistri Guillelmi de Sancto Amore Opera omnia, quæ reperiri potuerunt*. Coutances, 1632.

William of Puy-Laurens. "Cronica." Ed. Beyssier. *BFL* 18 (Paris, 1904), 85–175.

Wilms, Hieronymus. *Geschichte der deutschen Dominikanerinnen*. Dülmen i. W., 1920.

———. "Das älteste Verzeichnis der deutschen Dominikanerinnenklöster." *QF* 24. Leipzig, 1928.

———. *Das Beten der Mystikerinnen. QF* 11. Leipzig, 1916.

Zanoni, Luigi. *Gli Umiliati nei loro rapporti con l'eresia, industria della lana ed i communi nei secoli XII e XIII*. Bibliotheca historica italica, 2nd series, vol. 2. Milan, 1911.

Zarncke, Lilly. *Der Anteil des Kardinals Ugolino in der Ausbildung der drei Orden des heiligen Franz*. Beiträge zur Kulturgeschichte des Mittelalters und der Renaissance 42. Leipzig; Berlin, 1930.

Zeller-Werdmüller. See Ötenbach, nuns' book.

Zoepf, Ludwig. *Die Mystikerin Margaretha Ebner*. Beiträge zur Kulturgeschichte des Mittelalters und der Renaissance 16. Leipzig; Berlin, 1914.

Index